NOVELL'S

GroupWise® 6 Administrator's Guide

TAY KRATZER

Novell Press, San Jose

Best-Selling Books • Digital Downloads • e-Books • Answer Networks • e-Newsletters • Branded Web Sites • e-Learning

New York, NY ◆ Cleveland, OH ◆ Indianapolis, IN

Novell's GroupWise® 6 Administrator's Guide

Published by
Hungry Minds, Inc.
909 Third Avenue
New York, NY 10022
`www.hungryminds.com`

Library of Congress Catalog Card Number: 2001093700

ISBN: 0-7645-3563-3

Printed in the United States of America

10 9 8 7 6 5 4 3 2

1B/QU/QR/QS/IN

Distributed in the United States by Hungry Minds, Inc.

Distributed by CDG Books Canada Inc. for Canada; by Transworld Publishers Limited in the United Kingdom; by IDG Norge Books for Norway; by IDG Sweden Books for Sweden; by IDG Books Australia Publishing Corporation Pty. Ltd. for Australia and New Zealand; by TransQuest Publishers Pte Ltd. for Singapore, Malaysia, Thailand, Indonesia, and Hong Kong; by Gotop Information Inc. for Taiwan; by ICG Muse, Inc. for Japan; by Intersoft for South Africa; by Eyrolles for France; by International Thomson Publishing for Germany, Austria, and Switzerland; by Distribuidora Cuspide for Argentina; by LR International for Brazil; by Galileo Libros for Chile; by Ediciones ZETA S.C.R. Ltda. for Peru; by WS Computer Publishing Corporation, Inc., for the Philippines; by Contemporanea de Ediciones for Venezuela; by Express Computer Distributors for the Caribbean and West Indies; by Micronesia Media Distributor, Inc. for Micronesia; by Chips Computadoras S.A. de C.V. for Mexico; by Editorial Norma de Panama S.A. for Panama; by American Bookshops for Finland.

For general information on Hungry Minds' products and services please contact our Customer Care department within the U.S. at 800-762-2974, outside the U.S. at 317-572-3993 or fax 317-572-4002.

For sales inquiries and reseller information, including discounts, premium and bulk quantity sales, and foreign-language translations, please contact our Customer Care department at 800-434-3422, fax 317-572-4002 or write to Hungry Minds, Inc., Attn: Customer Care Department, 10475 Crosspoint Boulevard, Indianapolis, IN 46256.

For information on licensing foreign or domestic rights, please contact our Sub-Rights Customer Care department at 212-884-5000.

For information on using Hungry Minds' products and services in the classroom or for ordering examination copies, please contact our Educational Sales department at 800-434-2086 or fax 317-572-4005.

For press review copies, author interviews, or other publicity information, please contact our Public Relations department at 317-572-3168 or fax 317-572-4168.

For authorization to photocopy items for corporate, personal, or educational use, please contact Copyright Clearance Center, 222 Rosewood Drive, Danvers, MA 01923, or fax 978-750-4470.

Credits

Acquisitions Editor
Katie Feldman

Project Editor
Michael Kelly

Technical Editors
Eric Raff
Ernie Riedelbach

Editorial Manager
Ami Frank Sullivan

Senior Vice President, Technical Publishing
Richard Swadley

Vice President and Publisher
Mary Bednarek

Project Coordinator
Nancee Reeves

Graphics and Production Specialists
Beth Brooks, Gabriele McCann, Betty Schulte, Jacque Schneider

Quality Control Technicians
Andy Hollandbeck, Angel Perez, Carl Pierce, Linda Quigley

Permissions Editor
Carmen Krikorian

Media Development Specialist
Gregory Stephens

Proofreading and Indexing
TECHBOOKS Production Services

About the Author

Tay Kratzer works as a Novell Premium Service — Primary Support Engineer for some of Novell's larger customer sites. Tay is the co-author of two other GroupWise specific books, and he writes for the "Tay Kratzer's Hot Docs" section of *GroupWise Cool Solutions* magazine. Tay has supported Novell GroupWise for nine years, and he is a Novell Master CNE. Tay is the recipient of the Software Support Professional Association's Year 2000 "Outstanding Superstar" award. Tay lives in Utah with his wife, Dr. Irina Kratzer, and their four children, Wesley, Dallin, Lindy, and Anastasia.

To my wife, Irina Kratzer — you are simply the best!

To my mother and father, Venice and LeRoy Kratzer. Dad, thanks for teaching me things such as Basic programming before PCs ever hit the market. Mom, thanks for teaching me word processing in the WordStar days.

Preface

Novell GroupWise is an *integrated* e-mail and collaboration tool with a rich feature set and hundreds of options. The GroupWise Windows client appeals to first-time users along with power users, and administering a GroupWise system can be quite straightforward.

GroupWise 6 administration is simple for several reasons, but mostly because GroupWise is stable and easy to troubleshoot. This book makes that troubleshooting easier by helping you understand the structure of the data you'll be working with, as well as the tools you'll have at your disposal. True, GroupWise cannot be administered by a legion of trained monkeys, but it will only take a few intelligent and well-informed people to administer a very large GroupWise system. This fact is one of the major reasons why Novell GroupWise has kept a strong presence in organizations that take productivity, cost-effectiveness, and return-on-investment factors into account when evaluating collaboration solutions.

As users and administrators look to wireless and Windows-independent solutions, GroupWise 6 is unparalleled by any competitor in its offerings. GroupWise 6 is also strongly integrated with Novell's eDirectory. With GroupWise 6 and LDAP-directory authentication, users only need to remember the Novell eDirectory password. I appreciate that if I access my GroupWise account on my PalmPilot, or on a Macintosh-, Linux-, or Windows-based computer, I only need to remember one password: my Novell eDirectory password.

I learned a long time ago that if I write something down, and I know where I put it, I don't have to memorize a lot of information. I can't stand having to remember mundane facts, so I just write them all down. Over the nine years that I have supported Novell GroupWise, I have had to cook up some elaborate solutions in an effort to modify or fix my customer's systems. You are the beneficiary of my efforts to document hundreds of facts and solutions, which I just did not want to have to keep in my head!

When I sit down to a technical book, I like specifics. That's what I have provided to you in this book; I try to be specific. The other thing that makes this book unique is that it explains how to do many things that programmatically there are no solutions for. For example, moving a GroupWise post office is a popular theme from a customer's standpoint, but nothing in GroupWise administration allows for this task.

This book has five major parts:

- *Part I: Understanding GroupWise Architecture* — Part I reviews the GroupWise architecture. Even if you are among the ranks of the many GroupWise experts, you will find newer ways to understand GroupWise architecture.
- *Part II: Using the Administration Interface* — The second part of this book focuses on how to use ConsoleOne to administer your GroupWise system.
- *Part III: Agents and Clients* — The third part of this book explains installing and configuring the major elements in a GroupWise system.
- *Part IV: Practical Administration* — Part IV focuses on practical approaches to building and maintaining your GroupWise system.
- *Part V: Applied Architecture* — Finally, in Part V, you can find practical advice for fitting the GroupWise system to meet your needs. It's in this part of the book that you find detailed instructions on how to do things with your GroupWise system that are either undocumented or have no programmatic solution.

Acknowledgments

Thanks for the big contributions to this book by the following four employees at Novell: Howard Tayler, Ross Phillips, Eric Raff, and Tim King.

Thanks to Danita Zanre and the folks at www.caledonia.net for the large excerpt from Chapter 6 of the *GroupWise 6 Upgrade Guide* that they allowed me to reprint in this book.

Thanks to Sean Kirkby of www.concentrico.net for contributing Chapter 25 of this book.

Thanks to Eric Raff and Ernie Riedelbach for a fine of job of technical editing this book, and to my eagle-eyed editor, Michael Kelly, for helping to make this book extremely accurate.

Contents at a Glance

Contents

PART I

Understanding GroupWise Architecture

CHAPTER 1

Understanding the Basics of GroupWise Architecture

This chapter examines the Novell GroupWise architecture. Some terms are defined, and the way some components interact is briefly discussed. This chapter prepares you for a more thorough discussion of architecture in the next three chapters. To help you understand some of the naming conventions used, this chapter also discusses the evolution of the GroupWise product.

Understanding a Basic GroupWise 6 System

The word *GroupWise* is a Novell, Inc., trademark. It refers to a collection of applications and data-stores that, taken together, provide e-mail (and a lot more) to a community of computer users. GroupWise is properly categorized as collaboration software, or as a *groupware* product. Groupware defines software that helps people to collaborate outside of just sending e-mail to one another. An example of a collaboration feature in GroupWise 6 is shared folders. Figure 1.1 shows a view of GroupWise from a user's perspective in the GroupWise 32-bit Windows client.

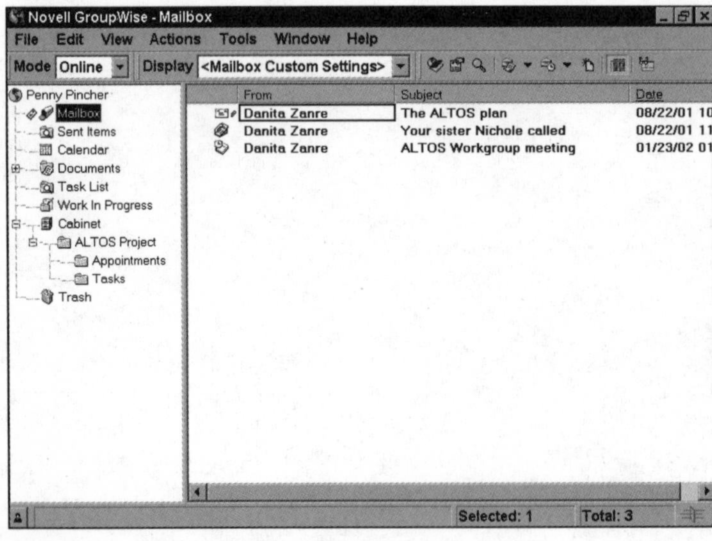

FIGURE 1.1 *The GroupWise 32-Bit Client*

GroupWise User

The term *GroupWise user,* or sometimes just *user,* refers to a mailbox that has been assigned to an end user on a GroupWise system. As an analogy, consider the United States Postal Service: A GroupWise user is similar to a post office box. Just as various mail items are delivered to a P.O. box, e-mail and other items are delivered to a GroupWise user.

GroupWise Post Office

Just as a P.O. box exists at a USPS post office, a GroupWise user exists at a *GroupWise post office.* Figure 1.2 shows a GroupWise post office object in ConsoleOne. A post office may also contain resources, libraries, and other GroupWise objects.

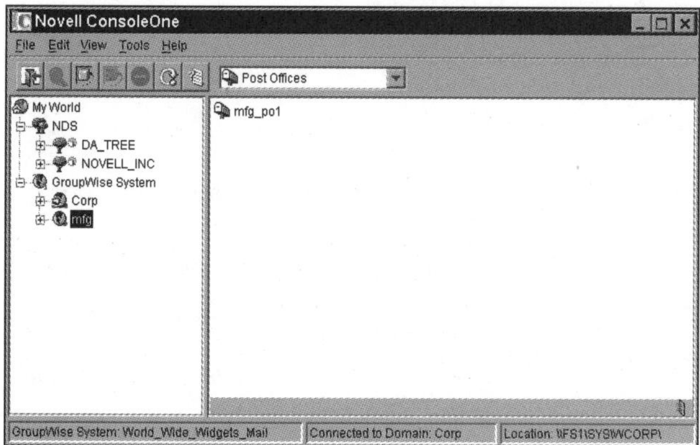

FIGURE 1.2 *A GroupWise Post Office*

Physically, every GroupWise post office exists as a collection of directories and data files on a file server. One of the most important attributes of a post office is the path to the root of these directories, the UNC path, as shown in Figure 1.3.

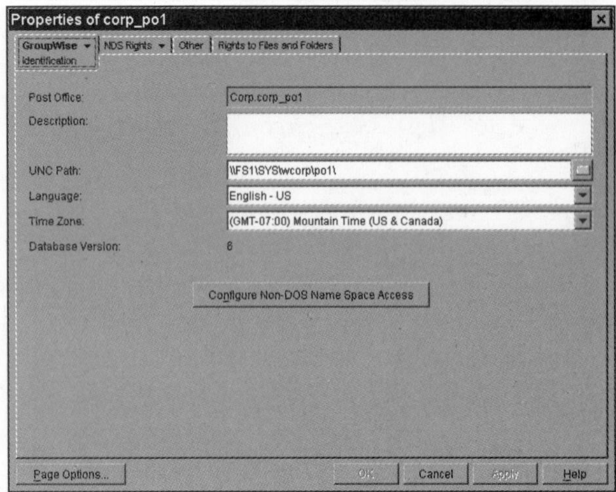

FIGURE 1.3 *The Details of a GroupWise Post Office*

GroupWise Domain

If GroupWise users are like P.O. boxes, and GroupWise post offices are like USPS post offices, then the *GroupWise domain* (see Figure 1.4) is like the distribution center at the airport, where trucks shuttle mail to various USPS post offices. At this point, the analogy gets a little difficult to follow, so domains will be discussed in terms of their functions. Domains exist to do the following:

- Transfer items between GroupWise post offices
- Transfer items to other GroupWise domains (which in turn deliver to their post offices)
- Provide a point of administration for all GroupWise objects, such as users, post offices, and libraries

Although post offices are where most of the action is, GroupWise domains are necessary because post offices cannot be administered by themselves. Just as with post offices, every GroupWise domain has a physical location, or UNC path (see Figure 1.5). This domain directory is the root of a complex directory structure containing files that are critical to the administration and proper functioning of a GroupWise system.

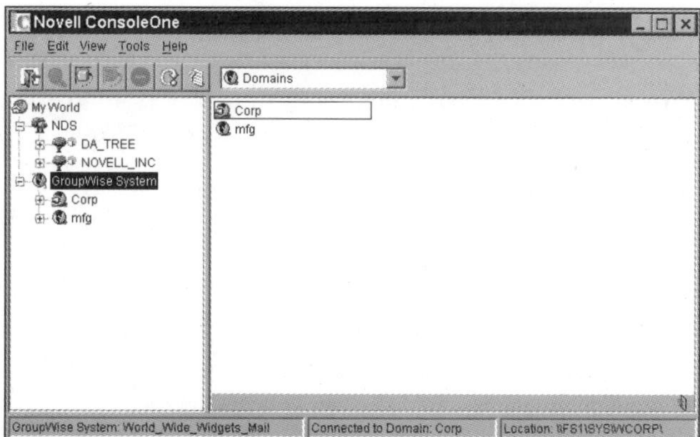

FIGURE 1.4 *A GroupWise Domain*

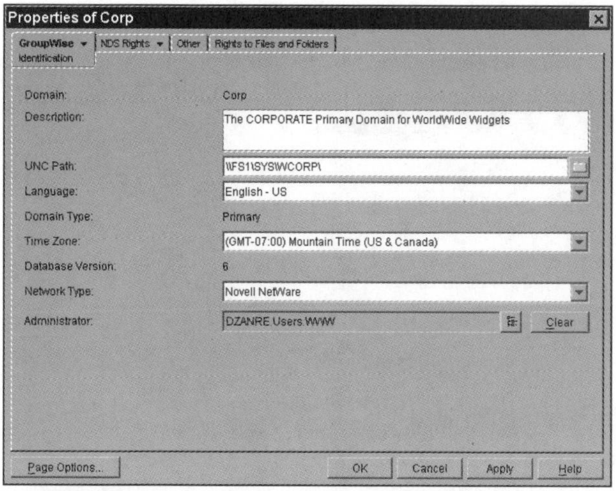

FIGURE 1.5 *The Details of a GroupWise Domain*

Primary Domain

Every GroupWise system must have a GroupWise *primary domain.* There can be only one primary domain in a GroupWise 6 system. All other domains established within a GroupWise system are either secondary domains or external domains.

There's also a thing called an *IDOMAIN*, or an *Internet domain*. The IDOMAIN refers to the Internet domain name for your organization, for example, `worldwidewidgets.com`. When you create IDOMAINs in your GroupWise system, these domains are not synonymous with regular GroupWise domains that are discussed in this chapter. The first domain you create in a GroupWise system is your primary domain.

The primary domain can function like any other GroupWise domain with post offices, users, and so on. Figure 1.6 shows the properties of a GroupWise primary domain; notice that properties of the primary domain indicate that the *Domain Type* is *Primary*. The difference is that the primary domain is the "supreme authority" within a GroupWise system. This means that any change made from any domain in a GroupWise system must be cleared through that system's primary domain. The GroupWise primary domain is responsible for replicating changes to all other domains, and in the event that a secondary domain database is damaged, the primary domain can be used to completely rebuild that secondary domain's database.

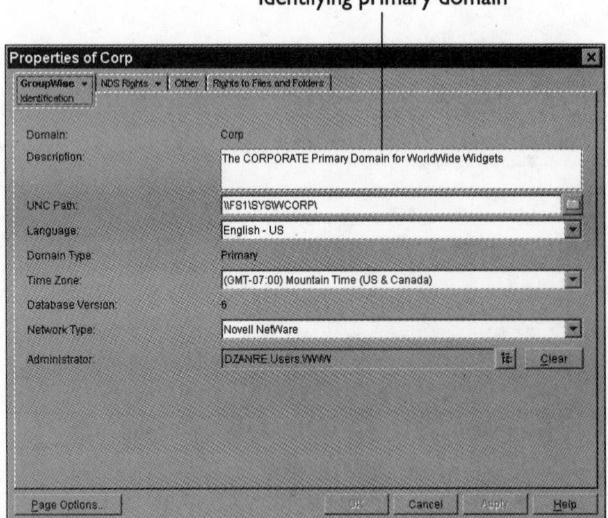

FIGURE 1.6 *The GroupWise Primary Domain Says Primary Next to It*

Secondary Domain

Most GroupWise domains are *secondary domains* (see Figure 1.7). When a change is made from a secondary domain, that change must be transmitted to the primary domain before it can be replicated to the rest of the GroupWise system.

Mail messages do not move in this manner. Secondary domains do not need to route ordinary mail messages through the primary. Only administrative changes must be routed in this way.

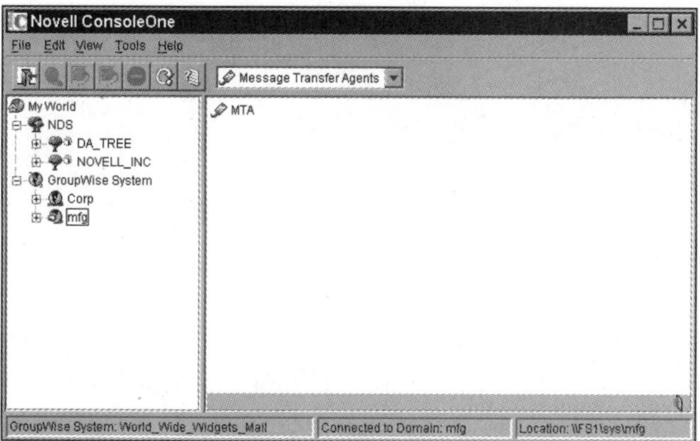

FIGURE 1.7 *A GroupWise Secondary Domain*

GroupWise System

The very top-level component of GroupWise is called the *GroupWise system*. It is not a true component, however, in that it does not have its own directory structure, or even its own object screen like domains and post offices do.

The GroupWise system is basically the name assigned to the collection of domains, post offices, and users (and more) that are managed from a particular primary domain. The system is represented by the icon shown highlighted in Figure 1.8, and the system name is World_Wide_Widgets_Mail.

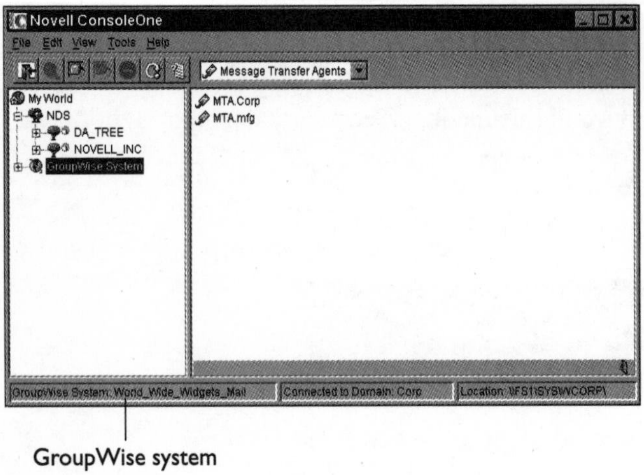

GroupWise system

FIGURE 1.8 *The GroupWise View with Just a GroupWise System Showing*

GroupWise Client

The *GroupWise client* is an application that allows a computer user to access a GroupWise mailbox. There are two kinds GroupWise 6 clients:

- The Windows client, shown in Figure 1.9, which runs on any Windows 32-bit platform.
- The GroupWise WebAccess/Wireless client that can run on a variety of browser platforms. Figure 1.10 shows this client for the Windows CE platform.

The GroupWise client typically talks to a post office agent (POA) in order to access the mailbox.

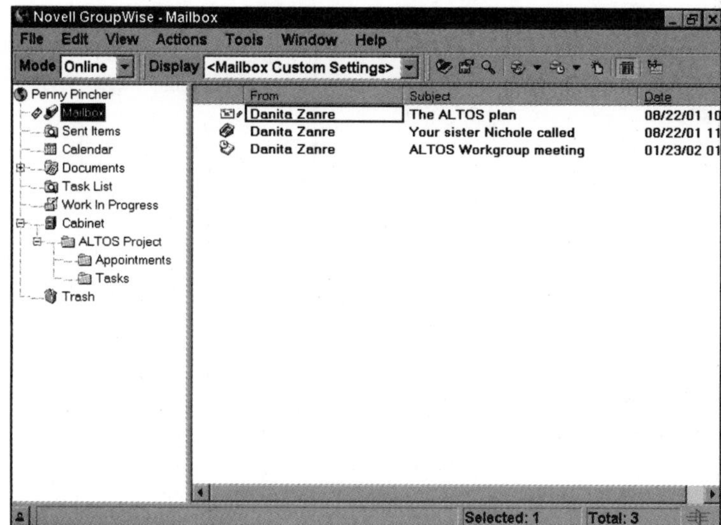

FIGURE 1.9 *The GroupWise 6 32-Bit Client*

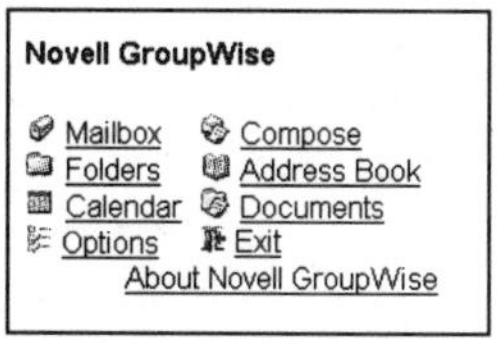

Novell GroupWise

Mailbox Compose
Folders Address Book
Calendar Documents
Options Exit
About Novell GroupWise

FIGURE 1.10 *The GroupWise 6 WebAccess Client for the Windows CE Platform*

Post Office Agent (POA)

Every GroupWise 6 post office must have a *post office agent (POA)* associated with it. Figure 1.11 shows a GroupWise POA object in ConsoleOne. A POA is a software process that typically runs on the same file server that houses the GroupWise post office. Figure 1.12 shows the interface of a POA process running as a NetWare NLM. The POA updates user mailboxes on that post office. A GroupWise POA also updates its GroupWise post office with administrative changes made from a domain in the GroupWise system. These changes may be address book changes or changes relevant to end users' interaction with the GroupWise system, like rights to libraries or membership in distribution lists.

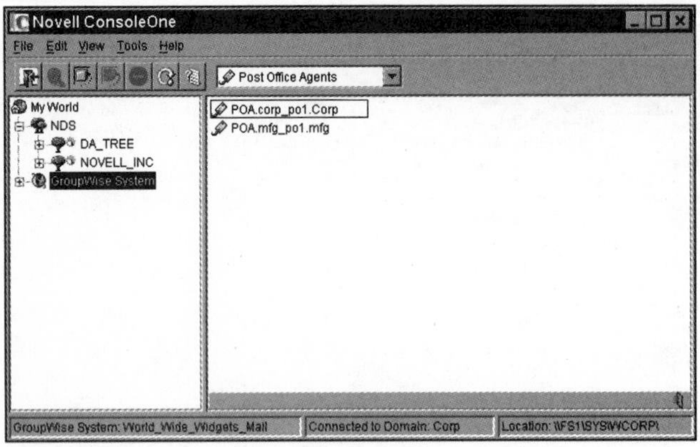

FIGURE 1.11 *A GroupWise POA Object*

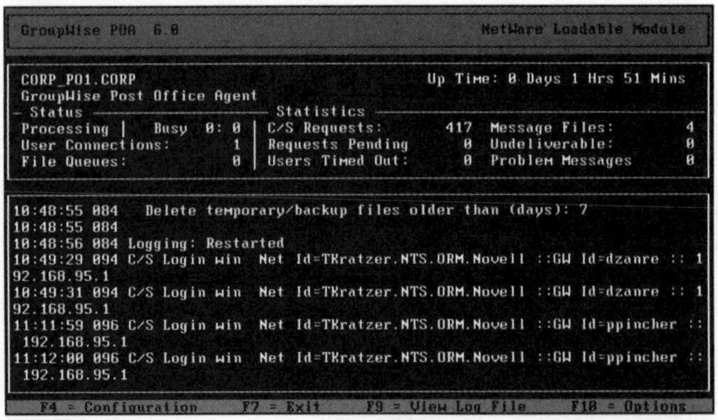

FIGURE 1.12 *A GroupWise POA Running as a NetWare NLM*

The post office agent is discussed in more detail in Chapter 8.

Message Transfer Agent (MTA)

Every GroupWise 6 domain must have a *message transfer agent (MTA)* associated with it. Figure 1.13 shows a GroupWise MTA object in ConsoleOne. The MTA is a software process that typically runs on the same file server that houses the GroupWise domain. Figure 1.14 shows the interface of a MTA process running as a NetWare NLM. It services the domain and each of the entities (post offices or gateways) associated with that domain.

The MTA is the agent that transfers messages between the post offices owned by the domain. It also transmits and receives with other domains on the GroupWise system, or even with domains outside of your GroupWise system, if you let it.

The MTA does not deliver messages to user mailboxes. The MTA drops messages off to the POA at a post office, and the POA does the actual delivery to the user mailbox databases.

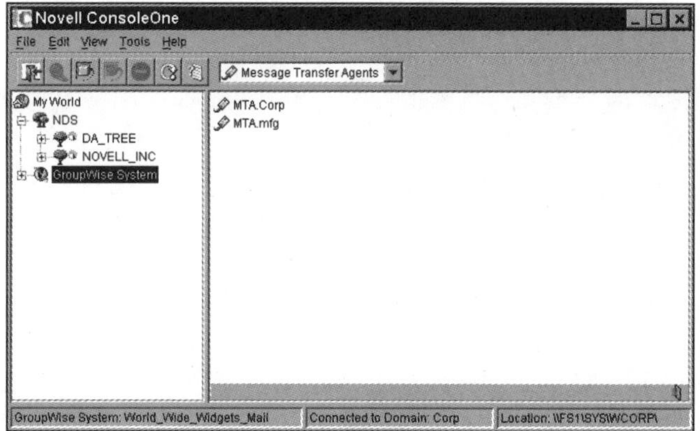

FIGURE 1.13 *The GroupWise MTA Object*

```
GroupWise MTA  6.0                                      NetWare Loadable Module

 Corp                                              Up Time: 0 Days 0 Hrs 1 Mins
 GroupWise Message Transfer Agent
 — Status ——————————————————————— Statistics ——————————————————————————
 \             Total  Closed  |                        Total     10 Minutes
 Domains           2       0  | Routed                    44              7
 Post Offices      1       0  | Undeliverable              0              0
 Gateways          1       0  | Errors                     0              0

08-22 12:44:06 DIS: MTA configuration loaded
08-22 12:44:10 DIS: MTA restart in progress
08-22 12:44:10 DIS: No configuration changes detected
08-22 12:44:10 DIS: MTA restart request ignored
08-22 12:44:46 DIS: MTA restart in progress
08-22 12:44:49 DIS: MTA restart completed
08-22 12:44:58 DIS: MTA restart in progress
08-22 12:44:58 DIS: No configuration changes detected
08-22 12:44:58 DIS: MTA restart request ignored
    F6 = Restart     F7 = Exit     F9 = View Log File     F10 = Options
```

FIGURE 1.14 *The GroupWise MTA Running as a NetWare NLM*

GroupWise Administrator

The *GroupWise administrator* application is a collection of snap-in modules for ConsoleOne. ConsoleOne is the latest general administration software that Novell has designed to manage Novell specific products in your computing environment.

Because GroupWise administrator requires ConsoleOne (see Figure 1.15), the GroupWise system must include at least one server with Novell Directory Services (NDS) or eDirectory. GroupWise uses NDS for a portion of its administrative directory.

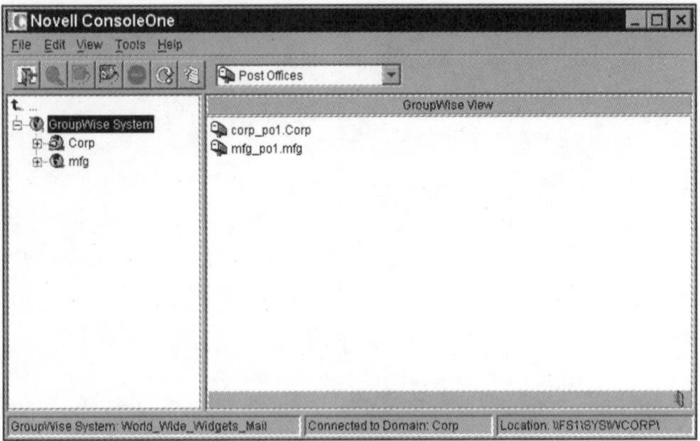

FIGURE 1.15 *The GroupWise View in ConsoleOne*

GroupWise Directory

The *GroupWise directory* is the collection of databases that defines the GroupWise system's domains, post offices, users, and other objects. The GroupWise directory has two major components:

- eDirectory/Novell Directory Services (NDS)
- GroupWise domain and post office databases

eDirectory/Novell Directory Services

eDirectory/Novell Directory Services is Novell's network directory solution. eDirectory is what Novell Directory Services has evolved into. For simplicity, this book refers to NDS and eDirectory simply as *NDS*. NDS is commonly used to define user accounts on file servers across enterprise networks, and it provides for simple, centralized administration. NDS has become an open solution beyond the Novell NetWare platform and as such NDS is now referred to as eDirectory. NDS has been extended to allow for the administration of user workstations, network applications, and even file servers.

NDS provides GroupWise administrators with the ability to manage their user's GroupWise mailboxes and network accounts from the same interface, ConsoleOne.

GroupWise Domain and Post Office Databases

The largest portion of the GroupWise Directory is in the GroupWise domain and post office databases. These database files are named WPDOMAIN.DB and WPHOST.DB. Every domain has a WPDOMAIN.DB file, which is that domain's database. Every post office has a WPHOST.DB file, which is that post office's post office database.

When ConsoleOne is loaded with the GroupWise Administrator Snap-ins, the GroupWise Administrator Snap-ins update the WPDOMAIN.DB file. When a GroupWise Domain's MTA is loaded, it must be pointed at the domain's WPDOMAIN.DB file.

Every post office has a WPHOST.DB file located at the root of the post office. Every post office POA is pointed at the path to the WPHOST.DB file in order for the POA to load. The WPHOST.DB file is often referred to as the *address book*. This file is the file GroupWise clients read in order to see other users and objects in their GroupWise system.

The GroupWise Message Store

A *GroupWise message store* is contained at each GroupWise post office. This is where a user's mailbox, with all its attendant messages and other data, is contained. The message store is the heart of what users interact with while they are running the GroupWise client.

A GroupWise message store can also exist in the form of GroupWise cache mode mailbox, remote e-mail, or in a GroupWise archive mailbox. Chapter 4 discusses the message store in much more detail.

Other GroupWise Objects and Services

This chapter has discussed users, post offices, domains, and systems, and it's also touched on the agents and the directory. The discussion of the basic GroupWise architecture is complete, but there are several types of GroupWise objects that have not been discussed. These will be covered in later chapters.

- Gateways (Chapter 10)
- Libraries (Chapter 5)

- Resources (Chapter 5)
- Distribution lists (Chapter 5)
- Nicknames (Chapter 5)

GroupWise Evolution

GroupWise 6 is a sixth-generation product. The original ancestor of GroupWise 6 was WordPerfect Office 1.0. When Novell bought WordPerfect Corporation, and later sold it to Corel, Novell retained the GroupWise product line. Prior to GroupWise 6, there are six major versions of GroupWise that are of interest in this book: GroupWise 4.1, GroupWise 5.0, GroupWise 5.2, GroupWise 5.5, and GroupWise 5.5 Enhancement Pack.

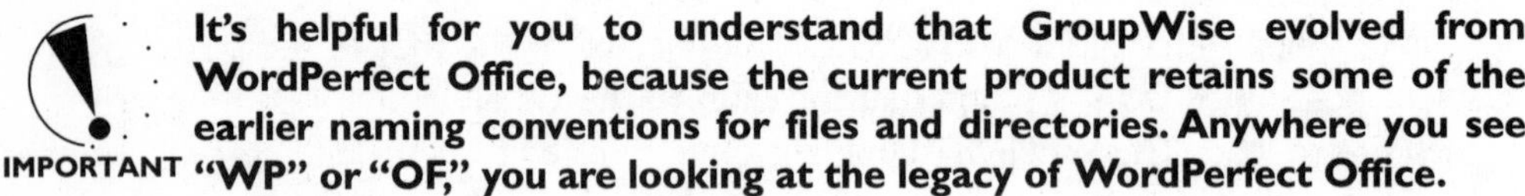
IMPORTANT **It's helpful for you to understand that GroupWise evolved from WordPerfect Office, because the current product retains some of the earlier naming conventions for files and directories. Anywhere you see "WP" or "OF," you are looking at the legacy of WordPerfect Office.**

- **WP:** The GroupWise domain database is called WPDOMAIN.DB. You will also find WPHost.DB, WPGATE, WPCSIN, and WPCSOUT.
- **OF:** All GroupWise post offices have directories called OFUSER, OFFILES, AND OFMSG.

Novell retained the WordPerfect and Office naming conventions to provide backward compatibility with older versions of GroupWise and WordPerfect Office. As new components have been added to GroupWise, the names of these components have followed the new GroupWise or Novell GroupWise names. For example, note the following:

- **GW:** The name of a GroupWise 6 domain dictionary file is GWDOM.DC. Look for GW in the names of GroupWise NetWare loadable modules, too.
- **NGW:** Every GroupWise post office has an important file called NGWGUARD.DB.

Summary

A GroupWise system is a combination of logical and physical components that work in harmony with one another. These components are the following:

- **GroupWise administrator:** The snap-in software in conjunction with ConsoleOne
- **GroupWise directory:** The combination of GroupWise domains and post offices, and Novell Directory Services (NDS)
- **Message transfer system:** The GroupWise MTA and POA
- **GroupWise message store:** The collection of files and directories in a GroupWise post office that contains all the mail messages and other items in user mailboxes
- **GroupWise client:** Your end-users' tools for reading mail, sending new mail, and collaborating with each other

Chapters 2–4 provide information on each of these components from an architectural standpoint.

The GroupWise online documentation discusses the components of a GroupWise system. Go to `www.novell.com/documentation/lg/gw6/index.html` **to have a look at the administration section of this guide.**

CHAPTER 2

Creating a GroupWise System

This chapter traces the creation of a GroupWise system. The goal is to explore the architecture in a way that will better help you understand it. There are some aspects of GroupWise architecture that are easier to explain as a GroupWise system evolves.

For the purposes of this chapter, GroupWise 6 is going to be installed at the fictional WorldWide Widgets Corporation. This fictional company is used for many examples throughout the book.

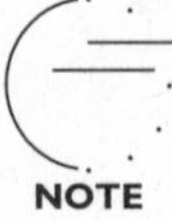

NOTE

Don't take this chapter as license to start installing your GroupWise system yet! First learn the architecture. You will want to carefully plan your system using the considerations offered throughout this book, and especially in Chapter 18. Chapter 18 gives you pointers on how to build your system correctly.

Installing GroupWise

WorldWide Widgets has a mixture of NetWare 5x, NetWare 6x, Windows NT, and Windows 2000 servers on its network. The company also has met one of the most important criteria to installing GroupWise 6, which is that its network supports Novell Directory Services (NDS). To install GroupWise, the administrator runs SETUP.EXE from the root of the GroupWise 6 CD. Figure 2.1 shows the screen that comes up after running SETUP.EXE.

Allowing for Extending the NDS Schema

The first thing you are asked for is an NDS tree in which GroupWise will *extend the schema.* Figure 2.2 shows that the setup wants to extend the NDS schema. NDS comes with a basic set of definitions for objects and their attributes. When GroupWise extends the schema of NDS, it adds new definitions, allowing NDS to contain new objects and new attributes for existing NDS objects. NGW: Post Office is a new object type that the GroupWise schema extension defines. The NGW: Object ID is a new, GroupWise-specific, attribute to the existing NDS user object.

The NDS schema definitions are added to NDS via standard developer APIs. You can find the GroupWise schema definition information in an ASCII file in the ADMIN folder of the GroupWise 6 CD. The name of the file is GwSchema.sch.

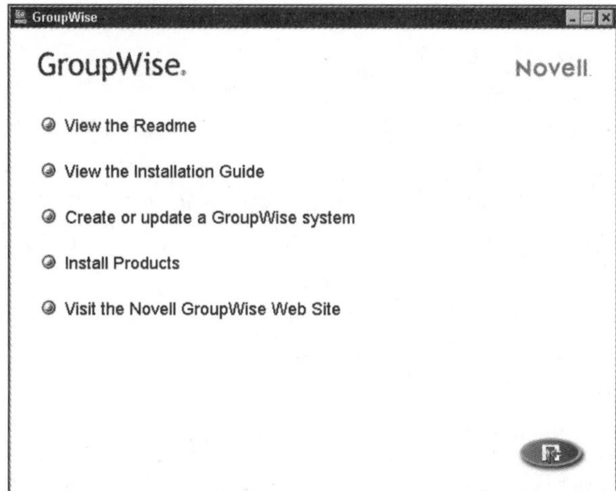

FIGURE 2.1 *GroupWise Installation Begins*

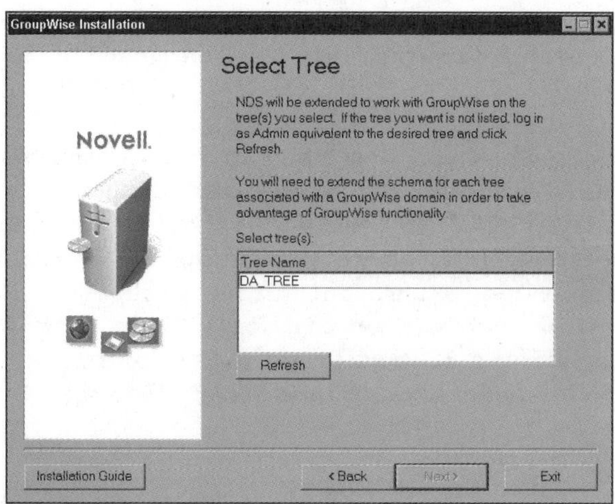

FIGURE 2.2 *Prompting to Extend the NDS Schema*

Defining the ConsoleOne Path for GroupWise Administration

As mentioned in Chapter 1, GroupWise is administered through snap-ins to ConsoleOne. With this design, if you have already implemented NDS, you have a single administration point for your network and the GroupWise system.

The installation routine now prompts you for the path to ConsoleOne. The snap-ins must be copied by the setup software to this directory structure so that ConsoleOne can work with the new objects and attributes available to NDS. They are also required to allow ConsoleOne to "connect" to a GroupWise domain database.

The GroupWise snap-ins are installed by the setup software to the NOVELL\CONSOLEONE\<VERSION>\SNAPINS\GROUPWISE directory at the location you specify to install the ConsoleOne snap-ins.

NOTE

The installation program only installs the GroupWise Administrator software to one location for one instance of ConsoleOne. If your system has multiple locations from which you run ConsoleOne, you will want to install the GroupWise snap-in software to those computers. Chapter 19 goes into detail on how to do this.

ConsoleOne is designed so that any *.JAR files found in a folder off of the NOVELL\CONSOLEONE\<VERSION>\SNAPINS folder is considered a snap-in. The GroupWise snap-ins are contained in the GROUPWISE folder.

TIP

There are some occasions when you may need to run ConsoleOne "unsnapped" from GroupWise. To do this, simply copy the NOVELL\CONSOLEONE\<VERSION>\SNAPINS\GROUPWISE folder and its contents to another location. Then delete the GROUPWISE folder temporarily. When ConsoleOne is unsnapped from GroupWise, all GroupWise objects show up with an icon that looks like a question mark on the right hand side of a 3D box. To get the snap-ins back in place, copy the GROUPWISE folder back into the SNAPINS folder.

Creating a Software Distribution Directory

A GroupWise software distribution directory (SDD) is a directory containing GroupWise applications. It is also an object in the GroupWise directory that allows various GroupWise components to find new software when it is available.

The installer prompts you to create the SDD on a file server. I recommend doing the following:

1. Copy the entire GroupWise 6 CD manually to a directory on the file server.
2. When prompted in the install for the path to the SDD, select a temporary location, which you will promptly delete later. When prompted for what software to install, just select GroupWise ConsoleOne Snapins.

WARNING

You probably know better, but I will give you some advice anyway. Don't indiscriminately delete files from your software distribution directory, unless you *know exactly what you are doing*. By deleting files, you could very easily cause yourself to have to place a support call when some piece of GroupWise software won't work correctly.

Creating a GroupWise System

To create a GroupWise system, you must launch ConsoleOne. When you ran the GroupWise setup software, you selected to either create or update a GroupWise system. If you indicated that you want to create a new GroupWise system, ConsoleOne will automatically launch, and Tools ➪ GroupWise Utilities ➪ New System will be executed by a wizard.

To create the GroupWise system and GroupWise primary domain for WorldWide Widgets Corporation, the administrator chooses Tools ➪ GroupWise Utilities ➪ New System.

There is a set of prompts that ask the administrator for information regarding the creation of a GroupWise system. Here's a close look at the ones that are relevant to understanding GroupWise architecture.

Selecting the Software Distribution Directory

Fill in the software distribution directory prompt shown in Figure 2.3, with the path where you installed the GroupWise software. Earlier in this chapter, I instructed you to copy the GroupWise 6 CD manually to a directory on a file server. The location where you copied the GroupWise 6 CD is the location you should select for the software distribution directory.

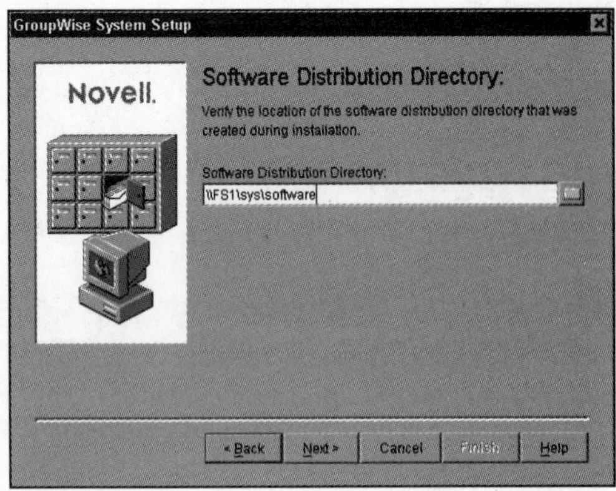

FIGURE 2.3 *Prompting for the Software Distribution Directory*

Selecting an NDS Tree

You can only create GroupWise in a tree that has had its schema extended with the GroupWise schema extensions (see Figure 2.4). The GroupWise schema extensions are added to the tree when running the SETUP.EXE from the GroupWise 6 CD or a copy of the GroupWise 6 CD.

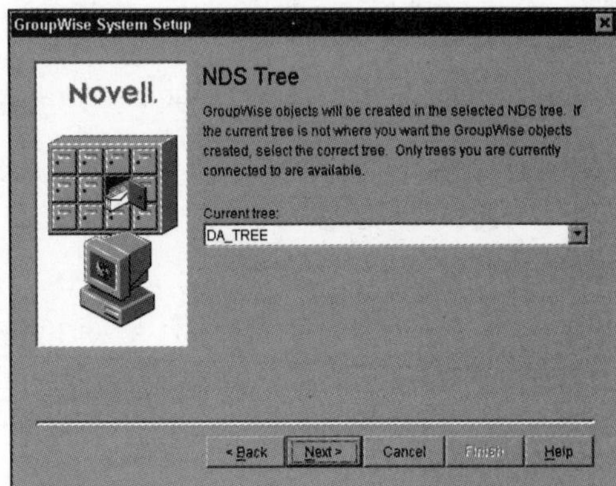

FIGURE 2.4 *Prompting for the NDS Tree*

Choosing a System Name

Now you need to decide on a name for your GroupWise system (see Figure 2.5). The GroupWise system name is rarely referenced again, but it will always be visible in the GroupWise system view in ConsoleOne. If WorldWide Widgets ever wants to enable a feature called *external system synchronization,* then it will have to share its GroupWise system name with its partner. Chapter 6 talks more about external system synchronization.

NOTE

Beyond external system synchronization, the GroupWise system name rarely becomes a point of interest.

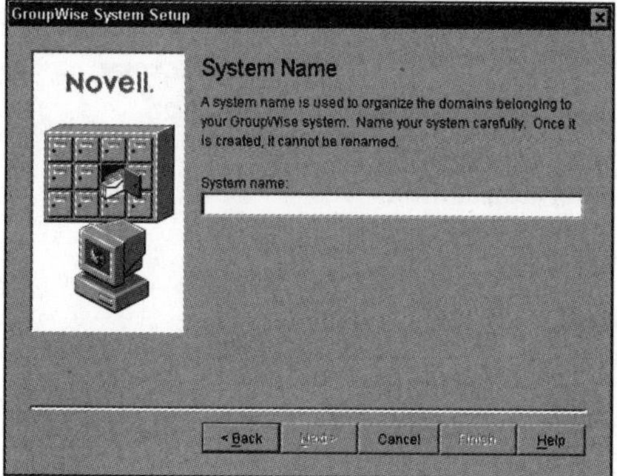

FIGURE 2.5 *Prompting for the System Name*

Creating the GroupWise Primary Domain

The primary domain was created as WorldWide Widgets installed its GroupWise 6 system. Remember that not all screens related to the install are mentioned in this section. The only screens that are mentioned are the ones related to understanding GroupWise architecture.

The primary domain is the first thing that actually denotes the physical creation of a GroupWise system.

The primary domain serves as the following:

- Plays a specific role in the newly created GroupWise system. The primary domain is the "master" of the GroupWise system.
- An object in NDS.
- A set of files and directories/folders that are needed for any GroupWise domain, physically located at a specific UNC path on a file server.

Choosing Your Primary Domain Name

Choose domain names carefully, because you may not change domain names once you've created them. Figure 2.6 shows the prompt for the primary domain name. I suggest using naming conventions that mirror those used in your NDS tree and server environment.

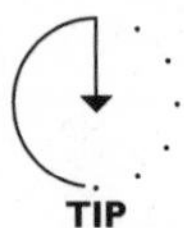
TIP

If possible, keep domain and post office names equal to or shorter than eight characters in length. This makes it easy to have directory names that match the name of the domain and helps avoid confusion.

WorldWide Widgets will call its primary domain CORP.

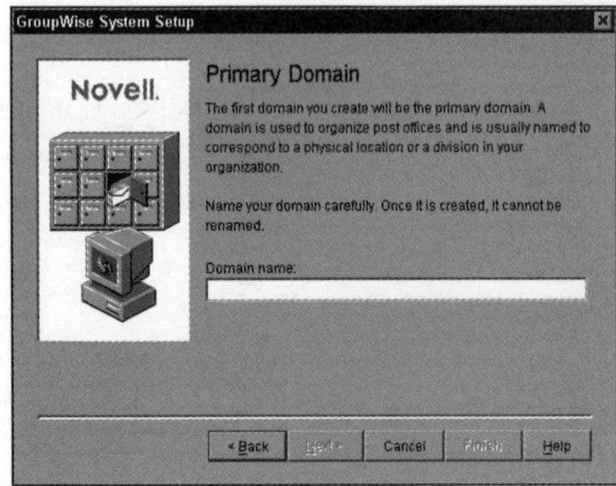

FIGURE 2.6 *Naming a Primary Domain*

Selecting a Primary Domain Directory

This is where the primary domain will physically reside. This directory must be on a file server, but it need not be on a NetWare server. As a matter of practice, though, it is best to place the GroupWise primary domain on a NetWare server.

The NLM versions of the GroupWise agents (MTA and POA) run much faster than NT applications. Because the primary domain is the center of all GroupWise directory updates, you will likely want the best performance possible.

WARNING

Never give your end users file access to a domain directory. They don't need it, and if they arbitrarily delete files, you may be in a world of hurt.

Specifying the Domain Context

This is where you place the GroupWise primary domain object in your NDS tree. The domain context is only important from an administration standpoint. If your company implements security controls on NDS objects, for example, then you may want to have a container for GroupWise objects. You may want to use organizational role objects to administer trustee assignments to the GroupWise system. In this way, you can control which of the system administrators can perform GroupWise administration operations.

WorldWide Widgets has decided to make its GroupWise domain structure match its NDS OU structure. In large systems, where operators all over the network are making changes in NDS, creating a GroupWise OU helps non-GroupWise administration personnel understand the separate purpose of the GroupWise objects.

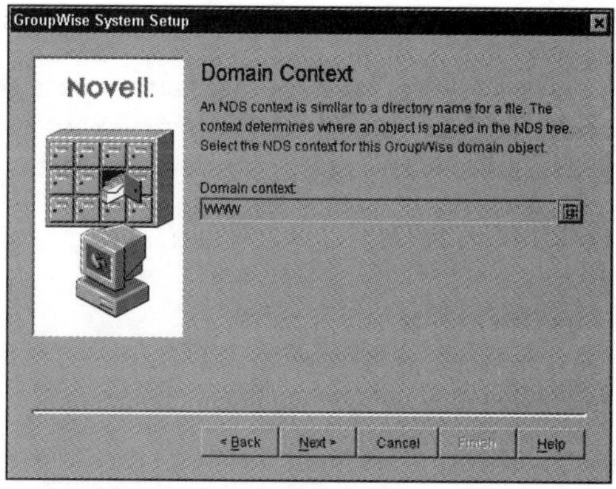

FIGURE 2.7 *Primary Domain NDS Context*

NOTE

If you need to move a GroupWise domain or post office to a new NDS container, refer to Chapter 21.

Letting GroupWise Know Your Time Zone

By specifying the time zone a GroupWise post office or domain is in, you effect how appointment and status message time stamps are created. Make sure to specify the correct time zone information or people will miss appointments. The time zone for the primary domain will be the time zone for the location where the file server is that will house the GroupWise primary domain. Chapter 6 covers time zone administration in more detail.

Giving the Post Office a Name

Although you may not want to create a post office yet, the installation wizard requires you to do so. The name of a post office cannot be changed, so choose wisely!

Giving the Post Office a Home: The Post Office Directory

The post office directory is the physical location for the GroupWise post office. Figure 2.8 shows the prompt for where to place the GroupWise post office. A GroupWise post office is a set of files and a directory structure that denotes a GroupWise post office. All GroupWise post offices have the same kind of structure.

IMPORTANT

There are significant risks involved in giving users file-system access to the post office directory. Fortunately, if you use the client/server access mode (see the following section), your users do not need file-system rights.

Selecting Your Post Office Access Mode

The GroupWise client can access the GroupWise Post Office in two different manners. They are the following:

- **Client/server:** This method is the best way to have your clients access the post office. The GroupWise client never touches the post office databases. The GroupWise client opens up a session with the GroupWise POA. The GroupWise POA is then the only process that accesses the GroupWise message store. GroupWise 4.1 did not have client/server access mode capabilities. GroupWise 4.1 customers constantly struggled with post office message store corruption. GroupWise 5x and GroupWise 6x customers that have implemented client/server access have seen about a tenth of the corruption they saw in GroupWise 4.1. Most customers will want to implement client/server access only.

- **Direct access:** This method of access is generally not recommended for customers to implement. Accessing a post office directly allows GroupWise client workstations to read from, and write to, a post office message store. You are looking for trouble if you do this.

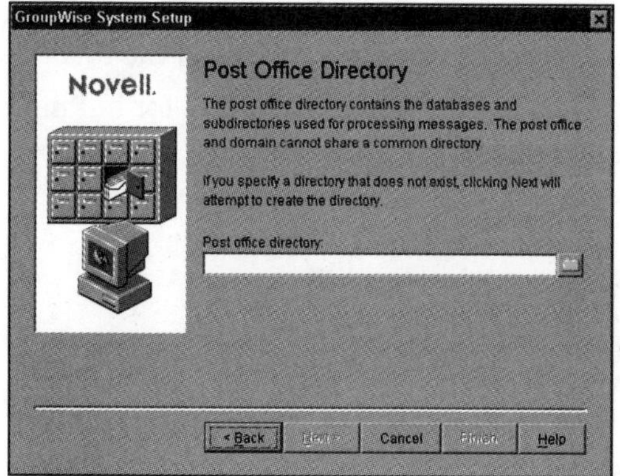

FIGURE 2.8 *Post Office Directory*

Establishing the Post Office Context

This is where the Post Office object will be placed in your NDS tree. This context is important to your end users, for reasons explained further in Chapter 12. The GroupWise client uses NDS to authenticate users to their mailboxes; having the post office in the same context as your users, speeds up authentication. If you place post offices in contexts where end users have no trustee assignments, you will create administration headaches for yourself later.

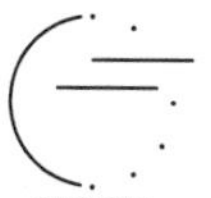

NOTE

There is no security risk inherent in allowing users to browse post office objects in the NDS tree.

Defining a Post Office Link

Each post office communicates with the rest of the GroupWise system through the domain's MTA. In order for the MTA to "talk" with a post office, it needs a way to hand messages to the post office. An MTA can either drop-off and pick-up files at the post office via a UNC connection, or it can transmit files via TCP/IP to the POA servicing the post office. Figure 2.9 shows the post office link prompt. A UNC link is called a *direct link* in this figure. A TCP/IP link is just as direct however, and almost always preferred.

- **Direct link:** This method of linking a domain to a post office requires that the MTA have file-system rights to the UNC path where the post office is. A direct link is sometimes used, particularly if your GroupWise post office is on the same file server that houses the domain that owns the post office. In most cases, even if a domain and post office are on the same file server, it is better to configure a TCP/IP connection between the MTA and the POA.
- **TCP/IP link:** This method of linking is the preferable method for linking the domain's MTA with a post office's POA.

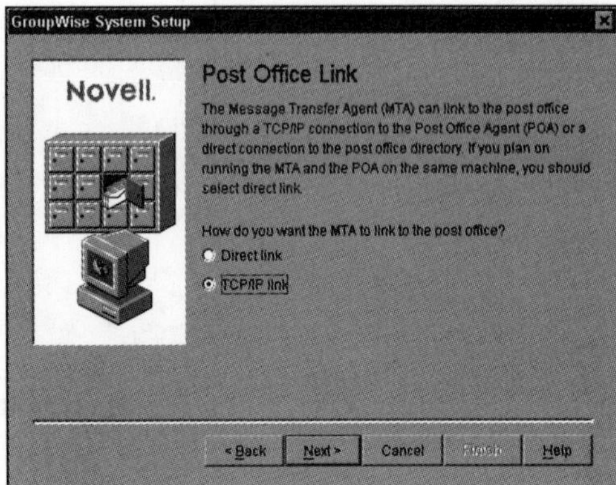

FIGURE 2.9 *Post Office Link*

Selecting Post Office Users

You may select users to be associated with this post office at this point. You can always do this later as you create additional users.

Summary

This chapter walked you through the creation of a GroupWise system. Here's the GroupWise system so far as shown in Figure 2.10.

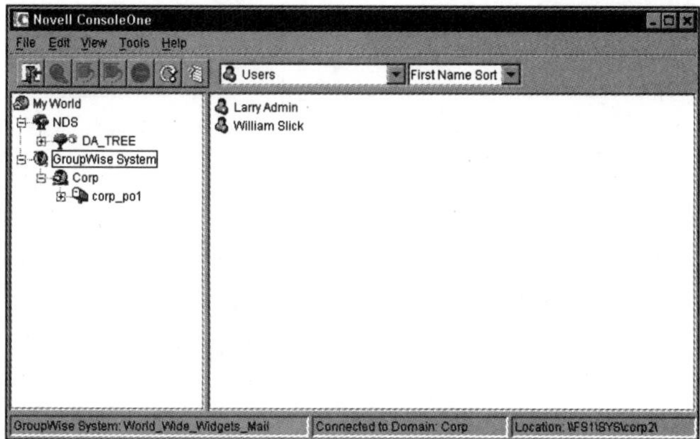

FIGURE 2.10 *WorldWide Widget's Beginning GroupWise System*

You can get some more details about this system by doing the following:

1. Open the GroupWise view (shown in Figure 2.10).
2. Highlight the GroupWise system.
3. With a right-mouse click, select the Information option (see Figure 2.11).

Doing these steps for WorldWide Widgets shows that it has created the following:

- One domain
- One post office
- One library
- Two users

If you call Novell Technical Support, you'll often be asked questions such as, "How many users are there in your system?" This information screen is where you'll find the answer quickly.

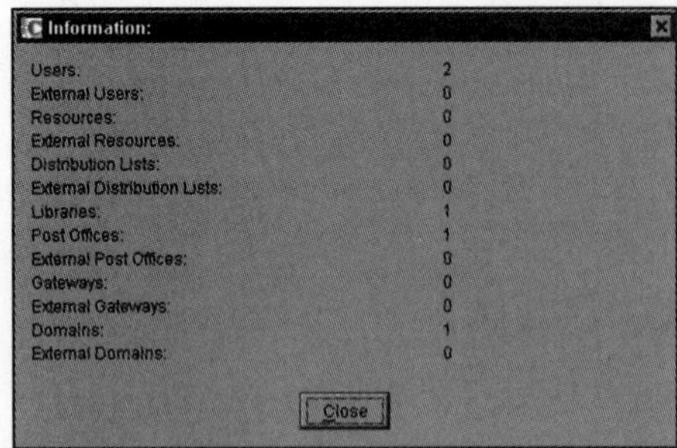

FIGURE 2.11 *The GroupWise System Information Screen*

This chapter discussed creating a GroupWise system, domain, and post office. You should now be fairly secure in your understanding of the general architecture of a GroupWise system. The next chapter explores the GroupWise directory in greater detail.

CHAPTER 3

Understanding the GroupWise Directory

This chapter explores how the various components of the GroupWise directory fit together. It examines some principles of administration and the flow of administrative messages through the GroupWise system, and it lays the groundwork for a very detailed discussion on troubleshooting and fixing the GroupWise directory in Chapter 22. The GroupWise directory refers to the databases used to manage GroupWise objects.

Understanding GroupWise Directory Components

As mentioned in Chapters 1 and 2, the GroupWise directory uses both Novell Directory Services and the GroupWise domain and post office databases. NDS and the GroupWise domain database (WPDOMAIN.DB) together provide the administration-level directory databases.

The portion of the GroupWise directory that is replicated for GroupWise clients to use is the post office database (WPHOST.DB).

GroupWise domain, post office, and message store databases use an underlying architecture called *FLAIM,* which allows for billions of extensible records. Until 1999, NDS used a different architecture that was also extensible, but did not work as well for large numbers of records. In 1999, Novell released NDS Version 8, which also uses FLAIM as its underlying architecture. Despite the fact that the lowest-level structures are now similar, the two systems are still separate.

Figure 3.1 shows some important architectural concepts that need to be explored:

- When administering GroupWise objects, most of the information goes into the GroupWise FLAIM databases.
- Information in NDS is moderately important to GroupWise administration.
- Every GroupWise domain database is essentially identical with every other record in other GroupWise domain databases.
- GroupWise post office databases only accept information that has first flowed through their owning domain.
- Not all information written to a domain database is written to a GroupWise post office database.
- GroupWise post office databases are not modified by GroupWise administration.

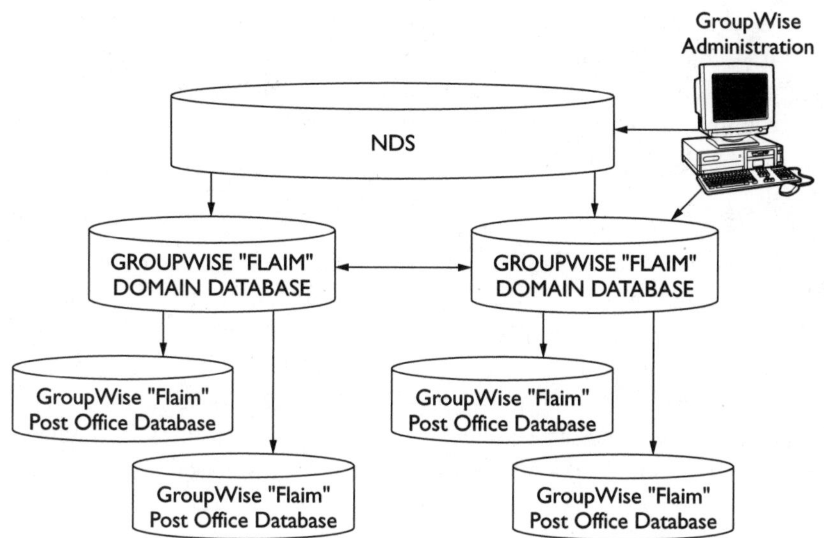

FIGURE 3.1 *The GroupWise Directory Databases*

How Novell Directory Services Is Used

It is important to understand that GroupWise evolved from WordPerfect Office. Before a heavy-duty, industry-recognized directory such as NDS came along, many applications had to have their own directory. With the release of GroupWise 5x, Novell began the process of merging the GroupWise directory with NDS. GroupWise administration requires NDS, but the primary domain database is still the ultimate authority in a GroupWise system.

Channeling GroupWise administration through NDS gives GroupWise 5x and GroupWise 6 two major improvements over previous versions (and over many other applications that do not leverage NDS):

- **Authentication security:** In older versions of GroupWise, if users could get into GroupWise administration, they could exert control over any object. With GroupWise 5 and later, access to individual GroupWise objects and their properties can be controlled through NDS.
- **Single point of administration:** Most GroupWise customers have already implemented an NDS directory tree. Having GroupWise mailboxes associated with their NDS user objects makes administration much easier. A phone number change or a name change has to be done only once.

Grafting GroupWise Objects with NDS

The process of controlling GroupWise objects through NDS is referred to as *grafting*. There are menu options in GroupWise administration that allow administrators to graft a domain, post office, or users into the NDS tree. The term graft may build a mental image in which a branch is taken from one tree and put on another tree.

Grafting GroupWise objects creates new objects in NDS, but those objects are fully contained in the WPDOMAIN.DB file. Most GroupWise objects in an NDS tree should be regarded as *aliases*, or *pointers*, to the actual object in the GroupWise FLAIM databases. Grafting objects into NDS allows objects to then be controlled through NDS.

Now that you know that the GroupWise directory is largely contained in the FLAIM databases, how often would you run DSREPAIR (the NDS database repair tool) to fix a GroupWise directory problem? You probably wouldn't! FLAIM databases have their own repair and analysis tools, which are discussed in Chapters 17 and 22.

The Role of the GroupWise Domain Database

A GroupWise domain directory contains a critical file: WPDOMAIN.DB, shown in Figure 3.2. This is the domain database.

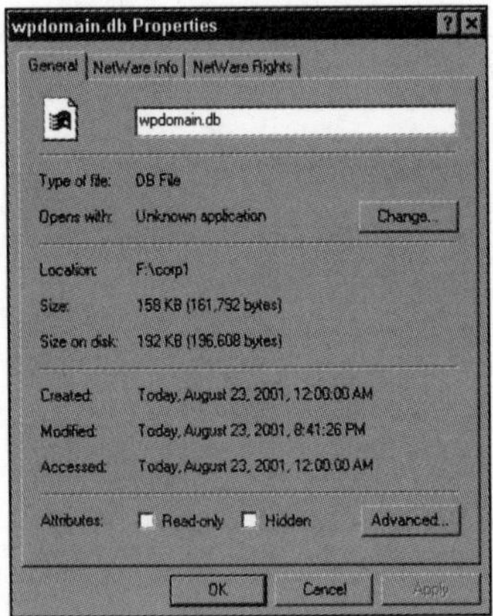

FIGURE 3.2 *A GroupWise WPDOMAIN.DB File in a Domain Directory*

Creating the First WPDOMAIN.DB File (the Primary Domain)

When a GroupWise system is created, a WPDOMAIN.DB file for the primary domain is created based upon the following:

- Information that the Administrator inputs
- Information from NDS
- Information from the domain structure, or *dictionary file,* called GWDOM.DC

The GWDOM.DC file is located at the root of any domain's directory. The GWDOM.DC file is an ASCII text file that defines the structure for all GroupWise 6 domain databases. The GWDOM.DC file should never be edited or modified.

Creating Secondary Domains

When a GroupWise secondary domain is originally created, it is created from information in the WPDOMAIN.DB file from the primary domain and the generic GWDOM.DC file. The information in a GroupWise secondary domain is an exact duplicate of the information in the primary domain. The only thing that makes a primary domain "primary" is that the "Domain Type" field, shown in Figure 3.3, for the primary domain reads as follows:

```
Domain Type: Primary Domain
```

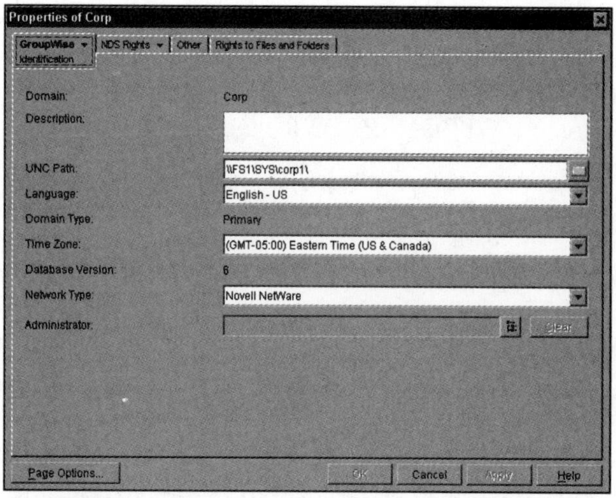

FIGURE 3.3 *The Domain Type for the Primary Domain*

A secondary domain's domain type, shown in Figure 3.4, reads like this:

```
Domain Type: Secondary Domain
```

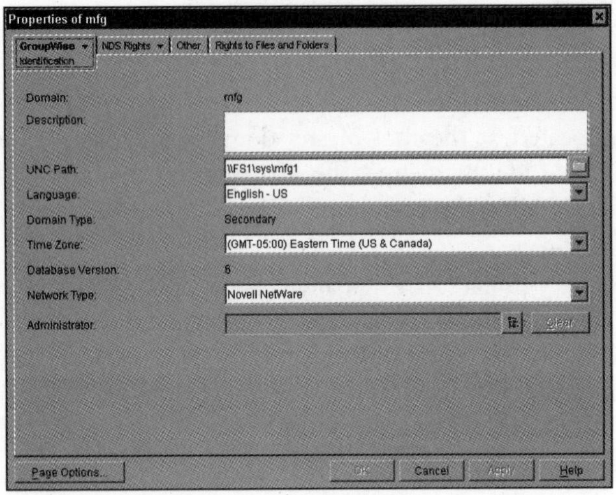

FIGURE 3.4 *The Domain Type for a Secondary Domain*

Understanding How a WPDOMAIN.DB File Changes and Increases in Size

As new objects and users are added to a GroupWise system, those objects are replicated to every WPDOMAIN.DB file in a GroupWise system. Deletions of objects are also replicated to every WPDOMAIN.DB file in a GroupWise system. The only two entities that write to a WPDOMAIN.DB file are the following:

- GroupWise administration snap-ins in ConsoleOne
- The *admin* thread of the GroupWise MTA

Suppose a GroupWise directory update message is sent from the CORP domain to the SALES domain. The administrator who makes the change is connected to the CORP domain, so GroupWise administration snap-ins write the changes to WPDOMAIN.DB for CORP. The CORP MTA sends the update to SALES. Now the SALES domain's MTA will be responsible for updating the SALES domain database (WPDOMAIN.DB) file.

Knowing the Role of Domain Databases and Information Replication

Ideally, each GroupWise domain database has a record for every object in the GroupWise system. When a GroupWise domain adds an object, it transmits a copy of that object to the primary domain, to be replicated to all other domains. Larger GroupWise systems are in a constant state of change. A change to a GroupWise object should take a short while to replicate to all other domains, but on a large system, "a short while" may mean 15 minutes or more.

This means that if for some reason one of your domain databases is damaged, you should recover it from tape backup or rebuild it, which is always done from the primary domain's database. Recovering a domain database from a backup tape that is more than a day old can result in serious synchronization problems with other domains.

Understanding the Directory Role of the Domain Database

The administration role of the WPDOMAIN.DB is to contain GroupWise objects in a database. With the help of GroupWise administration snap-ins, GroupWise objects in the WPDOMAIN.DB file can be created and modified. Whenever you administer your GroupWise system, GroupWise administration is connected to any one of the WPDOMAIN.DB files in your system. One WPDOMAIN.DB file exists for each domain. GroupWise administration allows you to connect to any one of your domains.

The GroupWise directory is a fully replicated directory. This means the following:

- Every object that **DOMAINA** has ownership of is replicated to DOMAINB and DOMAINC.
- Every object that **DOMAINB** has ownership of is replicated to DOMAINA and DOMAINC.
- Every object that **DOMAINC** has ownership of is replicated to DOMAINA and DOMAINB.

If GroupWise administration is connected to DOMAINA, you can still modify almost all of the objects that DOMAINB owns (as long as you have the NDS rights to that object). This process is explained in the section titled "Understanding Object Ownership." For those familiar with NDS, this object modification model may seem different. It is! The GroupWise replication model is different from NDS in these two ways:

- NDS uses a partitioned architecture. Although a server may contain NDS databases, the objects in those databases do not necessarily represent all the objects in an NDS tree.
- NDS allows that only servers with replicas of a particular partition are allowed to accept changes to the objects.

Understanding Object Ownership

Every user must be associated with a post office. Every GroupWise post office must be associated with a GroupWise domain. Consider the following scenario:

DOMAINA owns a post office called POST1, and POST1 has WESLEY JONES associated with it. In this scenario, you would say that

- DOMAINA owns POST1
- WESLEY JONES is associated with POST1
- DOMAINA must own the object WESLEY JONES

Ownership is an important role because it plays a key part in seeing that an object is properly synchronized across all domain databases (WPDOMAIN.DB files).

Understanding How GroupWise Objects Stay Synchronized

Only the GroupWise domain that owns a particular object can officially approve a change to an object. Another domain may propose a change to an object, but that proposal must be approved by the object's owning domain. Here's an example where the whole process of GroupWise directory changes is really drawn out.

Consider the following scenario: DOMAINB owns WESLEY JONES. The GroupWise administration snap-ins for ConsoleOne are connected to DOMAINC (a domain that does not own the object being modified) and changes the phone number on WESLEY JONES.

- DOMAINC — SECONDARY DOMAIN
  - Phone number changed on WESLEY JONES
  - The record for WESLEY JONES in DOMAINC's WPDOMAIN.DB file is changed from "safe" to "modify"
  - The proposed change is sent to DOMAINB by DOMAINC's MTA
  - The proposed change is viewable to the administrator while connected to DOMAINC by selecting Tools ➪ GroupWise System Operations ➪ Pending Operations
- DOMAINB — SECONDARY DOMAIN
  - DOMAINB's MTA receives the change information from DOMAINC and accepts the change and changes the user object's phone number in its WPDOMAIN.DB

- DOMAINB increments the *record version* of this object from version 1 ("version 1 was initial creation") to version 2. The fact that the record version value increments to "2" is not propagated to other domains.
- DOMAINB's MTA creates a message destined to the primary domain telling the primary about the change to object WESLEY JONES.
- DOMAINB's MTA creates a message destined for the post offices that it owns, indicating the change to object WESLEY JONES.

- DOMAINA — PRIMARY DOMAIN
  - DOMAINA's MTA receives from DOMAINB the change to object WESLEY JONES to its WPDOMAIN.DB
  - DOMAINA's MTA creates a message and sends this message to all other domains (except DOMAINB), telling all other domains to re-write this entire user object record with the information that the primary domain is sending about this object record.
  - DOMAINA's MTA creates a message and sends this message to each of its own post offices indicating the change to WESLEY JONES
- DOMAINC — SECONDARY DOMAIN
  - DOMAINC's MTA receives from DOMAINA, the change to object WESLEY JONES to its WPDOMAIN.DB
  - DOMAINC changes the record on object WESLEY JONES from "modify" to "safe"
  - DOMAINC sends a message to each of its own post offices indicating the change to the object WESLEY JONES
- ALL OTHER SECONDARY DOMAINS
  - DOMAINX's MTA receives from DOMAINA, the change to object WESLEY JONES to its WPDOMAIN.DB
  - DOMAINX's MTA sends a message to each of its own post offices indicating the change to object WESLEY JONES

From the preceding synchronization detail, the following conclusions can be drawn about how objects are synchronized to the GroupWise directory:

- If an administrator has NDS rights to do so, they can be connected to any domain in the system and modify objects associated with another domain.

- The only domain that can approve an object change is the domain that owns the object.
- The only domain that can propagate object changes to an entire GroupWise system is the GroupWise primary domain.
- Each domain is responsible for propagating directory changes to the post offices that it owns.

Knowing the Agent Information Role of the Domain Database

When a GroupWise MTA loads, it must be "pointed at" the root of the domain directory, which contains the WPDOMAIN.DB file. The WPDOMAIN.DB file provides three basic types of information for the MTA:

- **Configuration information:** When to connect, how many threads to load, and so on
- **Link information:** How to establish a connection with the other domains on the system
- **Routing information:** Discovering the correct route to use to send messages to their destination

The MTA specifically reads the MTA object record associated with the domain that the MTA is pointed to. Under Tools ➪ GroupWise Diagnostics ➪ General Edit, this record is found in the Message Transfer Agents by domain section.

The other processes that access the WPDOMAIN.DB file directly are the GroupWise Internet agent (GWIA), WebAccess, and the various GroupWise gateways. They all need the same basic kinds of information:

- **Configuration information:** When to connect, how many threads to load, and so on
- **Addressing information:** Looking up users to deliver inbound mail to them

The Role of the GroupWise Post Office Database

Every GroupWise post office must have a WPHOST.DB file. The WPHOST.DB file for a post office provides the following:

- The GroupWise client address book
- Lots of information for the GroupWise client and POA that isn't readily apparent to an end user

How a WPHOST.DB File Is Created

A GroupWise WPHOST.DB file is created when a post office is created. The WPHOST.DB file is created by the following:

- Information from the WPDOMAIN.DB file of the GroupWise domain that owns the post office
- The dictionary file called GWPO.DC located in all GroupWise domain and post office directories

How a WPHOST.DB File Is Modified

When a change needs to be replicated down to a post office, the domain MTA for the domain that owns the post office needing the replication sends the object update information to the POA servicing the post office. The POA has an admin thread that updates the WPHOST.DB file with the change.

The only entity that updates a WPHOST.DB file is the GroupWise POA. This is different from how a WPDOMAIN.DB file is modified. The WPDOMAIN.DB file is modified by the GroupWise MTA and by GroupWise administration. So when an administrator makes changes that affect GroupWise, those changes are written to the WPDOMAIN.DB that GroupWise administration is connected to. The administrator's workstation actually commits those changes to the GroupWise WPDOMAIN.DB. In the case of post offices, an administrator's workstation never touches the WPHOST.DB file. The only time an administrator's workstation touches a WPHOST.DB file is when the administrator uses Tools ⇨ GroupWise Utilities ⇨ System Maintenance routines on a post office.

Understanding the Contents of a WPHOST.DB File

A WPHOST.DB file is not a mirror of the entire GroupWise system. There are records related to domains that do not need to be replicated to a WPHOST.DB file. Because the WPHOST.DB file is not a general depository file like the WPDOMAIN.DB file, the content of a WPHOST.DB file is far tighter than a WPDOMAIN.DB file.

Using the WPHOST.DB as an Address Book

When users go into the GroupWise address book and access the Novell GroupWise Address Book tab, they are accessing information contained in the WPHOST.DB file. The information accessible in any of the other tabs of the GroupWise address book is not contained in the WPHOST.DB file.

Using the WPHOST.DB File for Identity Purposes

The WPHOST.DB file is read by the GroupWise client in order to help the GroupWise client to create an appropriate environment for the end user. The

WPHOST.DB file helps the client and the POA to identify which USERXXX.DB file in the message store is the end-user's database. The WPHOST.DB file helps to hold administrator-defined settings that control how GroupWise preferences are to be configured. A WPHOST.DB file has a hidden password within it, that password is given to all databases below a post office. The password read from the WPHOST. DB file helps a GroupWise POA gain access to all the other message store databases off of a post office.

What the WPHOST.DB File Provides to the POA

The POA reads its configuration information from the WPHOST.DB file. So when a POA is configured in ConsoleOne, those changes are replicated down to the WPHOST.DB file for the POA to read.

The POA discovers many other things from the WPHOST.DB. Some of these are the following:

- The administrator for the domain that owns this post office, which is important so that problems can be reported by the POA to the administrator.
- The IP addresses and ports of the POAs that services the other post offices in the GroupWise system. This helps when a POA needs to hand a user off to another post office so that it can proxy into a user's e-mail on a different post office.
- The names of all mail recipients (users and resources), gateways, domains, and post offices. This way if a user types in an incorrect name, the POA can immediately tell the user of the error.
- The TCP/IP port and address of the domain MTA that owns this post office.

Summary

The GroupWise directory is a fully replicated directory. All objects are broadcast to all other GroupWise domains. The GroupWise directory is separate from NDS but integrated with NDS to use the administration strengths of NDS.

CHAPTER 4

Understanding the GroupWise Information Store

The GroupWise information store consists of messages in post offices and documents in libraries. The GroupWise information store follows a *distributed* or *partitioned* model, in which different store files contain different portions of the entire store.

This chapter looks at these store files individually. It also details their relationships with each other and considers the information store as a whole, spanning multiple post offices. The objective of this chapter is to help you understand GroupWise architecture well enough to effectively troubleshoot your system. The concepts discussed here in Chapter 4 will be applied in Part IV and Part V, and especially in Chapter 17.

Identifying Components of the Post Office Directory Structure

The information store is entirely contained in the post office directory and its subdirectories. If you have more than one post office, then your information store spans post offices, with each local store containing items particular to the users belonging to that post office.

Figure 4.1 shows a post office directory.

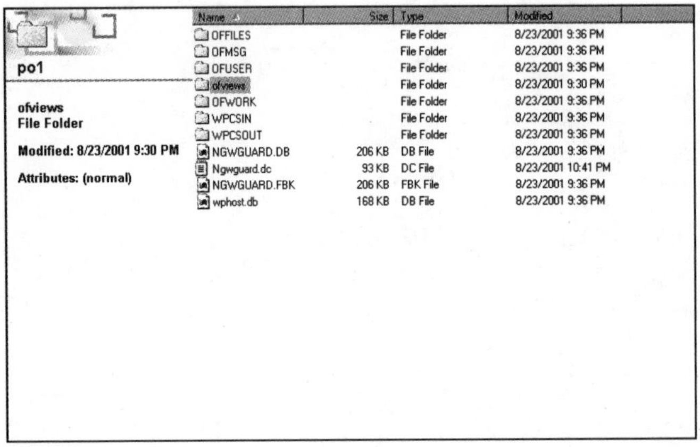

FIGURE 4.1 *Post Office Directory Structure as Viewed through Windows Explorer*

There are four types of directories here to focus on. These are:

- Input and output queues
- The OFUSER and OFMSG directories
- The OFFILES directories
- The GWDMS directory structure

How Input and Output Queues Are Used

There are three different queue directory structures in a GroupWise post office. These queues store message files that are coming into the post office from another location, or that are outbound to another location.

The WPCSIN Directory

This directory, shown in Figure 4.2, whether you see it at the post office level or under a domain directory, always does the same thing. It is the input queue for a GroupWise MTA.

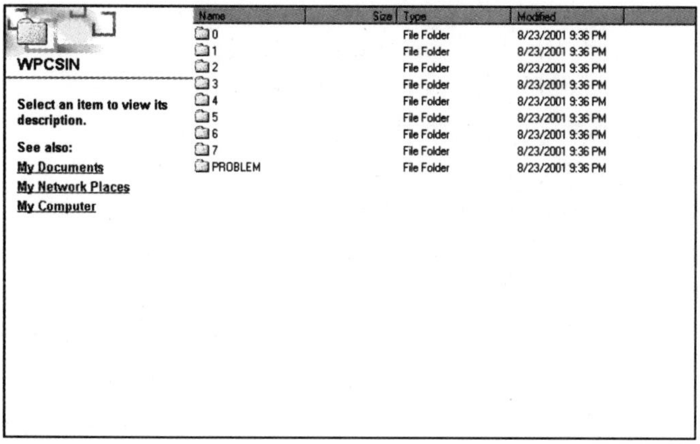

FIGURE 4.2 *The WPCSIN Directory under a GroupWise Post Office*

The 0-7 directories under WPCSIN hold message transport files that need to be transferred to another location (domain, post office, or gateway) by the GroupWise MTA. This means all the files here are outbound messages, from the perspective of the post office.

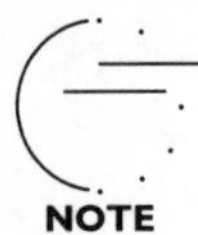
NOTE

Remember, the naming convention here is a holdover from the old WordPerfect Office days. This directory name is really an abbreviation for WordPerfect Connection Server INput.

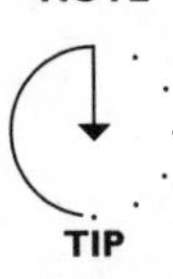
TIP

The queue directories were named from the perspective of the MTA. So no matter what level you see the WPCSIN or WPCSOUT directories, think of their functions from the perspective of the MTA. Hence, the WPCSIN directory at the post office level is the MTA's input queue, and the WPCSOUT directory is the MTA's output directory.

Aside from the 0-7 queues, you may see a PROBLEM directory. This directory is for files that could not be processed for some reason, with the exception of files that could not be processed because a link was down. These files go into a holding queue elsewhere.

The 0-7 Directory

Following is an explanation of the subdirectories of WPCSIN. Each of these numbered directories serves a different purpose.

0: Live, interactive request messages (busy searches, remote library queries, agent restart)
1: GroupWise remote mode, mailbox synchronization requests
2: Administration updates and high-priority mail messages
3: Status messages from high-priority mail
4: Normal priority mail messages
5: Status messages from normal priority mail
6: Low priority mail messages
7: Status messages from low priority mail

You will find these directories in many places on the GroupWise system. Everywhere you find them, the queue assignments for each directory remain the same.

The WPCSOUT Directory

You should now be able to guess at the meaning behind the name of this directory! Here it is: **W**ord**P**erfect **C**onnection **S**erver **OUT**put. This directory, shown in Figure 4.3, contains things that the MTA (long, long ago known as the *connection server*) has dropped off. This directory contains messages that are inbound for the post office.

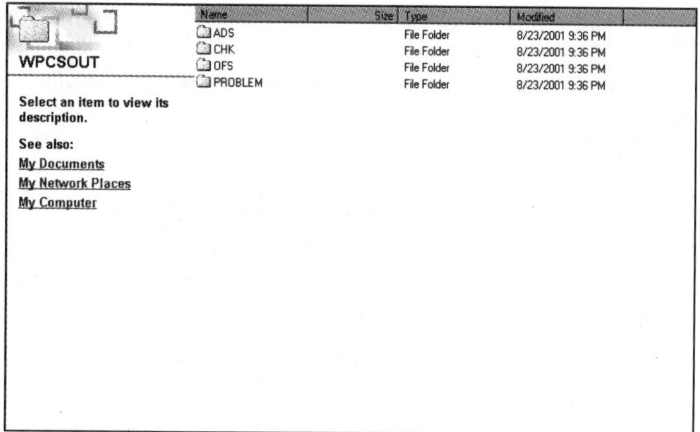

FIGURE 4.3 *The WPCSOUT Directory under a GroupWise Post Office*

There are four subdirectories off of WPCSOUT: ADS, CHK, OFS, and PROBLEM. The ADS, CHK, and OFS directories contain the familiar 0-7 queues. The CHK directory is new to GroupWise 6. It only has directories 0-3 and the DEFER directory.

- ADS: Administration updates
- CHK: GWCHECK jobs sent to the POA
- OFS: Information store updates (user e-mail, notes, tasks, and so on)
- PROBLEM: Where problem messages go

Remember, though, that these are queues. User e-mail does not exist in the OFS/0–7 structure for very long. It gets dropped there by the MTA, or by the POA's MTP thread, and then the POA moves it into the information store.

The OFWORK Directory

Finally, there is the OFWORK directory. In previous versions of GroupWise, this directory had more subdirectories, because it was used for more than it is used for now. In GroupWise 6, it only has the OFDIRECT subdirectory.

The OFWORK/OFDIRECT directory is used by the GroupWise remote client. Queue directories are created for each remote user, and these directories serve as input and output queues for remote requests, which then move through the WPCSIN\1 or WPCSOUT\OFS\1 directories for processing.

NOTE

The GroupWise 5.5 enhancement pack and GroupWise 6 versions use this OFWORK\OFDIRECT directory much less now when the GroupWise client is in remote mode. Updated remote technology (live remote) bypasses this directory most of the time, which facilitates much quicker access for remote users.

The Function of the OFUSER and OFMSG Directories

The core of the GroupWise information store is found in the OFUSER and OFMSG directories. These directories contain the user and message databases in which all mail items are stored as database records. The section of this chapter titled "Understanding the Core of the Messaging System" covers the user and message databases.

The Purpose of the OFFILES Directories

In most GroupWise systems, the majority of the disk space (often up to 80 percent) that is used by the information store is actually used by attachment files and BLOB files (*B*inary *L*arge *OB*jects) in the OFFILES directory structure. The OFFILES directory has up to 248 subdirectories, hexadecimally numbered. Figure 4.4 shows an OFFILES directory structure.

OFFILES

Select an item to view its description.

See also:
My Documents
My Network Places
My Computer

FD0 FD1 FD10 FD11 FD12 FD13 FD14 FD15 FD16 FD17 FD18 FD19 FD1A FD1B FD1C FD1D FD1E FD1F FD2 FD20 FD21 FD22 FD23 FD24 FD25
FD26 FD27 FD28 FD29 FD2A FD2B FD2C FD2D FD2E FD2F FD3 FD30 FD31 FD32 FD33 FD34 FD35 FD36 FD37 FD38 FD39 FD3A FD3B FD3C FD3D
FD3E FD3F FD4 FD40 FD41 FD42 FD43 FD44 FD45 FD46 FD47 FD48 FD49 FD4A FD4B FD4C FD4D FD4E FD4F FD5 FD50 FD51 FD52 FD53 FD54
FD55 FD56 FD57 FD58 FD59 FD5A FD5B FD5C FD5D FD5E FD5F FD6 FD60 FD61 FD62 FD63 FD64 FD65 FD66 FD67 FD68 FD69 FD6A FD6B FD6C
FD6D FD6E FD6F FD7 FD70 FD71 FD72 FD73 FD74 FD75 FD76 FD77 FD78 FD79 FD7A FD7B FD7C FD7D FD7E FD7F FD8 FD80 FD81 FD82 FD83

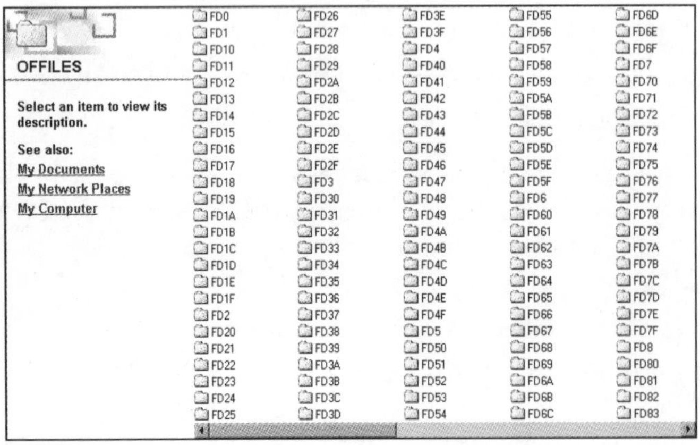

FIGURE 4.4 *The OFFILES Directory Structure Found under a GroupWise Post Office*

Storing Libraries in the GWDMS Directory Structure

The GWDMS (GroupWise document management system) directory and its subdirectories are the home for any GroupWise libraries that have been created under this post office.

In Figure 4.5, two library subdirectories have been expanded to illustrate the deeper structure. More discussion about the files found in this directory under the GroupWise document management system is in the section titled "Understanding the Structure of the GroupWise Document Management System."

For now, though, look at the DOCS directory, shown in Figure 4.6, and see what's there:

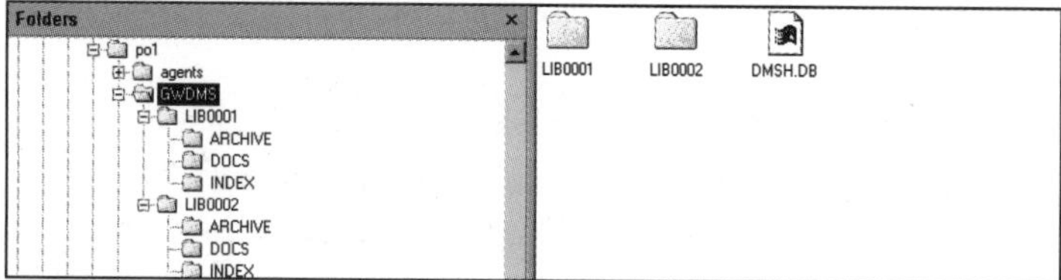

FIGURE 4.5 *The GWDMS Directory Structure Found under a GroupWise Post Office*

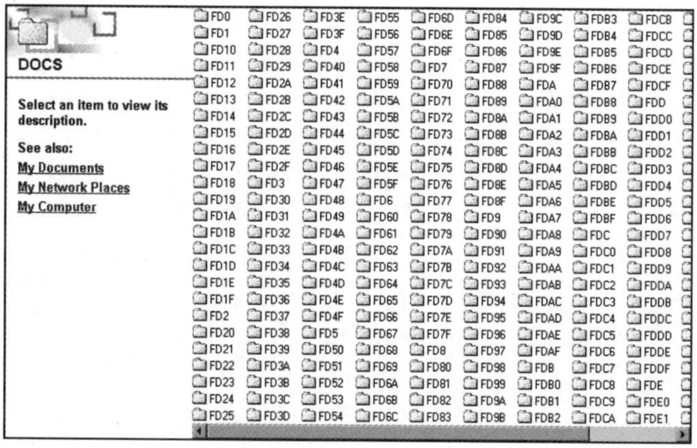

FIGURE 4.6 *The DOCS Directory Structure Found under a GroupWise Library*

Note that this structure looks very similar to the structure found beneath OFFILES. The numbering scheme for these 255 subdirectories is the same, and just like OFFILES, these directories contain binary large objects. In the DOCS directory, though, each BLOB file corresponds to a document in a GroupWise library.

Understanding the Core of the Messaging System

The exploration of the post office directory structure earlier in this chapter glossed over the relationships between the various files found. This section covers these relationships in detail.

What Is Contained in the User Database

Each and every user mailbox in the GroupWise system is assigned to a unique user database. These files are found in the OFUSER directory. They follow the naming convention USERxxx.DB, where *xxx* is replaced with the three-character file ID for the user.

NOTE

Customers who have migrated from WordPerfect Office days may on occasion have users with a two-character file ID.

This *file ID*, or *FID*, is alphanumeric, which means that you can have up to 46,656 uniquely named user databases on each GroupWise post office. The FID must be unique at the post office level, but no such restrictions exist system-wide. Users are also assigned a *globally unique ID*, or *GUID*, to ensure uniqueness system-wide, but this string is far too long to be conveniently used as part of a filename.

Understanding the Contents of a User Database

The user database contains the following types of records:

- Pointers
- Personal Items
- Personal Address Books
- Preferences

Pointers

When you open a user mailbox, you will see a list of folders, and in each folder you will see different items. What you are looking at here are simply database records. Each item record contains enough data to make the display meaningful, but the item itself usually exists in a different database. The item records found in the user database serve as *pointers* to the items in message databases.

There are also special pointers, called *document references,* that point to records in GroupWise libraries.

Personal Items

Some items are completely contained in the user database, however. These *posted* or *personal* items do not have recipients or senders. Personal notes, tasks, and appointments, as well as posted discussion items in shared folders, fall into this category.

Personal Address Books

Addresses that users enter, and groups that users create, exist in the *personal address books.* One such book is the *frequent contacts list,* which is populated automatically with the addresses of individuals you send mail to.

Preferences

Many user settings and preferences are kept in the user database. These include rules, send options, button bars, proxies, signature options, and the user password. Other settings, such as window positions, are kept in the Windows registry.

What Is Contained in the Message Databases

On every GroupWise post office, you find up to 25 message databases. These files follow the naming convention MSGn.DB, where *n* is a number from 0 to 24. Message databases contain group items — items that have been sent from one user to another user or users.

When a message is delivered to a user, that user gets a pointer in his/her user database pointing to the actual message item record in a message database. When a user reads a subject line from the Mailbox folder, the text comes from the item record in the user database. When that user double-clicks on the message to open it, the pointer is followed, and the resulting window is populated from the appropriate item record in a message database.

Understanding the User Database/ Message Database Relationship

When a GroupWise user sends a message, the complete item record is first written to the sender's message database. Next, a pointer is written to the sender's user database. This shows up as a sent item. If the message was sent to a user in the same post office as the sender, then the recipient's user database gets a pointer to the message, which exists in the message database. If the recipient exists in a post office different than the sender's, then when the message arrives at the destination, it is written first to the same message database as the sender's, then the destination user's user database receives a pointer to the local message database.

Every message a user sends will be written to the same message database. Each user is assigned to a message database for sending based on the user FID. This means that the 46,656 possible FIDs map down to 25 possible message databases.

Item records in message databases contain all data pertaining to that item, including status information — when it was delivered, opened, deleted, or any other action performed against it. If items are attached to a message, they will also be included as part of that item record, unless the item is larger than 2K. Attachments, message bodies, or other item fields that exceed 2048 bytes in length are written as separate records called *binary large objects* (*BLOBs*).

Understanding Binary Large Objects (BLOB Files)

In the OFFILES directory, there are 248 subdirectories. Each of these may contain binary large object files. These BLOB files are stand-alone records. They are referenced as records by pointers in user and message databases, and they contain any field data for item record fields that exceed 2048 bytes in length. Following are just a few examples of how your BLOB files are created:

- **With attachments:** If you attach a 2MB file to a mail message, you end up creating a BLOB file in the OFFILES structure, as well as a message record in your assigned message database. If your attachment is less than 2K, however (say, a 1000-byte autoexec.bat file), the attachment is encoded as a field in that message record, and it exists entirely within your assigned message database.
- **With long messages:** If you type a ten-page message and send it, your mail item exists as a record in the message database you are assigned to, but the text of that message is now in a BLOB file somewhere in the OFFILES structure.

- **With multiple addressees:** If you address a message to every user in your company, your TO: field will very likely exceed 2048 bytes in length. Thus, your message record will exist in your assigned message database, but the distribution list for that message will be in a BLOB file.

BLOB files are given hexadecimal names with alphanumeric extensions. They are encrypted using GroupWise's native 40-bit encryption, and they are compressed as well. BLOB files in the OFFILES structure cannot be read independently; they must be opened by following the appropriate item pointers via the GroupWise client.

Understanding the Purpose of the Deferred Message Database

In the OFMSG directory, there is a 26th message database, used for delayed delivery messages and for special item lists used by the system when GroupWise mailboxes are moved between post offices. This file is named NGWDFR.DB, and is called the *deferred message database.*

There are two different operations a user can perform that will result in records being written to this database:

- Sending a message with Delayed delivery checked
- Sending a message with Expiration date checked.

Both of these options may be checked for individual items from the File ➪ Properties menu of the item. These settings may be made for all items by going to Tools ➪ Options ➪ Send in the GroupWise client.

Delayed Delivery

When delayed messages are sent, GroupWise must write to three places:

- **Message database:** The message database assigned to this user for send operations gets the item record.
- **User database (of the sender):** The user database gets a pointer, as usual.
- **Deferred message database:** NGWDFR.DB gets a pointer to that item record, along with a date indicating when the item should be delivered to its recipients.

Messages with Expiration Dates

When a message is sent with an expiration date, it is sent normally. That is, records exist in the sender's user database, the recipient's user database, and the sender's assigned message database. An additional record is placed in

NGWDFR.DB: a pointer to the message database record, along with the date that record should be deleted if it has not yet been opened by the recipient.

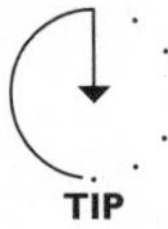

Although you can set expiration date options globally, this is a very poor way to try to manage mailbox size. Expired items are only deleted if they are unread, and the NGWDFR.DB database file will grow to be quite large if it must keep track of every message sent.

Understanding How Prime User Databases Are Made

To explain the function of a prime user database try to think of variables in high-school algebra.

A prime variable is one that represents a new iteration of the original variable. A prime user database is a new iteration of the original user database, containing only a subset of the contents of that original database.

Now, if you are not mathematically inclined, that example may not work. Here's an approach to the prime user database in terms of functionality.

When a user shares a folder or address book with a user on another post office, a prime user database will be created on that post office. This database will contain any shared folders or address books the user has shared with anyone on that post office.

The items that go into a shared folder will be written either to the appropriate message database on the sharee's post office, or, in the case of personal and posted discussion items, will be written directly to the prime user database.

Prime user databases cannot be named the same way user databases are. On large systems, the ability to create uniquely-named databases would be compromised. Thus, they are named as follows: "PUnnnnnn.DB," where "nnnnnn" is a six-digit number. This number is in two-byte hexadecimal pairs, beginning with 020101.

The first shared folder to arrive at a post office will arrive in PU020101.DB, regardless of which user shared the folder. The next user who shares a folder or an address book with that post office will end up creating PU020102.DB.

Remember, though, that PU databases are only created for folders or address books that are shared across post offices. If they are shared with users on the same post office only, they will be accessed through the sharing user's USERxxx.DB file.

Using the Mailbox Index to Find Mailbox Items

Every item on the GroupWise system is full-text indexed. This allows the powerful Find feature of the GroupWise client to locate items in your mailbox, even if you have forgotten which folder you filed them in. This full-text index is created by the post office agent during the QuickFinder Indexing process.

There are actually two sets of indexes in a GroupWise post office. The *mailbox index* is found in OFUSER/INDEX. There is a *library index* as well, which will be discussed a little later in this chapter.

In the OFUSER/INDEX directory, there are two types of files:

- ***.IDX:** These are the *permanent index files.* They are updated and renamed at the end of each day. There is typically one of these for each user mailbox.
- ***.INC:** These are the *incremental index files.* They are created during each QuickFinder Indexing run, and at the end of each day they are appended to the appropriate *.IDX files.

The names of these files are based on the time they were created or updated. The filenames are in hexadecimal format, so the file 000000F1.INC was created before the file 000000FF.INC. Index files are discussed further when GroupWise document management is fully explained in Chapter 14.

Keeping Track of Databases with the Guardian Database

With all the various files floating around in a GroupWise post office directory, a central naming authority is required. The NGWGUARD.DB file, or the *guardian database,* is the central naming authority. This file contains a catalog of every database in the GroupWise information store on this post office. Any process that needs to work with a GroupWise database must first hook into the guardian database.

Because NGWGUARD.DB represents a potential single-point-of-failure, the GroupWise post office agent backs this file up each time it loads, as well as at midnight. Here's how the process works:

1. The POA loads and checks the structure of NGWGUARD.DB.

   If it checks out okay, go to step 5.
2. The POA renames the bad NGWGUARD.DB to NGWGUARD.DBA.
3. The POA copies the last backup, NGWGUARD.FBK, to NGWGUARD.DB.
4. The POA writes all transactions from NGWGUARD.RFL (the guardian roll-forward log) to NGWGUARD.DB.

   The POA now has a clean NGWGUARD.DB, with all transactions made since the last backup rolled back into it.

5. The POA copies NGWGUARD.DB to NGWGUARD.FBK and to OFMSG\GUARDBAK\NGWGUARD.FBK
6. Delete NGWGUARD.RFL and create a fresh, blank version of this file.
7. When changes are made to NGWGUARD.DB, write these changes to NGWGUARD.RFL.

   This is how the changes between guardian backups are stored for recovery.

Exploring the User and Message Database Relationship

It may be helpful at this point to illustrate the way the user and message databases work together, as in Figure 4.7.

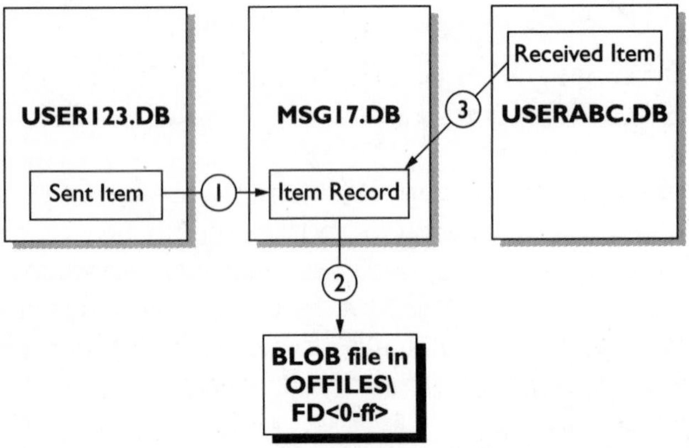

FIGURE 4.7 *The Relationship between User and Message Databases*

In the example in Figure 4.7, the user assigned to USER123.DB has sent a message to another user. USER123.DB is assigned to send through MSG17.DB, and has sent to USERABC.DB. The following numbers correspond to the numbered arrows in Figure 4.7:

- **1:** In the USER123.DB file, there is a record for a sent item. This record has a pointer to the message item record in MSG17.DB.

- **2:** In MSG17.DB, there is an item record that was created by USER123. This item contains an attachment that is larger than 2048 bytes, so that attachment data is written to a BLOB file. The item record contains a pointer to this BLOB file in the OFFILES directory structure.
- **3:** In USERABC.DB, there is a record for the item received from USER123. This record contains a pointer to the message item record in MSG17.

From this simplified illustration, you should be able to see that even if a dozen users on a post office have a copy of a message in their in-box, that message record exists only once in the appropriate message database. Similarly, an attachment sent to several people is written to only one BLOB file.

Understanding the Structure of the GroupWise Document Management System

If a GroupWise post office has no libraries, then the GroupWise document management system (GWDMS) directory will not contain any data. Once libraries have been created, though, the structure beneath GWDMS becomes fairly complex.

Shared Document Management Services Database (DMSH)

This file, DMSH.DB, exists at the root of the GWDMS directory structure. It contains lookup tables for document type and other administrator-defined document property fields, as well as a list of the libraries defined under this post office. It does not contain any document data, but it is critical to the functionality of the document management system on this post office.

Library Directories and Naming Conventions

Regardless of what you name your library, the library directories created under the GWDMS directory follow a numeric naming convention, beginning with LIB0001 and hexadecimally numbered through LIB00FF.

The last two characters of the directory name become the *library number.* This number is used throughout the library directory structure for the naming of files found in library directories.

Notice in Figure 4.8 that the last two characters of every file in the LIB0001 directory are 01 (excluding the .DB extensions, of course). Here's a look at these databases in turn.

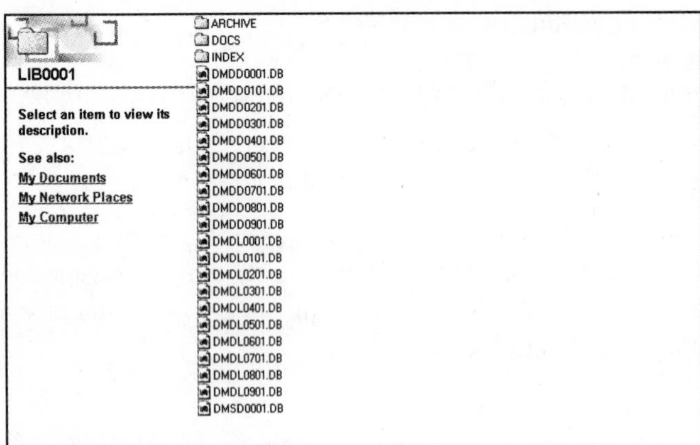

FIGURE 4.8 *The Library Directory Name Is Reflected in the Name of Each of the Files Contained Therein*

Library Database

DMSD00xx.DB is the library database, where *xx* is replaced with the 2-digit hexadecimal library number. This database contains the table of document numbers, as well as property-sheet field layout information for this library. It contains no document data but is critical to the function of the library.

Document Properties Database (DMDD)

There are ten document properties database files. They should be treated as a single database that has been partitioned into ten files. The naming convention is DMDDppxx.DB, where *pp* is replaced by the partition number 00 through 09, and *xx* is replaced by the library number.

The document properties database contains all information entered into document property sheets. This includes document subject, author, type, associated application, and much more. The property sheet is one of the key benefits to the GroupWise document management system, because it allows information about the document to be stored and searched for independently of the document itself, while maintaining a relationship to the document.

Each document record contains three kinds of pointers. The first is to the document BLOB file (discussed later in this chapter in the section, "Document BLOB Files"). The second is to the document's activity log (discussed in the next section). The third pointer points to any user database that contains a document reference to this document. This pointer is used to provide the mailbox indexing process with a word-list file for this document. In this way, a search for full-text of the document returns the document reference, even if the user did not specify a search of GroupWise libraries.

The last digit of the document number indicates in which DMDD partition the document's property sheet record resides. For example, document 1762 in this library is referenced in DMDD0201.DB, and document 21265's properties are in DMDD0501.DB.

Document Logging Database (DMDL)

There are also ten document logging database files. Again, they should be treated as a single database spread across ten partitions. The naming convention is DMDLppxx.DB, where *pp* is the partition number 00 through 09, and *xx* is the library number.

The document logging database contains all activity logs for documents in the GroupWise libraries. Any action that affects a document is logged in this database, including opening, closing, viewing, downloading, uploading, and deleting. Also recorded in the DMDL files is the file name for the document BLOB upon which the logged action was performed. When a document is viewed, the BLOB filename does not change, but any action that changes document content (closing it and, hence, checking it back in with possible changes) results in a new BLOB file being created.

Document BLOB Files

Although the DOCS directory structure is very similar to OFFILES, the contents of the 255 DOCS subdirectories are very different from the OFFILES BLOBs.

Document BLOB files are created for every document, regardless of document size. While OFFILES BLOBs are only created when field data exceeds 2048 bytes in length, document BLOBs are created for even a 0-byte document.

Word-List Files There is another kind of BLOB in the DOCS subdirectories. *Word-list files* are created for each document when that document is indexed. These files contain, as their name suggests, a list of every word in that document. These files are used to build the .INC files (incremental index files), and are also used to provide mailbox indexes with the full-text information for any document references they may contain.

Document Compression Document BLOB files are encrypted and compressed, just like OFFILES BLOBs, but they contain information that allows them to be manually opened by certain GroupWise users. The GroupWise client can read a BLOB file directly and determine if the GroupWise user is supposed to have access to this BLOB (a user with the manage right for this library, or a user who has edited the document in the past). If the user is cleared for the document, it will be re-imported, and a new BLOB and property sheet created. This may be useful for restoring documents that have been deleted, but whose BLOB files exist on backup media.

Document BLOB files are typically about 50 percent smaller than the documents would be in their native formats. Pure text documents may be reduced to 10 percent of their original size, while compressed graphic formats (such as GIF or JPEG documents) may not be reduced at all.

Document Index

All documents are full-text indexed. This is another selling point of GroupWise document management as a solution for document storage. Documents may be found using the GroupWise client to search for words they contain, or for field data recorded in their property sheets.

Inside the INDEX subdirectory, there are ten active and permanent index files. These files have an .IDX extension. There are also many .INC files, containing the incremental indexes. Just like the mailbox index, the document index is created by the POA QuickFinder Indexing process. The .INC files are created from the word-list BLOB files discussed earlier. At the end of the day, all .INC file content is written into the .IDX files, and the .IDX filenames are updated.

Exploring Document Reference Relationships

It may now be helpful to look at the diagram in Figure 4.9 that explores the relationships between the various GroupWise information store databases when document references are being employed.

The following is a discussion of Figure 4.9:

- The user assigned to USER123.DB creates a document in a GroupWise library. It is the ninth document created in this library, and it has been assigned document number 9.
- This library is the first one created on this post office, and it is in the LIB0001 directory.
- USER123 has also created a document reference, a pointer in his Documents folder allowing him to quickly find document number 9.
- USER123 attaches this document reference to a mail message and sends it to another user.

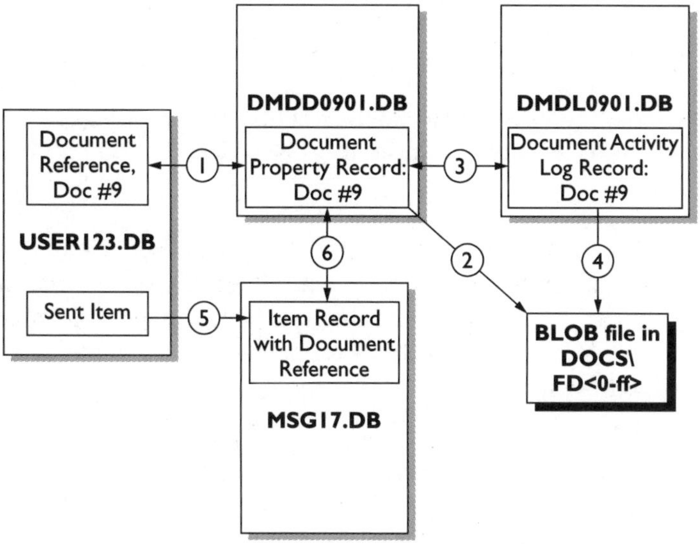

FIGURE 4.9 *The Complex System of Pointers Created When Document References Are Employed*

The following numbered items correspond to the numbered arrows in Figure 4.9.

- **1:** The document reference is a pointer to the document property record. The document property record has a back link to this document reference (the arrow points both ways). Because this is document number 9, library 1, its property sheet is in DMDD0901.DB.
- **2:** The document property record has a pointer to the actual document BLOB file in the DOCS directory structure.
- **3:** The document property record has a pointer to the activity log record for this document. The activity log has a back link to the property record (again, the arrow points both ways).
- **4:** The activity log record for this document is in DMDL0901.DB, because this is document number 9 in library 1. This record has a pointer to the BLOB file for this document.
- **5:** When the user sends the document reference, a message item record is created in MSG17.DB. USER123.DB has a pointer to this item record.

- **6:** The item record in MSG17.DB contains a document reference, which means it has a pointer to the document property record in DMDD0901.DB. That document property record has a back link to MSG17.DB.

NOTE

For simplicity's sake, the recipient's mailbox is not shown in Figure 4.9. That mailbox would have only a pointer to MSG17.DB for the received item.

As you can see, the document property record "knows" more about this document than any other database or record shown. When the POA needs to index this document, it reads this property record to find all document references and makes sure that the word list generated for this document is accessible when the mailboxes containing those references are indexed.

Summary

The GroupWise information store employs a mixture of strategies. Partitioning is used on user mailboxes so that message items are not unnecessarily replicated. A different sort of partitioning is used on document property and activity databases, in order to keep these files at manageable sizes even on large libraries. A third type of partitioning is used for document files and for long strings of field data; the binary large object files can be considered partitions of the message databases or the document databases, depending on their content.

Replication is used across post offices. Shared folders and address books are replicated to prevent unnecessary network utilization when users access these items. Messages sent between post offices are replicated once per post office, again, so users reading these messages do not need to open client/server connections to the sender's post office.

This replication across post offices is managed through database record numbers (DRNs) and globally unique identifiers (GUIDs). Items replicated to other post offices are linked back to the original item record. When users get moved, or folders get shared, and another copy of an item ends up on a post office, the duplicate DRN or GUID tells the delivery process to create a pointer to the existing item, instead of writing the item again.

PART II

Using the Administration Interface

CHAPTER 5

Working with GroupWise Objects

ConsoleOne is the tool you use for most of your GroupWise administration. This chapter looks at how some of the GroupWise entities — domains, post offices, and so on — are represented as objects in ConsoleOne.

Calling Up the GroupWise View

From ConsoleOne, access GroupWise View by doing the following:

1. Choose Edit ➪ Preferences.
2. Check the Show View Title option.

   By doing this, it is easy to distinguish when you are in GroupWise View.
3. Now select the GroupWise System icon, which displays the window shown in Figure 5.1.

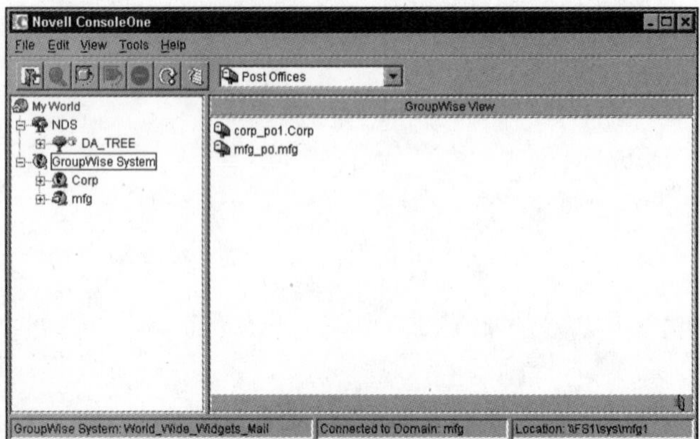

FIGURE 5.1 *The GroupWise View*

This window displays your GroupWise system and does so in a way that clearly illustrates the relationships between domains, gateways, post offices, and other objects. The window is divided into two side-by-side panes.

The System pane, on the left in Figure 5.1, displays the GroupWise System and the domains and post offices. The display follows the GroupWise domain and post office hierarchy: domain icons are at the first level, and post offices are at the second level.

The Object pane, on the right in Figure 5.1, displays all possible GroupWise objects, including domains and post offices. Because all GroupWise objects must be owned by either a domain or a post office, these objects are only viewable on the Object pane on the right.

Filtering the GroupWise View

The Object pane cannot display all types of GroupWise objects at once, however. An object filter drop-down menu determines the types of objects that are viewable.

The drop-down filter shown in Figure 5.2 provides up to ten types of filters for easily maneuvering between GroupWise objects.

FIGURE 5.2 *The GroupWise View Drop-Down Filter*

Creating GroupWise Objects

Creating objects in GroupWise 6 is much easier than it was in previous versions of GroupWise. It used to be that you had to go over to the NDS view of the tree in order to create most GroupWise objects. This is no longer the case. You can create GroupWise objects, especially user objects, from either the GroupWise View or the NDS View in ConsoleOne.

To create a GroupWise object from the GroupWise View, do the following:

1. Highlight the GroupWise System, or a domain or post office, click the right mouse button, and select New.

   For example, you may want to create a new user and immediately associate that user with the CORP_PO1 post office.
2. Select the CORP_PO1 post office, and click the right-mouse button.
3. From the New menu item, select User.
4. Proceed through the object-specific dialogs.

Viewing the Domain Object

If you highlight a domain, right-mouse click, and select Properties, you get a window such as the one shown in Figure 5.3.

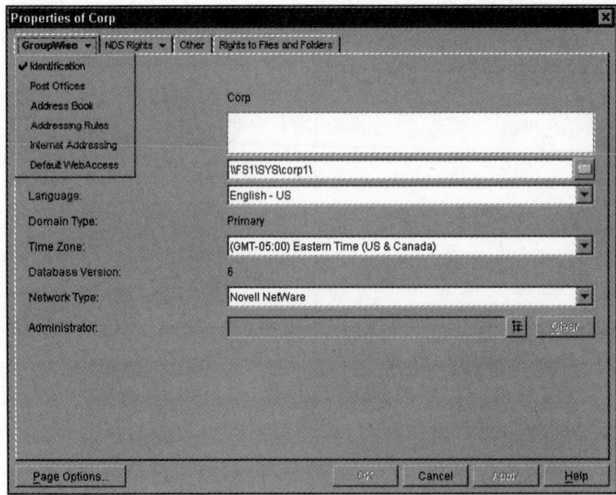

FIGURE 5.3 *The Domain Object Properties Window*

The domain object properties window has six properties pages, selectable by clicking on the word on the GroupWise tab. These properties pages are the following:

- Identification
- Post Offices
- Address Book
- Addressing Rules
- Internet Addressing
- Default WebAccess

The following sections offer a discussion of each of these pages in turn.

The Domain Information Property Page

This page displays all the general information about this domain. There are nine fields, as shown in Figure 5.3, but only six of them may be edited.

- **Domain:** The domain name may not be changed once the domain has been created. If naming conventions at your organization require you to change a domain name, you must create a new domain by that name and move users to it. Refer to Chapter 13 for more information.
- **Description:** The optional text you place in this field may be used to help other administrators contact you. This text is never visible to users, or from the server console.
- **UNC Path:** This field should be populated with the Universal Naming Convention (UNC) path to the domain database for this domain. The syntax for a UNC path is `\\<server name>\<volume>\<path to domain database>`. When you use the System Connection tool to switch domains (more fully covered in Chapter 6), ConsoleOne requires the UNC path value.
- **Language:** This drop-down menu is populated with the available languages.
- **Domain Type:** A domain that is part of your GroupWise system will show either as Primary or Secondary (and only one domain will be the primary!). Domains belonging to other systems that your system sends messages to will show as External or perhaps Foreign.
- **Time Zone:** This field is populated from a drop-down menu containing all of the widely recognized time zones worldwide. This field is critical if your organization spans multiple time zones, or if you share e-mail with organizations in other time zones.

- **Database Version:** In this field, you see 4.1, 5.0, 5.5, or 6. The 4.1 identifies a GroupWise 4.1 domain. The 5.0 value applies to any version of GroupWise 5.0, 5.1, or 5.2. If a domain is running GroupWise 5.5 or GroupWise 5.5 Enhancement Pack, this field reads 5.5. For a GroupWise 6 domain, this field reads 6. This field is important to keep an eye on if you are upgrading from an earlier version of GroupWise.
- **NetWork Type:** This field is a holdover from WordPerfect Office 4.0 days and can be ignored.
- **Administrator:** The Browse button for this field allows you to choose an NDS user object to serve as the GroupWise administrator. The object you select must have a valid GroupWise mailbox associated with it. Any error messages generated by GroupWise agents are e-mailed to this user.

The Post Offices Property Page

Simply put, this tab lists the post offices that belong to this domain. Post offices cannot be moved or renamed, however, so the information in this tab is not editable. Post offices can be deleted from this page, however. Post offices may only be deleted if they do not own any objects (such as users, resources, distribution lists, libraries, POAs, and so on).

If you want to know what post offices are owned by a particular domain, it is often easier just to expand the hierarchy under this domain in the System pane of the GroupWise View. All the post offices will appear there.

The Domain Address Book Property Page

This is the interface for administering the way the system address book appears to your users. In the Windows client, this address book appears under the Novell GroupWise Address Book tab.

Using this tab, you can change the sort order, the field order, and the field labels in the address book for this domain.

WARNING

This whole feature set is somewhat limited, though. For example, if you change the sort order from a system level, users may change the sort order to whatever they like, and you can't dictate it.

- **Sort address book by:** This tool has only two available values: Last Name, First Name or First Name, Last Name. As expected, the first option would put "Zachary Abrams" above "Allan Zane"(sorting alphabetically by last name). The second option would put "Allen Zane" above "Zachary Abrams."

- **Address Book Fields and Available Fields:** The interface, shown in Figure 5.4, is a little tricky.
  - The left- and right-pointing arrows move fields into and out of the address book, respectively.
  - The up- and down-arrows change the order of the fields by moving the selected field up or down, respectively.
  - The Edit Label button allows you to change the field label of the selected field.

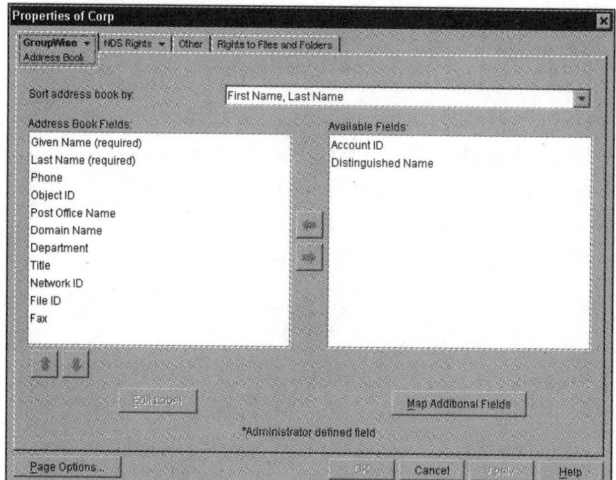

FIGURE 5.4 *The Domain Object Address Book Property Page*

The Domain Addressing Rules and Internet Addressing Property Pages

The Addressing Rules property page allows you to enable and test existing addressing rules. It does not allow for the creation of addressing rules, however. You create addressing rules from the System Operations window. Chapter 6 goes into more detail on creating addressing rules.

The Internet Addressing property page allows you to override system-wide Internet addressing settings at the domain level. Internet addressing is a very powerful tool, and like any good power tool, it can take your fingers off. Chapter 16 discusses Internet addressing. For now, leave it unplugged and put it back down between your table saw and your lathe.

The Default WebAccess Property Page

Use this property page to select the WebAccess agent (gateway) that processes requests for users located in this domain. This page applies only if you have multiple WebAccess agents installed in your GroupWise system. If you have only one WebAccess agent, that WebAccess agent services users in all domains.

- **Default WebAccess:** When you have multiple WebAccess agents and a user logs in to GroupWise WebAccess, the GroupWise provider (running on the Web server) checks to see whether a default WebAccess agent has been assigned to the user's post office (Post Office object ➪ GroupWise tab ➪ Default WebAccess page). If so, the provider connects to the assigned WebAccess agent. If not, it connects to the default WebAccess agent assigned to the post office's domain or to one of the WebAccess agents in its association list (GroupWise provider object ➪ Provider tab ➪ Environment page).

  If possible, you should select a WebAccess agent that has the best network level access to the domain's post offices to ensure the best performance. Each post office will use the domain's default WebAccess agent unless you override the default at the post office level (Post Office object ➪ GroupWise tab ➪ Default WebAccess page).
- **Override:** Check this box to indicate that you want to assign a default WebAccess agent to the domain. The domain's default WebAccess agent overrides the list of WebAccess agents associated with a GroupWise provider (GroupWise provider object ➪ Provider tab ➪ Environment page).
- **Default WebAccess Gateway:** Browse for and select the WebAccess agent you want to use as the default.

Viewing the Post Office Object

Here's a detailed look at the post office details window in Figure 5.5.

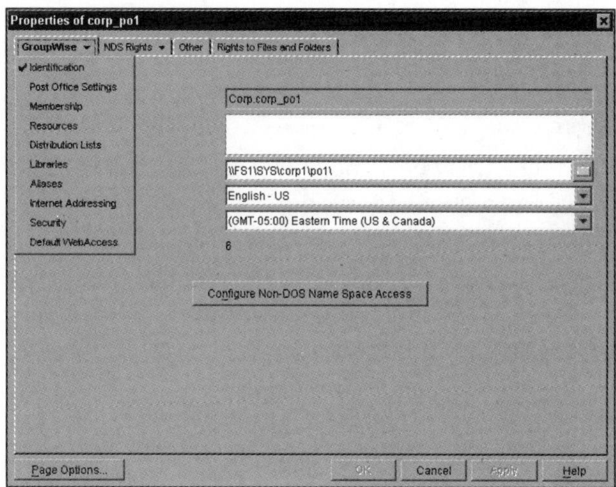

FIGURE 5.5 *The Post Office Object Properties Page*

As with the domain properties window, the post office properties window has several properties pages. They are the following:

- Identification
- Post Office Settings
- Membership
- Resources
- Distribution Lists
- Libraries
- Aliases
- Internet Addressing
- Security
- Default WebAccess

The Post Office Identification Property Page

The fields on this property page are shown in Figure 5.5. Only two fields are non-editable. The remaining four fields on this identification property page will generally stay the same.

- **Post Office:** This field displays the post office's GroupWise object ID (or "name" to you and me). Post offices cannot be renamed once they have been created. As with domains, if you need to rename one for some reason, you will have to create a new post office and move your users between the two. Moving users is covered in Chapter 13.
- **Description:** This optional field may be a good place to enter your pager number, or perhaps special instructions for system operators. The text here is visible through this window only.
- **UNC Path:** This field shows the path to the post office database, WPHOST.DB. Incorrect information here can foul network links and can prevent you from successfully running system maintenance on the post office database.
- **Language:** This field shows the language for this post office.
- **Time Zone:** This is the time zone for this post office. Changing this setting will result in chaos among the users on this post office, as all the appointments on their calendars at the time of the change will move. Time zones should be carefully selected when you create the post office, and then you should leave them alone.
- **Database Version:** As explained before in this chapter, in the section titled "The Domain Information Property Page," this will be 4.1, 5.0, 5.5, or 6.
- **Configure Non-DOS Name Space Access:** If you are running in direct access mode, *and* if you have GroupWise clients running on platforms that do not recognize UNC paths, *and* you want those clients to obtain the post office path from NDS, then you'll need to use this button. Enter the path style that your clients prefer into the appropriate field in the resulting dialog box. This setting is really here to be backwards compatible to GroupWise 5.x level post offices.

The Post Office Settings Property Page

The Post Office Settings page is packed with features specific to a post office. Here's an explanation of each of the options you will see on this page:

- **Network Type:** This field is obsolete and can be ignored.
- **Software Distribution Directory:** This pull-down menu is populated with the names of each of the software distribution directories (SDD) you have created in this system. Assigning an SDD to a post office provides the

GroupWise client with a UNC path for client updates. Chapter 12 discusses software distribution directories in more detail.

- **Access Mode:** There are three options here. Novell recommends the first option, Client/Server Only, be used almost exclusively.
  - **Client/Server Only:** The client "talks" via IP (Internet protocol) to the post office agent (POA). The POA handles all message store transactions. Users do not need any file system rights to the message store to run in client/server mode. (This is the preferable mode for running the GroupWise client.)
  - **Client/Server and Direct:** The client attempts a client/server connection, and if that fails, attempts to connect in direct access mode. This mode is not a hybrid. Clients always connect in only one manner. All this mode offers is the flexibility to support a mix of machines with and without IP addresses.
  - **Direct Access:** The client performs all mailbox transactions directly on the message store.
- **Delivery Mode:** This setting only applies if users are allowed to use the direct connection. For users with direct access connections, the setting applies as follows:
  - **Use App Thresholds:** The client writes to the sending user's USER and MSG databases, and if the threshold is not exceeded, will also write to each recipient's USER database.
  - **Client Delivers Locally:** The client writes to the sender's USER and MSG database, as well as to the USER database for every recipient on the local post office.

WARNING

Novell recommends that clients connect to the post office only in client/server mode. Direct mode, regardless of the delivery mode selected, poses a security and a stability risk to the message store. In direct mode, users must have file system rights to the message store, and store files are subject to corruption every time a workstation GPFs or is cold-rebooted.

- **Disable Logins:** If checked, users will not be able to log in to their GroupWise mailboxes on this post office. This option does not kick users out, however, if they are already logged in.

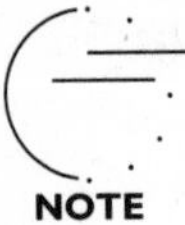
NOTE

If you need to kick users out in order to perform server or system maintenance, it helps if you are in client/server only mode. In this mode, you can simply unload the POA from the server console to kick everyone off — another reason to choose client/server only mode over the alternatives!

- **Disable Live Mode:** Select Disable Live Move to turn off the improved move-user capabilities available in GroupWise 6.0.

  A live move uses a TCP/IP connection to move a user from one post office to another. In general, it is significantly faster and more reliable than earlier move-user capabilities in GroupWise 5x. However, it does require that both post offices are running GroupWise 6.0, and that TCP/IP is functioning efficiently between the two post offices.

  The original move-user capability is required if you are moving a user to a post office that has not yet been upgraded to GroupWise 6.0, or if you are moving a user across a WAN link where TCP/IP may not be efficient. The original move-user capability uses the transfer of message files rather than a TCP/IP link between the two POAs.

  Moving users, and live mode user moves are both discussed in detail in Chapter 13.
- **Enable Intruder Detection:** Select Enable Intruder Detection to configure the POAs for the post office to detect system break-in attempts in the form of repeated unsuccessful logins.
- **Incorrect Logins Allowed:** Specify how many unsuccessful login attempts trigger a lockout. The default is 5. Valid values range from 3 to 10.
- **Incorrect Login Reset Time:** Specify how long unsuccessful login attempts are counted. The default is 30 minutes. Valid values range from 15 to 60 minutes.
- **Lockout Reset Time:** Specify how long the user login is disabled. The default is 30 minutes. Valid values range from 15 to 60 minutes.
- **Restore Area:** Displays the directory in your GroupWise system that has been designated as the restore area for this post office. If a restore area has not yet been set up, use Tools ➪ GroupWise System Operations ➪ Restore Area Management to create a restore area. You use a restore area to provide a backup copy of the post office, from which users can restore messages that have already been purged from your active GroupWise system.
- **Remote File Server Settings:** Use the remote file server settings to provide POA a login id to use in order to connect to another file server in order to

access to a remote machine where a GroupWise library or a document storage area is located.

- **Remote User Name:** Specify the network login ID for the POAs of this post office to use when accessing the remote file server. For example, GWMAIL.EMAIL.ACME identifies the remote login ID.
- **Remote Password:** Specify the password associated with the login ID provided in the preceding point.

The Post Office Membership Property Page

As shown in Figure 5.6, this page provides a list of those users assigned to this post office.

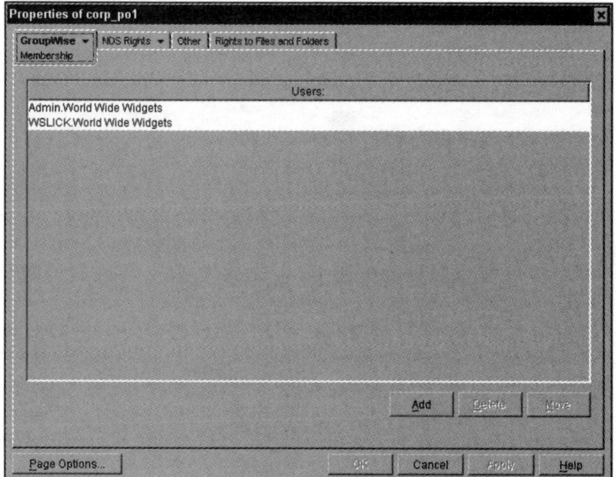

FIGURE 5.6 *The Post Office Membership Property Page*

This tab comes equipped with tools to add existing NDS users to this post office, delete users from the post office, and move users between post offices.

The Post Office Resources, Distribution Lists, and Libraries Property Pages

These pages provide lists of the various non-user objects associated with this post office. None of these objects can be created from the post office details window, so there are no Add buttons. Refer back to the section earlier in this chapter titled "Creating GroupWise Objects" for instructions on creating GroupWise objects.

Creating a Post Office Alias

Post office aliases (see Figure 5.7) provide one way for a post office to be given a different Internet address than the rest of your organization.

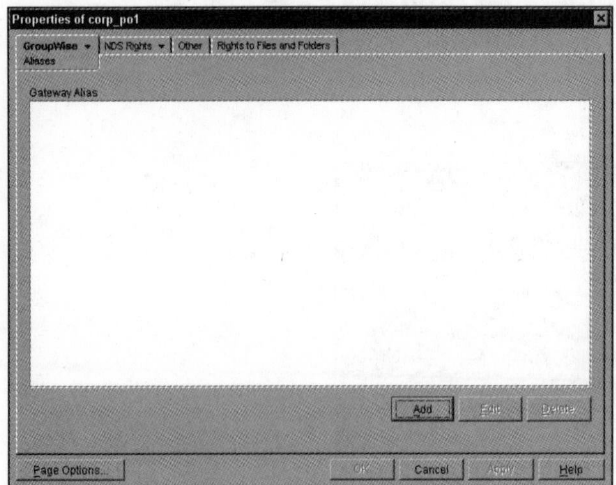

FIGURE 5.7 *The Post Office Aliases Property Page*

Clicking Add brings up the dialog shown in Figure 5.8.

For example, WorldWide Widgets has a post office whose users all want to be addressed a little differently than the rest of the company. Instead of being `user@wwwidgets.com`, they want to be `user@skippy-widgets.com`.

- **Gateway Alias Type:** This option brings up a list of all available gateway alias types on the system. In this example, the gateway alias type associated with the GroupWise Internet agent has been chosen.
- **Gateway Alias Address:** Setting this field to `skippy-widget.com` gives every user on this post office the desired e-mail address at `skippy-widgets.com`.

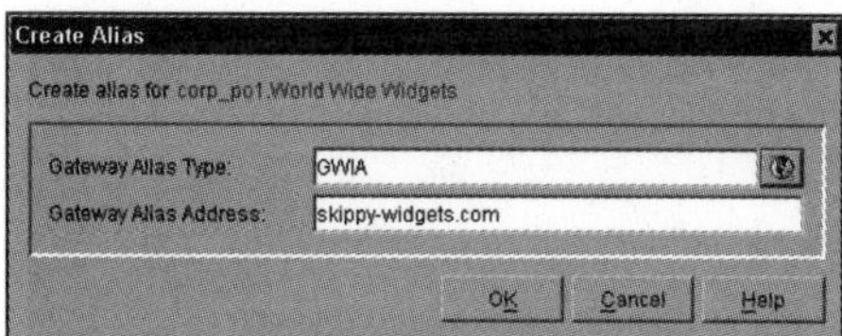

FIGURE 5.8 *The Create Alias Dialog Box*

The Internet Addressing Property Page

Just like on the domain details screen, this tab exists to allow you to make exceptions to the system Internet addressing configuration. Chapter 16 covers Internet addressing in detail.

The Security Property Page

There are two possible security values for a post office:

- **Low:** Users' network logins are not checked to see if they correspond to the mailbox they are using. In this mode, mailboxes should be password protected. If they are not, then any user can log in as any other user by placing the `/@u-<userID>` switch on the GroupWise command line (without the greater than and less than symbols).
- **High:** Users' NDS passwords are checked before allowing users to access their GroupWise mailbox. There are two methods that GroupWise can use to get the NDS password. They are *NDS authentication* and *LDAP authentication*. You can have both NDS authentication and LDAP authentication enabled at the same time. Here's a discussion of both of these options:

High – NDS Authentication

With NDS authenticaton enabled, if a user has a Novell client that is authenticated to an NDS tree, the GroupWise 32-bit client queries the Novell client using the WnetGetUser network API call. If a user is logged in as one person, but trying to open GroupWise as someone else, that user will be prompted for the mailbox password, which is not contained in NDS and requires that the mailbox truly have a GroupWise password.

High – LDAP Authentication

With LDAP authentication enabled, if users do not have the Novell client on their computers, or a user is using GroupWise WebAccess through a Web browser, they can still use an NDS password. The POA queries NDS via LDAP in behalf of the user. A prerequisite to this functionality is that your implementation of NDS be version 8.5 or better, with LDAP services enabled. Here are the steps to enable LDAP authentication:

1. For Security Level, select High.
2. In the High Security Options box, select LDAP Authentication.
3. Click the pencil icon.
4. Specify the IP address or DNS host name of the LDAP server.
5. Specify the port number that the LDAP server listens on.
6. Click OK.
7. Specify the user name that the POA can use to log in to the LDAP server in order to authenticate GroupWise users.

   This approach to LDAP authentication is faster and requires fewer connections to the LDAP server than if each GroupWise client user authenticates to the LDAP server individually.
8. If the LDAP user name requires a password, click Set Passwords, type the password twice for verification, and then click Set Password.

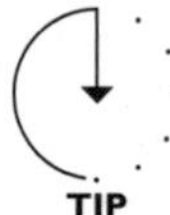
TIP

The syntax on the LDAP user line is CN=,OU=,OU=,O, as in, for example CN=ECORNISH,OU=ITS,O=ACME.

9. If the LDAP server uses SSL, select Use SSL and then browse to and select the SSL key file generated by the LDAP server.
10. Click OK to save the LDAP settings.

ConsoleOne then notifies the POA to restart so the new settings can be put into effect.

The Default WebAccess Property Page

Use this property page to select the WebAccess agent (or gateway) that will process requests from this post office's users. This page applies only if you have multiple WebAccess agents installed in your GroupWise system. If you have only one WebAccess agent, that WebAccess agent will service all post offices.

When you have multiple WebAccess agents and a user logs in to GroupWise WebAccess, the GroupWise provider (running on the Web server) checks to see if a default WebAccess agent has been assigned to the user's post office. If so, the provider connects to the assigned WebAccess agent. If not, it connects to the default WebAccess agent assigned to the post office's domain (Domain object ⇨ GroupWise tab ⇨ Default WebAccess page) or to one of the WebAccess agents in its association list (GroupWise provider object ⇨ Provider tab ⇨ Environment page).

If possible, you should select a WebAccess agent that has good network level access to the post office to ensure the best performance.

Check the override box to indicate that you want to assign a default WebAccess agent to the post office. The post office's default WebAccess agent overrides the default WebAccess agent assigned to the post office's domain (Domain object ⇨ GroupWise tab ⇨ Default WebAccess page). Browse for and select the WebAccess agent you want to use as the default.

Configuring Library Objects

If you want to use document management, you will be creating *library objects.* Figure 5.9 shows the Library Identification property page.

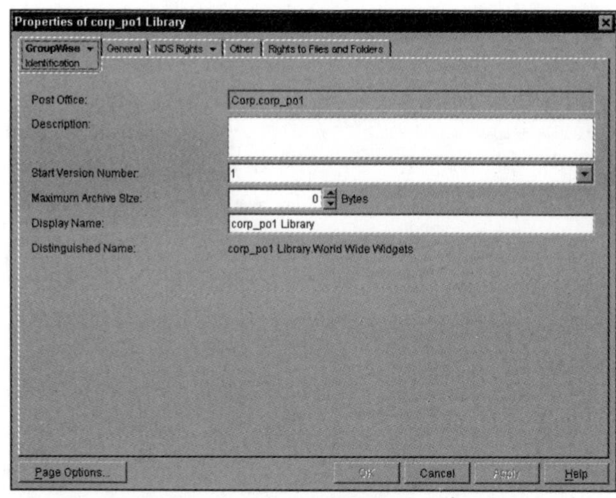

FIGURE 5.9 *The Library Identification Property Page*

The Library Identification Property Page

This section includes a discussion of the fields in the property page in Figure 5.9.

- **Post Office:** This field is the GroupWise domain and post office to which this library belongs. Libraries cannot be moved from one domain and post office to another, but with mass-change operations, the documents in one library can be moved to another. This topic is discussed in Chapter 14.
- **Description:** This is an optional field. The text here is not visible to users and is only useful to you as a way to describe the library object to other system administrators.
- **Start Version Number:** Document version numbers may begin at either 0 or 1. If you enter 0, then the first version of each document will be 000. If you enter 1, then the first version number will be 001. Most people count in ordinal terms, so it may be better to enter 1 here.
- **Maximum Archive Size in Bytes:** This is the number of bytes per library archive directory. The value you enter should be compatible with your backup medium. For example, you could make it 90 percent the size of a tape backup's capacity to allow for the tape's file storage data. Then you will be able to back up one archive directory per tape.

  It is usually best to keep the archive directories small in comparison to the size of the backup medium, especially if the backup medium is measured in gigabytes. This way you can back up the archive directories often enough to keep your hard disk space from being chewed up too quickly between backups. For example, if your backup medium is 1 GB, limit your archive directories to 200 MB.
- **Display Name:** Like domains and post offices, GroupWise libraries cannot be renamed. Fortunately, the display name for a library can be changed. This is visible to users when they select a library to save documents in.
- **Distinguished Name:** This is the name and context of the GroupWise library object in NDS.

The Storage Areas Property Page

As described in Chapter 4, GroupWise libraries are made up of document property databases (and other databases), and the documents themselves are stored as compressed, encrypted files called BLOB files. By default, all of the databases and BLOBs are kept in subdirectories of the post office directory.

The Storage Areas page (see Figure 5.10) allows you to choose other locations, whether they be on different volumes or even different servers, for the BLOB files. The document databases will always remain under the GWDMS structure, however.

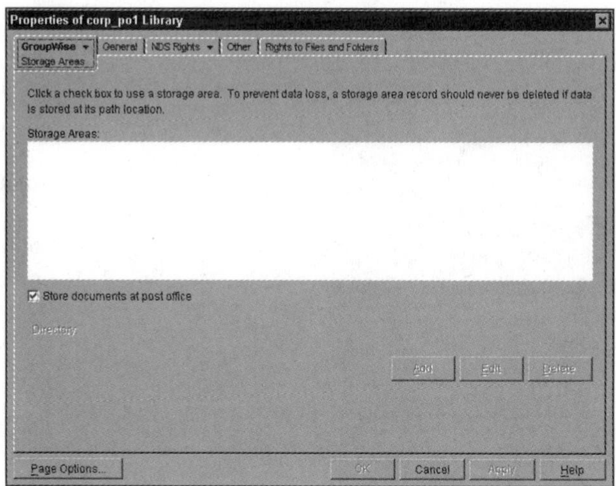

FIGURE 5.10 *The Library Storage Areas Property Page*

By default, the box labeled Store documents at post office is checked. You can uncheck it preparatory to adding a storage area for documents. You can not add document storage areas while this box is checked.

Clicking Add calls up the dialog box shown in Figure 5.11.

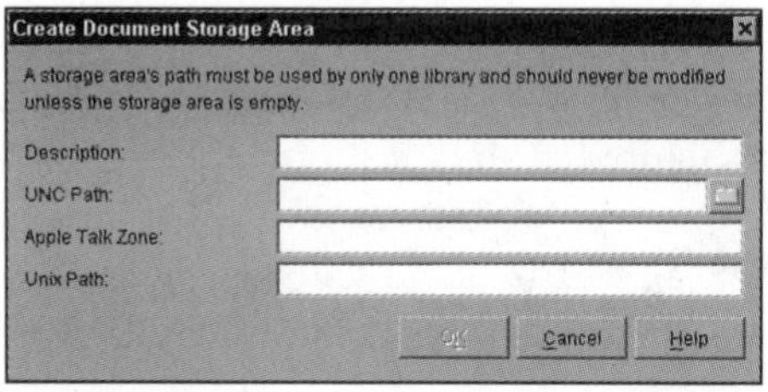

FIGURE 5.11 *The Create Document Storage Area Dialog Box*

By default, all of the fields in this dialog box are empty. In this example, WorldWide Widgets has begun the process of adding a new storage area, creatively naming it "New Storage Area." The UNC path was manually entered, but there is a browse button. This button allows you to surf out to a mapped drive and choose a directory. If you use the browse button, the field may be populated with a non-UNC path (such as `m:\docs`). Don't worry about this, though; the UNC path will be discovered correctly from your mapping.

As noted in Figure 5.12, the new storage area has been added.

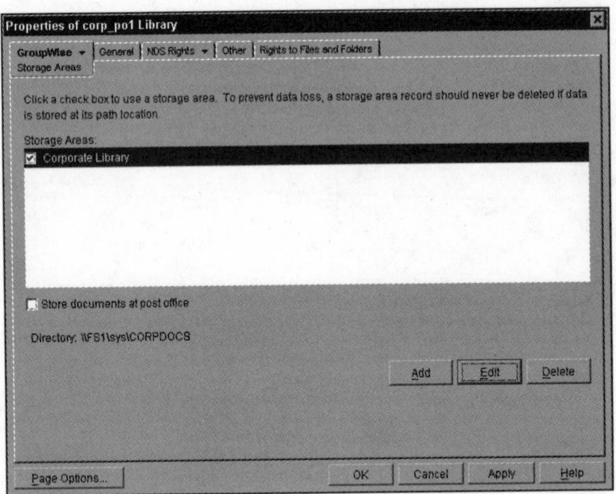

FIGURE 5.12 *The Library Storage Areas Page, with a New Document Storage Area in Place*

NOTE

The Directory field shows the UNC path that was entered.

Once a storage area has been created and the Library details window "Okayed," all documents created in this library will be stored at the location with the check box next to it. If that area fills up, you can create another storage area, and enable that one with the check box. At that point, all of the documents in the original storage area stay right where they are, and new documents go into the newly activated storage area.

Be careful working with storage areas, though. If the post office agent cannot access a storage area you have created, it will fail to load. Storage areas should be on servers with high availability.

Configuring the Rights Property Page

By default, all users are given rights to all libraries. This means that they can save documents in any library you create, and access any document they have been given document rights to.

If you wish to restrict library rights to a group of users, or if you need to assign a user to be the librarian (which you really should do), then you'll use the Library Rights tab shown in Figure 5.13.

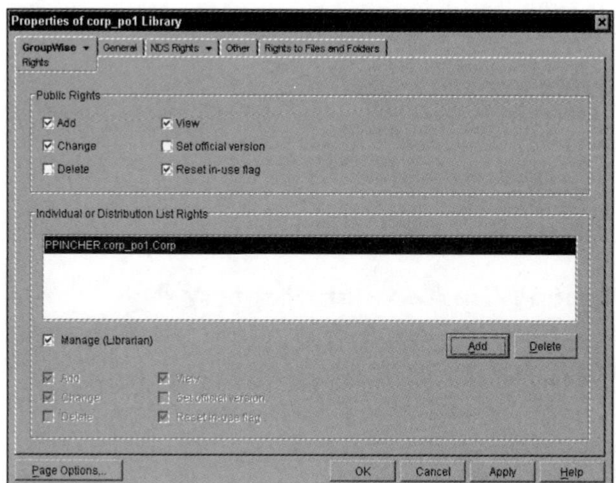

FIGURE 5.13 *The Library Rights Property Page*

By default, all of the check boxes in the upper portion of this tab are checked, and all those in the lower portion [except Manage (Librarian)] are grayed out. In this example, the administrator decided not to let just anybody delete or set the official version of documents in this library, however.

The user PPincher has been added. Now PPincher can have rights assigned to her that are denied to everyone else. She could also be assigned the Manage right, making her a GroupWise librarian.

GroupWise 6 Agent and Gateway Objects

The GroupWise post office agent, message transfer agent, as well as each of the GroupWise gateways, are represented in the GroupWise view that allows it to be configured from ConsoleOne. This chapter does not spend a lot of time showing you how to configure agents and gateways, because these objects each need their own chapter to be discussed in sufficient detail.

The post office agent object: This will be covered in Chapter 8.

The message transfer agent object: This will be covered in Chapter 8.

Gateway objects: because each gateway is a little different, this book covers two of the heavy-hitters, GWIA and WebAccess, in Chapters 10 and 11.

Administering User Objects

Administering GroupWise user objects is the most common task you will be doing with GroupWise administration in ConsoleOne. This section fully explains all the attributes that can be administered on a GroupWise object.

The User Object's GroupWise Account Property Page

If you have worked at all with Novell Directory Services and ConsoleOne, you are probably quite familiar with the User Object Details window. With GroupWise 6 installed to your tree, the user object has some new property pages available to it. The one you'll likely use the most is the GroupWise Account property page. Figure 5.14 shows this page.

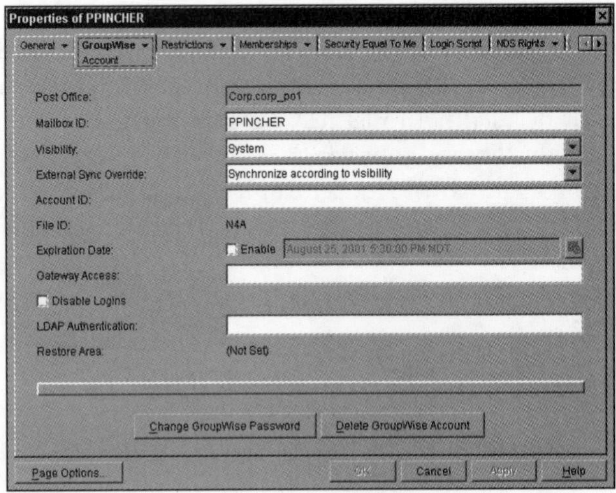

FIGURE 5.14 *The User Object's GroupWise Account Page*

This tab offers three major administrative tools:

- Changing GroupWise information for this user
- Changing this user's GroupWise password
- Deleting the user's GroupWise account

The following offers a discussion of each of the fields:

- **Post Office:** This is the name of this user's post office, with the name of the domain tacked on before the post office name with a period delimiting the domain and post office names.
- **Mailbox ID:** This is the user's GroupWise user ID. Changing this value will *rename* the user. A rename operation is actually a user-object move, but within the same post office.
- **Visibility:** This field defines which users elsewhere in the GroupWise system can find this user in the GroupWise address book. The options for this pull-down menu are as follows:
    - **Post Office:** This user can only be seen by users in the same post office.
    - **System:** Anyone on this GroupWise system can see this user in the address book.
    - **Domain:** This user can only be seen by users in the same domain.
    - **None:** This user does not appear in the GroupWise address book.

      Just because a user cannot be seen in the address book does not mean that user cannot be sent to. If you know the domain, post office, and user ID, you can enter those items in the TO field (for example, corp.corp_po1.ppincher), and the e-mail will reach the user.

      Similarly, if GroupWise Internet addressing is enabled, you can reach this user by entering the user's user ID and IDOMAIN (that is, `PPincher@wwwidgets.com`) in the TO field.
- **External Sync Override:** If you have connected your GroupWise system to another organization's GroupWise system, and are using external system synchronization, you may want to make some users invisible outside of your GroupWise system. This field allows you to override the setting in the Visibility field for this user.
- **Account ID:** This field is used for GroupWise gateways that offer accounting features so that users can be charged for, say, sending faxes or transmitting data across an expensive line.

- **File ID:** This is the three-character string that uniquely identifies this user's USER database in this post office directory. In the example in Figure 5.14, the File ID is *N4A*, which means that the mailbox for user PPincher is in USERN4A.DB.
- **Expiration Date:** If you have temporary or contract employees, you may choose to set an expiration date for them. After the date has passed, the user will not be able to log in to his or her GroupWise mailbox. Other users can still send mail to an expired user, however. Clearing the date out of this field after that date has passed will, in effect, un-expire the user, allowing them to log in again.
- **Gateway Access:** This is an obscure feature that was used in older GroupWise gateways. Use this field if instructed to do so when configuring a specific GroupWise gateway.
- **Disable Logins:** If you need to prevent a user from logging in, you can check this box. Note that this change, as with any changes made in ConsoleOne, takes time to propagate down to the post office. Try to plan a few minutes ahead in order to ensure that the user doesn't successfully log in before the update takes place.
- **LDAP Authentication:** This option applies only if you are using LDAP to authenticate users (see "The Security Property Page" section earlier in this chapter) and the LDAP server is not the Novell LDAP server. If so, enter the user's LDAP authentication ID.
- **Restore Area:** Restore Area displays the restore area, if any, that the user could access to restore deleted items from backup.

  To set up a restore area, choose Tools ➪ GroupWise System Operations ➪ Restore Area Management. Restore area management is covered more in Chapter 6.
- **Change GroupWise Password:** Clicking this option displays the Security Options window shown in Figure 5.15.

  The GroupWise password (managed with this Security Options window) is independent of the user's NDS password. So changing this password will not change the user's NDS password.
  - **Enter new password:** If a user forgets a GroupWise password, you can provide the user with a new password to access GroupWise. You should advise the user to change the new password to a personal one.

- **Retype password:** If you retype the password correctly, it is set; otherwise, you need to reenter the password in both fields.
- **Clear user's password:** If a user forgets a personal password, check this box to clear the password. The user can then enter a new password at his or her discretion. In a high security post office, it may be necessary to set a new password after clearing the old one.
- **Allow password caching:** This option is selected by default, allowing the user to select the Remember My Password option under Tools ➪ Options ➪ Security in the GroupWise client. This option lets the user restart GroupWise without reentering the password. The password is stored in the Windows password list on the current computer.
- **Allow NDS authentication instead of password:** This option lets users select the No Password Required with NDS option under Security options in the GroupWise client. When selected, this option lets the user access his or her mailbox without requiring a password if he or she is already logged in to NDS. Mailbox access is granted based on NDS authentication, not on password information.
- **Enable Novell Single Sign-on:** This check box lets the user select the Use Novell Single Sign-on option under Tools ➪ Options ➪ Security in the GroupWise client. When selected, this option lets the user access his or her mailbox without reentering the password. The GroupWise password is stored in NDS for the currently logged-in user.

  Novell Single Sign-on must be installed on user workstations in order for this option to take effect.

- **Delete GroupWise Account:** This selection deletes a user's GroupWise account, but not the user's NDS account.

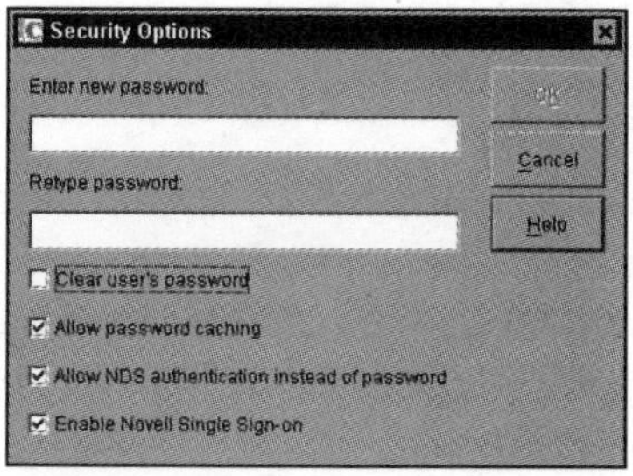

FIGURE 5.15 *The Security Options Window*

The User Distribution Lists Property Page

This page displays all of the distribution lists that this user appears on, and it allows you to add this user to additional GroupWise distribution lists.

The Participation button allows you specify if the user is a TO, CC, or BC recipient of messages sent to the distribution list you are highlighting.

The User Nicknames Property Page

A nickname is a way for a user to exist in two places at once. Nicknames added through this tab may be placed in any GroupWise post office. This is a handy way to overcome some of the limitations of the visibility feature, and can also allow the user to be known by more than one user ID.

Assume, for example, that PPincher is the webmaster for WorldWide Widgets. If you create a nickname for her of "webmaster" then anyone who addresses e-mail to `webmaster@worldwidewidgets.com` will reach user PPincher.

The User GroupWise Aliases Property Page

Earlier, in the section titled "Creating a Post Office Alias," you learned that Post Office aliases can be used to give every user a new "host" field for their Internet address. Similarly, a User alias can be used to change the "user" field for a single user's Internet address. It can also be used to change the entire address.

If you set the gateway alias address to a value with no @ sign, you are only changing the user portion of the Internet address. If you include the @ sign, then you have changed the entire address for that user.

If you assign a gateway alias to a user, that alias appears as the reply-to address on all mail they send through that gateway. In an example mentioned in the preceding section, Ms. Pincher wants inbound e-mail that is addressed to `webmaster@worldwidewidgets.com` to come to her. If you create a gateway alias called "webmaster" for her, then not only will she get mail addressed to "webmaster," but also all the mail she sends will appear as if it is *from* "webmaster."

If Internet addressing is enabled, you will probably want to use the Internet addressing tab to make exceptions such as this, which is all covered in Chapter 16.

The User GroupWise X.400 Information Property Page

If you need to connect your system to an X.400 system, then each of your users may need an X.400-style address. In most situations, however, it is much more convenient for X.400 systems and GroupWise systems to communicate via the SMTP, or *Internet e-mail* protocol.

If your users do need X.400 addresses, the X.400 system's administrator can assist you as you populate these fields.

The User GroupWise Internet Addressing Property Page

Internet addressing exceptions can be configured at the domain, post office, and user level. On the user object's details window, this tab allows you to make exceptions at the user level.

Understanding Resource Objects

A GroupWise resource is nothing more than a mailbox used to represent a physical entity, such as a conference room or a data projector. Resources are typically used to allow GroupWise users to schedule the use of these physical entities in the GroupWise calendar.

The Resource Identification property page, with the Identification tab shown, is in Figure 5.16. This section explores the fields this page presents.

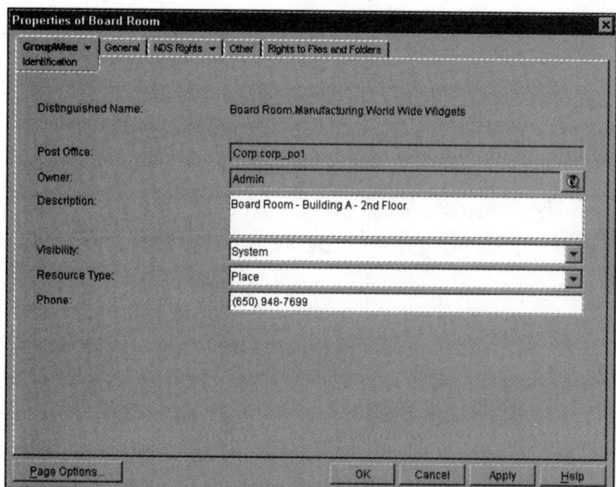

FIGURE 5.16 *The Resource Object Properties Window*

- **Distinguished Name:** This is the NDS name of the resource object, complete with the object's context. This field is not editable, but the resource may be moved to another NDS context using the NDS console view.
- **Post Office:** This shows the GroupWise domain and post office that contains the resource. You cannot change the post office that a resource is a member of from this window. But if you go to the GroupWise view, you can right-mouse click on the resource and use the move option. Resource moves are very similar to (and every bit as complex as) user moves. Chapter 13 talks about moving users.
- **Owner:** This is the GroupWise user ID of the owner of this resource. This user is responsible for assigning proxy rights for the resource, managing the resource's calendar, and responding to mail received by the resource. All of these tasks will be performed through the GroupWise client's proxy function. The owner of the resource automatically has proxy rights to the resource object.

  A resource owner should be someone who is comfortable using GroupWise, and who has responsibility over the actual physical entity. For instance, the secretary who keeps the overhead projector at his desk should own that projector's resource object.
- **Description:** This description field is unlike several of the others discussed in this chapter in that it is actually going to be very useful to your user community. The text entered here will appear in the Comments field in the GroupWise address book's entry for this resource. For instance, for a conference room resource, you could populate this field with directions to the room, descriptions of the seating and white-board arrangements, and the telephone number of the individual with the key to the room.
- **Visibility:** This field works exactly like it does for the user object. Restricting visibility prevents the resource from appearing in some users' address books. This is a good way to prevent users from trying to schedule a resource that they should not have access to.
- **Resource Type:** There are two possible entries in this field:
  - **Resource:** Used to denote all types of physical objects that can be checked in or out by employees, from handheld radios to company cars.
  - **Place:** Used to denote conference rooms or other locations at your physical plant. When you schedule an appointment for a group of people and include a place resource, the appointment's Place field will be populated with the name of the resource.

The Resource Distribution Lists Property Page

Just like you saw in the User Object's Details window, this tab provides a list of the GroupWise distribution lists that this resource is included in. (See "The User Distribution Lists Property Page" earlier in this chapter.) The resource may be added to or removed from a mailing list using this tab.

The Resource Nicknames Property Page

This also works exactly like the nicknames interface for the user object. (See "The User Nicknames Property Page" earlier in this chapter.)

The Distribution List Object

The GroupWise distribution list is simply a mailing list, and it is sometimes called a mailing list or even just a group. NDS group objects can also be used like GroupWise distribution lists. An NDS group object functions in the normal manner in which users can inherit rights. A GroupWise distribution list does not give users NDS rights. GroupWise distibution lists are more flexible as mailing lists than NDS groups though. For example, with a GroupWise distribution list, you can specify whether recipients are TO, CC, or BC recipients; with NDS groups, you cannot.

Like every other GroupWise object, the distribution list has a Details window in ConsoleOne (see Figure 5.17).

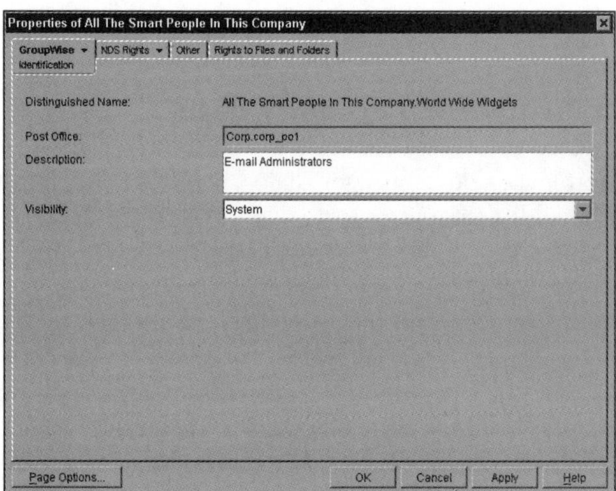

FIGURE 5.17 *The Distribution List Object Properties Window*

The Distribution List Identification Property Page

As shown in Figure 5.17, this page has only a few fields to examine:

- **Distinguished Name:** This is the NDS name and context for this distribution list object.
- **Post Office:** This is the name of the GroupWise domain and post office that contains this distribution list. This field cannot be edited.
- **Description:** This field appears in the GroupWise address book, and may therefore be very helpful for your users. Distribution list descriptions can explain the purpose of the mailing list, and even whom to contact to change the membership list.
- **Visibility:** Distribution list visibility, though populated with the same values as the visibility for users and resources, works a little bit differently. If you know the GroupWise address of a user, you can send mail to that user even though the user does not show up in the address book. A distribution list cannot be sent to in this way.

  The Visibility field is extremely useful for preventing unauthorized users from using a single distribution list to send to the entire company. Simply restrict the visibility to "Post Office" and only users on the same post office as the distribution list may send to the list.

The Distribution List Internet Addressing Property Page

Internet addressing is covered in Chapter 16. Even then, there will be little use for the Internet addressing tab.

The Distribution List Membership Property Page

Figure 5.18 shows the interface you use to change a distribution list.

Clicking on the Add button gives you a browser dialog box from which you may browse and select users to add them a list.

The Participation button allows you to change a user's participation in the list from TO to CC or even BC (blind copy).

Obviously, the Delete button removes the selected user or users from the distribution list.

As with almost all details window operations, membership changes are not committed to the domain database until the details window is dismissed with the OK button.

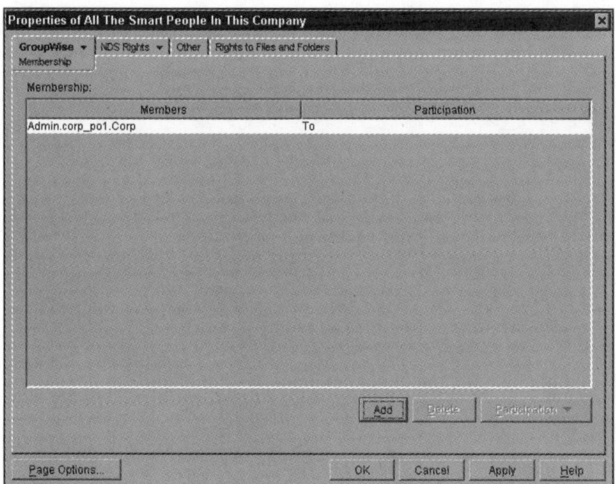

FIGURE 5.18 *The Distribution List Membership Property Page*

The Distribution List Nicknames Property Page

If you have restricted visibility to a distribution list, you may find it inconvenient that only users in a single post office can use the list. The Nicknames tab allows you to work around this. By adding a nickname for this list in another post office, you can allow users on that post office to use the list as well.

Summary

You should now be familiar with the GroupWise view and with the GroupWise object interfaces. Each of the objects has a different purpose, and each details screen is a little different, but they all work in much the same way.

A large portion of your time as a GroupWise system administrator will be spent working with the objects described in preceding pages. That won't be all you'll need to do, however.

CHAPTER 6

Using GroupWise System Operations

If you pull down the Tools menu and select GroupWise System Operations, you will be presented with the menu shown in Figure 6.1.

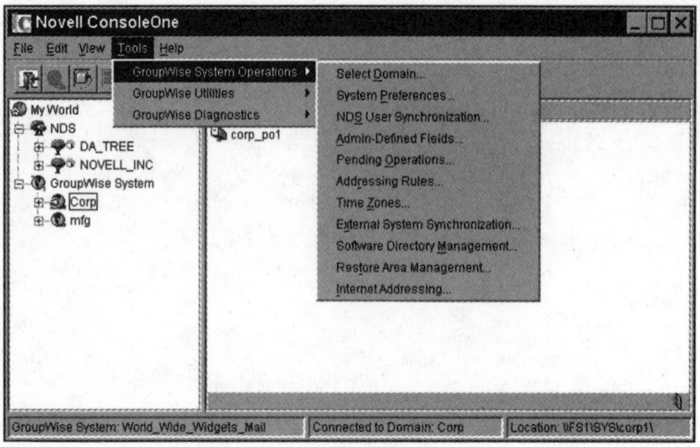

FIGURE 6.1 *The GroupWise System Operations Menu*

These operations all have one thing in common: They affect GroupWise objects system-wide. (The only menu option that does not affect all domains is the Select Domain menu option. So it's a little out of place!) This means they may affect multiple domains, post offices, and users, and you'll want to know what it is you are doing before you experiment. These operations will be discussed in turn.

Changing Connections with Select Domain

The GroupWise System Connection window allows you to change ConsoleOne's connection to a different GroupWise domain, or even a completely different GroupWise system. Figure 6.2 shows the dialog box that comes up when using the Select Domain menu option.

This "connection" is simply the GroupWise domain database that ConsoleOne is reading from and writing to. This window shows the path for the domain to which ConsoleOne is currently connected.

Some administrative operations are best performed from the primary domain. If you are performing system operations, it is best to be connected to the system's primary domain. If you are adding users to a secondary domain, however, you may want to be connected to the domain to which the user will belong. The select domain window gives you this flexibility.

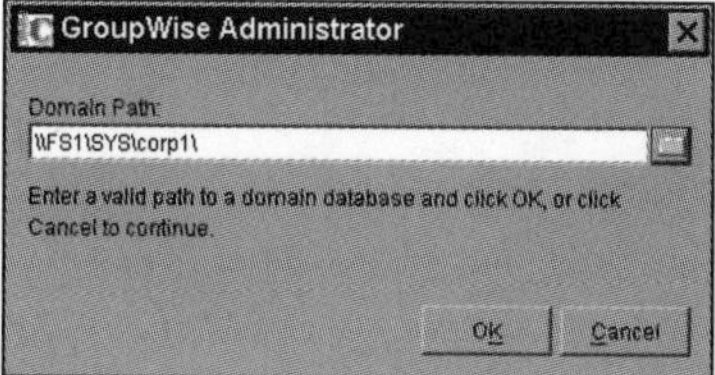

FIGURE 6.2 *The GroupWise Select Domain Box*

System Preferences

The window shown in Figure 6.3 allows you to set administrative preferences. In the upper portion of this window, you may set preferences pertaining to user creation.

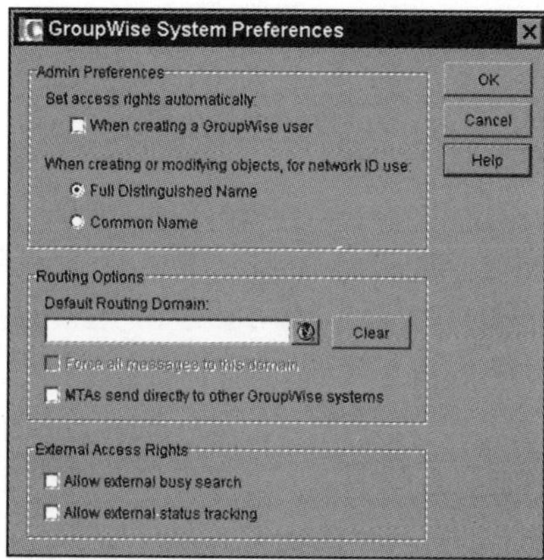

FIGURE 6.3 *The GroupWise System Preferences Box*

- **Set access rights automatically:** By checking the box labeled When creating a GroupWise user, you allow ConsoleOne to make trustee assignments automatically for new users. These assignments include rights to the PO and POA objects hosting the user's mailbox, as well as file-system rights if you are using direct access mode (which you should not be, as discussed in Chapter 5). If the post office is set to allow only client/server connections, the GroupWise client always chooses a client/server connection, even if the user has file-system rights. The only problem is this: Do you really want users to have file-system rights, someplace they don't need it? Generally not, so don't check this option.

- **. . . for network ID use:** The two options here apply only to objects created after this preference has been set. To modify the network ID for existing GroupWise users, you must open their user object and make a modification. Any modification will do — the network ID will be changed in the background. Do not change this option unless you really know what you are doing. It is generally best to keep the setting at Full Distinguished Name.
  - **Full Distinguished Name:** The GroupWise post office records the fully-distinguished NDS name for users, and it associates that name with the appropriate GroupWise user ID. Use this setting on post offices whose users authenticate to NDS.
  - **Common Name:** The GroupWise post office records only the common name for users, and it associates that name with the appropriate GroupWise user ID. Use this setting for post offices whose users do *not* authenticate to NDS. (Generally, you will not use the Common Name selection.)
- **Routing Options:** This allows you to specify a default routing domain. Chapter 16 gives a full discussion of how to use this.
- **External Access Rights:** Your GroupWise MTA can be enabled to send messages across the Internet to another GroupWise system. By doing this, GroupWise messages can retain their native GroupWise format. This feature was was introduced in GroupWise 5.5. The only flaw to this feature was that in GroupWise 5.5, with MTA to MTA connectivity, outside Internet users could do busy searches and status tracking even if you did not want to allow for that. This system preference was created to control that.

NDS User Synchronization

NDS user synchronization is a process by which information is pulled from NDS into the GroupWise directory. Ordinarily, it is not necessary to set this preference. When you run ConsoleOne with the GroupWise snap-ins, your changes are being written to both directories simultaneously.

Suppose, however, that the administrators in human resources do not have file-system rights to a GroupWise domain database. They may change phone numbers, mail-stops, or titles for users, and the changes will never propagate into the GroupWise address book where they will be really useful — unless NDS user synchronization is correctly configured. Figure 6.4 shows the NDS User Synchronization Configuration box.

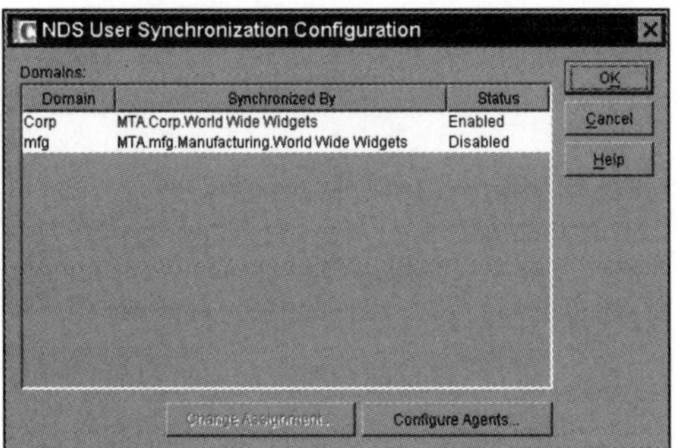

FIGURE 6.4 *The NDS User Synchronization Configuration Window*

By default, NDS user synchronization is not enabled. In the example shown in Figure 6.5, the status for the highlighted domain indicates that there is no NDS access. This means that the MTA does not have the necessary rights to read information from NDS.

Other possible statuses include Disabled and Enabled. To change the NDS synchronization status, click Configure Agents, which will bring up the box shown in Figure 6.5.

This window displays every message transfer agent object in the GroupWise system. The state of each agent is either Enabled or Disabled. Before an agent can be Enabled as an NDS Sync agent, it must have rights to read information from NDS.

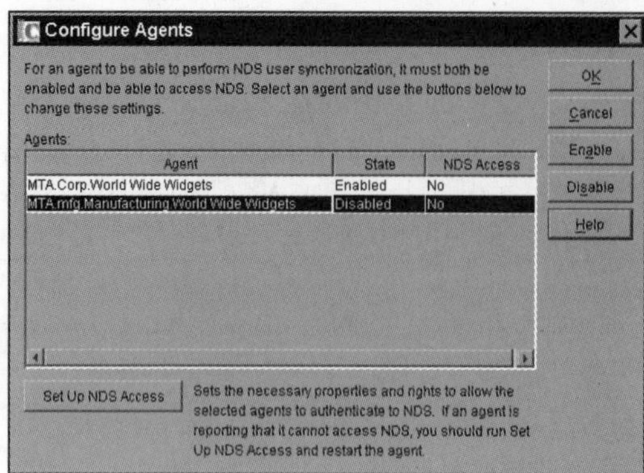

FIGURE 6.5 *The Configure Agents Box from the NDS User Synchronization Window*

Clicking Set Up NDS Access gives the highlighted MTA object the necessary trustee assignments to authenticate to and read from NDS. Before the rights are effective, however, the agent must be restarted. After clicking Set Up NDS Access, you'll observe the NDS Access field change from No to Restart Required.

With one or more agents enabled for NDS sync, you may then make agent assignments. From the NDS User Synchronization Configuration window, highlight a domain and click Change Assignment to get to Figure 6.6.

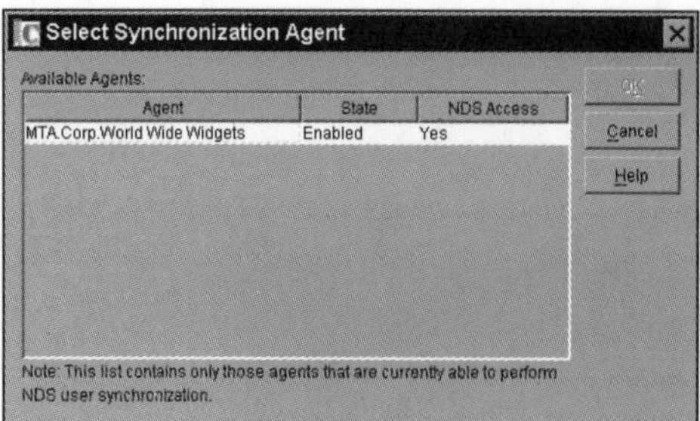

FIGURE 6.6 *The Select Synchronization Agent Box*

TIP

It is interesting to note that an MTA may perform synchronization for more than one domain. Configuring an MTA this way may result in unnecessary GroupWise administration traffic. Novell recommends

that every MTA be assigned to perform NDS synchronization for the domain to which it belongs, unless it is not possible for that MTA to authenticate to NDS for some reason.

Two more things must be configured before NDS user synchronization can occur. An event must be activated under the message transfer agent's Scheduled Events tab. Chapter 9 talks about the NDS user synchronization event in more detail. Also, the GroupWise MTA must have the /user and /password switches enabled and configured in its startup file. The MTA uses these switches in order to log in to NDS to compare NDS to the GroupWise WPDOMAIN.DB.

Admin-Defined Fields

This tool allows you to define new fields for the GroupWise address book. This is done by mapping schema attributes of the NDS user class object to the GroupWise user class object. This tool is also available when you select Map Additional Fields from the Address Book tab of the domain object's details window. Here is what you must do to add Admin-Defined fields:

1. Add the attribute you want to the NDS tree that will be associated with the user class object.

   This is done under Tools ➪ Schema Manager. You must have NDS rights to extend your NDS tree's schema.

WARNING

Make sure that you know what you are doing when using Schema Manager and extending your NDS schema. Schema Manager is not a GroupWise-specific utility; it comes natively with ConsoleOne. For further instructions on using Schema Manager, click the Help button or go to Novell's documentation site at www.novell.com/documentation and look up documentation for ConsoleOne.

2. Choose Tools ➪ GroupWise System Operations ➪ Admin-Defined Fields.
3. Highlight an unused Admin-Defined field and click Edit.
4. Highlight the Mobile attribute that you defined in Schema Manager and click OK twice.
5. Edit the properties of a domain with post offices whose address books you want the Mobile attribute to show up in.
6. From the GroupWise tab, select the Address Book property page.

7. Move the Mobile attribute from the Available Fields pane to the Address Book Fields pane, apply the changes, and go back to the main ConsoleOne screen.
8. Repeat Steps 5–7 for each domain where you want the Mobile field to appear.
9. Highlight a post office where you want the Mobile attribute to show up.

   This must be a post office that is owned by a domain that is designed to use the Mobile attribute. Choose Tools ➪ GroupWise Utilities ➪ System Maintenance.
10. Select Rebuild Indexes for Listing and then click Run.
11. Repeat Steps 9 and 10 for each post office where you want the Mobile field to appear.

    Now you can enable the Mobile attribute so that you can add mobile phone numbers to users.
12. Edit the properties of a user object where you want to add a mobile phone number by selecting the Other property page.
13. Select Add, add the Mobile attribute, and fill in the mobile phone number in the Mobile field.

Now, in the GroupWise address book, the Mobile field should show up under the Advanced button when looking at a user.

There's a product called Reach for NDS by Concentrico.net that does what this feature does and a whole lot more. Reach for NDS is available on the CD that comes with this book.

Pending Operations

When changes are made that involve multiple domains, it is possible for these changes to take several minutes (or even several hours) to complete. While connected to a particular domain, the Pending Operations box shown in Figure 6.7 lists all operations that this domain still has marked as unsafe.

Suppose you move a user from one domain to another. Regardless of which domain you are connected to when you make the change, that domain must wait for the other domain to acknowledge that the record to be modified exists. Until that acknowledgement is received by the domain you connected to, the operation you performed will show up in the Pending Operations box.

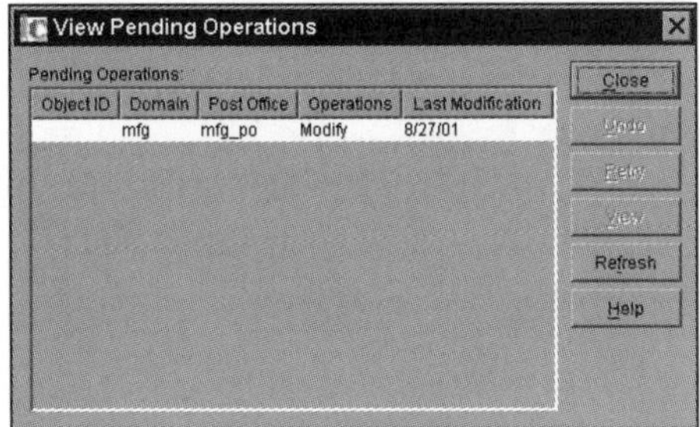

FIGURE 6.7 *The View Pending Operations Box*

If you suspect synchronization problems, you may try using some of the buttons in this window to solve your problem. Unfortunately, this seldom works. Typically, when an operation has gone pending for an extended period, the problem is not a simple one.

- **Undo:** Restores the object record in this database to its original state and sends a request to the other domain or domains to do the same.
- **Retry:** Resends the transaction request. This is only likely to work if the original request somehow got lost in transit — something that seldom happens — or if domain databases have been rebuilt to repair problems.
- **View:** Displays the transaction in more detail.
- **Refresh:** Re-reads the list of pending operations.

Addressing Rules

Addressing rules are find-and-replace operations that act on the addresses that users enter in the To, CC, and BC fields in mail messages they send. This feature was introduced in earlier versions of GroupWise so that Internet-style addresses could be entered without adding a gateway prefix.

In GroupWise 4.1 and 5.2, a user sending to `ppincher@worldwidewidgets.com` would have to enter a string such as `domain.smtp:ppincher@worldwidewidgets.com` or `INTERNET:ppincher@worldwidewidgets.com`.

With addressing rules, the prefix can now be added automatically by the system, making things simpler for the user. Configuring the addressing rules correctly is anything but simple, however.

Fortunately, GroupWise 5.5 and 6 include a much better alternative to using addressing rules: native Internet addressing. If you have a need for an addressing rule for other conditions, then you will want to set up addressing rules for your users. For example, if your users send a message to FAX:8015551212, perhaps you'll want to have the FAX: changed to TOBIT:8015551212. You could do this with an addressing rule (see Figure 6.8).

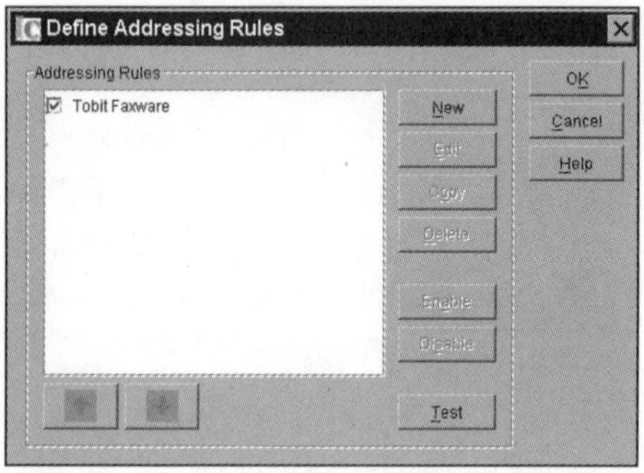

FIGURE 6.8 *The Define Addressing Rules Box*

By default, there are no addressing rules defined. Clicking New will bring up the dialog box shown in Figure 6.9, where you can create new addressing rules.

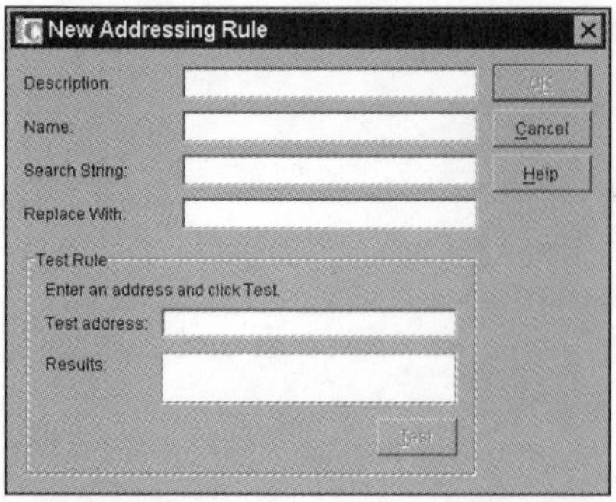

FIGURE 6.9 *The New Addressing Rule Box*

- **Description:** Enter a brief description of the rule.
- **Name:** Name the rule.
- **Search String:** Enter the search string that will trigger the rule.

  For example, FAX:* searches for any address that is preceded with FAX:.
- **Replace With:** Enter the string to replace the address line. Be sure to include all necessary elements of the original address string, as in the following example:

  ```
  GATEWAY_DOM.TOBIT:%1
  ```
- **Test address:** Enter an address that a user might enter, for testing your rule, such as the following:

  ```
  FAX:8015551212
  ```
- **Results:** After clicking the test button, this field will be populated automatically:

  ```
  GATEWAY_DOM.TOBIT: 8015551212
  ```

NOTE

When you create an addressing rule from system operations, it is not enabled at the domain level yet. You must then go to the properties of the domain, and from the GroupWise tab, select the Addressing Rules option. From here, you will see all addressing rules that have been defined from system operations. You can now enable them at the domain level and they will be active. Addressing rules are activated or deactivated at a domain level only. They are created at the system level through system operations.

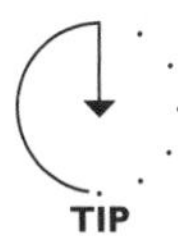
TIP

Addressing rules are processed in order from top to bottom. If you have multiple addressing rules defined, be aware that the format may have been altered by a previous addressing rule by the time it is acted upon by a lower addressing rule. You can rearrange the order of the addressing rules by clicking on the up and down arrows.

Time Zones

In a GroupWise system with post offices in more than one time zone, it is critical that the time zones be correctly configured. If you do business via e-mail with users on the Internet, you will also want to make sure your time zones are configured correctly so that time stamps on your e-mail messages reflect reality.

The time zones that are pre-defined in GroupWise 6 should cover every real time zone on the planet. Most GroupWise 6 shops find that once the correct time zone has been selected at the domain or post office level, time stamps system-wide are accurate.

In Figure 6.10, the list of pre-defined time zones is visible. In Figure 6.11, the Moscow time zone has been selected. The Daylight Savings Time settings for this time zone are displayed at the bottom of the window.

Configure Time Zones
Time Zones:
(GMT) Casablanca, Monrovia
(GMT) Greenwich Mean Time; Dublin, Edinburgh, Lisbon, Lond
(GMT+01:00) Amsterdam, Berlin, Bern, Rome, Stockholm, Vienn
(GMT+01:00) Belgrade, Bratislava, Budapest, Ljubljana, Prague
(GMT+01:00) Brussels, Copenhagen, Madrid, Paris, Vilnius
(GMT+01:00) Sarajevo, Skopje, Sofija, Warsaw, Zagreb
(GMT+02:00) Athens, Istanbul, Minsk
(GMT+02:00) Bucharest
(GMT+02:00) Cairo
Close
Add...
Edit...
Delete
Help
Daylight Saving Time
Start Date/Time:
End Date/Time:

FIGURE 6.10 *The Configure Time Zones Box*

Suppose, though, that you have a need to edit this time zone. (Novell does not recommend this, but the functionality is here for you.) Clicking Edit calls up the box shown in Figure 6.11.

All aspects of the time zone are available to be edited, including the rather tricky algorithm for determining when Daylight Saving Time begins and ends.

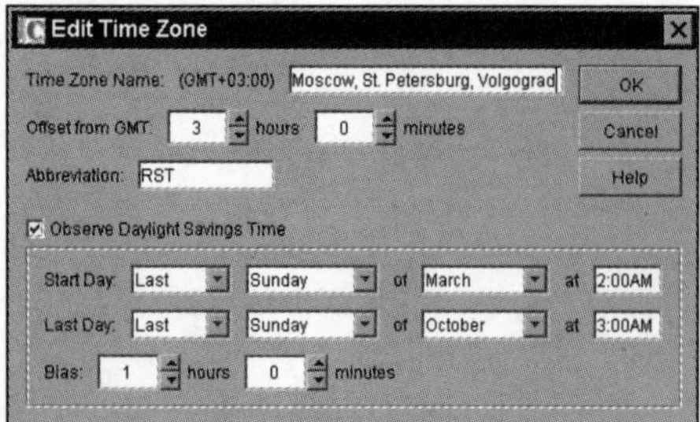

FIGURE 6.11 *The Edit Time Zone Box*

Numerous administrators have made a mistake using this interface. Suppose you have offices in Las Vegas and Phoenix — Las Vegas observes Daylight Saving Time, and Phoenix does not, but both cities observe the same offset from GMT. You have assigned both domains to the Mountain Time time zone. If you connect to the Phoenix domain and edit this time zone (to turn Daylight Saving Time off, of course), you are making that change system-wide. You have just turned Daylight Saving Time off for Phoenix and for Las Vegas.

The mistake was a simple one, and the solution is equally simple. Don't edit time zones. Put Phoenix in a different time zone than Las Vegas. There is even a pre-defined time zone, Arizona, that will suit your needs perfectly in this case. Remember, you are performing system operations in this chapter — if you edit a time zone, you do it for the whole system.

Do not edit time zones, unless you really intend to do so. Editing time zones affects any other entities in the time zone that you edited.

External System Synchronization

If your organization has partners that use GroupWise, you may wish to synchronize your address books with theirs. This synchronization must be set up on both sides, and requires you to choose a single domain on the external system as your point-of-contact.

When configured correctly, external system synchronization (see Figure 6.12) is a powerful collaborative tool. Users in your organization will see members of the external system as entries in the Novell GroupWise address book and will be able to communicate and share with those users just like they do with users on their home system.

This window is blank by default, even if you have defined some external domains in the GroupWise view. To synchronize with these domains you must click Add, at which point you will be presented with the dialog box in Figure 6.13, where you can synchronize your external domains.

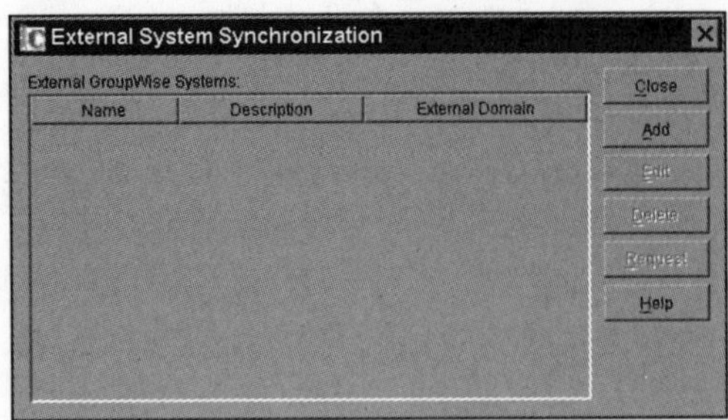

FIGURE 6.12 *The External System Synchronization Box*

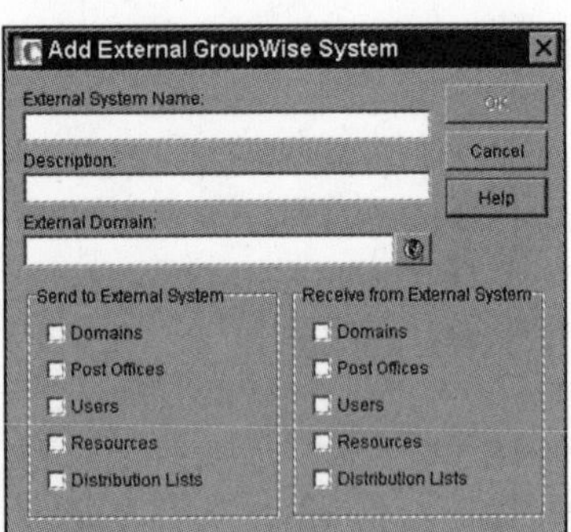

FIGURE 6.13 *The Add External GroupWise System Dialog Box*

- **External System Name:** This is the system name of the external GroupWise system with which you wish to synchronize. You must collect this information from the administrator of that system. In GroupWise 5x, the GroupWise system name is the name that appears at the very top of the GroupWise view when that administrator is connected to one of his or her domains. In GroupWise 6, the GroupWise system name is in the status bar at the bottom of the ConsoleOne administration view. You must highlight the GroupWise system object in order to see the system name at the bottom of the ConsoleOne window. See Figure 6.14 where the system name is noted.

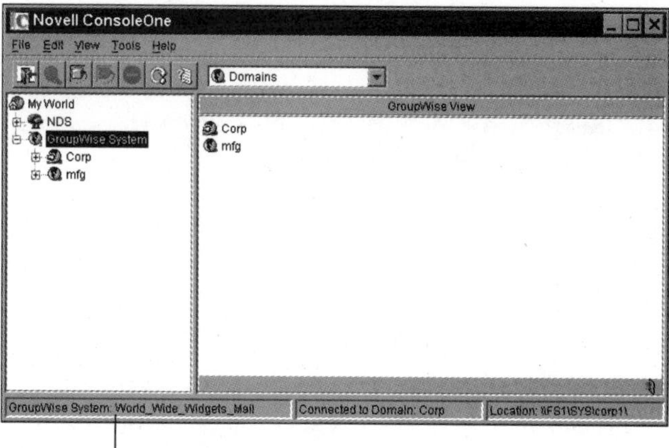

FIGURE 6.14 *The Name of the GroupWise System*

- **Description:** This optional field is best populated with contact information for the administrator of the external system.
- **External Domain:** This field is populated with the GroupWise Browse button to the right. This means that before you can add an external system to your synchronization list, you must define that system in the GroupWise view. To do this, you must right-click the GroupWise system object and choose New ➪ External domain. The resulting dialog box may only be used to define GroupWise objects that are external to your system
- **Send to External System:** This is a list of the classes of objects in your system that will be sent to the external system. If you choose to send something that the external system's administrator does not choose to receive, those object records will be discarded by the external system's MTA.
  - **Domains:** If checked, all domains defined in your system will appear as External GroupWise domains in the external system's GroupWise View.
  - **Post Offices:** If checked, all post offices defined in your system will appear as External GroupWise post offices in the external system's GroupWise view. They will appear hierarchically beneath their domains, if domains have also been selected to be sent.

- **Users:** If checked, all users defined in your system will appear in the external system's address book, except for those users whose visibility has been restricted.

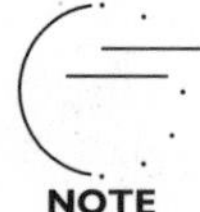

NOTE

A user's object can be kept from synchronizing by editing the user and making selections in the External Sync Override field.

- **Resources:** If checked, all resources defined in your system will appear in the external system's address book, except for those resources whose visibility has been restricted.
- **Distribution Lists:** If checked, all distribution lists defined in your system will appear in the external system's address book, except for those lists whose visibility has been restricted. Note that while invisible users and resources may still be addressed by users who know the object's ID, distribution lists cannot be sent to in this way.

▸ **Receive from External System:** This is a list of the classes of objects in your system that will be sent to the external system.

- **Domains:** If checked, you will see all of the external system's domains in your GroupWise view. This will allow you to specify network links to these domains, which may be helpful if the two systems also share some network infrastructure.
- **Post Offices:** If checked, all of the external system's post offices will appear in your GroupWise view. They will appear hierarchically beneath their domains, if Domains has also been selected.
- **Users:** Check this to have all of the external system's users appear in your GroupWise address book. Note that you will not receive address book records for those users with limited visibility.
- **Resources:** Check this to have all of the external system's resources appear in your GroupWise address book. Note that you will not receive address book records for those resources with limited visibility.
- **Distribution Lists:** Check this to have all of the external system's distribution lists appear in your GroupWise address book. Note that you will not receive address book records for those distribution lists with limited visibility. Your users will not be able to use any of the external system's distribution lists that do not appear in their address book.

Software Directory Management

The software directory management feature (see Figure 6.15) is a powerful tool. A software distribution directory object represents a directory on a file server that contains GroupWise software. These objects may be assigned to post offices, but each post office may only be assigned to one software distribution directory.

Your scheme for managing software distribution directories can have a huge impact on your successful rollout of the GroupWise client, or on upgrading the GroupWise client. Chapter 12 goes into more detail on leveraging the software distribution directories to your advantage.

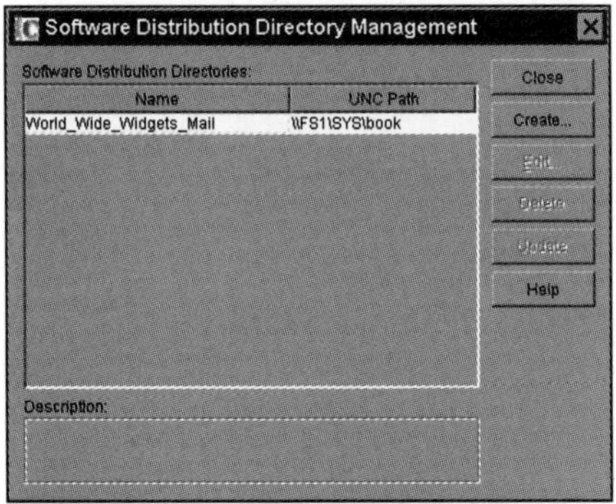

FIGURE 6.15 *The Software Directory Management Window Dialog Box*

There are several things you may want to do with software distribution directories as part of your GroupWise administration:

- Create a new directory
- Move an existing directory to a new path
- Patch or update an existing directory
- Delete an existing directory

Creating New Software Distribution Directories

Clicking the Create button results in the dialog box in Figure 6.16. Software distribution directories give a description to a directory that typically exists already. The largest purpose for defining a SDD is to associate the SDD to post offices so that the users of that post office can update their GroupWise clients when upgrades happen.

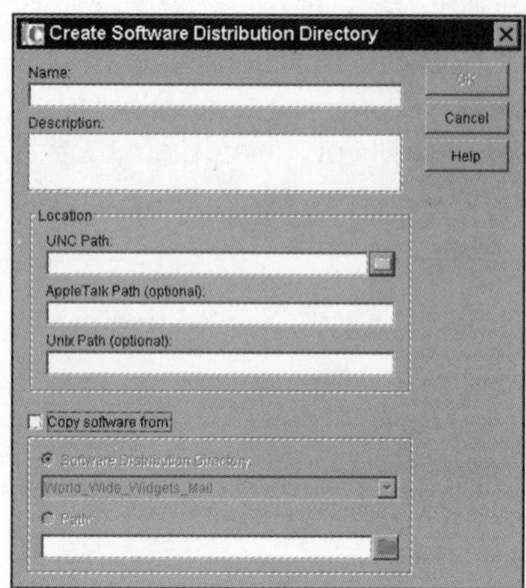

FIGURE 6.16 *The Create Software Distribution Directory Dialog Box*

- **Name:** You must assign a unique name to each software distribution directory object. You may choose to name the object based on the server upon which it will reside.
- **Description:** This optional field may be populated with the name and number of the individual responsible for maintaining the software in this directory. Input a detailed description. This description is used when assigning a software distribution directory to a GroupWise post office.
- **UNC Path:** This is the path to the directory. If a drive has been mapped already, you may browse to the directory. The field will be populated with a drive-based path, but when you click OK, GroupWise administrator converts that path to UNC format.
- **AppleTalk Path:** This optional path will be used only by users of the GroupWise 5.2 Macintosh client who cannot browse to UNC paths.
- **Unix Path:** This optional path will be used only by users of the GroupWise 5.2 Unix client who cannot browse to UNC paths.

- **Copy software from:** If you check this box, you are telling the GroupWise administrator to populate the UNC path that you specified from another software distribution directory or from an unassigned directory.

NOTE

The process responsible for this copy operation is ConsoleOne, running on your workstation. It may not be wise to use this feature to populate software distribution directories across a wide area network. In these cases, you should not use the Copy software from feature; instead, have someone local to that server manually copy the GroupWise 6 software from CD into the directory you specified.

Editing or Moving Existing Directories

All of the attributes of a software distribution directory may be edited, as shown in Figure 6.17.

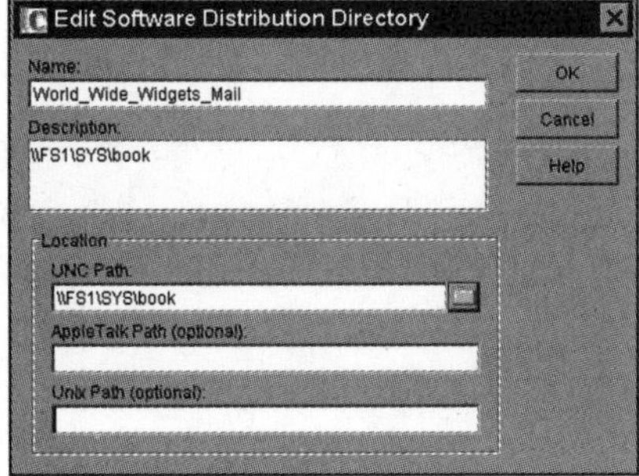

FIGURE 6.17 *The Edit Software Distribution Directory Dialog Box*

Moving a software distribution directory is simple:

1. Using Explorer or a command prompt, move or copy the software from the current location to the new location.
2. Edit the UNC path field and the Name field in the dialog box shown in Figure 6.17 to reflect the new location of the directory.

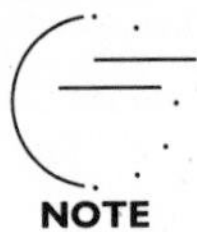

NOTE

Be careful about editing software distribution directories; this causes a number called the *bump number* to be incremented on all post offices that point to this defined software distribution directory. This could cause users to start receiving prompts that there is new GroupWise software available. More about this is covered in Chapter 12.

Deleting Existing Directories

This interface may be used to delete the software distribution directory object, but the directory itself must be deleted manually. This action prevents accidental deletion of software in cases where SDD objects share physical directories.

Patching or Updating Existing Directories

This tool (see Figure 6.18) is used only *after* a patch or upgrade has been applied to a software distribution directory somewhere on the system. For instructions regarding applying patches, refer to the readme file or files associated with that particular patch.

FIGURE 6.18 *The Update Software Distribution Directory Dialog Box*

Once one directory on the system has been updated, you may use this interface to copy the updated files from the updated directory to other directories.

Note: Again, be careful about using this to distribute software across the WAN. It is probably a wiser use of bandwidth to patch or update remote software distribution directories while on location.

The Force auto-update check by GroupWise components check box exists to alert the GroupWise client that new software is available. When you check this box and click OK, the new software bump number associated with this SDD is incremented by one. This is not something to be undertaken lightly! Every

GroupWise client that attaches to any post office assigned to this SDD must browse to the UNC path and check to see if the code in the directory is newer than the code on the user's workstation. If the UNC path is not available (that is, the user has no rights to the directory), then an error will be reported.

This subject will be covered completely in Chapter 12.

Using Restore Area Management

A restore area is a location where a post office has been restored from backup. There's no set procedure on how you might configure restore areas. You may want to create one per post office. Or you could just create restore areas on demand. When there's a need to restore something, and you've brought a post office off of backup, you would come in here to define a restore area.

- **Restore Area Directories:** Displays the directories in your GroupWise system that have been designated as restore areas for post offices.
- **Description:** Select a restore area directory to display any information entered in the Description field when the restore area was created. To modify or add a description, click Edit.
- **Create:** To create a restore area, click Create. You can create multiple restore areas.
- **Edit:** Select a restore area directory and then Edit to modify the name, description, or location of the restore area.
- **Delete:** Select a restore area directory and then click Delete to delete the restore area.

Restore areas is part of a whole new backup and restore system that is new to GroupWise 6. An even fuller explanation of how to use the GroupWise backup and restore features is fully explained in Appendix A.

Internet Addressing

Since the early 1990s, GroupWise has used a proprietary addressing format, commonly called *UPD format* for User.PostOffice.Domain. With GroupWise 5.5, Novell made it possible for the administrator to change the internal addressing algorithms. GroupWise 5.5 and GroupWise 6 can be configured to use Internet-style addresses natively (see Figure 6.19).

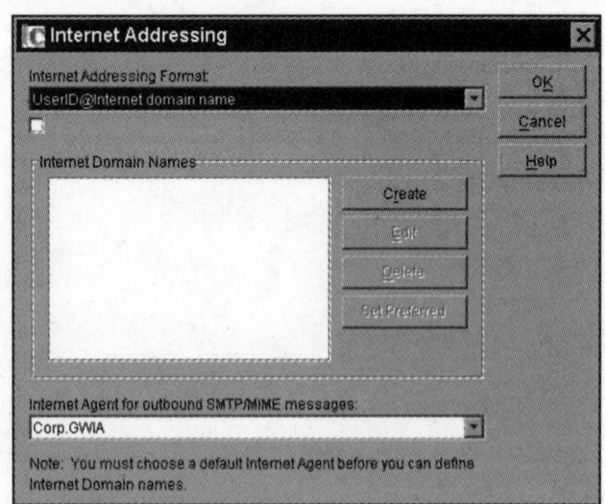

FIGURE 6.19 *The Internet Addressing Window*

Because of the significant impact of this change, there's an entire chapter devoted to Internet addressing. Refer to Chapter 16 for more information.

Summary

This chapter explored how to use a number of tools that apply changes to your entire GroupWise system. Now that you are familiar with each of them, it is time to move into the GroupWise utilities in Chapter 7.

CHAPTER 7

Using GroupWise Utilities and Diagnostics

There are still quite a few GroupWise administration tools you need to be introduced to. This chapter discusses the GroupWise Utilities menu and the functionality it presents. This chapter also shows you the GroupWise diagnostics.

The GroupWise Utilities Menu

Much of the work you will do administering the GroupWise system will be done from the GroupWise Utilities menu. Here you find the tools to maintain and repair libraries and user mailboxes, set global defaults for users' GroupWise client preferences, define links between your GroupWise servers, and more.

NOTE

The GroupWise Utilities menu is context-sensitive. The available menu items change depending on which view is active and what type of object has been selected. This documentation is based upon the original shipping version of GroupWise 6. It is expected that improvements will be made to the original GroupWise 6 shipping code, and so some menu options will change.

The GroupWise Utilities menu shown in Figure 7.1 illustrates the functions that can be performed on a particular object.

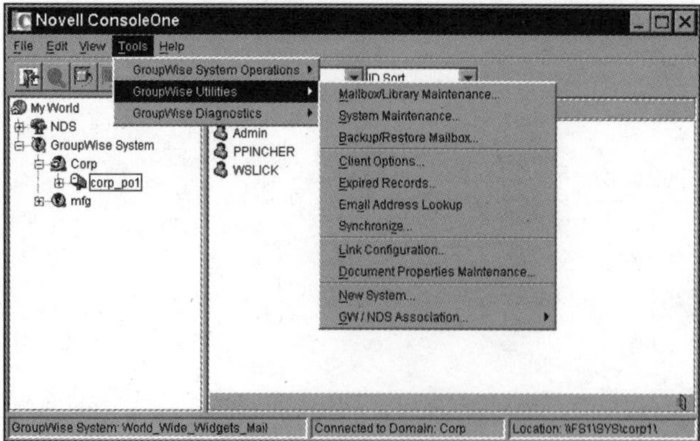

FIGURE 7.1 *The GroupWise Utilities Menu*

For some of the options on the GroupWise Utilities menu, this chapter gives only a brief description, because these utilities will be discussed further in other chapters.

Mailbox/Library Maintenance

These are the tools you will use to repair the GroupWise information store. Mailbox/Library Maintenance is just another name for the GroupWise check utility, or GWCHECK. When you issue a Mailbox/Library Maintenance job from ConsoleOne, the selections that you make are sent to the POA for the post office you selected. Then the POA runs the job using the GWCHECK code, which is embedded right into the POA. In Chapter 17, you can find much more detail on using Mailbox/Library Maintenance.

System Maintenance

These tools are for the repair of the GroupWise directory domain and post office databases. Chapter 17 gives practical circumstances under which to use System Maintenance.

Backup/Restore Mailbox

This is a menu item that is a piece of the Smart Purge and Backup/Restore system in GroupWise 6. By using this feature, you can manually specify that a post office's user databases have been backed up, and a backup timestamp should be put into the user databases. Selecting this menu option, and selecting Backup or Restore, will send a message to the POA to complete this function. Appendix A gives a thorough explanation on how to use this Backup/Restore Mailbox, along with other features related to Backup/Restore Mailbox.

Client Options

Figure 7.2 shows that the Client Options window looks very similar to the interface found under the Tools ➪ Options interface in the 32-bit GroupWise client. Settings here may be made and specified as defaults or even locked down as defaults for users, post offices, or entire domains.

A double-click on the Environment button shows the dialog box in Figure 7.3.

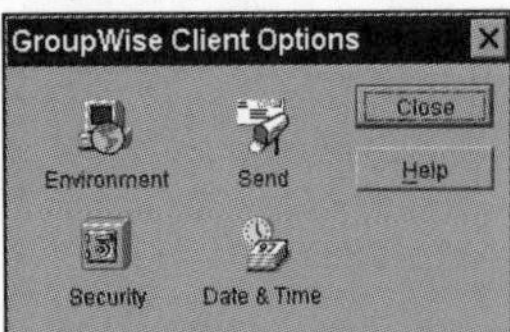

FIGURE 7.2 *The GroupWise Client Options Dialog Box in ConsoleOne*

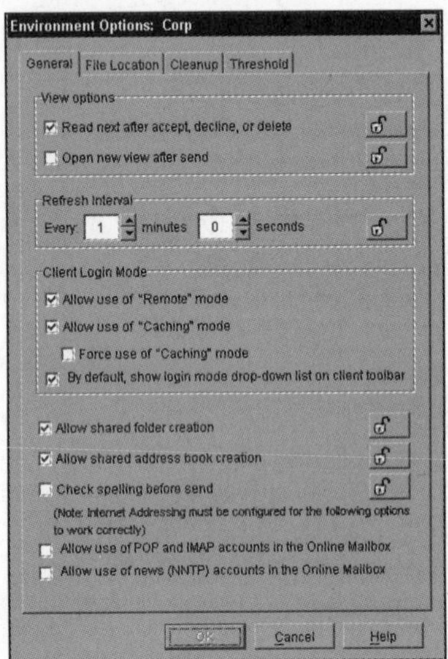

FIGURE 7.3 *Administering GroupWise Client Environment Options in ConsoleOne*

Client Environment Options

This dialog box looks somewhat similar to the Tools ➪ Options ➪ Environment dialog box as seen from the GroupWise 32-bit Windows client. The View Options and Refresh Interval sections are identical to the GroupWise 32-bit client. Imagine, for example, that you did not want the user's mailboxes to refresh every one minute, but instead every two minutes by default. Changing the Refresh Interval to a value of 2 would accomplish your design. Users can change this back to 1 or to 3 or whatever else they would like. Take note, however, of the set of padlock buttons on the right-hand side. If you want to make sure that the user's mailboxes refreshes only every two minutes, you could set the padlock button, which would lock down this setting so that users cannot make a change.

IMPORTANT

Client options can be set, and/or locked, on a user, post office, or domain level. If you want to set an option on an entire post office, make sure to highlight that post office, and then choose Tools ➪ GroupWise Utilities ➪ Client Options. If you want to set the client options for an entire domain, you would highlight the domain object, and choose Tools ➪ GroupWise Utilities ➪ Client Options.

You can change any setting listed in this dialog box, which will effectively change the default options for users who have not changed their defaults. Clicking on the adjacent padlock puts a locked setting in place. This will prevent users from changing their individual default, and it will also force the setting down to users who may have already changed it. If a user were to view these settings after the administrator has locked them down, they would be grayed out, and they would not be able to modify them.

NOTE

The settings you configure in client options do not carry over for GroupWise users that are in GroupWise remote mode or GroupWise caching mode.

Client Login Mode With the selection in this section of the Environment options, you can control how much flexibility GroupWise has to make copies of a user's mailbox for additional speed or functionality. GroupWise has always had a remote mode. With GroupWise 6, caching mode has been added. The caching mode really does all that remote mode ever did, and even more. The caching mode allows the GroupWise client to receive regular automatic updates to the caching mailbox, as well as keep a live connection with the GroupWise POA, which is necessary for functions such as busy search or cross-post-office proxy. Another advantage to caching mode is that the GroupWise client needs to chat far less with the GroupWise POA in order to read data from the GroupWise information store. Also, if the POA goes down for some reason, when the GroupWise client is in caching mode, the GroupWise client doesn't even blink.

WARNING

The caching mode feature replicates a user's entire mailbox down to that user's local hard drive. If in your GroupWise system you do not have a message expiration policy, and the GWCHECK-Mailbox/Library Maintenance procedures to enforce the expiration policy, your users could have more data than can be contained on their local hard drive.

The GroupWise 6 client can interact with the GroupWise user's mailbox when it is in one of three different locations. These locations are the following:

- The post office
- A copy of the user's mailbox in caching mode
- A copy of the user's mailbox in remote mode

If you do not want your users to use caching mode, make sure that the Allow use of "Caching" mode check box is unchecked.

The GroupWise client is capable of establishing a *live remote* connection with an MTA. This MTA then opens a link down to the user's post office, and the post office agent accesses the user's mail. Because of this, you can have remote users running in caching mode even if they are not physically on your company's network.

NOTE

The GroupWise client in caching mode cannot establish a live remote with an MTA. For this purpose, you may still need to support users' ability to use GroupWise remote.

For example, imagine that you have a couple of users that connect over a slow WAN link to their post office. Since the caching mode is much less chatty than a normal client/server connection to the POA, you could force some users to use caching mode. To do this, highlight the individual, then go into Tools ⇨ GroupWise Utilities ⇨ Client Options and select the check box, Force use of "Caching" mode.

The option, By default, show login mode drop-down list on client toolbar, is useful for this reason. If your users were GroupWise 5x users before, they never saw the online or caching options in their GroupWise client. Rather than confuse your GroupWise 5x users, or leave them to make the decision to go to caching mode, you can just hide this feature by unchecking the option, By default, show login mode drop-down list on client toolbar.

Allow Shared Folder Creation This option lets you take away the ability, or enable the ability, for users to share folders. This option should generally be enabled.

Allow Shared Address Book Creation This option lets you take away the ability, or enable the ability, for users to share address books. If you are using another address book solution, then you would want to take away the ability to share address books. This will encourage users to use another address solution for sharing addresses. For example, if you were to implement Reach for NDS by Concentrico.net, you would most likely want to disable shared address book creation. Appendix B introduces Concentrico.net's Reach for NDS product.

Check Spelling before Send This option is not enabled by default, but since good spelling is a dying art in this modern era of spell-checking computers, it may be a good idea to enable it.

Allow Use of POP/IMAP/NNTP Accounts in the Online Mailbox This option is not enabled by default, which is a good idea. If you allow users to POP their mailboxes from other e-mail accounts, they could bloat your message store beyond what you may have expected. The same goes for IMAP and NNTP. Generally, you will want to enable this feature on a user-by-user basis. If you enable the POP/IMAP feature, your users will see the Accounts menu option right next to the Tools menu. Figure 7.4 shows an account for which POP/IMAP has been enabled. If NNTP is enabled, then when a user goes to create a folder, one of the options on the folder will enable them to define NNTP specific information.

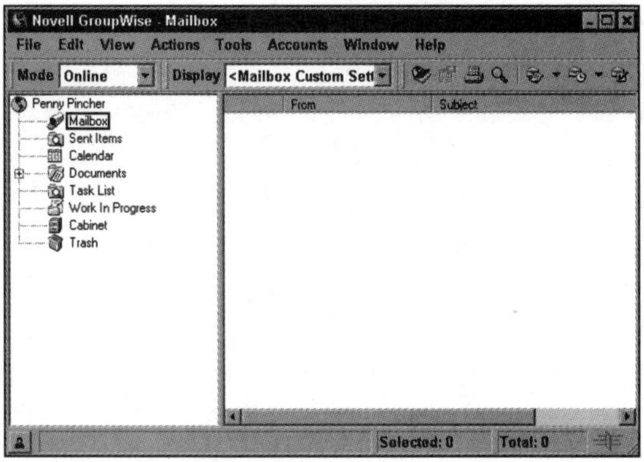

FIGURE 7.4 *The GroupWise Client with POP3/IMAP4 Enabled*

If a user is in caching mode or remote mode, that user has the ability to access POP3, IMAP4, and NNTP accounts, even if you have locked those features down. The reason for this is that the GroupWise POA cannot exert control over a GroupWise information store that is on a user's hard drive. So, these features cannot be controlled.

File Location – Archive Moving to the File Location tab in the Environment Options box, GroupWise users can archive their messages off to a location different from their mailbox. This way, if you have a message expiration policy of 90 days, users have recourse for saving messages that are important enough to them to retain beyond 90 days. There are some organizations that don't want the legal liability with archived messages. If your organization does not want users to archive, keep the path blank, and click the padlock button.

File Location – Custom Views This is part of a somewhat obscure but useful feature. If a user has a standard message, or even a template message that they often send, that user can save that message in the form of a View file. The File Location tab simply indicates where custom views should be saved by default.

Cleanup In this tab in the Environment Options box, you can specify just how mail messages should be cleaned up. The options in this tab can be useful for implementing a message retention policy. Using Mailbox/Library Maintenance jobs is a more effective method for implementing a message retention policy though. All of the cleanup options, except the archive options, are performed by the POA during a process called *nightly user upkeep*. If the auto-archive feature has been selected, then the archiving operation takes place when the GroupWise client logs in each day. The client must do the archiving because the POA would usually not have rights or even access to the user's archive path.

Cleanup – Allow Purge of Items Not Backed Up With GroupWise 6 and the Smart Purge and Backup/Restore system, GroupWise can be configured to not automatically purge items that are deleted from the trash. Thus, before a backup has been done, nothing will truly be purged from the information store.

This is a powerful feature, but if your organization does not intend to use this, it's useless to have this feature enabled. In fact, if you have this feature enabled, and you don't use it correctly, your information store will just grow and grow, at a rate you've never seen before! It's best to leave this option checked, until you are sure you've completely implemented the software for the Smart Purge and Backup/Restore system. Configuring and using these systems is explained in Appendix A.

Threshold The Threshold tab in the Environment Options box has to do with when users are connected directly to their post office via a drive letter mapping using direct mode, which is a connectivity mode you can set on any post office. When a user is connected in direct mode, the threshold value determines just how many recipients of a message within the post office the sender is on will have their user databases written to by the sender's GroupWise client.

WARNING

Do not regularly allow your users to connect directly to their post office via Direct mode, this opens you up for all kinds of corruption if used on a regular basis.

Send Options – Disk Space Mgmt All other client options mirror 32-Bit Windows client's options, except the Disk Space Mgmt feature. With this feature, you can specify just how much disk space users are able to take up with their mailbox, as well as the largest message that users are able to send.

- **Mailbox Size Limits:** This is the maximum amount of space allocated to users for their messages and the attachments associated with those messages. Chapter 4 discusses how in GroupWise even address lists can be spun off as attachments. Those address lists do affect the size of the message store, so even long attachment lists will impact a user's mailbox size limit.
- **Threshold for Warning Users:** When a user is getting close to the quota of disk space, with this feature, the GroupWise client warns the user that allocated disk space is getting low.
- **Maximum Send Message Size:** What if you don't want your users to send messages over a certain size. This option is the way you control users from using e-mail as an FTP utility!

Understanding the Architecture behind the Client Options Interface

As Part I of this book noted, the GroupWise administration snapins write changes directly to the GroupWise domain database to which it is connected. For client options to take effect, however, the changes must propagate all the way down to the GroupWise user database, USERxxx.DB. Here is the flow of events:

1. The administrator makes a change to client options.

   For example, imagine that you have unchecked the box labeled Allow shared folder creation, and then locked that setting. Assume that the post office object was selected at the time you made the change. This means that the setting will apply to the entire post office.
2. The GroupWise administrator snapins write the change to the GroupWise domain database and create an administration update file to propagate this change to the post office.
3. The MTA transmits this file to the POA.

4. The POA administration thread writes this change to the Post Office database.
5. A POA writes the change to the preferences capsule of the user database, or to user databases that are affected by the changes in client options.

Using Client Options to Lock Down the GroupWise Archive

The following scenario walks through the process of editing a client option. Here is the scenario:

A company policy has been established that all GroupWise mailbox archives must be created on the network. All users have home directories mapped to the root of drive U:, and GroupWise administrators need to enforce the policy and force all archives for all users into their home directories.

1. From ConsoleOne, select a domain object.

   If there are multiple domains in this system, perform Steps 1-8 for each domain.
2. Pull down the Tools menu and choose GroupWise Utilities ➪ Client Options.
3. Double-click the Environment button.
4. Click the File Location tab to get to Figure 7.5.
5. In the Archive Directory field, enter the following:

   ```
   U:\GWArchive
   ```
6. Click the padlock button to lock this option.

   Because you are doing this with a domain selected, the option will be locked for all users on this domain.
7. Click OK and close out of the Environment Options dialog box.

At this point, all you need to do is wait for this option to propagate. The next time users log in, they will find that their archives must be created in their home directories.

Now, suppose users already had archives on the local drives. In this case, you would have to move the archives manually, visiting each workstation. There is no central administration tool for working with existing GroupWise archives. If you want to administer an archive location, it would be wise for you to decide this before users begin using the archive feature of GroupWise. Otherwise, they may lose access to the archives on their local drives.

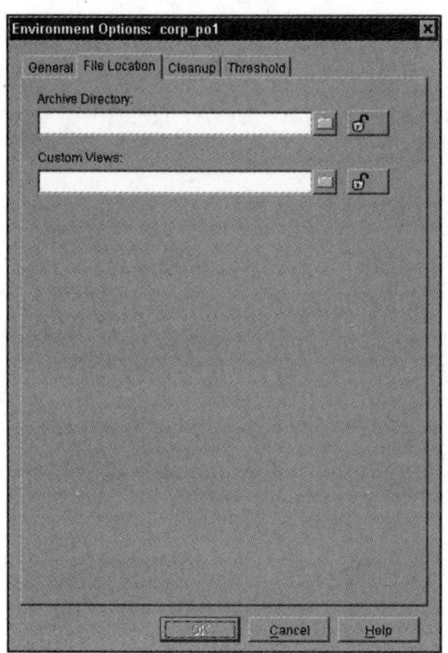

FIGURE 7.5 *The Environment Options File Location Tab*

If the user's archive path does not exist, then the GroupWise client will not be able to run the auto-archive operation. In other words, using the preceding example, when the administrator defines the archive path to U:\GWArchive and locks this down, the end user's client will not auto archive the first time they log in. This is because their unique archive directory does not exist under the U:\GWArchive directory. They will simply need to manually archive something, or go to File ⇨ Open Archive, and then close the archive. This will create the unique user directory with a couple of archive databases in the U:\GWArchive\ofFIDarc directory. Now the next time the user logs into GroupWise from the GroupWise client, the auto-archive function will run. Remember that this applies only if you have enabled auto archiving from the Cleanup tab. Any manual archives will work just fine, of course.

Expired Records

Returning to the GroupWise Utilities menu, GroupWise administration allows you to set an expiration time on a GroupWise user's account. This tool allows you to easily see accounts that have expired (see Figure 7.6).

If users have been assigned an expiration date, you may need a way to determine which users are expiring when. Users who have expired can still receive mail, but they cannot open their mailboxes. Expiration is a useful way to deal with temporary or contract employees without having to commit to deleting their mailboxes.

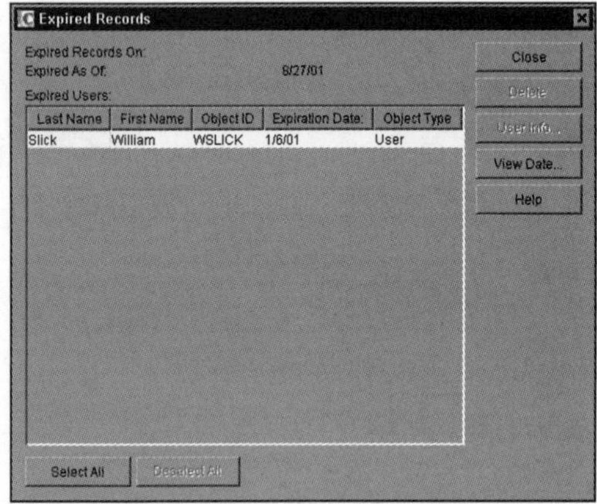

FIGURE 7.6 *The Expired Records Box*

Email Address Lookup

Many organizations want to make sure that their GroupWise user IDs are unique throughout the system. With this nifty feature, you can type in your proposed name and see if it has already been used. You can enter the name in many different formats to perform the lookup. It can be simply a user ID, `first.last` name, `last.first` name, or any of the these with the `@domain.x` applied as well.

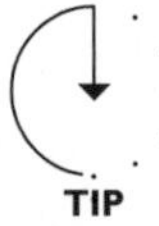

The Email Address Lookup option will also find alias records. The search window must match exactly what a user has defined as an alias, however. This will be helpful to quickly search for an address that you think may be coming from an alias record.

Synchronize

The synchronization dialog box shown in Figure 7.7 is a little misleading.

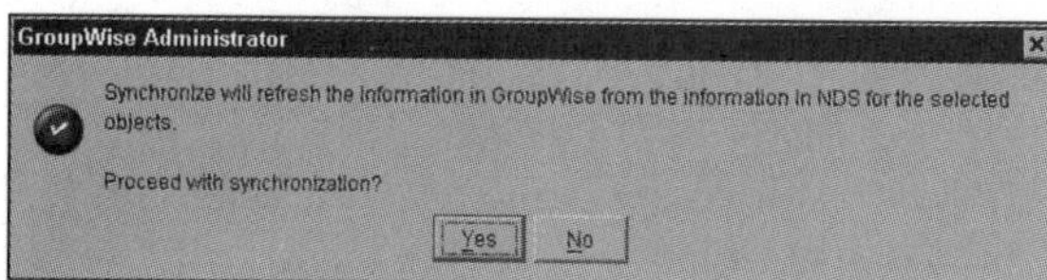

FIGURE 7.7 *The Synchronize Object Dialog Box*

The synchronization process is nowhere as simple as the description in this dialog. Assuming that ConsoleOne is connected to the primary domain, and the administrator synchronizes a user belonging to a secondary domain, here's what happens:

1. NDS-specific information in the user object is rolled into the synchronization request.
2. The synchronization request is sent to the secondary domain that owns this user.
3. The secondary domain updates the user object with information that was extracted from NDS.
4. The secondary domain bundles the GroupWise-specific information about the user object into another synchronization request.
5. The secondary domain propagates the new information to its post offices.
6. The secondary domain sends the request from step 4 to the primary domain.
7. The primary domain propagates this information to all other secondary domains.
8. All other secondary domains propagate the information to their post offices.

Synchronize only synchronizes the object that you have highlighted. For example, if you highlight a post office, it sends a message to the entire system regarding the post office object itself. All of the users on that post office are not synchronized, just the post office object itself.

The synchronization process initiated here is nearly identical to the process of updating or creating objects — the only difference being that no "new" information is created. The record is simply being re-propagated through the GroupWise directory.

Link Configuration

This tool allows you to define the connections and routes for messages on your GroupWise system. For example, how a post office connects to its domain, or how one domain connects to another domain.

The Link Configuration tool is used to define the connections, or links, between the domains and post offices on your GroupWise system. These links govern the way that the GroupWise message transfer agent (MTA) routes messages.

Before exploring the Link Configuration interface, you need to be familiar with some terms.

- **Link type:** Link types describe the type of route between two domains. A link type may be direct, indirect, gateway, or undefined.
- **Direct:** A direct link between two domains means that those domains' MTAs "talk" directly to each other. There is no domain or gateway intervening.
- **Indirect:** An indirect link between two domains means that a third domain is involved in any communication between them. For instance, if Domain A has an indirect link with Domain C through Domain B, then the Domain A MTA will send to the Domain B MTA, and the Domain B MTA will route the message to Domain C.
- **Gateway:** A gateway link between two domains indicates that the domains must communicate through a gateway, such as Async or GWIA. In this case, both domains must have the same type of gateway installed at their systems. For instance, if Domain A has a gateway link to Domain B through the Async gateway, then the Domain A MTA will hand the message to the Async gateway. This gateway will then dial Domain B's Async gateway to hand the message off again. Finally, Domain B's Async gateway will hand the message off to the Domain B MTA.
- **Link protocol:** Link protocols describe the type of connection between two domains. Differentiating between link type and link protocol is easy. Think of a trip on a U.S. highway. Link type is like your route — your

choice of roads. Link protocol is like your choice of vehicles — it is your transport mechanism. The protocol choices you are offered are mapped, UNC, and TCP/IP.

- **Mapped:** A mapped link is typically used by an MTA on an NT box. That machine must have a drive mapped to the link target. Mapped links to post offices require the MTA to actively poll the post office WPCSIN queues for mail to be transported. Mapped links take the form of `<drive letter>:\<path>`.
- **UNC:** A UNC link is similar to a mapped link, in that an MTA with a UNC link to a post office must poll the post office WPCSIN queues. UNC links do not require drive mappings, however, and for that reason are preferred over mapped links. UNC links take the form of `\\<server>\<volume>\<path>`.
- **TCP/IP:** TCP/IP links are preferred over both UNC and mapped links. With TCP/IP, the MTA need not poll post office directories. The post office agent (POA) will poll the structure and will only open a connection with the MTA when there are items to be transferred.

The window shown in Figure 7.8 has four main components:

- The toolbar
- The domain drop-down menu
- The Outbound Links pane
- The Inbound Links pane

The Link Configuration Toolbar

This toolbar has eight buttons on it. These buttons allow you to perform operations without accessing menu items. Here's a description of these buttons from left to right:

- **Open:** The first button is the Open Domain button. It allows you to connect to a different domain database for configuring links. You will be prompted for the path to a domain database.
- **Save:** The second button is the Save button. This saves all changes you have made to link configuration in the current domain database.
- **Undo:** If you have made changes but have not saved them yet, you can use the third button to revert to the original link configuration.

- **Help:** The fourth button opens the help file to the Link Configuration Contents page.
- **Find:** The fifth button allows you to find a domain link by entering a domain name. This is useful for very large systems.
- **Link:** The sixth button opens the highlighted link for viewing or editing. This will be discussed further under the "Editing Links" section later in this chapter, as well as in Chapter 9.
- **Domain Links:** The seventh button changes the display of the tool so that only domain links are displayed.
- **Post Office Links:** The last button changes the display of the tool so that only post office links are displayed.

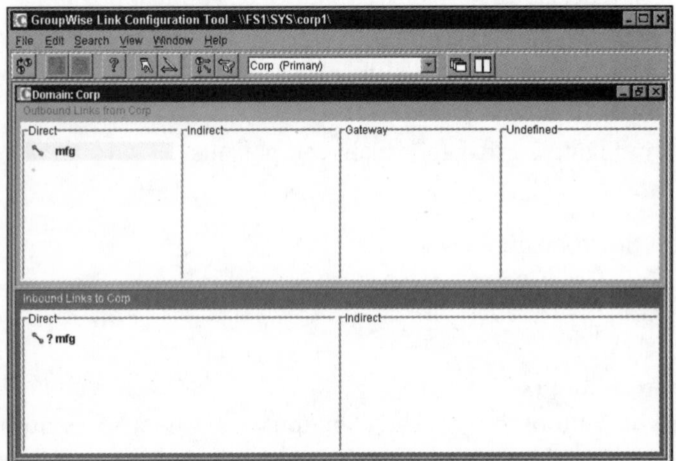

FIGURE 7.8 *The Link Configuration Tool with Domain Links Displayed*

The Domain Drop-Down Menu

In Figure 7.8, this menu reads "Corp (Primary)." This means that it's the primary domain's links being examined. Changing this to another domain does not change the system connection, however. Remember that all domains have copies of each other's records — you can be connected to one domain and change the links for a different domain.

To change the system connection, use the first button on the toolbar, or go to the File menu and select Open.

The Outbound Links Pane

This pane displays each of the outbound links, or "send" connections for this domain. Notice that domains displayed here are listed by link type, which is either direct, indirect, gateway, or undefined. The View menu can also be used to display links to this domain's post offices instead of links to other domains.

The Inbound Links Pane

This pane displays each of the inbound links, or "receive" connections for this domain. The sales domain's outbound link to Corp will be the same as the Corp domain's inbound link from sales. Outbound links can be edited — inbound links are edited by changing the corresponding outbound link somewhere else.

Again, use the View menu to expand this display to include gateway and undefined links, or to switch to post office links.

Editing Links

If you have created your domains and post offices properly, assigning IP addresses and ports right away, you may not need to edit links. The default links are probably going to work well. On complex systems, however, you will do quite a bit of link configuration.

To change a link type or a link protocol, simply double-click on a link in the outbound links pane. You may also highlight the link and click on the Link button on the toolbar. The resulting interface allows you to change the type and the protocol of the link. Chapter 9 discusses this even further, as part of a detailed exploration of the GroupWise MTA.

Document Properties Maintenance

This menu option is available only when a post office is selected, and it allows you to customize default property sheets for documents in GroupWise libraries (see Figure 7.9). Chapter 14 goes into much more detail on how and when to use the document properties maintenance tool.

If document management figures in to your GroupWise strategy, then you will want to become familiar with this tool. With a post office object selected, the menu item is available under the GroupWise Utilities menu.

This tool allows you to do the following things:

- Change the property sheet fields for documents for each GroupWise library
- Create or edit lookup tables for populating certain property sheet fields
- Add or edit document types to fit your document retention strategy
- Create relationships between fields and between lookup tables

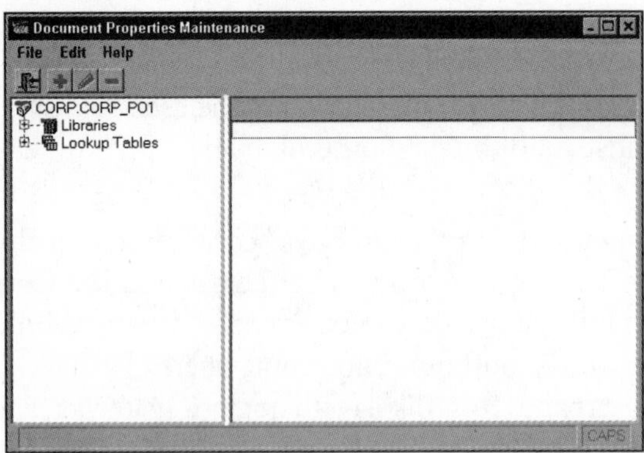

FIGURE 7.9 *The Document Properties Maintenance Tool*

New System

If you have already created a GroupWise system, it is unlikely that you will want to use this tool. Most organizations fare better with a single GroupWise system spanning multiple domains than with multiple GroupWise systems.

When you launch ConsoleOne for the first time after installing the GroupWise snapins, this wizard loads automatically. It walks you through the process of creating a GroupWise system, gathering domain and post office names from you, creating those objects, and then installing the necessary agent software.

This chapter does not this discuss this interface, but you can find information about the interface in Chapter 2.

GW/NDS Association

This section discusses your options when you select the GW/NDS Association option under the GroupWise Utilities menu.

Graft GroupWise Objects

The Graft Wizard helps you add GroupWise attributes to NDS user objects, and add GroupWise objects to the NDS tree. Recall that GroupWise has its own directory independent of NDS. The graft function is used on the occasions that a GroupWise object isn't in NDS, or is somehow not associated with its NDS object. Throughout this book, you can find instances in which you will be told to use the graft function. If you are creating a GroupWise 6 system from scratch, you will not need to use this tool, since your NDS user objects will automatically be grafted to the GroupWise mailboxes you create.

Disassociate GroupWise Attributes

This feature is the opposite of a graft. This feature is used when you want to disassociate a GroupWise object from its NDS object. This is often used for troubleshooting purposes. For example, you suspect that an NDS object has some corruption in it, and you want to delete the object from NDS, but not from GroupWise; this is a perfect scenario to disassociate the NDS object from its GroupWise object.

As illustrated in Chapter 3 and in Chapter 5, when GroupWise is first installed into a network, it adds attributes to, or *extends,* the NDS user object. This makes administration of user accounts much simpler.

Unfortunately, the synchronization between NDS and the GroupWise domain and post office databases is not perfect. Sometimes, particularly after a user moves, the NDS user object contains inaccurate GroupWise attributes, and the user mailbox can no longer be administered from ConsoleOne.

Enter the Disassociate GroupWise Attributes tool! This tool strips all of the GroupWise information from the highlighted user's NDS object.

Using the Disassociate GroupWise Attributes Tool

This tool has no interface window of its own. To remove GroupWise attributes from a user, do the following:

1. Select the user object in the NDS view.
2. Pull down the Tools menu and choose GroupWise Utilities ➪ GW/NDS Association ➪ Disassociate GroupWise Attributes.

If you were to use Display Object on a user whose GroupWise attributes had been removed, you would find that none of the attributes with NGW in their names (the GroupWise schema extensions) were populated. Also, "GDS" (GroupWise directory services) information appears. The NDS object would no longer be linked to a GroupWise object.

When GroupWise attributes have been removed, the user's mailbox still exists. All that has happened, in practical terms, is the link between the GDS and NDS systems has been broken for this user.

GroupWise Diagnostics

This section discusses your options when you select the GroupWise Diagnostics option under the GroupWise Utilities menu.

Display Object

One of the most useful tools the developers had for debugging was the display object tool. This window bypasses the usual object details windows and displays all record data as straight text.

This is a useful tool for viewing all the information about any object in your GroupWise system in one simple view. GroupWise diagnostics is particularly helpful because it allows you to see some information that is not available to be seen any other place. GroupWise diagnostics is an information gathering tool, but it in no way does a health-check type diagnosis of a GroupWise system or object. At various points throughout this book, you'll be told to use GroupWise diagnostics to garner some little piece of information.

In the example in Figure 7.10, a distribution list called CorpUsers is highlighted. The top window pane shows the GDS (GroupWise directory store) information. The bottom window pane establishes the context and class of this object record in NDS. Then you are given a flat list of attribute names and values.

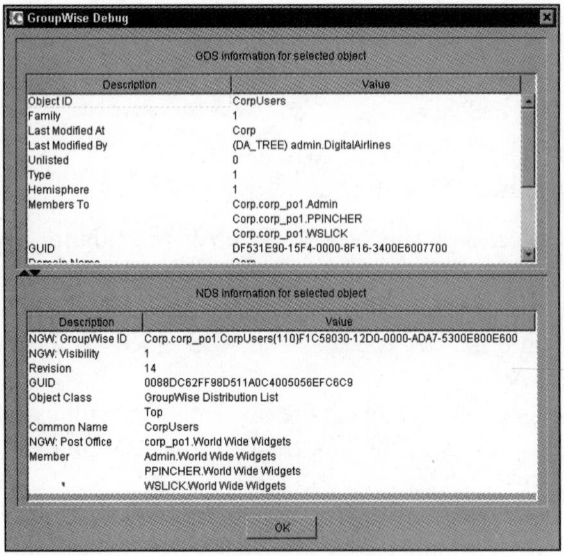

GroupWise Debug

GDS information for selected object

Description	Value
Object ID	CorpUsers
Family	1
Last Modified At	Corp
Last Modified By	(DA_TREE) admin.DigitalAirlines
Unlisted	0
Type	1
Hemisphere	1
Members To	Corp.corp_po1.Admin Corp.corp_po1.PPINCHER Corp.corp_po1.WSLICK
GUID	DF531E90-15F4-0000-8F16-3400E6007700

NDS information for selected object

Description	Value
NGW: GroupWise ID	Corp.corp_po1.CorpUsers{110}F1C58030-12D0-0000-ADA7-5300E800E600
NGW: Visibility	1
Revision	14
GUID	0088DC62FF98D511A0C4005056EFC6C9
Object Class	GroupWise Distribution List Top
Common Name	CorpUsers
NGW: Post Office	corp_po1.World Wide Widgets
Member	Admin.World Wide Widgets PPINCHER.World Wide Widgets WSLICK.World Wide Widgets

OK

FIGURE 7.10 *Display Object Window*

Here's a comparison of the values for GDS Object Start and NDS Object Start:

- **GDS Object Start:** Corp.corp_po1.CorpUsers
- **NDS Object Start:** CorpUsers.Corp.World_Wide_Widgets

The GDS value lists the GroupWise domain, post office, and finally the object name. The NDS value lists the object name, its container(s), and the root container. In both cases, the object name is the same, but the contexts are different.

This illustrates one of the differences between the WPDOMAIN.DB (or GDS) and NDS systems: GDS objects are addressed in `<domain>.<post office>.<object>` format, while NDS objects are addressed in `<object>.<container>.<container>.<organization>` format. NDS is ultimately more flexible, because it allows more than three levels of hierarchy.

General Edit

The name of this tool is counter-intuitive. No actual editing is allowed through this interface; it is read-only. This tool is similar to the display object tool, but it only shows information from the GDS system, as read from the connected GroupWise domain database.

Unlike display object, general edit shows the same information regardless of what was selected when the tool was activated. General edit is a window into the "guts" of the domain database, and from the Record Enumeration box in Figure 7.11, any record may be selected.

What's presented is a concise but complete display of the GDS information about this object.

Like the display object tool, general edit is typically useful when troubleshooting synchronization problems.

Information

This tool (see Figure 7.12) is available when highlighting the GroupWise system, a GroupWise domain, or a GroupWise post office.

This is a quick way to find out how many of which kinds of objects exist in a GroupWise system, domain, or post office. It can also be used to display the record state of users and other objects.

Record Enumeration

This dialog allows you to enumerate all records of a selected type in the domain database. Choose the record type that you are interested in.

Record type: All objects by GUID

GUID	External GUID	Domain Name	Post Office Name	Object ID
030308C0-1436-...		Corp	GWIA	
1C23F270-12D2-...		Corp	corp_po1	Admin
1FEF0710-1439-...		Corp	corp_po1	Board Room
35C482C0-1337-...		Corp	corp_po1	JUDY
413F7BD0-12DA-...		mfg	mfg_po	LIB
423E23F0-12D6-...		mfg		
42EF7290-12D6-...		mfg		
42F40670-12D6-...		mfg		
42F58D10-12D6-...		mfg		
43725B00-12D2-...		Corp	corp_po1	WSLICK
58D4EDC0-12DA...		mfg	mfg_po	LIB2
678D6400-143D-...		Corp	corp_po1	All The Smart Peo...
7A86D560-12D9-...		mfg	mfg_po	
7B4BFA20-12D9-...		mfg	mfg_po	
7DFB89C0-12D9...		mfg	mfg_po	mfg_po Library
99EB0700-12D9-...		mfg	mfg_po	MFG_LIBRARY1
A09766C0-12D9-...		mfg	mfg_po	MFG_LIBRARY2
B0BBE9C0-1434-...		Corp	corp_po1	3b87db55
D6571CB0-1437-...		Corp	corp_po1	PPINCHER

Info OK

FIGURE 7.11 *The General Edit Record Enumeration Box*

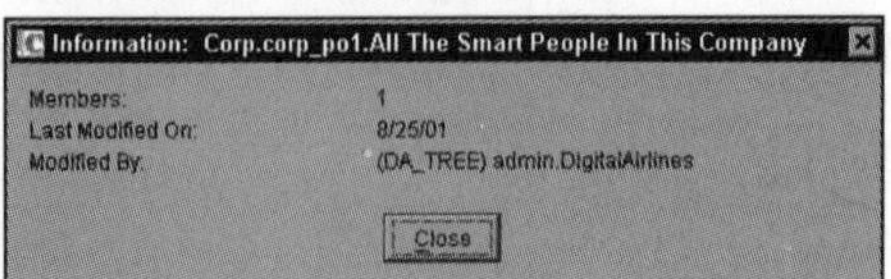

FIGURE 7.12 *The Information Dialog Box*

Summary

This chapter covered the GroupWise Utilities and GroupWise Diagnostics menus. The rest of this book will weave you in and out of many of these tools a lot. You will use them for maintenance, troubleshooting, and all kinds of configuration.

PART III

Agents and Clients

CHAPTER 8

Configuring the Post Office Agent

The post office agent is the workhorse of the GroupWise system. It is responsible for delivering mail to users, providing them with access to their mailboxes in client/server mode, indexing mailboxes and libraries, maintaining and repairing the message store, and redirecting users to other post offices for proxy or login.

It can be complicated to correctly configure the post office agent. After all, there is a lot for it to keep track of, and if your POA cannot accomplish everything with the CPU cycles the server gives it, your users will notice. This chapter explores all of the settings and console commands for the POA, and offers you some best practices to help you design and configure your system correctly.

Loading the Post Office Agent

The GroupWise post office agent requires certain information before it will load properly. Simply typing `LOAD GWPOA.NLM` from the server console will result in an error message stating that required parameters are missing. There are two ways to provide the required parameters.

Loading the POA Using the Startup File

When the agent installation program was run on this server, you were prompted for some information. This information was used by the installer to create a startup file with all the information the POA needs. The name of this file is the name of the post office, truncated to eight characters, followed by the .POA extension (for example, CORP_PO1.POA). If the installer was run more than once, the extension of the startup file will be changed to .PO1 .PO2, and so on (depending on how many times you installed).

To use the startup file, load the POA with the @ switch as follows:

```
LOAD GWPOA @<filename.POA>
```

For the CORP_PO1 post office, the command would be

```
LOAD GWPOA @CORP_PO1.POA
```

This command assumes that the GroupWise POA software is installed into the SYS:SYSTEM directory, and the CORP_PO1.POA file is also in the SYS:SYSTEM directory. The name of the *.POA file is not particularly important, it could be called MICKEY.POA or MICKEY.TXT; the POA doesn't care.

Loading the POA with Command-Line Switches

Another way to provide the POA with the information it needs is to use command-line switches. These switches take the general format of `/<parameter>=<value>`. Neither the parameter nor the value strings are case-sensitive. Any number of switches can be placed on the command line used to load the POA, and they can even be used in conjunction with the @ switch described in the preceding section.

The only required switch for the POA is the Home switch, which gives the agent the path to the post office to be served. The syntax is as follows:

```
LOAD GWPOA /HOME=<volume>:\<path>
```

For a post office residing in the PO directory on the MAIL volume of this server, the command line would look like this:

```
LOAD GWPOA /HOME=mail:\po
```

Learning the Switches

Almost all of the switches the POA will recognize are listed in the startup file. There is a blank startup file on your GroupWise 6 CD, in the \AGENTS\STARTUPS\LANGUAGE STRTUPUS.POA file. By now you've probably figured out that the startup file is just a shortcut for passing command-line switches to the POA. Any switch found in this file can be entered on the command line used to load the agent.

There are some undocumented POA switches described in the section later in this chapter titled "Undocumented POA Commands and Switches." Included in that section are switches to enable diagnostic logging, detailed IP logging, specification of the message transfer port, and more.

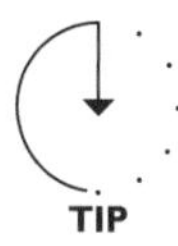

TIP

You can discover most of the switches for the GroupWise NLM POA by loading the GroupWise POA with the /? switch, as in the following example:

```
LOAD GWPOA /?
```

When to Use Switches

When loading a GroupWise POA, you usually do so with a command line such as this:

```
LOAD GWPOA @CORP.POA
```

The CORP.POA file is just an ASCII file that contains a listing of all the documented GroupWise POA switches that can possibly be enabled. Ideally, the only switch that should be enabled is the home switch:

```
/home-vol1:\CORPPO
```

Some of the switches have a location in ConsoleOne where the functionality that the switch is mapping to in the GroupWise POA code is configurable from ConsoleOne. For those switches, use ConsoleOne. By managing the features that are mapped to settings in ConsoleOne, it's much easier to make changes to how the POA functions, and most of the changes can happen on the fly when you make changes from ConsoleOne. With the GroupWise POA, however, when you make a change to the startup file (CORP.POA, in this example), you must manually bring down the POA and restart it. The only downside to ConsoleOne is that the switches are so well explained as they are in the *.POA file (although the switch is commented out with a semicolon), that it is easier to configure the POA through switches in the *.POA file.

Configuring the Post Office Agent

The numerous startup switches are probably a poor choice of tools for configuring the post office agent. You must have file system access to the SYS volume to apply them, and the values they represent will only be visible to those with server console or SYS volume access.

The solution is to administer the POA through ConsoleOne. Each post office object has a child object representing its POA. Double-clicking this object from the GroupWise view (or selecting Properties from the right-mouse-click menu) opens the window shown in Figure 8.1.

The rest of this section examines each of the four property pages on the GroupWise tab of the post office agent: Identification, Agent Settings, Log Settings, and Scheduled Events.

The Identification Property Page

The information on the Identification property page is not critical to the tuning of the POA, but it does help identify the POA as a unique object within the system. This page is the one that is visible when the POA object is first opened, and it is shown in Figure 8.1.

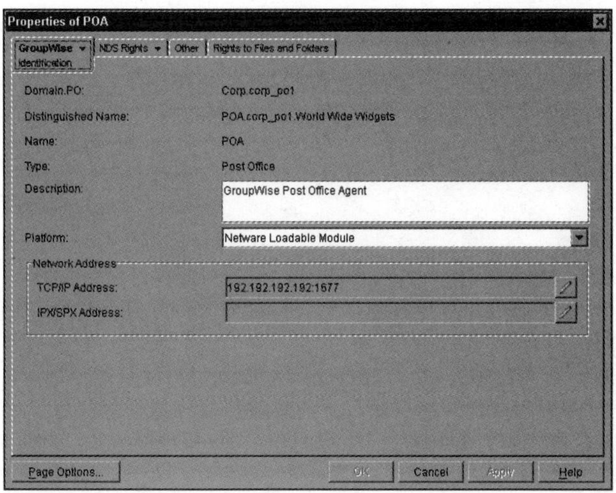

FIGURE 8.1 *The Post Office Agent Property Page in ConsoleOne*

- **Description:** The string entered in this field will be visible at the top of the POA screen on the server console.
- **Platform:** The pick list here offers four choices.
  - **NetWare Loadable Module:** Use this if you have GWPOA.NLM running on a NetWare file server.
  - **NT/OS2:** Use this if you are running GWPOA.EXE on a Windows NT or Windows 2000 box.
  - **Unix:** GroupWise 6 does not have Unix agents. This field is available for backwards compatibility to GroupWise 5x, which did have Unix agents.
  - **Unknown:** There is probably no use for you to use this entry. It is here for possible future compatibility.
- **Network Address Button:** The fields in this window, shown in Figure 8.2, are needed for the GroupWise POA to listen for client/server connections from a GroupWise client, and for the POA to listen for messages from the MTA servicing the domain above the post office the POA is running for.
  - **TCP/IP Address:** The uppermost field should display the TCP/IP address for this POA. This is the TCP/IP address of the server where the

POA is running. You may also fill in the DNS name for the POA rather than the IP address.

If the POA needs to be moved to another server, or the server's IP address must be changed, be sure to change the IP address for this POA to match the IP address of the server.

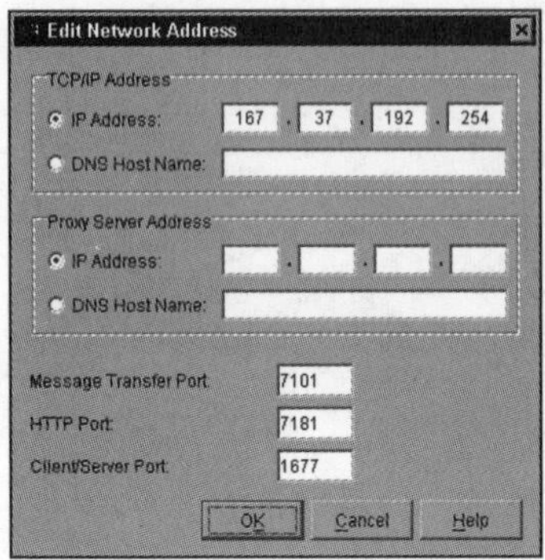

FIGURE 8.2 *The Post Office Agent Network Address Window*

- **Client/Server Port:** Enter the client/server port for this POA at the bottom of this window. If you are unsure of this value, use the default port, 1677. If there are multiple post offices on a single server, each of the POAs will need a unique port. You might use sequential numbering in this case (for example, 1677, 1678, 1679, and so on).

Filling in the IP address and client/server port for a POA isn't all that's needed for a POA to accept client/server connections. To fully configure the POA for client/server connections, make sure that the POA has the Enable TCP/IP (for Client/Server) check box checked on the Agent Settings property page.

- **IP Address:** If you intend to make your POA accessible outside of your firewall, fill in the IP address of your organization's proxy server.
- **Message Transfer Port:** The Message Transfer Port field identifies the port that will be used for communication from the domain MTA for the domain that owns this post office, down to the POA process that is running for this post office. If this field is not populated, the MTA will

require direct file access to the post office directory structure. If there is a port number here, however, the MTA will be able to transfer files to the POA using a TCP connection.

The default value for message transfer port is 7100. Again, if there are multiple post offices on this server, each of them must be assigned a unique message transfer port. You might use sequential numbering in cases like this (for example, 7100, 7101, 7102, and so on). Also, if there is an MTA running on the same server as the POA, the MTA by default will listen on port 7100. You would need to use a port other than the default 7100 for the POA when the MTA is running on the same server as the POA.

IMPORTANT **Filling in the message transfer port on the POA isn't all that's required for the MTA to communicate with the POA. In Tools ⇨ GroupWise Utilities ⇨ Link Configuration, you must enable TCP/IP communication between the MTA and the POA.**

- **HTTP Port:** The HTTP port is used by the POA and the GroupWise monitor utility. This port tells the POA what port to listen to for Web-browser monitoring. This GroupWise monitor utility reads the HTTP port value from the domain database, in order to monitor the POA.

IMPORTANT **To enable HTTP monitoring, you must also enable the HTTP user name and the HTTP password. To do this, go to the Agent Settings property page and fill in the HTTP User Name and HTTP Password fields.**

The steps in this section are sufficient to get the POA communicating with GroupWise clients and the MTA. But if the more advanced settings of the POA are not configured correctly, GroupWise end users could experience serious performance problems.

The Agent Settings Property Page

This is where most of your POA configuration will be done. This section starts with the settings in Figure 8.3, which shows this window with the scroll bar at the top.

- **Enable Automatic Database Recovery:** When checked, this setting allows the POA to rebuild damaged databases it encounters while processing messages or client/server requests.

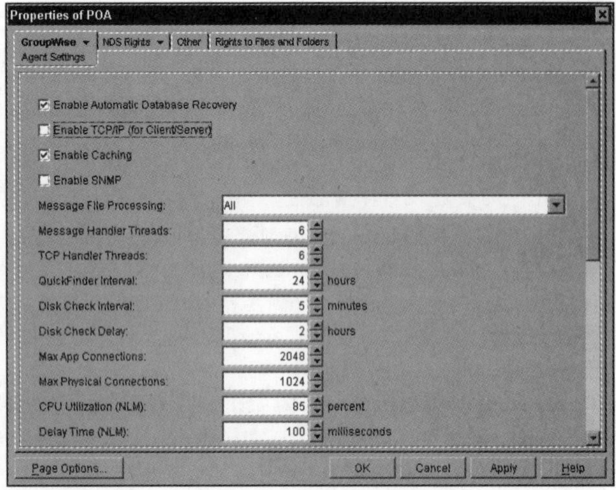

FIGURE 8.3 *The Post Office Object Agent Settings Property Page*

- **Enable TCP/IP (for Client/Server):** When checked, this allows the POA to listen and respond to client/server requests. This is required for the client/server access mode described a little later in this chapter.
- **Enable Caching:** When checked, the POA will store the last several database files it has "touched" in memory for quick access. This is in addition to any caching done by the operating system, and it typically improves agent performance.
- **Enable SNMP:** If checked, the POA will "publish" SNMP information for any management agents that may be listening. If GroupWise monitor is in use, then this option is required. Otherwise, it should be turned off for a nominal performance gain.
- **Message File Processing:** There are four available settings here. They roughly correspond to the WPCSOUT queues, and determine what priorities of messages this POA will process.
  - **All:** The default setting, the POA will poll all WPCSOUT queues for message files.
  - **High:** The POA will only process messages in the 0, 1, 2, and 3 (high priority) queues.
  - **Low:** The POA will only process messages in the 4, 5, 6, and 7 (normal and low priority) queues.

- **None:** The POA will not do any message-file processing at all.

WARNING

All mail coming into this post office from the rest of the system or from the Internet will arrive in one of these queues. Do not restrict the POA from processing these queues unless more than one POA has been created and launched to service this post office.

- **Message Handler Threads:** This setting determines the number of threads the POA will devote to the message file processing. This should not be more than half the number of TCP handler threads (see the next bullet). Generally, one message handler thread for every 40 users on the post office is sufficient. The lowest number of message handler threads you should allocate is 3.
- **TCP Handler Threads:** This determines the number of threads the POA will devote to handling client/server requests. Increasing this number may improve client/server performance, but only to a point. As a rule of thumb, you should have one TCP handler thread for every 20 users on the post office. The lowest number of TCP handler threads you should allocate is 6.
- **QuickFinder Interval:** This is the number of hours the POA will delay between spawning the QuickFinder index update process. This setting is best used in conjunction with Start QuickFinder Indexing, discussed later in this section. Generally, the default of 24 hours is the best setting. By setting the QuickFinder interval for every 24 hours, and coupling the Start QuickFinder Indexing setting to happen in the nighttime, the CPU-Intensive QuickFinder indexing process will not kick in during business hours.
- **DiskCheck Interval:** This is the amount of time, in minutes, that the POA will wait before re-checking the amount of disk space available. The DiskCheck may trigger a scheduled DiskCheck event. These events have *thresholds* of remaining disk space, and if the POA DiskCheck determines that the GroupWise volume has dropped below that threshold, it spawns that DiskCheck event. These will be covered in more detail in Chapter 17.
- **DiskCheck Delay:** Should a DiskCheck event be triggered by a DiskCheck, it may take some time for that event to free up some space. The DiskCheck delay is the amount of time the POA will wait, regardless of thresholds that have been tripped, before spawning another DiskCheck event.
- **Max App Connections:** This is the maximum number of application, or virtual, connections that the POA will allow to be open at any given time. If this number is reached and a client attempts to open another application

connection, the oldest connection in the table will be dropped. The client whose connection has been dropped may attempt to re-open it, however, so reaching this threshold may cause a serious performance hit as dropped connections cascade through the clients.

Novell recommends setting this to at least four times the number of users on the post office.

- **Max Physical Connections:** This is the maximum number of physical connections, or ports, that the POA will allow to be open simultaneously. If this number is reached, and a new user attempts to log on, that user will receive an error message and will not be able to connect. Set this to be equal to or slightly higher than the total number of users on this post office. Be sure to take into account users running GroupWise from more than one machine, or users who are proxied to from other post offices.

Scrolling down in this window, the rest of the options available to view are shown in Figure 8.4.

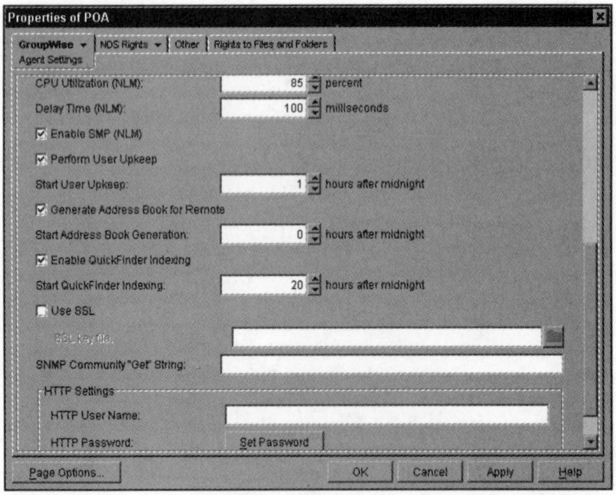

FIGURE 8.4 *The Post Office Agent Settings Property Page, Scrolled to the Bottom*

- **CPU Utilization:** This value is a trigger based on server utilization, and it is used in conjunction with Delay Time (discussed next). Should utilization climb above this number, the POA waits for the specified Delay Time before spawning a new thread. This throttles back the POA, perhaps preventing server utilization from sticking at 100 percent for extended periods.

- **Delay Time:** Used with CPU Utilization, this is the amount of time, in milliseconds, that the POA waits before spawning a new thread. These two settings apply only to the POA on the NetWare platform.
- **Enable SMP:** If checked, this setting allows the POA to load threads on additional processors if the NetWare 5 or NetWare 6 server has multiple processors installed.
- **Perform User Upkeep:** If enabled, this allows the POA to do the following:
  - Advance uncompleted tasks to the next day
  - Delete expired items from users' mailboxes
  - Empty expired items from trash
  - Synchronize users' frequent contacts books with the system address book
- **Start User Upkeep (hours after midnight):** As the name suggests, this setting allows you to determine at what hour of the day the POA performs the User Upkeep. A value of 2 results in a 2 a.m. run, while a value of 22 results in a 10 p.m. run.
- **Generate Address Books for Remote:** If enabled, this allows the POA to generate a WPROF.DB file for GroupWise remote users. This file is the remote address book. This setting is used in conjunction with the Start Address Book Generation" setting.
- **Start Address Book Generation (hours after midnight):** Again, a value of 2 results in a 2 a.m. run, while a value of 22 result in a 10 p.m. run.
- **Enable QuickFinder Indexing:** If enabled, the QuickFinder indexing process launches at the hourly interval specified under the QuickFinder Interval setting (discussed earlier). The first launch takes place as scheduled under Start QuickFinder Indexing.
- **Start QuickFinder Indexing (hours after midnight):** Because the QuickFinder process is CPU-intensive, it may be useful to schedule it to happen only outside of business hours. To do this, set Start QuickFinder Indexing to 4, and set QuickFinder Interval to 12. The first indexing run will execute at 4 a.m., and the second will execute at 6 p.m. The second run will be more intensive than the first, catching all of that day's mail. The next 4 a.m. run will pick up any messages that were created in the late evening or early morning.

Note: The POA settings can be confusing. Don't worry — later on in this chapter, I offer some "best practices" to help you tune the POA appropriately.

- **Use SSL:** This feature tells the POA to allow only HTTPS (HTTP Secure) connections to monitor the POA agent through a web browser. If you do not use SSL, and you monitor your GroupWise POA across the Internet, potential hackers could determine the username and password you are using to monitor your GroupWise POA.
- **SSL Key File:** This is the location where the SSL key file is located that the GroupWise POA will use if you have SSL enabled. Browse to the *.DER SSL key file. The *.DER file should be located on the same file server that the POA is running from so that the POA always has easy access to the file.
- **HTTP User Name / Password:** This is the password you intend to use when monitoring your POA through a web browser. This feature of monitoring the POA with a browser is detailed even further towards the end of this chapter.
- **SNMP Community "Get" String:** The fields for SNMP community strings are not required, unless you are using a third-party simple network management protocol (SNMP) product.

The Log Settings Property Page

This tab allows you to control the amount of information captured in the POA log, as well as the amount of disk space that old logs will take up (see Figure 8.5).

- **Log File Path:** By default, this field is left blank. POA logs are put in the WPCSOUT\OFS directory under the post office directory. If you choose to keep logs elsewhere, enter the path here. I don't recommend that you put logs on a separate server — performance may suffer, and if that server goes down the POA will not function.
- **Logging Level:** There are three menu items in this pick-list:
  - **None:** No logging.
  - **Normal:** The POA tracks "major" events in the log, but most of the detail will be gone.
  - **Verbose:** The log contains useful detail and is the recommended setting.
- **Max Log File Age:** This is the oldest that any log file on disk will be allowed to get before being automatically deleted by the POA. The default is seven days, and this is typically sufficient.

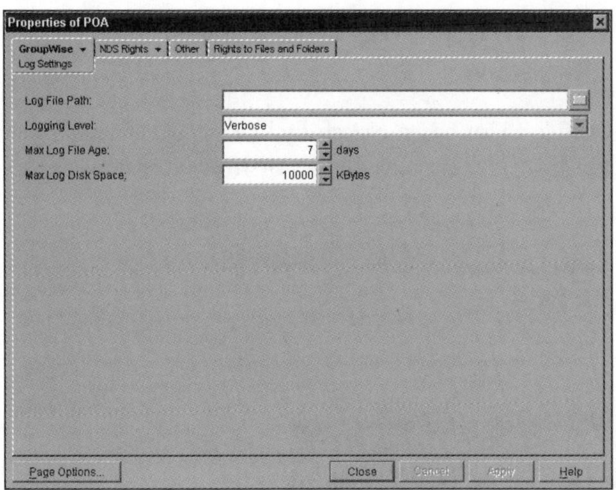

FIGURE 8.5 *The Post Office Agent Object Log Settings Property Page*

- **Max Log Disk Space:** This is the maximum amount of disk space that all of the log files together will be allowed to take up. If the logs reach this limit, the oldest log file will be deleted. If you choose to set the Max Log File Age beyond seven days, you will want to raise this limit to make sure that you actually get to keep your oldest logs for the time that you specify. Unfortunately, this can be very difficult to estimate. Just crank this up to 50,000 KB and that ought to do ya! The POA will generate a new log file when the old one reaches 256K in size. You should never see a single log file that has seven days of information in it or that is larger than 256K.

The Scheduled Events Property Page

You will use the Scheduled Events tab to automate message store maintenance. Scheduled events is a way in which the POA can be configured to run mailbox/library maintenance (GWCHECK) on a post office at some kind of a time interval. One of the best things about scheduled events is that they can be configured to happen when the system is being used the least. Chapter 17 discusses scheduled events in even more detail.

Monitoring and Configuring the POA at the Console Screen

Once the GroupWise post office agent has successfully loaded, the screen shown in Figure 8.6 will be available from the server console or from a remote console session.

TIP

Remember, to load the POA, type in LOAD GWPOA @STARTUPFILENAME.POA.

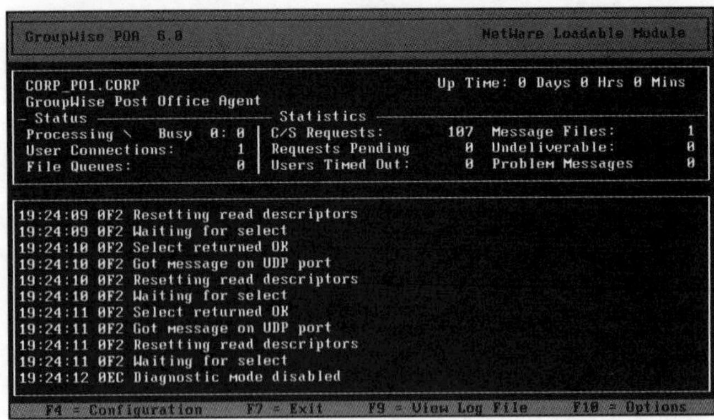

FIGURE 8.6 *The Post Office Agent Console on a NetWare 5 Server*

The POA may be controlled, to some extent, with keyboard commands you issue. The commands available from the main screen are the following:

- **F4:** Configuration
- **F7:** Exit
- **F9:** View Log File
- **F10:** Options

The F7 and F9 keystrokes need little explanation: Pressing the F7 key unloads the post office agent. If client/server connections are active, or if the QuickFinder indexing process is running, you will be prompted to confirm your decision to exit.

Pressing the F9 key allows you to browse through the currently active log file.

The Configuration Menu

When you select the F4 key, the menu shown in Figure 8.7 appears.

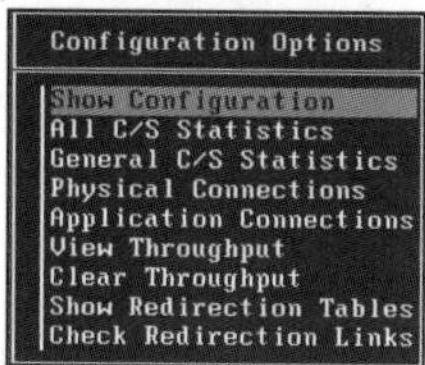

FIGURE 8.7 *The Post Office Agent Configuration Options Menu*

Each of the menu items here is going to pump information into the active log file when executed.

- **Show Configuration:** This option lists the configuration values and settings currently in memory. The settings you learned about in the section of this chapter titled "Configuring the Post Office Agent" are listed here. This list is identical in nature to the list of settings that the POA displays when it is first loaded. This list is not displayed in its own static window; rather it is dumped into the current active log of the POA. To review the configuration, press F9 to view the log file.
- **All C/S Statistics:** As the name suggests, this menu option dumps a list of all of the client/server statistics into the current log file. Each of the options that follow in this list is a subset of this option, so those individual statistics will be covered there.
- **General C/S Statistics:** This menu option creates a section in the log file titled *TCP Configuration.* Beneath this, you will find values for the configured limits of application and physical connections (*Max*), as well as the current number of those connections that are active (*Cur*) and the highest the current value has reached (*High*).
- **Physical Connections:** This lists the IP address and GroupWise user ID for each user that has a physical connection to the post office agent. A physical connection is a memory address for the transmission and receipt of TCP packets and will correspond to a port number. The port number used by the client and the POA for each connection is unfortunately not displayed. The numbers range from 1024 to 2048 or higher, depending on the number of users currently logged in.

- **Application Connections:** This lists the IP address and GroupWise user ID for each user that has an application connection to the post office agent. Most users will have more than one application connection, because these connections represent the windows or applications within the GroupWise client that are sharing the user's current physical connection. For example, a user with only the Inbox window open may have only one or two application connections. A user reading a mail message, running Notify, and browsing a shared folder will have at least three, and perhaps as many as six.
- **View Throughput:** This displays the client/server TCP/IP throughput for the POA. It does not include message transfer throughput, or files processed from the WPCSOUT queues.
- **Clear Throughput:** Use this option to clear the throughput count. When view throughput is executed, the throughput calculations will be based on the last time the throughput was cleared, or the last time the agent was loaded.
- **Show Redirection Tables:** This option shows each of the post office agents on the system, and their configured IP addresses and ports. The redirection table is used by the POA to connect users to other post offices for proxy purposes, for connections to libraries, or for redirected logins. The list shown here is from the perspective of this post office. Discrepancies between addresses shown on this list and addresses configured from ConsoleOne indicate a synchronization problem.
- **Check Redirection Links:** This option is the same as the Show Redirection Tables option, except that after each entry is listed, the POA attempts to connect to the POA at that address and shows the results of that attempt.

  This tool is especially valuable — with one keystroke, you can find out which POAs on your system are responding, and which are not.

The Options Menu

Selecting the F10 key pulls up the menu shown in Figure 8.8.

- **View Log Files:** This option is similar to the main screen's F9 keystroke, but it offers more utility. It brings up a pick-list from which you may choose to browse not only the current log file (marked with an asterisk) but also any of the POA logs that reside on disk.
- **Logging Options:** This option brings up the screen shown in Figure 8.9.

Use the up- and down-arrow keys to navigate and Enter to edit the selected logging option. The Esc key takes you back to the main screen.

Options

View Log Files
Logging Options
Configuration Options
Admin Status
Message Transfer Status
Cycle Log
Actions
Edit Startup File

FIGURE 8.8 *The Post Office Agent Options Menu*

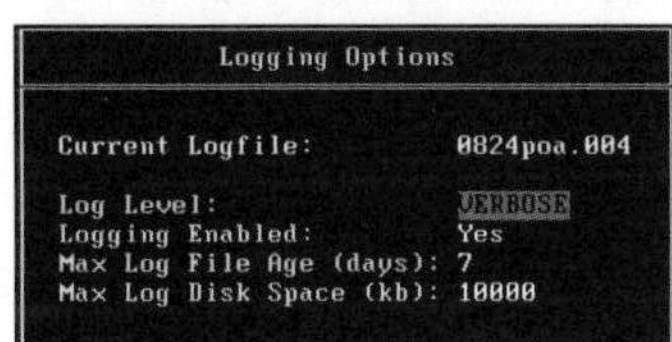

FIGURE 8.9 *The Post Office Agent Logging Options Menu*

It is better to configure the POA logging from ConsoleOne. In this way, the POA always starts with the settings you have selected. Making changes from the POA's console screen should be reserved for temporary situations and troubleshooting. When you make changes from the POA's console screen, those changes don't stick after the POA has been unloaded and reloaded.

- **Configuration Options:** This menu option is identical to the main screen's F4 keystroke.
- **Admin Status:** Selecting this option brings up the submenu shown in Figure 8.10.

  There are four available actions or configuration options in this dialog box. Again, use the up- and down-arrow keys to navigate, and Enter to edit. Two of these options are especially useful:

  - **Perform DB Recovery:** Executes an immediate recovery of WPHOST.DB.

- **Status:** Allows you to suspend processing of administration tasks (very useful if you are currently rebuilding this database off-line and want to keep things in sync).

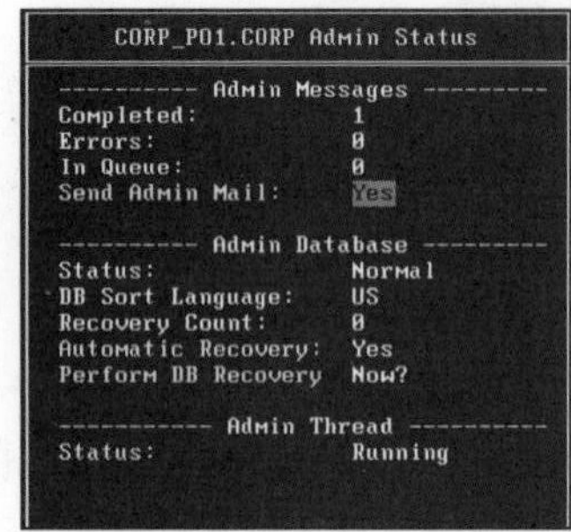

FIGURE 8.10: *The Post Office Agent Admin Status Screen*

Selecting the Esc key takes you back to the Options menu.

- **Message Transfer Status:** This menu item calls up the Message Transfer Status screen shown in Figure 8.11.

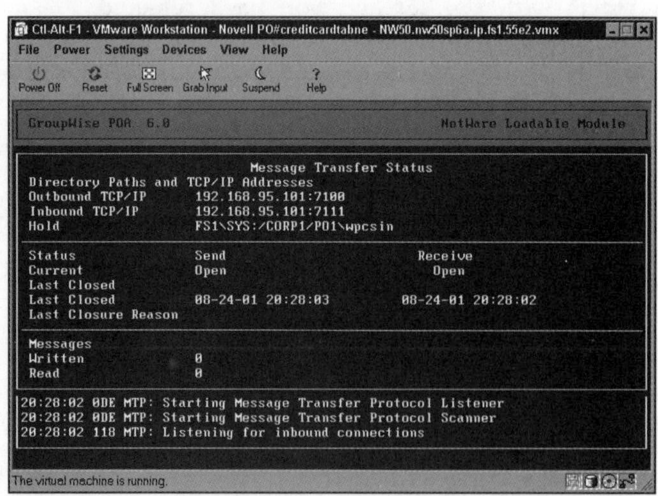

FIGURE 8.11 *The Post Office Agent Message Transfer Status Screen*

- **Outbound TCP/IP:** Displays the IP address and port of this post office's domain MTA.
- **Inbound TCP/IP:** The IP address and message transfer port of this POA.
- **Hold:** This is the directory where this POA queues up messages if the connection to the MTA is blocked for some reason.
- **Last Closure Reason:** Shows why the POA could not connect to the MTA. It may not tell you exactly what's wrong, but it can give you a good idea where the problem is.

As with the Admin Status dialog box, selecting the Esc key takes you back to the Options menu.

- **Cycle Log:** Cycling the log dumps the current log into a file and begins a new log file. This is useful when you are getting ready to use the Configuration Options menu to list some TCP information, and you want it to be at the top of the log file for easy access later.
- **Actions:** This option calls up the Actions menu shown in Figure 8.12.
  - **View MF Queues:** Allows you to see, at a glance, how many files are waiting in the WPCSOUT directory structure. These files are waiting for processing by the POA. The list is dumped into the current log file.
  - **Disable Auto Rebuild:** This tells the POA not to attempt to rebuild damaged databases that it encounters in the course of message delivery or client/server processing.

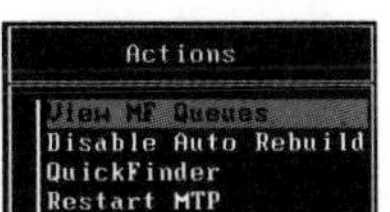

FIGURE 8.12 *The Post Office Agent Actions Menu*

- **QuickFinder:** This calls up the four-option dialog box shown in Figure 8.13.
- **Update QuickFinder Indexes:** This option launches the indexing process. All indices served by this POA, including the mailbox index and all library indexes, will be updated.

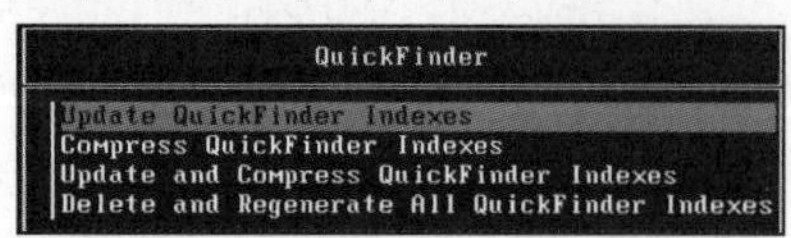

FIGURE 8.13 *The Post Office Agent QuickFinder Menu*

- **Compress QuickFinder Indexes:** This merges all incremental indexes with the permanent index. The permanent index files will be renamed to reflect the time the operation was performed.
- **Update and Compress QuickFinder Indexes:** This performs both of the preceding operations, beginning with the update.
- **Delete and Regenerate All QuickFinder Indexes:** This deletes all the *.INC and *.IDX files in the post office\ofuser\index directory, and launches the indexing process to re-index all databases in the post office.

WARNING

Kick off the Delete and Regenerate All QuickFinder Indexes option only when the POA has a lot of time to spare; for example, on a Friday night. Depending upon the amount of data you have, it could take more than a day to re-index all of your data.

- **Restart MTP:** The MTP process is the process on the POA that sends and receives messages from the MTA. Often in troubleshooting connectivity problems between a POA and the MTA on the domain above the post office, it's helpful to restart the MTP process.

Undocumented POA Commands and Switches

There are a few things that you can make the POA do that are not listed in the menu items, and which are not even listed in Novell's shipping or online documentation. These commands are typically used by Novell's technical support personnel to resolve sticky problems, or for troubleshooting. There are other undocumented POA commands; however, the two listed here are the ones you are most likely to need for troubleshooting.

- **Ctrl+Z (diagnostic logging keystroke):** This keystroke toggles *diagnostic* logging on and off. Diagnostic log files are much larger than *verbose* log files, but may contain information that is critical to correctly diagnosing a problem (hence the name). Running the POA in diagnostic mode for extended periods is not recommended. Performance degrades slightly in this mode. If your log level has been set to verbose from ConsoleOne, and you enable diagnostics logging by pressing the Ctrl+Z key on the system console, when you disable diagnostics logging by pressing Ctrl+Z again, the log level for the POA does not revert back to its setting of verbose, but instead reverts to normal logging. Be aware of this if you ever toggle diagnostics logging on and off from the POA screen. You may need to manually go into the logging options to set the log level back to verbose. The next time the POA is started, it will read the logging level from the WPHOST.DB and run with verbose logging.

- **/DIAGNOSTIC or /DEBUG startup switch:** Placed in the startup file or the startup command line, this switch launches the POA with diagnostic logging as described in the preceding paragraph.
- **/IPLL-DIAG startup switch:** This switch launches the POA with very detailed IP transaction logging, useful in conjunction with sniffer traces to isolate network problems.

Understanding the Agent Log

The GroupWise post office agent is a multi-threaded server application that performs large numbers of operations each second. The log files can be confusing. An entry indicating that something was received for processing may not be immediately followed by an entry indicating that the spawned process was completed.

Log Line Format

To help make sense of this, each line in the agent log is divided into four main parts.

The first of these is the time stamp. Anyone who can read a 24-hour digital clock can make sense of this — it is in HH:MM:SS format. This is the hour, minute, and second of the day that the event in this log entry occurred.

The second part is the process number. This is more complex. The process number is typically a three-digit number identifying the process or *thread* that performed the operation described in this log entry. If you are trying to follow a thread in the log, you must do so by finding the next occurrence of this number. If process 118 attempts to deliver a message, and the next line indicates that process 244 encountered an error, the error was not with the message in the previous line. Look for the next occurrence of process 118 to see if the message was delivered.

The third part, which is not always present, is the process type. This is a three-letter string, which identifies either the admin engine or the message transfer engine. When the POA processes updates to the post office database (administration messages), the string is *ADM*. Message transfer events (connections to the MTA for transmitting or receiving messages of any type) use the string *MTP*.

The fourth part of the log entry is the event description. This may be short and cryptic, but after you have seen a few of them, you can easily make sense of them. It may be an error message, or it could announce the user ID of the user who just logged in.

Common Log Entries and Explanations

This section offers a look at some examples of log entries. In all of these examples, the log level was set to *verbose*, so that the maximum amount of useful information was captured without overburdening the POA.

Message Delivery

The following sequence tracks delivery of a mail message from *tkratzer* to *ecornish*.

```
14:06:13 462 Processing 47d66d45.vz0
(37D6C1A2.204:3588161547:3588235330)
14:06:16 462 Distribute message from: tkratzer
14:06:16 462 Begin distribution to 1 users
14:06:16 462 Distributed: ecornish
14:06:16 462 Processed OK
```

The first entry is the most cryptic, but don't let that throw you off. It says that the file named *47d66d45.vz0* was picked up for processing. You can ignore the parenthetical information.

Notice that all five entries have the same process number, *462*. That's how you know that the file described in the first entry contained the transactions described in the next four. And fortunately, the rest of the event descriptions are short and easy to understand.

Administration Update

This next sequence is the result of the administrator changing the telephone number for user *ecornish*.

```
14:02:12 464 ADM: Completed: Update object in Post Office -
User WWWIDGET-DOM.SALES-PO.ECORNISH (Administrator:
(WWWIDGET-INC) TKRATZER.IS.WWWidget, Domain: WWWIDGET-DOM)
```

It looks confusing, but only because so much information has been packed into the event description. Server process 464 performed an ADM (administration) type of transaction. The object updated was user ECORNISH in the SALES-PO post office of the WWWIDGET domain.

The bit in parentheses is especially useful. With this information, you can audit your administrators, ensuring that they are accountable for the changes they make to your system. The administrator who made the change was authenticated to the WWWIDGET-INC tree and used the TKRATZER account in the IS.WWWidget context. You can also see that the operation was performed while ConsoleOne was connected to the WWWIDGET-DOM domain database.

QuickFinder Indexing

These next sequences are made up of excerpts of log entries captured during the QuickFinder Indexing Process.

```
14:07:13 478 Starting QuickFinder Index Update
14:07:13 478 Performing disk space check for QF index job
14:07:14 478 Processing Pending Work, Lib2 on Po2, Partition
0: dmdd0002.db
14:07:17 478 End Pending Work, Lib2 on Po2, Partition 0:
dmdd0002.db
14:07:17 478 Processing Pending Work, Lib2 on Po2,
Partition 1: dmdd0102.db
```

So far, so good, right? Process 478 begins the indexing process at 2:07:13 p.m. The first order of business is to check and make sure that there is sufficient disk space for the temporary files required. Then, a second later, it begins to index Partition 0 of Lib2. Three seconds after that, process 478 announces that it is done with Partition 0, and it begins work on Partition 1.

What is this pending work mentioned? The POA is looking through the indexing queue in each partition to see if there are documents that have been updated or created in that partition since the last indexing run.

Now, skipping ahead in the log to the point where all of the indexing queues have been read, you find the following:

```
14:07:24 478 Updating QuickFinder Index, Lib2 on Po2,
Partition 0: dmdd0002.db
14:07:27 478 Indexed 2 versions, Lib2 on Po2, Partition 0
14:07:27 478 Updating QuickFinder Index, Lib2 on Po2,
Partition 1: dmdd0102.db
14:07:31 478 Indexed 7 versions, Lib2 on Po2, Partition 1
```

The log file here says that the POA is performing the actual updates to the indexes. There were two documents needing indexing in Partition 0, and seven documents in Partition 1.

Skipping ahead again:

```
14:08:34 478 Updating QuickFinder Index: pu020101.db
14:08:37 478 Updating QuickFinder Index: pu030101.db
14:08:41 478 Updating QuickFinder Index: userd95.db
14:08:41 478 CPU utilization above threshold
14:08:41 478 CPU utilization below threshold
```

Now the POA has begun indexing user mailboxes. This run occurs in alphanumerical order, so the log starts with the PU*.DB databases and moves on to the USER databases.

Note that at 2:08:41 p.m., process 478 gets "slapped." CPU utilization on the server has climbed above the threshold, and thread 478 is forced to pause in his work for a moment. Within a second, utilization is back below the threshold.

```
14:08:41 478 QuickFinder: 10 items indexed
14:08:41 478 QuickFinder: 20 items indexed
14:08:41 478 QuickFinder: 30 items indexed
...
14:08:47 478 QuickFinder: 980 items indexed
14:08:51 478 QuickFinder Indexing Thread Finished
```

Here, the POA has begun compressing the old IDX and INC files into a new set of IDX files. As it does so, it counts by tens. (I skipped over everything between 30 and 980 to save space in the book!) This portion of the process went by quickly — it took seven seconds to compress the indexes for almost a thousand items.

Best Practices

Post office agent performance is important to your users. If the agent does not have the resources it needs to quickly process client/server requests, your users will notice. The client will be sluggish, non-responsive, and users may think their workstations have locked up. It is, therefore, critical that the system be built and configured so that the POA is always performing well for your users.

Limit the Size of the Post Office

The first mistake made by many administrators is overloading the post office. Unfortunately, it is very difficult to determine exactly how many users can belong to a single post office. Performance depends more on what the users are doing than on how many of them there are. In practice, GroupWise administrators have seen that having more than about 700 users in client/server (online mode on the client) on a GroupWise post office often results in poor performance.

If users are not living in GroupWise or if your users are all using caching mode, you may be able to get away with many, many more than 700 users on a post office. With caching mode enabled, it's quite feasible that a GroupWise 6 post office can support a couple of thousand users.

Limit the Size of the Message Store

Post office agent performance degrades, and memory requirements increase, as the size of the message store grows. Performance problems are intensified if users keep too much mail in their master mailboxes. For a 700-user post office, I recommend purging mail older than 180 days. This should ensure good performance.

One Post Office Per Server

If you have a choice between putting two 350-user post offices on a single server, and putting one 700-user post office on that same server, I recommend the 700-user option. The POA will load-balance in favor of client/server threads, but if there are two POAs running on one CPU, they cannot "talk" to each other to determine the best allocation of the limited resources. Placing more than one post office (and, therefore, more than one POA) on a single file server is not recommended. That said, putting 100-user post offices on the same server will generally not cause problems, and is in fact a common practice. It's the larger post offices that have problems with two on a server.

As with the size of the post office, the number of post offices per server is an area where you may be able to ignore my advice and get away with it — especially on heavy-hitting hardware. Just be sure to consider my recommendations.

Dedicate the Server to GroupWise

If you have more than 200 users in the post office, don't use this server for other applications. User home directories, NDS authentication, APPS volumes, and Web servers should be on separate hardware. Your users will grow to depend on GroupWise more than almost any other application they run. They will demand good performance out of it, so GroupWise deserves to be treated as a mission-critical application. If another application can steal CPU slices out from under your POA, your users may eventually rise in revolt.

Tune the POA for Maximum Performance

Setting certain numbers too low can be disastrous. Setting them too high can cause the server to run low on memory. These guidelines should help you find the happy medium.

- Set application connections to four times the number of users on the post office.
- Set physical connections to the same number as the number of users on the post office.
- Set TCP handler threads so that you have one thread for every twenty users.
- Set message handler threads so that you have one thread for every sixty users.
- Disable SNMP, unless you are using GroupWise monitor or a third-party SNMP agent.

Read Appendix A for more fine-tuning ideas.

Monitoring Your POA through a Web Browser

The GroupWise POA can be monitored through a Web browser. In fact, you can even suspend and restart some processes on the GroupWise POA. You can find lots of information about how your POA is functioning that you cannot find out in any other manner. For example, with the Web-browser monitoring interface of the POA, you can determine what version and date of the GroupWise client users are using. You'll still find it useful to use the POA's console interface on your NetWare or NT server, but as for monitoring the POA, nothing beats the Web-browser interface of the POA.

Simple Configuration

The GroupWise POA needs three settings tweaked in order to support HTTP monitoring of the POA. They are the following:

- An HTTP port specified
- An HTTP monitoring user name specified

- An HTTP monitoring password for the user name specified

All of these settings can be configured in ConsoleOne.

HTTP Port

To specify your HTTP port, go to the properties pages of your POA object in ConsoleOne.

On the GroupWise Identification property page, you can find a TCP/IP Address field. Click the pencil button to the right of the field to bring up the Edit NetWork Address dialog box shown in Figure 8.14.

Fill in the HTTP port with a value that you know is unique. Don't use the same port as the client/server port or message transfer port.

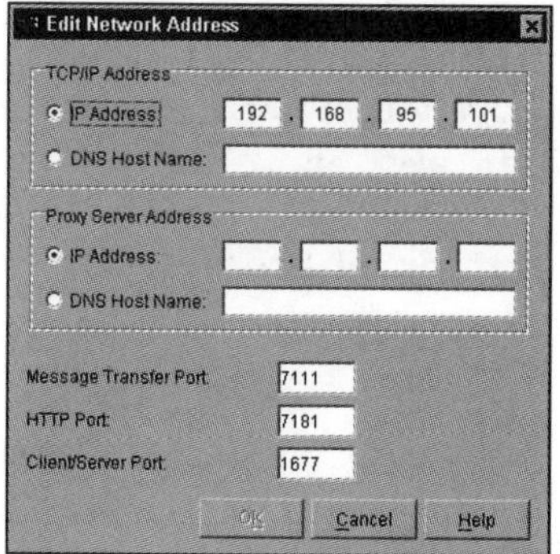

FIGURE 8.14 *The Edit Network Address Dialog Box*

HTTP User Name/Password

To specify your HTTP user name and password settings, go to the properties pages of the GroupWise POA object.

At the bottom of the GroupWise Agent Settings property page, fill in the HTTP User Name field and the HTTP Password fields.

Monitoring the POA with a Web Browser

Fill in the IP address or DNS name of the server running the POA, along with a colon and a port name. For example:

```
http://192.168.95.101:8100
```

You will be prompted for the user name and password with a dialog box like the one in Figure 8.15.

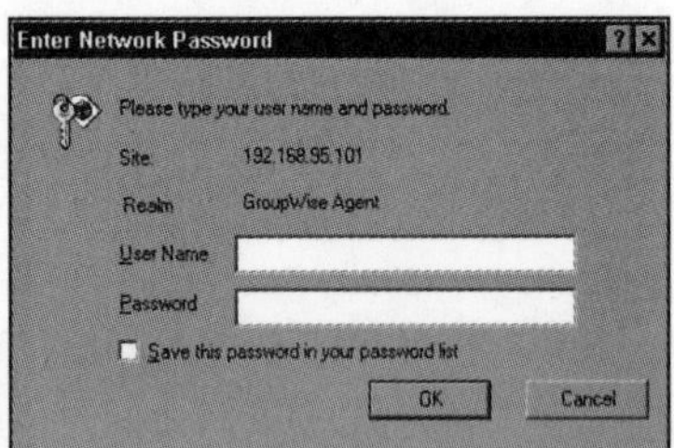

FIGURE 8.15 *The GroupWise POA HTTP Authentication Dialog Box*

Once you are in the GroupWise POA HTTP monitoring screen, you'll see a bevy of information.

TIP

When monitoring the GroupWise POA through a browser, if you do not remember the HTTP port number, you can also enter through the client/server port. This is usually 1677, and the client/server port will redirect the browser to the correct HTTP port for monitoring.

Advanced Configuration

The HTTP monitoring piece of the GroupWise POA has some powerful features that can be enabled if you would like, including the following:

- HTTP refresh interval control
- HTTPS support (secure SSL monitoring of the POA)
- GroupWise client version/release date flagging

HTTP Refresh Interval Control

To take advantage of this feature, you need to edit the startup file for the POA. This setting cannot be made from ConsoleOne.

To enable the switch, type the following:

```
/httprefresh
```

If you want to have the refresh take place every 20 seconds, the line would read the following:

```
/httprefresh-20
```

HTTPS Support

The POA can use an SSL key file so that the authentication, and the information on the POA screen, is secure. To enable this feature, do the following:

1. Edit the properties of the GroupWise POA object.
2. Go to the GroupWise Agent Settings property page.
3. Select the Use SSL check box.
4. Specify the path to a SSL key file. (These files have a *.DER extension, and you must generate this file.)

   This should be a path on the same server that the POA is running on. This way the POA will always have access to this file.
5. Restart your POA for the settings to take effect.

When you monitor your POA now, use the following command line:

```
https://192.168.95.101:8100
```

GroupWise Client Version/Release Date Flagging

When monitoring the GroupWise POA, you can see the GroupWise client version and code release date. This doesn't take any special configuration. The GroupWise POA can be configured to change the font color on client version and release date, if the values you specify are below a particular threshold. Here are the switches that you would use:

```
/gwclientreleaseversion
```

and

```
/gwclientreleasedate
```

So for example, if you wanted to know which users had a version older than the GroupWise 6.0.1 client and/or older than 4/6/2001, you would use the following parameters:

```
/gwclientreleaseversion-6.0.1
/gwclientreleasedate-04-06-2001
```

When monitoring the POA, and looking at the C/S Users section, you can see the information on the line titled *GroupWise Client Release*. Figure 8.16 shows an example of this.

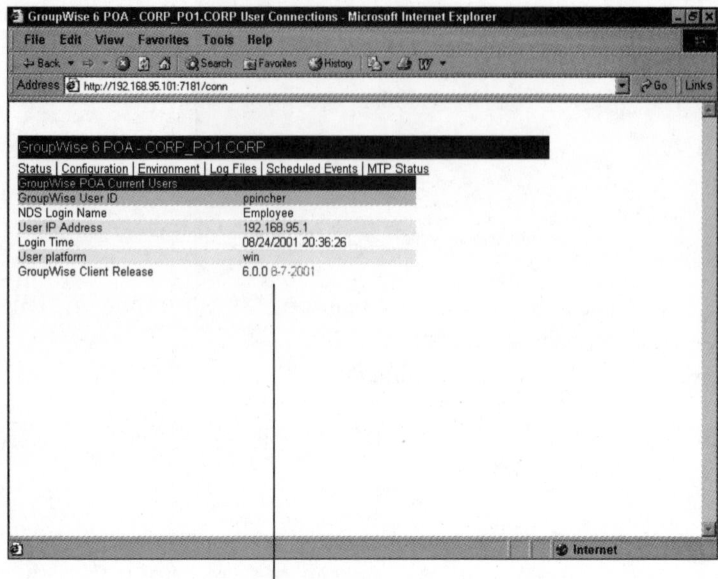

FIGURE 8.16 *The GroupWise Client Release*

Summary

This chapter discussed loading, configuring, tuning, and monitoring the GroupWise post office agent. This chapter also took a close look at the POA object in ConsoleOne and examined the options available to from the POA's server console.

CHAPTER 9

Configuring the Message Transfer Agent

The message transfer agent (MTA) has three major responsibilities in the GroupWise system.

- Transferring messages between post offices and domains
- Writing administrative changes to the domain database (WPDOMAIN.DB)
- Transferring messages to or from gateways for transport to or from other mail systems

This chapter discusses operation and configuration of the MTA and explores link configuration for the GroupWise system. At the end of the chapter, you can find some best practices to help you design and configure your system correctly.

Loading the Message Transfer Agent

The GroupWise message transfer agent requires certain information before it loads properly. Simply typing **LOAD GWMTA.NLM** from the server console results in an error message stating that required parameters are missing. There are two ways to provide the required parameters.

When the agent installation program was run on this server, you were prompted for some information. This information was used by the installer to create a startup file with all the information the MTA needs. The name of this file is the name of the domain, truncated to eight characters, followed by the .MTA extension (for example, CORP.MTA). If the installer was run more than once, the extension of the startup file will be changed to .MT1, .MT2, and so on (depending on how many times you installed).

To use the startup file, load the MTA with the @ switch as follows:

```
LOAD GWMTA @<filename.MTA>
```

For the CORP domain, the command would be the following:

```
LOAD GWMTA @CORP.MTA
```

Loading the MTA with Command-Line Switches

Another way to provide the MTA with the information it needs is to use command-line switches. As was explained about the POA in Chapter 8, these switches take the general format of `/<parameter>=<value>`. Neither the parameter nor the value strings are case-sensitive. Any number of switches can be placed on the command line used to load the MTA, and they can even be used in conjunction with the @ switch described earlier.

The only required switch for the MTA is the `Home` switch, which gives the agent the path to the domain to be served. The syntax is as follows:

```
LOAD GWMTA /HOME=<volume>:\<path>
```

For a domain residing in the CORP directory on the MAIL volume of this server, the command line would look like this:

```
LOAD GWMTA /HOME=mail:\corp
```

Learning the Switches

Almost all of the switches the MTA will recognize are listed in the startup file. There is a blank startup file on your GroupWise 6 CD, AGENTS\STARTUPS \LANGUAGE\STRTUPUS.MTA. Any switch found in this file can be entered on the command line used to load the agent.

The section, "Undocumented MTA Commands and Switches," found later in this chapter, includes switches to disable the admin thread and to turn off the Message Logging feature.

As indicated in Chapter 8, startup switches and startup files should only be used when a particular setting cannot be made in ConsoleOne. Administer the MTA through ConsoleOne.

Configuring the Message Transfer Agent

Each domain object has a child object representing its MTA. Double-clicking this object from the GroupWise view (or selecting Properties when right-mouse-clicking the MTA object) opens the window shown in Figure 9.1.

The rest of this section explores each of the six property pages available from the GroupWise tab.

The Identification Property Page

The MTA Identification property page is shown in Figure 9.1, and as you can see, there is not much critical configuration data here.

- **Description:** The text entered in this field will be visible at the top of the agent screen on the server console. It may be useful to enter the phone number or pager number of the administrator responsible for configuring the MTA in this field.
- **Platform:** This window allows you to select the server platform on which the MTA will run. You will most likely want to select either the option for NLM (NetWare loadable module) or NT/OS2.

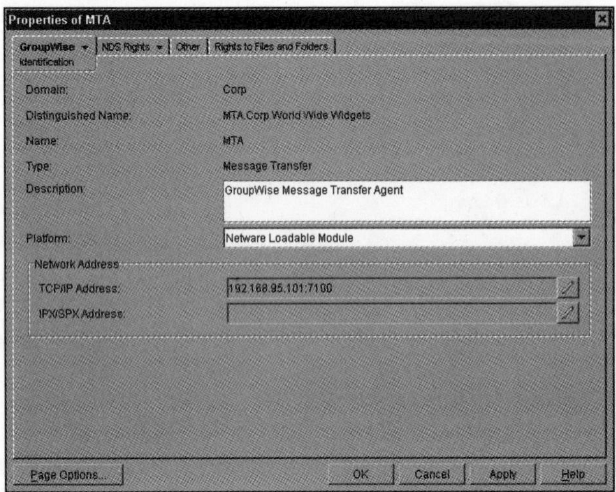

FIGURE 9.1 *The MTA Object Details Property Page in ConsoleOne*

- **Network Address Button:** The information found on the MTA Network Address button is absolutely critical to proper communication across your GroupWise system. When creating a new domain (and hence a new MTA object) you will want to do the following:

1. Click the button labeled TCP/IP Address.
2. Enter the IP address or DNS name of the server upon which this MTA runs.
3. Enter the message transfer port for this MTA.

   If you are unsure of this value, use the default port, 7100. If there are multiple domains on a single server, each of the MTAs will need a unique port. Perhaps you could use sequential numbering in this case (such as 7100, 7101, 7102, and so on). You may also need to renumber ports if there are POAs on this server that are communicating with their MTA via IP — as is explained in Chapter 8, the POA also defaults to port 7100 for the message transfer port.

The HTTP port is used by the MTA and the GroupWise monitor utility. This port tells the MTA what port to listen to for Web-browser monitoring. This

GroupWise monitor utility reads the HTTP port value from the domain database, in order to monitor the MTA.

To enable HTTP monitoring, you must also enable the HTTP user name and the HTTP password. To do this, go to the Agent Settings property page and fill in the HTTP User Name, and HTTP Password fields.

If the IP address for the domain file server must be changed, it is critical that the change also be reflected in the MTA object's network address panel. All other domain databases have a copy of this object record and use this information when communicating with this MTA. If the information is inaccurate, other MTAs will be unable to connect with this MTA to transfer messages.

This chapter discusses the best way to make changes to IP addresses and ports on a live system in the section called "Best Practices."

The Agent Settings Property Page

If you recall the available agent settings for the POA, you'll probably be relieved to see how little there is to worry about on this page for the MTA (see Figure 9.2). Here, you control four aspects of MTA operation: scan cycles, database recovery, additional threads, and HTTP monitoring.

- **Scan Cycle:** This is the interval, in seconds, that each normal-priority thread waits before scanning its assigned queues. The queues that the MTA scans are the WPCSIN/4 through 7 subdirectories of the domain directory. Also, if the MTA is linking to a post office via a UNC path, this is the interval between scans of the WPCSIN/4 through 7 subdirectories of the post office directory.

  As you can imagine, an MTA with UNC links to multiple post offices could become seriously burdened just with polling directories if this value is set too low. Novell recommends that all post offices (except those local to the MTA) be linked with IP addresses to avoid this potential problem.
- **Scan High:** This is the interval, in seconds, that each high-priority thread waits before scanning its assigned queues. The high-priority queues are WPSCIN/0 through 3. Again, if this number is too low and there are lots of post offices linked via UNC, the MTA could be overtaxed just with file-polling.

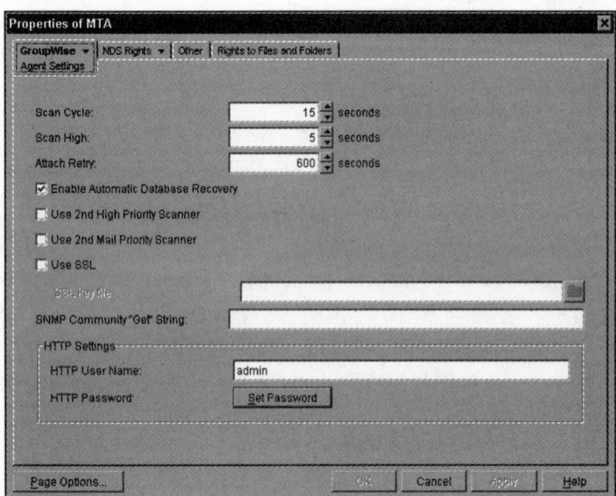

FIGURE 9.2 *The MTA Object Agent Settings Property Page*

- **Attach Retry:** If for some reason the MTA is unable to connect to another server, whether via TCP/IP links or UNC mappings, it will wait for the attach retry interval to expire before attempting another connection. The default value of 600 seconds (five minutes) is good, because mail won't wait too long in the hold directories between attempts, and the MTA shouldn't bog down with consecutive reconnect attempts.
- **Enable Automatic Database Recovery:** This is the second aspect of MTA operation you'll control from this tab. If checked, this setting allows the MTA to perform a *recover* operation on a damaged domain database. If this is not enabled, then damage to the domain database will result in the MTA shutting down.

  If your domain databases are getting damaged regularly (probably through unstable workstations being used for GroupWise administration), then you should disable this feature and resolve the problem. This will help prevent certain kinds of record loss.
- **Use 2nd High Priority Scanner:** Each link the MTA must service is assigned its own threads. There are two — a high priority routing thread and a normal, or mail, priority routing thread. If there are 10 links to be serviced, there will be 20 threads. Checking this box will spawn a second

thread for high-priority routing for each link, which means you'll now have 30 threads (10 mail priority and 20 high priority). This should only be used if you have a significant amount of users using the busy search feature, and scheduling users off of their post office.

If you find bottlenecks at an MTA, consider using the queue assignment or link scheduling features described later in this chapter.

- **Use 2nd Mail Priority Scanner:** Like the preceding setting, this option spawns an additional thread for every link. The additional threads service queues 2–7. This option allows the MTA to process the 2–3 queues separately from the 4–7 queues. The end result is that messages in the 2–3 directories move more quickly through your MTA. Checking this option is particularly helpful for larger GroupWise systems, which have a lot of administrative changes.
- **Use SSL:** This feature tells the MTA to only allow HTTPS (HTTP secure) connections to monitor the MTA agent through a Web browser. If you do not use SSL, and you monitor your GroupWise MTA across the Internet, potential hackers could determine the user name and password you are using to monitor your GroupWise MTA.
- **SSL Key File:** This is the location of the SSL key file that the GroupWise MTA will use if you have SSL enabled. Browse to the *.DER SSL key file. The *.DER file should be located on the same file server that the MTA is running from, so that the MTA always has easy access to the file.
- **HTTP User Name / Password:** This is the password you intend to use when monitoring your MTA through a Web browser. When you click on the Set Password button, you get the window shown in Figure 9.3.

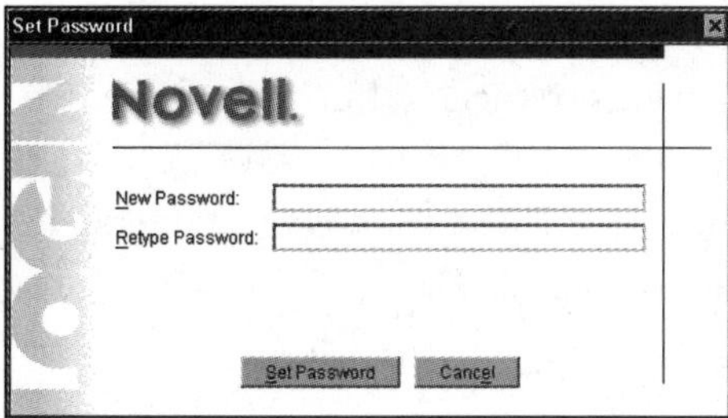

FIGURE 9.3 *The Set Password Dialog Box*

The Log Settings Property Page

This tab, shown in Figure 9.4, allows you to control the amount of information captured in the MTA log, as well as the amount of disk space that old logs take up.

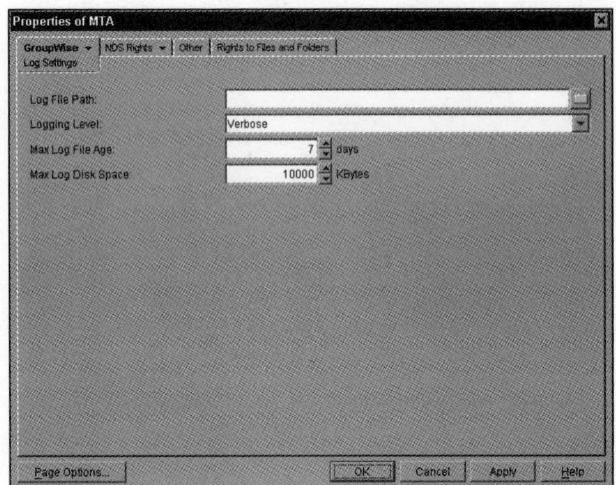

FIGURE 9.4 *The MTA Object Log Settings Property Page*

- **Log File Path:** By default, this field is left blank. MTA logs are put in the MSLOCAL directory under the domain directory. If you choose to keep logs elsewhere, enter the path here. I do not recommend that you put logs on a separate server — performance may suffer, and if that server goes down the MTA will not function.
- **Logging Level:** There are three menu items in this pick-list:
  - **None:** No logging.
  - **Normal:** The MTA tracks major events in the log, but most of the detail is gone.
  - **Verbose:** The log contains useful detail. This option is recommended.
- **Max Log File Age:** This is the oldest that any log file on disk will be allowed to get before being automatically deleted by the MTA. The default is seven days, and this timeframe is typically sufficient.
- **Max Log Disk Space:** This is the maximum amount of disk space that all of the log files together will be allowed to take up. If the logs reach this limit, the

oldest log file will be deleted. If you choose to set the Max Log File Age option beyond seven days, you will want to raise this limit to make sure that you actually get to keep your oldest logs for the time you specify. Unfortunately, this can be very difficult to estimate. Just crank this up to 50,000 KB.

The Message Log Settings Properties Page

Message logging is an integral part of the search feature of the HTTP monitoring piece on the GroupWise MTA. With message logging enabled, you can search for messages that passed through the MTA. In GroupWise 5x, customers were discouraged from turning on message logging; however, this is no longer the case. In GroupWise 6, message logging has been totally revamped. The MTA no longer uses a proprietary database, but the message log files are simple text files. The filename is in the format of MMDDMSG.00X, and message log files are located by default at the DOMAIN\MSLOCAL\MSGLOG directory. The MTA will cycle to a new MMDDMSG.00X just as it does with the traditional log files.

One advantage to enabling message logging is to hook into a couple of report-gathering features that are available in the GroupWise 6 monitor utility. For example, you can generate reports that will tell you how much data has been transmitted and received between two domains. This is very useful when a company has WAN links involved between the GroupWise agents. GroupWise 6 message logging is not the terrible performance-degrader that it is in previous versions of GroupWise.

Figure 9.5 shows the GroupWise Message Log Settings property page.

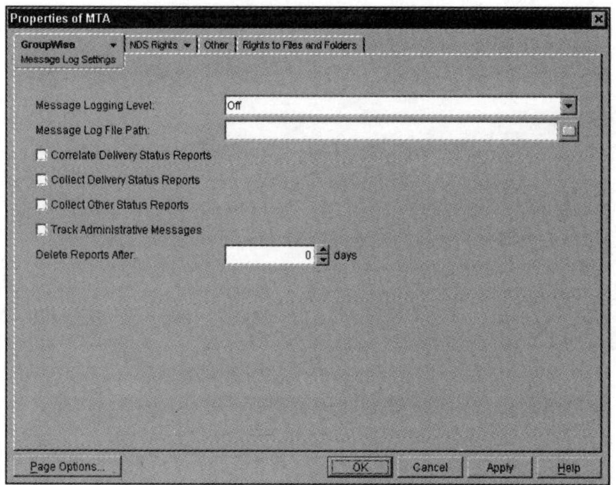

FIGURE 9.5 *The MTA Message Log Settings Property Page*

The Scheduled Events Property Page

There is only one kind of scheduled event that a GroupWise 6 MTA can run, and that is an NDS user synchronization event. The MTA is able to scan NDS for *deltas*, changes to NDS user objects that are not correctly reflected in the domain database.

The Default NDS User Synchronization event is configured as shown in Figure 9.6. Click the Edit button to get to the dialog box shown in Figure 9.7.

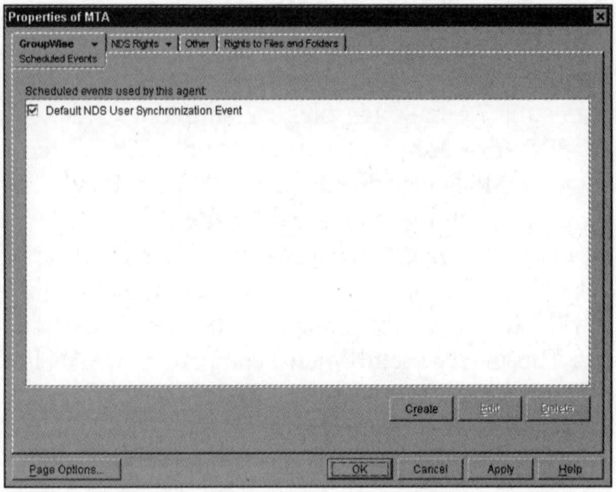

FIGURE 9.6 *The MTA Scheduled Events Property Page*

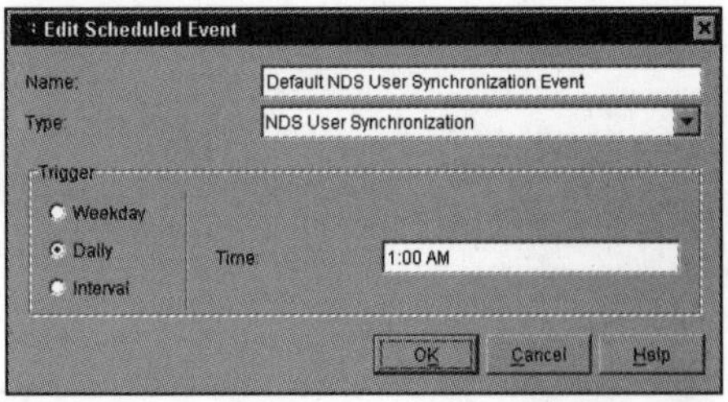

FIGURE 9.7 *Editing the Default NDS User Synchronization Event*

- **Name:** This is the name of the event, and it is displayed in the window shown in Figure 9.6.
- **Type:** Currently there is only one available option for this field: NDS User Synchronization.
- **Trigger:** This option is where all the configuration work is. You may choose to trigger the event at any hour and minute of the day, and you may choose to have the event run daily, or on a single specified day of the week. You can also trigger NDS synchronization to happen on an hour-based interval. For example, you could have NDS synchronization happen every hour. Hourly NDS synchronization could be useful if your users have been given rights to update their own information through products such as Concentrico's Reach for NDS product. With the Weekday radio button selected, you have the option to choose which weekday the event runs.

On most systems, the event is not CPU-intensive and does not cause a noticeable performance hit. Schedule the event so that it does not conflict with planned outages or backups, and you should be just fine.

This scheduled event is enabled by default on the MTA. If running the MTA on an NT server, you may need to disable this event if the NT server does not have access to NDS to log in to the tree. Leaving this enabled in this situation can cause problems with the MTA.

In order for your GroupWise MTA to access NDS, it must log in to NDS. The MTA must have the /user and /password switches enabled in its startup file to allow the MTA to log into NDS.

The Routing Options Property Page

This tab offers you the ability to override certain Internet addressing and default routing settings made at the system level. On large systems, this tool is critical to the proper administration of GroupWise Internet addressing, as well as configuration of MTA-to-MTA direct connectivity with other GroupWise systems. Chapter 16 discusses when to use this tab, shown in Figure 9.8.

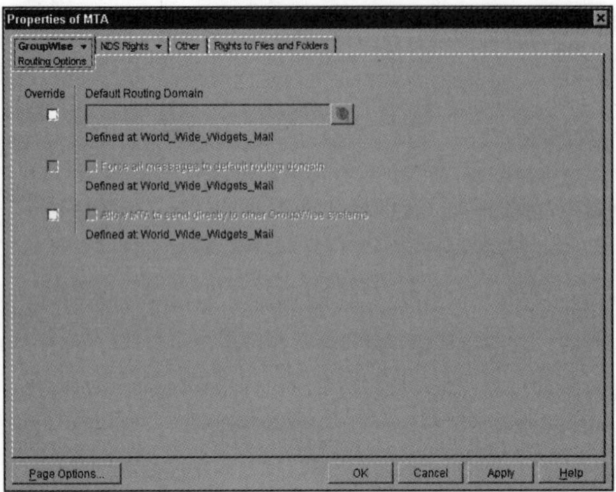

FIGURE 9.8 *The MTA Object Routing Options Properties Page*

Link Configuration and the MTA

On large GroupWise systems, you will likely have to spend some time with the link configuration tool, optimizing or otherwise tweaking the connections between different domains, and between domains and post offices.

In the example in Figure 9.9, there are four domains. Three are listed under Direct Links (*mfg, Sales,* and *uww*), and one is the domain to which ConsoleOne is currently connected (*Corp*). How do these domains communicate with one another? Are messages routed directly between all of them?

The Link Hop utility (see Figure 9.10), with indirect connections between domains, answers these questions.

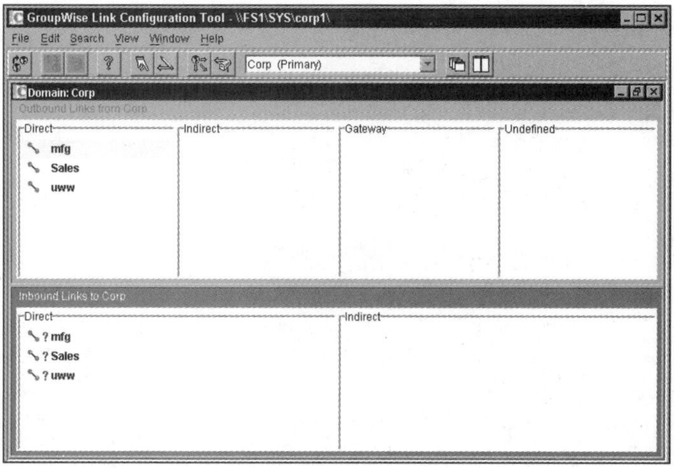

FIGURE 9.9 *The Link Configuration Tool Found under Tools ➪ GroupWise Utilities*

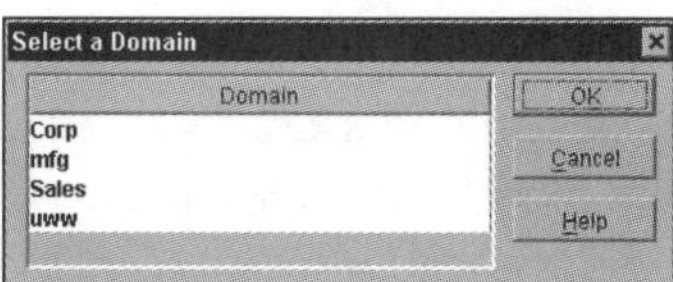

FIGURE 9.10 *Selecting a Domain to See What Indirect Links It Supports*

The dialog box asks you to select a filter. Essentially, you are going to tell the link configuration tool to display any indirect connections that pass through the domain selected here. Highlight Corp and click OK to display the window shown in Figure 9.11.

This window shows that mfg "talks" to Sales via the Corp domain and vice versa. In fact, every domain seems to route through Corp.

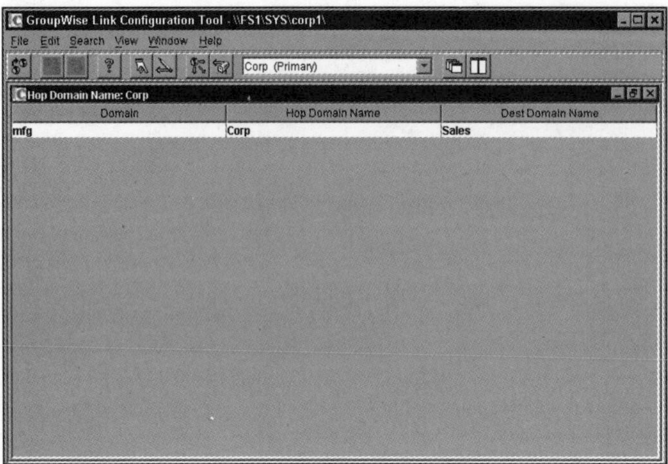

FIGURE 9.11 *The Link Hop Display for the Corp Domain*

Creating an Indirect Connection

Imagine you want to route messages from Sales to mfg through Corp. Perhaps the Corp domain sits at a physical hub on the wide area network, and all traffic passes through there anyway. In this case, having the Corp MTA store-and-forward all messages that pass by it may ease the load on the physical network, and may prevent TCP timeout errors across the WAN.

Consider the following scenario:

- Sales connects directly to mfg.
- The Sales MTA gets 8912 or 8913 errors (TCP time-outs), sometimes during business hours. These errors occur only when connecting to mfg.
- Since Sales has no problem communicating with Corp, and Corp has no problem communicating with mfg, Corp should be used to connect Sales with mfg.

The following steps create an indirect connection between Sales and mfg:

1. Connect to the domain whose MTA you want to affect.

   In this scenario, it's the Sales domain, which is done from GroupWise system operations, under Select Domain.

2. Select the appropriate domain object (Sales, in this case), pull down the Tools menu, and choose GroupWise Utilities ➪ Link Configuration.
3. Double-click the link you want to edit.
   In this scenario, it is the mfg domain link (see Figure 9.12).

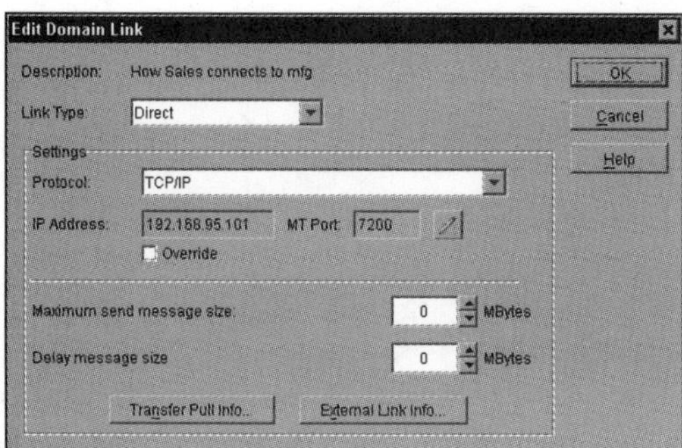

FIGURE 9.12 *Direct Link from Sales to Mfg*

   Here the link type is Direct. Since this is what needs to be changed, grab that drop-down menu.
4. Select Indirect, as in Figure 9.13, and everything changes.

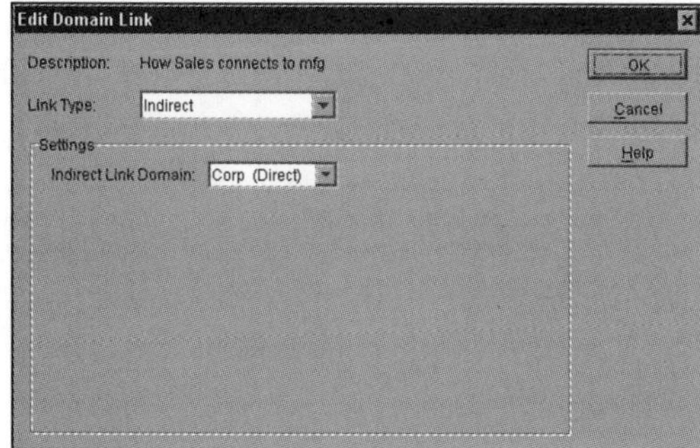

FIGURE 9.13 *Indirect Link from Sales to Mfg*

No longer are there IP Addresses and ports. With an indirect or gateway connection, the only thing to specify is the domain or gateway, respectively, through which to connect. In this scenario, Corp has been used.

5. Click OK and exit the link configuration tool.
6. When prompted to save changes to links, answer Yes.

Overriding Links with the Link Configuration Tool

In some circumstances, it may be necessary to use the link configuration tool to override the IP address that has been specified for an MTA or POA object. Here's the process:

Consider the following scenario:

- The mfg domain's MTA object is on a different IP address than the one listed in ConsoleOne.
- For some reason, the IP address on the MTA won't change correctly. The change does not propagate, and the link is now down between the domain Corp and mfg.

With the following steps, you can override the address:

1. Connect to the domain whose MTA needs to be affected, which in this scenario is Corp.
2. Select that domain object, pull down the Tools menu, and choose GroupWise Utilities ➪ Link Configuration.
3. Double-click the problem link that needs to be edited; in this scenario, it's the mfg domain link (see Figure 9.14).
4. Check the box labeled Override.
5. Notice that there are now new fields for the IP address and port for this link. Enter the correct IP address and port here.
6. Click OK.
7. Exit the link configuration tool, responding Yes to the prompt to save changes.

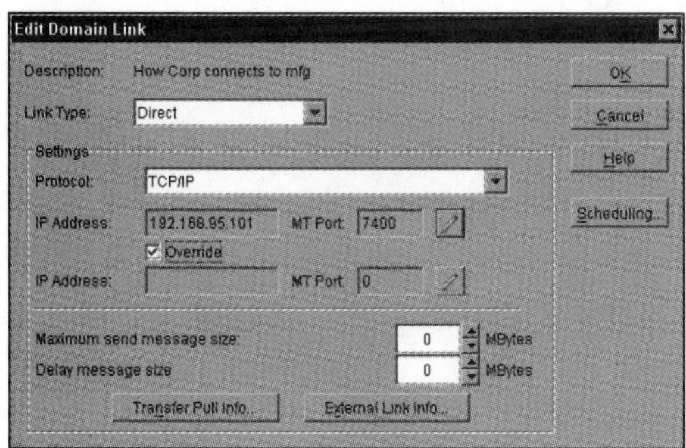

FIGURE 9.14 *The Mfg Link from the Corp Domain Is a Direct Link, with an IP Address and Port Listed*

Configuring a Transfer Pull Link

Transfer pull assumes that two domains connect via UNC paths, but that one MTA is not going to be given any file system rights to the other MTA's domain directory. In this situation, the MTA that does have rights is going to have to "pull" messages from the non-trusted MTA's domain directory.

To configure this, both MTAs must have their links changed. You will give the non-trusted MTA an override link to a new UNC path. This path will be on the non-trusted MTA's server. You will give the trusted MTA a transfer pull path to this new UNC path.

Consider the following scenario:

- Mfg is the non-trusted MTA. The path it will use is `\\WIDGET_CORP1\DATA\XFERPULL` (on the mfg MTA's server).
- Sales is the trusted MTA. It will use the transfer pull path of `\\WIDGET_CORP1\DATA\XFERPULL`.
- The Sales MTA has already been assigned a login ID and password for the mfg server. This was done with the `/USER` and `/PASSWORD` switches in the startup file.

The following steps allow to configure the links:

1. Make a directory under on the WIDGET_CORP1 server on the DATA volume called XFERPULL.
2. Under the XFERPULL directory, make a directory called WPCSIN.
3. Under the WPCSIN directory, make individual directories 0 through 7.

4. Connect to the mfg domain and highlight that domain object.
5. Pull down the Tools menu and choose GroupWise Utilities ➪ Link Configuration.
6. Double-click on the link to the Sales domain.

   Make sure the link type is direct and the link protocol is UNC.
7. Check the Override box.
8. Enter the new UNC path (**\\WIDGET_CORP1\DATA\XFERPULL**) in the UNC Override field.
9. Exit the link configuration tool and save all changes.
10. Connect to the Sales domain and highlight that domain object.
11. Pull down the Tools menu and choose GroupWise Utilities ➪ Link Configuration.
12. Double-click on the link to the mfg domain.

    Make sure the link type is direct and the link protocol is UNC.
13. Click on the Transfer Pull Info button to get to Figure 9.15.

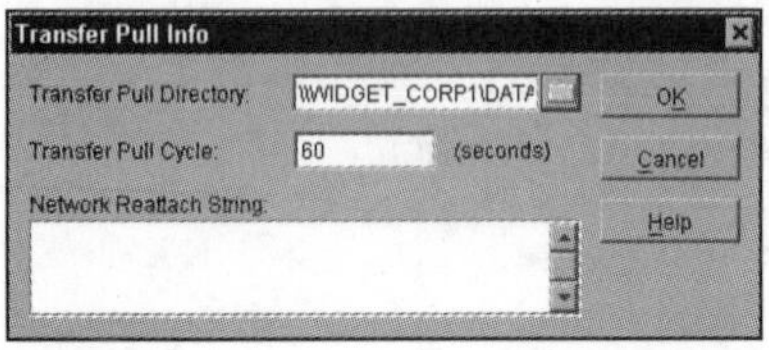

FIGURE 9.15 *The Transfer Pull Info Dialog Box*

14. Enter the new UNC path (**\\WIDGET_CORP1\DATA\XFERPULL**) in the Transfer Pull Directory field.
15. Enter a polling interval, in seconds.

    Remember that polling across a slow or untrusted link can be a performance hit for the MTA. Sixty seconds is usually fast enough to satisfy users whose mail traverses the link.

16. Click OK to dismiss the Transfer Pull Info dialog box, and click OK again to finish editing the link.
17. Exit the link configuration tool and save your changes.

The mfg MTA really has no idea what is going on. The MTA is simply re-directing any messages for Sales into a directory on its own file server.

The Sales MTA, however, is doing double duty. When the Sales MTA sends to the mfg domain, he sends as usual, dropping files in the directory specified as the mfg UNC path. But every 60 seconds, he polls the new UNC path, the transfer pull directory, to see if mfg has anything to send.

Cutting Down on WAN Traffic by Scheduling Links with the Link Configuration Tool

Now here's a situation where even a TCP/IP link may need a little additional help. Suppose you have a TCP/IP WAN link to a particular domain, and during the day there is heavy traffic on that link. You have decided that GroupWise traffic should not be sent over this connection during the day, unless there are high-priority messages, or lots of files have queued up. Here's a walk through on this scenario:

- The mfg domain lies across a WAN link that is exceptionally busy from 8 a.m. to 5 p.m., Monday through Friday, because of a mainframe inventory program.
- The Corp MTA, which connects to mfg, is not to connect during the day, unless there are high-priority messages, a large volume of messages, or messages that have been waiting a long time.

The following steps will help you work through this scenario:

1. Connect to the domain for which the link schedule will apply.
2. Select that domain object, pull down the Tools menu, and choose GroupWise Utilities ➪ Link Configuration.
3. Double-click the link you want to edit.

   In this case, it's the mfg domain link.
4. Click the Scheduling button to get to the Link Schedule window (see Figure 9.16).

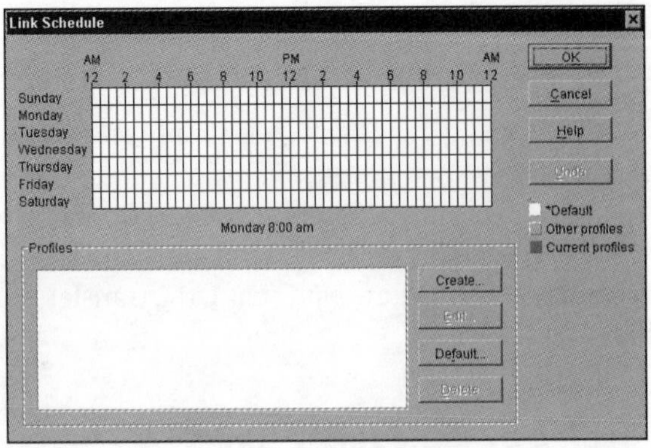

FIGURE 9.16 *The Link Schedule Window*

Now, two profiles need to be created. One is the default profile, which will be in force after hours. The other will be the daytime profile, which will be in force during business hours.

5. Click the Default button and click OK to get to the Edit Profile window (see Figure 9.17).

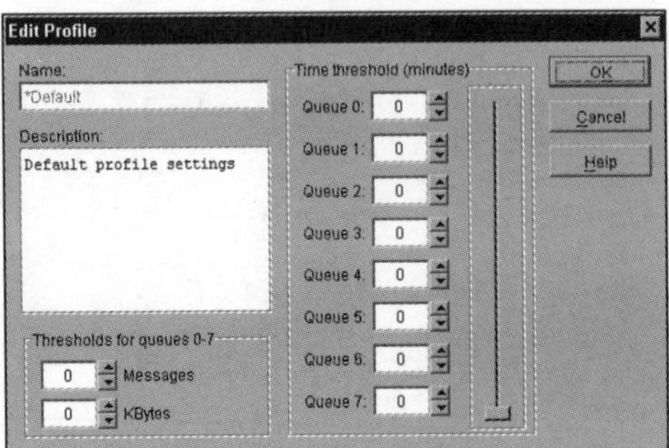

FIGURE 9.17 *The Edit Profile Window*

6. Now click the Create button in the Link Schedule window to get to Figure 9.18.

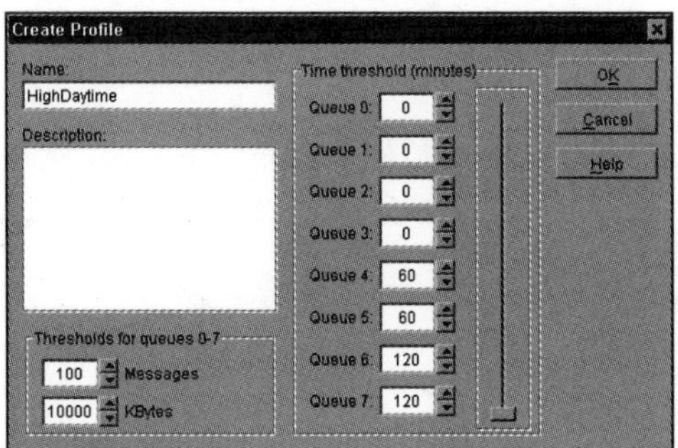

FIGURE 9.18 *The Create Profile Window, with Changes Made for Aggressive Link Scheduling*

7. Name this profile.

Now you are creating the profile for link scheduling during the day.

In this example, the profile is set so that high priority queues (0–3) are processed immediately. Normal priority queues (4–5) are processed only after the oldest item in them has waited 60 minutes. Low priority queues (6–7) are processed only after the oldest item has waited two hours.

This example has also been set up so that if a total of 100 messages exist across all queues, regardless of their age, the MTA will open the link. Also, if there is 10,000K (10Mb) of files across all queues, the MTA will open the link.

8. Click OK.

9. With this new profile selected, drag the mouse across the schedule pane to create a rectangle.

The one in the example runs across the 8 to 5 block, Monday through Friday (see Figure 9.19). This is the schedule for which the selected profile will be active. At all other hours (the white space), the default profile will be active.

10. Click OK to dismiss the Link Schedule window, and click OK again to close the Edit Link window.

11. Exit the link configuration tool and save your changes.

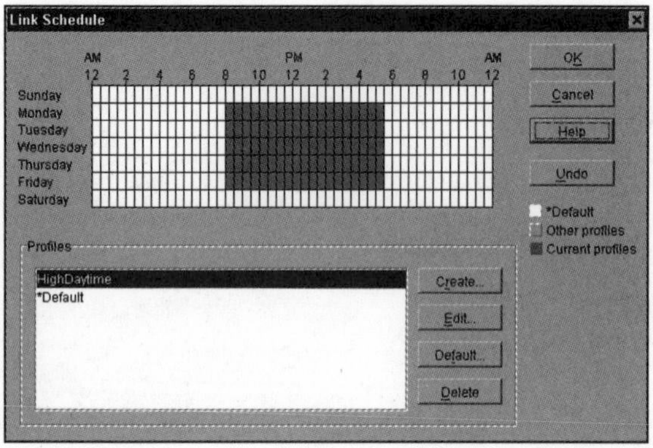

FIGURE 9.19 *The Link Schedule Window with Profiles Created and Scheduled*

Message Transfer Agent Console Commands

As mentioned earlier, the message transfer agent typically runs on a NetWare or Windows NT file server. It has its own interface, and this section discusses that interface. When the message transfer agent has been successfully loaded, you see the screen shown in Figure 9.20.

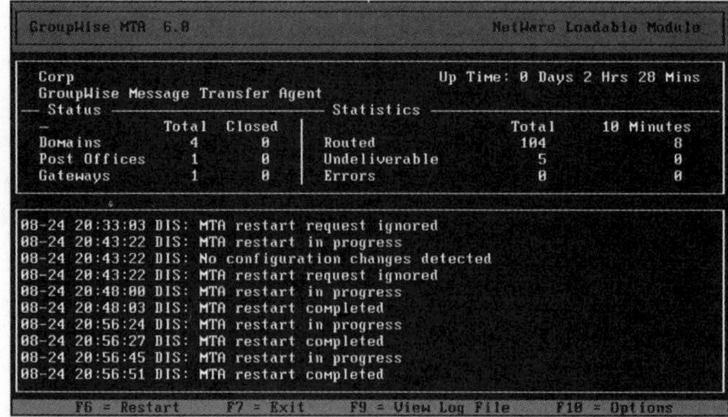

FIGURE 9.20 *The GroupWise Message Transfer Agent Console on a NetWare 5 Server*

The MTA may be controlled from this screen with keyboard commands. Commands available from the main screen are the following:

- **F6**: Restart
- **F7**: Exit
- **F9**: View Log File
- **F10**: Options

Restarting and Exiting

This section offers a brief discussion on the difference between the F6 – Restart option and the F7 – Exit option.

When you hit F6, you are prompted to confirm the restart. After confirmation, the agent closes its connections to other servers, stops all processing of transfer files on this server, and re-reads configuration information from the domain database. The MTA does not, however, re-read the MTA startup file. The MTA startup file is the ASCII file with configuration switches in it.

When selecting F7, you are prompted to confirm the exit command. After confirmation the agent closes all connections, stops processing messages, and GWMTA.NLM (GWMTA.EXE on NT servers) unloads. If you then reload the agent from the server console, the MTA will re-read the startup file and the configuration information from the domain database.

The F7 keystroke does exactly the same thing that the UNLOAD GWMTA.NLM command does on a NetWare server. If you have made changes to the MTA startup file, and you want them to be applied, you must use F7 to exit (or the UNLOAD command), and then reload the MTA manually.

TIP

When running the MTA as a service on NT, and it has been set to interact with the desktop, the F7 option will be grayed out. This is because it is running as a service. To shut down the MTA when it is running as a service, you will need to stop that service from running. This is done by opening the Services option from the Windows NT Control Panel. From here, you can start and stop the MTA that is running as a Windows service.

The Options Menu

Hitting F10 from the main screen presents you with the menu shown in Figure 9.21.

Options

Configuration Status
Admin Status
Active Log Window
View Log Files
Log Settings
Cycle Log
Live Remote Status

FIGURE 9.21 *The Message Transfer Agent Options Menu*

Here's an explanation of each of these options in turn.

Configuration Status

The Configuration Status tool is one of the most powerful troubleshooting tools you have. It allows you to look at the status of the MTA's connections with other GroupWise domains, post offices, and gateways, and it tells you why those connections are down if there are problems. It even allows you to suspend connections should you want to prevent communication with another domain, post office, or gateway for some reason.

In Figure 9.22, you find four columns of information, but the interface provides no column headers. From left to right, the column headers would be the following:

- Link Name
- Link Class
- Link Status
- Link Path

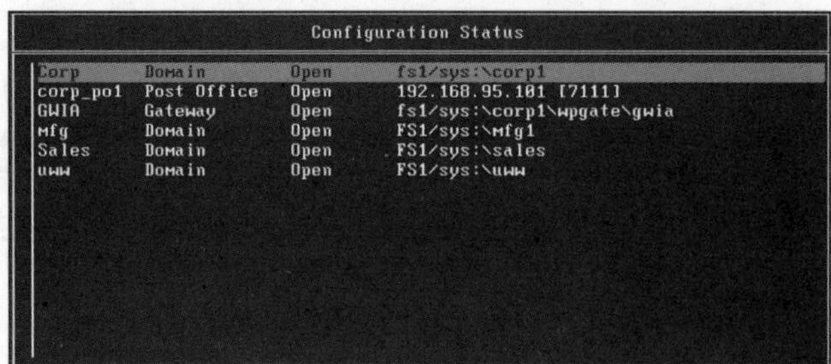

Configuration Status
Corp Domain Open fs1/sys:\corp1
corp_po1 Post Office Open 192.168.95.101 [7111]
GWIA Gateway Open fs1/sys:\corp1\wpgate\gwia
mfg Domain Open FS1/sys:\mfg1
Sales Domain Open FS1/sys:\sales
uww Domain Open FS1/sys:\uww

FIGURE 9.22 *The Message Transfer Agent Configuration Status Screen*

Consider the first line of text. The link name here is Corp, and the link class is Domain. This means that this line represents this MTA's link to the Corp domain. The link status is Open, and the link path is `fs1/sys:\corp1`. This means that this MTA can successfully write to this path on the fs1 file server.

Now this first line of text is a special one. It defines this MTA's link to its home directory. This MTA is running against the Corp domain database, servicing the Corp domain, so the Corp link is listed first.

In Figure 9.23, the Corp link is highlighted, and I pressed the Enter key.

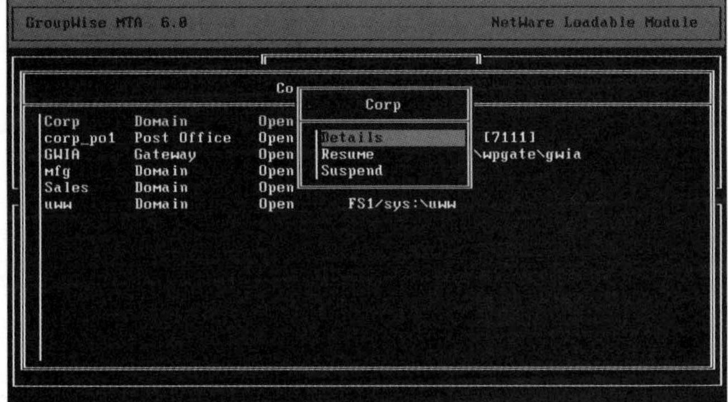

FIGURE 9.23 *The Message Transfer Agent Link Options Menu*

There are three options presented on this menu:

- **Details:** This option brings up a window showing the details for the selected link.
- **Resume:** This option resumes service for this link, if someone previously suspended it, or the link was closed because of communication problems of some sort.
- **Suspend:** This option discontinues service for this link. Service will not be resumed until Resume is selected or the MTA is restarted.

Figure 9.23 shows that the link status for domain mfg is open. Here's how to check out a link. Selecting Details for the mfg link presents the screen shown in Figure 9.24.

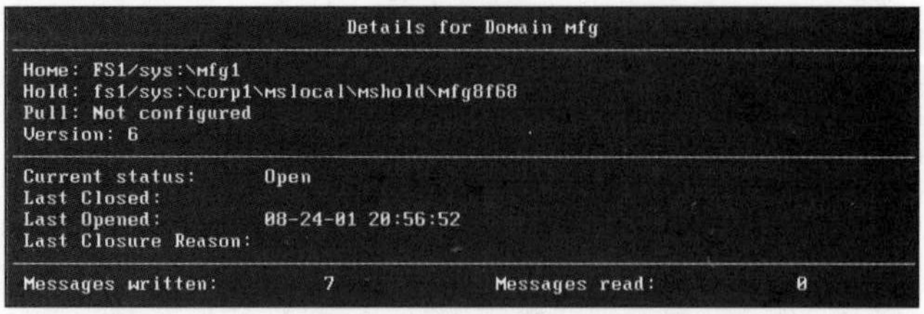

```
                    Details for Domain mfg
Home: FS1/sys:\mfg1
Hold: fs1/sys:\corp1\mslocal\mshold\mfg8f68
Pull: Not configured
Version: 6

Current status:         Open
Last Closed:
Last Opened:            08-24-01 20:56:52
Last Closure Reason:

Messages written:           7          Messages read:          0
```

FIGURE 9.24 *The Message Transfer Agent Link Details Window*

Here's a look at each of the fields available in this window:

- **Home:** This field shows the home directory, or link path, for this link. This may be a server path, or it could be an IP address and port. If it is an IP address, the line that reads Home in Figure 9.24 will say MTP instead, for message transfer port information.
- **Hold:** This field displays the directory that the MTA uses to queue up files destined for this domain if the home path is not accessible (that is, the link is down). Large numbers of files may queue up in this hold directory if the link stays down for an extended period of time.
- **Pull:** If you have configured the MTA for transfer pull, as described earlier in this chapter, the transfer pull path is listed here.
- **Version:** This field shows the version of the domain, post office, or gateway that the MTA is connecting to. This information is required so that the MTA can properly format transfer files for older versions of GroupWise.
- **Current status:** Here you see what you already saw from the other screen. This link is open.
- **Last Closed:** This field displays the date that this link was closed last. If the link has not been closed since the MTA was last restarted, this field is blank.
- **Last Opened:** This field is the date that this link was last opened. Again, it is only tracked since this MTA was last restarted.
- **Last Closure Reason:** Here is a big reason for visiting this screen in the first place. The MTA will tell why a link is closed. For example, an MTA could complain that it cannot create files, which means it has insufficient rights to the directory in question, or perhaps the directory in question does not exist.
- **Messages written:** This field shows the number of messages written to this path.

- **Messages read:** This field is the number of messages received on this link. It will typically be 0 unless the connection is via TCP/IP. Messages delivered to this MTA via UNC paths are not tracked on this screen.

From the information here, you should be able to quickly determine the nature of a link problem. You will still need to do some troubleshooting, but this screen will narrow your field of possibilities quite nicely.

As another example of this screen, Figure 9.25 shows the details when highlighting the corp_po1 post office link and checking out the details.

```
                    Details for Post Office corp_po1
MTP:  192.168.95.101 [Port 7111]
Hold: fs1/sys:\corp1\mslocal\mshold\cor8685
Version: 6

Current status:        Open
Last Closed:
Last Opened:           08-24-01 20:56:52
Last Closure Reason:

Messages written:          0           Messages read:           0
```

FIGURE 9.25 *The Message Transfer Agent Link Details Window for a Post Office Connected via TCP/IP*

In this window, you can see that the Home field has been replaced with an MTP field. The TCP/IP address for the corp_po POA is shown, as is the message transfer port, 7111. Note also that this link has never been closed, so the Last Closed and Last Closure Reason fields are blank.

Admin Status

When Admin Status is selected from the options menu, a window similar to the one shown in Figure 9.26 appears.

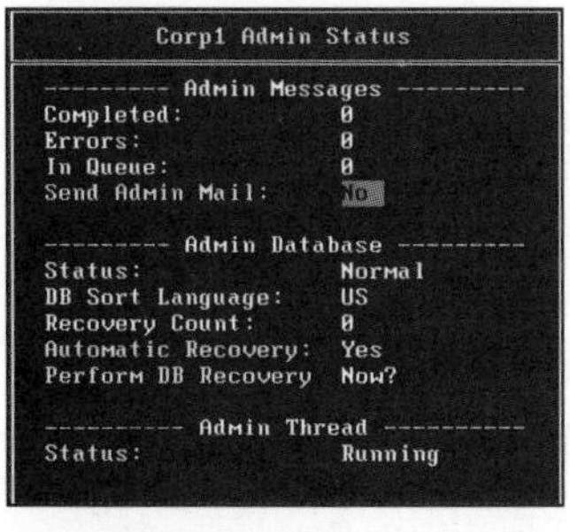

```
           Corp1 Admin Status
--------- Admin Messages ---------
Completed:              0
Errors:                 0
In Queue:               0
Send Admin Mail:        No

--------- Admin Database ---------
Status:                 Normal
DB Sort Language:       US
Recovery Count:         0
Automatic Recovery:     Yes
Perform DB Recovery     Now?

---------- Admin Thread ----------
Status:                 Running
```

FIGURE 9.26 *The Message Transfer Agent Admin Status Window*

Some of the lines in this window allow user interaction, while some are purely informative.

- **Completed:** This first line, listed under the Admin Messages heading, tells how many admin messages have been successfully written to the domain database since the MTA was loaded.
- **Errors:** This entry tells how many errors have occurred when attempting to perform administrative transactions on the domain database. Errors in this column are not typically associated with domain database damage, though. They usually occur when domains are out of sync, and this domain receives a transaction that it cannot perform — adding a user who already exists or deleting a non-existent user, for instance.
- **In Queue:** This line is a count of the admin messages awaiting processing. If lots of administration traffic is taking place (say, you just imported 2,000 users), then you can expect a positive number here for a while. Usually, it should be 0.
- **Send Admin Mail:** This line is interactive. Pressing Enter allows you to toggle between No and Yes. This option governs whether or not the MTA sends e-mail to the administrator of this domain when there are errors.
- **Status:** There are two status lines. This one, under the Admin Database heading, tells the status of the domain database. During an automatic recovery, the database may be locked against changes. This status should always read Normal.
- **DB Sort Language:** This is the language used to sort the address book.
- **Recovery Count:** This is the number of times since the MTA has been loaded that the MTA has run a recovery against the domain database. This number should always be 0. If it is not, then you have had domain database damage at some point (or perhaps you have manually triggered a recovery, described later in this section).
- **Automatic Recovery:** This line is interactive. Pressing Enter allows you to toggle between Yes and No. In most cases, you will want to leave this set to Yes, allowing the MTA to recover the domain database if it encounters a structural error during transactions. If the MTA is restarted, this setting is not remembered; it is re-read from the domain database. Permanent changes to this setting should be made to the MTA object from ConsoleOne.
- **Perform DB Recovery Now?:** Another interactive line, pressing Enter here allows you to spawn a database recovery. This option may be useful if you suspect the database is damaged.

- **Status:** This second status line indicates the status of the admin thread of the MTA. This line is interactive; press Enter to toggle between Running and Suspended. One common reason to suspend the admin thread is to prevent updates from taking place during an off-line rebuild of the domain database. While the fresh database is being created, you want administrative changes to be queued up. Otherwise, they will be written to the current database, which is going to be replaced.

Active Log Window

The main screen for the MTA shows what appears to be an active log, but all that is logged to the main screen are global sorts of messages. To see the blow-by-blow log, you need to select Active Log Window from the Options menu (see Figure 9.27).

```
GroupWise MTA  6.0                                   NetWare Loadable Module

                              Active Log
21:28:30 0A8 RTR: Corp: 00000867.001 Priority 10  :0:0 : Transfer to uww
21:28:30 0A8 RTR: Corp: 00000867.001: Message queued: fs1/sys:\corp1\mslocal\m
shold\uww1a70\2\00000867.001
21:28:30 0A8 RTR: Corp: 00000867.001 Priority 10  :0:0 : Transfer to Sales
21:28:30 0DC uww: Releasing message: fs1/sys:\corp1\mslocal\mshold\uww1a70\2\0
0000867.001
21:28:30 0DC uww: Message queued: FS1/sys:\uww\wpcsin\2\ab86c6fe.000
21:28:30 0A8 RTR: Corp: 00000867.001: Message queued: fs1/sys:\corp1\mslocal\m
shold\sal1a5b\2\00000867.002
21:28:30 0A8 RTR: Corp: 00000867.001 Priority 10  :0:0 : Transfer to mfg
21:28:30 0CC Sales: Releasing message: fs1/sys:\corp1\mslocal\mshold\sal1a5b\2
\00000867.002
21:28:30 0CC Sales: Message queued: FS1/sys:\sales\wpcsin\2\ab86c6fe.000
21:28:30 0A8 RTR: Corp: 00000867.001: Message queued: fs1/sys:\corp1\mslocal\m
shold\mfg8f68\2\00000867.003
21:28:30 0ED mfg: Releasing message: fs1/sys:\corp1\mslocal\mshold\mfg8f68\2\0
0000867.003
21:28:30 0ED mfg: Message queued: FS1/sys:\mfg1\wpcsin\2\ab86c6fe.000
```

FIGURE 9.27 *The Message Transfer Agent Active Log Window*

This is the active log for the MTA. Log entries here indicate the time of the operation, the thread name that performed the operation, and a description of the operation. This chapter discusses the interpretation of the MTA logs in the section titled "Understanding the MTA Log."

View Log Files

If the information you are looking for in the MTA log is not in the currently active log, you will need to select View Log Files to get to the window shown in Figure 9.28.

```
View Log Files

0824mta.006  08-24-01 18:28:14     6220 bytes
0824mta.007  08-24-01 18:28:46     4501 bytes
0824mta.008  08-24-01 18:29:46     5208 bytes
0824mta.009  08-24-01 19:05:48     2848 bytes
0824mta.00a  08-24-01 20:27:24     6105 bytes
0824mta.00b  08-24-01 20:28:12     4099 bytes
0824mta.00c  08-24-01 20:48:02     3684 bytes
0824mta.00d  08-24-01 20:56:26     5681 bytes
0824mta.00e  08-24-01 20:56:50    18592 bytes
*0824mta.00f 08-24-01 20:56:50        0 bytes
```

FIGURE 9.28 *The Message Transfer Agent View Log Files Window*

Selecting one of the log files listed here and pressing Enter brings up a viewing window, as shown in Figure 9.29.

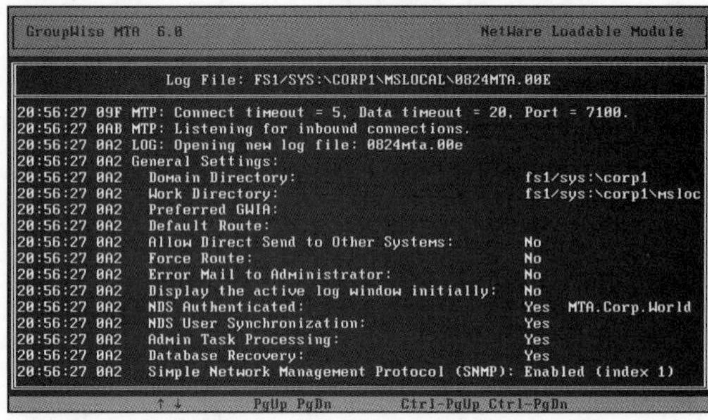

GroupWise MTA 6.0
NetWare Loadable Module
Log File: FS1/SYS:\CORP1\MSLOCAL\0824MTA.00E
20:56:27 09F MTP: Connect timeout = 5, Data timeout = 20, Port = 7100.
20:56:27 0AB MTP: Listening for inbound connections.
20:56:27 0A2 LOG: Opening new log file: 0824mta.00e
20:56:27 0A2 General Settings:
20:56:27 0A2 Domain Directory: fs1/sys:\corp1
20:56:27 0A2 Work Directory: fs1/sys:\corp1\msloc
20:56:27 0A2 Preferred GWIA:
20:56:27 0A2 Default Route:
20:56:27 0A2 Allow Direct Send to Other Systems: No
20:56:27 0A2 Force Route: No
20:56:27 0A2 Error Mail to Administrator: No
20:56:27 0A2 Display the active log window initially: No
20:56:27 0A2 NDS Authenticated: Yes MTA.Corp.World
20:56:27 0A2 NDS User Synchronization: Yes
20:56:27 0A2 Admin Task Processing: Yes
20:56:27 0A2 Database Recovery: Yes
20:56:27 0A2 Simple Network Management Protocol (SNMP): Enabled (index 1)
↑ ↓ PgUp PgDn Ctrl-PgUp Ctrl-PgDn

FIGURE 9.29 *A Log File Viewing Window*

It is much easier to view the log files from the HTTP interface to the GroupWise agents, rather than from the MTA console screen. You will find it more readable and interactive. You can also use the browsers "find" functionality to find specific information that you may be looking for when you use the HTTP option to View log files.

Log Settings

The Log Settings dialog box can be used to change the logging level, age of log files, and space taken up by log files on the fly.

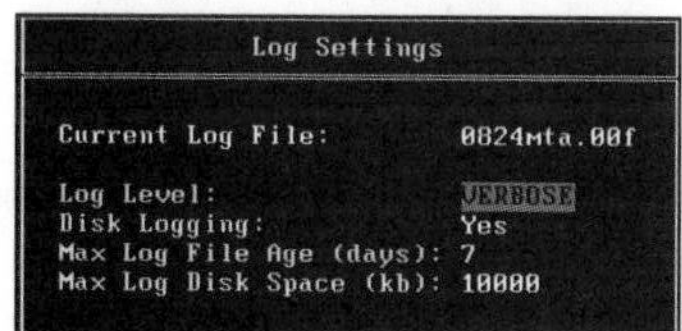

FIGURE 9.30 *The Message Transfer Agent Logging Options Dialog Box*

These settings will not be retained after a restart, however. If you want to change the logging options permanently, make your changes from ConsoleOne, and then execute a restart (F6) on the MTA to force it to re-read configuration information in the domain database.

Cycle Log

This command forces the MTA to begin writing to a new log file. This option is useful if the current log file needs to be moved or edited by another application (that is, opened in WordPad so that a Find operation can be performed).

Live Remote Status

This option lists GroupWise remote or cache client users who are connected to the MTA, along with the post offices and domains that the MTA communicates with in order to service the remote or cache client users. If you have more interest in live remote, read later in this chapter the section called "Configuring the MTA to Support Live Remote."

Undocumented MTA Commands and Switches

There are several console command-line options that offer functionality that is not documented in the GroupWise MTA interface. These should be used as troubleshooting tools, rather than as part of day-to-day operations.

- /NOMSGLOG: This switch prevents the MTA from accessing or creating the message log files in the <domain>\MSLOCAL\MSGLOG directory. If the MSGLOG directory is renamed and MTA is reloaded with this switch, it re-creates the MSGLOG directory, but not the message log files. This option should be used if the message logging log files have become corrupt and the MTA fails to load while those files are in place.

- **F4 or Ctrl+D keystrokes:** These keystrokes execute an immediate NDS user synchronization operation. If you use these keystrokes while MTA is running, you will be presented with a confirmation prompt.

Understanding the MTA Log

The message transfer agent keeps two kinds of logs. This section focuses on the MTA log, which keeps track of the actions performed by the MTA, including error messages, administration updates, and connections to other GroupWise agents.

Message logging is a system whereby messages are tracked in a series of text files that are updated by the MTA. The tool for reading utilizing this information is the message tracking feature of the HTTP monitoring piece on the GroupWise MTA.

You can browse the MTA logs from the MTA console using the View Logs tool under the Options menu. This tool does not allow for searching, however, and may be less convenient for you than using your favorite word processor would be.

MTA logs for a given domain's MTA are found at the root of the domain MSLOCAL directory. The log files have names such as 0125mta.003, which indicates the month and day that the log file was created. The 003 in this example indicates that this was the third log file created, and of course, the file name shows that it was created on January 25th.

If a log file is a 0-byte file, the MTA is probably currently working with it, and you will not be able to open it without using the Cycle Log command under the Options menu.

The Top of the Log File

At the top of each log file, the MTA writes the settings that it is running with. These settings, as discussed at the beginning of this chapter, could have been passed to the MTA through the command line, the MTA startup file, or the domain database.

Here's a look at a sample log file. Following are log entries from the MTA for the Corp domain.

General Settings

This first few blocks of text tell which domain the MTA is running against, what the Internet addressing and routing settings are, and some of the other general settings.

```
13:43:50 General Settings:
13:43:50   Domain Directory: widget_corp1/data:\www\corp
13:43:50   Work Directory: widget_corp1/data:\www\corp\mslocal
```

The last two lines in the preceding example show parameters that came from either the command line or the startup file. The domain directory came from the /home switch and the work directory came from /work.

```
13:43:50   Preferred GWIA: Corp.GWIA
13:43:50   Default Route:                              Corp
13:43:50   *corp.www.com
13:43:50   *mfg.www.com
13:43:50   *sales.www.com
13:43:50   *worldwidewidgets.com
13:43:50   *www.com
13:43:50   Allow Direct Send to Other Systems:         No
13:43:50   Force Route:                                No
```

This set of settings deals with Internet addressing (covered in Chapter 16). Internet addressing has been enabled on this system. The preferred GWIA and default routing domain are listed, and then each of the IDOMAINs defined on this system is listed with a preceding asterisk.

```
13:43:50   Error Mail to Administrator:                Yes
13:43:50   Display the active log window initially:    No
13:43:50   NDS Authenticated: MTA.Corp.Corp.           Yes
World_Wide_Widgets
13:43:50   NDS User Synchronization:                   Yes
13:43:50   Admin Task Processing:                      Yes
13:43:50   Database Recovery:                          Yes
```

The preceding are some of the operational settings for the MTA. This MTA has been authenticated to the directory, and NDS user synchronization is on. The admin thread is running, and if the MTA encounters domain databases damage, it will attempt to repair it.

TCP/IP Settings

An important part of your troubleshooting, should you have problems getting the MTA to "talk" to other GroupWise agents, is found here in the TCP/IP settings portion of the MTA log:

```
13:43:50 TCP/IP Settings:
13:43:50    Maximum Inbound TCP/IP Connections:        40
13:43:50    TCP Port for Incoming Connections:         7100
13:43:50    TCP/IP Connection Timeout:                 5
13:43:50    TCP/IP Data Timeout:                       20
```

The IP address of the MTA is not given here, because this parameter is defined at the server level. The inbound port is reported here, however. Also significant are the connection timeout and data timeout settings. These settings tell how many seconds the MTA will wait on an attempted connection or transmission. The values here are the defaults, and may be changed with the `/tcpwaitconnect` and `/tcpwaitdata` switches in the MTA startup file.

Logging and Performance Settings

Here are the logging settings for this MTA. Log files will not be kept for more than seven days, and may be deleted sooner than that if more than 1MB of disk space is being taken up by all of the logs.

```
13:43:50 Logging Settings:
13:43:50    Log Level:                                     VERBOSE
13:43:50    Disk Logging:                                      Yes
13:43:50    Log Directory: widget_corp1/data:
\www\corp\mslocal
13:43:50    Maximum Logfile Age:                            7 Days
13:43:50    Maximum Log Disk Space:               1024 Kilobytes
13:43:50 Performance Settings:
13:43:50    Additional High Priority Routing Thread:         No
13:43:50    Additional Mail Priority Routing Thread:         No
13:43:50    Low Priority Scanning Cycle:              15 Seconds
13:43:50    High Priority Scanning Cycle:              5 Seconds
```

In the performance settings section, it shows that there are no additional threads that have been spawned, and the scanning cycles for the MTA queues (WPCSIN\<0-7>) are every five seconds for the high-priority queues, and fifteen seconds for mail priority.

```
13:43:50 Message Logging Settings:
13:43:50   Message Logging Directory: widget_corp1/data:
\www\corp\mslocal\msglog
13:43:50   Message Logging Settings:
13:43:50 Scheduled Event Settings:
13:43:50   Today's NDS User Sync Event Times:
```

Finally, the log says that message logging is not enabled, and there are no NDS user sync events scheduled for today.

The Body of the Log

Each line in the body of the MTA log is divided into three major sections: The time-stamp, the process, and the statement. For example:

```
16:13:56 MTP: mfg-ipS0: Connection established. 10.10.106.59
```

In this example, the time-stamp reads 16:13:56 (56 seconds after 4:13 p.m.), the process is MTP, and the statement is mfg-ips0: Connection established. 10.10.106.59.

The Process Column

If you are to make sense of the MTA log, you must first understand the acronyms and abbreviations in the process column. This section defines them:

- **DIS:** The dispatch process is responsible for (drumroll, please) dispatching other processes. You will see the DIS process when the MTA receives a restart command.
- **RTR:** The router process is responsible for moving files from one directory to another, as part of the whole message transfer operation. It is also the receive process when another MTA or POA transmits a file to this MTA via TCP/IP. If you have UNC links, RTR is going to be both send and receive, because RTR handles movement between directories.

- **MTP:** The message transfer process is responsible for connecting to another GroupWise MTA or POA and transmitting a message file to it via TCP/IP. This is the send process for the MTA.
- **MLG:** The message logging process is responsible for writing to the message log database. Even with message logging disabled, you will see the MLG process announcing the results of RTR and MTP operations.
- **SCA:** The scanner process is responsible for polling gateway directories under the domain directory, as well as any post office directories where TCP/IP connectivity has not been set up.
- **ADM:** The administration process is responsible for updating the domain database with any GDS (GroupWise directory services) information that is being propagated around the system. Add a user while connected to one domain, and you should see the ADM process on every other domain's MTA add that user there. (You'll also see the ADM process in the POA logs as the user gets added to the post office database.)
- **SNMP:** The simple network management protocol process shows up when SNMP is enabled. It periodically announces that it has obtained the necessary parameters to publish MTA operational information to any SNMP-aware query agent on the system.

The following sections examine a few examples of these threads in action.

Scenario 1

In this scenario, the MTA has just loaded and is beginning the process of scanning its input queues.

```
16:43:54 Corp: Begin opening Domain
16:43:54 Corp: Domain now open
16:43:54 SCA: Corp: Begin high priority routing
16:43:54 SCA: Corp: Begin normal priority routing
```

In these first four lines, the MTA is reporting that the Corp domain is opened and the SCA process launched for high and normal priority queues. When the MTA opens a scanning connection, it checks to make sure that it has the necessary file-system rights to work with the transport files.

```
16:43:54 SCA: corp_po1: Begin high priority routing
16:43:54 SCA: corp_po1: Begin normal priority routing
```

Now the SCA process is launched for the corp_po1 post office. The link protocol for this post office is UNC, so the MTA must scan the WPCSIN directory under the post office directory for files to pick up and process.

```
16:43:54 GWIA: Begin opening Gateway
16:43:54 GWIA: Begin opening Gateway
16:43:54 WEBACC55: Begin opening Gateway
16:43:54 WEBACC55: Begin opening Gateway
```

Threads must be spawned to take care of each gateway under the domain directory. The preceding shows that the GWIA and WEBACC55 directories are being opened.

```
16:43:54 GWIA: Gateway now open
16:43:54 SCA: GWIA: Begin normal priority routing
16:43:54 SCA: GWIA: Begin high priority routing
16:43:54 WEBACC55: Gateway now open
16:43:54 SCA: WEBACC55: Begin normal priority routing
16:43:54 SCA: WEBACC55: Begin high priority routing
```

Finally, the MTA reports that the GWIA and WEBACC55 directories are successfully opened and the scanning threads launched against them.

Scenario 2

In this scenario, an administrative change has been made to the Corp domain database. This change was made directly from NetWare administrator, so the ADM process never enters into the picture in the MTA log. The change does need to be broadcast to other domains and post offices, however.

```
16:14:55 MLG: Arrived (0x108B)
16:14:55 RTR: Corp: 0000108b: Routing
widget_corp1/data:\corp\mslocal\gwinprog\2\0000108b (1 kb)
16:14:55 RTR: Corp: 0000108b: Originator: Corp.Domain Message
Server [ADS]
16:14:55 RTR: Corp: 0000108b Priority 10  :0:0 : Transfer to
Corp.corp_po1:ADS
16:14:55 RTR: Corp: 0000108b: Message queued: widget_corp1/
data:\corp\mslocal\mshold\cora517\2\0000108B.001
```

The following steps show you what has happened thus far (numbers do not represent line numbers, but logical steps in the message flow):

1. The MLG process announces the arrival of a new file to be processed.
2. The RTR process announces that it is routing the file and gives the full path to the file and its approximate size.
3. The RTR process then moves the file to the holding queue for the Corp_PO1 post office. This directory is named using the first three characters of the domain or PO name (cor) followed by four characters of hexadecimal hash (a517). Note that the file goes into the 2 directory.

```
16:14:55 RTR: Corp: 0000108c: Routing
widget_corp1/data:\corp\mslocal\gwinprog\2\0000108c (1 kb)
16:14:55 RTR: Corp: 0000108c: Originator: Corp.Domain Message
Server [ADS]
16:14:55 RTR: Corp: 0000108c Priority 10  :0:0 : Transfer to
mfg
16:14:55 RTR: Corp: 0000108c: Message queued: widget_corp1/
data:\corp\mslocal\mshold\mfga59b\2\0000108C.001
```

4. The RTR thread is still busy here. The file name has been incremented, and RTR is now transferring to the mfg domain. This is the point at which the administration update file is replicated to other domains. The file is copied to the holding queue for the mfg domain (hashed name is mfga59b).

```
16:14:55 RTR: Corp: 0000108c Priority 10  :0:0 : Transfer to
sales
16:14:55 RTR: Corp: 0000108c: Message queued:
widget_corp1/data:\corp\mslocal\mshold\sala601\2\0000108C.002
16:14:55 corp_po1: Releasing message:
widget_corp1/data:\corp\mslocal\mshold\cora517\2\0000108B.001
16:14:55 sales: Releasing message:
widget_corp1/data:\corp\mslocal\mshold\sala601\2\0000108C.002
16:14:55 corp_po1: Message queued:
WIDGET_CORP1/DATA:\corp_po1\wpcsout\ads\2\a82aeb7f.000
16:14:55 sales: Message queued: WIDGET_CORP1/DATA:\sales\
wpcsin\2\a82aeb7f.000
```

5. RTR transfers to the sales domain in the first three lines of this block, dropping the file in the holding directory

6. The "Releasing message" lines indicate that the RTR let go of the files in the holding directory, which basically means the files are done being written to, and may be picked up by another process.
7. Now, the messages bound for sales and for corp_po1 are going to go out over UNC connections. This means RTR must make the transfer. This can be seen in the last two lines of this block. Instead of writing to the corp\mslocal structure, RTR writes to sales\wpcsin (the input queue for the sales MTA) and corp_po1\wpcsout\ads (the input queue for the corp_po1 POA's ADM thread).

```
16:14:55 MLG: Arrived (0x108C)
16:14:55 MLG: Queued for all next hops (0x108B)
16:14:55 MLG: Queued for all next hops (0x108C)
16:14:55 MLG: Transferred (0x108B)
16:14:55 MLG: All hops transferred (0x108B)
16:14:55 MLG: Transferred (0x108C)
```

8. Now the MLG process announces what has happened. This is not the most helpful information in the world — it really only reports the file names, and the fact that they have been queued and transferred.

```
16:14:56 MTP: mfg-ipS0: Transmitting file
widget_corp1/data:\corp\mslocal\mshold\mfga59b\2\0000108C.001,
Size: 750
16:14:56 MTP: mfg-ipS0: End-of-file confirmation packet
received
16:14:56 MLG: Transferred (0x108C)
16:14:56 MLG: All hops transferred (0x108C)
16:15:44 MTP: mfg-ipS0: Disconnect packet sent.
```

9. The link to the mfg domain is a TCP/IP link, so the MTP thread must transmit the file that the RTR dropped off in step 4 earlier. Notice that the mfg domain connection is defined by a different hash name than the mfg holding queue is. This is confusing at first, but these names will be constant while the MTA is loaded.
10. The MTP sends confirmation that the whole file has been transmitted.

11. MLG announces success in transfer of the file.
12. MTP sends a disconnect packet, closing the connection about a minute after the transmission was completed. This lag before the disconnect makes the MTA more efficient if large numbers of files must be transmitted between domains. The connection will not need to be reopened every time a file goes across, as long as the files are not sent too far apart.

In this scenario, all that was reported was that the MTA was distributing a transport file to other GroupWise agents on the system. The ADM thread wasn't in action, because the administrative change had already been made to this MTA's domain database by GroupWise administrator.

Scenario 3

This scenario examines an administrative change that has been passed to the MTA from somewhere else.

```
17:10:02 MLG: Arrived (0x109E)
17:10:02 RTR: Corp: 0000109e: Routing
widget_corp1/data:\www\corp\mslocal\gwinprog\2\0000109e (1 kb)
17:10:02 RTR: Corp: 0000109e: Originator: sales.Domain
Message Server [ADS]
```

The first three lines report the following:

1. The MLG thread announces that a new file has arrived: 0x109e.
2. The RTR process picks it from the GWINPROG directory.
3. The RTR process reads it and determines that it came from the sales MTA, and that it is an administrative message.

```
17:10:02 RTR: Corp: 0000109e Priority 10  :0:0 : Transfer to
Corp.Domain Message Server:ADS
17:10:02 RTR: Corp: 0000109e: Message queued: widget_corp1/
data:\www\corp\wpcsout\ads\2\B82af86a.00!
```

4. Now the RTR process decides that the message must be handed to the Corp MTA's administrative process.
5. RTR drops the file in the WPCSOUT\ADS\2 directory.

```
17:10:02 MLG: Transferred (0x109E)
17:10:02 MLG: Queued for all next hops (0x109E)
17:10:03 ADM: Completed: Update replica Link sales
(Administrator: (WWW_TREE) admin.worldwidewidgets,
Domain: sales)
```

6. The MLG process announces that the file has been transferred to the appropriate queue, and that the routing for the file has been established ("queued for all next hops") — in this case the Corp MTA ADM thread is going to be the last hop.
7. The ADM thread announces that it has completed a transaction. This domain's replica for the link configuration for the sales domain has been changed. The original change was made by an administrator logged into the WWW_TREE NDS tree, using the admin.worldwidewidgets account. The administrator was connected to the sales domain database when he or she made the change.

Configuring the MTA to Support Live Remote

Prior to GroupWise 5.5 Enhancement Pack and GroupWise 6, the MTA never "talked" directly with the GroupWise client. Now, however, the GroupWise MTA can communicate with the client, if the client is a GroupWise 5.5 Enhancement Pack (5.5E for short) or GroupWise 6 client running in remote or cache mode. This may sound like a funny thing for an MTA to do, but it's a great idea. This feature was added to allow GroupWise systems to better support remote-user connections over the Internet.

Increasingly end users have their own connections to the Internet. It is natural for GroupWise users to want to connect to their organization's GroupWise system in order to download their GroupWise mail to their GroupWise remote mailbox. Prior to GroupWise 5.5E and GroupWise 6, the only way administrators could enable this functionality was to allow Internet hosts to contact each post office's POA and speak with the POA at any port. This raised all sorts of security issues. Because of this, most organizations opted not to allow users to access their POA from outside their organization's firewall.

Now the GroupWise MTA will accept a connection from a GroupWise client at the live remote port configured for the MTA. The GroupWise MTA can then open up a virtual live remote session with the POA that supports the user's post office. The effect then is that system administrators can tell users that if they have a connection to the Internet they can configure GroupWise to connect to `MTA.WORLDWIDEWIDGETS.COM` using port 8100.

The MTA must have two lines enabled in the startup file of the MTA. They are the following:

```
/liveremote-[port number]
/lrconn-100
```

The first line specifies the port that the MTA will listen on for live remote connections. The second line specifies the maximum number of live remote connections that the MTA will allow at once. Each remote user will require one connection for the duration of their upload and download sequence.

For the MTA to be able to support live remote, every link between this MTA and the rest of the system must be a TCP/IP link. There can be indirect links, but the entire path must be TCP/IP, all the way down to the POA. This applies even if your POA and MTA are on the same file server.

Take the following scenario:

- USERA = Live remote user
- POSTOFFICEA = USERA's post office
- DOMAIN1 = USERA's domain
- DOMAIN2 = Another domain in the GroupWise system whose MTA is configured to receive live remote connections

The message flow will run as follows:

1. USERA establishes a live remote connection with the DOMAIN2 MTA.
2. The DOMAIN2 MTA establishes a live remote connection with DOMAIN1 on behalf of USERA.
3. The DOMAIN1 MTA establishes a live remote connection with the POSTOFFICEA POA.
4. The POSTOFFICEA POA accesses the information store on behalf of USERA and passes responses back along the live remote chain to the user.

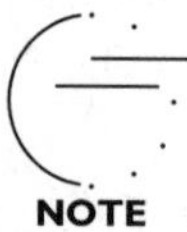
NOTE

Live remote connections can be monitored on the MTA. The DOMAIN2-MTA will register USER1 as a live remote user under F-10, live remote status. The DOMAIN1-MTA will register DOMAIN2-MTA as a live remote user under F-10, live remote status. The POSTOFFICEA-POA will register USER1 in the log as the live remote user.

The GroupWise remote client does not need a special new kind of connection type of live remote. The GroupWise remote client would just specify another TCP/IP connection as though the MTA that is listening for live remote connections is a POA.

Best Practices

Following are some practices that have been observed to improve the performance and stability of the GroupWise MTA. They are not hard-and-fast rules, however, and anything published by Novell should probably take precedence.

System Design

Keep in mind that you can only have an MTA where you have a domain. This means that if your system has some natural transfer points (such as on the segment with an edge-router, or at the firewall), you may want to consider putting a domain there so that there will be an MTA at that point.

Assume that you will be building a large system, and will be using occasional indirect connections. Here are a couple of rules of thumb:

- Don't put any post offices under the primary domain, and don't use the primary domain as a hub for indirectly connected domains.
- If you have more than one domain on a LAN, those domains should all connect directly via IP. The MTAs can handle this easily. Thus, LAN connections should be mesh-style.
- If you have multiple LANs as part of a wide area network, consider having one domain at the edge of each LAN acting as a hub for indirect connections between that LAN's domains and others.
- If you have busy gateways (such as the GWIA, which will be covered in the next chapter), you may want to consider devoting a domain (and, therefore, an MTA) to those gateways.

Remember, even though MTAs can communicate directly with any other MTA with a valid IP address, this is not always the best way to connect — especially where there are lots of router hops between them. Since packets are going to be stored and forwarded anyway on these long routes, you should consider having the MTA store and forward the messages (by using indirect connections). This way you will be less likely to have problems with TCP connection time-outs, and your message transfers will be more efficient.

Moving MTAs to New IP Addresses or Ports

First of all, if you are moving an MTA to a new IP Address, it is probably because you are moving the entire domain directory to a new server. If that is the case, review Chapter 20 for the complete procedure.

Perhaps, though, all you are doing is moving the file server to a new LAN segment and assigning it a new IP address. Here is the procedure you should follow:

1. Connect to the domain that is being moved.
2. Change the MTA object's network address to reflect the new address or port.

   Connections between other domains and this one will now start to drop off. Other domains, and this domain's post office, will show this domain as closed.
3. Unload the MTA.
4. Move the server to the new address and/or port, making the appropriate address or port changes at the server level (such as from NWCONFIG on a NetWare 5 server, or from the Network control panel item on an NT server).
5. Reload the MTA.

   Check the connection to this MTA from other MTAs on the system, and from this domain's post office's POAs. The connections should begin opening up, now that they "see" this MTA at the new address and/or port.

Tuning the MTA

Typically, a busy MTA needs little tuning to keep up with its queues. If TCP/IP links are used exclusively, the MTA will not need to waste CPU cycles polling or maintaining idle connections and will have the resources it needs.

You may find, however, that some types of messages need to be moved faster than others. Remote users and users making busy searches both use the high-priority queues. To weight these queues a little more heavily, check the Use 2nd High Priority Router box found on the Agent Settings tab of the MTA detail window. This will spawn an additional thread for the 0 and 1 subdirectories. The more connections the MTA services, the more threads will be spawned. If the server is having trouble keeping up with queues, this will mean that the mail priority queues (2 through 7) will back up even further, while the 0 and 1 get processed more quickly.

On large systems, an MTA on a Pentium II-class server should be able to process at least 100,000 messages each day without noticeable backups in any of the queues. Some administrators have seen MTAs that process three times that many messages in a day.

Monitoring Your MTA through a Web Browser

Just like the GroupWise POA, the GroupWise MTA can be monitored through a Web browser.

Simple Configuration

The GroupWise MTA needs three settings tweaked in order to support HTTP monitoring of the MTA. They are the following:

- An HTTP port specified
- An HTTP monitoring user name specified
- An HTTP monitoring password for the user name specified above

All of these settings can be configured in ConsoleOne.

HTTP Port

To specify your HTTP port, go to the properties pages of your MTA object in ConsoleOne.

On the GroupWise Identification property page, you can find a TCP/IP Address field. Click the pencil button to the right of the address field to bring up the Edit Network Address dialog box shown in Figure 9.31.

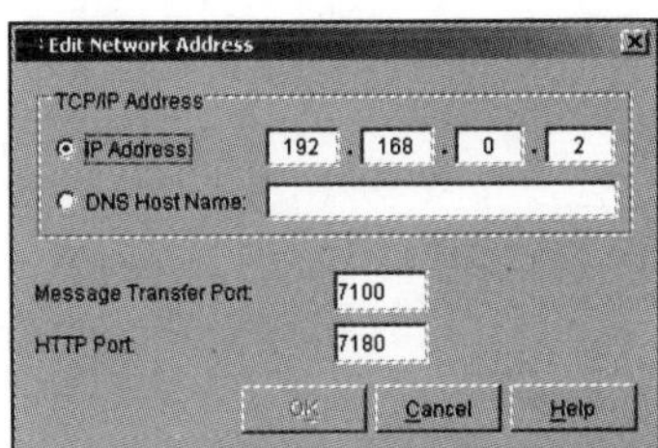

FIGURE 9.31 *The Edit Network Address Dialog Box*

Fill in the HTTP port with a value that you know is unique. Don't use the same port as the message transfer port.

HTTP User Name/Password

To specify your HTTP user name and password settings, go to the Agent Settings property page of the GroupWise MTA object. At the bottom of the GroupWise Agent Settings property page, fill in the HTTP User Name field and the HTTP Password field.

Monitoring the MTA with a Web Browser

Fill in the IP address or DNS name of the server running the MTA, along with a colon and a port name. For example:

```
http://192.168.0.2:7180
```

You will be prompted for the user name and password with a dialog box.

Once you are in the GroupWise MTA HTTP monitoring screen, you'll see a bevy of information.

Summary

This chapter covered all aspects of the GroupWise message transfer agent, from the details window found in ConsoleOne to the logs found in the MSLOCAL directory. This chapter also discussed the link configuration tool and walked you through its use.

CHAPTER 10

Installing and Configuring the GroupWise Internet Agent

The GroupWise mail format is a proprietary format. GroupWise supports many open standards, but is not itself an open system. This means that in order to communicate with other systems, some sort of translation is required.

The GroupWise Internet agent is the most popular translator for GroupWise, because it allows GroupWise users to send e-mail messages to recipients via the Internet. It does much more than that, however. It provides access to the GroupWise system from five different open-standard protocols.

In this chapter, you get a glimpse of the architecture of the GroupWise Internet agent and the protocols it supports. You also explore the installation, configuration, and operation of the GroupWise Internet agent, otherwise known as the GWIA.

GroupWise Internet Agent Architecture

GWIA architecture — the way in which the GWIA works with the rest of the GroupWise System — is best understood in terms of general gateway architecture. All GroupWise gateways perform one or more of the following functions:

- Translation
- Transport
- Mailbox access

The functions performed by the gateway determine the way in which the gateway connects to the rest of the system. The GWIA performs all three of these functions. The following sections look at each of them in turn.

Translation

The GWIA translates messages from simple mail transfer protocol (SMTP) format or multipurpose Internet mail extensions (MIME) format into GroupWise format. It also translates GroupWise messages from the proprietary GroupWise format into SMTP or MIME format. This allows messages sent by GroupWise users to be read by users of other e-mail systems, assuming that system can receive SMTP or MIME e-mail messages.

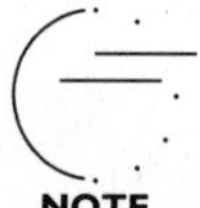
NOTE

Other gateways that perform translation include the GroupWise API gateway and the GroupWise gateways for MSMail, Exchange, Notes, cc:Mail, and Tobit FaxWare.

The translation function requires that the GWIA be able to receive messages from the GroupWise system. The MTA handles this, dropping Internet-bound messages into the GWIA's input queues. When messages are sent to the GroupWise system from the Internet, the MTA handles transferring those messages once the GWIA has translated them into GroupWise format.

Transport

Translated messages originating in the GroupWise system must be transported to the correct mail host on the Internet. The GWIA performs this function independently of the GroupWise MTA. The GWIA functions as a sendmail host, which means it can communicate with any other sendmail host on the Internet (assuming a connection can be established).

This transport is performed via TCP/IP on port 25, which is the industry-standard sendmail TCP port. The GWIA performs the appropriate domain name services (DNS) lookup to locate the recipient's mail host, and then connects and transfers the translated message. For inbound messages, the GWIA is always "listening" for similar connections from other sendmail hosts.

Mailbox Access

The GWIA has the ability to give users access to their mailboxes from alternate clients, such as Eudora, Netscape Messenger, or Microsoft Outlook Express, as well as other POP3 clients on handheld computers. The GWIA supports two forms of mailbox access: post office protocol (POP3) and Internet message access protocol (IMAP4). The GWIA also allows users to access the GroupWise address book via the lightweight directory access protocol (LDAP).

In order to do this, the GWIA must be able to connect directly to the post office directory, or via TCP/IP to the post office agent, for every user who needs POP3 or IMAP4 access. Typically, the GWIA connects to the POA in client/server mode and thus acts as an intermediary between the POA and the third-party mail client.

LDAP address-book access is provided a little differently. The GWIA reads the necessary address-book information directly from the domain database. The GWIA is hard-coded to look to its parent domain directory for the necessary domain database file.

Architecture Summary

When the GWIA is functioning in its capacity as a sendmail host (translation and transport), it connects with the GroupWise system via the MTA and standard file-polling. When the GWIA functions as a POP3 or IMAP4 host (mailbox access), it connects with the GroupWise system via the POA in client/server or direct access mode. When the GWIA functions as an LDAP host, it connects with the GroupWise system via a UNC mapping to the domain database.

Installing the GroupWise Internet Agent

The GWIA is not installed, by default, when you create your GroupWise system. It is not required for users to be able to send messages to each other. Of course, because it is required for users to send Internet e-mail, a GroupWise system without a GWIA is a little bit like a Harley that you only take to and from the grocery store.

This section walks through the process of installing the GWIA, so users can send e-mail to their biker friends in Sturgis, South Dakota, or anywhere else in the world.

1. First, locate the GWIA installation program.

   It is found in the GWIA directory, under the Internet directory at the root of your GroupWise CD or the software distribution directory.

2. Double-click on `<SDD>\Internet\GWIA\Install.EXE`.

   The welcome screen comes up, explaining what this installation program is going to do, as shown in Figure 10.1.

3. Click Next.

   Next comes the prompt for the software platform screen in Figure 10.2. This example shows the GWIA being installed as a NetWare loadable module (NLM) version of the GWIA, so NetWare is selected as the platform.

4. After making the selection, click Next.

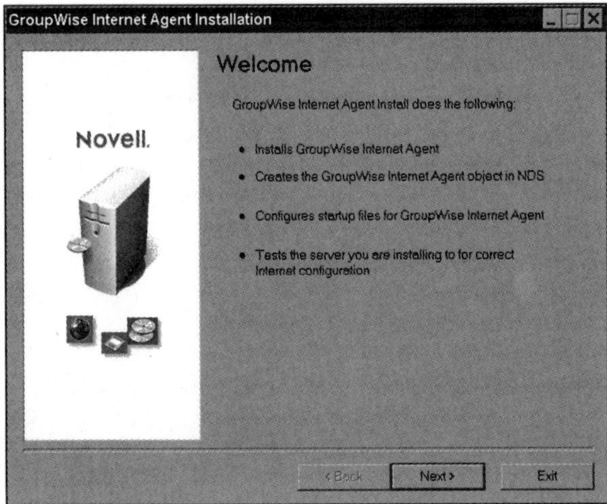

FIGURE 10.1 *The GWIA Installation Welcome Screen*

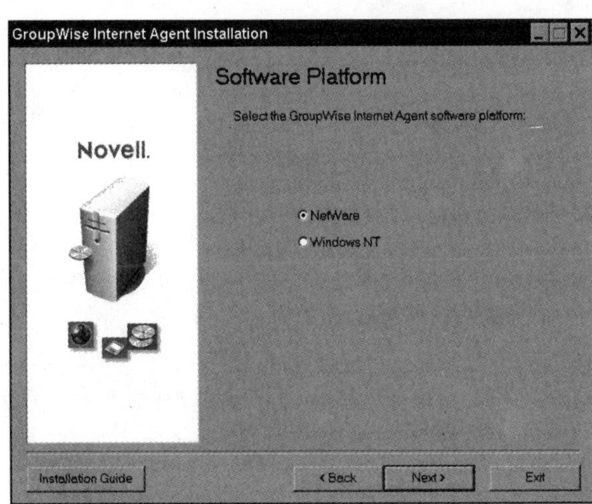

FIGURE 10.2 *Choosing a Platform for the GWIA*

As Figure 10.3 shows, the installation needs the paths for the NLMs and the NetWare load script (it's talking about an *.NCF file) that the GWIA will use. This should be the system directory on the SYS volume of the server where the GroupWise domain that owns this GWIA resides.

5. After making the selection, click Next.

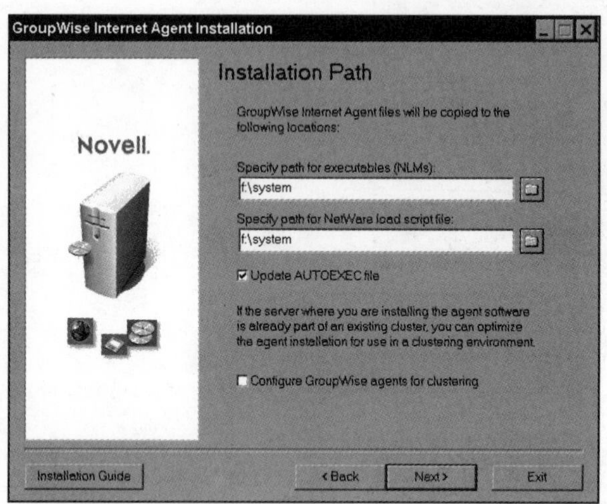

FIGURE 10.3 *Specifying the Path for the NLM and NCF Files*

6. The GWIA, like all GroupWise agents, can be monitored via a Web browser. Figure 10.4 shows the installation prompting for the port that the GWIA should listen to for Web-browser monitoring requests, as well as the user name and password to use. You should fill in the user name and password. The user name and password are essential for monitoring the GroupWise GWIA through a Web browser. The user name and password are also important to the GroupWise monitor agent.

   At this point, the installation asks whether the GWIA is going to send directly to the Internet or if it is going to use a relay host (see Figure 10.5). Relay hosts are commonly used on large, heterogeneous systems where Internet access must be tightly controlled at the firewall.

7. If a relay host is needed, provide the installation program with the IP address of the relay host machine and click Next.

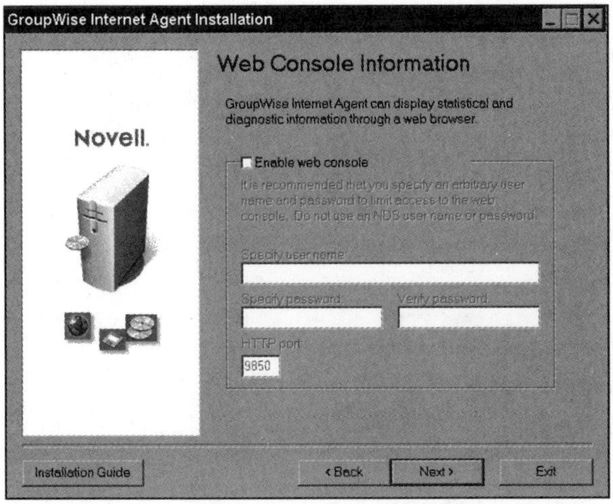

FIGURE 10.4 *Web Console Configuration Information*

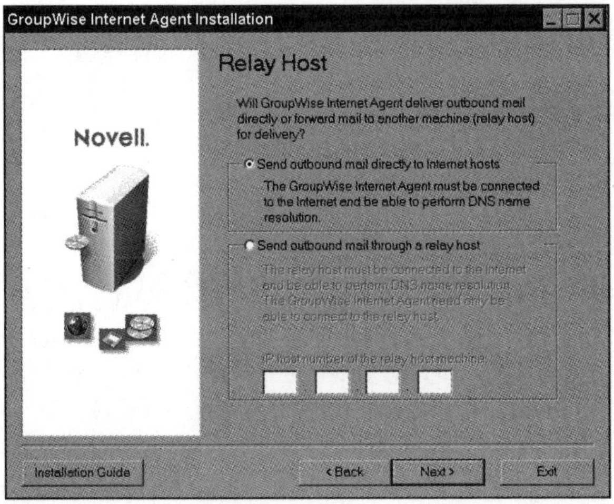

FIGURE 10.5 *Choosing between Direct Connection to the Internet and Connection via a Relay Host*

8. Figure 10.6 shows that you need to tell the installation which domain to connect the GWIA to.

You should have made this decision well in advance of this step, because in Step 4 you selected the server to which you are installing the software. The GWIA will be most efficient if it runs on the same server where the GroupWise domain resides. This server should also be running the GroupWise MTA for that domain. The installation also prompts for a name for the subdirectory for the GWIA. The default is GWIA. Because that name is pretty intuitive, it's a good default.

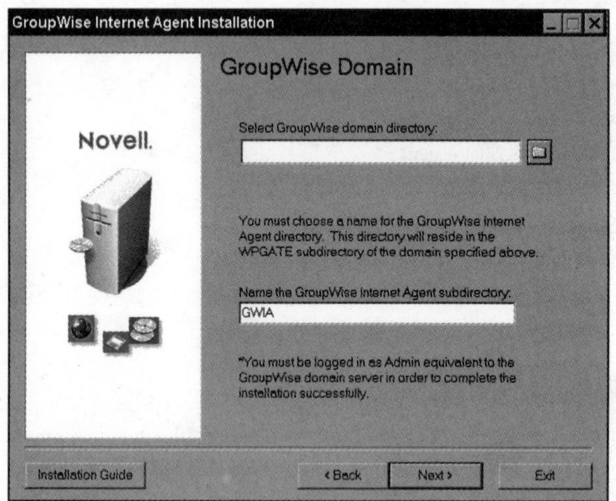

FIGURE 10.6 *Choosing the GroupWise Domain and Naming the GWIA Subdirectory*

9. In yet another case of intuitive naming, the installation asks for the name of the object that will be used to represent the GWIA in the GroupWise system and in NDS (see Figure 10.7). This object will appear as a child object of the domain selected in an earlier step. You may name it GWIA or some other name that works for you, such as SMTP.
10. After clicking Next, the installation program spawns a quick test from the server to find out if it has a connection to the Internet and if it can query a DNS. If your GWIA server meets these two requirements, the installation wizard moves ahead until you see the step in Figure 10.8.
11. Now the install needs the Internet mail domain name. This is the name by which your GroupWise system will be known on the Internet.

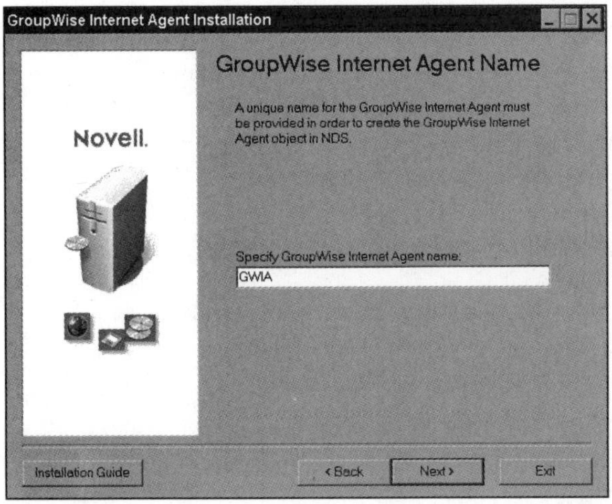

FIGURE 10.7 *Naming the GWIA Object*

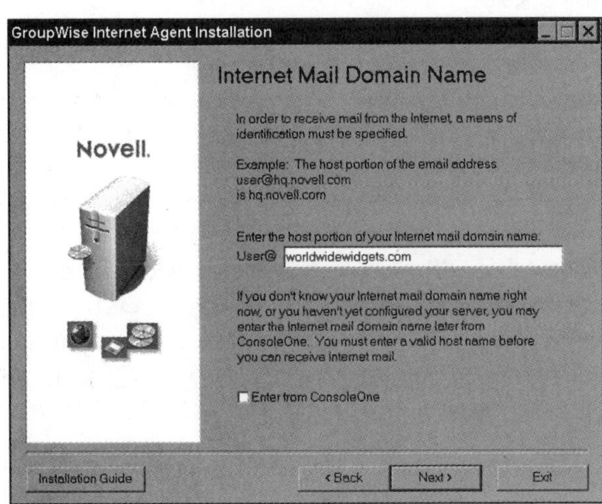

FIGURE 10.8 *Internet Mail Domain Name*

12. Armed with all the information provided during the installation, the wizard, shown in Figure 10.9, is now ready to actually install something. If you reach this point and decide you want to change something, you can use the Back button as many times as you want. When you are ready, click Install.

FIGURE 10.9 *The Installer Is Ready to Go. Are You?*

WARNING

While the GWIA software is being installed, a fairly standard installation bar comes up. Using the Stop button will result in an incomplete (and therefore broken) installation.

When the installer finishes, it does an interesting thing, without asking for permission. It launches the GWIA. Even if there are problems with the configuration, the GWIA will be loaded. It may not be able to correctly send Internet e-mail, but it is up and running. If during the installation problems came up that you decided to "fix later," now may be a good time to unload the GWIA so that it does not start generating undeliverable messages.

Loading the GroupWise Internet Agent

The previous two chapters discussed how the message transfer agent and post office agent must be provided with certain startup parameters in order to load correctly. The GWIA needs the same sorts of parameters, but they are not provided to the GWIA the same way they are to the MTA or POA.

Loading the GWIA

To load the GroupWise Internet agent once it has been installed and configured, enter the following at the server console:

```
GWIA
```

Novell has very thoughtfully provided an NCF file for the GWIA, called GWIA.NCF. NCF.

That was pretty painless, wasn't it? No startup parameters needed to be passed to the GWIA manually, because it is hard-coded to look in its startup directory (typically SYS:\SYSTEM) for a file named GWIA.CFG. In the case of the NCF file, the GWIA was passed a parameter telling it where to look for the configuration file, but it wasn't necessary.

This assumes, however, that you are using the default installation directory for the GWIA (SYS:\SYSTEM on the server where the domain resides). If you need to move the GWIA to another directory, or to another server, you may have some extra work to do before it will load correctly.

Understanding GWIA Configuration Files

GWIA.CFG should be in the same directory as GWIA.NLM (or GWIA.EXE, for NT servers). This is just a text file.

ConsoleOne "finds" GWIA.CFG using a different text file, EXEPATH.CFG. This second file exists in the WPGATE\<GWIA> directory under the domain directory. Because ConsoleOne knows the path to the domain, EXEPATH.CFG can always be found.

Here's why this is significant: Suppose you want to run the GWIA on a separate box from the domain. In this case, ConsoleOne cannot "guess" where the GWIA.CFG file is. You would use EXEPATH.CFG to tell ConsoleOne where to find GWIA.CFG, and then you would need to make sure that GWIA.CFG and GWIA.NLM were in the same directory.

Configuring the GroupWise Internet Agent

Just like the MTA and POA, the GWIA should be configured using ConsoleOne. The GWIA object is found under the domain object under the Gateways drop-down list in ConsoleOne. After right-clicking on the GWIA object and selecting Properties, the window shown in Figure 10.10 opens.

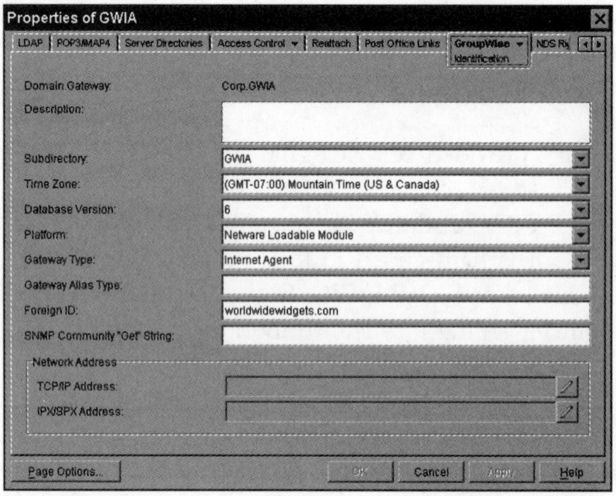

FIGURE 10.10 *The GroupWise Internet Agent Object Identification Property Page*

Along the top are a series of property pages. There are quite a few of them! Some of the property pages have arrows/triangles pointing down. This means there's more to select under this property page by clicking on the property page. The GWIA does quite a bit, so more configuration information is required. Fortunately, on each property page (and on most of the dialog boxes that can be spawned from those property pages) there's a Help button. The online help for the GWIA is very informative and should keep you on track if you find yourself editing your GWIA without this book at your side.

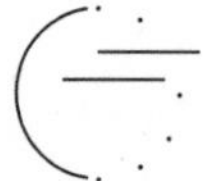

NOTE

Almost all of the settings changes you make on the GWIA are held in the GWIA.CFG file, and not in the WPDOMAIN.DB or NDS.

Understanding the GroupWise Identification Property Page

This page is most likely over to the right, and it's labeled GroupWise. This section starts here, because this is the most basic information on the GWIA.

This page, shown in Figure 10.10, is where some general information about the GWIA is configurable. These fields are common to all GroupWise gateways, which is why some of them may seem a little out of place for the GWIA.

- **Domain.Gateway:** This is the GroupWise name of the gateway. In the example in Figure 10.10, the value Corp.GWIA means that the agent belongs to the Corp domain and is named GWIA.
- **Description:** This is flavor text; you could use this for the pager number of the GWIA administrator, or perhaps a warning to not change the GWIA object without permission from so and so.
- **Subdirectory:** This field is populated by a pick-list. It shows where the queue directories for this gateway are. In the case of the GWIA, you should pick GWIA (or whatever you named your GWIA subdirectory during installation).
- **Time Zone:** By default, the GWIA has the same time zone as its parent domain. There may be reasons to change this, but not usually. This setting is used to time-stamp inbound and outbound SMTP/MIME messages.
- **Database Version:** For the GroupWise 6 GWIA, this should be set to 6. This setting tells the MTA whether or not it needs to convert messages back to a 4.x or 5.0 format (for compatibility with older gateways).
- **Platform:** In the example for this chapter, the NLM version of the GWIA was installed, so NetWare Loadable Module is selected.
- **Gateway Type:** For the GWIA, the only valid value here is Internet Agent. Obviously, with other gateways, other values would be appropriate.
- **Gateway Alias Type:** This field is used to associate this GWIA with user or post office aliases. If you have more than one GWIA, you will need to have more than one gateway alias type, because each GWIA (and each GroupWise gateway) must have its own unique gateway alias type.

  Gateway aliases are really useful and very common. You should use them as part of your overall Internet addressing scheme. See Chapter 16 for more details.
- **Foreign ID:** This is the name by which your GroupWise system will be known on the Internet. It is critical that this value match the domain portion of the To line for all messages that are destined to your users. If the GWIA receives a message that is addressed to a domain that does not match one of its foreign domains, the message will be rejected.

  The Foreign ID field can have several different domains on it. The names simply need to be separated by a space. For example:

  ```
  Worldwidewidgets.com sales.worldwidewidgets.com
  ```

  The default Internet domain name should be listed first. All others should be listed afterwards.

The Foreign ID field can hold only 124 characters. To accommodate more domain names, the GWIA is hard-coded to look in the <DOMAIN>\WPGATE\<GWIA> directory for a file called FRGNAMES.CFG. This is an ASCII text file that you can create with a listing of all the Internet domain names. The names should each be on a line by itself, and the last line of the file should be blank. Here's an example:

```
Worldwidewidgets.com
Sales.worldwidewidgets.com
Newyork.worldwidewidgets.com
Widgetsoftheworld.com
Eva-Cornish.com
```

- **SNMP Community "Get" String:** Enter the SNMP community string that the gateway should use for all SNMP GET commands. The community name is case-sensitive.
- **Network Address:** Fill in the TCP/IP address, and also fill in the HTTP port, but do not fill in the TCP port. This window is re-used by all the agents, but the need to use these fields is dependent on the agents itself. This window is just a generic window used by all GroupWise agents. The TCP port is used by the MTA and the POA, but the GWIA has no use for this field. The GWIA uses the standard ports for SMTP, POP3, IMAP4, and LDAP services. For example, SMTP uses port 25, POP3 services uses port 110, and so on.

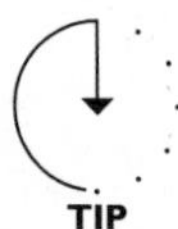

Do not fill in the IPX/SPX Address field; it's of no use.

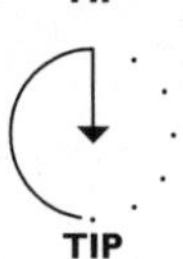

The TCP/IP address and HTTP port on any agent is not only used by the agent itself, it's also used by the GroupWise monitor agent. The monitor agent reads this information in order to monitor the particular agent. In writing this book, and in testing, I found that when you change the HTTP port on the GWIA, it does not write this change to the GWIA.CFG. So make sure that the value in the HTTP port on the GWIA in ConsoleOne and the value in the GWIA.CFG match. The GWIA.CFG file is an ASCII file. For the HTTP port information, look for the line "/HTTPPORT-<port number>" in the GWIA.CFG file.

Configuring the GroupWise Gateway Time Settings Property Page

The Gateway Time Settings property page shown in Figure 10.11 is used to configure the polling intervals and operational cycles for the GWIA. This page is available on the drop down list of the GroupWise page.

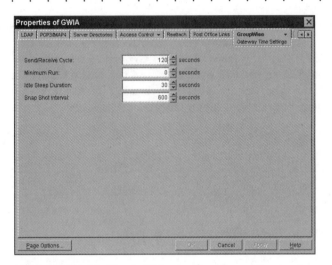

FIGURE 10.11 *The GWIA Gateway Time Settings Property Page*

- **Send/Receive Cycle:** This is the number of seconds that will be split between the GWIA's send and receive cycles. In the example in Figure 10.11, the 120 seconds specified will give the send and receive cycles each 60 seconds to complete processing. If a message file is being processed when the time expires for that process, the process will complete before swapping out.
- **Minimum Run:** This is the minimum amount of time, in seconds, that the gateway will be "awake" once the idle sleep duration has passed. Typically, this is best set at 0, but if you pay more to open a connection than to maintain the connection, you may choose to set this value higher. This may catch some additional messages and send them on the current connection, rather than opening a new one for them later.

A minimum run of more than *nn* seconds is probably only going to be meaningful in conjunction with dial-up connectivity.

- **Idle Sleep Duration:** This is the amount of time, in seconds, that the GWIA will "sleep." During this time, messages could be accumulating in the <DOMAIN>\WPGATE\<GWIA>\WPCSOUT\<GWIA-FID>\0-7 directories. This setting allows you to reduce the amount of CPU time spent supporting polling.

NOTE

The SMTP portion of the GWIA is actually two separate parts. They are the gateway and the daemon. The gateway translates messages from GroupWise format to ASCII and from ASCII to GroupWise format. The daemon listens on port 25 to receive messages and sends the ASCII files generated for it by the gateway as SMTP messages on the Internet. Although the gateway has an idle sleep duration, the daemon never sleeps.

- **Snap Shot Interval:** This is a sliding window for statistical purposes. The default, 600 seconds, results in 10 minutes of GWIA statistics being shown on the GWIA console. Regardless of the size of this window, it slides forward every 60 seconds.

Configuring the GroupWise Log Settings Property Page

The page in Figure 10.12 looks just like the Log Settings pages for the POA and MTA.

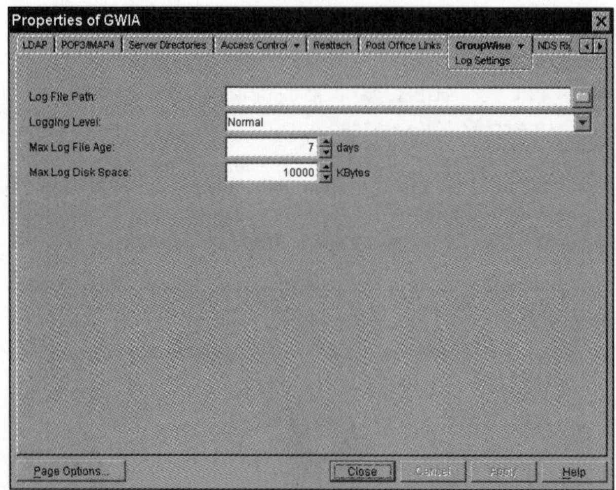

FIGURE 10.12 *The GWIA Log Settings Property Page*

- **Log File Path:** By default, this field is left blank. GWIA logs are put in the <DOMAIN>\WPGATE\<GWIA>\000.PRC directory. If you choose to keep logs elsewhere, enter the path here. It's not recommended that you configure the GWIA to put logs on a separate server. Performance will suffer, and if that server goes down, the GWIA will not function.
- **Logging Level:** There are four menu items in this pick-list:
  - **Off:** No logging.
  - **Normal:** The GWIA will track "major" events in the log, but most of the detail will be gone.
  - **Verbose:** The log will contain useful detail. Although this is not the default, it is the recommended logging level.
  - **Diagnostic:** This is typically used when troubleshooting the GWIA. It's very detailed! Only run this for troubleshooting purposes.
- **Max Log File Age:** This is the oldest that any log file on disk will be allowed to get before being automatically deleted by the GWIA. The default is seven days, and this is typically sufficient.
- **Max Log Disk Space:** This is the maximum amount of disk space that all of the log files together will be allowed to take up. If the logs reach this limit, the oldest log file will be deleted. If you choose to set the maximum log file age beyond seven days, you will want to raise this limit to make sure that you actually get to keep your oldest logs for the time you specify. Crank it up to 50,000 and feel the power!

Configuring the GroupWise Optional Gateway Settings Property Page

Figure 10.13 shows the Optional Gateway Settings page. This page is the same for all GroupWise gateways; there are options here that do not apply to the GWIA. The Directory Sync/Exchange field, for instance, is not supported by the GWIA.

- **Accounting:** If set to Yes, the GWIA creates an accounting file, ACCT, in the 000.PRC directory, that describes all traffic it processes. This file is e-mailed each day to the user specified as the Accountant under the Gateway Administrators property page.
- **Convert Status to Messages:** This setting does not apply to the GWIA.
- **Outbound Status Level:** This setting does not apply to the GWIA
- **Enable Recovery:** This setting allows the GWIA to restart itself or attempt to reconnect to a foreign host, if a connection is interrupted.

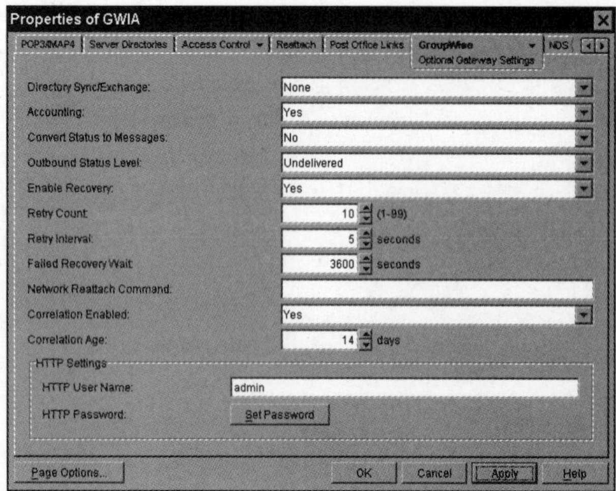

FIGURE 10.13 *The GWIA Optional Gateway Settings Property Page*

- **Retry Count:** The GWIA does not read this value; it has hard-coded values it complies with for retries.
- **Retry Interval:** The GWIA does not read this value; it has hard-coded values it complies with for retries.
- **Failed Recovery Wait:** The GWIA does not read this value; it has hard-coded values it complies with for retries.
- **Network Reattach Command:** Populate this field with a command line or with the file name of a batch file for mapping drives to reattach the GWIA to a domain file server. It only applies to the GWIA running on an NT server. If the GWIA is running on a NetWare server, use the Reattach Settings property page.
- **Correlation Enabled:** Set this to Yes.
- **Correlation Age:** Set this to 14 days.
- **HTTP Settings:** This area has two options.
  - **HTTP User Name:** Fill this in with the user name that you will use to monitor the GWIA through a Web browser.
  - **HTTP Password:** Fill this is in with the password you will use when monitoring the GWIA.

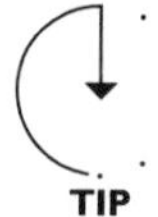
TIP

The HTTP information on any agent is not only used by the agent itself but also by the GroupWise monitor agent. The monitor agent reads this information in order to monitor the particular agent. In writing this book and testing, I found that when you change the HTTP name and HTTP password on the GWIA, it does not write this change to the GWIA.CFG. So make sure that the value in the HTTP port on the GWIA in ConsoleOne and the value in the GWIA.CFG match. The GWIA.CFG file is an ASCII file. For the HTTP port information look for the line "/HTTPPORT-<port number>" in the GWIA.CFG file.

Configuring the GroupWise Gateway Administrators Property Page

The page in Figure 10.14 is what you will use to take care of the *RFC Compliance* task, in which you specify a postmaster.

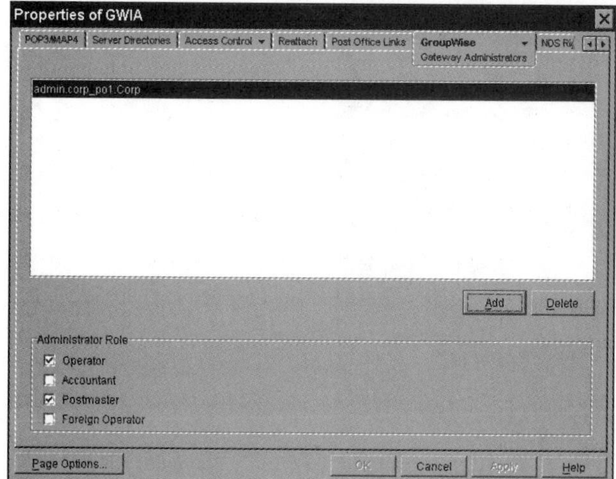

FIGURE 10.14 *The GWIA Gateway Administrators Property Page*

Later in this chapter, you will learn about the process of creating a postmaster. For now, here is an explanation of what each of the administrator roles are:

- **Operator:** Administrators specified as operators will receive certain kinds of GWIA errors in their mailboxes.
- **Accountant:** Administrators with this role will receive gateway accounting and statistical logs each day.

- **Postmaster:** Administrators with this role will receive any message that comes in to the GWIA addressed to `postmaster@<GWIA Foreign ID>`.
- **Foreign Operator:** This role has no functionality for the GWIA. With other gateways, it allows you to specify a user on a foreign mail system who can e-mail certain commands to the gateway. This field is very useful for gateways that provide direct connectivity between GroupWise and third-party mail systems.

Configuring the GroupWise Gateway Aliases Property Page

This page, shown in Figure 10.15, gives a listing of all users who have a gateway alias associated with this GWIA. This is a great feature for seeing which user has which gateway alias. Chapter 16 talks more about using gateway aliases for the GWIA. Consult this chapter before using aliases widely.

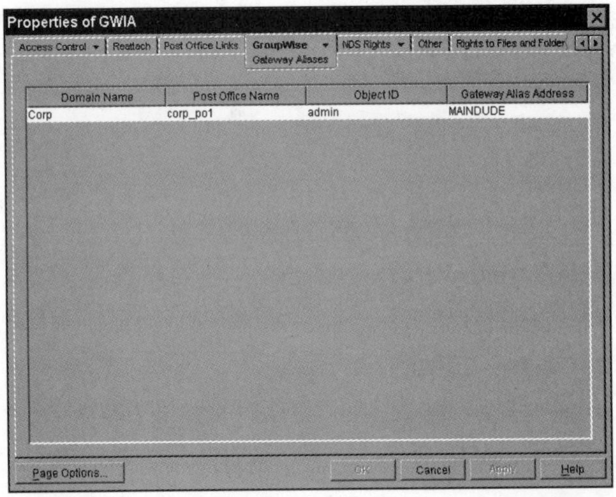

FIGURE 10.15 *The GWIA Gateway Aliases Property Page*

Configuring the SMTP/MIME Settings Property Page

There is an awful lot of configuration control offered you through the SMTP/MIME Settings property pages. This is where you govern address handling, message formatting, SMTP dial-up, and other assorted SMTP/MIME-related communications settings.

This GWIA SMTP/MIME Settings page, shown in Figure 10.16, has six fields, which govern some global settings.

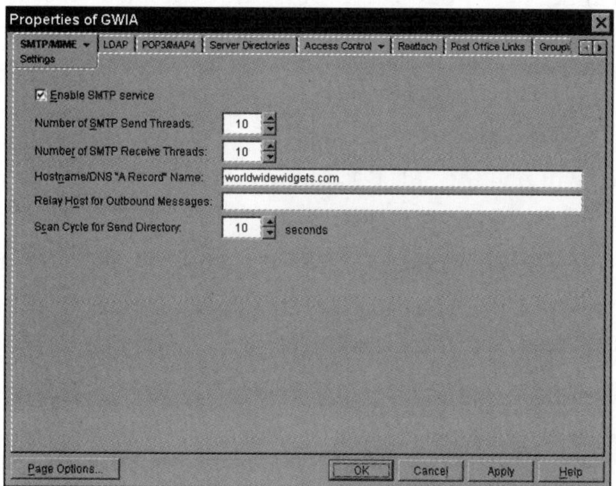

FIGURE 10.16 *The GWIA SMTP/MIME Settings Property Page*

- **Enable SMTP service:** This box must be checked before users can send or receive Internet e-mail messages through the GWIA.
- **Number of SMTP Send Threads:** This is the number of server processes, or threads, that will be devoted to SMTP send operations. If the GWIA runs out of threads (that is, all of them are busy), then messages waiting to be sent to Internet recipients will have to wait until a thread is freed up.
- **Number of SMTP Receive Threads:** This is the number of server processes that will be devoted to SMTP receive operations. When a sendmail host on the Internet tries to communicate with the GWIA, one receive thread will be dedicated to managing that communication. If there are no threads available, the sendmail host will determine that the GWIA is busy or not responding and will retry the transmission according to its own configured preferences.
- **Hostname/DNS "A Record" Name:** This is the name of the GWIA, as it is known on the Internet. Populate this field with a valid DNS name only. This is the name that will be returned to any SMTP service that connects into port 25 on the GWIA. If this name does not match a valid DNS name,

you may have problems receiving mail if other SMTP sendmail hosts do reverse-DNS lookups on your GWIA's IP address.

- **Relay Host for Outbound Messages:** Some administrators are only able to expose a very few machines to the Internet through their firewalls. In cases like this, the GWIA can be configured to relay all outbound SMTP/MIME messages through another machine. Populate this field with the DNS name of the relay host (for example, `unixmailer.worldwidewidgets.com`).
- **Scan Cycle for Send Directory:** This is the interval, in seconds, at which the SMTP send threads will poll the SMTP send directory for messages to be transmitted to Internet hosts.

Configuring the SMTP/MIME Address Handling Property Page

The Address Handling property page (see Figure 10.17) is generally a place where you make settings and then leave them as they are.

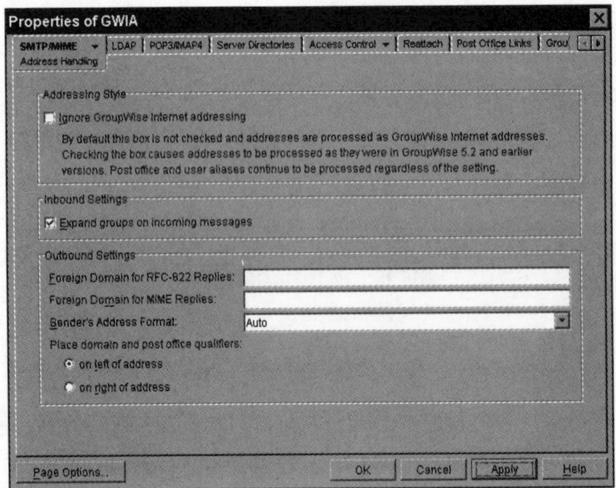

FIGURE 10.17 *The SMTP/MIME Address Handling Property Page*

- **Addressing Style:** This setting allows the administrator to revert to old-style GroupWise address parsing. When you use this option, all replies to Internet mail must go back out the same GWIA they came in. Also if you use this option, then the GWIA will only receive mail to domains defined in the Foreign ID field. It will *not* read the IDOMAIN list of domain names from the domain database. Leave this box unchecked unless you have been told to check it by Novell technical support. The default is that this setting is unchecked.

NOTE

Checking the Ignore GroupWise Internet addressing option enables the /dia switch in the GWIA.CFG file.

For a complete discussion of Internet addressing, refer to Chapter 16.

- **Inbound Settings:** The Expand groups on incoming messages check box allows some very powerful functionality. If Expand groups on incoming messages is checked, then Internet users may send to distribution lists on your GroupWise system. They will need to know the name of the list, and would simply address it as **<groupname>@<host>**. For example, to send to the CorpUsers distribution list on our example system, an Internet e-mail user would address the message to **corpusers@worldwidewidgets.com**. The GWIA would then expand the address of the message, adding each of the mailboxes listed under the CorpUsers distribution list.
- **Outbound Settings:** The Outbound Settings options become obsolete when GroupWise Internet addressing is enabled. For more information on Internet addressing, see Chapter 16.
  - **Foreign Domain for RFC-822 Replies:** This field will be used to build the TO line when a GroupWise user replies to an RFC-822 (SMTP) message that came in through the GWIA.
  - **Foreign Domain for MIME Replies:** This field will be used to build the TO line when a GroupWise user replies to a MIME message that came in through the GWIA.
  - **Sender's Address Format:** This setting is only enabled if Ignore GroupWise Internet addressing has been checked. It allows you to choose how the GroupWise user's reply-to address will be built from the various components of his or her GroupWise address.
  - **Place domain and post office qualifiers:** These radio buttons allow you to choose where domain and post office components go if they are included in the Sender's Address Format field you selected. If they are on the left, then the address would be `user.po.domain@host`. If they are on the right, the address would read `user@po.domain.host`.

Configuring the SMTP/MIME Dial-up Settings Property Page

Later in this chapter, there's a section called "Configuring Dial-up Internet Access" that talks about how to use the Dial-up Settings page.

Configuring the SMTP/MIME ESMTP Settings Property Page

ESMTP stands for *extended SMTP.* The ESMTP protocol is a special new protocol, through which enhancements to the SMTP protocol, called *service extensions,* can be created. The GroupWise 6 GWIA supports two ESMTP service extensions. The two that the GWIA supports are the following:

- DSN
- STARTTLS (secure SMTP over TLS/SSL)

DSN DSN is short for delivery status notification. This protocol is described in the Internet RFC 1894. By enabling this protocol, the GWIA can give confirmation to the sender of a message that the message was truly delivered to the intended recipient. Before the DSN protocol, the GWIA would only report if there was a problem getting a message to its recipient. The sender had to assume that the recipient got the message, because they never got a response back saying that it wasn't received. The DSN protocol makes it so that a sender no longer has to guess or assume whether a recipient received a message; they get confirmation of the fact.

With the DSN Hold Age option, you select the number of days that you want the Internet agent to retain information about the external sender so that status updates can be delivered to the sender. The default hold age of four days causes the sender information to be retained for four days. If the Internet agent does not receive delivery status notification from the GroupWise recipient's post office agent (POA) within that time period, it deletes the sender information and the sender does not receive any delivery status notification.

STARTTLS The GWIA supports sending messages over the Internet via SSL. This is a rather new protocol, and the GWIA will only send SSL encrypted messages to SMTP hosts that will receive via the STARTTLS protocol. The STARTTLS protocol is described in RFC 2487.

WARNING

Make sure to be using the latest version of the GroupWise GWIA for these ESMTP features. There are bound to be quirks that need to be worked out, as these are the newest features of the GWIA, and this is a newer protocol.

Configuring the SMTP/MIME Message Formatting

Here you will set the inbound and outbound for conversion of messages to and from GroupWise format.

Under Inbound Settings, shown in Figure 10.18, there are only two available fields for you to edit:

- **Number of Inbound Conversion Threads:** This is the maximum number of server processes the GWIA will devote to converting messages from SMTP/MIME format to GroupWise format.
- **GroupWise View Name for Incoming Messages:** This is the name of the view (the embedded name, not the actual file name) that the GroupWise client will be told to use when displaying a message that was received from the Internet. This field should not be edited unless you are designing your own views with the GroupWise SDK. GroupWise views are the *.VEW files off of a post office OFVIEIWS\WIN directory. This feature can be used if you want all inbound Internet mail to be displayed using a custom view file from the GroupWise client. You could add a note to the view that says this file was received from the Internet as an SMTP message or something to this effect, if desired.

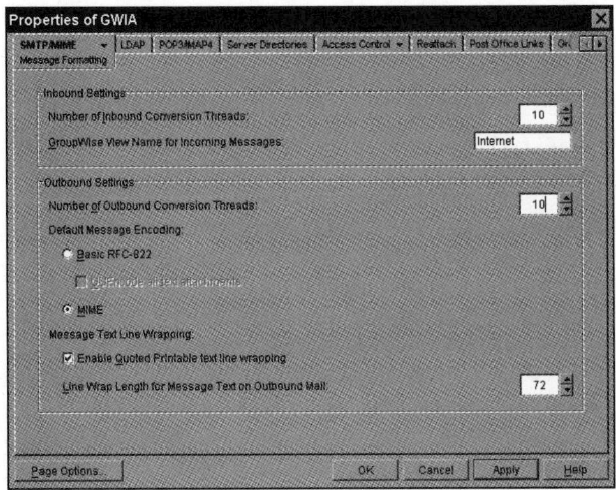

FIGURE 10.18 *The SMTP Message Formatting Property Page*

Under Outbound Settings, you have a few more fields to focus on. These settings are more likely to have an effect on your users' Internet e-mail experience.

- **Number of Outbound Conversion Threads:** This is the maximum number of server processes the GWIA will devote to converting messages from GroupWise format to SMTP/MIME format.
- **Default Message Encoding:** There are two options here. *Basic RFC-822* is the older (and generally more compatible) message format. *MIME* is the newer standard, and it is generally more efficient when binary files (executables, images, and so on) need to be transmitted. When RFC-822 encoding is selected, binary attachments must be encoded in the 7-bit UUEncode format. The UUEncode all text attachments option will force text attachments to also be encoded.

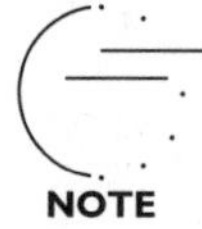
NOTE

If your users complain that people that they send Internet e-mail to cannot read the messages they send, you will likely need to force RFC-822 encoding on all messages.

- **Enable Quoted Printable text line wrapping:** This check box allows you to select the quoted printable MIME standard for text line wrapping. If this is not checked, outbound messages will wrap text according to the Line Wrap Length setting that follows this one.
- **Line Wrap Length for Message Text on Outbound Mail:** This is the number of characters after which the GWIA inserts a soft return. This prevents messages entered with no returns at all from appearing all on the same line. Of course, the recipient's mailer may need to be "told" to respect the soft return character.

Configuring the SMTP/MIME Scheduling Property Page

The GWIA SMTP/MIME Scheduling property page is used to define the times of the day and days of the week that the GWIA will process SMTP/MIME messages. Scheduling cannot be employed for POP3, IMAP4, or LDAP services. If those services are enabled, the GWIA will attempt to provide them all the time, regardless of the settings made on the Scheduling property page.

The Scheduling property page is especially useful when configuring the GWIA for dial-up access to the Internet, using the SMTP/MIME Dial-up Settings property page. This will be covered later in this chapter, under "Configuring Dial-up Internet Access."

Configuring the SMTP/MIME Security Settings Property Page

Security is an important part of any Internet strategy. Since the GWIA may be exposed to the Internet in order to receive messages, it is critical that it be protected against certain kinds of attacks. The SMTP Security dialog box in Figure 10.19 allows you to defend the GWIA from two kinds of common e-mail attacks: spam and mailbombs.

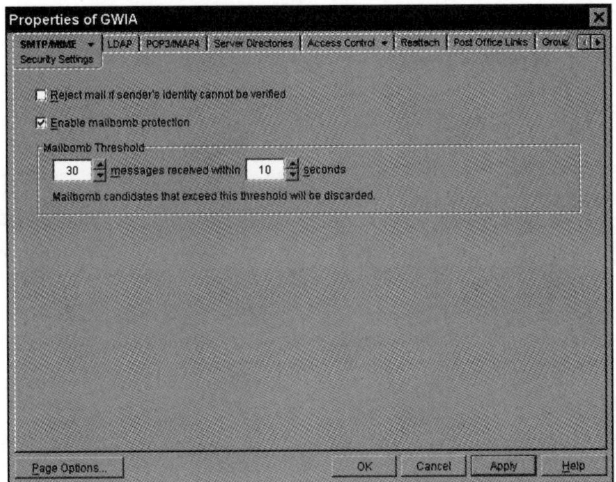

FIGURE 10.19 *The GWIA SMTP/MIME Security Settings Property Page*

- **Reject mail if sender's identity cannot be verified:** This setting prevents the GWIA from accepting e-mail from anonymous sendmail hosts. While some legitimate e-mail is routed in this manner, anonymous mailers are more often used for mass-mailings, also known as spam. The GWIA will do a reverse-DNS lookup on the name of the sending sendmail host to verify that its given name is in the DNS tables on the Internet. If it cannot find the name, it will not accept mail from this host.
- **Enable mailbomb protection:** If checked, the GWIA will use the mailbomb thresholds to prevent a single host from tying up the GWIA inbound threads with a mass mailing. Some mass mailings are actually designed not to deliver large numbers of messages, but to tie up the receiving host. The default mailbomb threshold of 30 messages received in 10 seconds is typically sufficient to identify a mailbomb attack before any harm has been done.

Configuring the SMTP/MIME Timeouts Property Page

Each of the fields is populated with the number of minutes (not seconds) that the GWIA will wait before timing out on a particular operation. This timeout could be due to a noisy line, an unresponsive host, or some other loss of connectivity.

Configuring the SMTP/MIME Undeliverables Property Page

This page, shown in Figure 10.20, is where you will tell the GWIA how to handle inbound messages that could not be delivered.

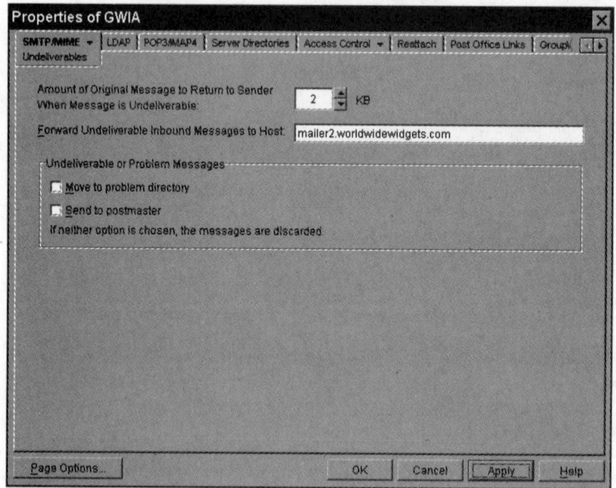

FIGURE 10.20 *The GWIA SMTP Undeliverables Property Page*

NOTE

Undeliverable messages that are outbound are handled by the destination mail host. That host may choose to reply, may forward the message to the configured postmaster, or may simply discard the message. As a GroupWise administrator, you have no control over how other e-mail administrators choose to handle undeliverable e-mail.

- **Amount of Original Message to Return to Sender When Message is Undeliverable:** This is the amount of the original message, in kilobytes, that will be returned to the sender if the message could not be delivered. Typically, it is not necessary for a sender to have more than a few lines of his or her message to identify it. This allows you to save a little bit of bandwidth.

- **Forward Undeliverable Inbound Messages to Host:** If you are operating a heterogeneous mail system, you may have a single DNS name but multiple mail hosts. If the GWIA is the default inbound mail host, you can configure it to forward any undeliverable messages to another mail host on your system. This other mail host may then be able to find the desired recipient of the e-mail message. This could be used if you are using NIMS (Novell Internet messaging system) with the same domain name as your GroupWise users.
- **Move to problem directory:** If this option is checked, undeliverable messages will be put in the GWPROB directory in the GWIA subdirectory.
- **Send to postmaster:** If this option is checked, the user who has been configured as the postmaster will receive the full text (and attachments) of any undeliverable messages. This allows the postmaster to straighten out addressing problems, as well as to manually forward messages to the correct recipients.

Configuring the LDAP Settings Property Page

The property page in Figure 10.21 allows you to configure the LDAP service provided by the GWIA. In order to complete configuration of the LDAP service, however, you must allow LDAP access from the Access Control property page, described a little later in this chapter.

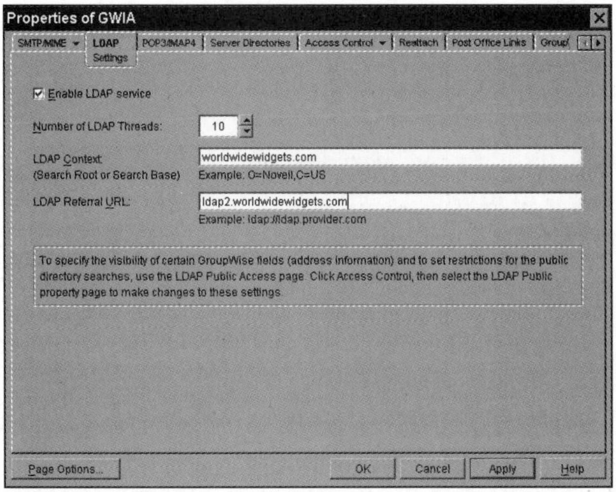

FIGURE 10.21 *The GWIA LDAP Settings Property Page*

- **Enable LDAP service:** This must be checked for the GWIA to be able to provide LDAP service to browsers and e-mail clients.
- **Number of LDAP Threads:** This is the maximum number of server processes that will be devoted to handling LDAP requests.
- **LDAP Context:** This context must be set to match the Search Root entry in your users' browsers' or e-mail clients' LDAP setup information. (*Search Root* is the term used by Netscape Communicator. *Search Base* is the term used by MS Outlook Express.) If you do not want to limit the context of LDAP searches, you can leave this field blank.
- **LDAP Referral URL:** This setting allows you to define a secondary LDAP server to which you can refer queries that the GWIA was unable to resolve. Obviously, the secondary LDAP server would be configured and managed separately from the GWIA. For this feature to work, the client performing the LDAP lookup to the GWIA must support the tracking of referral URLs.

Configuring the POP3/IMAP4 Settings Property Page

If you want your users to be able to use a POP3 or IMAP4 e-mail client to access their GroupWise messages, you will need to begin by enabling POP3 and IMAP4.

- **Enable POP3 service:** This must be checked before the GWIA will respond to POP3 requests from e-mail clients.
- **Number of threads for POP3 connections:** This is the maximum number of server processes that the GWIA will devote to servicing POP3 mailbox connections. Each connection will tie up one thread, but connections are usually cleared fairly quickly. A small number of threads can support a large user community, depending on how often users download e-mail via POP3.
- **Enable IMAP4 service:** This must be checked before the GWIA will respond to IMAP4 requests from e-mail clients.
- **Number of threads for IMAP4 connections:** This is the maximum number of server processes that the GWIA will devote to servicing IMAP4 mailbox connections. Each connection will take up one thread, and connections are more latent than POP3 connections are. This is due to the fact that with IMAP4, the user mailbox always exists on the server, and the client must re-request items that the user wants to re-read.

For more information about setting up POP3 or IMAP4 access for your users, refer to the section titled "Configuring Access Control," later in this chapter.

Configuring the Server Directories Settings Property Page

If you decide to run the GWIA on a different server than the domain that hosts it, you will need to use the Server Directories Settings property page shown in Figure 10.22 to relocate the directories that the GWIA uses to process SMTP/MIME messages. Typically, these directories are located under the domain directory, in the GWIA structure under WPGATE.

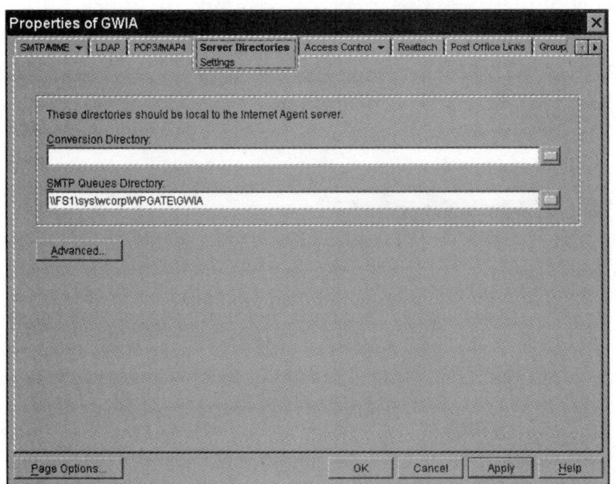

FIGURE 10.22 *The GWIA Server Directories Settings Property Page*

- **Conversion Directory:** This path becomes the GWIA's "work" directory. By default, this is found at <domain>\WPGATE\<GWIA>\000.PRC\GWWORK. The GWIA uses this directory for storage of temporary files used during message conversion.
- **SMTP Queues Directory:** This path becomes the parent directory for the SMTP SEND, RECEIVE, and RESULT directories, which are the input and output queues for the SMTP inbound and outbound threads.
- **Advanced:** Clicking on this button brings up the SMTP Service Queues Directory dialog box. This dialog box is used for trapping messages between the SMTP daemon and the gateway. If you populate this field with a path, all inbound and outbound messages will be dropped in subdirectories of this directory. They will remain here until another process moves them to the appropriate SMTP queue directory.

This feature is useful if you have a third-party e-mail virus scanning tool. That tool must be able to scan the files found under the Advanced path you specify, and then move the files into the appropriate SMTP queue.

Configuring the GWIA Access Control Property Pages

The GWIA Access Control property pages, Settings, SMTP Relay Settings, and LDAP Public Settings, are used to configure POP3, LDAP, IMAP4, and SMTP relay access for the GWIA. These property pages allow for the creation of classes of service and memberships. Each membership may be assigned to one or more classes of service.

This property page in Figure 10.23 is explained and utilized in the section titled, "Configuring Access Control," later in this chapter.

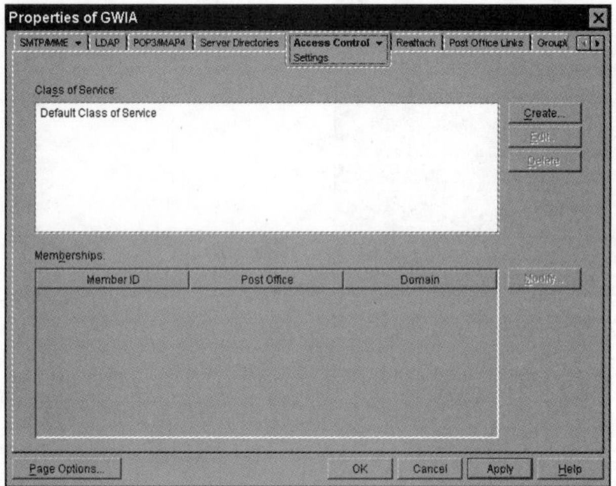

FIGURE 10.23 *The GWIA Access Control Settings Property Page*

Using the Access Control Testing Property Page

The GWIA Access Control Testing property page in Figure 10.24 allows you to test the memberships and classes of service created with the Access Control property page. The display here may be changed to include domains, post offices, distribution lists, or users.

Clicking on View Access displays a dialog box that shows the GWIA access allowed for the selected object. The Access Control Testing property page will be used in an example later in this chapter.

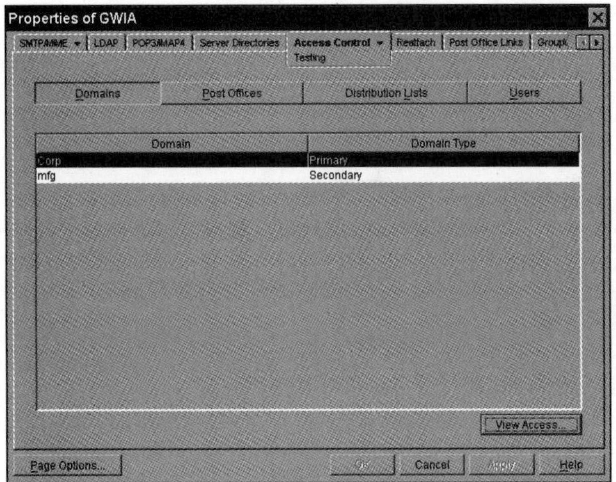

FIGURE 10.24 *The GWIA Access Testing Property Page*

Using Access Control Database Management Property Page

The GWIA does not use the domain database for access control. The access control database is called GWAC.DB, and it's in the <DOMAIN>\WPGATE\<GWIA> directory. Thus, a separate tool, shown in Figure 10.25, has been provided for maintaining and repairing the GWIA access control database.

- **Validate Database:** This button checks the physical structure of the database, essentially making sure that all records can be read correctly. Clicking Validate Now displays a live validation window, showing the validation process's progress.
- **Recover Database:** The recover option should only be used after the validation report has been generated and reviewed. Recovery is not a perfect process. If records have been damaged and cannot be read, they cannot be regenerated. They will be removed, and the new, recovered access database will not re-create the removed records.

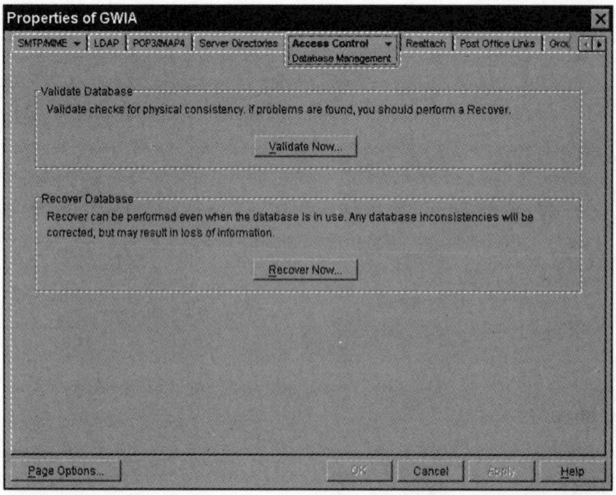

FIGURE 10.25 *The GWIA Access Control Database Management Property Page*

Understanding the Reattach Settings Property Page

When the GroupWise GWIA acts as a POP3 or IMAP4 server, it must access the POP3/IMAP4 user's mailbox. In the Post Office Links property page, the links to post offices can either be UNC or TCP/IP. The TCP/IP link is generally preferred, but if UNC is chosen, then the GWIA must log in to the server using a user ID and password in the fields showed in Figure 10.26. This is where you configure this information.

- **Tree:** This is the name of the NDS tree that the GWIA is logging into.
- **Context:** This is the NDS context for the user that the GWIA will attempt to connect as.
- **User ID:** This is the NDS user object that the GWIA will attempt to connect as.
- **Password:** This is the password that the GWIA will use when logging in.

Using the Post Office Links Property Page

The Post Office Links property page is used to define the connection between the GWIA and each of the post offices to which it must connect to provide users with POP3 or IMAP4 access.

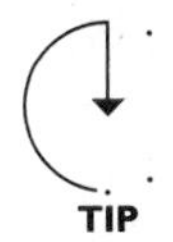
TIP

If you do not intend to enable POP3 or IMAP4 features on your GWIA, don't worry about configuring the link to the post offices.

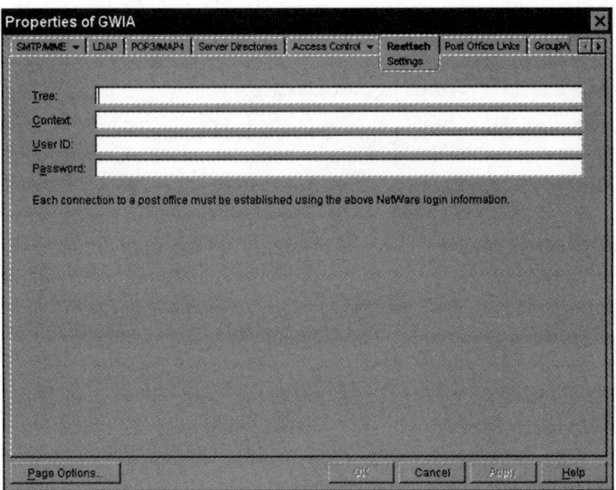

FIGURE 10.26 *Reattach Settings for the GWIA*

Configuring Access Control

By default, everyone in your organization has full access to all features you enable on the GWIA. This includes the ability to collect their e-mail via POP3 or IMAP4 service, as well as the ability to send and receive messages of unlimited size via SMTP/MIME.

This section assumes that you want to restrict this access. Here are the security requirements for this scenario:

- No POP3 or IMAP4 mailbox access
- SMTP relay access may only be allowed to users within our domain (`worldwidewidgets.com`)
- No rule-generated messages may be sent through the GWIA
- Inbound messages are to be refused from the host `eslime.com`

Imagine that you want to be able to make exceptions to this. Some users will eventually need POP3 access, and there are one or two users competent enough in their creation of GroupWise rules, that they can be trusted with rule-generated responses on the Internet.

1. Open up the GWIA object's properties window and go to the Access Control property page.
2. To the right of the Class of Service pane, click Create.

   You should be presented with the dialog box shown in Figure 10.27.

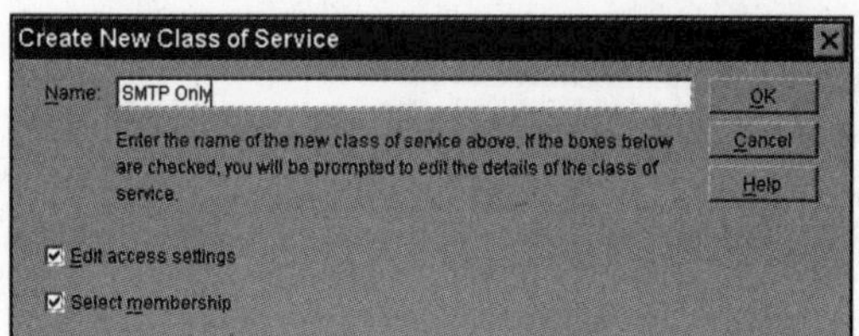

FIGURE 10.27 *Creating a New Class of Service*

3. Enter a name for this class of service.

   In this scenario, the class is called SMTP Only. After clicking OK, you get the screen shown in Figure 10.28.
4. From the SMTP Incoming tab, click Allow incoming messages.
5. Under Prevent messages from, click Create.
6. Enter the host name **eslime.com** in the resulting dialog box.
7. Click the SMTP Outgoing tab shown in Figure 10.29.

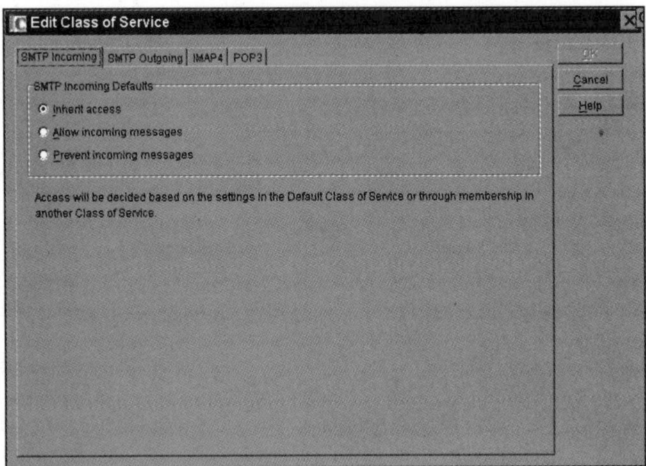

FIGURE 10.28 *The Edit Class of Service Box*

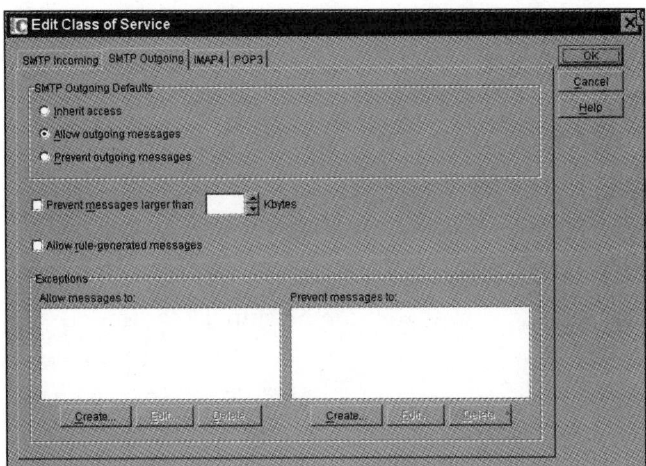

FIGURE 10.29 *Defining SMTP Outgoing Access for a New Class of Service*

8. Click Allow outgoing messages.

Make sure that the Allow rule-generated messages check box is not selected.

9. Click the IMAP4 tab shown in Figure 10.30.

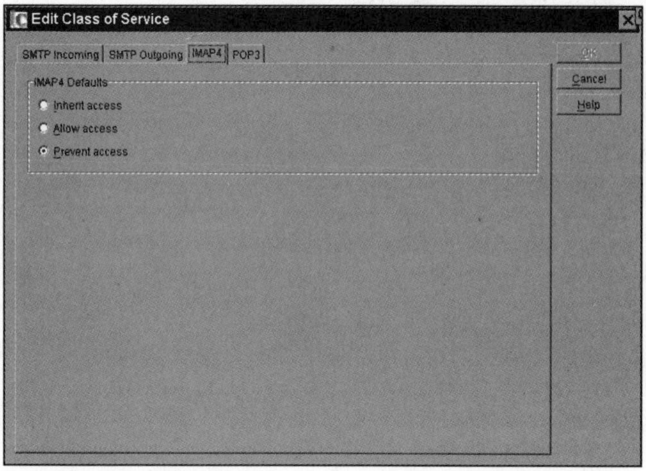

FIGURE 10.30 *Defining IMAP Access for a New Class of Service*

10. Click the Prevent access radio button.
11. Click the POP3 tab.
12. Click the Prevent access radio button.
13. Click OK.

    You should now be presented with the dialog box shown in Figure 10.31.

14. Click the Domains button, highlight each domain, in turn, and click Add. This adds all users on each domain to the membership list for this class.
15. Click OK.
16. Click the SMTP Relay Settings under the GroupWise Access Control drop-down tab (see Figure 10.32).
17. Under SMTP Relay Defaults, click the radio button labeled Prevent message relaying.

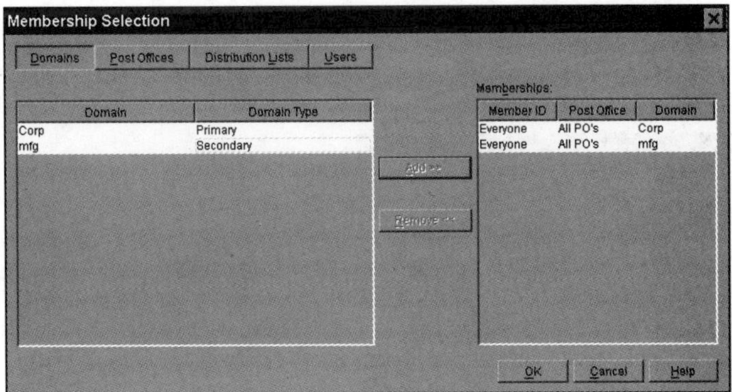

FIGURE 10.31 *Defining the Membership List for a New Class of Service*

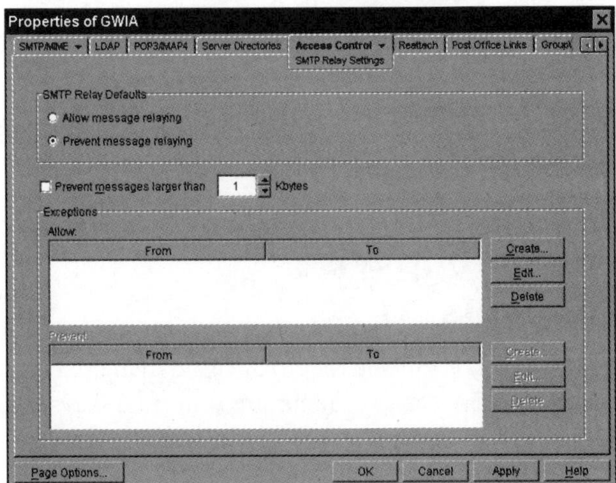

FIGURE 10.32 *Defining SMTP Relay Access for a Selected Class of Service*

18. Under Exceptions, and to the right of the Allow pane, click Create.

19. Enter the host name for From addresses that will be allowed to relay through the GWIA. In this case, it is **worldwidewidgets.com**. You do not need to specify a To address.

20. Click OK, and you will see the new exception as shown in Figure 10.33. Then click OK again to save all changes.

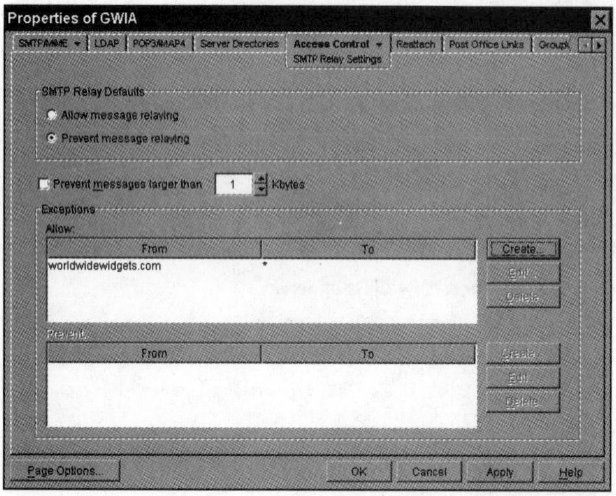

FIGURE 10.33 *Adding an Exception to the SMTP Relay Access*

Understanding the GroupWise Internet Agent Console

The GWIA console (see Figure 10.34) is much easier to navigate than the GWIA object details screen is. From the GWIA console, there are only four keystroke commands:

- **F7 - Exit:** This option presents you with the following prompt: Terminate Agent (Yes/No). Pressing Y unloads the GWIA module.
- **F8 - Info:** This option reports the settings from GWIA.CFG, the GroupWise Internet agent configuration file, into the current log file. This is helpful for determining what settings the GWIA is currently observing.
- **F9 - Browse Log file:** This option allows you to browse the current log file.

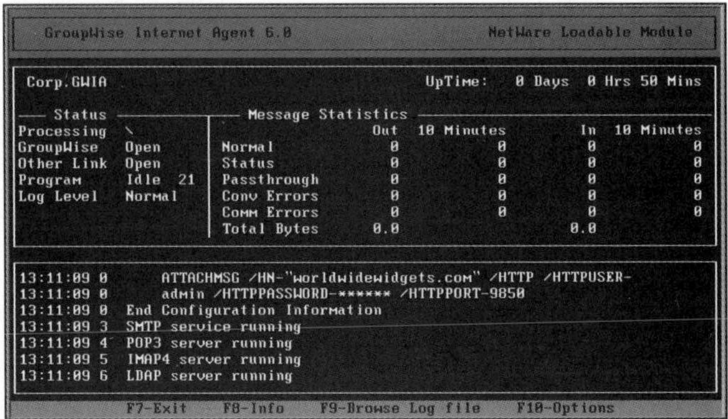

FIGURE 10.34 *The GWIA Console*

- **F10 - Options:** This option brings you into the GWIA Options menu, where you have the following further choices.
  - **F1 - Exit Options:** This option exits the Options menu, taking you back to the main screen.
  - **F2 - Log Level:** This option toggles the log level through the various settings: Low, Normal, Verbose, and Diagnostic.
  - **F6 - Colors:** This option changes the color scheme for the GWIA console. None of the color schemes are especially attractive, but if you get tired of the white-on-blue, this at least gives you some options.
  - **F8 - Zero Stats:** This option resets to zero all the statistics that the GWIA has been keeping. This is useful if you want to note current traffic levels.
  - **F9 - Stats:** This option cycles the upper-right pane of the GWIA console between each of the five= statistical panes: Message Statistics, SMTP Service Statistics, POP3 Service Statistics, LDAP Service Statistics, and IMAP4 Service Statistics.

The balance of this section looks at these statistics a little more closely.

- **Message Statistics:** These are general statistics that have to do with mail messages that are converted by the gateway process. Each statistic is reported in two ways: the total for the time that the GWIA has been loaded and the total for the preceding ten minutes.
  - **Normal:** The number of mail messages that the gateway has processed.
  - **Status:** The number of status messages that the gateway has processed. These are typically transferred statuses sent back to users on this GroupWise system.
  - **Passthrough:** The number of messages that were sent from external GroupWise domains through a gateway link. These messages retain their original message formatting, unlike messages sent across the Internet.
  - **Conv Errors:** The number of errors the gateway has encountered attempting to convert messages from GroupWise format to other formats, and vice-versa.
  - **Comm Errors:** The number of communication errors the gateway has encountered while attempting to communicate with other hosts.
  - **Total Bytes:** The total number of bytes transferred through the GWIA.
- **SMTP Service Statistics:** These statistics pertain to the SMTP services provided by the GWIA. Some of these statistics are incorporated into the general message statistics described earlier, but for the real story, you want to be looking at this screen.
  - **Messages Sent:** The total number of messages sent to sendmail (SMTP or MIME) hosts on the Internet.
  - **Send Threads:** This is the number of server processes actively processing SMTP/MIME send operations. The number on the left of the colon is the number of threads being used. The number on the right of the colon is the maximum number of threads allocated for sending messages.
  - **MX Lookup Errs:** The number of errors the GWIA has encountered when looking up DNS mail exchange (MX) records. Before the GWIA can send to an Internet host, it must first find that host's MX record in DNS.
  - **TCP/IP Read Errs:** The number of errors the GWIA has encountered attempting to read from a TCP socket. Errors here could indicate problems with internetworking segments that carry Internet traffic, or they could be indicative of network problems within your organization.

- **Hosts Down:** If the GWIA finds a hosts MX record, but cannot contact the host, that host is down, and this number will be incremented by one.
- **Messages Received:** The number of SMTP/MIME messages received by the GWIA from hosts on the Internet.
- **Receive Threads:** This is the number of server processes actively processing SMTP/MIME receive operations. The number on the left of the colon is the number of threads being used. The number on the right of the colon is the maximum number of threads allocated for receiving messages.
- **Unknown Hosts:** When a sendmail host sends to the GWIA, but that host does not identify itself, this number is incremented. Mail from unknown hosts can be rejected if you configure the GWIA to do so. (This setting is found on the SMTP/MIME Settings property page, under the Security button.)
- **TCP/IP Write Errs:** The number of errors that the GWIA has encountered attempting to write data to a TCP socket. As described earlier, errors here could indicate a problem local to you, or a problem somewhere out on the Internet.
- **Connections Denied:** Connections denied because the reverse-DNS lookup on the host was not correct.
- **Relaying Denied:** If your GWIA is configured to not allow message relaying, and someone attempts to relay a message off of your GWIA, this number will increment each time someone does. Relaying is a common practice for POP3 and IMAP4 clients that need to send mail.

- **POP3 Service Statistics:** These statistics pertain to the GWIA's POP3 service and can help you gauge the amount of traffic your organization is generating by accessing user mailboxes via POP3.
  - **Total Sessions:** The total number of POP3 mailbox sessions since the GWIA was loaded. A POP3 session is defined as a *download* of POP3 mail. If a user keeps his or her POP3 mailer open all day, and downloads GroupWise e-mail three times, that user will increment this count by three.
  - **Active Sessions:** The total number of POP3 mailbox sessions currently active.
  - **Sessions Avail:** The number of server processes available to service POP3 mailbox connections. The active and avail numbers should add

up to the number of POP3 threads you specified under the GWIA POP3/IMAP4 Settings property page.

- **Store Login Errs:** The number of errors that the GWIA has encountered attempting to connect to post office information stores. If you see this number incrementing, it's time to look at the Post Office Links property page of the GWIA and make sure that the links to your post offices are correct.
- **Unknown Users:** The number of errors in which the user name furnished was invalid. A high number here may be indicative of a hacker attempting to guess mailbox IDs.
- **TCP/IP Read Errs:** The number of errors that the GWIA has encountered attempting to read data from a TCP socket.
- **Messages Sent:** The number of messages downloaded to users' POP3 mailers and uploaded to their master mailboxes.
- **Retrieval Errs:** The number of errors encountered retrieving messages from post office information stores.
- **Conversion Errs:** The number of errors encountered converting messages from GroupWise format to clear text format for POP3 download.
- **Pass Auth Errors:** The number of errors that the GWIA has encountered due to users entering invalid passwords. A high number here may be indicative of a hacker with a correct user name attempting to guess at the mailbox password.
- **Denied Access Cnt:** The number of times that the GWIA has denied mailbox access to a user attempting to authenticate. A high number here may indicate hackers guessing at mailbox IDs and passwords.
- **TCP/IP Write Errs:** The number of errors that the GWIA has encountered attempting to write data to a TCP socket.

- **LDAP Service Statistics:** The statistics here pertain to the GWIA's LDAP service.
  - **Public Sessions:** This is the number of LDAP sessions that the GWIA has opened for users who were not authenticated.
  - **Auth Sessions:** This is the number of LDAP sessions that the GWIA has performed for authenticated users.

- **Sessions Active:** This is the number of LDAP sessions currently active. Each active session requires its own LDAP thread.
- **Sessions Avail:** This is the number of LDAP threads available to service LDAP sessions. The active and avail numbers should add up to the number of LDAP threads that you specified from the GWIA's LDAP Settings property page.
- **Search Requests:** This is the total number of search requests that the GWIA has processed.
- **Entries Returned:** This is the number of address entries that the GWIA has provided via LDAP.

- **IMAP4 Service Statistics:** The statistics here are very similar to those seen under the POP3 Service Statistics screen, but of course these are specific to IMAP4 service, which has much higher overhead than POP3.
  - **Total Sessions:** The total number of IMAP4 mailbox sessions since the GWIA was loaded. If a user keeps his or her IMAP4 mailer open and connected all day, this number will only increment by one.
  - **Active Sessions:** The total number of IMAP4 mailbox sessions currently active.
  - **Sessions Avail:** The number of server processes available to service IMAP4 mailbox connections. The active and avail numbers should add up to the number of IMAP4 threads that you specified under the GWIA POP3/IMAP4 Settings property page.
  - **Store Login Errs:** The number of errors that the GWIA has encountered attempting to connect to post office information stores. If you see this number incrementing, it's time to look at the Post Office Links property page of the GWIA and make sure that the links to your post offices are correct.
  - **Unknown Users:** The number of errors in which the user name furnished was invalid. A high number here may be indicative of a hacker attempting to guess mailbox IDs.
  - **TCP/IP Read Errs:** The number of errors that the GWIA has encountered attempting to read data from a TCP socket.
  - **Messages Sent:** The number of messages downloaded to users' IMAP4 mailers and uploaded to their master mailboxes.

- **Retrieval Errs:** The number of errors encountered retrieving messages from post office information stores.
- **Conversion Errs:** The number of errors encountered converting messages from GroupWise format to clear text format for IMAP4 download.
- **Pass Auth Errors:** The number of errors that the GWIA has encountered due to users entering invalid passwords. A high number here may be indicative of a hacker with a correct user name attempting to guess at the mailbox password.
- **Denied Access Cnt:** The number of times that the GWIA has denied mailbox access to a user attempting to authenticate. A high number here may indicate hackers guessing at mailbox IDs and passwords.
- **TCP/IP Write Errs:** The number of errors that the GWIA has encountered attempting to write data to a TCP socket.

Understanding the GroupWise Internet Agent Log

This section shows you some sample sections of GWIA log files, and it shows you how to interpret them. The goal is to help you understand what you see in your own GWIA logs, so that you can more effectively administer your system.

Log Line Format

Each line in the agent log is divided into four main parts. The first of these is the date and time stamp, that is, the date, hour, minute, and second that the event in this log entry occurred.

The second part is the process number. This number identifies the server process or thread that performed the operation described in this log entry. If you are trying to follow a thread in the log, you must do so by finding the next occurrence of this number. If process 12 claims to be processing an outbound message, and then process 17 reports an MX lookup error, the error was not with the message in the previous line. Look for the next occurrence of process 12 to see if the outbound message was processed correctly. Look for the previous occurrence of process 17 to see what it was doing before it got the MX lookup error.

The third part, which is not always present, is the process type. This string identifies the service engine that is currently active. When the GWIA is servicing

POP3, IMAP4, or LDAP connections, this string will be POP3, IMAP4, or LDAP, respectively. SMTP processing is not identified with a process type string.

The fourth part of the log entry is the event description. This may seem a little bit cryptic, but after you have seen a few of them, you will be making sense of them easily. Events you may see described include error messages, login IDs for POP3 or IMAP users, or descriptions of the conversion and transfer of SMTP/MIME messages.

Configuration Information in the GWIA Log

Here's the first block of text you will see in the GWIA log, the GWIA configuration:

```
11-23-01 13:14:41 1  Begin Configuration Information
11-23-01 13:14:41 1    Platform= NLM
11-23-01 13:14:41 1    Domain and Agent= CORP.GWIA
11-23-01 13:14:41 1    Foreign Name= worldwidewidgets.com
11-23-01 13:14:41 1    Description= Corp domain GWIA
11-23-01 13:14:41 1    Alias Type= GWIA_Alias
11-23-01 13:14:41 1    Root Directory= MAIL:\CORP\WPGATE\GWIA
11-23-01 13:14:41 1    Work Directory=
MAIL:\CORP\WPGATE\GWIA\000.prc\gwwork
11-23-01 13:14:41 1    Log File=
MAIL:\CORP\WPGATE\GWIA\000.prc\1123log.00e
11-23-01 13:14:41 1    Directory ID= gwi94b6
```

These first ten lines show that process 1, at 1:14 p.m. on November 23, 2001, began reading configuration information. These lines correspond to information you may recall entering from the GWIA's Information property page. The GWIA tells what directory it is working from. The log also tells the name of the current log file, as well as the directory ID for the GWIA. This directory ID is a directory off of the DOMAIN\WPGATE\GWIA\WPCSOUT directory that the MTA will use to queue messages up for the GWIA to send out.

```
11-23-01 13:14:41 1    Directory Synchronization= NO
11-23-01 13:14:41 1    Directory Exchange=        NO
11-23-01 13:14:41 1    Accounting=                YES
11-23-01 13:14:41 1    Convert GroupWise Status to Messages=
NO
11-23-01 13:14:41 1    Outbound Status Level= UNDELIVERED
```

The preceding five lines come from the GWIA's Optional Gateway Settings property page under the GroupWise drop-down tab. You can see that accounting has been enabled, and users whose outbound messages cannot be transferred will get an Undeliverable status back.

NOTE **The GWIA cannot track messages once they have been successfully transferred.**

```
11-23-01 13:14:41 1     Log Level=      Verbose
11-23-01 13:14:41 1     Log Max Age=    7 days
11-23-01 13:14:41 1     Log Max Space= 1024 kb
11-23-01 13:14:41 1     Enable Recovery=       YES
11-23-01 13:14:41 1     Retry Count=           10
11-23-01 13:14:41 1     Retry Interval=        60   seconds
11-23-01 13:14:41 1     Failed Recovery Wait= 3600 seconds
11-23-01 13:14:41 1     Network Reattach Command= <none
specified>
11-23-01 13:14:41 1     Correlation DB Enabled= YES
11-23-01 13:14:41 1     Correlation DB Age=     14 days
11-23-01 13:14:41 1     Correlation DB Directory=
MAIL:\CORP\WPGATE\GWIA
11-23-01 13:14:41 1     Send/Receive Cycle=  2   minutes
11-23-01 13:14:41 1     Minimum Run=         0   minutes
11-23-01 13:14:41 1     Idle Sleep Duration= 30  seconds
11-23-01 13:14:41 1     Snap Shot Interval=  10  minutes
11-23-01 13:14:41 1     Time Zone=  MST
11-23-01 13:14:41 1     GMT Offset= -7 hours, 0 minutes
11-23-01 13:14:41 1     Hemisphere= NORTH
11-23-01 13:14:41 1     Daylight Saving Change= 1 hours,
0 minutes
11-23-01 13:14:41 1     Daylight Saving Begin=  4/4
(month/day)
11-23-01 13:14:41 1     Daylight Saving End=    10/31
(month/day)
```

The preceding set of lines show the logging level, recovery and retry settings, gateway correlation settings, polling intervals, and time-zone information in effect for the GWIA. Some of these settings came from the Optional Gateway Settings property page, some came from the Log Settings property page, and the time-zone information was read from the appropriate time-zone definition in the domain database.

```
11-23-01 13:14:41 1    SMP Off
11-23-01 13:14:41 1    SNMP On
11-23-01 13:14:41 1    Startup Switches=
/Home-\\WIDGET_CORP\MAIL\CORP\WPGATE\GWI
11-23-01 13:14:41 1      A /DHome-
\\WIDGET_CORP\MAIL\CORP\WPGATE\GWIA /SMTP /LDAP
11-23-01 13:14:41 1       /MIME /MUDAS=2 /MailView-
Internet /SD-16 /RD-8 /P-10
11-23-01 13:14:41 1       /TE-2 /TG-5 /TC-5 /TR-5 /TD-3
/TT-10 /PT-30 /IT-30 /
11-23-01 13:14:41 1      LdapThrd-10 /ST-4 /RT-4
/IRFOUID /SMP /LDAPcntxt=CN=U
11-23-01 13:14:41 1      S /POP3 /IMAP4
11-23-01 13:14:41 1  End Configuration Information
```

In this last set of configuration entries, the log says that the GWIA will not use a second processor (SMP Off), and it will publish simple network management protocol (SNMP) information. The log also shows all the startup switches that have been written to the GWIA.CFG file. These switches govern the number of threads for the various services, among other things.

Message Processing Log Entries

When the GWIA processes a message that was sent from a GroupWise user to a recipient on the Internet, the log entries will look a lot like this:

```
11-23-01 13:15:12 17 Processing outbound message...
11-23-01 13:15:12 17   Sender: DZanre@worldwidewidgets.com
11-23-01 13:15:12 17   Building message: s83a9360.033
11-23-01 13:15:12 17   Recipient: glenn@brown.com
11-23-01 13:15:12 17   Queuing message to daemon
```

In these five lines, we see the sender's address, the message filename, the recipient's address, and then the announcement that the message has been queued. This does not mean that the message has been successfully sent, however. In this case, the message has simply been converted from GroupWise format to clear-text SMTP format. Now the SMTP service must contact the brown.com host. Unless there is an error, however, this action will not be logged.

As you can see, from the GWIA log you will be able to tell exactly which users on your system are sending mail to Internet users, and you can capture every address. You can also tell which Internet users are sending e-mail to which users on your system. We know of at least one case where information from GWIA log information has been used to expose users who were selling company secrets to the competition. Your users may consider this to be an infringement on their privacy, so you should be sure to word your organization's e-mail policy in such a way as to allow you to scan GWIA logs freely.

Here's a look at what happens with an SMTP error:

```
11-23-01 13:54:13 0  Analyzing result file: r83a9c7e.084
11-23-01 13:54:41 0  Analyzing result file: r83a9c5d.083
11-23-01 13:54:41 0       Command:  stribling.com
11-23-01 13:54:41 0       Response: 250 ok
11-23-01 13:54:41 0       Command:  HELO
mail.worldwidewidgets.com
11-23-01 13:54:41 0       Response: 250 Hello
mail.worldwidewidgets.com [10.10.10.59], pleased to meet you
11-23-01 13:54:41 0       Command:  MAIL
FROM:<DZanre@worldwidewidgets.com>
11-23-01 13:54:41 0       Response: 250
<DZanre@worldwidewidgets.com>... Sender ok
11-23-01 13:54:41 0    Detected error on SMTP command
11-23-01 13:54:41 0       Command:  RCPT
TO:<darren@stribling.com>
11-23-01 13:54:41 0       Response: 420 TCP read error
```

This file shows that process 0 analyzed a result file named r83a9c7e.084. This result file corresponds to an SMTP communication. Because there's no more information about this result file, you know that the communication was error-free.

In the second line, process 0 picks up another result file to analyze, and this one has an error in it. Scanning through the available information, you can see that user `DZanre@worldwidewidgets.com` sent a message to `darren@stribling.com`. The GWIA was able to look up and then open a connection with the `stribling.com` mail host. You can tell this from the successful HELO commands and the success of the first MAIL command. Unfortunately, the GWIA got a TCP read error trying to transmit the recipient address. This indicates that the connection between `worldwidewidgets.com` and `stribling.com` is too noisy, was dropped, or timed out.

Unfortunately, the result file does not tell what time these events occurred. What is visible is the GWIA's analysis of the SMTP daemons actions after the fact.

POP3 Connection Log Entries

Each time a user initiates a POP3 connection with the GWIA, that action is logged. Here is a sample of such a connection:

```
11-23-01 13:53:59 8  Accepted POP3 connection with:
10.10.40.232
11-23-01 13:53:59 8  POP3 Command: USER kathywascheck
11-23-01 13:53:59 8  POP3 Command: PASS
11-23-01 13:53:59 8  POP3 Command: STAT
11-23-01 13:53:59 8  POP3 Command: QUIT
11-23-01 13:53:59 8  POP3 Session ended: 10.10.40.232
```

Process 8 handled the entire connection, which is what is to be expected, as the GWIA can only have as many simultaneous POP3 sessions as it has POP3 threads. The log shows the IP address of the user workstation that is running the POP3 mailer, and then the log tells which POP3 commands were issued. The entire POP3 connection lasted only a second, and then process 8 was free to service another connection or return to the pool of idle threads.

Designating a Postmaster for RFC-822 Compliance

To complete the task list you were given when you installed the GWIA, you will need to specify one user as a *postmaster.* Document RFC-822, which defines the simple mail transfer protocol, directs that every mail host must have a valid mailbox for mail addressed to `postmaster@<mail host>`.

Here is how to do it:

1. Edit the properties of the GWIA, by selecting the Gateway Administrators page under the GroupWise tab.

2. Click the Add button.
3. Browse to the NDS user object you wish to specify as the postmaster for this GWIA and click OK.

   Note that the NDS user you specify must be associated with a valid GroupWise mailbox.
4. Check the box next to Postmaster under Administrator Roles.
5. Click OK.

Configuring Dial-up Internet Access

Some organizations may not have the luxury of a permanent connection to the Internet. In these cases, the GWIA can be configured to dial an Internet service provider (ISP) for temporary connectivity. The requirements for such a connection are as follows:

- The ISP must provide ETRN service, as per RFC-1985.
- The ETRN host name provided by the ISP must have a static address
- The IP stack on the GWIA server must be able to dial the ETRN host. This could be accomplished with BorderManager on NetWare servers.

If these requirements have been met, the procedure for configuring dial-up SMTP access for the GWIA is as follows:

1. Open the SMTP/MIME Settings property page on the GWIA and click the Dial-up Settings page.

   The dialog box shown in Figure 10.35 appears.
2. Check the box labeled Enable dial-up.
3. Under ETRN Host, enter the name of the ISP's ETRN host.

   This is the name of the host that will be receiving e-mail for your GWIA when your GWIA is not connected.
4. Under ETRN Queue, enter the foreign name of the GWIA.

   This must be the same as the domain name that your ISP has assigned you. This is the queue the ETRN host will use to identify the GWIA when the GWIA connects to collect messages.

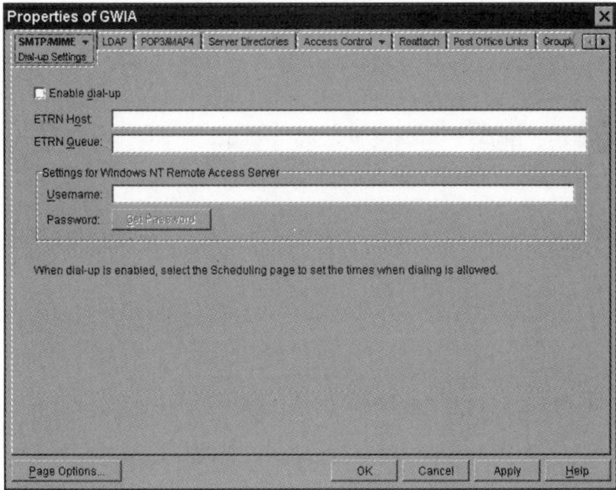

FIGURE 10.35 *Enabling Dial-up Access from the SMTP/MIME Dial-up Settings Property Page*

5. Click OK.
6. Go to the Schedule property page
7. Click Create.

   The dialog box shown in Figure 10.36 should appear.

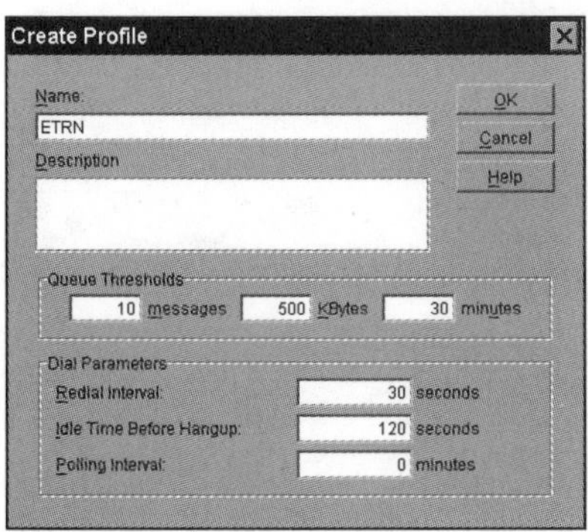

FIGURE 10.36 *Creating a New Profile from the GWIA Schedule Property Page*

8. Name the new profile ETRN, or something similarly descriptive.
9. Enter the appropriate thresholds.

   In Figure 10.36, the GWIA has been configured to dial the ETRN host if there are 10 messages queued, if there is at least 500KB of mail queued, or if the oldest item queued has been waiting at least 30 minutes.
10. Set the polling interval, under Dial parameters, to the minimum amount of time you want the GWIA to wait before checking the ETRN host for inbound mail.
11. Click OK.
12. As shown in Figure 10.37, with the new profile selected, block out the hours of the day that you want this profile to be in force.

    You should probably select all hours of the day, on all days of the week. You may choose to create additional profiles for lower frequency dialup after hours or on weekends.

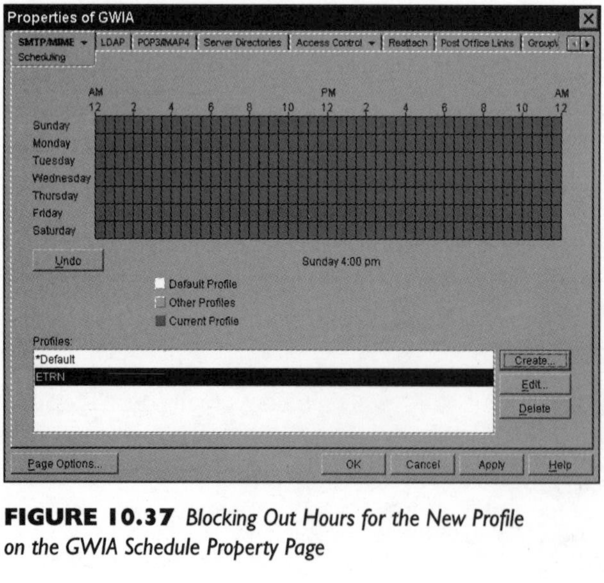

FIGURE 10.37 *Blocking Out Hours for the New Profile on the GWIA Schedule Property Page*

Monitoring the GWIA through a Web Browser

The GWIA allows you to monitor it though a Web browser. The following switches must be enabled in the GWIA.CFG file. This file is most likely in the SYS:SYSTEM directory of the file server that your GWIA is running on. Here are the switches to add, or to make sure they are enabled in the GWIA.CFG file:

```
/HTTP
/HTTPUSER-<USERID>
/HTTPPASSWORD-<PASSWORD>
/HTTPPORT-<PORT NUMBER>
```

For example, here is one sample string:

```
/HTTP
/HTTPUSER-admin
/HTTPPASSWORD-notell
/HTTPPORT-9800
```

Once these switches are enabled, and the GWIA has restarted, if necessary, you may monitor the GWIA using the following syntax:

```
http://<gwia IP Address or DNS Name>:<HTTPPORT value as
specified in the GWIA.CFG file>
```

For example, here is one sample string:

```
http://192.168.95.101:9800
```

You will be asked to authenticate to the GWIA using the userid and password specified in the GWIA.CFG file. Then you will see a screen such as the one in Figure 10.38.

The monitoring shows things such as statistics. But what's really neat is that the entire configuration of your GWIA is all laid out on the Configuration page. It's easier to see how your GWIA is configured in the HTTP monitoring screen than it is through ConsoleOne.

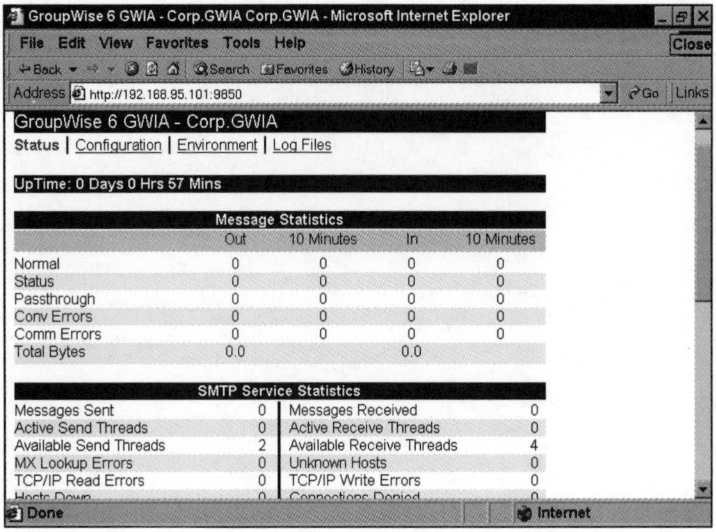

GroupWise 6 GWIA - Corp.GWIA Corp.GWIA - Microsoft Internet Explorer

File Edit View Favorites Tools Help

Address http://192.168.95.101:9850

GroupWise 6 GWIA - Corp.GWIA

Status | Configuration | Environment | Log Files

UpTime: 0 Days 0 Hrs 57 Mins

Message Statistics	Out	10 Minutes	In	10 Minutes
Normal	0	0	0	0
Status	0	0	0	0
Passthrough	0	0	0	0
Conv Errors	0	0	0	0
Comm Errors	0	0	0	0
Total Bytes	0.0		0.0	

SMTP Service Statistics			
Messages Sent	0	Messages Received	0
Active Send Threads	0	Active Receive Threads	0
Available Send Threads	2	Available Receive Threads	4
MX Lookup Errors	0	Unknown Hosts	0
TCP/IP Read Errors	0	TCP/IP Write Errors	0

Done Internet

FIGURE 10.38 *Monitoring the GWIA through a Web Browser*

Best Practices

It is difficult to make recommendations for GWIA implementation without first discussing GroupWise Internet addressing. Because Chapter 16 will be covering Internet addressing in detail, I suggest that you review the best practices there before installing or configuring the GWIA. There are a few recommendations to make here, however.

- **Dedicate a domain to the GWIA.** I discuss default GWIAs and routing domains more in Chapter 16. For now, it is enough to say that if you have lots of Internet traffic (more than 30,000 messages per day), you may want to offload that traffic from your other production domains. Create a domain with no post offices, and dedicate a machine to running just that domain's MTA and the GWIA.
- **If POP3 or IMAP4 access is strategic for your organization, install a GWIA on the same box as the post office for speedier POP3 and IMAP4 access.** This GWIA need not be supporting SMTP/MIME traffic. It can be

devoted to providing POP3 and IMAP4 mailbox access to users on this post office. While it may not be feasible for large organizations to put a GWIA on every post office, if POP3 or IMAP4 mailbox access is being used heavily, this configuration will improve performance.

- **Monitor GWIA statistics, and adjust threads accordingly.** If you see more than 80 percent of the total threads for a given service active at any given time, you should increase the number of threads for that service by 25 percent. This will ensure that the GWIA is able to request additional server resources to meet the demands of your user community. Of course, if server utilization regularly climbs over 70 percent, you should consider upgrading your server hardware, or perhaps using more than one GWIA. (See Chapter 16 for a discussion on configuring multiple default GWIAs.)

Summary

The GroupWise Internet agent is a critical piece of any GroupWise system. Without the GWIA, your GroupWise users don't have Internet e-mail, and they don't have the ability to use their POP3 or IMAP4 mail programs. This chapter shows you how to install and configure the GWIA. This chapter also explains the meaning behind the entries you will find in the GWIA log files.

CHAPTER 11

Configuring GroupWise WebAccess

This chapter explores the aspects of WebAccess in relation to a GroupWise system. GroupWise provides several options for users to access their mailboxes via the Internet. Having a good understanding of WebAccess will prepare you to setup and maintain a reliable implementation of WebAccess in your GroupWise environment.

Understanding WebAccess Architecture

To understand the WebAccess component of your GroupWise system, it is important to understand the components of WebAccess architecture. This will help with installation, configuration, and troubleshooting of the WebAccess components.

Understanding the WebAccess Agent

WebAccess can be thought of as being composed of two main pieces. The first piece is referred to as the *WebAccess agent,* and it is the piece that is responsible for requesting and receiving data from a user's mailbox. The GroupWise agent can run on NetWare as an NLM (GWINTER.NLM) or on NT as either an executable (GWINTER.EXE) or a Windows NT service. You can think of the WebAccess agent as a client that communicates directly via TCP/IP with a POA via its client/server port such as 1677, or via a mapped drive where it would touch the user and message databases directly.

Understanding the WebAccess Application

The second piece is referred to as the *WebAccess application* and is responsible for taking the data received by the WebAccess agent and delivering it to the Web browser that is being used to access WebAccess. The WebAccess application runs on a Web server as a Java servlet. It runs on any of the following supported Web-server platforms:

- NetWare running the NetScape Enterprise Web server
- Windows running IIS 4 or later Web erver
- Windows running Netscape FastTrack/Enterprise Web server
- Solaris running Apache Web server

The WebAccess application communicates with the WebAccess agent via TCP/IP. By default, the WebAccess agent listens on port 7205 for information coming from the WebAccess application. The data that is exchanged between the agent and the application is encrypted using an encryption key. This is not your standard SSL type of encryption, but simply an encryption key that each piece (agent and application) uses to encrypt data between them. The encryption key is discussed even further in this chapter in the section titled "Configuring the GroupWise WebAccess Gateway"

Here is a quick walkthrough of what a request coming in from a Web browser to log into a GroupWise mailbox would look like. This will help to explain the flow of information through a WebAccess system, as well as help you see the relationship between the WebAccess application and agent:

1. A user sits down at a Web browser and enters the URL to GroupWise WebAccess in their browser. For example, the URL may be `http://groupwise.worldwidewidgets.com`.
2. The browser is directed to the Web server that DNS resolves them to. Once here, the user sees the GroupWise WebAccess Login screen. (There are lots of options as to what you will have your users doing; for simplicity, the Web server at `groupwise.worldwidewidgets.com` goes directly to the GroupWise 6 Login screen.) This screen is a standard HTML document that the Web server is displaying. Figure 11.1 shows this screen.

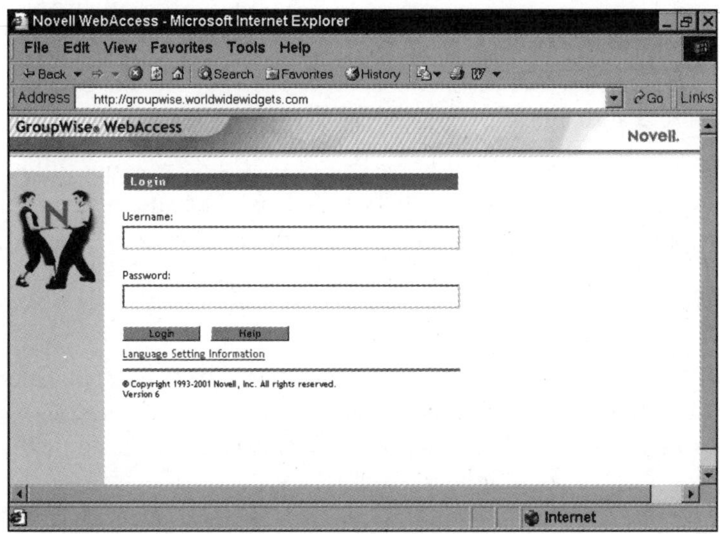

FIGURE 11.1 *The GroupWise WebAccess Login Screen*

3. The user enters a user ID and password and clicks Login.
4. The Web server hands this information over to the WebAccess application that is running as a servlet on the Web server. The servlet also detects the platform and manufacturer of the browser that is hitting it, and then creates a session for this user.
5. The WebAccess application takes the user ID and password and does some quick lookups on which WebAccess agent it should route the request to. It discovers that it needs to send the request to an IP address of X.X.X.X on port 7205.
6. The WebAccess application encrypts the data using the encryption key found on the local Web server and sends the user name and password to the WebAccess agent running on a NetWare or NT server via port 7205.
7. The WebAccess agent receives the data, decrypts it using the same encryption key that was used to encrypt the data, and then does a lookup in the WPDOMAIN.DB to identify the domain and post office that this user is located in.
8. Once the user's domain and post office are located, the WebAccess agent checks how it will communicate to this particular post office. It discovers that it must communicate via TCP/IP.
9. The WebAccess agent sends the user ID and password down to the POA object for the user's post office, and acts like a traditional GroupWise client, in that it connects to the POA via client/server port 1677. The POA picks up the request and authenticates the user into their mailbox.

Simple, right? This is a quick and simple outline of how a user's request flows from an actual browser into a GroupWise mailbox. At this point, the return path of the data from the post office to the Web browser will not be discussed. Basically, the return path for the data coming from the post office is in reverse order, minus a few of the lookups, because a session ID is in place to route the data back from the agent to the application.

This should give you a basic understanding of how the WebAccess application and the agent work together to access the user's mail via WebAccess. Now that you have an understanding of GroupWise WebAccess architecture, next comes an explanation of the installation of GroupWise WebAccess.

Installing the GroupWise WebAccess Gateway

This section offers a walkthrough of a simple GroupWise WebAccess installation to get you a little more familiar with the basic install of WebAccess. Pay attention to this section; I have tried to make it a little more in depth than your standard "How to install something, read this, then-click-next" section. You will find some behind-the-scenes information in this section that should be beneficial to you.

Before you can install WebAccess, you need a functional Web server that is up and running. The supported Web servers were listed in the previous section.

In this example, you see a simple installation of the WebAccess agent and application being installed onto a single NetWare server. In the section titled "Advanced Installation Options for WebAccess," you can find additional information about installing the agent and application on different servers. For now, this will give you a good understanding of the install options for the agent and application.

1. To begin with, launch the SETUP.EXE from the INTERNET\WEBACCESS directory located in your GroupWise software distribution directory or GroupWise 6 CD.

   You will be prompted as to what components you can install, as shown in Figure 11.2. You have three options: WebAccess agent, WebAccess application, and WebPublisher application.

   The WebAccess agent and application were discussed earlier. The WebPublisher application is used to access documents stored in GroupWise document management libraries. If you are using GroupWise document management, you may want to enable the WebPublisher application piece. This example does not include installing the WebPublisher application.

2. Check the agent and application components and select Next.

   As shown in Figure 11.3, you are then prompted as to what type of server the WebAccess agent will be installed on, as well as the path to place the install files. The agent can run either on a NetWare or a NT/2000 server. This step determines what code the install script will install. If you select NetWare as the platform, the GWINTER.NLM gets installed for the agent.

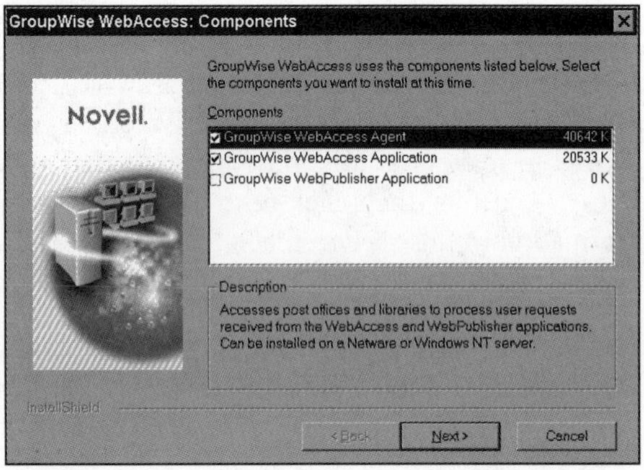

FIGURE 11.2 *Choosing Which GroupWise WebAccess Components to Install*

If you select Windows NT, then the GWINTER.EXE gets installed. (There are, of course, additional files that are installed, but the GWINTER is the main workhorse for the agent piece) The path that you define here will be where the agent files are installed. You may make this path anything you choose. The directory specified here must be eight characters or less.

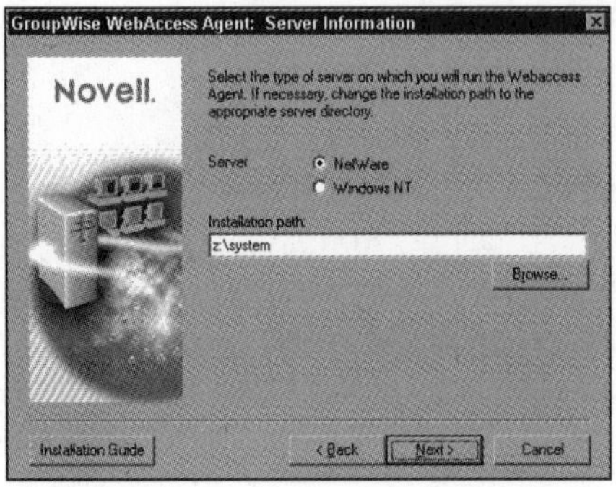

FIGURE 11.3 *Choosing the Web-Server Platform*

3. Select the server platform, enter the path, and then click Next.

Now you are prompted to enter the IP address or DNS name of the server that you are installing the agent on. The install script tries to auto-detect this information for you and displays it, as seen in Figure 11.4. Before this screen though, the first thing the script does is query the server that you defined to verify whether any GroupWise modules are loaded. If they are, you are prompted to unload the GroupWise modules.

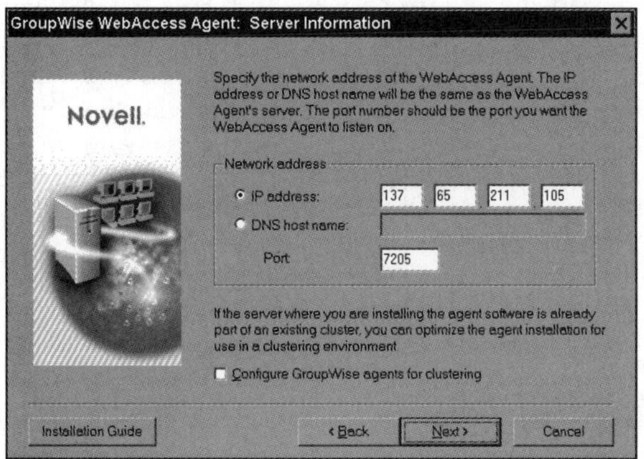

FIGURE 11.4 *GroupWise WebAccess Agent Server Information*

The install tries to determine the DNS name and IP address of the server.

TIP

On NetWare, the DNS host name comes from the HOSTS file found in the SYS:\ETC directory. Before proceeding, make sure that the local HOSTS file on the Web server has the local IP address and a Web-server name defined in it. This information can be anywhere in the HOSTS file.

```
192.168.95.101 webmail.worldwidewidgets.com
```

So if the DNS name is incorrect, the HOSTS file is where this information is coming from.

The information about the DNS name and IP address of the server is used to help create a binary file on the Web server called COMMGR.CFG, which the WebAccess application reads in order to find out what server and port the WebAccess agent is installed on. This information is also placed into the GroupWise WPDOMAIN.DB to tell the WebAccess agent what port it should listen on for connections coming from the WebAccess application.

TIP

If you notice in the installation, there is an option to cluster enable the WebAccess agent. Checking this box simply changes the definition of the path to the WebAccess agent when the agent loads. You will see an example of what checking this cluster option does in the next section, which talks about how to load the WebAccess agent. If you are installing this WebAccess agent into a Novell cluster, then you will want to check this box. If you do check the option to configure the GroupWise agent for clustering, and you are *not* running in a cluster environment, don't worry. The agent will load just fine on a non-clustered server if you check this option.

4. After confirming the server information, click Next, and you will see the screen shown in Figure 11.5.

FIGURE 11.5 *GroupWise WebAccess Agent Gateway Directory*

You are now prompted for the path to the domain. Once again, the install script tries to fill this information out for you; however, it may not be correct. The path to the domain that you see here comes from the workstation's registry that you are running the install from. Notice that it gives you the full path of where the gateway directory will be. GroupWise stores all the gateway directory structures under the domain\wpgate\ location. Hence, you will see this in the gateway directory, full path information.

Keep this directory within eight characters or less. The install script will check to make sure that the directory exists; if it does not, it will prompt you to create it. If it does exist, you may be prompted that the directory is already being used and ask whether you are sure you want to use this directory.

5. After specifying the gateway directory, click Next.

   You are now asked what you would like the WebAccess agent gateway object to be called. This is the object that you will see from ConsoleOne under the GroupWise domain defined earlier. For simplicity, it is recommended to keep these names the same.

If you entered something different in Step 5 here, the install should reflect this name at this point. If you would like to give them different names, keeping the WebAccess agent name within the eight-character limit is not critical here.

The next step, shown in Figure 11.6, may have you wondering why this is necessary. It is asking you for a user name and password so that it can access the WPDOMAIN.DB for the domain the WebAccess agent is being installed under. I like to recommend that you have the domain and WebAccess agent on the same server. Hence, a user name and password are not necessarily required. However, the install requires you to enter a user name and password here. The root reason for this is that if your domain is on FS1, and you are installing the WebAccess agent on FS2, the agent *must* be able to directly access the WPDOMAIN.DB to read some of its configuration information from. Because of this, the agent must log into the FS1 server in order to access the domain database. This is the reason for this prompt during the install of the agent. Also, if the agent must communicate to post offices via a direct link, it will use this user name and password to authenticate to the post office server. You should enter an NDS user name and password of a user that has read, write, create, erase, modify, and file-scan rights to the domain directory. You should enter the fully distinguished name starting with a leading period. This user name and password are written to the STARTWEB.NCF file, which will be discussed when loading the WebAccess gateway in the next section.

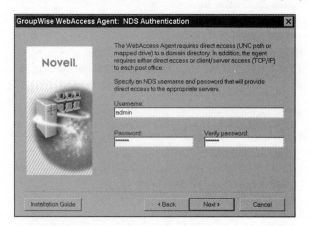

FIGURE 11.6 *Username and Password*

6. Enter the user name and password and click Next.

   The next screen gives you the option to monitor the WebAccess agent through a standard HTTP browser. This gives you some great functionality in checking in on your WebAccess agent to see how it is running without having to actually look at the agent console screen. The user name and password here are *not* an NDS user name and password. You can select any user name and password.

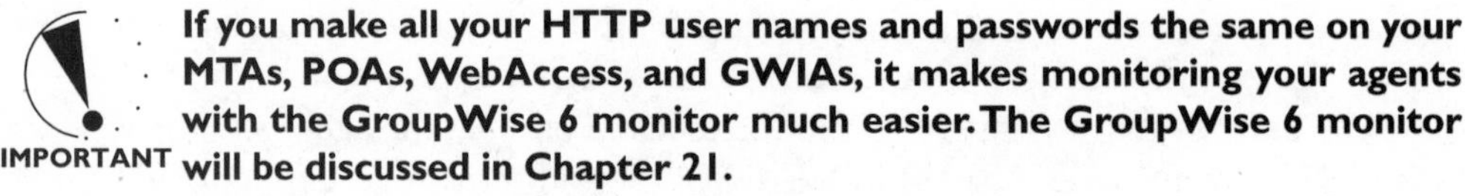

IMPORTANT

If you make all your HTTP user names and passwords the same on your MTAs, POAs, WebAccess, and GWIAs, it makes monitoring your agents with the GroupWise 6 monitor much easier. The GroupWise 6 monitor will be discussed in Chapter 21.

7. Check the Enable Web Console option, enter the user name and password, and then click Next to proceed to the summary screen.
8. At the end of the installation wizard you will see the summary screen like the one in Figure 11.7.

   You now get a summary of the WebAccess agent setup information. Verify that all information is entered correctly.

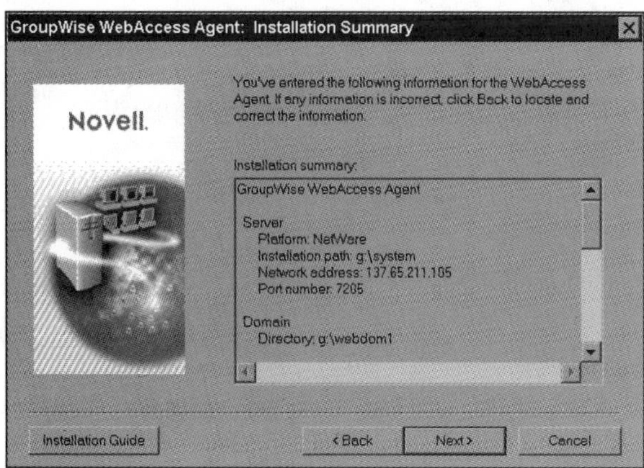

FIGURE 11.7 *WebAccess Agent Installation Summary*

9. Click Next to proceed to the GroupWise WebAccess agent portion of the installation.

   This concludes the WebAccess agent portion of the install. The wizard now takes you directly into the WebAccess application wizard.

   In this step of the installation, shown in Figure 11.8, the wizard takes you through the WebAccess application install.

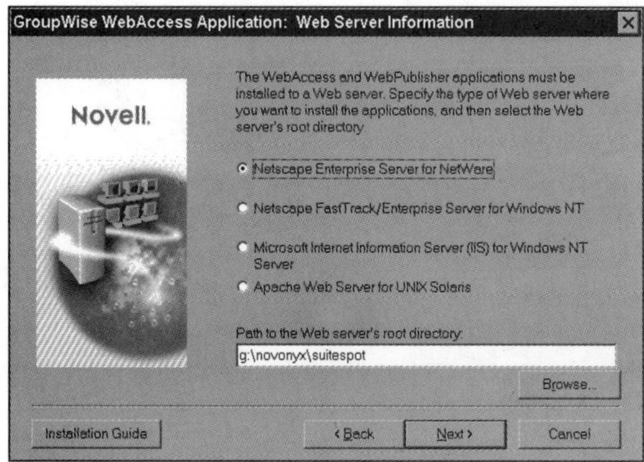

FIGURE 11.8 *WebAccess Application Install*

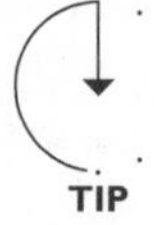

The application is the piece that runs as a servlet on a Web server and communicates to the WebAccess agent via TCP/IP.

The first thing you are prompted for is what type of Web server you will be installing the application on.

10. Select the Web server platform, verify that the path to the root of the Web server is correct, and then click Next.

Now you get to enter the IP or DNS name of the Web server, and whether or not it is using SSL. WebAccess install defaults to use SSL.

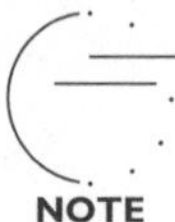

If you do select to use SSL, then you must have your Web server configured to support SSL connections. Your Web server will need to be configured to use a certificate to encrypt the data to and from the browser.

This chapter talks more about certificates in the advanced configuration section of this chapter.

11. Indicate whether or not you will use SSL, and then select Next.

The next screen (Figure 11.9) prompts whether or not you want to replace your Web server's default Web page. This may or may not be desired. If you do select to replace your Web server's default Web page, the default Web page will be renamed so that you will not lose it.

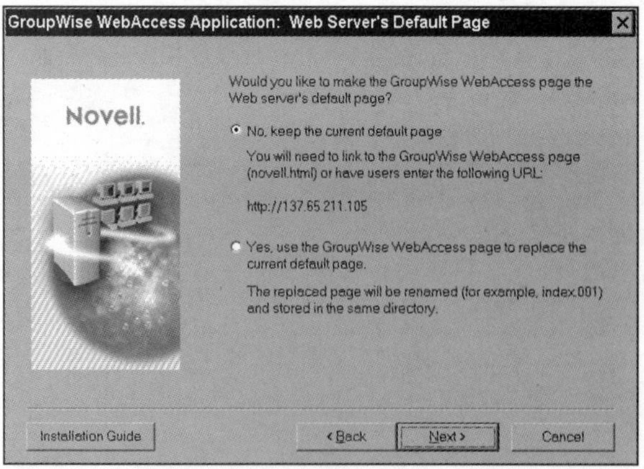

FIGURE 11.9 *Prompting What to Do with the Default Web Page*

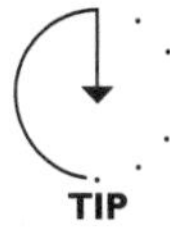

If you do keep the existing default Web page for your Web server, you may want to add a link on it that points to `http://<your Web server DNS name>/servlet/webacc`**. This will allow users to click on this link and be sent directly to the language page to select their language after which they can log into WebAccess.**

12. Select the Web server default Web page option you prefer, and click Next.

    You are then prompted as to where you want the configuration files for the WebAccess application to be located. This defaults to the <\\<SERVER NAME>\SYS\NOVELL directory for NetWare. The install creates a WebAccess directory under the specified directory where the configuration files are actually placed. These configuration files should exist on the same server as the Web server.

If this directory does not exist, you will be prompted to create it.

13. Enter the path for the configuration files and click Next.

    You will then be prompted as to what Java servlet gateway you will be using (Figure 11.10). I recommend the use of the Novell servlet gateway. You may, however, use a different servlet gateway. If you are running in this mode, you must know the path to the Java servlet directory.

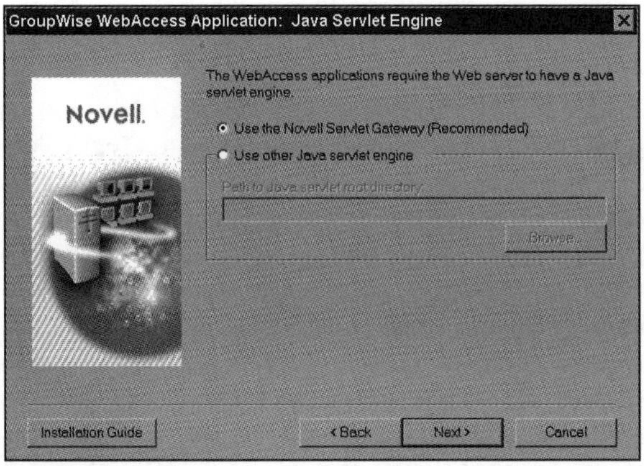

FIGURE 11.10 *Java Servlet Gateway*

14. Select the Novell Java servlet gateway and then click Next

IMPORTANT

This is *not* an NDS user name and password. This user name and password is used if you want to actually configure the Novell servlet gateway. Rarely will you need to configure the Novell servlet gateway, so this chapter won't even discuss it.

15. Enter a user name and password for the servlet gateway, then click Next.

    The installation asks what you want the default language selection to be for WebAccess users. The default is English. This is the first thing a user will see when they hit the `http://<yourWeb server DNS name>/servlet/webacc` link.

NOTE

Later in this chapter, there's a section ("Skipping the GroupWise WebAccess Language Page") that discusses how to design your Web server so that users are not prompted for the language to use.

16. Select the default language and click Next.

    This next option (Figure 11.11) asks you in what context of your NDS tree should the application objects be created. These application objects consist of the GroupWise WebAccess object, the GroupWise provider object, the LDAP provider object, and the NovellSpeller object. These objects, and the services they perform, are discussed more in the section titled "Configuring the GroupWise WebAccess Gateway." The default context is the context of the domain object. This is usually sufficient, as these objects should exist close to the domain for administration purposes.

NOTE

It may be a bit confusing to see the name of the GroupWise domain listed at the beginning of the context. Even though a GroupWise domain object is not considered an NDS organization or organization unit, which are your traditional container objects that would contain NDS leaf objects, the domain NDS object has an attribute that defines it as a container object. Because of this, you can actually create *some* objects under the domain. However, the only NDS objects that are allowed to be created under a domain are GroupWise gateways, service providers, and application objects. When you understand this, it makes sense to have the context listed as the domain object. This makes it nice because in NDS you can then simply click the domain NDS object to see all the associated objects.

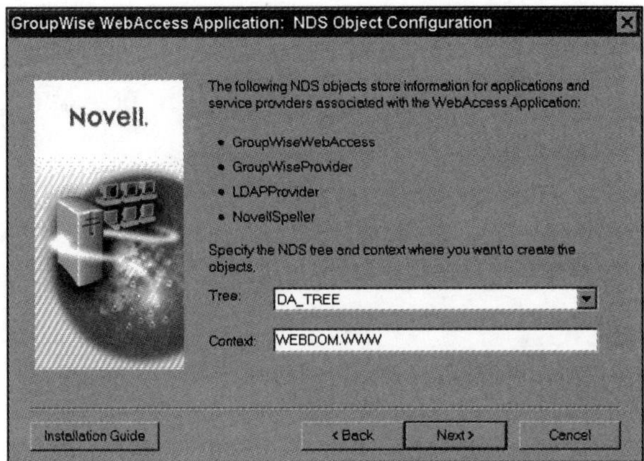
GroupWise WebAccess Application: NDS Object Configuration
Novell.
The following NDS objects store information for applications and service providers associated with the WebAccess Application:
GroupWiseWebAccess
GroupWiseProvider
LDAPProvider
NovellSpeller
Specify the NDS tree and context where you want to create the objects.
Tree:
DA_TREE
Context:
WEBDOM.WWW
Installation Guide
< Back
Next >
Cancel

FIGURE 11.11 *Choosing an NDS Context for WebAccess Applications*

17. Verify that the context is correct and click Next.
18. You will then be given the summary of the WebAccess application information that you entered. Verify this and click Next.

    If you already have a Novell servlet gateway running, you may be prompted about overwriting it with a different version, or that it is already the same version. If it is the same version, you can click No to overwrite it. Otherwise, you should replace your existing servlet gateway. If Java is already loaded, you must unload it. The install will prompt you to either unload it, or give you the option to let it unload Java.

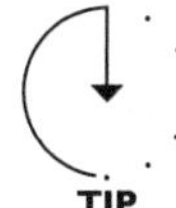

To unload Java manually, from the NetWare console prompt, enter the following command:

```
java -exit
```

The install will then proceed to install the WebAccess agent and application. You may be prompted to overwrite older files. If so, you will want to keep the newest file.

The last thing that you see is a summary screen with information on how to load the components that were just installed. The launch installation summary gives you a test file that contains all the input options that you entered during the wizard walkthrough portion of the install.

In the next section, you learn more about how to launch the WebAccess agent and the application. If you leave the last options checked, then the Install wizard launches the WebAccess agent and restarts the Web server for you. This gives you a functioning WebAccess system up and running. There you have it; pat yourself on the back for successfully installing WebAccess.

Loading the GroupWise WebAccess Agent and Application

This section discusses how to start the WebAccess agent and WebAccess application.

Loading the GroupWise WebAccess Agent

To start the GroupWise WebAccess agent when it is running on a NetWare server, you will need to run the STRTWEB.NCF file. From the NetWare console prompt, type the following:

```
strtweb
```

You will learn more about how to start the WebAccess agent running on NT in the "Advanced Installation Options for WebAccess" section. For now, this section covers the information on how to start the agent and application on a NetWare platform. As mentioned before, you are going to want to run the STRTWEB.NCF file from the system console of your NetWare server. The STRTWEB.NCF file is located in the SYS:\SYSTEM directory.

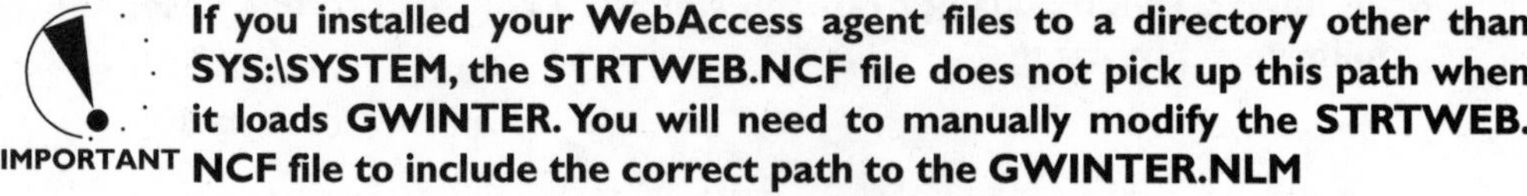

If you installed your WebAccess agent files to a directory other than SYS:\SYSTEM, the STRTWEB.NCF file does not pick up this path when it loads GWINTER. You will need to manually modify the STRTWEB.NCF file to include the correct path to the GWINTER.NLM

Here's an explanation of what's in the STRTWEB.NCF file. Following is a sample STRTWEB.NCF file:

```
load SYS:system\gwinter /ph=fs1\mail:do2\WPGATE\WEBAC60A
/user=.webaccuser.webaccess.apps /password=password /http
```

NOTE

If when you installed the agent, you selected the option to install in a cluster environment, the STRTWEB.NCF file will look like this. (The # symbol acts as a remark, so the first load line does not load.)

```
#load SYS:system\gwinter /ph=fs1\mail:do2\WPGATE\ WEBAC60A
/user=.webaccuser.webaccess.apps /password=password
# FOR CLUSTER ENABLED VOLUME
load SYS:system\gwinter /ph=mail:do2\WPGATE\ WEBAC60A
/user=.webaccuser.webaccess.apps /password=password /http
```

Notice that the only difference is how the /ph switch is formatted. In a clustered environment, the path simply references the volume name. This way if a node running GWINTER fails over to another node, it will still be accessing the same volume, and is not tied to a specific server.

The first command line parameter in the STRTWEB.NCF file is the /ph switch that contains the path to the gateway directory. Next is the /user and /password switches. Remember you had to enter these during the install.

When you load the WebAccess agent, you may notice that the GWINTER.NLM auto loads several other NLMs, starting with VS*.NLM. These NLMs are used when a user views an attachment that may be some sort of document type from the WebAccess client. These VS*.NLMs take very little server memory as only a small piece of them loads when you load the agent. When a user needs to actually view a document, the entire viewer NLM loads at that point.

The install also creates a STOPWEB.NCF file, which will shut down the WebAccess agent. It simply contains the line `Unload gwinter`, which will unload the WebAccess agent.

Following are all the switches that can be used in the strtweb.ncf or strtweb.bat (if loading the agent on an NT box):

- **@filename:** This switch allows you to place all startup switches in a particular file. This is similar to when a domain or post office agent is loaded. This switch is not used by default.
- **/help:** If the GWINTER.NLM or GWINTER.EXE are loaded with the /help switch, then all startup switches are displayed with a brief description of each.
- **/home- or /ph-:** This is a required switch and tells the agent the path to the WPDOMAIN.DB file.
- **/http:** This switch enables the HTTP monitoring ability of the agent.

- **/httpuser-:** Enter a user name to protect the HTTP monitoring port.
- **/httppassword-:** Enter a password that is used with the /httpuser- switch.
- **/logdiskon:** This switch enables the agent to log information to disk. By default, disk logging is not enabled.
- **/log-:** Enter the path that the log file will be stored in. You must have the /logdiskon switch enabled also.
- **/loglevel-:** Enter the logging level desired. Options are Normal, Verbose, or Diagnostic.
- **/logdays-:** Enter the number of days that the log files will be kept for the agent before being deleted by the agent.
- **/logmax-:** Enter the maximum size that all log files will consume.
- **/maxusers-:** Enter the maximum number of concurrent users that the agent will support. The default is 250 users.
- **/user-:** This switch is only used for the NLM version of the agent. Enter an NDS user name that has rights to the domain directory here. The /user- switch is also used when the NLM version of the agent is configured to link to a post office via a UNC connection.
- **/password-:** This switch is only used for the NLM version of the agent. Enter the password for the NDS user that is defined with the /user- switch.
- **/port-:** Enter the port that the agent will listen on for requests coming in from the WebAccess application.
- **/ip-:** Enter the IP address that the agent will bind to. The agent will bind to the first bound IP address of the server by default.
- **/threads-:** Enter the number of threads available for the agent to use to process user requests.
- **/work-:** Enter the path that the agent will use to perform work. This switch is useful if the agent is running on a different server than where the domain database is located. The work switch should point to a directory on the same server as where the agent is running.

Loading the GroupWise WebAccess Application

With just the WebAccess agent running, you only have one piece to the entire WebAccess system running. You need to also get the WebAccess application up and running.

Loading the GroupWise WebAccess application is done by restarting the Web server where you installed the WebAccess application. The Web server is responsible for loading the WebAccess application, and does so when it loads. The reason for this is because the WebAccess application is tightly integrated with the Web server, and cannot run on its own. It is a Java servlet process that the Web server calls and starts up.

To restart a NetScape Enterprise Web server running on NetWare, you can issue this command at the NetWare console prompt:

```
NVXWEBUP
```

To unload the NetScape Enterprise Web server running on NetWare, you can issue this command at the NetWare console prompt:

```
NVXWEBDN
```

To unload a Netscape Enterprise Web server and the administration components for Netscape Enterprise Web server, issue this command at the NetWare console prompt:

```
NSWEBDN
```

And then to reload NetScape Enterprise Web server and the Netscape Enterprise Web server administration components, issue this command at the NetWare console prompt:

```
NSWEB
```

When the Web server loads, you should see it starting two servlets: <GroupWise WebAccess Spell Checker> Spell Servlet is ready for work and <GroupWise WebAccess> WebAccess Servlet is ready for work. If you choose to select a screen to view on the NetWare server, you can see the activity of these servlets when you switch to the Java Interpreter: com/novell/application screen. The WebAccess application should be up and running at this point and ready to communicate with the WebAccess agent.

So there you have it. You know all the nitty gritty details of how the WebAccess agent and application pieces are loaded and unloaded.

Logging In to the GroupWise WebAccess Client

Now that you have the application and the agent up and running, you are ready to read mail. In this section, there will not be a lot of time spent on the actual

WebAccess interface and all the options that are available here. To begin with, you must launch your Web browser and point it to the Web server that you installed the WebAccess application on. If you replaced the default home page, you can simply enter **http://<yourWeb server DNS name>**, and the language page for WebAccess should be displayed. If you did not replace your default Web page, you can enter **http://<yourWeb server DNS name>/servlet/webacc**, and the login page will be displayed. You can then enter a GroupWise user ID and password and click Login.

IMPORTANT

WebAccess users are required to have passwords on their GroupWise Accounts in order to log in via the WebAccess client. If your POA is configured to query NDS via LDAP, then users may also use their NDS password if they have not assigned a password to their GroupWise mailbox.

You should now be viewing your GroupWise master mailbox from the WebAccess client. Figure 11.12 displays a screen shot of a GroupWise 6 user's mailbox as viewed from the WebAccess client.

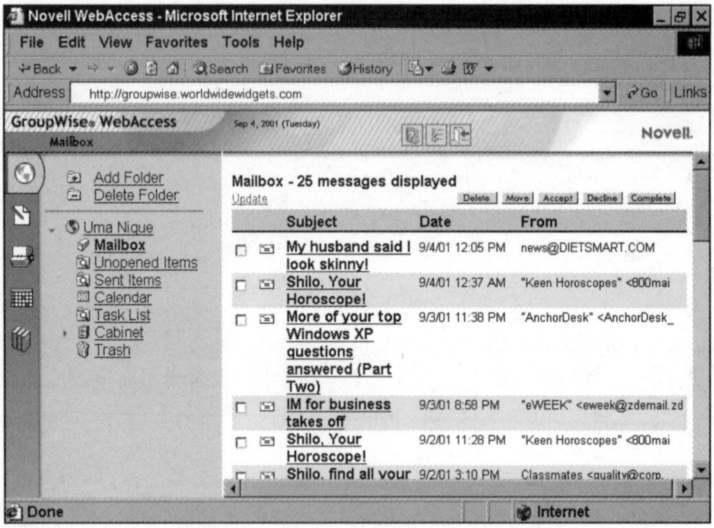

FIGURE 11.12 *The GroupWise WebAccess Client*

Configuring the GroupWise WebAccess Gateway

In this section, you learn about some of the new NDS objects that are associated with the WebAccess gateway, what functions they perform, as well as how to configure all aspects of the WebAccess gateway. This section goes through each configuration screen, discussing most of the options and how they affect the overall performance or functionality of the WebAccess gateway. This section does not discuss every option, because some of the options are self-explanatory and make minor changes to the functionality of WebAccess. Also, there are a few generic gateway options that are of minimal consequence that will not be discussed.

The WebAccess Agent

This is the object that you can see associated with a domain when you select to view gateways. It is the only object associated with a WebAccess gateway that is directly associated to a domain. When you go to the details of the WebAccess agent, you can configure the settings associated with this agent.

- **Subdirectory:** This is the directory under the WPGATE directory of the owning domain for the agent. If you select the drop-down button, you will see all the gateway directories under this gateway. This should be the directory that the WebAccess agent uses for some of its configuration files.
- **Time Zone:** This allows you to enter the default time zone that this agent is in.

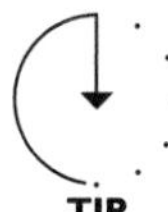

End users can adjust the time zone from the WebAccess client so that appointments will show up in their local time zone.

- **Platform:** You should specify what platform this WebAccess agent will be running on. If you are running the agent on an NT platform, you will need to change this to reflect Windows NT/2000.

The Unix platform is left over from GroupWise 5.2 days. GroupWise 6 currently does not have a WebAccess agent that will run on Unix. The WebAccess application is the piece of WebAccess that is able to run on Unix, however.

- **Gateway Alias Type:** For the WebAccess gateway, you should not need an alias type. This field is active on any of the GroupWise gateways.
- **Foreign ID:** For the WebAccess gateway, you should not need a foreign ID either. Again, this field is active on any of the GroupWise gateways and is primarily used with a GWIA.
- **SNMP Community "Get" String:** If you are using SNMP monitoring software to monitor the WebAccess gateway, this field allows you to set the get string to match your software that is doing the monitoring. Blank is default.
- **Network Address:** When you click on the pencil to the right of the Network Address field, you get the screen shown in Figure 11.13.

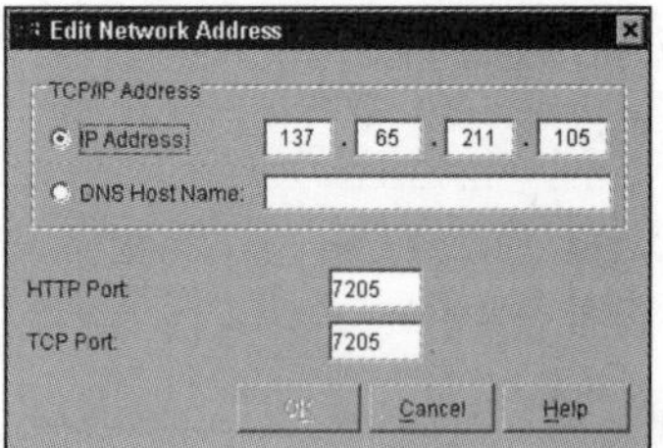

FIGURE 11.13 *The GroupWise WebAccess Agent Network Address Dialog Box*

This is where you can enter the IP address or DNS name of the server where the WebAccess agent is running. The HTTP port is the port that the agent will listen on for Web-browser monitoring. Like all other GroupWise agents, the WebAccess agent can be monitored through a Web browser. The TCP port is the port that the WebAccess application running on the Web server will use to communicate data to the WebAccess agent. In other words, the agent will listen on this port for data coming from the application. The HTTP port should allow you to configure a different port for the agent to listen on for HTTP monitoring of the agent. However, in the released version of GroupWise 6, the HTTP port does not appear to do anything. It is best to leave them the same, then when you want to monitor the agent, you select the defined HTTP and TCP port, which will be the same thing.

The IPX/SPX addresses are no longer used in GroupWise 5.5 or 6.

Configuring the GroupWise Optional Gateway Settings Property Page

Most of these optional gateway setting are generic gateway settings that do not apply to the WebAccess gateway. The help file regarding them should suffice. You can leave them to default without any problems.

Configuring the GroupWise Gateway Administrators Property Page

Here you can define a GroupWise user or group as the administrator for the GroupWise agent. The roles are generic roles for all gateways. The one role that you may be interested in setting is the operator role.

The operator role allows the defined user(s) or group(s) to receive mail messages when errors occur at the GroupWise agent. This helps alert you if there are problems with the gateway.

NOTE

The user that you add as an administrator must be a GroupWise user. Also, if you add a group or distribution list, its visibility must be set to system.

Configuring the WebAccess Settings Property Page

Shown in Figure 11.14, this page is quite important to enabling the application and agent to communicate properly between themselves. Both settings here are stored in the domain database and the COMMGR.CFG file, which is located in two places. It is located in the DOMAIN\WPGATE\<WEBAC60A directory for the WebAccess agent. A copy of this file is made available to the WebAccess application on the Web server, the default of which is \NOVELL\WebAccess. On a NetWare server, the NOVELL\WebAccess directory is generally off the root of the SYS:volume. On a Windows 2000/NT server, it's usually off the root of the C:\ drive. The COMMGR.CFG file is encrypted and cannot be manually manipulated.

NOTE

The COMINT.CFG file located in the DOMAIN\WPGATE\WEBAC60 directory is basically a live backup of the COMMGR.CFG file. If your COMMGR.CFG file becomes damaged or corrupt, you can rename the COMINT.CFG file to COMMGR.CFG.

The only way to access this information is through the ConsoleOne interface with the GroupWise 6 snapins in place. When you make changes to the maximum threads or encryption key settings, it will update three files. They are the

COMINT.CFG and COMMGR.CFG files located at the DOMAIN\WPGATE\WEBAC60A directory, as well as the COMMGR.CFG file, which is located on the Web server in the \NOVELL\WebAccess directory.

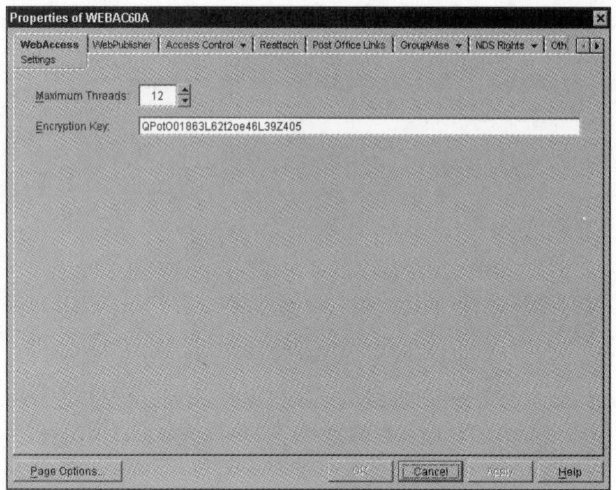

FIGURE 11.14 *The WebAccess Settings Property Page*

- **Maximum Threads:** This setting allows you to increase or decrease the maximum number of threads that the WebAccess agent will use for communication. If you find that your users are seeing a slow response using WebAccess, you may need to increase this number. You can monitor your agent to see if it is hitting the maximum number of threads. You will learn how to identify how many threads the WebAccess agent is using in the upcoming section titled "Understanding the GroupWise WebAccess Console."
- **Encryption Key:** The encryption key value that is defined here is used to encrypt data that is sent between the WebAccess agent and the WebAccess application provider. This ensures that communication between these two WebAccess components is encrypted and secure. As mentioned earlier in this section, this encryption key is stored in the COMMGR.CFG file. Because both the WebAccess agent and application provider must use the same encryption key, the COMMGR.CFG file is accessible to both the application and the agent.

You can accept the default encryption key that the install generates, or you can use your own encryption key, if desired. If you have problems where the application cannot talk to the agent, it is good to double-check the COMMGR.CFG file on both the Web server where the application is running and the server where the agent is running. You can manually copy the COMMGR.CFG file from the DOMAIN\WPGATE\WEBAC60A directory to the \NOVELL\WEBACCESS directory if you do have a communication problem between these two agents.

Configuring the Access Control Settings Property Page

This configuration page (Figure 11.15) allows you to set up who can use the WebAccess gateway to access their GroupWise mailbox. You can define multiple classes of service with corresponding members. The default class of service contains everyone and allows everyone access to the WebAccess agent.

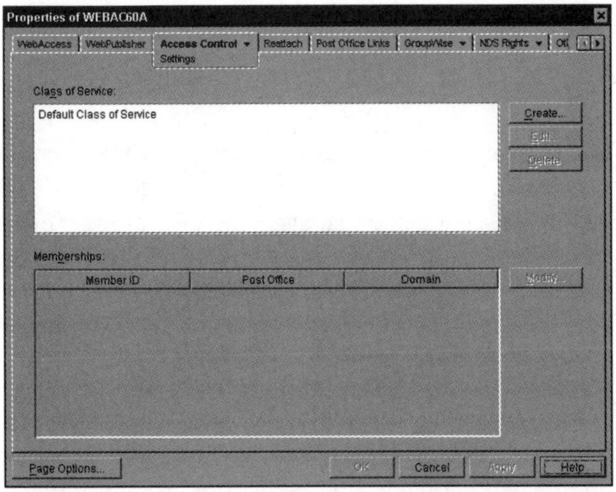

FIGURE 11.15 *The WebAccess Access Control Settings Property Page*

You can modify or create additional classes of service if you want to exclude users from accessing GroupWise WebAccess.

The following steps walk you through a quick scenario when you may want to do this. In this example, a group of users should not be allowed access to the WebAccess client. To restrict access to these users, you must define a new class of service.

1. Click Create to create a new class of service.
2. Give the new class a name something like **Restricted Access**, leave the edit access settings and select membership options checked, and then click OK.
3. Next, choose Prevent Access and click OK.

   You are now brought to the screen where you can assign the membership to this class of service. You can add specific users, distribution lists, or entire post offices or domains to the membership list.
4. Select who you would like to be included in this membership list and then click OK.

   If all the users that should be denied access to WebAccess are across multiple post offices, you should create a group that contains all these users. Then add this group as a member of the class of service you created.

There you have it. You can create multiple classes of service if you want to control who can or cannot have access to the GroupWise system through the WebAccess gateway.

Understanding the Access Control Database Management Properties Page

All of the access control settings regarding classes of service and membership are stored in a database called GWAC.DB. This database is located in the DOMAIN\WPGATE\WEBAC60A directory. This database management tab allows you to validate and recover this database.

- **Validate Now:** Clicking this will basically run a structure check on the GWAC.DB file and report back if there were any inconsistencies found in the database. It also tells you how many bytes, fields, and indexes it validated. If inconsistencies are found, you should perform a recover now on the database.
- **Recover Now:** Clicking this will basically run a structural rebuild of the GWAC.DB that will repair any structural damage in the database. The GWAC.DC file is used as a template file on how to structurally build the new GWAC.DB file.

Configuring the Reattach Settings Property Page

This tab is used when you are running the WebAccess agent on an NT platform, *and* the links to the post office are direct (or UNC) links (post office links are discussed in the next section). If you are running the WebAccess agent on a NetWare platform, this tab is not needed, or if the post office links are TCP/IP, you do not need this information. Remember that the WebAccess agent acts like a client when it access the user's user and message databases. If the agent is running on NT, and you have defined direct links to post offices, the NT server running the agent must log into the server where the post office is located in order to access the message store. This facilitates the need to supply the following information.

- **Tree:** Enter the name of the NDS tree that the server that houses the post offices is located.
- **Context:** Enter the full context of the NDS user that will be used to log in to the post office server.
- **User ID:** Enter the NDS user ID that has rights to the post office directory. (This user ID must have read, write, create, erase, modify, and file scan rights to the post office directory.)
- **Password:** Enter the password for the NDS user here.

Configuring the Post Office Links Settings Property Page

This tab is very important. It defines exactly how the WebAccess agent will actually communicate to the post offices in the GroupWise system. Remember that the agent acts like a client in that it must access the post office message store to retrieve a user's mail.

- **Domain column:** This defines the domain that the post office is under.
- **Post Office column:** This identifies the name of the post office.
- **Access Mode:** This defines how the WebAccess agent will access the post office. You have four options here.
  - Client/server and direct
  - Client/server only
  - Direct only
  - Follow P.O. (use current post office access)

If the access mode is set to Follow P.O., then it depends on what the post office object access mode is set to. If it is set to client/server only, then you will see an IP address or DNS name in the Link column. If it is set to direct only, you will see the UNC path to the post office in the Link column. If it is set to client/server and direct, you may see either an IP address or UNC path. As already discussed in Chapter 5, you are going to want client/server access from the WebAccess agent to each post office.

WARNING

It's not possible to have a post office set to allow client/server only on the access mode, but have the WebAccess agent set to a direct connection. If this were the case, then user's using the WebAccess client would not be able to log in to their post office as the post office would reject direct connections coming from the WebAccess agent.

You can edit any of the post office links from this interface if they are not configured correctly. Simply highlight the post office you would like to edit and click the Edit Link button. This will give you the screen shown in Figure 11.16.

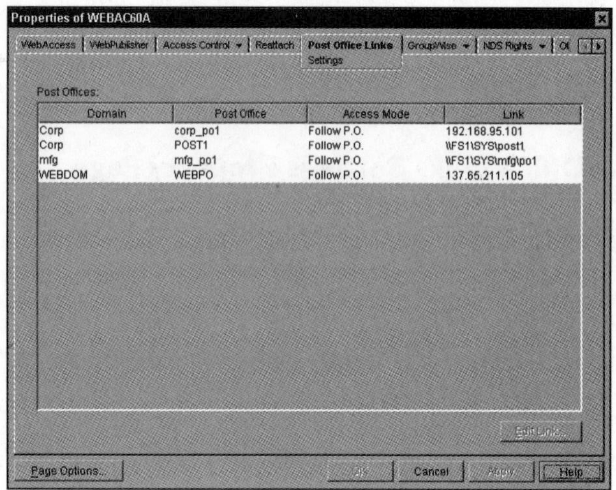

FIGURE 11.16 *The WebAccess Post Office Links Property Page*

Notice that the Post Office Links Settings window defines what the access mode for the post office is currently set to so that you don't have to pull up the details of each post office object to find this. Also, when you have Follow P.O. selected, you cannot modify the links; they are grayed out. This is because it will read the UNC path and IP address from the POA object record in the WPDOMAIN.DB and use it. If you select any of the other three options, you will be able to modify either the UNC path or the IP address and port.

IMPORTANT **When troubleshooting WebAccess to POA connectivity problems, come to the Post Office Links property page first. Quite often, WebAccess will have the incorrect IP address or port for the POA. Somehow, when a POA's IP information, or a post office's access method, does not get communicated well enough to WebAccess, coming in here and manually making changes is often the solution.**

Configuring the WebPublisher Settings Property Page

These settings are used only if you installed the WebPublisher piece of WebAccess during the initial install of the gateway. Here's an explanation of these options so that if you are running GroupWise document management you will be able to configure this piece of the WebAccess gateway.

- **WebPublisher Proxy User Mailbox ID:** This is the GroupWise mailbox ID of a GroupWise user that will actually be retrieving documents in the GroupWise system. Document management users must share their documents with this particular proxy user in order for them to view these documents from WebPublisher. The proxy user is just a GroupWise user that you create in your system, for the express purpose of supporting WebPublisher.
- **WebPublisher Proxy User Mailbox Password:** Enter the Proxy user's GroupWise password here.
- **Library Access:** Here is where you define what libraries will be visible from WebPublisher. If you have multiple libraries in your GroupWise system, you can allow or restrict access to these libraries for the WebPublisher agent.
- **Assign General User Access to WebPublisher Users:** If you enable this option, then documents in the available libraries that are accessible to general users are available through WebAccess. In other words, if a user creates a document and this particular document type is accessible by all users, then the WebPublisher proxy user would be able to see it, so the document would be available through WebPublisher. The owner of the document would not need to explicitly share it with the WebPublisher proxy user.

- **Disk Cache Size:** This setting determines the size of the disk cache where cached documents will reside. When a user retrieves a document from a GroupWise document management library from within WebPublisher, the document will be cached. This setting determines how large this cache can grow to.
- **Cache Synchronization Interval:** This value in seconds determines how often the WebPublisher application will synchronize the document(s) in the cache with the real document sitting in the GroupWise library.
- **Disk Cache Path:** This defines the location of the cache for documents that are retrieved via WebPublisher. It is recommended to have this directory located on the same server as the one where the WebAccess agent is running. The default location for this cache on a NetWare server is SYS\SYSTEM\CACHE; for NT, it is C:\GROUPWISE\CACHE.

You should now be comfortable in configuring the WebAccess agent and understand how these settings can affect the performance and functionality of your WebAccess agent.

The next section discusses the NDS objects that got created with the WebAccess application installation. It is through these NDS objects that you administer the remaining components of the WebAccess gateway.

Configuring the WebAccess Agent Sub-Components

As already explained, there are two main components of WebAccess: the agent and the application. To be technically correct, the WebAccess application refers to a couple of sub-components that work together to make up the WebAccess application. One of these components is referred to sometimes as the servlet component, and the others are referred to as the service provider components. These two sets of components work together in regards to the WebAccess application. Also, when you started the installation program, you noticed that there was an option called the WebPublisher application. Think of the WebPublisher application as a mirror piece to the WebAccess application with minor differences. They both perform the same functions, and they both talk to the same WebAccess agent(s). The WebPublisher application is used strictly for GroupWise document management access through a Web interface. It does *not* retrieve user's mail, appointments, tasks, and so on.

Before discussing the next few components of the WebAccess gateway, here's a list of what these additional objects are actually called:

- GroupWise WebAccess object
- GroupWise WebPublisher object
- NovellSpeller object
- GroupWise document provider object
- GroupWise provider object
- LDAP provider object

These six objects exist exclusively in the NDS tree and are located in the context specified during the install of the WebAccess application or WebPublisher application. (Remember that this context may be under the GroupWise NDS domain object. They are not necessarily associated with a domain and do not exist in the WPDOMAIN.DB databases.) These objects are used to configure and administer the GroupWise application pieces of WebAccess. Because GroupWise 6 offers many more features in WebAccess than previous versions, these objects needed a better way to manage these functions. Also, because GroupWise 6 WebAccess allows you to service multiple WebAccess agents from a single WebAccess application install, there has to be a way to manage just the WebAccess application pieces of the picture. So having said that, here's a discussion of the GroupWise WebAccess objects that will help you understand how these all relate to the big picture of WebAccess.

GroupWise WebAccess Object

The GroupWise WebAccess object is the main component of the WebAccess application. You could think of this object as being the WebAccess application object that loads as a servlet on the Web server. Through this object, you configure all the settings that will affect an end user's connection to WebAccess. This is the object that allows you to configure how an end user interacts with the WebAccess gateway. Feel free to pull up the properties of your own GroupWise WebAccess object in your NDS tree and follow along. To find the GroupWise WebAccess object, go into your NDS tree and highlight the GroupWise domain that you installed GroupWise WebAccess to. The GroupWise WebAccess sub-components discussed in this section are not available from the GroupWise view in ConsoleOne.

- **Application / Environment:** Here you define some of the basic environment settings for the WebAccess application object.

- **Configuration File:** This is the path to the WEBACC.CFG file. The WEBACC.CFG file contains all the configuration information regarding the GroupWise WebAccess object. This is a text file and can be viewed from any text editor. It is not recommended that you manually edit this file, because if you do, the changes would not be reflected on the GroupWise WebAccess object when you went to the details of it from ConsoleOne.
- **File Upload Path:** This is the path to which attachments are uploaded to the Web server when a user attaches a file to a newly composed e-mail from WebAccess. As soon as the user hits OK to attach a file, then WebAccess begins uploading it to this directory. This allows the upload to be taking place in the background while the user may continue to compose the mail message. After the message is sent or cancelled, the uploaded file is deleted from this upload directory.
- **Logout URL:** Here you can enter a URL that a user will be sent to when logging out of the WebAccess client. You can enter any URL here, and the user's browser will be directed there upon logging out. Very handy if you want to send the user to a particular Web site upon exiting.
- **Timeout for inactive sessions:** This setting allows you to configure how many minutes of inactivity must pass before a user's connection becomes disconnected from the application.
- **Path for inactive sessions:** Imagine that you were in the middle of composing an e-mail from the WebAccess client and were interrupted for several minutes. The inactive session timeout value kicks in, and you get disconnected. Have you lost that e-mail you were in the middle of composing? No! The WebAccess application saves your session before disconnecting you to this location. When you come back and re-authenticate to WebAccess, you can resume your e-mail that was half composed.
- **Use client IP in securing sessions:** If this option is checked, then the WebAccess application uses the client's IP address to help construct the hash value used to identify the user's browser session within the WebAccess application. Be aware, however, that if a user's browser is configured to use a proxy server, then there is a chance that the proxy server can use different IP addresses during the same session. This would cause *invalid hash* errors to appear on the WebAccess application. If you see this type of problem, you will want to disable this option.

- **Application / Log Settings:** This is where you may configure the log settings for the WebAccess application. Configuring log files is covered in even more detail in the section, "Understanding the GroupWise WebAccess Log Files."
- **Application / Services:** Here is where you can define what services are available through the WebAccess application by listing what are called GroupWise providers. These providers are discussed in just a bit. For now, think of this service tab as the ability to configure whether or not the WebAccess application can access either a WebAccess agent or an LDAP server. The reason for the LDAP server portion is because, from the WebAccess address book, you can query other LDAP servers to look up names and addresses in their directories. Without the LDAP provider defined as an active service on the GroupWise WebAccess object, LDAP lookups from the WebAccess client address book would fail. Similarly, if you did not have the GroupWise provider listed here as an active service, then the application could not physically talk to a GroupWise agent.

  You cannot have multiple instances of the same provider listed here. If you choose to edit a listed provider, it takes you to the properties of that particular provider, which you will read about shortly. Deleting a listed provider does not actually delete the provider from the system, but simply deletes it from the GroupWise WebAccess object, so that this service is not active from the GroupWise WebAccess object's point of view.
- **Application / Templates:** Here is where you can define where and what type of interface an end user sees when accessing WebAccess. It may be helpful for you to understand what *templates* are, first of all.

  You can think of templates as being the container that holds or displays the data that is retrieved from a user's mailbox located at the post office. Templates are associated with the type of browser or device being used to access WebAccess. For example, if you were to access your GroupWise mailbox from a standard Web browser such as Internet Explorer or Netscape, you would be using the standard HTML templates to view the contents of your mailbox. If you were to access your mailbox from a Windows CE device running a browser, you would probably want to use a different set of templates called *simple HTML* templates. Or if you were to access your mailbox from a wireless cellular phone, you would need to view your mail by using a different set of templates called *WML (wireless markup language)*. Templates are explained much more in Chapter 24. Just remember that templates are the key to how flexible the GroupWise

WebAccess system is as far as supporting and displaying the contents of a user's mailbox across many different types of devices. For now, this chapter talks about some of the basic configuration options that are available for the WebAccess application.

- **Template Path:** This defines where all the template directories exist. If you were to look in the actual directory defined here, you would see several subdirectories beneath these, one representing each set of templates that WebAccess supports.
  - **Java Package:** A Java package name is a directory path that uses the period (.) instead of a slash (\) to separate components of the path. This is really just a path that you are looking at here. This identifies the location of where the template string tables are located. Unless you are an HTML developer and creating your own custom templates, you will never need to modify this path.
  - **Images URL:** This is the path to the actual images that you see from the WebAccess client. These images are *.GIF files that make up the icons and buttons that you see from the browser.
  - **Applets URL:** This identifies the path to the WebAccess Applets. This should be blank unless you have moved the applets to a different server. You would then enter the path to another root directory. The default location of applets is beneath the Web server's document root directory.
  - **Help URL:** This is the path to the help HTML files. If WebAccess users want to pull up the online help, then they are directed to the INDEX.HTM file here.

TIP

Under this help directory, there is a subdirectory that represents the language that the user is using. For example, if the language is English then you will see an EN directory under the HELP directory, which would contain the INDEX.HTM. You could then create your own help files, if desired.

- **Enable Template Caching:** This option allows the WebAccess application to cache the templates in RAM the first time they are used. This increases performance.
- **Cache Size:** This value determines how much RAM the Web server will use to cache the templates. The default setting is large enough to contain all of the default templates. Unless you have created custom templates, you should not need to modify this setting.

- **Default Language:** This identifies the default language that will be presented to end users when they hit your Web server's home page and you have selected to use the default WebAccess home page.
- **Define User Interfaces:** Clicking this button allows you to set up custom user interfaces. This may be useful if you have users using different types of devices to access their mailboxes. More about this will be discussed in Chapter 24.
- **Application / Settings:** Here is where you can enable or disable options that end users will see from the WebAccess client. If you disable them, then the interface for that particular option will be missing for all WebAccess users hitting this particular WebAccess application.
- **Spell check items:** Here you can either enable or disable the end user's ability to spell-check newly composed e-mail messages before sending them.
- **Search LDAP directories:** If this is disabled, users will not be able to search the admin-defined LDAP servers for e-mail addresses. More about setting up LDAP servers will be discussed in the upcoming section, "Configuring an LDAP Address Book for WebAccess."
- **Change Passwords:** This allows end users to be able to change their GroupWise master mailbox password from WebAccess.
- **Access document management:** This allows or disallows an end user from accessing documents from within GroupWise libraries.
- **View attachments in HTML format:** This will be useful if you do not want to give end users the ability to view attachments from within WebAccess. It totally removes the view option from mail with attachments when they read them.
- **View documents in HTML format:** This option performs the same functionality as the preceding function. It will not allow documents from document management libraries to be rendered in HTML format for viewing.
- **Customize Settings in XML:** This button launches an XML editor that can be used to modify the settings on the WebAccess application as well.

NovellSpeller Object

The NovellSpeller object basically represents the GroupWise speller servlet object. It is created when you install the WebAccess application object. The speller servlet object automatically starts when the WebAccess application is loaded by the Web server.

- **Application / Log Settings:** From here, you can configure the log settings for the speller. Speller-logging is discussed in even more detail in the upcoming section, "Understanding the GroupWise WebAccess Log Files."
- **Application / Environment:** This is really the only thing that you can configure on the speller object, other than the logging.
- **Configuration File:** This is the path to the spell checker's configuration file. It is a text file and contains all of the configuration information regarding the spell checker.
- **Dictionary Path:** This is the path to the dictionary files that contain the word lists and suggestions when spell checking something.
- **Maximum Suggestions:** Here you can enter the maximum number of suggestions to give when a misspelled word is encountered during a spell check.
- **Customize Settings in XML:** Here you can also modify these settings from and XML configuration editor.

GroupWise Provider Object

The GroupWise provider object works in conjunction with the GroupWise WebAccess object or the WebAccess application. Think of it as the actual transport provider that is responsible for carrying the data between the WebAccess agent and the WebAccess application. This may sound a bit confusing because the entire chapter has been saying that the GroupWise WebAccess application will talk directly to the WebAccess agent. Basically it does, but for administration purposes, it has been broken out into providers.

A user's Web browser talks to a servlet running on the Web server. This servlet functions as the default WebAccess application. The application then looks up what providers it has access to and hands the request over to the appropriate provider. This all happens on the same server. There is not an actual separate program that acts as the provider; it is all bundled into the WebAccess application but it acts as a separate, configurable sub-process of the WebAccess application. The provider then communicates directly to the agent. If you think of it this way, then it will be much easier to understand how the provider objects relate to the WebAccess application or servlets.

- **Provider / Environment:** Configuring the GroupWise provider object is really quite simple and straightforward. Below are the properties of the GroupWise provider object.

- **Timeout for Busy Search:** This value sets the number of minutes that the provider waits when doing a busy search to the WebAccess agent. This allows the administrator to have some control over how soon busy searches are cancelled through the WebAccess client.

NOTE

A busy search is a feature that allows you to check when other GroupWise users may be available for scheduling an appointment with them through the GroupWise calendar.

- **Configuration File:** This simply points to the COMMGR.CFG file that the provider uses to determine both where the WebAccess agent is (the IP address and port) and how to encrypt the data in transit using the encryption key embedded in the COMMGR.CFG file.
- **GroupWise WebAccess Agents:** This is where you list all of the WebAccess agents that the provider will be able to communicate with. You must have at least one agent defined here, but you can have multiple agents defined. This gives you a level of fault tolerance in regards to the WebAccess agent. More information regarding fault tolerance with WebAccess is discussed in the section titled "Configuring GroupWise WebAccess for More Scalability and Stability."

LDAP Provider Object

The LDAP provider object basically serves the same function as the GroupWise provider object; the WebAccess application sends requests for LDAP lookups to it, and then the LDAP provider does the looking up and hands the results back to the GroupWise WebAccess object. The LDAP provider does *not* communicate with the WebAccess agent like the GroupWise provider object does. Instead, it queries whatever LDAP servers have been configured for lookups directly.

- **Configuration File:** This points to the path to the LDAP configuration file. This is a text file that contains all the configuration information for the LDAP provider. This file would contain the settings for the LDAP servers, for example.
- **LDAP Servers:** This lists the configured LDAP servers that would be available to search from the WebAccess client. In the upcoming section, "Configuring an LDAP Address Book for WebAccess," you learn how to set up additional LDAP services here.
- **Customize Settings in XML:** Once again, you can configure these settings from the XML configuration editor, if desired.

You should now be comfortable in configuring most of the aspects of the WebAccess gateway, including the WebAccess agent and application. In future sections, you will learn how to leverage these settings to create a highly reliable, and scalable, GroupWise WebAccess gateway for your environment.

Understanding the GroupWise WebAccess Console

This section discusses what each of the options mean when you view the WebAccess console. This section goes through each statistic, as they are very helpful in knowing the status of the WebAccess agent. Figure 11.17 shows the WebAccess agent console for a WebAccess agent running on the NetWare platform.

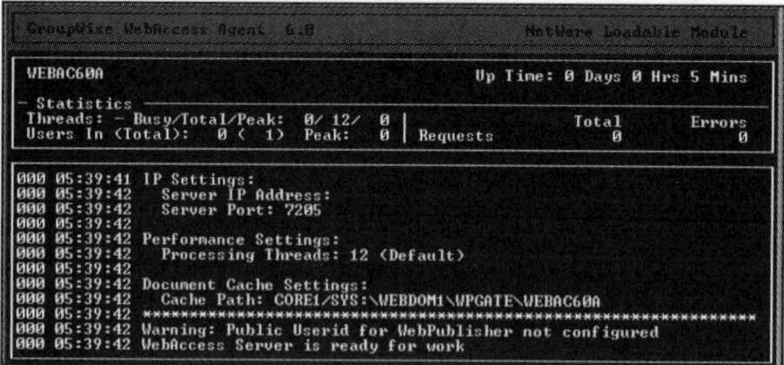

FIGURE 11.17 *The WebAccess Agent Console Screen on NetWare*

- **Statistics – Threads:** Here are some of the most valuable statistics you can gather from the WebAccess agent. There are three different thread values here. The Busy value represents how many WebAccess threads are currently in use. The Total value represents how many total threads are available to service requests. This would be the maximum number of threads available total. The Peak value represents the maximum number of concurrent threads that have been active at the same time.
- **Users In (Total) – Peak:** There are three values here as well. The Users In value lists the number of currently logged in users at this moment in time. The Total value is the total number of users that have logged in since the agent has been up. (Up Time is in the upper right corner of the WebAccess

agent to help you determine how long the agent has been running.) The Peak value represents the maximum number of users that have been logged in at the same time.

- **Requests:** There are two statistics here. The Total request value represents how many total requests have come into the WebAccess agent since it has been up. The Errors value shows how many errors have occurred since the agent has been up. You can view the log files to find out what errors may have occurred. In the upcoming section, "Monitoring GroupWise WebAccess through a Web Browser," you will learn how to search these log files.
- **Logging Box:** This is the window directly under the Statistics window, and it displays the activity that is occurring on the WebAccess agent. The far left value represents the thread number that is performing the task. Next is the time that the event occurred, and last is the information associated with the particular request being logged. The logging level determines how much information is displayed here.
- **F9 = Browse Logfile:** Pressing F9 from the agent console screen brings up a static copy of the current log file. Notice that at the beginning of each log file is the basic configuration information of the agent. It may be helpful information to verify what settings the agent is using.
- **F10 = Options:** Pressing F10 brings up a dialog box with two options: View Log files and Logging Options. If you select to view log files here, you are given a list of all the log files that the WebAccess agent has created over a period of time. You can select any of the log files and view their contents. If you select the Logging Options option, then you can change the current log settings that the agent is using. These log settings will be discussed further in the upcoming section, "Understanding the GroupWise WebAccess Log Files."

TIP

When you change these log settings here, they are active only during the timeframe that the WebAccess agent is up and running. When the WebAccess agent gets restarted, it will pick up the log settings from either the startup file or the setting defined through the properties of the WebAccess agent object in ConsoleOne.

If you are running the WebAccess agent on Windows NT, the console screen is quite different. Figure 11.18 shows the console screen of an agent running on Windows NT.

```
Novell GroupWise WebAccess
000 00:12:35 ***** WebAccess Configuration Information *****
000 00:12:35
000 00:12:35 General Settings:
000 00:12:35   Gateway Home Directory: d:\do3\wpgate\do3_wac1
000 00:12:35   Work Directory: d:\do3\wpgate\do3_wac1
000 00:12:35   Server Platform: Windows NT 5.0 Build 2195 Service Pack 2
000 00:12:35
000 00:12:35 IP Settings:
000 00:12:36   Server IP Address: ERAFF_LAP
000 00:12:36   Server Port: 7205
000 00:12:36
000 00:12:36 Performance Settings:
000 00:12:36   Processing Threads: 12 (Default)
000 00:12:36
000 00:12:36 Document Cache Settings:
000 00:12:36   Cache Path: D:\do3\WPGATE\Do3_Wac1
000 00:12:36
000 00:12:36 SNMP Enabled for the WebAccess Agent
000 00:12:36 ****************************************************************
000 00:12:36 Warning: Public Userid for WebPublisher not configured
000 00:12:36 WebAccess Server is ready for work
_
```

FIGURE 11.18 *The WebAccess Agent Console Screen on Windows*

You do have some function keys that help to control the console screen from within Windows. Here are the commands you can issue from the console when running on Windows NT/2000.

- **F1 or F7:** Pressing F1 or F7 from the agent screen will exit the WebAccess agent.
- **F2:** Pressing F2 will cycle the log level on the WebAccess agent. The available levels are normal (default), verbose, and diagnostic. Normal is usually adequate unless you are troubleshooting a particular problem with the agent and need additional logging information.

TIP

Using F2 to set the log level is active only as long as the WebAccess agent is up. If it is restarted, the log level is set to what has been defined in either the startup file, or the WPDOMAIN.DB through ConsoleOne.

- **F12:** Pressing F12 will display the statistics and thread activity of the agent. This is exactly the same thread information that you get from the agent when it is running on NetWare as an NLM. The values mean the same thing. It also gives you the current log level, whether disk logging is enabled, and the name of the current log file.

TIP

The F12 functionality does not exist in previous versions of the NT WebAccess agent, only in the GroupWise 6 version.

As you can see, there are not a lot of different statistics or configuration pieces to the WebAccess agent compared to some of the other agents or gateways.

Understanding the GroupWise WebAccess Log Files

This section explains how to access and understand the different log files that are generated by the components that make up the WebAccess gateway. Having log files being generated can be invaluable in troubleshooting and resolving problems with any GroupWise component, not just WebAccess. The log files are generated by the following pieces of the GroupWise WebAccess gateway:

- WebAccess agent
- WebAccess application
- WebAccess speller application
- WebPublisher application.

To begin with, here's a definition of some of the standard logging settings that most of the components in WebAccess share:

- **Log File Path:** This defines the path where the log files will be located for a particular agent or application. If this path is blank, then the agent uses the default logging location for the log files.
- **Logging Level:** This setting defines what the logging level is set to for the agent or application. The valid settings are generally normal (default), verbose, diagnostics, or off. The higher the level of logging, the more detailed the log files will be. Diagnostic logging should only be used if troubleshooting a problem and you need very detailed information as to what is happening at the particular agent or application level. You should not run diagnostic logging as a standard practice. Normal or verbose will suffice.
- **Max Log File Age:** This setting allows you to set the number of days that log files will be kept. If, say, this is set to seven days (the default), then when a log file reaches an age of seven days, the agent or application will automatically delete this log file. I like to increase this setting to around 30 days if possible, as you never know when you may need to dig back through a few weeks' worth of log files to help track down and troubleshoot problems.
- **Max Log Disk Space:** This setting determines how much disk space that *all* of the log files for a particular agent or application can consume. It is *not* how large a single log file can grow to. All the individual log files will be

256K in size, and then the agent or application will cycle into another log file. As mentioned, this setting allows you to control how much disk space is being used by the log files. The default is 1024K, or 1 MB worth of log files. I also like to increase this setting. It depends on your environment as to how large you set this value. I have seen systems where 10 MB worth of logs would keep only a couple of day's worth because of the volume of information that was being generated. You will want to take a baseline of your system to see what value would work best for you in your environment.

So basically either the max log file age or the max log disk space setting will take precedence over each other, whatever is reached first. Having these two settings together allow you to completely control how many and how long the log files stick around for your WebAccess processes. Now that you understand some of the shared characteristics of logging on the WebAccess processes, here's a discussion that points out any unique differences between the different processes.

WebAccess Agent Log Settings

By default, the WebAccess agent does not generate a log file to disk. You must enable this option by adding the /logdiskon switch to the STRTWEB.NCF file. This will enable disk logging for the WebAccess agent. Without this switch, the WebAccess agent will not log to disk any events. The default location of the WebAccess agent log files is the DOMAIN\WPGATE\WEBAC60A\000.PRC directory, but can be changed with the log file path setting on the agent.

There are also startup switches that allow you to set all the logging options from the command line when the agent is loaded. These switches would be contained in the STRTWEB.NCF file and are the following:

- **/log=:** Path to log files.
- **/logdiskon:** Enables disk logging.
- **/loglevel=:** Sets the log level. Values are normal, verbose, or diagnostic.
- **/logdays=:** Sets the number of days to keep logs. Enter a number that represents days.
- **/logmax=:** Sets the size of log files. Enter a size in kilobytes.

GroupWise WebAccess Object Log settings

The GroupWise WebAccess object log settings, or in other words, the WebAccess application settings, are configured by going to the properties of the

GroupWise WebAccess object and selecting Application / Log Settings. Figure 11.19 is a screen shot of what you will see.

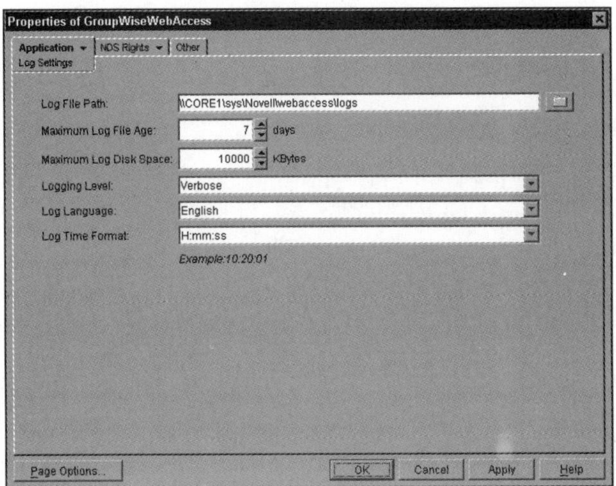

FIGURE 11.19 *The GroupWIse WebAccess Object Application Log Settings*

Notice that here you have a couple additional options above the standard settings:

- **Log Language:** This allows you to define the language that the log files will be written in.
- **Log Time Format:** This allows you to change the format of the time value displayed in the log file. The default is H:mm:ss for Hour:Minute:Second. If desired, you can change this order. You have the option of adding MM/dd or dd/MM for Month/Day or Day/Month to the logging, which may be useful.

TIP

The name of each WebAccess application log file will be in the format of MMDDWAS.XXX, where XXX is an incremented number throughout a 24-hour time period. The agent always cycles to a new log at 24:00 hours.

WebAccess Speller Application

Configuring the speller log settings is similar to the agent and application log settings. This can be done by going to the properties of the NovellSpeller object in NDS. For this agent, you do not have the options of setting the max log disk space and max log file age, however.

WebAccess WebPublisher Application

The WebAccess WebPublisher log settings are exactly the same as the GroupWise WebAccess object settings.

Configuring GroupWise WebAccess for More Scalability and Stability

For this section, the topic centers around shoring up and making the WebAccess system more scalable and fault tolerant. With only one WebAccess application and agent running, if either of these components has a failure, all users would be unable to access their mailboxes through WebAccess. There are lots of good reasons why GroupWise administrators would be interested in this section. Think of it, with multiple agents set up and running being serviced by multiple applications, the overall WebAccess availability will be greatly enhanced. It also allows you to bring down pieces of the WebAccess system, without interrupting all access to user's mailboxes. This is useful for upgrades, or maintenance on anything from the GroupWise system to servers to applications running on the servers. I have tried to lay the groundwork in the previous sections for this particular section. First, I begin by discussing what is involved with getting multiple agents and application services working together.

Configuring Multiple Agents and Application Servers for a Fault-Tolerant WebAccess System

With the introduction of GroupWise 6 WebAccess, administrators have the ability to set up multiple agents and applications that all work together. This section explores how to configure a single application to talk to multiple agents. It also discusses how configuring multiple agents can provide a very fault-tolerant WebAccess system. With a simple install of WebAccess, you have only one WebAccess application talking to a single WebAccess agent. There is very little that changes when you consider setting up multiple applications talking to multiple agents. Here is an example scenario that discusses how to make it all work together.

You want to have the WebAccess application on your Web server communicate with two different WebAccess agents that are installed in close proximity to the two major sections of your WAN. In this scenario, you will see how to configure and set this up.

Before explaining exactly how to configure and set up this scenario, it is very important that you understand how a WebAccess application knows what agent or agents it should communicate with. When there is more than one WebAccess agent installed in your GroupWise system, the application must check to see what agent the user should be directed to. If you read Chapter 5, it mentioned that you can configure a default WebAccess object for a domain or post office. Configuring a default WebAccess setting on users' domains or post offices is critical to setting up multiple agents in a GroupWise system. Here is the order that the application will check to see what WebAccess agent to log a particular user in to:

1. If there is an agent specified in the URL field that is entered when a request hits the Web server where the WebAccess application is running on, the application does no lookups and sends the user request directly to the agent that was defined in the URL. An example of what this URL may look like is the following:

   ```
   http://mail.worldwidewidgets.com/servlet/webacc?GWAP.ip=192.168.
   5.5&GWAP.port=7205
   ```

   The IP address would reflect the IP Address of the server where the WebAccess agent is running, and the port is the port the WebAccess agent is listening on.

2. If there was no agent defined in the URL, then the application does a lookup to see if there is a default WebAccess definition defined at this user's post office. If so, the user is routed to this agent.

3. If there was no default WebAccess defined at the user's post office, a lookup is performed on the user's domain for a defined default WebAccess object. If one is found here, the user is routed to this agent.

4. If there was no default WebAccess agent defined at the domain, the application will look at the service provider that it is associated with and route the user to the first agent defined in the GroupWise WebAccess agent's list.

5. If there are no defined agents for the service provider, then the application will read the COMMGR.CFG file located in the SYS:\NOVELL\WebAccess directory and route the request to this agent.

This list not only supplies the application with the information on what agent to send the user to but also what agents to fail over to if any agents are down. For example, if there was a default WebAccess agent defined at the domain level, but it was unavailable, the application would then roll over to the next lookup method, which would be the agents defined at the service provider level, and send the request to the first agent here. If this agent were down, it would cycle to the next defined agent for the service provider, if there were one. If none of the defined agents for the service provider are accessible, the last resort is to hit the agent listed inside the COMMGR.CFG file. If this agent is down, the user will not be able to log in.

Phew, that is quite a paragraph! The next section breaks all this down into a couple of examples to make sure you understand how the lookup/failover model works.

Lookup/Failover List: Scenario 1

Presume that you have three agents installed in your GroupWise system, all being serviced by one application.

DEFINITION	WEBACCESS AGENT
Entered URL	No agent defined in URL (`webmail.worldwidewidgets.com`)
Post office	Agent 1 defined as the default agent for this post office
Domain	No agent defined
Agents defined at service provider	Agent 2
	Agent 1
COMMGR.CFG file	Agent 3

With this configuration, when a user logs in, the application would build a list of WebAccess agents that it would use to send the user's request to. If any of these agents were down, the application would cycle to the next agent in the list. From the preceding table, the following table is what the application would build in regards to what agent this user should be sent/failed over to.

APPLICATION LIST VALUE	GENERATED FROM
Agent 1	Post office definition
Agent 2	Service provider list
Agent 1	Service provider list
Agent 3	COMMGR.CFG file

Because there was an agent defined for the user's post office, this was the first agent that the application would try to hit. If this agent were down, it would have sent the user to the first agent listed in the service provider's list. If both of these agents had been down, the last agent it would have sent the request to would be the agent listed in the COMMGR.CFG file.

Lookup/Failover List – Scenario 2

Assume that you have four agents installed in your GroupWise system now, all being serviced by one application.

DEFINITION	WEBACCESS AGENT
Entered URL	No agent defined in URL (webmail.worldwidewidgets.com)
Post office	No default agent defined for the post office
Domain	Agent 2 is defined as the default agent for this domain
Agents defined at service provider	Agent 1
	Agent 3
COMMGR.CFG file	Agent 3

From the preceding table, the following table is what the application would build in regards to what agent this user should be sent/failed over to.

APPLICATION LIST VALUE	GENERATED FROM
Agent 2	Domain agent definition
Agent 1	Service provider list
Agent 3	Service provider list
Agent 3	COMMGR.CFG file

In this scenario, you will see that potentially you can have the application trying to hit the same agent, depending on your setup and configuration. You should carefully plan how you will define the agents that the users will be directed to. With the understanding you now have, you should be able to now design a very reliable WebAccess system.

Here's one more additional little piece that is important. How does the application know whether there is a default WebAccess agent defined at the domain or post office level? This information is not stored on the Web server, and the application was never designed to talk directly to a GroupWise domain database to discover this information. Here is what happens.

In order to build the list of agents when a user logs in, the application must find out if there is a default WebAccess gateway defined at the domain or post office level for the user. When the user ID and password are entered at the Login page for WebAccess, the application sends this informtion to the service provider, and the service provider contacts the first agent defined here. It then queries this agent and asks the agent to look in the domain database for a default WebAccess agent defined at either the post office or domain level. This agent then returns the results back to the application through the service provider. Now that the application knows whether or not the user has a default WebAccess agent defined, it can build the correct list of agents to route the user too.

Now that you understand the lookup and failover model, here is how to configure this type of a setup.

Matching Encryption Keys

The first thing that must be considered here is that for a single WebAccess application to be able to talk to multiple agents, the encryption key between the application and all agents it communicates with *must* be the same. The WebAccess application will read the COMMGR.CFG file located by default in the \NOVELL\WebAccess directory of the Web server. Remember that this COMMGR.CFG file contains the encryption key that must match the encryption key stored in the COMMGR.CFG file located in the DOMAIN\WPGATE\WEBAC60A directory for *each* of the WebAccess agents. The easiest way to facilitate seamless communication from the application to each agent is to make the encryption key the same for all agents that a single WebAccess application will be configured to talk to. (A simple copy-and-paste procedure works great.) This is done by editing the WebAccess agent that is directly associated with a particular GroupWise domain and accessing the WebAccess settings. Figure 11.20 shows this screen.

From here, you should enter the exact same encryption key on all agents. This will update the COMMGR.CFG file on both the application and agents directories.

Configuring the Default WebAccess Agents for a Domain or Post Office

To configure a default WebAccess agent at the domain or post office level, you need to access the properties of the respective domain or post office object. From the respective property pages, choose the GroupWise ⇨ Default WebAccess properties page. From here, you click the override box in order to browse out through the NDS tree and select the appropriate WebAccess agent object.

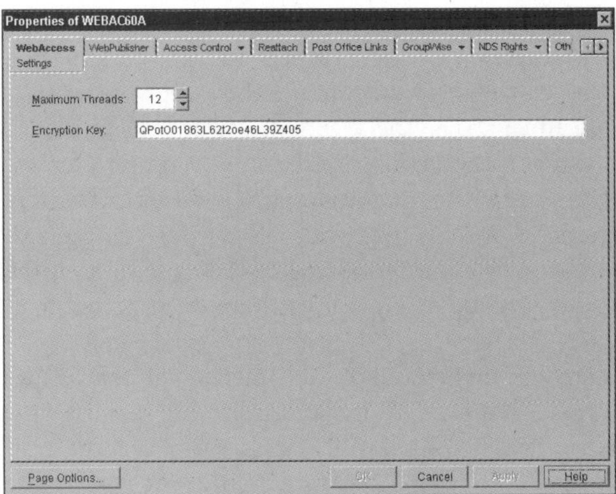

FIGURE 11.20 *Editing the WebAccess Encryption Key*

To configure the agents known by the service provider, you need to access the property page of the GroupWise provider object. From here, you can add, edit, or delete any WebAccess agents from the list. Remember that the application will start at the top of this list and work down when it builds its login/failover table for when a user logs in. You must add the agents to this list in the order that you want them searched.

You need to now double-check that the WebAccess application object has the correct WebAccess provider defined so that it knows what provider to look up the agents from.

This is configured by going to the details of the GroupWise WebAccess object and selecting the services option under the application tab. From here you can add, edit, or delete providers that are defined in your tree.

Running the WebAccess Agent on Windows NT/2000

This discussion talks about a good reason to run the WebAccess agent on Windows NT.

The WebAccess agent allows users to read their mail. Many times users have mail with all sorts of different types of attachments. If the user reads a message from WebAccess and there is, for example, a spreadsheet attached to a message, the user has the option of either viewing it or saving it to the local workstation. If the user decides to view the document, then the WebAccess agent must be able to render it into HTML format so that it can be displayed on the end user's browser. The viewer files that WebAccess uses for rendering attached documents are not written by Novell. WebAccess uses Inso Viewer technology to accomplish this task. To put it simply, the Inso Viewers are more stable when running on their native Windows platform versus running as NLMs that have been ported to the NetWare platform.

So if your users are frequently viewing complex attachments, you may want to consider running the WebAccess agent on an NT platform simply because of the viewing issue. From experience, the NT/2000 WebAccess agent is more stable when it comes to viewing attachments than the NetWare WebAccess agent. Novell does work with the company that produces the Inso Viewers to resolve known viewer problems. Because of this, there are updates that Novell receives to the viewer files. If you are having problems with the WebAccess agent, you will want to make sure that you are using the latest viewer files. On NetWare, you can identify the dates of your viewer files by looking in the SYS:\SYSTEM directory (or the directory you specified to install the agent files to) and look for files that start with VS*.NLM, as well as the SCC*.NLM files. On Windows NT, they have the same names — except they have .DLL extensions instead of .NLM extensions — and exist in the C:\WebAcc directory by default (or wherever you specified the agent files to reside when you installed the WebAccess agent on NT).

I do not recommend running the GroupWise WebAccess application on a Windows NT/2000 server. The GroupWise WebAccess application runs much better on a NetWare server. Also, the servlet gateway, which is a Java application, works more reliably on the NetWare platform.

Installing the WebAccess Agent to Run on Windows NT/2000

This procedure assumes that you have either an NT 4 or Windows 2000 server that you will be installing the WebAccess agent to.

WARNING

The Novell client for Windows NT/2000 must be installed to the Windows NT/2000 server in order to do a successful installation. After installing and configuring the new GroupWise domain and WebAccess agent components, you may remove the Novell client for Windows 2000/NT. If you do not establish a GroupWise domain on the Windows 2000/NT server, you must keep the Novell client installed.

I recommend that before installing the GroupWise WebAccess agent for Windows NT/2000, where possible, to have the WPDOMAIN.DB on the hard drive of the Windows NT server that will be running the Windows NT WebAccess agent. To do this, you must first install a GroupWise domain to the Windows NT/2000 server.

Installing a GroupWise Domain on a Windows NT/2000 Server

The following are instructions on how to install a GroupWise domain on an NT/2000 server:

1. Be logged into your Novell NDS tree where your GroupWise system is involved using the Novell client, as well as at the Windows NT/2000 server that you will be configuring to run the GroupWise WebAccess agent for Windows NT/2000.
2. Connect to the primary domain for your GroupWise system.
3. Create a new GroupWise domain by highlighting the GroupWise system object, clicking the right-mouse button, and choosing New ➪ Domain. Establish the domain on the hard drive of the Windows NT server.
4. When the domain is created, in ConsoleOne, choose Tools ➪ GroupWise System Operations ➪ Select Domain to make sure that you are connected to the WPDOMAIN.DB file on the hard drive of the Windows NT server.
5. Edit the MTA object for the new domain on the NT server by filling in the IP information for the MTA.

   The IP address will correspond to the IP address of the NT server.
6. Now change the link information for the new GroupWise domain on the NT server, by choosing Tools ➪ GroupWise ➪ Link Configuration.

   Make sure that the new GroupWise domain connects via IP to at least one domain in your system.

7. Install the GroupWise MTA software for the Windows NT/2000 platform.

   This software is located in your <GroupWise 6 software distribution directory>\AGENTS folder.

8. Load the GroupWise MTA for your newly created GroupWise domain on the Windows NT/2000 server.

   Make sure that the MTA is communicating with the rest of the GroupWise system.

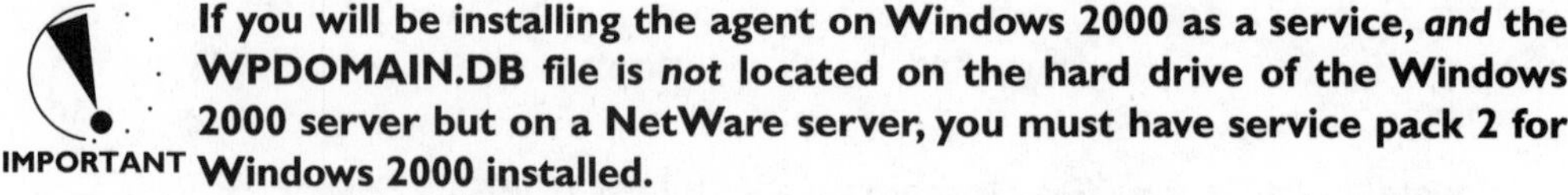

IMPORTANT **If you will be installing the agent on Windows 2000 as a service, *and* the WPDOMAIN.DB file is *not* located on the hard drive of the Windows 2000 server but on a NetWare server, you must have service pack 2 for Windows 2000 installed.**

Installing a GroupWise WebAccess Agent on a Windows NT/2000 Server

This section walks you through installing a WebAccess agent on an NT/2000 server:

1. Run **Setup.exe** from the INTERNET\WebAccess directory on the GroupWise 6 CD and accept the license agreement.
2. Select to install just the WebAccess agent and click Next.
3. Now select the platform, which will be Windows NT.

   If you need to modify that path to where the agent files will be copied to, you may do so here and then click next. When you click next, you will be prompted to create the directory if it already does not exist. You will also be prompted to shut down any agents that may be running on this Windows NT box.

IMPORTANT **The install for NT does not attempt to stop any GroupWise agents that may already be running on the NT server. You must manually perform this operation to shut down all GroupWise agents on the NT server.**

You are then prompted to enter the IP address or DNS name of the NT server. The install will try to discover this information for you. The IP address that is discovered is the static IP address that is assigned to the NT server. If you are installing the agent to a Windows NT workstation, it is highly recommended that you obtain a static IP address for the workstation.

4. Enter or verify the IP address or DNS name, as well as the port, and click Next.

   You then are prompted to enter the path to the domain database and define a gateway directory. You can accept the default gateway directory of WEBAC60A or enter a different gateway directory here.

5. Enter the correct path and gateway directory and click Next.

   Next you will define the name of the WebAccess agent object. This is the object that represents the gateway in NDS. It defaults to the same name as was entered in Step 5 for the WebAccess directory name. It is recommended that this name be the same as the directory name.

6. Verify or enter the object name and click Next.

   This next step is the first big difference between a NetWare install and a Windows install. You are asked whether or not you want to install and configure SNMP support for the WebAccess agent, as well as whether you want to run the agent as a Windows service. If you enable the option to install SNMP support, the install allows the agent to be monitored via SNMP. If you would like to run the agent as a service, you must select how the service will be configured for startup. The default is to automatically start the WebAccess agent service. The advantages of running the agent as a service is that it will load automatically when the Windows NT box is booted up. The disadvantage is that the shipping version of the WebAccess agent running on NT as a service does not allow you to actually view the console. This is termed Allow to interact with desktop when installing, say, an MTA or a POA to run as a service on an NT server. With at least the shipping version of GroupWise 5, if you feel you need to be able to see the WebAccess agent screen, you should not install the agent as a service.

7. Select the appropriate options and click next.

   If installing as a service, you are then asked to enter a user name and password. This user name and password allow the service to log into the Windows NT box in order to load. The install script does not allow you to use the system account for the service. If you are not installing as a service, this question is not asked.

8. If you get this prompt, enter a user name and password of a user that exists as a user that has rights to this particular NT server.

If the WPDOMAIN.DB file is located on a different server than the NT box, then this user name and password must be the same for the Windows account and the NDS account.

9. You now get the option to enable the WebConsole for the WebAccess agent, so go ahead and select to enable this, enter a non-NDS user name and password, and click Next.

10. At the following summary screen, review the information about how the agent will be installed, and click Next.

    The agent will begin copying the necessary agent files for the agent to run on Windows NT. The last thing that the install will do is to create the NDS object for the WebAccess agent under the domain object. You must have access to the NDS tree from the workstation you are running the install from. If you do not, then you will be prompted with an NDS login screen during this portion of the install. You will need to log in to complete the install.

Starting the GroupWise WebAccess Agent Service for Windows NT/2000

There are two approaches to starting the agent when it is running on Windows NT. If you installed the agent as a service, then you must start and stop the agent using the services manager. To access Windows NT services, open the control panel and select the services option. This displays all available services on the local NT box. You should see a service called *WebAccess <name of your agent>*. Just highlight this service, and you will be able to start or stop it. You can also configure how this service will start by default. Your options are Manual (you must manually load the agent), Automatically (the service will start with the Windows NT box is booted), or Disabled (the service will be disabled and cannot be started until enabled).

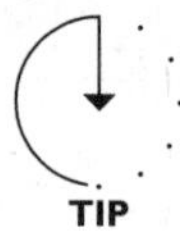

With the original shipping version of the GroupWise 6 agent running on Windows NT, if you set it up to run as a service, it will not allow you to see the console screen for the agent.

When you run the WebAccess agent as a service, elements such as the home path are all stored in the Windows registry, so there is not a STRTWEB.BAT file as there would be if you did not install the WebAccess agent as a service. Windows simply reads the appropriate information regarding the WebAccess agent service in order to load the agent up.

Starting the GroupWise WebAccess Agent from a Batch File

If when you installed your WebAccess agent, you did not install it as a service, the WebAccess agent is started with a batch file. This file is found in the C:\WebAcc directory (or the directory specified during the install of the agent). You will find a file called STRTWEB.BAT. Following is a sample of a default STRTWEB.BAT file:

```
title Novell GroupWise WebAccess
@echo off
cls
GWINTER.EXE /ph=D:\do3\WPGATE\Do3_Wac1
```

Starting the agent when running on Windows NT is as simple as running this batch file. You can modify this bat file to include additional switches, if desired. You may also want to add this batch file to the startup folder on the Windows NT server. This will cause the agent to start automatically *after* a user is logged into the NT server.

You should now be familiar with how to start both the NetWare and NT versions of the WebAccess agent.

Configuring an LDAP Address Book for WebAccess

This section explains how to configure an LDAP address book. The LDAP address book is used when a user logs into the WebAccess client and selects the address book. From here, the user can perform LDAP lookups on predefined LDAP servers. As an administrator, you have the flexibility of defining additional LDAP servers, allowing users to query LDAP compliant servers for addresses. The GroupWise Windows 32-bit client gives users the ability to define LDAP address books, and so this functionality has also been added to the GroupWise WebAccess client. By default, there are two LDAP servers created when the WebAccess application is installed. They are the popular public LDAP servers *BigFoot* and *SwitchBoard*.

Configuring additional LDAP servers is done through the LDAP provider object. This object was created when the WebAccess application was installed. Figure 11.21 shows the details of the LDAP provider object.

Here you will see the two default LDAP servers. You are presented with a configuration screen that allows you to set up the new LDAP server.

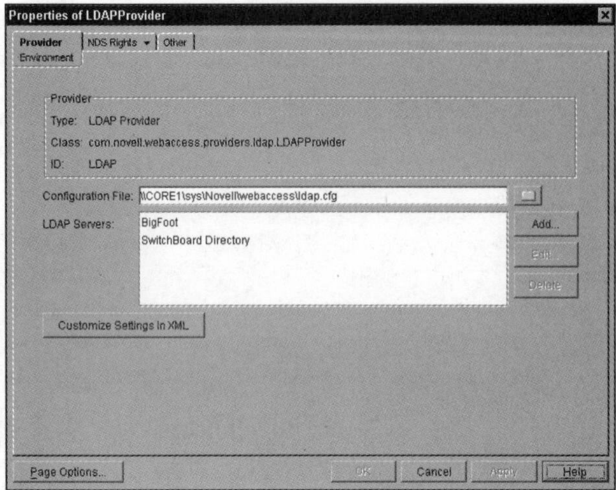

FIGURE 11.21 *The GroupWise WebAccess LDAP Provider Object Details*

- **Name:** Enter the name of the LDAP server. This is the name that the end user will see when selecting an LDAP server to search from the WebAccess client.
- **Server:** Enter the DNS name or IP address of the server that is servicing LDAP requests from clients.
- **Port:** The standard LDAP port is 389. If the LDAP server that you are defining here has been configured to use a different port, you should modify this field. If not, keep the default port.
- **Maximum Results:** Enter the maximum number of results that can be returned to the WebAccess client from the LDAP server. The default is 100.
- **Timeout:** The timeout value here represents how long the LDAP provider will wait on the configured LDAP server for a reply. The default is 30 seconds.
- **Search Base:** Enter the search base value here. LDAP servers allow you to configure a search base that sets limits on how many objects can be searched. When the LDAP server was set up, there should have been a search base defined. This search base should match up with the search base defined on the LDAP server.
- **Image URL:** This is the path to the image file that you would like displayed to represent the particular LDAP server you are defining. This path must be

defined off the root of the Web server DOCS directory. For the NetScape Enterprise Web server, this would be the SYS:\NOVONYX\SUITESPOT\DOCS directory. If using the NetScape Enterprise Web server and your GIF representing the LDAP server is physically located at SYS:\NOVONYX\SUITESPOT\DOCS\COM\NOVELL\WEBACCESS\IMAGES\YOURPIC.GIF, the image URL would be `/com/novell/webaccess/images/yourpic.gif`.

- **Web URL:** This is where users will be sent if they click on the image defined in the Image URL: value. This is a nice way to link a Web site to the LDAP server graphic.
- **Username:** Enter the LDAP user name that must be used to authenticate to the LDAP server you are defining.
- **Password:** Enter the LDAP user name's password here. This allows the LDAP provider object to authenticate to the LDAP server and perform the query, if necessary.
- **Define Field Mappings:** Click this option to set up field mappings. If your LDAP server is configured to return additional values for each user, you can map these fields to fields that will be displayed in the WebAccess client.

  The field mappings are default. If you need to add additional field mappings, click Add. This will add an additional row where you can then type in the LDAP and local fields.

Monitoring GroupWise WebAccess through a Web Browser

This section discusses the options you have for monitoring your WebAccess agent through any standard Web browser. In order to have this functionality, the WebAccess agent must be enabled to allow HTTP monitoring. This can be done during the install, with startup switches, or by modifying the WebAccess agent object from ConsoleOne.

Once you have the HTTP monitoring enabled for a WebAccess agent, you can browse to the agent using a Web browser. Figure 11.22 is a screen shot of a WebAccess agent that is being monitored from a Web browser.

Here's an explanation of some of the information shown in Figure 11.22:

- **Status:** The status page shows you the current status of the WebAccess agent. Here you can get a good idea of how the WebAccess agent is performing. Notice under the Statistics section that you can view how much memory the server has as well as the current processor utilization of the server.

NOTE

If the agent is running on an NT server, you do not get the processor utilization reading.

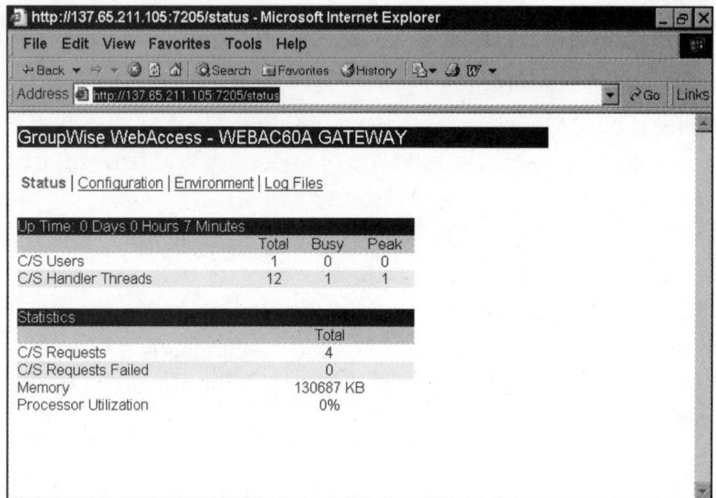

FIGURE 11.22 *Monitoring GroupWise WebAccess through a Web Browser*

- **Configuration:** The configuration tab shows you the current configuration of the WebAccess agent. This is helpful if you need to check how the WebAccess agent is configured. You can quickly check all configuration settings here.
- **Environment:** The Environment tab shows you different things if looking at an agent running on NetWare versus Windows. The NetWare Environment tab shows you the following information in regards to the server configuration:

```
Server      FS1
Company     Novell
O.S. Revision     NetWare 5.00h
```

```
O.S. Date  December 11, 1999
Memory     261757
Processor utilization    48%
Supported connections    17
Connections in use1
Clib version      5.0
Receive buffer max10000
```

It also shows all loaded modules on the NetWare server.

If you look at the Environment tab with the agent running on Windows NT, you get the following information in regards to the server configuration:

```
Company    Microsoft
O.S. Revision     Windows NT 5.0 Build 2195 Service Pack 2
Memory     523744 KB
```

Also, you get just the WebAccess components that are loaded on the Windows server.

- **Log Files:** The Log Files tab allows you to view the contents of the WebAccess log files. You will see a list of all the agent log files. You can highlight any one and select View Log to see the entire contents of that particular log file. If disk logging is not enabled with the /logdiskon switch, then you will get a message saying that disk logging is not enabled.

That is about it for monitoring the WebAccess agent through a Web browser. Remember that by default the HTTP port is the same port as the port the agent listens on for requests coming in from the WebAccess application.

Advanced Installation Options for WebAccess

In this section, you find out about some of the more complex and advanced installation options for WebAccess. These may or may not apply to your environment, but should be useful for many of the GroupWise administrators out there.

Distributed Installation Concepts

To begin with, it is important to review a few of the concepts to a distributed install for WebAccess. Distributed installation entails having the WebAccess application installed on one server and the agent(s) installed on different servers.

It may also mean having multiple WebAccess applications throughout an organization. In a nutshell, think of this as options on how to set up a large enterprise WebAccess solution.

Also, keep in mind that GroupWise 6 gives you the ability to have one entry point via a WebAccess application that will talk to multiple agents. You can also configure GroupWise domains and post offices to have a preferred WebAccess agent. This will come into play when you configure which agents will service which users.

Installing Additional WebAccess Agents

To install additional WebAccess agents, the procedure is exactly the same as was discussed in the section, "Installing the GroupWise WebAccess Gateway," earlier in this chapter. You only need to do the part of the section that talks about installing the WebAccess agent. Also, make sure the encryption key on the newly installed WebAccess agent matches the encryption key on all the other WebAccess agents. Also, when you run the GroupWise WebAccess installation, do not install the GroupWise WebAccess application. You will need to manually start the GroupWise WebAccess agent. You have already learned how to manually start the WebAccess agent in the section titled "Loading the GroupWise WebAccess Agent and Application." If you would like to view the installation summary, it will show you a text file that contains all the settings that you entered during the install wizard. If you leave the check in the "Start the GroupWise WebAccess agent" selected, the install script will load the WebAccess agent for you if desired.

Changing the GroupWise WebAccess Login Experience

This section talks about what the end user sees and experiences before actually seeing the mailbox from the WebAccess client. This section also covers any options that are available to access WebAccess by entering additional information on the URL line to access WebAccess.

To begin with, there are lots of ways that you can design access into a user's mailbox through WebAccess. Here is a list of a few of the more common approaches that I have seen implemented.

- You can have the end user simply enter a URL into a browser in order to access the language page for WebAccess. Once here, the user selects the language and then is prompted for a GroupWise user name and password.

- You can skip the language page altogether and send the user directly to the user name and password page.
- You could configure your WebAccess system so that users must enter a generic user name and password in order to get to the user name and password screen of WebAccess. This may help to deter would-be hackers from trying to guess GroupWise user names and passwords.
- Or maybe you want users to see some sort of company welcome page with FAQs and information about WebAccess on it. From here, they would need to click on some sort of link to get to the user name and password screen in order to log into WebAccess.

As you can imagine, there are many ways to approach what end users see before they actually get to their mail. The important thing to remember is that the last thing users must see in order to access their mailbox from WebAccess is the Login page. This is where they will enter their GroupWise user name and password. In order to get to this login page, the user must get to the following type of URL:

```
http(s)://<your Web server DNS Name>/servlet/webacc
```

Once users get here, they enter their user ID and password and are logged in to their GroupWise account.

Here is some additional URL information that can be entered that may help you determine how to set up access into users' mailboxes through WebAccess.

```
http://yourserverhere/servlet/webacc?GWAP.ip=10.1.1.1&GWAP.po
rt=7205&User.lang=en
```

This URL directs the browser to use a specific agent located at IP address 10.1.1.1 using port 7205, and to specify English as the language to use.

```
http://yourserverhere/servlet/webacc?User.html=Simple
```

This forces the WebAccess application to use the simple HTML templates to deliver the content to the browser. This may be helpful for testing purposes. Or if you had users using a very slow link, you may want to add this as a link from a main page they could click on. WebAccess is a bit quicker when the simple templates are used compared to the default frames.

You will see that after the `/servlet/webacc`, you must begin the operands with a ? symbol. Then you separate each operand with an & symbol. Knowing this, you can string together something like the following:

```
http://yourserverhere/servlet/webacc?GWAP.ip=10.1.1.1&GWAP.po
rt=7205&User.lang=en&User.html=Simple
```

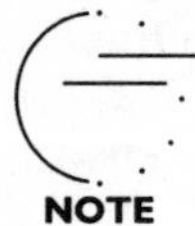
NOTE

These URL examples are case-sensitive. You cannot enter `user.lang` **or** `user.html=simple` **and have it work. It must follow the syntax keeping upper- and lowercase characters in place.**

Skipping the GroupWise WebAccess Language Page

When you install the WebAccess application and replace the existing default Web page, you are prompted to select your language when you log in to WebAccess. In many cases, you may want to simply skip this language page and send the user directly to the Login page.

If you are planning on setting up a Web page that gives users a jumping-off point before they get to the Login page, then it is very simple to skip the language page. For example, if when designing your company's WebAccess system, you may want the end users to get a welcome HTML page that may have company infomation or information about how to use the WebAccess system. You would add a link from this first default HTML page that would point to the WebAccess application running on your Web server. When you define the link into WebAccess, it would look something like this:

```
http://<your Web server's DNS name>/servlet/webacc
```

Because you specified the actual servlet that WebAccess is using, you skip the language page. The user then enters a user name and password and gets directed to the correct or default WebAccess agent.

Best Practices

In this section, I share some tips that will help you to better design or set up and maintain the WebAccess system.

- **Keep WebAccess agents as close to users as possible.** In other words, if you have a domain across a WAN link, it would be best to install a WebAccess agent under this domain, then define this WebAccess agent as the preferred agent for this domain.
- **For the greatest stability of the WebAccess agent, run it on Windows NT.**

- **When possible, keep the agent on the same server as the GroupWise domain.**
- **Monitor closely how heavily the WebAccess agent is being used.** You may need to increase the thread count to provide suitable performance for users.

Summary

This chapter has discussed many of the aspects of the WebAccess system. By reading and studying this chapter, you should be able to successfully implement a robust and scalable WebAccess system. By understanding some of the underlying concepts to how the WebAccess system works, you will also have the knowledge to provide solutions in your environment for users needing access to their GroupWise mailboxes from any web browser. Chapter 24 closely ties to this chapter, because GroupWise wireless just piggybacks GroupWise WebAccess.

CHAPTER 12

Administering the GroupWise Client

The GroupWise client is the end-user piece of the GroupWise system. It provides access to the user mailbox, documents in libraries, and archive and remote mailboxes. It offers the user tools for creating rules, sharing folders and address books, and of course doing all of those things normally associated with e-mail.

The GroupWise client also offers some tools that may be considered administrative, especially where document libraries are concerned: mass-change operations on documents, and for that matter, any operation that makes use of a user's administrator-assigned *manage right* to a library is going to be performed from the GroupWise client.

This chapter covers administration of the GroupWise 32-bit Windows client. Specifically, this chapter looks at deploying the client, updating the client, and administering logins and client options.

Understanding the GroupWise Windows Client Installation Process

The GroupWise 6 client is installed from the CLIENT\WIN32 directory of the GroupWise CD or software distribution directory. The user runs SETUP.EXE, and the familiar InstallShield setup program interface appears, walking the user through the process of installing the client. Unfortunately, this installation process prompts the user for several kinds of decisions the user may not be prepared to make.

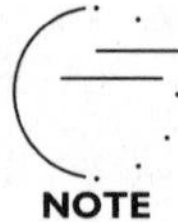

NOTE

The GroupWise 6 32-Bit Windows client runs on the following platforms: Windows 95, Windows 98, Windows ME, Windows NT/2000, and Windows XP. GroupWise WebAccess is also a GroupWise client. The GroupWise WebAccess and wireless client solutions help GroupWise to support practically any major platform.

Here are four different ways that you can have the GroupWise client installed:

- Install the GroupWise client by running SETUP.EXE from the GroupWise 6 CD.
- Install the GroupWise client by running SETUP.EXE from a GroupWise software distribution directory.
- Distribute one small executable called SETUPIP.EXE to users and have them run it from their workstation.
- Distribute the GroupWise client via a solution such as ZenWorks.

If your organization has implemented ZenWorks, then distributing the GroupWise 6 client can be pretty sweet. With ZenWorks, you can just blow down an image of GroupWise 6, configured in just the manner you would like.

If your organization has not implemented ZenWorks, then an *.EXE of some sort must be run, and the user is required to act in some manner to see that the GroupWise client is installed. The trick though, is to make sure that your end users have to answer as few questions as possible.

Your users can run the SETUP.EXE from a GroupWise 6 software distribution directory, but when they do so, they are confronted with a lot of questions that they may not know how to answer. It is best to design your GroupWise client installation in such a manner that users do not need to answer any questions regarding what to install and where to install it.

Rolling out the GroupWise client doesn't have to be all that hard. The initial rollout of the GroupWise client can be as simple as having users download one small executable and run it. Upgrading the GroupWise 5x client to GroupWise 6 is even easier.

GroupWise has over 25 million users. This chapter assumes that most people reading this book are upgrading to GroupWise 6, so this chapter discusses upgrading from GroupWise 5x to GroupWise 6. After discussing upgrading, this chapter discusses a strategy for rolling out the GroupWise 6 client for the first time.

Upgrading the GroupWise Client from GroupWise 5x to GroupWise 6

Upgrading the GroupWise client to GroupWise 6 can be done at whatever pace you may like. This chapter discusses solutions and ideas that you really cannot find adequately documented anywhere else. For example, wouldn't it be nice to upgrade the GroupWise client in an automated fashion? Or if you know how to do that, wouldn't it be nice to upgrade the GroupWise client for a controlled set of users, rather than an entire post office of 500 people in the same day? What if you wanted to audit whom has been upgraded to the GroupWise 6 client? All of these ideas are explained in this chapter.

This chapter discusses the *auto-update algorithm* that's built into the GroupWise client in detail. It is best to absorb all of the concepts regarding the auto-update algorithm before proceeding in any manner. Even if you have a slick software distribution solution, such as Novell's ZenWorks product, the auto-update algorithm is good to understand.

Here are four methods of upgrading the GroupWise clients to GroupWise 6 that will be explained in detail in this chapter:

- Upgrading all users belonging to a particular GroupWise post office. The users will have a mapped drive and rights to the GroupWise <SDD>\CLIENT folder. This is the default manner in which the GroupWise client is designed to upgrade.
- Upgrading all users belonging to a particular GroupWise post office using SETUPIP, which does not require that the users have a mapped drive to the SDD.
- Upgrading some of the users in a GroupWise post office to the GroupWise 6 client. The value of this is that if you have 700 users on a post office, you may not want to have all of them upgrade to the new GroupWise 6 client in one day. The help desk doesn't like that! This method is something that I cooked up for use at some of my customer sites. This assumes that your users are using the Novell NetWare client.
- Upgrading the GroupWise client by distributing the SETUPIP utility through an e-mail message. This is particularly helpful when you have GroupWise remote users whose clients need to be upgraded.

And finally, I discuss a way to audit the progress of your upgrade to see which users have actually managed to receive the new client through whatever method you choose for your client upgrade.

Understanding the Auto-Update Algorithm

The auto-update algorithm is how the GroupWise client, installed at end-users' computers, knows it should upgrade itself to a newer version of the GroupWise client. By using the auto-update algorithm to your benefit, you can automate the process of upgrading the GroupWise client with little or no interaction required by your end users.

Auto-Update Algorithm in a Nutshell (the Short Version!)

In a nutshell, here's how the process works, and then you'll learn just how to configure these components a little later.

- In ConsoleOne, you give the software distribution directory (SDD, for short) for a particular post office a *BUMP*. The BUMP number is not called as such in ConsoleOne, but its key is called *NewSoftwareBump* in the Windows registry.

- The next time that users launch the GroupWise client, it discovers the BUMP, which tells the GroupWise client that it must look for a file called SOFTWARE.INF for further information. A BUMP doesn't tell the GroupWise client it needs to update, it just tells the GroupWise client to investigate further. Looking for the SOFTWARE.INF is the first part of the investigation.
- The GroupWise client finds the SOFTWARE.INF file, which is in the SDD\CLIENT directory. The SOFTWARE.INF file, which is just an ASCII test file, has a *BUILD* value, actually called *BuildNumber,* in the SOFTWARE.INF file. The BUILD value in the SOFTWARE.INF corresponds to the version of GroupWise in the SDD. The GroupWise client that is currently installed has a BUILD value in the Windows registry. If the BUILD value in the SOFTWARE.INF file is higher than the BUILD value in the Windows registry, the GroupWise client keeps going and looks for a SETUP.CFG file.
- The SETUP.CFG file has a section called *AutoUpdate.* If the Enabled= line reads `Enabled=Yes`, then the GroupWise client kicks off the SETUP.EXE process to install the GroupWise client.
- The SETUP.EXE process reads the SETUP.CFG file for instructions on just how to install the GroupWise client, and which questions to ask the user in conjunction with the installation.

Fully Understanding the Auto-Update Algorithm (the Long Version!)

In a bit of a larger nutshell, this section elaborates a bit on the auto-update algorithm.

The Software Distribution Directory and the BUMP Number GroupWise has software distribution directories (SDD, for short; it'll save on so much typing). These directories house the GroupWise software after it has been installed from the GroupWise CD. When patches are released, they are applied to a GroupWise software distribution directory. A GroupWise SDD is not only a location for software, but also it can be defined in GroupWise administration and assigned to post offices. In GroupWise 6, the GroupWise software distribution directories are defined under Tools ➪ GroupWise System Operations ➪ Software Directory Management. Figure 12.1 shows the software distribution directory for WorldWideWidgets.

The GroupWise client is hard-coded to look for a home-base software distribution directory. The GroupWise client discovers its home-base SDD from information that is stored at the post office regarding the SDD associated with that post office. So each time the GroupWise client logs into a post office, it takes note of the home-base SDD for the post office.

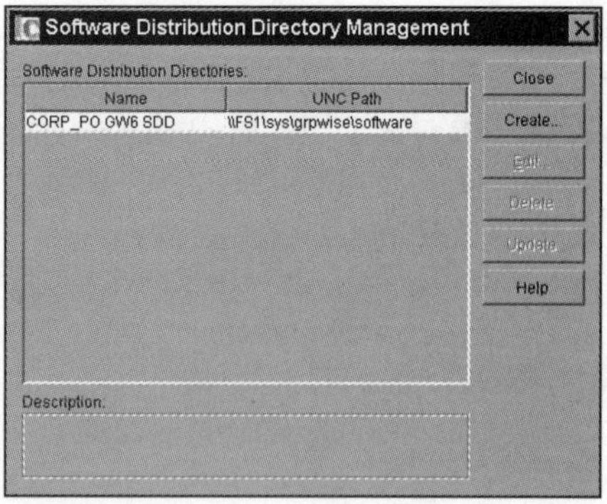

FIGURE 12.1 *GroupWise Software Distribution Directory Management*

A GroupWise SDD has a value called a *BUMP* number associated with it. The BUMP number starts at 0 and can be incremented to 1, then 2, then 3, and so on. Whenever the GroupWise client was installed or upgraded last on a computer, it put a BUMP value in the Windows registry that was identical to the SDD that the GroupWise client was upgraded from. Every time the GroupWise client logs in, it compares the BUMP value of the SDD to the BUMP value in its registry. Changing the BUMP number of an SDD prods GroupWise clients to look further and see if it's time to upgrade. Later on, this chapter discusses more on how and why to increment the BUMP number on an SDD. Controlling the BUMP number is essential to controlling the GroupWise client upgrade process.

Every GroupWise post office should have an SDD associated with it. In fact, when you go to create a GroupWise post office, one of the required fields is the SDD that will be associated with the post office. The SDD for a post office is required because any GroupWise client is hard-coded to look for a home-base SDD. The post office is the best mechanism for the GroupWise client to discover a home-base SDD, because it's a sure thing that a GroupWise client always needs a post office. You can configure an SDD that can be used by several post offices. For upgrade purposes, creating post-office-specific SDDs is often the best practice. Even if you intend to use a solution such as ZenWorks, GroupWise requires you to define an SDD for each post office. To see or change the SDD associated with a GroupWise post office, view the properties of that post office and select the GroupWise Post Office Settings property page. Figure 12.2 shows this page.

The GroupWise SDD should, and typically will, have the GroupWise 32-bit client installed into it. The GroupWise client is located in the <SDD>\CLIENT folder. Sites using the GroupWise SDD for GroupWise client software distribution must grant end users read and file scan rights to the <SDD>\CLIENT folder and its subfolders. Users should not have rights in any other location of the SDD.

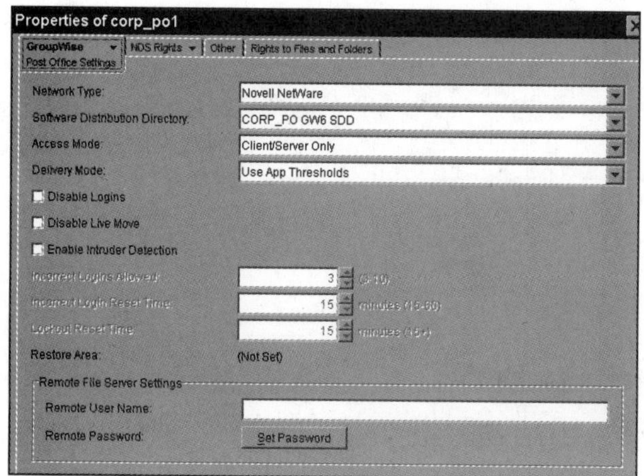

FIGURE 12.2 *The SDD Associated with a Post Office*

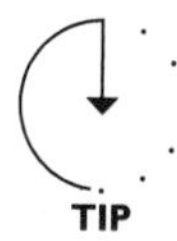

If you are using ZenWorks or a similar solution, or if you use SETUPIP, which is explained later in this chapter, it is not essential that end users have rights to the SDD.

In the <SDD>\CLIENT folder are the two other files that are an essential part of the GroupWise upgrade and auto-update algorithm. These files are SOFTWARE.INF and SETUP.CFG.

The SOFTWARE.INF File, the BuildNumber, and the SETUP.CFG File The SOFTWARE.INF file is an ASCII file containing a small amount of information. In fact, here are the entire contents of the SOFTWARE.INF file from the GroupWise 6 SDD.

```
[General]
BuildNumber=2017
```

That's it! The BuildNumber is really the version number in development terms. GroupWise development releases versions of the GroupWise software in versions that you and I typically know as 5.5 or 5.5.2 or 6.0.0. The BuildNumber of 2017 is the original shipping version of the GroupWise 6 client. The BuildNumber version of the GroupWise 6 Support Pack #1 client could very well be 2025 (we don't know this – this is just for the sake of discussion). This would mean that at Novell, before the GroupWise client was released for Support Pack #1, there were 8 build cycles of the GroupWise client.

Now here's what the BuildNumber means to the auto-update algorithm. Whenever the GroupWise client is installed, the BuildNumber of the GroupWise client is put into the Windows registry. Figure 12.3 shows this value in the Windows registry. (I'm sorry to expose you to the Windows registry. I know it gives some people the creeps.) The BuildNumber string value is kept in the following location:

```
HKEY_LOCAL_MACHINE\SOFTWARE\Novell\GroupWise
```

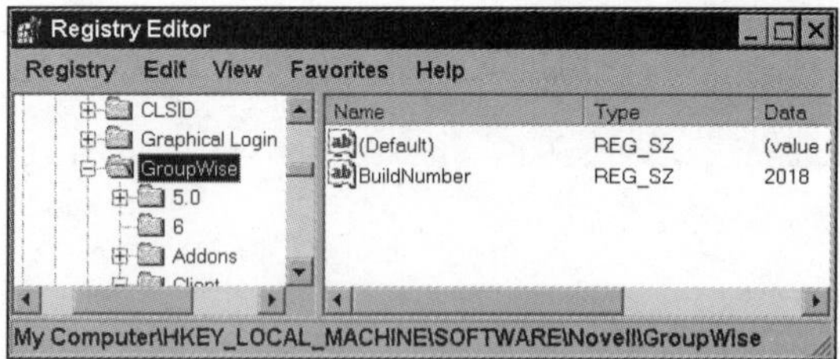

FIGURE 12.3 *The GroupWise BuildNumber in the Windows Registry*

Now I need to digress for a moment in order to fully explain the relevance of the BuildNumber. You may remember that every GroupWise post office has an SDD associated with it. The SDD has a BUMP number associated with it. Each time the GroupWise client loads, it asks for the BUMP number associated with the SDD for the end user's post office. This BUMP number is contained in the WPHOST.DB file. When the GroupWise client loads and contacts the POA, the conversation goes something like this:

CLIENT: Hi post office agent (POA) at IP address 192.168.100.237, port 1677. I need a client/server session with you. Here are my authentication credentials.

POA: Here's a client/server session, and here's the port we will speak at.

CLIENT: Hey POA, before I completely load the user interface of this client, what is the BUMP number for the SDD associated with my post office?

POA: It's 5.

CLIENT: Okay, let's see, the last time I installed the GroupWise client, the BUMP number was 4. This is held in the Windows registry at the following location:

```
HKEY_LOCAL_MACHINE\SOFTWARE\Novell\GroupWise\Client\5.0
```

The value is called:

```
NewSoftwareBump
```

In this example, the BUMP number for the SDD is different than the BUMP number in the Windows registry. If the BUMP numbers in the WPHOST.DB and the workstation's registry are the same, then the client stops the auto-update process here, and the user is logged into the mailbox.

NOTE

Remember that the BUMP number only has to be *different*. The client does not do a greater- or less-than comparison to determining whether to continue the auto-update process. It simply checks to see if the BUMP number is different or not.

So the GroupWise client sees that the BUMP numbers are different; thus, the GroupWise client must look further to see if it is essential to upgrade the GroupWise client.

CLIENT: Hey POA, what's the location of my SDD.

POA: It's in the DENVER\MAIL:DENPO\GW6 folder.

CLIENT: Okay, let me look at the DENVER\MAIL:DENPO\GW6\CLIENT folder, and look at the SOFTWARE.INF file. The BuildNumber is 2017 in the SOFTWARE.INF file, and the BuildNumber in the Windows registry on my machine is 1807. It seems like it's time to upgrade. Now let me check one more thing. I'll just look at the SETUP.CFG file in the <SDD>\CLIENT\WIN32 folder to see if the AutoUpdate section of this file has a line that reads `Enabled=Yes`. Yes, it does! It's upgrade time!

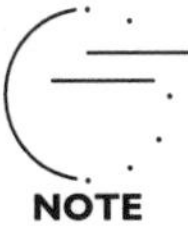

NOTE

If the user does not have the necessary rights to read the <SDD>\CLIENT directory, and you have not enabled SETUPIP, which is discussed later in this chapter, the end user will get a prompt that there is new software available, but they do not have rights to it. Be aware of this because even if you check the BuildNumber in the SOFTWARE.INF file, and it is lower than what the clients have, the end user still may get a confusing prompt because they do not have rights to read this file.

So here's a quick synopsis of what you just read:

1. If the BUMP for the SDD associated with a post office is *different* than the BUMP in the Windows registry, then the client compares the BuildNumber in the SOFTWARE.INF file with the BuildNumber in the Windows registry.
2. If the BuildNumber in the SOFTWARE.INF file is *greater than* the build in the Windows registry, then the GroupWise client looks at the SETUP.CFG file.
3. If the AutoUpdate section in the SETUP.CFG files contains `Enabled=Yes`, the GroupWise client will attempt to upgrade itself.

The GroupWise client will then upgrade itself by using one of the configurations that is detailed in the following sections.

Configuring the SETUP.CFG

The SETUP.CFG file is the end of the auto-update algorithm. This is a template file that allows the administrator to customize the way in which the GroupWise client is installed at the user's workstation. There's a line in the SETUP.CFG that, if present, tells the GroupWise client that it's time to upgrade and run the SETUP.EXE process. This line is the following:

```
Enabled=Yes
```

The SETUP.CFG file resides in the <SDD>\CLIENT directory. To use this file, copy it to the <SDD>\CLIENT\WIN32 directory. Then edit the file to make configuration changes to the file. The file must be copied to the <SDD>\CLIENT\WIN32 directory in order to work. No matter how the SETUP.EXE is activated, the GroupWise SETUP.EXE looks for the SETUP.CFG file and installs GroupWise 6 according to the instructions of the SETUP.CFG. Here is the factory SETUP.CFG that ships with the GroupWise 6 client:

```
[GroupWiseSetup]
Version=6
StandardInstall=Yes
Path=C:\Novell\GroupWise
Folder=GroupWise

[ShowDialogs]
HideAllDialogs=No
Welcome=Yes
SetupOptions=Yes
```

```
DestinationDirectory=Yes
SelectOptionalComponents=Yes
SelectProgramFolder=Yes
SelectStartUpFolderSoftware=Yes
LanguageSelection=Yes
SoftwareIntegrations=Yes
StartCopyingFiles=Yes
SetupComplete=Yes

[AutoUpdate]
Enabled=Yes
SetupIPEnabled=No
ForceUpdate=No
PromptUntilUpdated=No

[Startup]
Notify=No

[GWTIP]
Default=Yes
Hide=No
Workstation=Yes

[GWMAILTO]
Default=Yes
Hide=No
Workstation=Yes

[GWCHECK]
InstallGWCheck=Yes
GWCheckEnabled=No

[IntegrationApps]
Lotus WordPro=Yes
```

```
Microsoft Binder 97=Yes
Microsoft Excel 7.0=Yes
Microsoft Excel 97=Yes
Microsoft Excel 2000=Yes
Microsoft PowerPoint 97=Yes
Microsoft PowerPoint 2000=Yes
Microsoft Word 7.0=Yes
Microsoft Word 97=Yes
Microsoft Word 2000=Yes
Corel Presentations 7.0/8.0/9.0=Yes
Corel Quattro Pro 7.0/8.0=Yes
Corel Quattro Pro 9.0=Yes
Corel WordPerfect 7.0=Yes
Corel WordPerfect 8.0=Yes
Corel WordPerfect 9.0=Yes

[Languages]
Default=English
Arabic=No
ChineseSimplified=No
Chinese=No
Czech=No
BrazilianPortugese=No
Danish=No
Dutch=No
English=Yes
Finnish=No
French=No
German=No
Hebrew=No
Hungarian=No
Italian=No
Japanese=No
Korean=No
```

```
Norwegian=No
Polish=No
Russian=No
Spanish=No
Swedish=No
Thai=No
Turkish=No
```

The factory SETUP.CFG is broken up into the following different sections:

```
[GroupWiseSetup]
[ShowDialogs]
[AutoUpdate]
[Startup]
[GWTIP]
[GWMAILTO]
[GWCHECK]
[IntegrationApps]
[Languages]
```

NOTE

Your SETUP.CFG may have some lines that look different from the preceding example. As the GroupWise 6 client is revised, some of the contents and syntax of this file will change also.

Here's an explanation of each line items of the sections of the SETUP.CFG:

- **GroupWise Setup:** For the GroupWiseSetup line item, you have the following fields:
  - **Version:** This must match the version of the GroupWise client being installed, or the SETUP.EXE will end up ignoring the SETUP.CFG file.
  - **StandardInstall:** A standard install is an installation of the GroupWise client to the C:\ Drive. A non-standard installation is a *workstation installation.* A workstation installation is generally discouraged. A workstation installation keeps part of the GroupWise client on a server, and another part of the GroupWise client on the local machine.
  - **Path:** This is the path that GroupWise will be installed to when a standard install is selected.

- **Folder:** This is the name of the folder that contains GroupWise, the address book, and Notify, which will be created on the computer where GroupWise is installed.

- **ShowDialogs:** The ShowDialogs section has to do with which dialogs will show up when GroupWise is installing.
  - **HideAllDialogs:** This option is powerful; by using this, users will not be prompted with any of the dialog boxes mentioned in the ShowDialogs section.
  - **Welcome:** This determines whether a user sees the initial welcome screen for the installation of GroupWise 6.
  - **SetupOptions:** This determines whether the user sees the setup options screen for the installation.
  - **DestinationDirectory:** If set to Yes, users will be able to specify the location that the GroupWise software is installed to. If set to No, the installation will use the location specified in the `Path` line of the GroupWiseSetup portion of the SETUP.CFG file.
  - **SelectOptionalComponents:** GroupWise has components that don't need to be installed, but add extra functionality, for example, the Internet browser integration and the GroupWise tip of the day information files. This option controls whether or not the user will be prompted to install these components.
  - **SelectProgramFolder:** The program folder has to do with the folder on the Windows Start menu that GroupWise will be installed to. The actual folder name is specified on the `Folder=GroupWise` line of the GroupWiseSetup portion of the SETUP.CFG file.
  - **SelectStartUpFolderSoftware:** Does the user want GroupWise Notify in their Windows Startup folder? GroupWise Notify is a utility that gives users visual and audio notification of a new message item or an appointment alarm.
  - **LanguageSelection:** What language does the user want to install?
  - **SoftwareIntegrations:** This has to do with GroupWise document management. You will want this set to No unless you are truly using GroupWise document management. If this field is set to Yes, and users are not using document management, users will be prompted with annoying questions when they open or save files in their applications.

- **StartCopyingFiles:** This field determines whether the users will be asked to start the copy process of the installation of the GroupWise client.
- **SetupComplete:** This determines whether users will be shown a dialog box when the installation is complete.

- **AutoUpdate:** You find the following fields in the AutoUpdate line:
  - **Enabled:** This piece of the SETUP.CFG is part of the auto-update algorithm. If the Enabled field is set to No, then the auto-update algorithm just stops here, and a user is not prompted to upgrade. Even if No is set, then the SETUP.CFG will be used, but only if you manually launch SETUP.EXE from this SDD.
  - **SetupIPEnabled:** This tells whether or not a post office supports the SETUPIP functionality. SETUPIP is explained further later on in this update.
  - **ForceUpdate:** If this is set to No, the users are prompted whether or not they want to update their GroupWise client. If this is set to Yes, then users are told that they will be upgraded, and they get an OK or Cancel button. If they click Cancel, then GroupWise just won't launch. If they say OK, then the upgrade kicks off. You will be assimilated (sinister laugh)!
  - **PromptUntilUpdated:** If the ForceUpdate field is set to No, and the PromptUntilUpdated field is also set to No, users have the choice as to whether they will be prompted to update. If the ForceUpdate is set to No and PromptUntilUpdated to Yes, then users will be prompted to update every time they log in to GroupWise. If ForceUpdate is set to Yes, then PromptUntilUpdated doesn't have any purpose.
- **Startup:** The Startup line item just determines if Notify will be put in the Startup group for Windows, so it starts automatically on boot-up of the computer.
- **GWTIP:** With the GWTIP line item, you find the following fields:
  - **Default:** If set to Yes, the GroupWise tips are installed. If set to No, they are not.The tips are under Help ➪ Tip of the Day in the GroupWise client.
  - **Hide:** If you specify No, the Tip of the Day appears in the select components portion of the install. The default is No.

    The Hide entry allows the system administrator to force the user to install or not install a particular component. If Hide is set to Yes, then the component will not be listed in the Select Components dialog box, and the Default entry will determine if the component is going to be installed. For example, if Hide is set to Yes and Default is set to Yes, then the component will always be installed. However, if Hide is set to Yes and Default is set to No, then the component will never be installed.

Whether or not something is hidden, if the line HideAllDialogs, in the ShowDialogs section, is set to Yes, then users will not see an option to install anything. It's all decided for them.

- **Workstation:** If the GroupWise client is being installed in workstation mode — I suggest that it never is — then this field determines whether the tips will be installed in workstation mode. The idea is that if you are going to have the GroupWise client installed in workstation mode, which uses the least amount of space possible on the local computer's hard drive, then you may not want the GroupWise tips installed.

- **GWMAILTO:** The GWMAILTO functionality is the ability for users to send messages from their Web browser and have it use GroupWise for that send functionality.
  - **Default:** If you specify Yes, this feature is installed. If you say No, it is not installed.
  - **Hide:** The Hide entry allows the system administrator to force the user to install or not install a particular component. If Hide is set to Yes, then the component will not be listed in the Select Components dialog box, and the Default entry will determine if the component is going to be installed. For example, if Hide is set to Yes and Default is set to Yes, then the component will always be installed. However, if Hide is set to Yes and Default to No, then the component will never be installed.

    Whether or not something is hidden, if the line HideAllDialogs, in the ShowDialogs section, is set to Yes, then users will not see an option to install anything. It's all decided for them.
- **GWCHECK:** The GroupWise client has the ability to use GWCHECK. This was especially added to GroupWise because of the Caching mode of the GroupWise 6 client. This version of GWCHECK is a client-only version. End users will not be able to run this version against their post office. It is strictly used for cache or remote modes for the GroupWise client.

- **InstallGWCheck:** This determines whether or not GWCHECK will be installed.
- **GWCheckEnabled:** This determines whether the Tools ➪ Repair Mailbox option will be available to your users. This option is available only if they go into Caching or Remote mode.

- **IntegrationApps:** If you are going to use document mangement, this line determines which applications will use GroupWise integration. In order for any of these selections to be valid, the SoftwareIntegrations field needs to be set to Yes. SoftwareIntegrations is in the ShowDialogs section.
- **Languages:** This determines the default language to be installed.

Using the SETUP.CFG in an Example Scenario

Your CIO wants the GroupWise 6 upgrade to be easy for end users. These are the technical directives for the GroupWise 6 installation:

- Users should not be prompted for what to install with GroupWise, this creates too many questions that users don't understand.
- Users should be prompted to upgrade the GroupWise client for two weeks. After two weeks, they will be required to upgrade the GroupWise client.
- The GroupWise client should be installed as a standard installation.
- Users should have all the features of GroupWise enabled except document management. Document management is powerful, but it takes significant training, and will be activated later.
- Notify should not be in the startup group.
- GWCHECK should be installed and enabled.

Here's how to translate the CIO's directives into actions with the SETUP.CFG

DIRECTIVE	SETUP.CFG LINE ITEM
Users should not be prompted for what to install with GroupWise, this creates too many questions that users don't understand.	`HideAllDialogs=Yes`

continued

(continued)

DIRECTIVE	SETUP.CFG LINE ITEM

Users will be allowed to say yes or no to the installation, but they will be prompted to update each time they go into GroupWise. After two weeks, those people who did not update will be forced to update.	The AutoUpdate section takes care of this. For two weeks, have the following lines enabled:
	`Enabled=Yes`
	`ForceUpdate=No`
	`PromptUntilUpdated=Yes`
	Then in two weeks change it to:
	`Enabled=Yes`
	`ForceUpdate=Yes`
	The ForceUpdate will get the straggling few who haven't upgraded.

The GroupWise client should be installed as a standard installation.	`StandardInstall=Yes` (in the GroupWiseSetup section)
Users should have all the features of GroupWise enabled except document management.	`SoftwareIntegrations=No` (in the ShowDialogs section)
Notify should not be in the startup group.	That's easy; just keep the default `Notify=No` in the Startup section.

GWCHECK should be installed and enabled.	In the GWCHECK section, do the following:
	`InstallGWCheck=Yes`
	`GWCheckEnabled=Yes`

Upgrading All Users on a Post Office with a Mapped Drive to the Software Distribution Directory

The GroupWise administrator can fully configure what end users will see during the GroupWise client upgrade, as well as just what will be installed. Before getting into the steps of the upgrade, however, this section explains WorldWideWidget's technical directives with the upgrade of the GroupWise client.

- End users will be forced to update their GroupWise client.
- End users should not be asked any questions regarding components to install.

- GroupWise document management integration will not be enabled by default.
- GroupWise Notify will not be put in the Windows startup folder.
- GroupWise tips will be enabled.
- The Mail To functionality from the user's browser will be implemented.
- The client version of GWCHECK will be installed.
- The Language installed will be English.

Here are example procedures for upgrading a post office. The hope is that after reading this section, you can easily modify this scenario to match the needs of your organization.

1. Create a GroupWise 6 SDD.

   The SDD that you create needs only a full copy of the CLIENT folder and subfolders from a GroupWise 6 SDD.

2. Go to the <SDD>\GW6\CLIENT folder, find the SETUP.CFG file, and copy the SETUP.CFG file to the <SDD>\GW6\CLIENT\WIN32 folder.

3. Edit the SETUP.CFG file.

   When installed, this file defaults to a read-only file. You need to change this attribute. In Windows Explorer, you can remove the read-only attribute by changing the properties of the file and un-checking the read-only attribute. The technical directives numbered 1 through 7 at the beginning of this section can be fulfilled with the SETUP.CFG file as follows:

   ```
   [AutoUpdate] - ForceUpdate=Yes
   [ShowDialogs] - HideAllDialogs=Yes
   [ShowDialogs] - SoftwareIntegrations=No
   [Startup] - Notify=No
   [GWTIP] - Default=Yes; Workstation=Yes
   [GWMAILTO] - Default=Yes; Workstation=Yes
   [GWCHECK] - InstallGWCheck=Yes; GWCheckEnabled=Yes
   [Languages] - Default=English; English=Yes
   ```

4. Go into ConsoleOne and define the newly created SDD by choosing Tools ➪ GroupWise System Operations ➪ Software Directory Management and clicking the Create button.

Give the software distribution directory a name such as CORP_PO GW6 SDD, as shown in Figure 12.4.

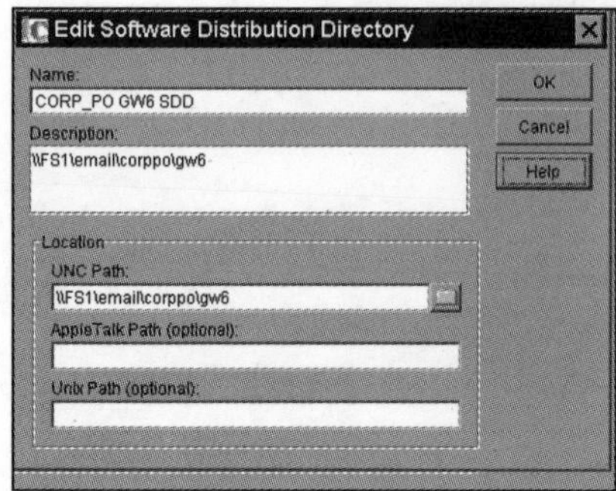

FIGURE 12.4 *A Newly Defined GroupWise 6 SDD*

WARNING

Taking the next steps can cause the GroupWise client to upgrade the next time that users log in to GroupWise.

5. To assign this new GroupWise 6 SDD to the post office, edit the properties of the post office and select the Post Office Settings page from the GroupWise tab.

6. In the Software Distribution Directory field, select the appropriate SDD for this post office (see Figure 12.5).

Step 5 may have been enough to kick off the auto-update process. But there's a chance that it didn't. Here's why. If the original GroupWise 5.x SDD for the post office you are upgrading had the same BUMP number as the SDD for the GroupWise 6 SDD you just created, then the GroupWise client doesn't pick up on a BUMP number change. A change in the BUMP number is the first part of the auto-update algorithm, so the BUMP number must change before GroupWise will discover the new GroupWise client it should upgrade to. You should identify the BUMP number of the GroupWise 5.x and GroupWise 6 SDD to see if you need to increment the GroupWise 6 SDD to kick off the upgrade process. Here's how you do this:

1. On the computer where you are using ConsoleOne, exit ConsoleOne.

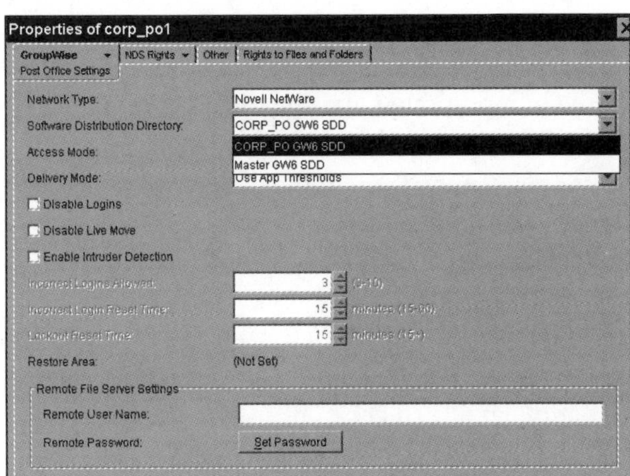

FIGURE 12.5 *Selecting a Newly Created GroupWise 6 SDD for a GroupWise Post Office*

2. Create a file at the root of the C: drive called GWSUPP.FIL.

   This file does not have to have anything special in it; it can just be an ASCII file with any characters inside it. Just make sure it has the exact name of GWSUPP.FIL.

3. Run ConsoleOne, and you should see in ConsoleOne the menu option GroupWise Diagnostics under the Tools menu.

4. Choose Tools ➪ GroupWise System Operations ➪ Software Directory Management and fill in the description field of the GroupWise 5.x that is currently assigned to the post office and the GroupWise 6 SDD that you are preparing for the post office.

   This will allow you to determine which SDD is which.

5. Choose Tools ➪ GroupWise Diagnostics ➪ General Edit, and in the drop-down list, select Areas by ID.

   Find the GroupWise 5.x SDD that was originally defined for the post office you are upgrading.

6. Compare the software version number (which is really the BUMP number) of the GroupWise 5.x and GroupWise 6 SDDs.

Are they different from each other? If they *are not* different, the GroupWise client will not know that it needs to upgrade. If they *are* different, and even if the GroupWise 6 SDD's software version is lower, the GroupWise client will detect the change in the bump number, which will factor into the auto-update algorithm.

7. If you need to increment the software version of the GroupWise 6 SDD (that is, if the GroupWise 5.x SDD and the GroupWise 6 SDD have the same software version number) go back to Tools ➪ GroupWise System Operations ➪ Software Directory Management and highlight the GroupWise 6 SDD.
8. Select the Update button, check the Force auto-update check by GroupWise components option, and then click OK.

   This action will increment the software version/BUMP number by one.

The next time that users try to log into GroupWise, the client will detect a change in the GroupWise client, which will begin the process initiated by the auto-update algorithm to upgrade the users.

Upgrading the GroupWise Client Using SETUPIP

Using the SETUPIP utility, users can upgrade the GroupWise client without needing a drive mapping to a file server. This solution is particularly useful for administrators who have post offices with users spread throughout the NDS tree, without easy file access to an SDD, or perhaps even GroupWise users who have no NDS accounts at all. Also, for customers who have implemented NetWare 6 and no longer use the NetWare client, SETUPIP is even more timely.

The SETUPIP functionality can exist alongside the mapped-drive solution discussed earlier in this chapter. Thus, if a user does have rights to the SDD for the post office, the GroupWise client will run the SETUP.EXE from the <SDD>\CLIENT\WIN32 directory. On the other hand, if a user does not have rights to the SDD, then the <SDD>\CLIENT\WIN32\SETUPIP.EXE utility will kick in, and the user will upgrade via an IP connection to the POA and a Web server.

This section discusses the architectural concepts behind SETUPIP. It is important that you have read the preceding sections of this chapter to fully understand the workings of SETUPIP.

When a GroupWise client detects that the BUMP number for the user's post office is different than the BUMP number in the Windows registry, it seeks the SOFTWARE.INF file, as well as a SETUP routine such as SETUP.EXE, in the <SDD>\CLIENT\WIN32 folder. If the GroupWise client determines that it does not have the capacity to get to a drive letter mapping to the SDD for the post office, it asks the POA to help the client get its hands on the SOFTWARE.INF file.

First, the POA sends the GWIPUPDT.DLL file from the <SDD>\CLIENT directory to the client. When the GWIPUPDT.DLL file makes it to the GroupWise client, the GroupWise client then re-requests that the POA retrieve the SOFTWARE.INF file from the <SDD>\CLIENT directory. The POA fetches the SOFTWARE.INF file for the client. The client then looks at the BuildNumber value and compares it to the BuildNumber in the Windows registry. If the BuildNumber in the SOFTWARE.INF file is greater than the BuildNumber in the Windows registry, the GroupWise client requests that the POA retrieve the SETUP.CFG from the <SDD>\CLIENT\WIN32 directory. The GroupWise client then looks for these lines in the SETUP.CFG file:

```
[AutoUpdate]
Enabled=Yes
SetupIPEnabled=Yes
```

Both of these lines must be set to Yes to allow for SETUPIP.EXE to be used as an upgrade method. If SETUPIP is enabled, the GroupWise client requests that the POA retrieve SETUPIP.EXE from the <SDD>\CLIENT\WIN32 directory. The GroupWise client then runs the SETUPIP.EXE utility, which is pre-configured by the GroupWise administrator to pull the GroupWise client from a Web-server location.

Configuring the Web Server for SETUPIP

These instructions enable SETUPIP functionality for your post office. The instructions for this procedure are based upon using a Netscape Enterprise Web server on a NetWare 5.0 server. If you are using another Web server, there may be some special things to take into consideration. For example, the Microsoft Windows IIS server may not allow downloading of files by default. This may be a right that you must assign in IIS administration.

1. Configure the Netscape Enterprise server to support downloads from a directory with about 2,500 files. To do this modify the MAGNUS.CONF file

located in the SYS:\NOVONYX\SUITESPOT\HTTP-<web_server_name>\ CONFIG directory by adding the following line:

```
MaximumFilesReturnedInIndex 2500
```

2. Restart the Web server for this setting to take effect.
3. On the server with the Netscape Enterprise Web server, make a folder under the SYS:NOVONYX\SUITESPOT\DOCS directory called GWCLIENT.
4. Locate your GroupWise 6 master SDD, and go to the CLIENT folder.
5. Copy the SOFTWARE.INF file to the SYS:NOVONYX\SUITESPOT\DOCS\GWCLIENT directory.

IMPORTANT

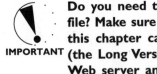

Do you need to increment the BuildNumber in the SOFTWARE.INF file? Make sure to do so, if needed. For more details, see the section in this chapter called "Fully Understanding the Auto-Update Algorithm (the Long Version!)." Make sure that the SOFTWARE.INF file on the Web server and the SOFTWARE.INF file in the SDD directory have identical values for the BuildNumber.

6. Copy the OFVIEWS folder and contents from the <SDD>\CLIENT folder to the SYS:NOVONYX\SUITESPOT\DOCS\GWCLIENT directory.

   So now there should be a folder off SYS:NOVONYX\SUITESPOT\DOCS\GWCLIENT called OFVIEWS.
7. Copy the <SDD>\CLIENT\WIN32 folder and contents to the SYS:NOVONYX\SUITESPOT\DOCS\GWCLIENT directory.

   So now there should be a folder off SYS:NOVONYX\SUITESPOT\DOCS\GWCLIENT called WIN32.
8. From your master GroupWise 6 SDD, copy the SETUP.CFG from the CLIENT folder to the SYS:NOVONYX\SUITESPOT\DOCS\GWCLIENT\ WIN32 folder.
9. Modify the SETUP.CFG mentioned in the prior step so that it matches the installation criteria for your GroupWise system. Make sure that the AutoUpdate section reads as in the following:

```
Enabled=Yes
SetupIPEnabled=Yes
```

Configuring the Post Office SDD to Support SETUPIP

The software distribution directory (SDD) associated with a GroupWise post office that will support SETUPIP should be accessible to the POA servicing the post office. The POA retrieves certain files from the SDD on behalf of the client. You will either want to put the GroupWise SDD for this post office on the same server where the POA is running, or your POA will need to have the `/user-<nds login name>` and `/password-<password>` switches enabled in its startup file.

TIP

When a NetWare server must log in and act as a client to another NetWare server, the server being logged in to must have a read/write or master replica of the partition containing the OU where the user in the `/user-<nds login name>` **resides.**

1. Completely configure the GroupWise 6 SDD for this post office, as explained in the section "Upgrading All Users on a Post Office with a Mapped Drive to the Software Distribution Directory."

   Do everything, but do not increment the BUMP number at this time.

2. Modify the SETUP.CFG file in the <SDD>\CLIENT\WIN32 folder for the SDD associated with the post office to be upgraded. Make sure that the AutoUpdate section reads as in the following:

   ```
   Enabled=Yes
   SetupIPEnabled=Yes
   ```

3. Access an SDD that has the ADMIN\UTILITY folder, go to the <SDD>\ADMIN\UTILITY\SETUPIP folder, and run the utility called WRITEIP.EXE.

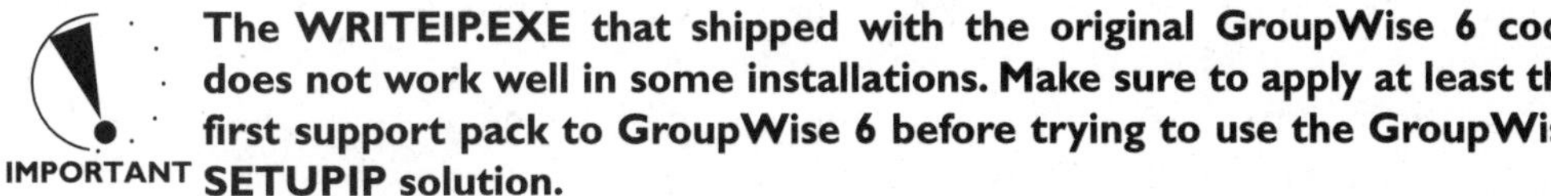

IMPORTANT

The WRITEIP.EXE that shipped with the original GroupWise 6 code does not work well in some installations. Make sure to apply at least the first support pack to GroupWise 6 before trying to use the GroupWise SETUPIP solution.

   Fill in the DNS name or IP address of the Web server with the appropriate location of the GroupWise 6 SDD on the Web server, as in the following example:

   ```
   http://www.worldwidewidgets.com/gwclient
   ```

   When you click on the OK button, WRITEIP.EXE will compile a new SETUPIP.EXE file. This file contains the information that you just entered using WRITEIP.EXE.

4. Copy the SETUPIP.EXE to the GroupWise 6 <SDD>\CLIENT\WIN32 directory associated with this post office.

   This is *not* the SDD on the Web server.

Now everything is in place for an upgrade of the GroupWise client via SETUPIP. You may increment the BUMP number for the post office you are attempting to upgrade. Go back to the section "Upgrading All Users on a Post Office with a Mapped Drive to the Software Distribution Directory" and increment the BUMP number as needed.

The next time your users log in to GroupWise, if they have file-system rights to the SDD, they will launch the SETUP.EXE process to upgrade the GroupWise client. Otherwise, they will launch SETUPIP.EXE to perform the upgrade from the Web server. The SETUPIP.EXE is sent to the user's machine by the POA just as the SOFTWARE.INF and SETUP.CFG files were sent. When SETUPIP.EXE kicks in, it does a download of the GroupWise client from the Web server and then launches into the SETUP.EXE when the download completes.

Upgrading Remote GroupWise Users with the SETUPIP Utility

What if you have GroupWise remote users who access the post office through GroupWise remote 100 percent of the time? How do you upgrade their GroupWise client? The GroupWise remote client is not designed to query the POA about the BUMP number of the post office. Because of this, the auto-update algorithm is never initiated, and the GroupWise remote client is oblivious to upgrades to the GroupWise client for the user's post office.

With the SETUPIP utility, upgrading GroupWise remote users can be much easier than shipping them a CD. Send them the SETUPIP utility that you generate. Here's what you might do.

- Follow the instructions in the section just prior to this one called "Upgrading the GroupWise Client Using SETUPIP." You do not have to increment the BUMP number on behalf of the users that you send the SETUPIP utility to.
- Take the utility that you generated called SETUPIP.EXE and e-mail it to the users who are remote GroupWise users. In the mail message, instruct the users to connect to the Internet and highlight the attached SETUPIP.EXE, click the right mouse button, and select Open.

The SETUPIP.EXE utility will proceed to download the GroupWise client. The entire download is quite large. That's the bad news. The good news, though, is that if the user exits the SETUPIP utility prematurely, when it is launched again it will pick up where it left off before the user exited.

Auditing the GroupWise Client Upgrade

The GroupWise 6 POA has a feature that can give you a quick look at who has upgraded the GroupWise client to GroupWise 6, or any other particular version of the GroupWise client. This ability falls back on the HTTP monitoring feature of the GroupWise POA, as described in Chapter 8.

Remember that it is usually a better idea to define these HTTP settings through ConsoleOne, rather than using switches in the startup file for the POA.

In order to enable HTTP monitoring, you could add the following switches in the startup file of the GroupWise 6 POA. Here are the switches, along with examples of how the switches might be configured:

```
/httpport-7181
/httpuser-admin
/httppassword-notell
```

After enabling these switches in the POA's startup file, restart the POA. Then go to the POA's HTTP port in this manner in your browser:

```
http://137.65.211.105:7181
```

You will be prompted for the user name and password. Once you've gotten into the POA via HTTP, go to the C/S Users link. From here, you can view the version of GroupWise client that your various users are using. Figure 12.6 shows an example of this.

Adding the following switch to the POA's startup file will highlight any user who is using a client older than the version you indicate.

```
/gwclientreleaseversion-[version number e.g. 6.0.0]
```

Adding this switch will put a red font on the information of any user whose client date is older than the date you indicate.

```
/gwclientreleasedate-[mm-dd-yyyy]
```

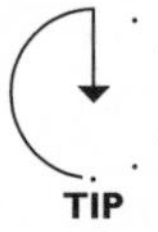

You must always bring the POA down and back up to have it re-read its startup file. These two switches must be added to the POA's startup file; they cannot be enabled from ConsoleOne in any manner.

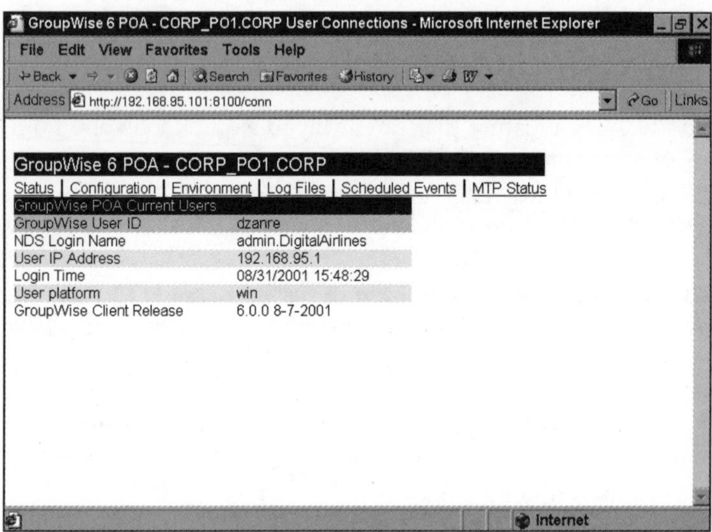

FIGURE 12.6 *The GroupWise POA's HTTP Monitoring Screen*

Understanding the GroupWise Login Process

Here is a look at the GroupWise client's login process. Understanding the login process is helpful to configuring your GroupWise system to support the GroupWise client login process. It's also helpful to understand the login process when troubleshooting login difficulties.

When you double-click on the GroupWise application, the client must successfully connect you with your mailbox. To do this, it consults several sources of information for "clues" to connecting:

- Other GroupWise code in memory
- Command-line options on the shortcut
- Login parameters in the Windows registry

- The registered network provider
- Novell Directory Services
- Domain Name Services
- User data entered in a login dialog box

The preceding list includes the order in which the client consults them. Here's a walkthrough on the login process.

Is GroupWise in Memory?

If a GroupWise component, such as Notify or the address book, is currently running, then that component has already connected with your mailbox. The GroupWise client will use that same connection. Sometimes you may quit GroupWise, and then try specifying a command-line option, only to get connected the same way you connected last time. This occurs because GroupWise was still unloading when you launched it again. Some code portions were still in memory, so the old connection was still used.

Command-Line Options

There are several command-line options you can enter on the GroupWise shortcut. These should be used as troubleshooting tools rather than administrative methods of using the GroupWise client, as they are not easy to globally administer. Figure 12.7 shows a command-line parameter that will force the GroupWise client to bring up the Login dialog box.

Here are the command-line switches that concern logging into GroupWise:

- `/@u-`: GroupWise user ID
- `/ipa-`: IP address for GroupWise POA
- `/ipp-`: IP port for GroupWise POA
- `/pr-`: Path to GroupWise remote data on local drive
- `/ph-`: Drive letter path to post office
- `/pc-`: Path to GroupWise cache data on local drive

During the GroupWise login process, two critical pieces of information are required. The GroupWise client needs answers to the following two questions:

- Whose mailbox do I connect to?
- How do I get to it?

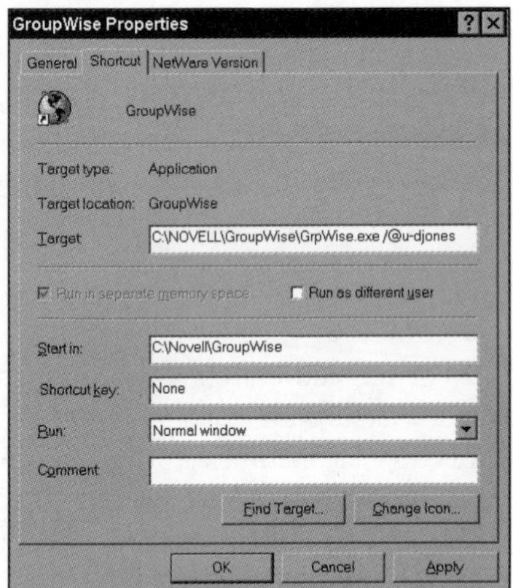

FIGURE 12.7 *Using the* `/@u-` *Command Line Switch*

This information could be provided via command-line options. Consider the following string:

```
C:\NOVELL\GroupWise\Grpwise.exe /@u-tkratzer /ipa-10.0.0.1
/ipp-1677
```

This tells the GroupWise client to log in as user tkratzer, and that the POA can be found on port 1677, at address 10.0.0.1.

If the `/@u-` switch has been set to a question mark, then the client will prompt the user with the Login dialog box. This can be a useful tool for an administrator who routinely checks multiple mailboxes and wants to be prompted each time. Here's the command line switch to use this option:

```
/@U-?
```

The Network Provider

The GroupWise client is going to make a call to the network provider. This call, WnetGetUser, will return the login name that this individual used to gain access to the network.

When the GroupWise client finally connects to the POA, it will check the security level of the post office. If the PO is set to high security, then the client will compare the network ID obtained through WnetGetUser with the network ID associated with the GroupWise mailbox (usually the NDS user ID). If these values do not match, the user will be prompted for a password.

If the security is set to High – NDS Authentication or High – LDAP Authentication, then the client will only allow matches with values it knows it obtained through Novell Directory Services or LDAP. This prevents users from setting up a private network to spoof the WnetGetUser security and hack into a GroupWise mailbox.

Novell Directory Services

The GroupWise client already consulted with Windows to see who the user was logged in as. With the WnetGetUser information in hand, the GroupWise client knows what kind of a network the user logged into. If it detects NDS, then the GroupWise client will attempt to discover GroupWise post office information from the NDS user object for this user.

This is the power of the directory at work. The NDS user object is associated with a post office object (from the GroupWise Account property page of the user object). That post office object has two attributes for the GroupWise client to check:

- Access mode
- Location

If the access mode is set to direct access, then the client will connect directly to the location (UNC path) specified.

If the access mode is set to client/server only or client/server and direct, then the GroupWise client will browse to the POA object, which is a child object of the PO object. That object will have one attribute for the GroupWise client to check, the network address, which will provide the GroupWise client with the IP address and port of the POA so that a client/server connection can be established.

This may seem very involved, but it is extremely fast. The Novell client for the Windows 32-bit platforms will have already pulled down most of the required information regarding the user object. If the PO object exists in the same physical partition as the user, or if the partition it is in is on the same server the user authenticated to, the discovery will take place in a fraction of a second.

The Windows Registry

Suppose that nothing is on the command line, and either the NetWare client is not logged in or is not even installed on the Windows machine. The client will now check the Windows registry at the following key:

```
[HKEY_CURRENT_USER\Software\Novell\GroupWise\Login
Parameters]
```

There are several possible parameters to be found underneath this key. If you were to export the entire key for a particular user, you would see something like the following:

```
[HKEY_CURRENT_USER\Software\Novell\GroupWise\Login
Parameters\Account Name]
@="tkratzer"

[HKEY_CURRENT_USER\Software\Novell\GroupWise\Login
Parameters\Mode]
@="Master"

[HKEY_CURRENT_USER\Software\Novell\GroupWise\Login
Parameters\Path To Remote Database]
@="c:\\gwremote"

[HKEY_CURRENT_USER\Software\Novell\GroupWise\Login
Parameters\PostOfficePath]
@=""

[HKEY_CURRENT_USER\Software\Novell\GroupWise\Login
Parameters\TCP/IP Address]
@="10.0.0.1"

[HKEY_CURRENT_USER\Software\Novell\GroupWise\Login
Parameters\TCP/IP Port]
@="1677"
```

In each of these lines, the value in quotation marks after the @ sign is the parameter value. In the preceding example, user tkratzer will be connected to the POA at 10.0.0.1:1677. If no network connection is available, he will be connected to his remote database at C:\GWREMOTE. The PostOfficePath parameter is blank because tkratzer's post office allows only client/server connections. A UNC path or drive mapping here is impossible.

These registry entries were written the last time that the GroupWise client connected to a mailbox. The implication here should be obvious: If you can get the client to connect once, it will "remember" how it did it when the time comes to connect again.

Domain Name Services

Now suppose that there are no command-line switches, network information, or Windows-registry information for the GroupWise client to use. In this case, the client will still not have discovered which post office to connect to.

At this point, the client falls back on DNS. The GroupWise client will do a DNS lookup for a server named NGWNAMESERVER first and then NGWNAMESERVER2 second. If the administrator has assigned that domain name to a valid GroupWise POA (any POA on the system), then the GroupWise client will connect to that POA at the port 1677.

IMPORTANT

The POA that the DNS server points to as NGWNAMESERVER must be configured to listen at port 1677.

NGWNAMESERVER Redirection

Now, suppose that this POA is not the right one for this user. On a large system, the odds are good that it will not be. In this case, the POA will ask the client who it is logging in as (information that the client got from WnetGetUser) and then will look in the address book. The POA will then check the redirection table to find the IP address for the correct POA for this user.

The user will be automatically redirected to the correct POA, and assuming reasonable network performance, this will happen in just a few seconds.

Prompting the User

Suppose, though, that the administrator has been lax in his/her responsibilities. Not only are NDS and LDAP authentication not available, but Domain Name Services has not been configured either. The NGWNAMESERVER lookup will time out (after a minute or so, which will be very long and painful for an impatient user), and then the user will see the screen in Figure 12.8.

This is a disaster. Have a look at the number of fields our lucky user gets to populate. Do you suppose this user will populate these correctly? Not likely. The user will pick up the phone and call you.

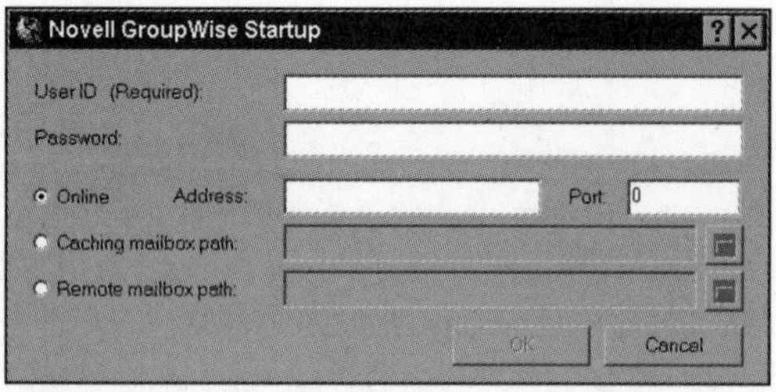

FIGURE 12.8 *The GroupWise Client Login Dialog Box*

You can provide the user with this information automatically in at least four ways before it came to this, and this chapter covered each of those. The next section walks you through the process of covering all of your bases, ensuring that users with new machines or toasted registries do not need to make that annoying phone call.

Administering the Login Process

This section teaches you how to ensure that the GroupWise client can get the necessary login parameters through Novell Directory Services or the DNS. This section also discusses registry entries to "push" to workstations, should you happen to be using a tool such as Novell ZenWorks.

Configuring NDS

All users of a GroupWise post office should have browse, read, and compare rights to the post office object itself, as well as to the POA associated to that post office. For simplicity, assign the rights to the post office object, and the POA object to the OU or OUs that the users for the post office are in.

The following steps provide you the tools to verify access modes and IP address when configuring NDS:

1. Open up the Post Office Settings page for the post-office object associated with the users whose GroupWise login you are administering.

   Figure 12.9 shows the Post Office Settings property page.

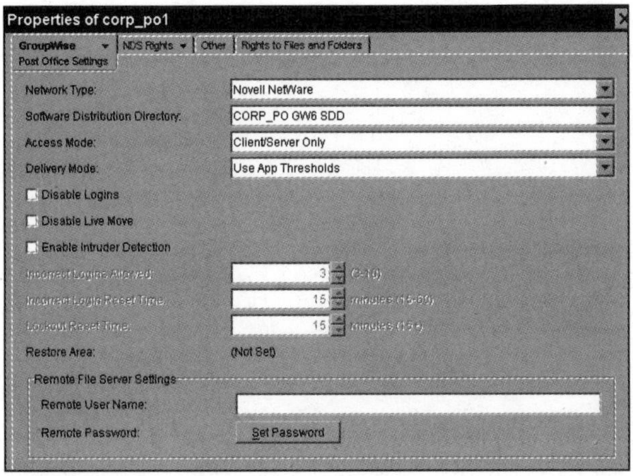

FIGURE 12.9 *The Identification Page of a GroupWise Post Office*

The Post Office Settings property page for a post-office object allows you to check on the access mode, among other things.

2. Verify that the Access Mode field reads either Client/Server and Direct or (preferably) Client/Server Only.

   Client/server access to mailboxes is much preferred over direct access.

3. Verify that the UNC path to this post office is correct on the Identification property page.

   This is not a big issue if you are running in client/server mode, but it is still good to be accurate here.

4. Make sure that Disable Logins is not checked.

   This option should be checked only if, for some reason, you want to keep users out of their mailboxes temporarily.

5. Close the details for the PO.

6. Open the Identification property page for the POA associated with this PO.

7. Go to the TCP/IP Address field and verify that the TCP/IP address and port here is accurate.

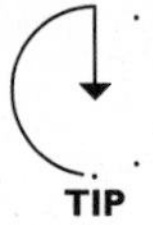

TIP

For NetWare, you may need to go to the server console and type CONFIG **to view the actual IP address of the server. From NT/2000, you can open a DOS window and type** IPCONFIG **to get the IP address of the NT/2000 server.**

8. Close the POA object.

In these eight steps, you have done two things:

- Ensured that the GroupWise client can get login parameters from NDS
- Ensured that those parameters are accurate

Configuring DNS

Now you need to choose a post-office agent, preferably one that is centrally located on the LAN, to serve as the NGWNAMESERVER agent. On very large systems, it may be advisable to create a dummy post office (no users) with a POA dedicated to NGWNAMESERVER redirection.

1. Make sure that this POA is listening on port 1677.

This is done from the Network Address field of the POA's Agent Settings property page.

2. Create a DNS record on your domain name server.

This server is not part of the GroupWise system and may be on almost any server platform, including NetWare 4, 5, or 6, Windows server platforms, or any flavor of UNIX or LINUX.

3. In your DNS server, enter the host name as NGWNAMESERVER.

4. Enter the IP address of the POA that you chose to act as NGWNAMESERVER.

In these four steps, you have ensured that any GroupWise client that looks for NGWNAMESERVER on your system will find a POA at the IP address specified. That POA will then redirect the client to the correct POA for connection to the user's mailbox.

Administering GroupWise Client Options

The GroupWise administrator snap-ins for ConsoleOne provide you with a powerful tool for controlling the way the GroupWise client works. If while selecting a domain, post office, or user, you choose Tools ➪ GroupWise Utilities ➪ Client Options, you will see the dialog box in Figure 12.10.

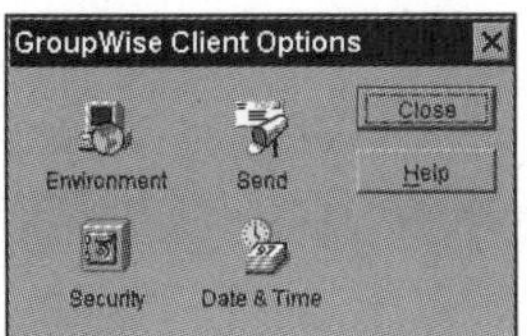

FIGURE 12.10 *The GroupWise Client Options Dialog Box in ConsoleOne*

After selecting Environment, you see the dialog box shown in Figure 12.11.

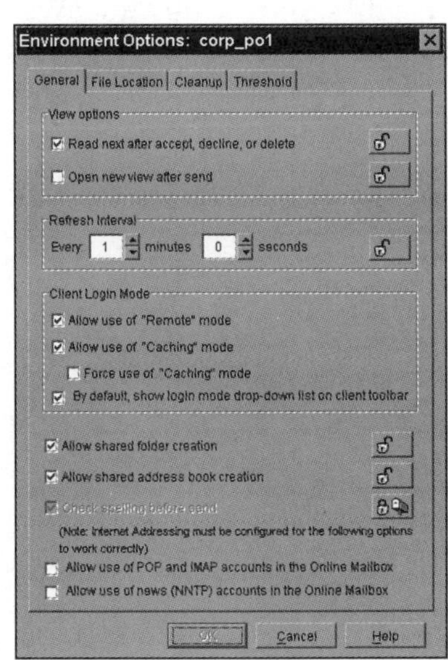

FIGURE 12.11 *Administering GroupWise Client Environment Options in ConsoleOne*

This dialog box looks similar to the Options dialog box as seen from the GroupWise 32-bit Windows client. Take note, however, of the set of padlock buttons on the right-hand side, as well as several other options.

You can change any setting listed in this dialog box, which will effectively change the default options for users who have not changed their defaults. By clicking on the adjacent padlock, you can also lock a setting in place. This will prevent users from changing individual defaults, and it will also force the setting down to users who may have already changed it.

As noted in Part I of this book, GroupWise administration writes changes directly to the GroupWise domain database to which it is connected. For client options to take effect, however, the changes must propagate all the way down to the GroupWise user database, USERxxx.DB. The following numbered list examines the architecture that makes this happen.

1. The administrator makes a change to client options.

   For example, imagine that you have unchecked the box labeled Allow shared folder creation and then locked that setting. In this scenario, a post office object was selected when going into Tools ➪ GroupWise Utilities ➪ Client Options. This means that the setting will apply to the entire post office.

2. The GroupWise administration snap-ins write the change to the GroupWise domain database and create an administration update file to propagate this change to the post office.

3. The MTA transmits this file to the POA.

4. The POA administration thread writes this change to the post office database.

   The POA then writes the preference changes to the preferences capsule of all USERxxx.DB files in the post office.

Using Clients for Non-Windows Platforms

This chapter focused exclusively on the GroupWise 6 32-bit client. Some organizations will require other client platforms, however. This section briefly evaluates each of these platforms in terms of feature parity, strengths, and weaknesses.

GroupWise 6 32-Bit Windows Client

This is the flagship client for GroupWise. All of the functionality available to any GroupWise user is typically available within this client. It requires a 32-bit Windows platform.

Strengths

The primary strengths of this client lie in the fact that it is the flagship client for Novell GroupWise. When new features or functionality are coded for GroupWise, they are coded for this platform first. The following list is hardly complete, but it does illustrate some of what is present (so that you can judge the other clients against this one):

- Notification of new messages
- Document administration features (see Chapter 14)
- Remote-access abilities (via GroupWise remote — requires a standard installation)
- Archive access
- Full-featured button-bars, menus, and quick-menus
- Full collaboration features, including folder sharing, GroupWise library access, item tracking, calendar viewing, and more

Weaknesses

The primary weakness of this client lies in the fact that it must be installed to every workstation that needs to run it. The GroupWise client also takes over 50MB of disk space.

GroupWise 5.2 32-Bit Macintosh Client

For Macintosh users, the GroupWise 6 system will support connections from the older GroupWise 5.2 Macintosh client. The primary weakness of this client lies in the fact that it is no longer receiving active development attention at Novell.

For those customers who purchase GroupWise 5.2, the Macintosh 5.2 client may be used against a GroupWise 6 post office. You must obtain the *.VEW files so that the Macintosh client can utilize a GroupWise 6 post office. Obtain the file GWMACVEW.EXE from Novell's support site for these *.VEW files.

NOTE

Novell's position on development for the Macintosh platform may change. Any press releases or announcements from Novell dated later than December 2001 will obviously supercede anything said in this book.

Strengths

Here are some of the Macintosh client's strong points:

- Native PowerPC support
- Notification of new messages
- Robust collaboration support, including shared folders, access to GroupWise libraries, calendar viewing, and full status tracking
- Remote mailbox support allows you to work offline

Weaknesses

The Macintosh client's primary weakness is that several features that are in the GroupWise 6 Windows client are not available in the GroupWise Macintosh client.

GroupWise 5.2 16-Bit Windows Client

The GroupWise 5.2 16-Bit Windows client is technically unsupported, but it works against a GroupWise 6 post office, in client/server mode. Some organizations still support a few legacy 486- or even 386-class machines, which lack the horsepower to support a 32-bit version of Windows. These machines, running Windows 3.1, will support the GroupWise 5.2 16-bit client. This client is no longer receiving development attention from Novell, and does not support the full suite of features found in the 32-bit client. This client is only available to those customers who have upgraded from previous versions of GroupWise.

Strengths

Here are the strengths for maintaining a 16-bit Windows client:

- Support for Windows 3.1 or Windows NT 3.5
- Out-of-the-box macro support (This is not available in any other GroupWise client. Some organizations choose to run the 16-bit client on a 32-bit platform for support of macros they created under earlier versions of GroupWise.)
- Collaboration support includes full status tracking and full calendar support

Weaknesses

The 16-bit Windows client's primary weakness is that several features that are in the GroupWise 6 Windows 32-bit client are not available in the GroupWise 16-bit client.

GroupWise 6 WebAccess Full-Featured Browser Support

Novell has long been touting the standards-based platform as the future alternative platform for GroupWise. If the 32-bit Windows client won't work for you, then any machine that can run a Web browser can access a GroupWise mailbox through the WebAccess gateway.

Strengths

WebAccess with full-featured browser support has several strong features:

- No installation required. Any Java-compliant Web browser can serve as the GroupWise client.
- Low bandwidth. This client will perform acceptably over a dial-up connection.
- Wide cross-platform support. This client performs the same on Windows, Macintosh, Unix, and Linux workstations.
- Support for SSL connections ensures security for mailbox access across the Internet.

Weaknesses

This platform also has its weaknesses:

- No notification of new messages
- No offline support
- No archive access

GroupWise 6 WebAccess Simple HTML Browser Support

The advent of handheld computers has brought back the need for simple HTML support, the stuff GroupWise WebAccess was made of, long ago. So, for example, an HP Jornada, with Internet Explorer 4.x or better, can access GroupWise 6 WebAccess. The interface is simpler and leaner, specifically for the popular handheld computer platforms. Figure 12.12 shows the GroupWise 6 WebAccess simple HTML browser support interface.

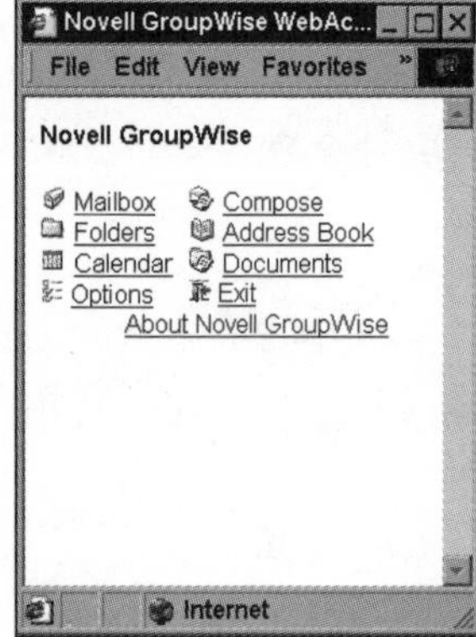

FIGURE 12.12 *GroupWise 6 WebAccess with Simple HTML Support*

Strengths

WebAccess with simple HTML browser support has several strong features:

- No installation required. Any Mozilla 4.x compatible browser or better can support this version of WebAccess.
- Low bandwidth. This client will perform acceptably over a dial-up connection.
- Wide cross-platform support.
- Support for SSL connections ensures security for mailbox access across the Internet.

Weaknesses

This platform also has its weaknesses:

- No notification of new messages
- No offline support
- No archive access

GroupWise 6 Wireless

GroupWise Wireless piggybacks on GroupWise 6 WebAccess to give users with devices such as PalmPilots and cell phones access to their GroupWise mailbox.

Chapter 24 of this book explains how to set up GroupWise Wireless support for your GroupWise system.

Strengths

This platform's primary strength is its very broad device support.

Weaknesses

These clients can read messages, not attachments, and you can compose simple messages. The weaknesses are not really in GroupWise Wireless, but in the devices themselves.

GroupWise Internet Agent POP3/IMAP4

Some of your users may want to access their GroupWise e-mail from home, using their Eudora, Netscape Mail, or Outlook Express mailers. Any mail application that supports POP3 or IMAP4 mail access can collect GroupWise e-mail through a correctly-configured GroupWise Internet agent. There are POP3 clients for almost any platform, including the very popular Palm OS devices.

NOTE

Chapter 10 talks more about where to configure POP3 and IMAP4 functionality on the GroupWise Internet agent.

Strengths

Following are the strengths for this support:

- Low user-education costs — they use the tool that they are familiar with
- Low bandwidth
- Mailbox may be worked with offline (POP3 only)
- Wide cross-platform support

Weaknesses

This configuration has some weaknesses:

- Limited collaboration support — all items show up only as e-mail items on the POP3 or IMAP4 mail application
- No archive access
- No GroupWise library access

Summary

This chapter explained the process of deploying the GroupWise client and administering it. This chapter also introduces the wide variety of platforms and formats in which your GroupWise mailbox can accessed.

PART IV

Practical Administration

CHAPTER 13

Moving Users

A casual survey of GroupWise administrators will reveal that moving users is one of the more problematic tasks they perform. This chapter exposes the architecture behind user moves and presents ways to avoid problems when moving users. This chapter also walks you through the move-user process and explores ways to troubleshoot user moves that have gone wrong.

The superstitious reader may associate ill omens with the fact that the move-user process is discussed in Chapter 13. While I cannot refute superstitions, I can assure you that it was not some sort of evil coincidence that this topic ended up on Chapter 13. I did it deliberately...

Understanding the Directory Level Move of a GroupWise User Object

A GroupWise move-user operation is both a GroupWise directory operation and a message-store operation. This section explores what happens in the GroupWise directory when a user object is moved from one post office to the next.

A move of a user is actually called a *rename* by the GroupWise directory processes. Look at this POA log of when a user called BSmith is moved from one post office to the next:

```
ADM: Completed: Rename object in Post Office - User
sales.sales_p1.BSMITH (Administrator: (WWW_TREE)
admin.World_Wide_Widgets, Domain: mfg)
```

The directory-level move of a GroupWise object rarely fails. If you make sure you connect to the destination domain when you perform the move, you will further reduce the likelihood for problems. Here is a look at the architectural principles behind a move user at work here.

In a move-user operation, the *owning domain,* as explained in Chapter 3, isn't readily apparent as in most operations. In a move-user operation in which a user is moved from DOMAIN1.PO1 to DOMAIN2.PO2, the destination domain immediately becomes the owning domain. This means that the destination domain must approve the move/rename operation before anything else will happen. The most important directory processes in a move-user operation are the directory processes at the destination domain and post office. To ensure a smooth move-user operation at the GroupWise directory level, an administrator should be connected to the destination domain's WPDOMAIN.DB database before issuing the move of the user.

Determining When a Move Is Pending

When a user is moved, NDS is updated with the post office change for an object, but the GroupWise directory may still be propagating the change. If NDS says that the user's post office is PO2, but the GroupWise directory says that the user's post office is PO1, the GroupWise snap-in will know that a move is pending. Or if NDS says that a user's post office is still PO1, but the GroupWise directory says that it's PO2, then the GroupWise snap-in will think that a move is pending.

This condition will exist until the GroupWise directory has successfully broadcast the user move to all other domains. Or this condition can exist if the NDS replica that you made changes to when moving the user is not the same replica that NetWare administrator is talking to at a certain moment in time. Until this condition no longer exists, the GroupWise directory is in a freeze state for the user's object. If you attempt to view the details or edit this user's object while in this freeze state, you will get a message as in Figure 13.1.

The freeze state to an object can be a two-edged sword at times. This freeze state sometimes means that the GroupWise directory is waiting to catch up to the NDS. Sometimes, however, it means that NDS is behind the GroupWise directory. Follow this fictitious scenario with the following players for an explanation of how this happens:

- USERA a user on DOMAINA
- DOMAINA
- DOMAINB
- NDS-PARTITION-A-REPLICA-1
- NDS-PARTITION-A-REPLICA-2

1. The state of things at the directory level
   - GroupWise administrator is connected to DOMAINB.
   - The NetWare client is communicating with NDS-PARTITION-A-REPLICA-1.

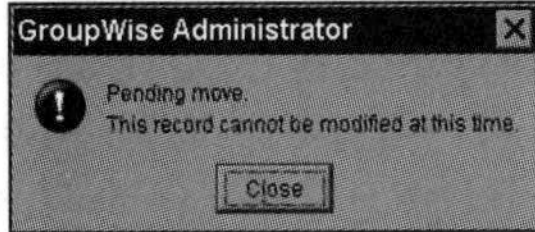

FIGURE 13.1 *Pending Move Warning*

2. The operation: GroupWise administrator moves USERA to DOMAINB.
3. The immediate state of things at the directory level
   - DOMAINB is the destination domain on the move operation, and so DOMAINB has approved the move operation.
   - NDS-PARTITION-A-REPLICA-1 knows about the change to USERA's post office.
   - DOMAINA doesn't know about the change to USERA yet; it's still replicating.
   - NDS-PARTITION-A-REPLICA-2 is not aware of the change to USERA; it hasn't synched with NDS-PARTITION-A-REPLICA-1 in order to get that information.
4. The error state
   - Another administrator, authenticated to NDS-PARTITION-A-REPLICA-2, launches GroupWise administrator.
   - GroupWise administrator is connected to DOMAINB.
   - The NetWare client is communicating with NDS-PARTITION-A-REPLICA-2.
   - NDS-PARTITION-A-REPLICA-2 hasn't received the change from NDS-PARTITION-A-REPLICA-1.

Now a condition exists in which there is a post office mismatch between GroupWise and NDS. The end result is that you'll continue to get the pending-move message from Figure 13.1.

Generally, this condition will rectify itself with time. Sometimes it doesn't, though. In this case, you will have to do something to clean up the directory. For example, you could delete the user's NDS account when you are not snapped into GroupWise. You could also try removing the link between GroupWise and NDS, which is called Disassociate GroupWise Attributes. This option is in ConsoleOne under Tools ➪ GroupWise Utilities ➪ GW/NDS Association.

Understanding the Chronology of the Move-User Process

The following is an investigation into how a user is moved. The user, USERA, is being moved from the SOURCE post office to the DESTINATION post office. The entire move-user process at both the directory level and the message-store level is mapped out in this section.

The GroupWise 6 POAs support a move-user method that is much faster than previous versions of GroupWise. The method of using a user's message store is called *live move*. The traditional, slower move method is called *message file move.* This chapter will first explain a move of a GroupWise user using message file move, and then a move of a GroupWise user using live move.

GroupWise message file move is the old standby architecture for a move-user operation. GroupWise 6 POAs prefer to use live move, and will attempt to use the live-move architecture first.

Moving a GroupWise User via Message File Move

When performing this move, you are connected to the destination domain, DOMAIN2.

SOURCE	
POST OFFICE	DOMAIN
PO1	DOMAIN1

DESTINATION	
POST OFFICE	DOMAIN
PO2	DOMAIN2

When moving a user from one post office to another, if the user will be moving to a new domain, make sure to be connected to the new domain when issuing the move-user operation.

1. In ConsoleOne, the GroupWise Administrator is connected to DOMAIN2 and moves USERA to DOMAIN2.PO2.

   The MTA for DOMAIN2 broadcasts the USERA move to PO2 for PO2's POA to approve the rename of USERA.PO1.DOMAIN1 to USERA.PO2.DOMAIN2.

DOMAIN2 does not broadcast the USERA move operation to the rest of the GroupWise system yet.

2. PO2 receives the USERA rename and the ADMIN thread of the POA updates its WPHOST.DB file with the USERA "rename" operation.

   The ADMIN thread of the POA creates a message to be sent back to its domain, DOMAIN2, indicating that PO2 has received and approved the rename of USERA.

3. DOMAIN2 receives the message from PO2 indicating an all-systems-go on the move user.

   DOMAIN2 broadcasts the rename of USERA to the entire GroupWise system by sending the rename operation to the primary domain and to all of the post offices in DOMAIN2.

4. DOMAIN1 receives the message from the primary domain indicating the rename of USERA.

   DOMAIN1's MTA-ADMIN thread updates the WPDOMAIN.DB file with the rename of USERA and DOMAIN1's MTA transmits the rename of USERA to PO1.

5. PO1 receives the USERA rename operation.

   PO1's POA updates the WPHOST.DB file with the rename of USERA.

6. PO1 sends an inventory list of USERA's mailbox to PO2.

   PO1's POA creates a message containing the inventory list of all the records in USERA's mailbox. PO1's POA log says the following:

   ```
   ADM: Completed: Rename object in Post Office
   Processing Admin task: Rename
   (.Move) Initiating: USERA
   (.Move) Sending Inventory List: USERA
   Created : COMM3\SYS:/DOMAINA/PO1\wpcsin\2\27eb13a7.000
   Admin task completed: OK
   Admin message processed: OK
   ```

7. The PO2's POA requests that PO1's POA send the inventory items.

   PO2's POA receives the inventory list and reports the following in its log:

   ```
   (Move.) Inventory List Received: USERA
   (Move.) Requesting User Data: USERA
   Created : COMM3\SYS:/DOMAINB/PO2\wpcsin\6\E7eb13c0.b30
   ```

8. The source post office sends all the user's inventory, one record at a time.

   PO1's POA receives the message requesting the inventory items from PO2's POA; the log says the following:

```
(.Move) Request for User Data Received: USERA
Created : COMM3\SYS:/DOMAINA/PO1\wpcsin\6\E7eb13e2.b30
Created : COMM3\SYS:/DOMAINA/PO1\wpcsin\6\E7eb13e2.b31
```

   Eleven lines such as the preceding ones are also sent.

```
(.Move) Bag Records Sent (11): USERA

Created : COMM3\SYS:/DOMAINA/PO1\wpcsin\6\E7eb13e2.b3b
 (.Move) Items Sent (1): USERA

Created : COMM3\SYS:/DOMAINA/PO1\wpcsin\6\E7eb13e2.b3c
Created : COMM3\SYS:/DOMAINA/PO1\wpcsin\6\E7eb13e2.b3d
(.Move) AddressBook Components Sent (2): USERA

Created : COMM3\SYS:/DOMAINA/PO1\wpcsin\6\E7eb13e2.b3e
Created : COMM3\SYS:/DOMAINA/PO1\wpcsin\6\E7eb13e2.b3f
(.Move) User Settings Sent (2): USERA
```

   The log tells you that USERA's inventory items were sent over to PO2, and the log file details further that when a user's mailbox is moved, every record is extracted and moved individually as its own file.

9. PO2 receives USERA's inventory.

   PO2's POA receives each record and reports the following in its log:

```
(Move.) Bag Record Received: USERA
(Move.) Bag Record Received: USERA
```

   Several other lines with this same syntax are reported in the POA log file.

10. If PO2 feels that it received all of the items on the inventory list, PO2 requests that PO1 purge USERA's inventory.

    PO2 received all the records indicated on the original inventory list, so it tells PO1 to purge USERA's mailbox from PO1. The log file for PO2 says the following:

```
(Move.) Transfer Complete. All Items Received: USERA
(Move.) Sending Purge Notification: USERA
Created : COMM3\SYS:/DOMAINA/PO1\wpcsin\2\27eb1f13.000
```

11. PO1 purges USERA's messages.

    PO1 receives the request to purge USERA and reports the following in its log:

```
Processing Update: item record
Delete user/resource: USERA
Purge item record
```

Several other lines are in the log indicating that the POA purged the user's records one by one.

NOTE

When a user's mailbox is purged, you should see the messages *Purge item record,* but you will not get a message that says something like *USERA deleted.*

Key Technical Factors in the Message File Move

Remember that a user move is a move of both a user's directory object and his or her messages. Moving the GroupWise user's message store tends to be much more problematic then moving the object in the GroupWise directory. An understanding of the move-user architecture can really help you out of a bind. The discussion in this next section will still refer to USERA and other terms introduced in the section.

The Twelve-Hour, Seven-Day Clock When the destination PO receives the inventory list, it puts this inventory list in the USERxxx.DB file for USERA.

NOTE

The xxx will be replaced with USERA's file ID, or FID, as explained in Chapter 4.

The USERxxx.DB file may not exist yet, so the POA just newly creates this file and places the inventory list within the USERxxx.DB file. The inventory list is also placed in the PO\OFMSG\NGWDFR.DB file (the deferred delivery database) on the destination post office. The inventory list in the deferred delivery database is a reminder to the destination PO to ask the source PO for the items on the inventory list for USERA every twelve hours for seven days. This reminder mechanism was designed to create a fail-safe for the message-store move operation. This fail-safe mechanism is good, but it can create problems also. Here are the contributing factors for potential problems:

- Message store items are moved one item at a time.
- The message store items are sent through the 6 directories.
- The POA is hard-coded to use only one thread to service the WPCSOUT\OFS\6 directory.

Now consider this scenario:

- An administrator moves 50 users from PO1 to PO2.
- The users have an average of 3,000 message items each, with lots of attachments.
- PO1 and PO2 are across the WAN from each other.
- The WAN link speeds are slow.

In this scenario, it is unlikely that PO1 and PO2, and the MTAs between them, will each be able to process 150,000 messages in 12 hours.

Here's the mess that will be created: The 12hour clock will pass, and PO2 will assess that PO1 has not sent all of the inventory items. The items may be in transit to PO2, and may even be waiting in PO2's WPCSOUT\OFS\6 directory. Since PO2 has not processed the items, though, PO2 has not acknowledged that the items have arrived. And so, PO2 requests the items from PO1 again. So another 150,000 items begin their journey across your WAN. Now you've got a real mess, and it is quite possible that neither post office will recover from the situation.

So, what cardinal rule will you use to prevent this scenario?

Don't move a lot of users at one time!

Some administrators have asked, "How many might I move?" If the move is across a WAN link, and your users have a bunch of messages, then move them one at a time. If your users have a small amount of e-mail, or you are moving them in a fast, LAN-type environment, you can usually get away with moving ten users at a time. If you move ten users at once, and the WPCSIN and WPCSOUT/OFS 6 directories don't back up, then your agents are up to the challenge, and you can consider moving more users at once. If the queues back up for more than an hour or so, then you are probably moving more users at once than you should be.

Integrity of the Message Store When a user is moved from PO1 to PO2, the integrity of the message store on both post offices is important. The most important is the integrity of the message store on PO1. If a customer is implementing routine message store maintenance routines on their GroupWise post offices, then there is generally little concern about the message store. The move-user task list (in the upcoming section, "Moving a GroupWise User") talks about what GWCHECK/ mailbox maintenance routines to run on a user to be moved.

Moving a GroupWise User via Live Move

Moving users from one post office to another has been enhanced to increase performance and reliability. At Novell, a benchmark test was done, moving an account with 47,000 items via live move and via message file move. The live move took 45 minutes. The message file move took over four hours.

Both source and destination post offices must have at least one new POA with an IP address and port defined for client/server processing in order for a live move to work.

In live-move mode, individual files containing each message in a user's mailbox are no longer transferred. Instead, a client/server thread is used to transfer information between the post offices. If a connection cannot be made by PO1's POA to PO2's POA, there will be a timeout of 15 minutes. The connection will be retried two more times, after which the message file move method of moving a user will be attempted. If a connection is made but the other POA does not support the live-move method, the old message file move method will be used without any retries.

After the inventory list is pushed to the PO2 POA, the PO2 POA will attempt to connect back to the PO1 POA using an IP connection to retrieve the data. If a connection cannot be made to the PO1 POA, there will be a timeout of 15 minutes. The connection will be retried four more times, after which the message file move method of retrieving data will be attempted. If a connection is made, but the other POA does not support the new method (because it is older), the old retrieve data method will be used without any retries.

With live moves, the recommendation is still to move one user at a time. Multiple simultaneous moves can be successful, but if all client/server threads on the target POA are being used, the previously mentioned timeouts could occur, and the old MF method will be used.

All GroupWise 6 POAs attempt a live move first, before falling back to a message store move. When you move a user, you cannot request a live move over a message store move. The POA is hard-coded to try and do a live move if everything is in place. If for some reason, you want to disable a live move, then do the following:

1. Go to the destination's post office object in ConsoleOne.
2. Go to the properties of the post office object.
3. Go to the GroupWise Post Office Settings property page.

4. Check the Disable Live Move checkbox, as shown in Figure 13.2.
5. Follow Steps 1 – 4 on the source post office object also.

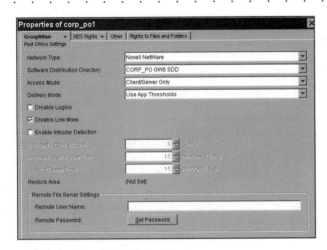

FIGURE 13.2 *Disabling Live Move*

Moving a GroupWise User

The following is an exhaustive task list for moving a user. If you are moving several users, then each step in the list can be done simultaneously for all users, except the step in which you actually change the user's post office from the source PO to the destination PO.

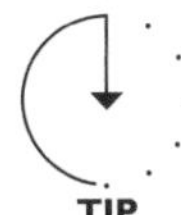

TIP

Do not proceed from one item to the next unless you have achieved success with the current task!

Here are some terms to keep in mind as you review the task list:

- **Destination domain:** The domain that owns the post office the user is being moved to
- **Destination PO:** The post office that the user is being moved to
- **Source PO:** The post office that the user is currently a member of
- **USERA:** The user being moved

1. In ConsoleOne, connect to the destination domain.

   To do this, choose Tools ➪ GroupWise System Operations ➪ Select Domain. Browse to the UNC path for the destination domain and select the WPDOMAIN.DB file.

IMPORTANT

Throughout the remainder of this checklist, always stay connected to the destination domain.

2. Check and clean USERA's message store with Mailbox/Library Maintenance routines.

NOTE

Avoid using the standalone GWCHECK (GWCHECK.EXE). It is slower compared to the POA routines spawned from Mailbox/Library Maintenance.

   Highlight USERA and select Tools ➪ GroupWise Utilities ➪ Mailbox/Library Maintenance. Then select the Structural Rebuild option and click Run.

   Issue an Analyze/Fix Databases command on the contents of USERA's user database (don't bother with the message database). You can issue this Mailbox/Library Maintenance job immediately after issuing the structural rebuild.

   Issue a Mailbox Statistics command on this user. You can issue this immediately after issuing the content analysis and fix just mentioned. Don't worry about the box limit value; just leave it at 500. It won't delete any mail. Just don't select the Expire Statistics radio button, unless you know what you are doing.

   Confirm that all three of these maintenance routines happened, and that there are no major problems with USERA's message store. Make sure you are set up as the GroupWise domain's administrator in ConsoleOne — this way you will receive a log from the POA indicating that the user's mailbox maintenance routine went through. To do this, edit the details on the domains you are dealing with in the move, and select yourself as administrator. Figure 13.3 shows where you configure the administrator for a GroupWise domain.

3. Make sure that USERA's object will synchronize to the source PO and destination PO.

When moving a large amount of people, it won't be feasible to take this step. Try and synchronize all of the users though. When moving multiple users, simply highlight the users to be moved with a Shift-Click or Ctrl-Click routine and choose Tools ➪ GroupWise Utilities ➪ Synchronize.

Temporarily change USERA's phone number.

Log in as a test user on the destination PO and confirm that USERA's phone number changed, and that the user shows up as a member of the source PO.

Log in as a test user on the source PO and confirm that USERA's phone number changed, and that the user shows up as a member of the source PO.

Change the phone number back on USERA.

If you are going to move USERA to another NDS OU, go to Step 4. If not, skip to Step 5.

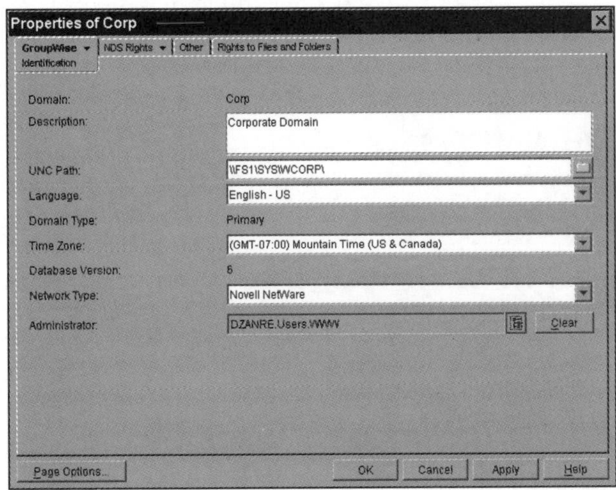

FIGURE 13.3 *Defining the Administrator to Get GWCHECK Logs*

4. Disassociate USERA's NDS object from the user's GroupWise object.

   Highlight USERA, select Tools ➪ GroupWise Utilities ➪ GW/NDS Association ➪ Disassociate GroupWise attributes, and move USERA to his/her new NDS OU.

5. View details on USERA and make note of the FID.

   Highlight USERA and edit the properties of USERA. Select the GroupWise Account property page to take note of the file ID.

6. Move USERA.

   Highlight USERA in the GroupWise view, right-mouse-click on the USERA object, and select Move. Select the world icon in the GroupWise Move dialog box and select the destination post office. Follow the remaining prompts to allow the user to move.

7. Associate USERA's NDS object with USERA's GroupWise object.

NOTE

Only do this step if you disassociated USERA's NDS object from USERA's GroupWise object in Step 4.

   Highlight USERA in the NDS View, not the GroupWise View. Edit USERA, and go to the GroupWise Account property page. Click on the world icon to the right of the Post Office field. Select the post office that USERA is now a member of. When you hit OK as though you want to finish the operation on USERA, a message should come up, like the one in Figure 13.4. Say Yes, if everything is correct.

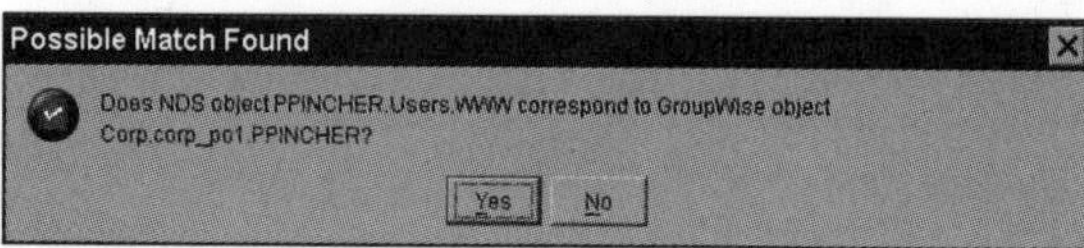

FIGURE 13.4 *Prompting to Associate an NDS User with a GroupWise User*

How to Assess the Success of a User Move

So you moved a user, and everything seems to be quiet on the POAs. You may now be asking, "Did everything get moved?" Here are some things to look for:

- **Are there purge messages?** The source PO should indicate that it is purging the messages for the moved users. This only happens if the destination PO received all the items it was expecting to. If you moved multiple users, though, this method is next to useless. You won't be able to assess the state of multiple users' moves without heavy perusal of log files. Also, you can check the source post office OFUSER directory to see if the USERxxx.DB still exists. If it does not, you should be safe to say the move went through and all mail is moved.

NOTE

Quite often, you will see the old USERxxx.DB in the old post office. This is not cause for alarm. If only one record did not get over to the destination post office, the USERxxx.DB file is retained. It's always possible that the source post office is not able to locate or access a record, and so the USERxxx.DB file is retained. When scheduled maintenance routines are run, those routines will clean up this database after a 14-day period.

- **What does mailbox maintenance tell you?** Before you moved the users, you ran a mailbox statistics. Now run a mailbox statistics and see if you have the same number of items (taking into account that a small number of items could have been delivered or deleted since the move took place).

When Something Goes Wrong Moving a User

There are a several kinds of move-user failures. Don't panic — you can generally dig your way out. This section looks at the most common kinds of failure, and how you'll solve those problems if you find yourself faced with them.

The User Moved, but Only a Part of the User's Messages Moved

This is the most common of the possible failures. In most cases, the user's messages will get to their destination on the second attempt (when the destination POA asks for the items it does not have yet). It is just a bit nerve-racking waiting for 12 hours, hoping the problem will remedy itself.

1. Wait for 12 hours and see if the mail comes through on the re-request. If the mail does not come through after the 12 hours, then go to Step 2. If you aren't patient enough to wait 12 hours (and I'll certainly understand!), then skip to Step 2 now.
2. Move the user back to the user's old post office.

IMPORTANT

When moving a user back to an old post office, make sure to connect to the domain that you are moving the user back to.

3. Make sure that USERA can get back into e-mail at the source PO.
4. Try and determine what caused the problem that messed up the move. Perhaps there was a problem with the message store at either of the post offices. It may be a good measure to run a structural check and fix of all user and message databases on both post offices. Follow this up by doing a contents check and fix on both post offices. You may also want to make a test user, create some e-mail for the test user, and move the user to the new post office and see if you have problems with the move.
5. Move USERA to the destination PO again, following the complete procedure listed in the section titled "Moving a GroupWise User."

The User Moved, but the User's Password Was Lost

This problem is actually identical to the problem mentioned in the section just prior to this one. A user's password is just another record in the User Settings section of the user database. The user settings are the last thing to be extracted by the source PO, and thus they are the last items inserted into the USERxxx.DB file at the destination PO. The password record will generally make it to the destination PO, but it may be 12 hours away.

To allow a user to get into the mailbox, without having to wait 12 hours, you may have to set a GroupWise password for the user from ConsoleOne. To do this, go to the properties of the user object, open the GroupWise Account property page, select Change GroupWise Password, and follow the prompts.

The User Moved, but *None* of the User's Messages Moved

There are a handful of things that can cause this problem. The problem could be related to USERA, or it could be related to some other element in the message store at either the source PO or the destination PO. Check the log files for error messages during the time of the move.

1. Move USERA back to their old post office. If they received new messages at their new post office, that's not a problem. The user will not lose these message items. These new messages will go back and forth with the user.

2. Now try and determine why USERA's e-mail did not move. Here's some things to think about:
   - Did you move other users successfully from the same source PO to the same destination PO? If so, the problem is most likely a problem with USERA's USERxxx.DB file. If USERA is the only user you are moving, perhaps you will want to make a test user on USERA's post office and move them to the destination post office. It's best to create a few messages in the test account also.
   - Set both POA's at both the source PO and the destination PO to diagnostic mode. To do this, go to the POA at the NetWare console and press Ctrl+Z. Create a test user on the source PO, send them e-mail, and try and move them to the destination PO. What does the POA report?

Summary

This chapter discussed moving users safely and troubleshooting user moves that have gone awry. To ensure safe user moves, do the following:

- Verify the user's message store before initiating the move.
- Don't move more than ten users at a time (unless you've carefully benchmarked the move process on your system!).
- Be connected to the destination domain when initiating the move.

When troubleshooting moves that have not gone well, remember these tips:

- Don't panic.
- Determine the extent of the failure of the move (messages missing, directory entries incorrect, and so on) before taking any action.
- Be prepared to move the user back to the original post office in order to solve the problem.

CHAPTER 14

Library and Document Administration

GroupWise provides powerful document-management functionality right out of the box. This allows users to work with documents in the same way that they work with e-mail messages, appointments, tasks, and reminder notes. Documents become just another item type in the GroupWise information store.

This chapter introduces you to basic document management concepts and shows you how document management is implemented in the GroupWise system. This chapter also walks you through some common library and document administration tasks.

Understanding the Role of Document Management

Imagine for a moment that all the documents in an organization are stored on workstation hard drives *and* as hard copies in file cabinets. Ask yourself how accessible these documents are to users that may need to view, revise, or copy these documents to perform their work? What if the user's hard drive becomes inaccessible? What if the key is misplaced for the file cabinet? What if the user that owns the document is out on sick leave?

In this situation, documents are likely accessible only to the user(s) that created them. For other users to access the document, they are dependent on the creator. If the user that owns the document is not accessible, then the process of accessing the document may break down.

Now ask yourself what process will ensure that the latest copy of the document is the copy that gets updated? And what process will ensure that the history of these documents is preserved so that all versions of the document are maintained? What process will create an activity log of users that have accessed the document? What process will be used to enforce security of the documents so that only authorized users can access the document?

Without a centralized electronic document-management system, these questions are difficult to answer. A lot of these document processes would require manual attention and thus would be subject to manual rates of completion.

With a document-management system, all these manual processes are handled automatically by document-management software. In a document-management system, documents reside in a centralized place where they can be managed by a document-management system and easily backed up. Version control, accessibility, security, and document life cycles are all handled by the document-management system.

Electronic document management first started in the legal and government industries and has been steadily spreading to other industries. Many organizations have recognized the value of document management. Today, many law firms use document-management systems from different vendors to store all their documents and typically have the documents organized by client and matter information.

A large law firm may create tens of thousands of documents a year and depend on a document-management system to organize and manage all its documents. Another example could be a research and development department that wants to keep track of design documents. Another may be a pharmaceutical company that wants to centrally manage product formulas.

To determine whether or not your organization would benefit from document management, ask yourself these questions:

- Are word processors, spreadsheets, or other document-creation applications used in my organization?
- Do users ever e-mail text documents, presentations, spreadsheets, or other files to each other as part of their day-to-day jobs?
- Does important information exist in text documents, spreadsheets, or other document files?

If you answered yes to any of these questions, your organization will benefit from document management. You may not need a million-document library, but you will definitely see productivity rewards when you implement a document-management system.

Working with GroupWise Documents

As alluded to in the preceding section, GroupWise documents are any electronic data that needs to be managed. They could be drafts of presentations, briefs, sales reports, pictures, or corporate policies. Even executables can be stored as documents in a GroupWise library.

End users will access documents through GroupWise mailboxes or through WebAccess or WebPublisher. From the GroupWise client, there are four ways to access documents:

- Document references in the Documents folder
- Query folders

- Document references in shared folders
- Find in GroupWise dialog boxes

The following sections offer fuller explanations of each of these:

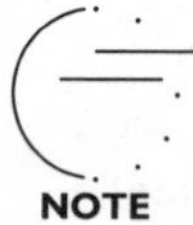

Most document-management features are available only in Windows 32-bit clients. Limited document-management functionality is available in the GroupWise Web client.

Document References

By default, when a user creates or accesses a document, a special pointer to that document is created in the Documents folder of the user's mailbox. This pointer is called a *document reference*. The Documents folder, with its collection of document references, can be considered a user's work list. Figure 14.1 shows a user's Documents folder.

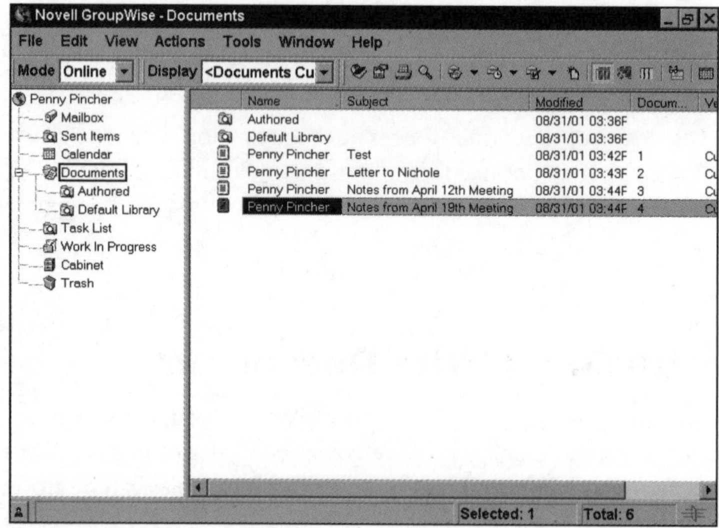

FIGURE 14.1 *Document References in a User's Documents Folder*

A document reference is a pointer that represents a document. Many users think a document reference is necessary to access a document, but in truth a document reference is nothing more than a handy shortcut to a document.

To open a document in a GroupWise library, simply double-click on the appropriate document reference.

A document reference that points to a document that has been deleted from the library is not very handy, because it points at something that no longer exists. It does have some use, however. The document reference still contains a link to the document activity log found in the appropriate DMDLppnn.DB file. This file has some very useful information about what happened to the document and where it was last located. For example, a dialog box like in Figure 14.2 will show up when trying to open a document reference to a document that no longer exists.

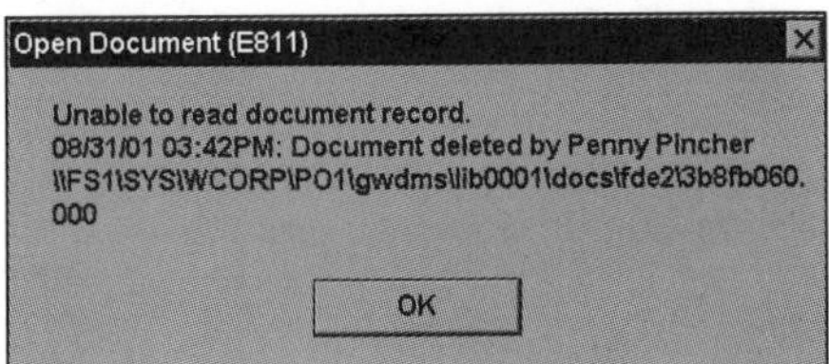

FIGURE 14.2 *An Error Reading a Document Reference*

Notice the path information given in this dialog box (the line beginning with \\FS1). This is the last known path for the document BLOB file. To get the actual document back, the document BLOB can be restored from tape, provided that the backup system has been working properly and the document BLOB can be restored. This BLOB file can be re-imported as a new GroupWise document by a user who previously accessed the original document, or by a user with manage rights to this library. The document will then be uncompressed and unencrypted and put into the library as a new document with a new document number.

Query Folder

A query folder can be created with predefined search criteria to locate documents. Each time the folder is accessed, the search is dynamically performed. This means that the user will always be getting the latest documents available that meet the search criteria as long as indexing is current.

For example, user Larry Admin in the IS department creates a query folder that searches for any document in any library. Each time he opens this folder, all documents in all libraries are displayed, assuming that Larry has been given at least view rights to the document or that Larry has the manage rights for these libraries and has applied that right in his search criteria.

Shared Folder

A shared folder can be used to hold document references. This creates a rather unique situation. Any user that has rights to the shared folder will have view rights, at least, to any documents that have references in the shared folder. The sharing list for the folder will take precedence over the sharing list for the document.

The document in the shared folder shown in Figure 14.3 will be viewable to any GroupWise user who has access to the shared folder, whether or not that user was included in the sharing list for the document itself.

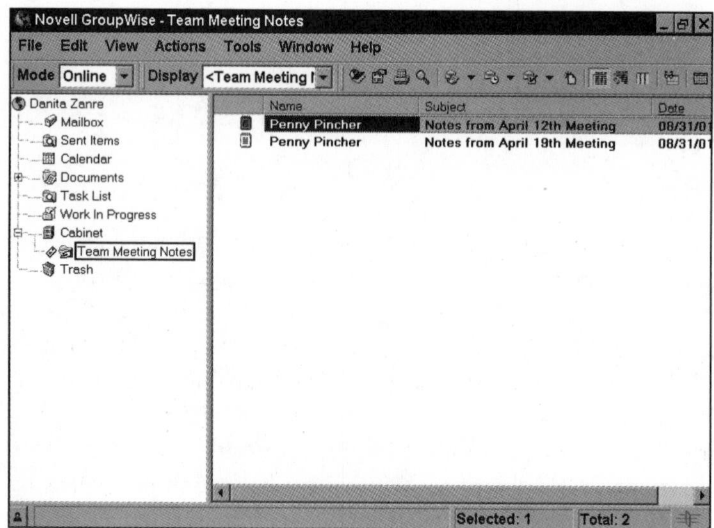

FIGURE 14.3 *A Document in a Shared Folder*

The Find Feature

Users may use the Find feature to locate documents. The Find Results window will display a list of pointers, similar to document references, that can be double-clicked to access documents. Any document that matches the criteria in the Find dialog box will show up in the Find Results window. The results can then be saved as a query folder if the query will need to be done again.

Document Management and Application Integrations

As mentioned earlier in this section, when a user double-clicks a document reference or a document pointer in a query folder or Find Results dialog box, that document is opened. This means that GroupWise must communicate with the application into which the document is opened.

The most common, and most effective, means of integrating your document applications with GroupWise is via the open document management API (ODMA). ODMA integrations occur when the integrated application calls the ODMA library on the workstation to see if an ODMA service provider is present. When the GroupWise client is installed, and application integrations are enabled, GroupWise shows up as an ODMA service provider.

ODMA integrations allow the GroupWise interface to be used in place of the application's usual Save or Open dialog boxes.

Document Management Security

Security is a key feature of GroupWise document management, and it is administered through a three-tier system. The three types of rights are the following:

- **Library rights:** Granted by the administrator, these apply to an entire library.
- **Document rights:** Granted by document creators, these apply to individual documents.
- **Document version rights:** Granted by document creators, these apply to individual versions of individual documents.

In order for a user to access a document, they must have all three types of rights in some form. If a user is given document rights but not library rights, the user will not be able to access the document. This is because the user will not be able to access the library in which the document is stored. Also, if a user is given library rights, but has no rights to an individual document, or a document version, the user will not be able to access the document or version.

Library rights

As shown in Figure 14.4, library rights include add, change, delete, view, set official version, and reset in-use flag, as well as the Manage rights (for users that you want to serve as GroupWise librarians). These rights are granted through ConsoleOne via the library object's Rights property page. They can be given per library to all users or to a few privileged users, or to a combination of the two.

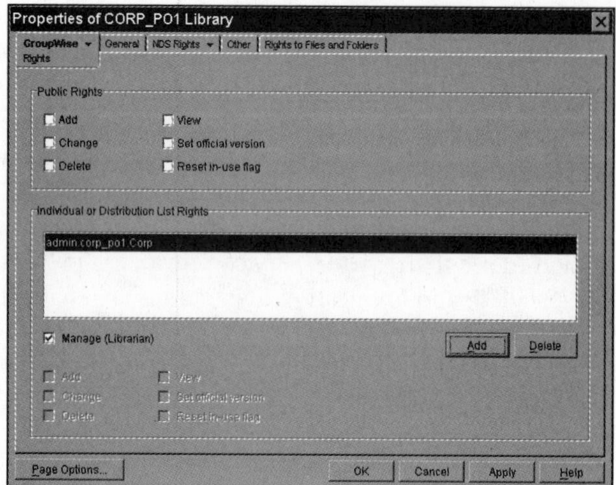

FIGURE 14.4 *The Rights Property Page on a GroupWise Library Object*

- **Add:** Allows a user to add a document to the library. A user with add rights can import a document and create a new document or new version if the user has add rights to the library.
- **Change:** Allows a user to edit documents that they create, or that they have been given edit document rights to. If users have not been given the change library rights, they will not be able to exercise the edit document rights.
- **Delete:** Delete rights allow a user to delete a document or version from a library. This right should be used sparingly because once a document version is deleted from the library the only way to bring it back is for you to get a copy of the document BLOB from a backup tape and have the document BLOB imported.

  If you wish to allow users to delete documents, but want to closely control the actual deletion process, here's a solution for you. Make a document type of delete in the Document Properties Maintenance tool. Then tell the users to set the document type to delete when they have a document or version number they wish to delete. A little later in this chapter, you will learn about how to use the Document Properties Maintenance tool.

Figure 14.5 shows a document that has been changed. In this case the delete document type has been created with criteria allowing documents that have not been accessed in 30 days or more to be deleted.

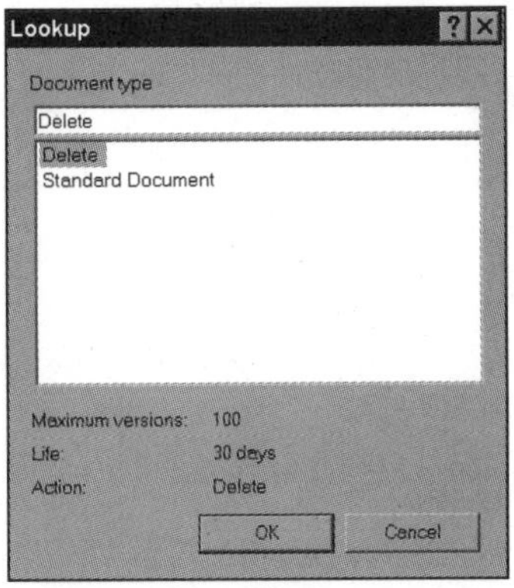

Lookup

Document type

Delete

Delete
Standard Document

Maximum versions: 100
Life: 30 days
Action: Delete

OK Cancel

FIGURE 14.5 *Changing a Document's Document Type to Delete*

When a user changes the document type to delete, the document will not be deleted immediately. The document will not get deleted until it meets the criteria to be deleted as configured in the Document Properties Maintenance tool, and an archive/delete documents maintenance action is run. This gives the administrator much more control over the deletion of documents.

- **Set official version:** This right allows a user to designate a particular version of a document as the official version of that document. There are three possible version types for a document:
  - **Official:** The version considered to be the official copy of the document
  - **Current:** The version with the highest version number
  - **Other:** Any version other than the current or official version

  Official versions and current versions will be returned on all searches for the official version of a document. For more information about using document versions, see "Document Version Rights," later in the chapter.

- **Reset in-use flag:** This right allows a user to change the in-use flag to available without checking the document back in to the library. If there is a copy of the document checked out, it will no longer be managed by GroupWise.

  For this reason, Reset in-use flag rights should be given out sparingly unless you know that your users will not abuse the right. If a user does not have rights to Reset in-use flag, they will see the error shown in Figure 14.6 when they try to access this feature. In the GroupWise client, Reset in-use flag rights correspond to the action of highlighting a document and choosing Actions ➪ Reset Document Status.

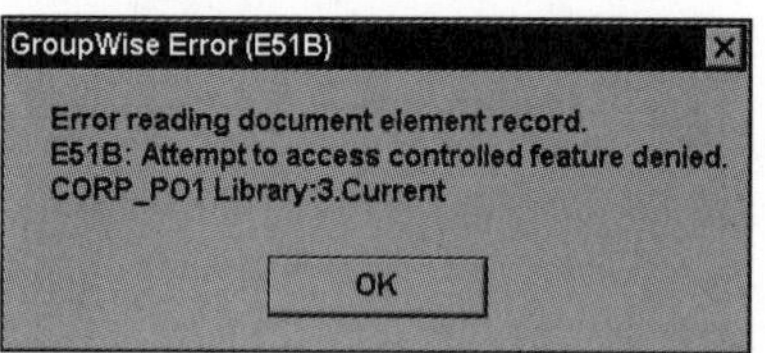

FIGURE 14.6 *The Reset In-Use Flag Rights Error Dialog Box*

- **Manage:** Manage rights cannot be granted for all users, as noted in Figure 14.4. It appears only in the lower portion of the Library Rights tab, and can only be checked when a specific user has been added to the library access list.

  Manage rights allow users to find any document in the library, even though the author or creator of the document may not have shared the document with anyone. Users with manage rights may alter the sharing list of any document in the library, granting themselves or anyone else full rights to documents. For this reason, manage rights should be reserved for system administrators or users who serve as GroupWise librarians.

Document Rights

This chapter has discussed the rights that can be set at the library level. These rights are set by the system administrator from the library object's details window. Document rights, however, are set by the users who create documents, and they are set from the Document properties page. They may also be set as defaults from the Documents page under Tools ➪ Options ➪ Documents ➪ Properties ➪ Sharing Defaults.

The library manage rights are applied by the librarian user, via the GroupWise client, and allow the librarian user more control over document rights than other users have.

The rights that can be set at the document level are the following:

- View
- Edit
- Delete
- Share
- Modify security

Document rights are rights specific to a document. By default, only the author or creator of a document will have any document rights to a document. Document authors or creators can choose to grant document rights to other users, and can even set a default so that other users have document rights to all new documents he or she creates. Remember, though, that a user without library rights (granted by the administrator) will not be able to exercise document rights. Also remember that the librarian user (the user or users with manage rights to this library) can change document rights independently of the author or creator of the document.

The difference between *author* and *creator* is simple. The creator of a document is the user who first imported the document into the GroupWise library. The author of a document is defined as the person who wrote the document. The creator gets to decide who is listed as the author.

- **View:** This right allows a user to view the document in the GroupWise viewer. The document may not be edited, but the user can create a new document by copying the original.
- **Edit:** This right allows the document version to be opened in edit mode. With edit rights, a user can delete all the content of a document and save it again. Thus, edit rights give users full power over the content of a document.

Edit rights cannot be exercised without change rights at the library level.

- **Delete:** Delete rights allow a user to delete the document version. This will remove the associated property sheets and BLOB files from the GroupWise library.

IMPORTANT

Delete rights cannot be exercised without delete rights at the library level.

- **Share:** This right allows a user to share a document via a shared folder. With this right, the user can put a copy of a document in a shared folder, giving all users with access to the shared folder access to the document.
- **Modify security:** This right allows a user to change the security settings on a document. This is like an admin equivalent right on the document. This right is also necessary if a user needs to create a new version of the document (unless a new version of the document is created indirectly through a GroupWise remote session). Figure 14.7 shows the dialog box that appears if a user attempts to create a new version of a document, but does not have modify security rights.

FIGURE 14.7 *When a User Does Not Have Modify Security Document Rights*

Document Version Rights

The rights granted at the document level may also be granted more granularly, at the document version level, with *version-specific rights.* To show how this would be useful, consider the following scenario:

Suppose that user Penny Pincher has created a spreadsheet for the WorldWide Widget fiscal 2000 budget. She needs to be able to make changes to the document and needs to allow other users to make changes, but at the same time she needs to be able to maintain a static, official copy of the document.

This is where version-specific rights come into play. Penny creates a new version of the document, and then designates the old version as the official version. Then she grants all users version-specific rights. Other users will be allowed to view and edit the current version, but will only be given view rights to the official verison. Penny will reserve edit rights to the official version to herself.

Version-specific rights are basically the same as document rights, but they are granted on each of the three version types: official, current, and other.

- **Document Storage Areas:** A document storage area is a location on disk where document BLOB files are stored. By default, all documents are stored under the post office directory structure in GWDMS\<LIBRARY>\DOCS. Additional document storage areas are administered from the Storage Areas tab of the library object's details window (see Figure 14.8). The storage area can be changed at any time to any path that the POA can access. Typically, administrators create document storage areas on separate servers or separate volumes from the post office in order to be able to manage the disk space separately.

NOTE

If the path of a library storage area is changed, existing document BLOBs in the old storage area will stay in the old storage area until they are accessed again. When an existing document in the old storage area is checked out and back in, a new BLOB file will be created in the new storage area.

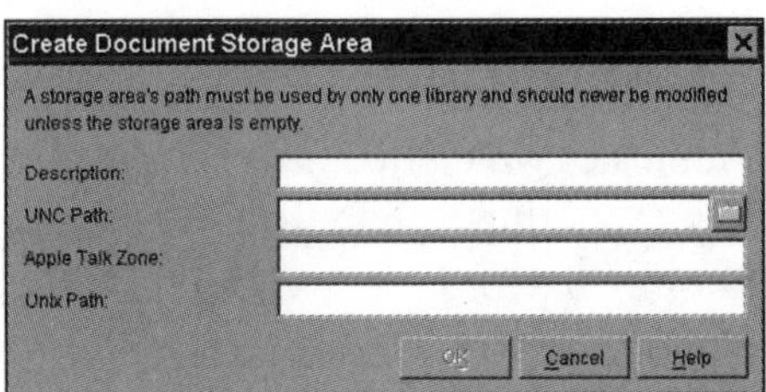

FIGURE 14.8 *Creating a New Document Storage Area*

The document storage area object exists in the domain and post office databases. It also exists in the guardian database, as well as the DMSH and DMSD databases specific to the GroupWise library. Once a document storage area is added to a library, the POA for the post office will not load unless the document storage area is accessible. Therefore, document storage areas located remotely from the post office server should only be placed on servers that are guaranteed to be up and accessible.

TIP

You can force a POA to load even if the library storage area is inaccessible by using the `/noconfig` switch in the POA load statement or startup file. The `/noconfig` switch tells the POA to disregard any POA configuration information in the post office database. Any settings that the POA requires will therefore not be available from WPHOST.DB, and will need to be specified in the POA startup file.

- **QuickFinder**: The QuickFinder indexing process is a low-priority POA process that indexes user mailboxes (including attachments and document references), as well as all documents in libraries on the post office. Chapter 8 shows a POA log file that includes some QuickFinder indexing .

NOTE

QuickFinder does not index images or .exe files. The property sheets of image or EXE document objects will be indexed, but any text contained in the actual binary file (image comments windows, for example) will not be included in the full-text index.

Understanding QuickFinder Indexing Process and Document Management

The QuickFinder indexing process proceeds as follows:

1. The POA begins the indexing run with the library found in the LIB0001 directory (this is the first library created on this post office). Processing continues through LIB00FF.
2. The POA checks the indexing queue found in the document property databases (DMDD*.DB). This queue indicates which documents have been added or updated since the last indexing run, thus telling the POA which documents need to be indexed or re-indexed.
3. The POA opens the document BLOB file for each document that must be indexed. From this BLOB file, it reads each unique word and adds that word to a word-list BLOB file unique to this document. Thus, for every document in the library, there will be two BLOB files: a document BLOB and a word-list BLOB.
4. If a document reference has been created by a user, the DMDD files will contain pointers to those document references. For each document reference, a copy of the word-list BLOB will be *hooked* to the mailbox indexing queue. If the mailbox is on a remote post office, the word-list BLOB will be sent to that PO's POA, for inclusion in the mailbox index.

TIP

Because each document reference on a remote post office generates BLOB traffic, I recommend that users not create large numbers of document references. Encouraging users to create query folders will help in this regard.

5. Once all the queued documents have had word-list BLOB files created, the word-list files are used to generate the incremental library index database. This database is found in the *.INC files in the GWDMS\<LIBRARY>\INDEX directory.
6. With the libraries indexed (remember, you began with LIB0001 and ran through LIB00FF), it is time to begin indexing mailboxes. The POA indexes user databases in alphabetical order, beginning with any prime user databases (PUxxxxxx.DB) in the OFUSER directory, and moving through the user databases (USERxxx.DB) in alphanumerical order.
7. The POA checks the indexing queue found within each PU or USER database. This queue tells the POA which items were added to the mailbox or shared folder since the last time the mailbox was indexed.
8. The POA opens each item found in the PU or USER database that it is indexing. The item content may be found in the PU or USER database, in a message database (MSGn.DB), or in a BLOB file in the OFFILES directory. The item data is indexed from the appropriate master record, wherever that record is located.
9. If the item being indexed is a document reference, the POA should now have a word-list BLOB file hooked to that document reference. This word-list file is used to generate the full-text index of the document reference. This prevents the POA from having to go back to the library and re-index the document (or, worse yet, index a document residing in a library in a remote post office).
10. All index data is written to the incremental index files (*.INC) found in the OFUSER\INDEX directory.
11. At the end of the last indexing run of the day, all *.INC file content is combined with the permanent index content found in the *.IDX files. This goes for both the library index and the mailbox index. The *.INC files are deleted, and the *.IDX files are renamed to reflect the fact that they have been updated with new content. All changes to the index databases are reflected in the database catalog in the guardian database (NGWGUARD.DB).

NOTE

Items only need to be indexed once, unless content changes. Once an item has been indexed, the appropriate indexing queue is updated to reflect that the item need not be indexed again. If the item is updated though, even if no changes were made, the item will be added to the indexing queue again. For instance, if a document is checked out and checked back in with no changes, it will still be re-indexed on the next run.

Intervening in the Indexing Process

Once the indexing process has begun, the only way to stop it from running is to unload the POA. Fortunately, I have not seen cases where it was necessary to call an immediate halt to the indexing process.

Sometimes, though, administrators want to trigger indexing manually. This must be done from the POA console. From the F10 ⇨ Actions ⇨ QuickFinder menu, you can find four options pertaining to QuickFinder indexing:

- **Update QuickFinder Indexes:** Launches the indexing process. All indexes served by this POA, including the mailbox index and all library indexes, will be updated.
- **Compress QuickFinder Indexes:** Merges all incremental indexes with the permanent index. The permanent index files will be renamed to reflect the time the operation was performed.
- **Update and Compress QuickFinder Indexes:** Performs both of the preceding operations, beginning with the update.
- **Delete and Regenerate All QuickFinder Indexes:** Deletes all the index *.IDC and *.IDX files in the OFUSER\INDEX directory and the LIBNNNN\INDEX directories. It then re-creates the *.IDX files. This option can also be activated by a hidden keystroke. You must be at the initial load screen of the POA and then hold down the Ctrl and Q keys at the same time.

WARNING

Delete and Regenerate All QuickFinder Indexes can take a very, very long time. Perhaps days, if you have a large post office and lots of documents. The index rebuild process will immediately delete all of the indexes for this post office and start to generate them again. Depending on CPU speed, I have observed that the POA can index between 10,000 and 30,000 documents an hour. If your post office supports a library with 500,000 documents, and has 500 users, each with 2,000 items in their mailbox, then you are looking at indexing 1,500,000 documents. At 10,000 per hour, this could take up to 150 hours, or a little over six days.

Dedicating a POA for QuickFinder Indexing

As mentioned in Chapter 8, you may find that a separate server needs to be dedicated to the process of indexing documents in large GroupWise libraries. For more information, refer back to Chapter 8, under the "Best Practices" section.

Planning Your Document-Management System

Even if you already have an established GroupWise e-mail system, you will want to take care in the way you implement document management. Consider this: In 1994, most companies that used GroupWise considered e-mail to be a convenience. By 1998, those same companies considered e-mail "mission-critical." It is not too much of a stretch to imagine the same sort of shift in the document-management arena. You may look at document management as a convenience today, but the odds are good that what you will really be building is a mission-critical system.

This section discusses the areas in which you will need to do some research. This section is designed to cause you to ask, and answer, some questions about your own organization so that you can effectively plan your document-management system.

Determining the Number of Users Requiring Library Access

The first thing you need to ask yourself is how many users are going to use the document-management system. It is possible that all of your users will need some sort of access, but you will want to be able to distinguish between those who will only use it occasionally, and those who will be actively creating documents every day.

Document management will obviously generate additional load to the server that hosts the post office and POA agent. This should be kept in mind when creating new post offices or planning to create a new library.

TIP

In the past, Novell has recommended that no more than about 500 to 750 users be placed on a GroupWise post office. With GroupWise 6, and caching mode on the GroupWise client, a post office can grow to support a few thousand users. This keeps the information store at a manageable size and helps ensure good performance. If document management will be heavily used, however, the post office supporting the library should probably not have more than 300 users on it. Keeping down the number of users on a post office will help to keep the processor utilization down and your users happy. Also, in the event that changes happen in the organization, you will likely be in a more flexible position to accommodate change if your servers are not already pushing capacity.

Library Location

Document management is most efficiently maintained when users reside on the same post office as the libraries they use the most. This eliminates the need for users to pull their documents across WAN links, and makes the indexing process more efficient, since document references for local libraries need not be sent across the wire. It also speeds up the query process for documents. Local libraries are queried directly by the same POA that services the GroupWise client in client/server mode. Remote libraries are queried via a store-and-forward system, guaranteeing at least a few seconds of additional lag before search results are returned to users.

There is some call for central library location, however. Corporate libraries could be created to house documents, such as ISO procedures, that most users will need only infrequently.

In this book's example company, WorldWide Widgets, the administrator selected to have all user libraries on the same post offices as the users they service. The Corp library, however, is centrally located on the Corp post office and houses documents that need to be accessed by the whole company. Users on the Corp post office are local to this library, which is good, since they are the ones who will be updating the documents there. Everyone else is remote to this library, which is fine, since they will only be accessing the corporate documents occasionally.

Disk Space for Document Management

Perhaps the most difficult challenge you will face as a GroupWise document-management administrator will be determining the amount of disk space your users' will require for their libraries.

Space Needed Today

Begin by determining how much space would be required to import all of the documents system-wide into GroupWise libraries. Add up the disk space taken up by all of the document directories on servers and individual workstations. The space required for these documents in GroupWise will be about 70 percent of their space on disk.

Remember, documents are compressed and encrypted. A pure text document may be a mere 20 percent of its original size. A compressed image file, however, will probably be right around 100 percent of its original size. If you assume that most of your documents will get about 50 percent compression, then the BLOB files for your existing documents will require about 50 percent of the space the documents currently require.

There are also the document property sheets, activity logs, and word-list BLOB files to consider. Typically, these files add about 40 percent to the space taken up by the document BLOB files (or 20 percent of the space taken up by uncompressed documents). So add 20 percent to the 50 percent, and you have the 70 percent figure.

If your documents are currently taking 20Gb of space, spread across several servers and a few hundred workstations, importing all of those documents into GroupWise libraries will require around 14Gb of space. This can be spread across multiple libraries, of course.

Space Needed in the Next Three Years

Now that you know how much space you need today, you need to plan for the future. Find out how many of your current collection of documents were created in the last year. Use this number to formulate a growth curve to estimate the amount of space needed for documents in the next two to three years.

If 30 percent of your 20Gb of documents were created in the last 12 months, then you should assume that your users are going to create at least 6Gb worth of documents per year. Taking 70 percent of that gives you a figure of 4.2Gb per year for growth of the GroupWise libraries.

Keep in mind that these numbers are very rough estimates. Your organization may have done business modeling that more accurately predicts document creation, or you may have access to benchmarks from organizations like yours that have implemented GroupWise document management. If this is the case, use your data rather than these ballpark figures.

Keep in mind, also, that with document management in place, you will see a much higher re-use of existing documents. Users will be better able to share the documents they create, so you may see a significant decrease in the growth of your libraries (coupled with an increase in productivity!).

Plan for Additional Hardware

Aside from the disk-space considerations previously discussed, you may need additional server hardware to support dedicated QuickFinder indexing. The QuickFinder server does not need to be a top-of-the-line server, however. In many cases, a workstation-class machine will suffice. The indexing process is a background process that users do not interact with directly. As long as the CPU speed is reasonably fast (300MHz or better), the POA on this machine should be able to keep up with your indexing needs. Of course, if you have 500,000 documents in your library, and the documents are changing frequently, you may want to consider using a powerful server to perform the QuickFinder process.

Dedicated servers are typically not required for the libraries themselves. Even if you plan to use additional document storage areas, these are usually best supported on separate volumes on the same server where the post office and the library reside.

User Training

For the users to become productive with document management, some end-user document-management training will likely be necessary. The online help included in the GroupWise client may be enough for some of your users, but they will likely be better served with some formal instruction.

Most users are reluctant to change the way they work. Document management represents a significant change, so steps should be taken to make things as easy as possible on your users. It has also been my experience that once users become accustomed to using document management, they wonder how they ever got along without it. The trick is getting your users to that point without upsetting them.

Selecting a Librarian User

One of the most important aspects of your document-management system will be choosing someone to work as a librarian. A user with manage rights to a library has the ability to find all documents in the library regardless of security, and can change the document security of any document in the library. The librarian user should generally be a system administrator who has post office administrative rights as well as library manage rights, but you may find it useful to give certain power users manage rights.

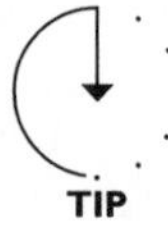
TIP

Anytime that manage rights are used to provide a user with access to a document, the system notifies the owner of the document of the security change message shown in Figure 14.9. So, although your librarian can read any document in the library, he or she cannot be sneaky about it.

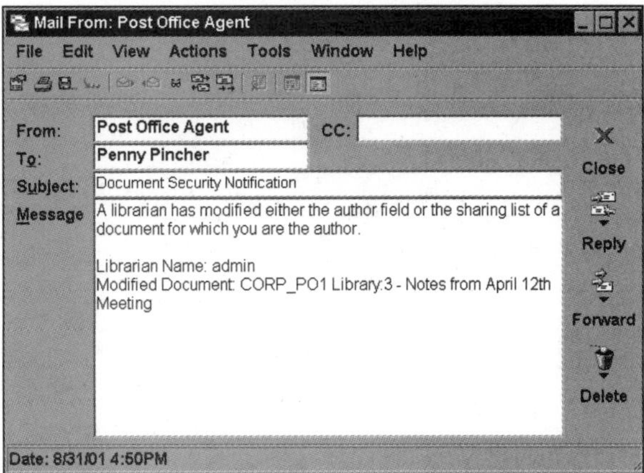

FIGURE 14.9 *Mail Notification Indicating That the Librarian Made a Change in the Security to a Document*

Creating a Library

This section walks you through the creation of a new GroupWise library. Before doing this, here are some points for you to remember:

- At least one library is created by default when installing a new GroupWise 6 system.
- After a new GroupWise system has been created, or an existing system migrated to GroupWise 6, library options will appear any time a new post office is created.
- Existing post offices can have new libraries added at any time.
- A post office can hold a maximum of 255 libraries

Before you create a library, you should verify that all agents are up and running and no connections are closed. You should also verify that administration changes are being propagated down to the post office. This can be done by changing a user's phone number from ConsoleOne, and then checking the address book from the GroupWise client to see if the change made it.

1. Create the library object in your system by highlighting the GroupWise post office that will host the library.

   Do this from the GroupWise view, not the NDS view. Also, make sure to be connected to the domain that owns the post office that will house the new post office.
2. With the post office highlighted, select the right mouse button and choose New ➪ Library.
3. Fill in the details of the library in the resulting dialog box, shown in Figure 14.10, and give the library a name, an NDS context, and check the Define additional properties box.

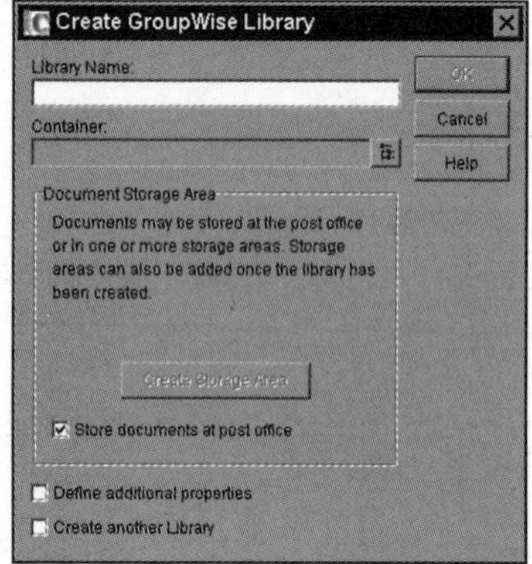

FIGURE 14.10: *The Create GroupWise Library Dialog Box*

NOTE

An external document storage location does not need to be created unless you expect production documents will take up more space than available on the post office volume. If you need to create an external document storage location, then start the process when you get to Step 12.

4. Click OK.

   You will now be presented with the library object's Identification property page, as seen in Figure 14.11, so that you can define additional library properties.

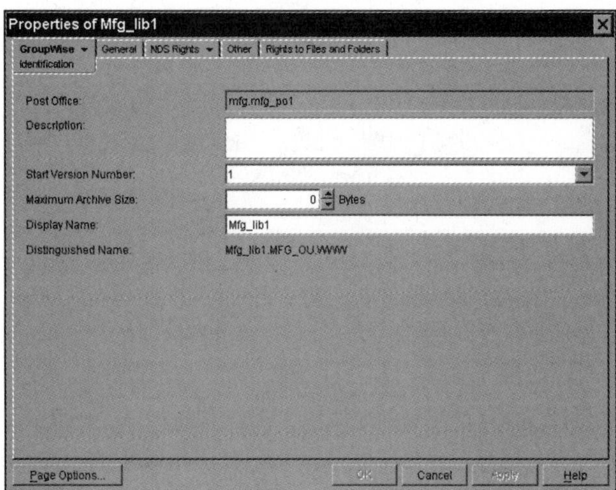

FIGURE 14.11 *The Library Object's Identification Property Page*

5. Fill in the Description field with the purpose of the library, the pager number of the library administrator, or some other useful information.
6. The Start Version Number field can be left as 1 or changed to 0.

   This value determines if the first version of a document is version 0 or version 1. Most people think in terms of ordinal numbers (for example, we count to ten starting with one, not zero), so it makes more sense to use 1.
7. The Maximum Archive Size field in bytes is the number of bytes allowed for archive sets, and the size should be smaller than the size of your backup media.

   For example, if your backup media is 6Gb, then you may want the maximum archive size to be 1.5Gb. This would have each archive set be 1.5Gb so that you would only need to wait for 1.5Gb of archive documents before you would have a complete archive set to move to backup tape. If you set the size to 6Gb, you would have to wait for 6Gb of archive documents before an archive set would be complete.

8. The Display Name field can be left at the default (the name of the library object) or changed to a longer name.

   The display name is the name that users will see in their library configuration list, so it should be something intuitive.

9. If you really need to create an external storage area, click the Storage Areas property page on the GroupWise tab and uncheck the Store documents at post office check box.

   If you do not need an external document storage area, skip to Step 14.

10. Click the Add button (it can only be selected after the Store documents at post office check box has been unchecked).

11. Fill in an appropriate description of the storage area.

12. Fill in the appropriate UNC path.

    A browse button is available, which will populate the UNC path field.

13. Click OK.

The path used must be unique for this library. If multiple libraries use the same path, document BLOB file maintenance cannot be run safely.

14. Click the Rights property page below the GroupWise tab and select to disable the public rights for Delete and Reset in-use flag.

See the "Library Rights" section earlier in this chapter for a full discussion on these settings.

15. Use the Add button to add at least one user.

    Assign that user manage rights. It is critical that every library have at least one librarian user assigned.

Using Document Properties Maintenance

Once a library has been created, you will likely want to begin customizing the way the properties sheets appear for documents in this library. This section walks you through the use of the Document Properties Maintenance tool.

Document properties maintenance is used to add or remove fields from libraries, to edit lookup tables, and to edit document type definitions. To use the tool, do the following:

1. From ConsoleOne, select the post office object for which document properties maintenance needs to be run (the post office that owns the library you just created).
2. Choose Tools ➪ GroupWise Utilites ➪ Document Properties Maintenance.

   You will be presented with the window shown in Figure 14.12.

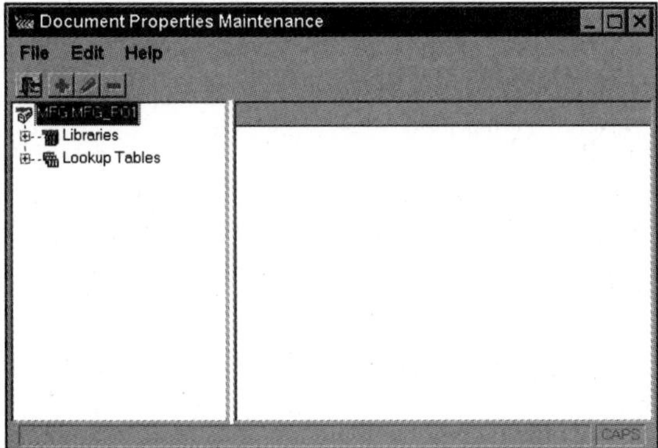

FIGURE 14.12 *The Document Properties Maintenance Interface*

In these steps, you create related fields for your document property sheets. This scenario shows how to create and populate lookup tables for automobile makes and models. This scenario also adds the Make and Model Property fields to the Mfg_lib1 property sheet.

3. Expand the Lookup Tables list, and then select the root Lookup Tables icon.
4. Click the + button on the toolbar to begin adding a lookup table.

   You will be presented with the dialog box shown in Figure 14.13.

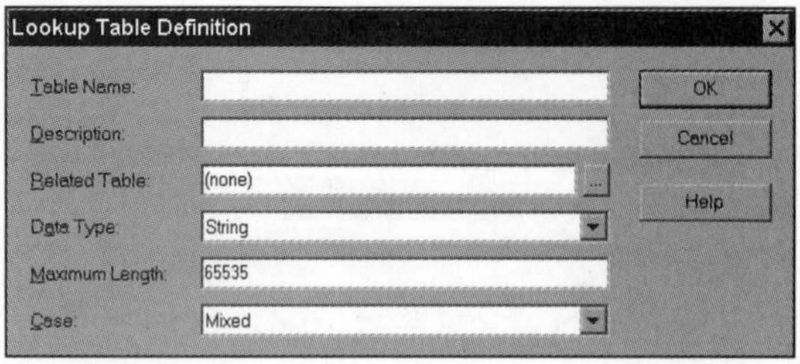

FIGURE 14.13 *The Lookup Table Definition Dialog Box*

5. In the Table Name field, type **MAKE Lookup Table,** and then add something like **Lookup Table for MAKE** to the Description field.
6. Leave the Related Table definition as (none).

   This is because Make is going to be the parent field for Model.
7. Leave the Data Type field as String, the Maximum Length field at 65535, and the Case field as Mixed.
8. Click OK.

   The Make table has now been created.
9. Highlight Make Lookup Table and click the + button to add values as shown in Figure 14.14.

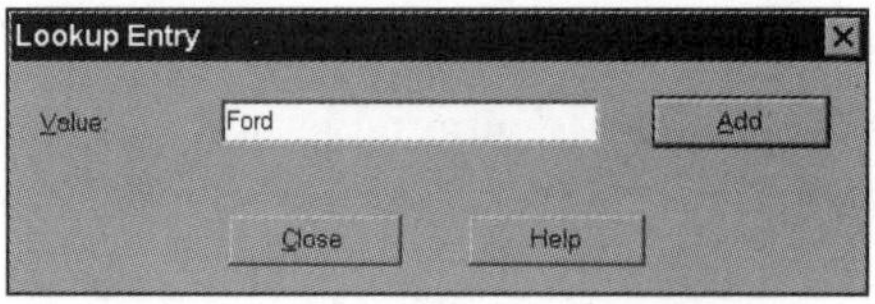

FIGURE 14.14 *Adding the Value "Ford" to the Make Lookup Table*

10. Add the lookup entries of Dodge, Chevrolet, and Ford by entering the value in the field and then clicking the Add button.

11. Click the Close button to dismiss the Lookup Entry dialog box.
12. Highlight the Lookup Tables icon again and click the Add button.
13. In the Table Name field, type **MODEL Lookup Table,** and then add something like **Lookup Table for MODEL** to the Description field.
14. Select MAKE Lookup Table from the browse button on the Related Table field.
15. Leave the Data Type field as String, the Maximum Length field at 65535, and the Case field as Mixed.
16. Click OK.

    The Model table is now created and is considered as a child of the Make lookup table.
17. Highlight Model Lookup Table and click the + button to add values.

    The dialog box shown in Figure 14.15 opens.

    The first value of the Make Lookup Table will appear as the Parent Value. In this example, the first parent value is Chevrolet. At this point, you would add values to the parent value Chevrolet by typing in the Value field and clicking the Add button.

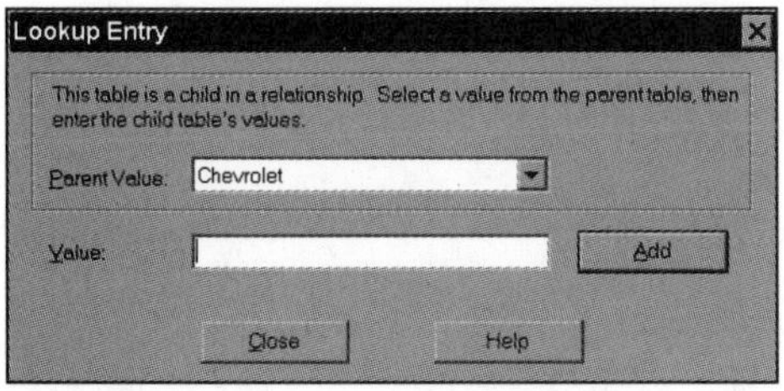

FIGURE 14.15 *Adding a Model Value That Relates to the Chevrolet Make Value*

18. Add the values Corsica and Impala to the parent value Chevrolet.
19. Now change the Parent Value field to Dodge and add the value Durango.

20. Now change the Parent Value field to Ford and add value F150.
21. Click the Close button.
22. Expand the Libraries icon and select the library to which you want to add the Make and Model fields.
23. Click the + button to begin add mode, and you will see the dialog box shown in Figure 14.16.

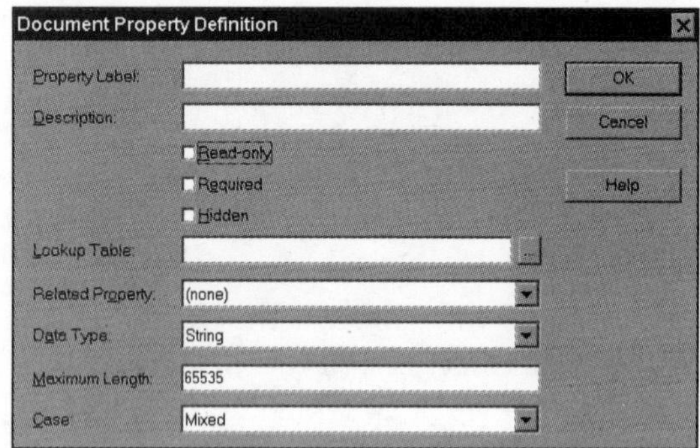

FIGURE 14.16 *Assigning the Make Field to Document Property Sheets for All Documents in a Library*

24. In the Property Label field, type **MAKE,** and add something like **MAKE of Automobile** in the Description field.
25. Check the Required check box.

    The Read-only check box should only be used if you need a field stamped on every document property sheet, for example, something like *Property of WorldWide Widgets — Internal Use Only.* The Hidden value should only be used if you need to have a value that is placed in the field but is hidden from the users.
26. Click the Lookup Table browse button, select MAKE Lookup Table from the list, and then close the dialog box.
27. Again, expand the Libraries icon, select the same library to which the Make field was added, and click the + button to begin add mode (see Figure 14.16).

28. In the Property Label field, type **MODEL,** and add something like **MODEL of Automobile** in the Description field.
29. Click the Required check box and assign it to the Model Lookup Table.
30. Leave the Related Property field as Make and click OK.

So, 30 steps later, what has been accomplished?

- The Make lookup table has makes of cars in it.
- The Model lookup table has models of cars in it, and the make that is selected determines which models are available.
- Both Make and Model are now available fields on document properties sheets.
- When a user creates a document, that document can now be related to a specific automobile with just a couple of clicks.

This process may be useful for a library at an auto dealership, but how can it be applied to your organization?

Related fields such as Client and Matter number or Customer and Contact can be used to organize documents based on attributes in their properties sheet. If all documents at a law firm have Client and Matter number fields populated, for example, it becomes a simple matter to locate all documents by querying the library based on the Client field. For involved cases, a query for both the Client and Matter number fields can be used to call up all documents specific to that particular case.

As shown in the example scenario, the Document Property Maintenance tool can be used to create related fields. It is also the tool you will need to use to create or edit document types.

The document type lookup table is just another lookup table, similar to the Make lookup table created in the preceding steps. It is populated with descriptive names for document types, as well as criteria for the expiration of these documents.

You will also use the Document Property Maintenance tool to add fields to property sheets. In the example scenario, you added the Make and Model fields to the property sheets. You linked them to lookup tables, but not all fields need to be linked to a static table. You could create a custom field called Customer, for instance, and allow users to populate it with the name of the customer or client for whom the document was created.

Maintaining GroupWise Libraries

Library maintenance is necessary to fix inconsistencies created by hardware, software, or user errors. Obviously, hard drive corruption can cause database inconsistencies. Scheduled events should be configured to routinely run library checks to keep your libraries in good working order and to alert of potential future problems.

Here is a discussion of the tools available to you for library maintenance. When a GroupWise library is selected, and mailbox/library maintenance is activated from the Tools ➪ GroupWise Utilities menu, you will find an Analyze/Fix Library option, as shown in Figure 14.17.

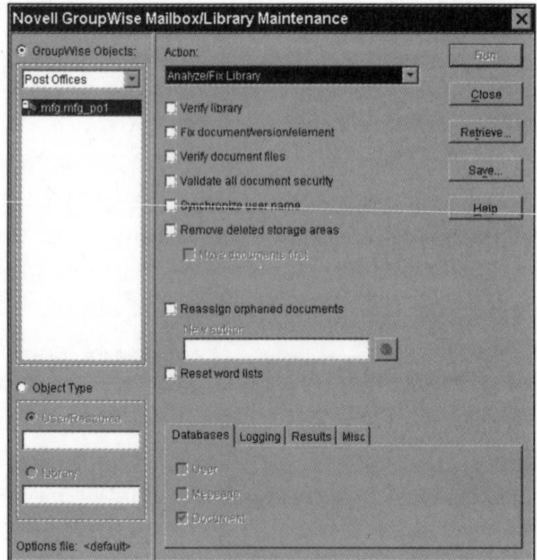

FIGURE 14.17 *The Mailbox/Library Maintenance Tool with Analyze/Fix Library Selected*

There are several check boxes available with this option selected:

- Verify library
- Fix document/version/element

- Verify document files
- Validate all document security
- Synchronize user name
- Remove deleted storage areas
- Reassign orphaned documents

This section discusses each of these options in turn.

- **Verify library:** The Verify library operation will clear up inconsistencies between a post office database and the DMSH.DB file. These two files are responsible for telling the POA and the clients which libraries are available on this post office.

  In cases where DMSH.DB does not know about a library, but the post office database does, *Problem 70 messages* will start to appear any time library maintenance is performed. The problem could also manifest itself in GroupWise clients by not showing the correct list of libraries under Tools ➪ Options ➪ Documents.

  Verify library fixes the cause of these Problem 70 messages. It also checks to make sure the document class schema is correct. The schema is re-applied if it is found to be invalid.

- **Fix document/version/element:** This check makes sure that every document, version, and element record has a match. This is similar to a contents check on a user mailbox (covered in Chapter 17). Where pointers do not line up correctly, this tool attempts to resolve the problem. In cases where the problem cannot be resolved, the tool reports the document number of the document that is problematic.

  This tool also reports the document number of every document BLOB file that was referenced in a properties sheet but not found on disk. It provides the administrator with the last known path to the document, which allows the administrator to find the document BLOB file on a tape backup system.

- **Verify document files:** Like Fix document/version/element, Verify document files reports the document number and last known path to every document BLOB file referenced in the library but not present on disk. It does not verify or fix the assorted document pointers in the library, however. If all you are looking for is a list of missing BLOB files, this option runs more quickly than the Fix document/version/element option.

This type of problem typically occurs when a user is deleted from the system and then re-imported later with the original FID. The problem stems from the fact that mailbox access can be granted based on the three-character FID, which can be specified in the import file, but document access is granted based on the 32-digit GUID. Security problems based on invalid GUID information may also occur when information-store files are damaged, but this is rare.

NOTE

A GUID is a system-level unique identifier of a GroupWise object. This 128-bit code is represented as a 32-digit hexadecimal number, and can have 3.4*1038 possible values (that's 34 followed by about 38 zeros, or over 340 times a billion times a billion times a billion times a billion). The GUID is created when a user object is created and never changes because it's guaranteed to be unique through out the system.

- **Validate all document security:** This option performs the same GUID check as the Validate author/creator security option but applies it to all users on the sharing list for the document, including the lists for version-level security.
- **Synchronize user name:** The Synchronize user name option goes through the author and creator fields and verifies that the display name is correct. This type of check should be run if the first or last name of a user changes, and that user is either the author or creator of documents in the library.
- **Remove deleted storage areas:** If a document storage area needs to be removed, the Remove deleted storage areas operation must be used.

1. Delete the storage area from the Library Storage Areas tab on the library object.
2. Select the post office to which this library belongs, pull down the Tools menu, and choose GroupWise Utilities ➪ Mailbox/Library Maintenance.
3. Select Analyze/Fix Library and check the boxes for Remove deleted storage areas and Move documents first.
4. Click Run.

This operation moves all document BLOB files from the deleted storage area to the currently active storage area, and updates all property sheets and activity logs with the new path. It also allows you to remove the physical directory structure.

If you delete a storage area, but do not run this operation, and then delete the physical directory structure (or otherwise make the deleted storage area unavailable to the POA), then the next time the POA attempts to load, it will fail. It is therefore critical that the POA be up and running throughout Steps 1 through 4. If you must delete a storage area, do not wait very long between deleting it from the library object and running this operation.

NOTE

If you need to move a storage area from one physical location to another, refer to "Moving a Document Storage Area," later in this chapter.

- **Reassign orphaned documents:** If a user has been deleted from the GroupWise system, and that user is the creator of documents in GroupWise libraries, those documents become orphaned. The Reassign orphaned documents operation allows you to specify a new creator for all orphaned documents in the library.

  If you plan to delete a user from the system, you should also plan to reassign that user's documents to someone else using this feature.
- **Reset word lists:** Allows the program to regenerate the document library word list the next time an index operation is performed. Documents stored in a library are indexed and inserted into a generated word list. This word list allows users to search for a document by keywords as well as any word contained within a document.

TIP

If you archive a document and then run this operation, users will not be able to find this document by performing a search. This is because the document was archived, hence when the reset word list operation runs, there was no source document to reference to regenerate the word list. As a result, users may not be able to find the document. Archiving documents is being used less and less, with this situation being one of the main reasons. A second reason is that disk space is cheap today, and the need to archive infrequently used documents is lessened.

Creating Library Maintenance Schedule Events

The prior section discussed each of the Analyze/Fix Library options found when you are running mailbox/library maintenance. These options may be run manually for troubleshooting purposes, but I recommend that they be scheduled to run automatically. This will ensure that database problems are caught quickly and help prevent the loss of document data.

1. Open the details window for the POA object and select the Schedule Events property page.

   If there are multiple POAs for this post office (that is, if you have a dedicated indexing POA), select the POA that performs message file processing.

2. Click the Create button.

   You will be presented with the dialog shown in Figure 14.18.

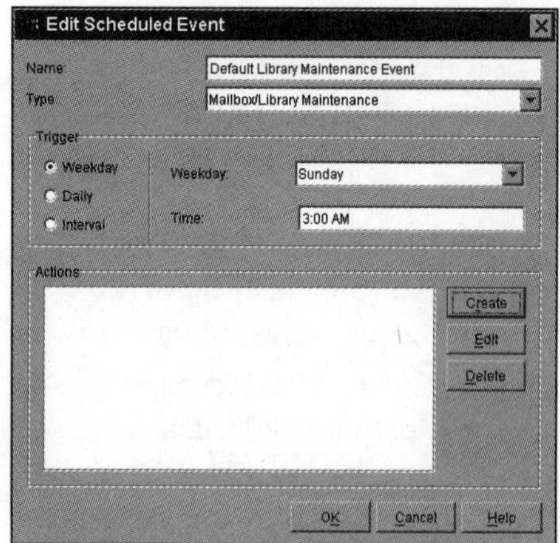

FIGURE 14.18 *Creating a New Scheduled Event for the POA*

3. Name the event Default Library Maintenance Event.
4. Change the type from Disk Check to Mailbox/Library Maintenance.
5. Leave the trigger at Weekday, and the weekday at Sunday.
6. Change the time to 3:00 AM.

   (This example scenario shows a time when no other scheduled events are running and backup jobs will be finished.)

7. Click the Create button and you get the dialog box shown in Figure 14.19.

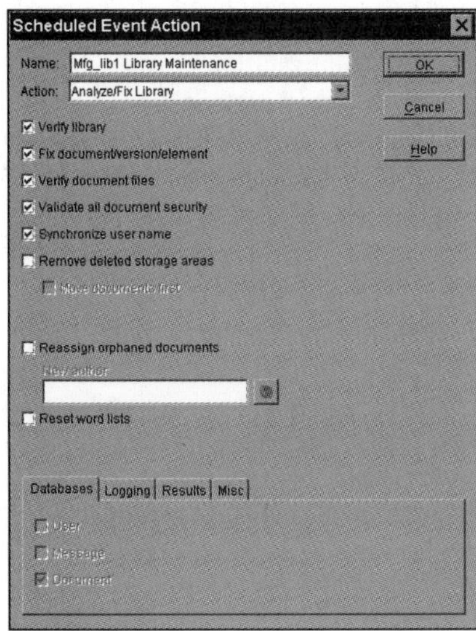

FIGURE 14.19 *Assigning Actions to the New Scheduled Event*

8. In the Name field, type **<Library Name> Library Maintenance** and change the Action field to Analyze/Fix Library.
9. Check the boxes for Verify library, Fix document/version/element, Verify document files, Validate all document security, and Synchronize user name.
10. Click OK.
11. Finally, enable the Default POA Mailbox/Library Maintenance Actions option and then click OK.
12. Click OK again, on the Edit Scheduled Event dialogue box, to save the new event.

    By default, the new event will already be enabled.

Next Sunday at 3:00 a.m., the POA will launch a thread to perform maintenance on all libraries owned by this post office. Monday morning, the administrator will have a log file from this operation waiting in his or her mailbox. The log file should be carefully reviewed to ascertain the current health of the libraries.

Performing a Mass Change to the Author Field

One of the more common document administration tasks involves making changes to the property sheets for large numbers of documents. In this scenario, Billy Bob is now taking over the responsibilities for Larry Admin, so the administrator needs to change all documents that were authored by Larry to be authored by Billy. Before beginning, here are a couple of things I would like to reiterate:

- All mass-change operations are initiated through the GroupWise client.
- Mass-change operations should be performed by users with manage rights. These users are the only ones who can be confident that all documents that need to be changed have been selected. This is because users with manage rights can find documents in the library that have not been shared.

1. Log in to the mailbox of a librarian user for the post office to which you will be making changes.
2. Pull down the Tools menu and select Mass Document Operations to get to the dialog box shown in Figure 14.20.

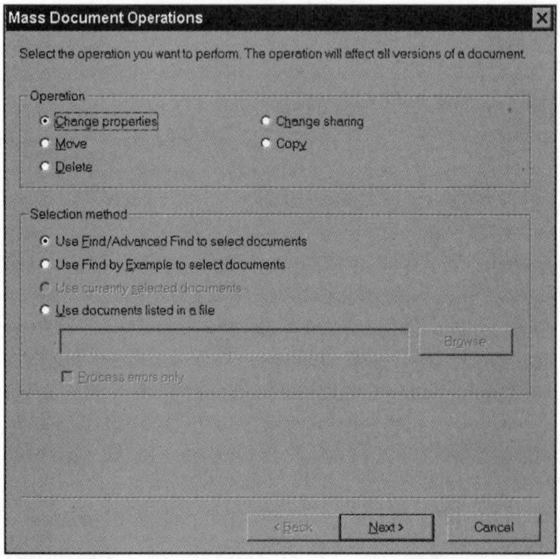

FIGURE 14.20 *The Mass Document Operations Dialog Box*

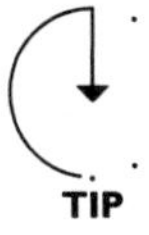

The Mass Document Operations option is available only if you are in online mode from the GroupWise 6 client. If you are running in cache or remote modes, you will not see this option.

3. Leave the Operation selection as Change properties.
4. Under Selection method, leave the Use Find/Advanced Find to select documents field as the method to select documents.
5. Click Next to get to the dialog box shown in Figure 14.21.

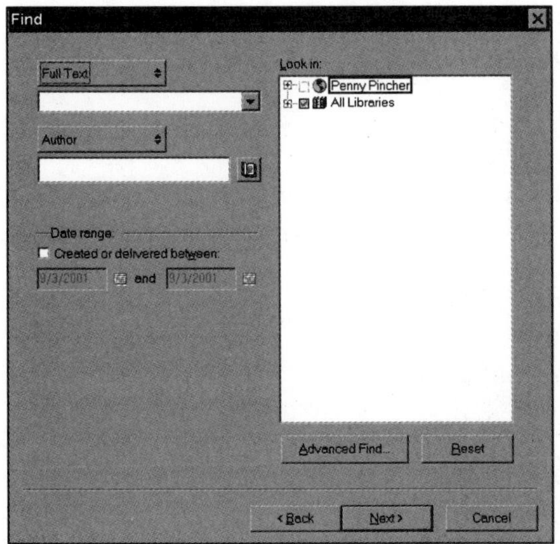

FIGURE 14.21 *Property Sheets to Find for Mass-Document Operations*

6. In the Author field, use the browse button to enter the name of the author that needs to be updated.

   In this case, the name is Larry Admin.
7. If you prefer to only change documents within a certain date range (perhaps you only need to change documents that Larry created after he transferred to the corporate office on 1/1/2001), select the Created or delivered between field and enter the appropriate date range.

8. In the Look in pane, you will need to specify which libraries to search for documents that meet your criteria.

   By default, only the library that this user has specified as their default library (under Tools ➪ Options ➪ Documents) will be checked.

NOTE

To do this properly, you must have manage rights for all libraries that are selected in the Look in pane. If you don't see the Apply Librarian Rights check box on the dialog box, then you definitely do not have manage rights for all libraries in the system. More specifically, you don't have manage rights to the default library of the mail account into which you are logged.

9. Click Next to get to the dialog box shown in Figure 14.22.

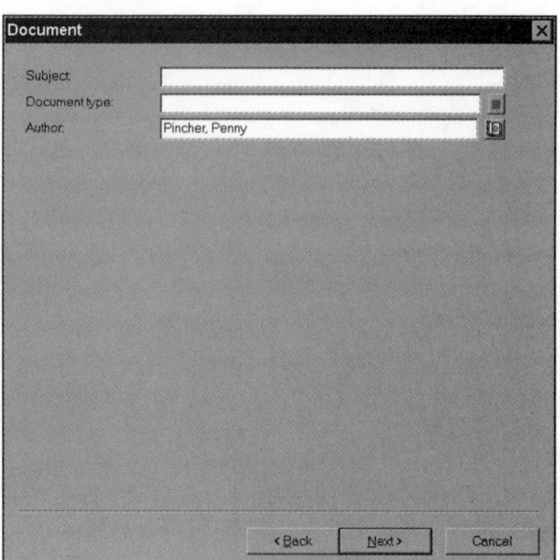

FIGURE 14.22 *Entering Target Values for the Mass-Document Operation*

10. Use the browse button to pick the new author value.

    In the example case, the new author value is Billy Bob.

11. Click Next and you will be presented with the dialog box shown in Figure 14.23.

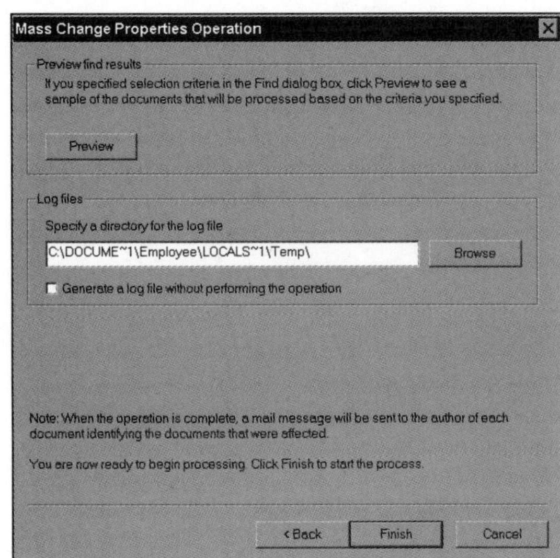

FIGURE 14.23 *Setting the Operational Parameters for the Mass-Document Operation*

12. Click the Preview button so that you can see exactly which documents will be changed by this operation.
13. If you want to make sure that all parties (authors) affected are okay with the changes, check the Generate a log file without performing the operation check box.

    If you click next with this option enabled, the utility will generate Mass0000.err and Mass0000.logs in your Windows Temp directory, as well as sending you a copy of the logs. The logs can then be sent to others to verify the changes are correct and approved. If this option is enabled, all the steps in the mass-change operation will need to be repeated to actually do the operation when the change is approved.

NOTE

If you decide to generate a log file without performing the operation, every document shown in the log file will show a *Not Processed error.* This is normal and tells you that the criteria were met but the operation was not actually performed.

14. Click Next.

A Mass Change Progress window will then appear and give a summary of the operation. If you checked Validate document property fields, then you may see a Validation Error dialog box after the operation is complete.

Performing a Mass Change on an Author's Name

In this scenario, Billy Bob now wants to be known as Bill Bob. To accommodate this, the administrator changed the First Name field of Billy Bob's NDS user object to Bill. Now Billy's name on his GroupWise mailbox has been updated to Bill Bob, but all of the documents for which Bill is the author still show Billy as the first name of the author. Figure 14.24 shows this situation; notice that his mailbox name is Bill Bob though.

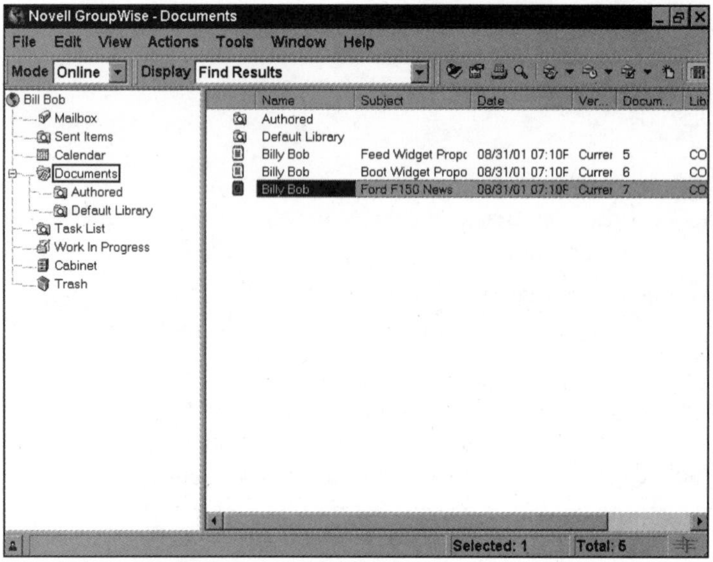

FIGURE 14.24 *Documents Showing Billy as Author*

This operation could be performed from the GroupWise client as a true mass-document operation, but in this case there is an administrative tool that is much easier to use. In order to get the document properties sheets synchronized with the address book regarding Bill Bob, you can run a synchronize user name library check. Here are the steps for doing this:

1. Launch ConsoleOne.
2. Highlight the library or libraries in which Bill Bob's documents are kept.

TIP

If you want to select all the libraries at once, select the GroupWise system icon. Click the libraries filter. All of the libraries in the system will appear. You may now select these libraries with a Ctrl+click mouse routine, multiple selections of libraries.

3. With the libraries highlighted, choose Tools ➪ GroupWise Utilites ➪ Mailbox/Library Maintenance.

   You will be presented with the window shown in Figure 14.25.

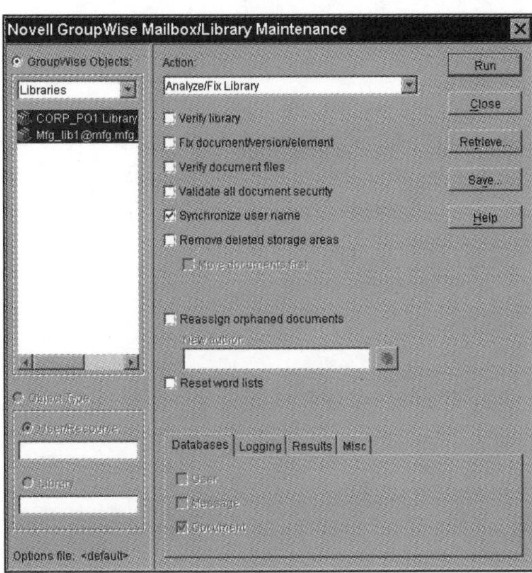

FIGURE 14.25 *The Mailbox/Library Maintenance Tool, with Multiple Library Objects Selected*

4. Change the Action field to Analyze/Fix Library.

5. Check Synchronize user name.

   You are not required to select a user to synchronize. The operation will synchronize all user names.

6. Click Run.

Each POA that services a library in the list will then synchronize user first and last names in document property fields with the user first and last names in the address book. Even if a user name has changed completely (such as if Billy Bob changed his name to Jim Dandy — a dubious improvement at best), the POA will be able to synchronize the change. This is because the user GUID remains the same through any number of name changes or post office moves.

Using Archive/Delete Documents

If you begin to run out of disk space on a server volume housing a GroupWise library, it may be time to run an archive/delete documents operation. This operation uses the criteria specified under document types to determine which documents are to archived, which get deleted, and which documents remain in the library.

Before beginning, this section discusses how document type information gets applied. In Figure 14.5, earlier in this chapter, the delete document type was presented. The following is an explanation of how to make the delete document type. These concepts can be applied to any document types.

1. Launch ConsoleOne.
2. Highlight a GroupWise post office where you want to create the delete document type.
3. Click the + sign next to the lookup tables to expand the lookup tables.
4. Highlight the Document Type icon.
5. Click the + sign on the menu to add a new document type.
6. Fill in the Value field.

   This is the name of the document type. When users create documents, they assign document types to them by selecting this value from a list on the property sheet.

7. Indicate the maximum versions.

   This is the maximum number of versions allowed for this document type. It has no bearing on the archive/delete operation.

8. Choose the expiration action.

   This is an action that is going to be taken on this document by the archive/delete operation. Possible values are archive, delete, and retain. Document types with an expiration action of retain will always remain in the library. For the delete document type you are creating, the action is going to be deleted.

9. Choose the document life (in days).

   This value is used to determine whether or not the expiration action is performed. If the value is 30, then this document will be eligible for the expiration action after it has been untouched for 30 days. This means that an actively viewed or edited document with a 30-day document life could remain in the library indefinitely. For the delete document type you are creating, the document life will be 30 days.

In the example scenario for the delete document type, when the archive/delete operation is run, all documents that have not been accessed within the document life time of 30 days defined for the delete document type will be deleted.

Moving a Document Storage Area

Moving a document storage area can be tedious, because the document storage area object is stored in multiple databases. Information about document storage areas appears in all domain databases, the post office database, DMSH.DB, and DMSD000n.DB. Because the information is contained in several places, care must be taken to ensure that the change correctly propagates. Remember, if the POA finds a document storage area object record, but cannot connect to the document storage area at the defined path, the POA will not load.

Before beginning, here are some things to consider when contemplating moving a document storage area.

- If you are going to move a document storage area to a new server, this should be done before the old server is decommissioned.

- Make sure that the new document path conforms to an 8.3 naming convention.
- If you are moving an entire post office, and documents are stored at the post office, there is no need to worry about the update. It will occur automatically.
- If you are moving an entire post office, and documents are stored in document storage areas, you should move the document storage areas before you move the post office.

Following is the procedure for moving a document storage area:

1. Create a test document in the library to verify that the current document storage area and library are working properly, and check the activity log on the property sheet of the document to be sure the document is being written to the path defined in the document storage area.

   You can see the path to where the document is stored by right-clicking on the columns and selecting Filename.

2. Disable logins on the post office by checking the Disable logins check box on the information screen on the post office.

   If users attempt to log in to that post office, they will see the dialog box shown in Figure 14.26.

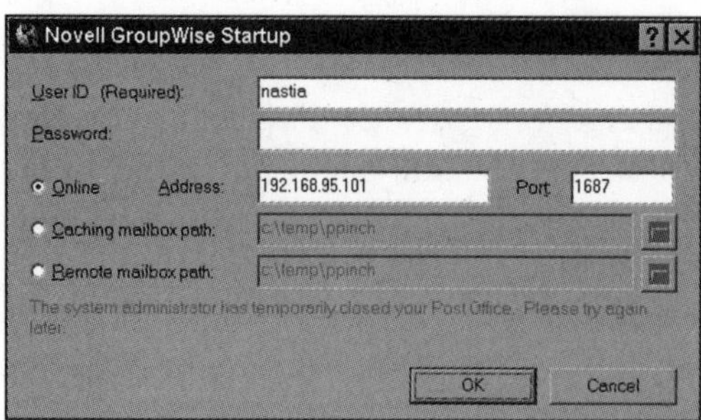

FIGURE 14.26 *Can't Log In to the Post Office*

3. Unload the POA.
4. Ensure that the POA has the necessary `/user` and `/password` switches to connect with full rights to the new document storage area and to the old document storage area.

   If the two locations are on servers in different NDS trees, you will need to create identically named accounts, and then provide appropriate bindery contexts so that the user name (without context) is all that is required for connection.
5. Reload the POA.
6. Verify that no users are connected to the POA by looking at the POA screen — the POA screen should show 0 user connections — and then attempt to log in to this post office, to be sure that the POA is not allowing connections.
7. Copy the document storage area to the new location, and verify that all of the directories and files were copied.
8. Launch ConsoleOne, and open the Identification property page for the GroupWise library.
9. Select the Storage Areas property page, edit the document storage area entry of the library object to reflect the new path on the new server, and click OK to save your changes.
10. Wait for the POA to process the change of the document storage area; you should see something in the POA's log file referencing the change to the document storage area.
11. From the post office object details window, uncheck the Disable logins box.
12. Make sure that the test document you created in Step 1 is still accessible (try opening or viewing it).
13. Create a new document in the library and look at the activity log of the property sheet to verify the document is being stored in the new path of the document storage area.

Troubleshooting Document Storage Area Move Problems

If you follow the procedures in the preceding section, you should not run into problems moving document storage areas. If you have managed to get yourself into trouble, however, the following troubleshooting steps may help:

- **Make sure the `/user` and `/password` switches are correct.** Ensure that the same user account can be used to access the old and the new storage location.
- **If the POA will not load, apply the `/noconfig` switch to the load statement or POA startup file.** This should be treated as a temporary fix that lets you get the POA up and running so that it can process the change.
- **Rebuild the post office database using the System Maintenance tool found under Tools ➪ GroupWise Utilities.**
- **Try toggling the UNC path for the storage area back to its original value.** Once that change has propagated, test to make sure the old path actually works by creating a new document and viewing its activity log. If the old path can be made to work, try the walkthrough procedure again to move the storage area to the new location.
- **Try running the Remove deleted storage area operation.**

If these troubleshooting steps fail, contact Novell support to get the problem resolved.

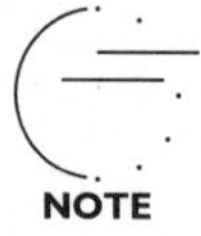

NOTE

I have seen situations where WPDOMAIN.DB and WPHOST.DB were correctly updated, but NGWGUARD.DB, DMSH.DB, and DMSD0001.DB were not correctly updated. In these cases, Novell had to be contacted so that they could manually edit the databases with secure Novell tools. Until the problem was resolved, the POA had to be loaded with the `/noconfig` switch.

Backing Up the GroupWise Document Management System

System backups are critical to the timely restoration of a mission-critical system, and this is especially true when you are using document management. If documents make up a large part of your business, you should spare no expense ensuring that the document-management system is backed up regularly.

The best solution currently is to use backup software that can handle backing up open files. This will ensure that all document-management databases and BLOB files are backed up, even if there is some activity on the system during the backup run.

As stated earlier, documents are stored in BLOB files, and every time a document is opened and subsequently brought back into the library, a new document BLOB is created and the old document BLOB is deleted. This architecture can interfere in the backup process.

Consider this: What if a user opens and closes a document between the time the backup agent has backed up the property sheet information and backed up the document BLOB? In this situation, the document BLOB that the backed-up property sheet points to is not the BLOB file that got backed up. For this reason, all users should be out of the post office to get a good backup of a library.

Fortunately, if the BLOB file has become orphaned in this manner, there is a solution. I cover this in the next section.

Exporting Orphaned Document BLOBs

If document BLOB files are restored from tape without their accompanying property sheets (the DMDD*.DB files), then some of these BLOB files may not be referenced by any property sheet. These document BLOBs are now orphaned. The trick is finding them. After all, there are thousands, perhaps tens or hundreds of thousands, of BLOB files, and there are only likely to be a few orphans.

Fortunately, the standalone GWCheck tool, GWCHECK.EXE, can be used to export all orphaned document BLOB files.

1. Run GWCHECK.EXE.
2. Select Library for the object type, and enter in the name of the library.
3. Select Analyze/Fix for the action, and check the options for Contents and Documents.
4. Click Run.

GWCHECK.EXE will look in each document storage area for document BLOB files that do not have a corresponding entry in the DMDD*.DB files. Any document BLOB files thus determined to be orphaned will be moved to an FDxx directory structure underneath the root of the directory from which GWCHECK.EXE was run.

The log file will list the pertinent information about each of the orphaned documents, including library name, original document number, version, original path to document BLOB, and author name. You can then use this information to return the document BLOB files to their author. The author of the document can then import the BLOB file as a new document by simply dragging and dropping the file onto the GroupWise client window.

Best Practices

I would like to reiterate some points made earlier in this chapter by identifying them as best practices. These principles or practices have been proven to improve the stability and or performance of GroupWise document management systems:

- **Use a dedicated indexing station.** This server could be used to index libraries on multiple post offices, and it will prevent the indexing process from competing with client/server services for CPU time.
- **Employ a *local library* model.** Users create the majority of their documents in a library housed on their post office, rather than on a different post office.
- **Try to limit library size to 500,000 documents.** Even though GroupWise architecture can handle over a million documents in a library, I have seen that performance begins to degrade with libraries of that size. Running a Fix document/version/element operation on a very large library may take over a week to complete. These limitations may change as faster hardware becomes available.
- **Provide users with document-management training.** This will save you enormous amounts of time by preventing the deluge of questions that typically follows the deployment of any new product.

Summary

This chapter discussed GroupWise document management. The chapter walked you through some key library and administration tasks, and explained how to best maintain a mission-critical document-management system.

GroupWise document management is a fourth-generation product, and is the most cost-effective document-management solution on the market today. The integration of document management with the user mailbox makes the tool as easy to use as e-mail, and reduces the cost of ownership by centralizing and simplifying administration.

CHAPTER 15

Administering Multiple GroupWise Systems

It is not uncommon, in this age of mergers, acquisitions, and outsourcing, for an administrator to be confronted with the task of administering more than one GroupWise system. This chapter covers the tasks that are common to multiple-system administration: merging systems, releasing systems, and synchronizing address books between systems.

Multiple-System Concepts

Before discussing the tasks that are common to multiple-system administration, here are some concepts to understand.

The Primary Domain Defines the System

If you are working with more than one GroupWise system, you are also working with more than one primary domain. The primary domain database, WPDOMAIN.DB, contains complete information about all objects contained in its GroupWise system.

In order to administer multiple systems, you need to know which primary domain owns which objects. You also need to know which system you are connecting to when you make changes.

External Domains Are Placeholders

A primary domain can contain a special kind of record — an external domain record. This is essentially a placeholder that allows the primary domain to be aware of the existence of another GroupWise system. Note, however, that this placeholder does not give the primary any control over objects that exist in the other system.

External domains allow you to manage the connectivity between your multiple GroupWise systems as if they were a single system — almost. You will use external domain records as you merge systems into a single system, or release domains into their own systems. You will also use external domain records to set up address-book synchronization between two systems that are external to each other.

Releasing Domains

When a domain needs to become its own system (as part of an outsourcing contract, perhaps), the administrator must tell the primary domain to *release* the domain that must be let go. That domain will then become a primary domain in its own, single-domain system.

Merging Systems

When two GroupWise systems need to be combined, the primary domain for one system will release all of its secondaries. This, in effect, creates several GroupWise systems, each with its own primary domain. Then the primary domain for the destination system must adopt each of these domains in turn. Thus, when merging two systems, you must first go through the process of releasing all the secondary domains on one of the systems.

When the merges are complete, all domains will belong to a single system, and there will be only one primary domain. Of course, partial merges are not uncommon — one department or division may get sold to another company. In this case, that division's domain would be released from the original system and merged with a new one.

Synchronizing Systems

When two GroupWise systems need to remain separate, but also need to share their address books, the administrator may enable external system synchronization. This can be a great boon to productivity.

The downside to external system synchronization is that it can potentially bloat the GroupWise directory, making rebuild times much longer. This is typically the case when two very large organizations (5,000 or more users) decide to synchronize their address books. Some customers choose to use an LDAP solution, or a product such as Concentrico.net's Reach for NDS, to create address-book solutions that do not bloat the GroupWise directory.

Releasing a Secondary Domain to Create a New GroupWise System

Now that the concepts are covered, here is a walkthrough of the first of the multiple-system scenarios discussed in this chapter.

The WorldWide Widgets Corporation has decided to outsource its manufacturing division. The manufacturing division will be its own separate company called ACME. They will have their own NDS tree, named ACME. The following is a discussion of how ACME and WorldWide Widgets pull this off.

ACME'S Pre-Domain Release Preparation

First of all, ACME is going to be getting new file servers as part of the outsourcing.

1. Install a new GroupWise software distribution directory to ACME's NetWare server.
2. Install the latest patches to the GroupWise software distribution directory.
3. Install the GroupWise agents so that they are ready to run on the ACME server.
4. Create an NDS OU, named APPS, to house the GroupWise system for manufacturing.
5. Create an NDS OU, named STAFF, to house the manufacturing staff.

   Figure 15.1 shows the ACME tree.

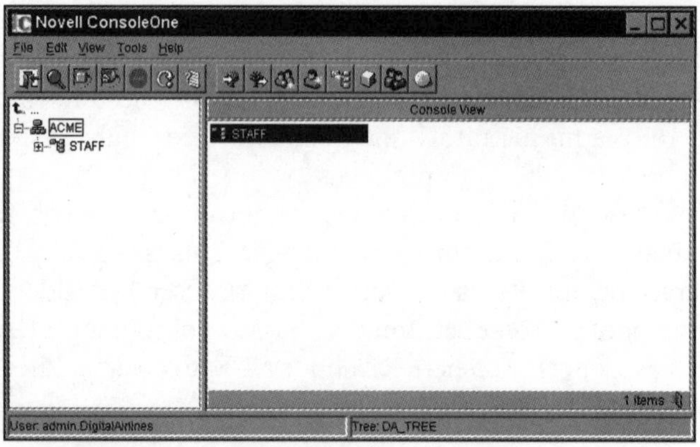

FIGURE 15.1 *The ACME Location*

   Figure 15.2 shows how the manufacturing division currently looks in the WorldWide Widgets system.

6. Move the mfg domain and the mfg_po1 post office to the ACME server so that they physically reside on the ACME server.

   This operation is covered in Chapter 20 of this book.

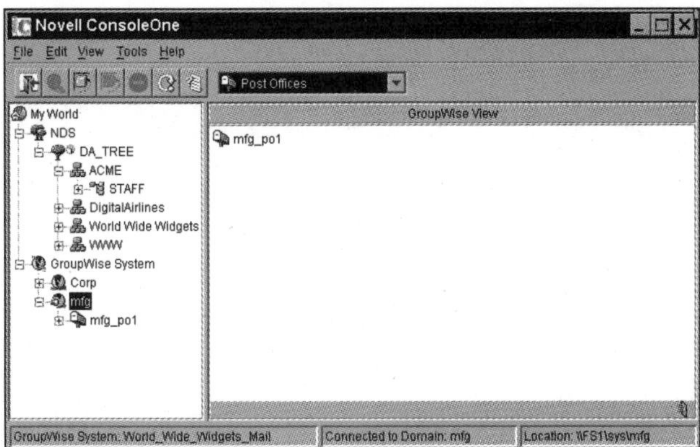

FIGURE 15.2 *The Manufacturing Division at WorldWide Widgets*

7. Check that the mfg domain has no pending operations. To do this, choose Tools ➪ GroupWise System Operations ➪ Pending Operations.

WorldWide Widgets — The Release

The WorldWide Widgets administrator is now all set to release the mfg domain.

1. Connect to the primary domain named Corp.
2. Select the mfg domain.
3. Choose Tools ➪ GroupWise Utilities ➪ System Maintenance.
4. In the System Maintenance screen, select the Release Secondary option, as shown in Figure 15.3, and click Run.
5. Specify a path to the mfg domain, as well as a new system name, called ACME_Mail.
6. The Release Domain wizard prompts you to update NDS objects, as in Figure 15.4.

   You will want to do this. This option takes the mfg and mfg_po1 objects out of the WorldWide Widgets NDS tree.

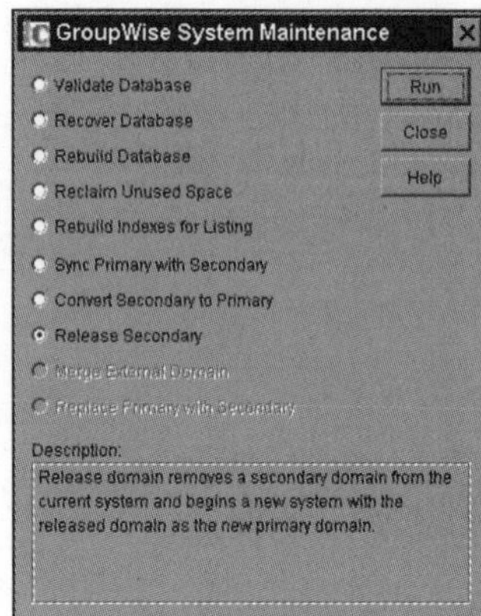

FIGURE 15.3 *The Release Secondary Option*

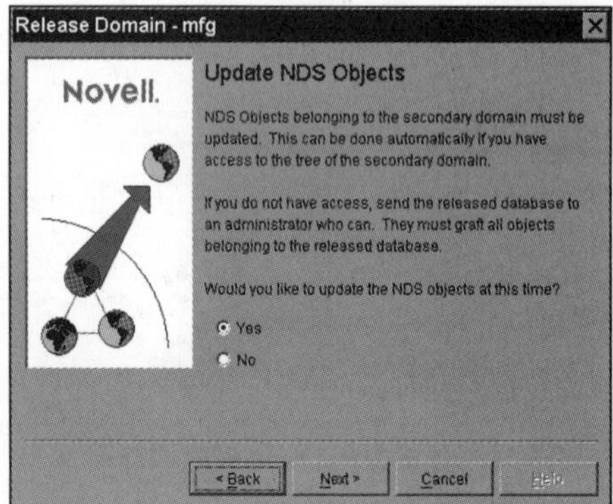

FIGURE 15.4 *Updating NDS Objects*

7. Follow the Release Domain wizard's prompts to unload the MTA on the primary domain, as well as on the mfg domain that is being released.
8. The final dialog box says that you are ready to release the domain, so click the Release button.

   The domain is released and becomes an external GroupWise domain in the WorldWide Widgets system. The mfg domain becomes its own primary domain over the ACME_Mail system.

TIP

When writing this section and following the steps outlined in this section, I got errors when trying to release a secondary domain. The errors seem to have been related to removing the Update NDS Objects selection that I made. The mfg domain was released, despite the error that I got, but I didn't know that until I actually connected to the domain that I released. When I did that, I saw that the old primary domain was a white earth icon, rather than a blue earth icon, which told me that the domain had in fact been released. Also when I edited the mfg domain, the domain type was primary.

The domain is now released, but that's not the end of the story. The mfg domain and the mfg_po1 post office still need to be grafted into the ACME tree. And three users, BHAUG, DHEYREND, and DJONES, still need to be created in the ACME tree. Here's the process to follow:

1. Connect to the mfg domain, which is now a primary domain.
2. Go into the NDS browser portion of ConsoleOne.

   You do not want to highlight anything in the GroupWise system portion of the ConsoleOne interface.
3. Choose Tools ➪ GroupWise Utilties ➪ GW/NDS Association ➪ Graft GroupWise Objects. The Graft GroupWise Objects wizard appears, as shown in Figure 15.5.
4. Select the Domains, post offices, and gateways option, and proceed through the wizard, but do not attempt to graft users.
5. Create each of the users in an NDS OU, or in a variety of NDS OUs, in the ACME tree, with only the NDS name and surname.

IMPORTANT

The NDS name must match the GroupWise mailbox ID, and the surname must match the last name of the GroupWise object. The requirement to make the NDS name match your GroupWise user object may not fall in with your naming standards. What you will have to do is rename the NDS object to the name you would really like. You must comply with the steps outlined in this section to get your GroupWise user objects into the NDS tree.

FIGURE 15.5 *Grafting GroupWise Objects*

6. From the NDS browser view, choose Tools ➪ GroupWise Utilties ➪ GW/NDS Association ➪ Graft GroupWise Objects to graft users, resources, and distribution lists.

   Follow the prompts of this wizard, making sure to specify the right NDS contexts, as well as the NDS contexts that the users who moved with mfg have been created in.

The graft utility will find that the GroupWise mailbox ID and the NDS login ID values correlate. The graft utility will then associate the GroupWise object, with its intended NDS user object.

Final Steps and Cleanup

The new GroupWise system needs to have a software distribution directory definition pointing to the newly installed GroupWise software distribution directory. Defining a software distribution directory is done under Tools ➪ GroupWise System Operations ➪ Software Directory Management, as outlined in Chapter 6.

The mfg_po1 post office needs to have its "software directory" pointing to the new ACME software distribution directory (see Figure 15.6).

The users in the ACME tree should be given browse, read, and compare rights to the mfg post office, as well as the POA below that post office object. This will allow users' GroupWise clients to dynamically discover their new POA IP address.

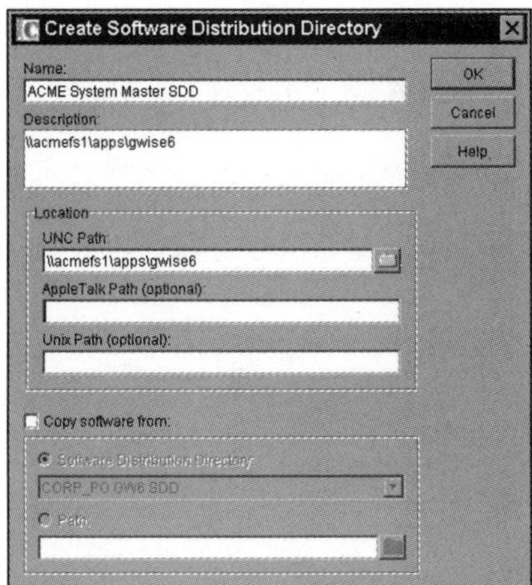

FIGURE 15.6 *Creating a New Software Directory*

In this example, WorldWide Widgets and ACME do not need to reference each other anymore. Both sides will delete any reference to one another. This means that the WorldWide Widgets administrator will delete the external domain for manufacturing, and the administrator for the ACME_Mail system will delete all external domains left over from the WorldWide Widgets system.

The manufacturing division's NDS user objects should also be deleted from the WorldWide Widgets NDS tree.

Synchronizing External Systems

Continuing the WorldWide Widgets and ACME Manufacturing scenario, imagine that WorldWide Widgets acted a little hastily. They have deleted all user objects and external references to manufacturing, but now they discover their users need to exchange address books.

For the balance of this chapter, the GroupWise system for WorldWide Widgets will be called System 1; ACME's system will be called System 2.

Creating System Definitions for Synchronizing

First, from System 1, you need to create a definition for System 2.

1. Highlight the GroupWise system object as shown in Figure 15.7.

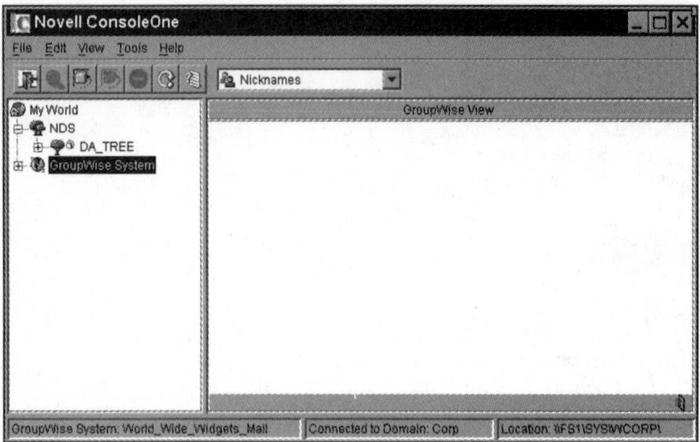

FIGURE 15.7 *Highlighting the GroupWise System Object*

2. Click the right mouse button and choose New ➪ External Domain.
3. Fill out the information in the next dialog box, shown in Figure 15.8, that will be appropriate for System 2.

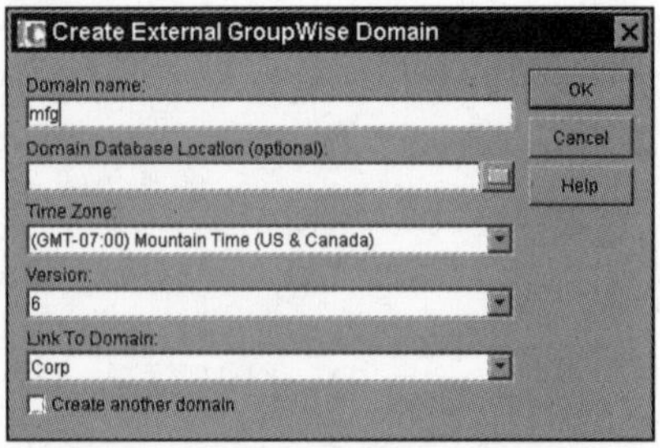

FIGURE 15.8 *Defining the mfg Domain*

At this point, the mfg domain again exists in the WorldWide Widgets system, but only as an external domain, as shown in Figure 15.9.

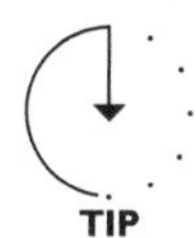

TIP

External domains will use a white earth icon, rather than a blue earth icon.

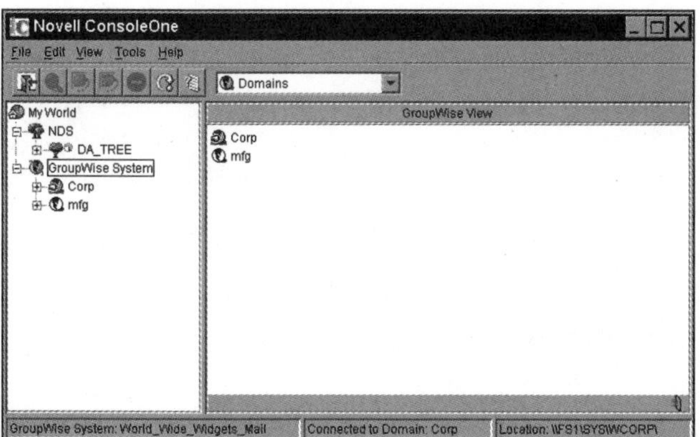

FIGURE 15.9 *Mfg Defined in the WorldWide Widgets System*

IMPORTANT

When defining an external GroupWise system for synchronization purposes, define the primary domain for that system. Defining a secondary domain in another system, rather than the primary domain, is fine, but a secondary domain does not support external system synchronization.

To create a definition for System 1 from System 2, you need to repeat the procedure in the previous section, but from System 2's perspective.

1. Connect to System 2 and highlight the GroupWise system object in the GroupWise view.
2. Click the right mouse button, select Create, and then select External Domain.
3. Fill out the information in the next dialog box that will be appropriate for System 1.

At this point, the Corp domain exists in the ACME_Mail system, but only as an external domain, as shown in Figure 15.10.

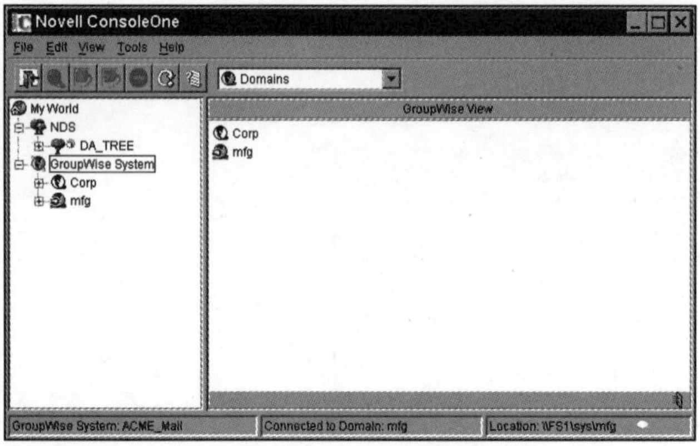

FIGURE 15.10 *Corp Defined in the ACME System*

Creating MTA Connectivity

To create MTA connectivity between System 1 and System 2, you need to define how System 1's MTAs deliver messages to System 2's MTAs, and vice versa.

1. While connected to System 1, choose Tools ➪ GroupWise Utilities ➪ Link Configuration.
2. Edit the link to the external domain for System 2.

   Fill in the correct information so that the MTA on System 1 can contact the MTA on System 2, as shown in Figure 15.11.
3. While connected to System 2, choose Tools ➪ GroupWise Utilities ➪ Link Configuration.
4. Edit the link to the external domain for System 1.

   Fill in the correct information so that the MTA on System 2 can contact the MTA on System 1.

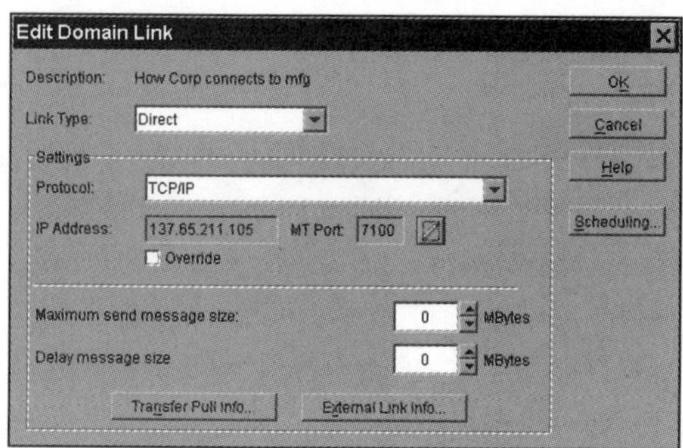

FIGURE 15.11 *Link Configuration for MTA Connectivity*

Now the MTAs for both systems know how to transfer messages between systems.

Testing System Connectivity

Before enabling external system synchronization, you need to test the connection. Otherwise, you may end up with thousands of address-sync messages queued up in <DOMAIN>MSHOLD directories.

1. Send an e-mail from a user on System 2 to a user on System 1.

   To do this, compose a message in this manner: On the To line, type in the name of the external domain followed by the post office and user name all separated with dots.

   For example, you want to send to the user Admin on the post office corp_po1 off of the Corp domain in System 1. The To line of the message should read `corp.corp_po1.admin`. Figure 15.12 shows this syntax.

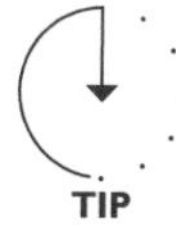

Suppose that the Corp primary domain did not have a post office under it. There is a post office under the Sales domain though. You can still send from System 2 to System 1. You can utilize the connection to Corp to route a message to the Sales domain. Here's how the To line would read: `corp:sales.sales_p1.tkratzer`**.**

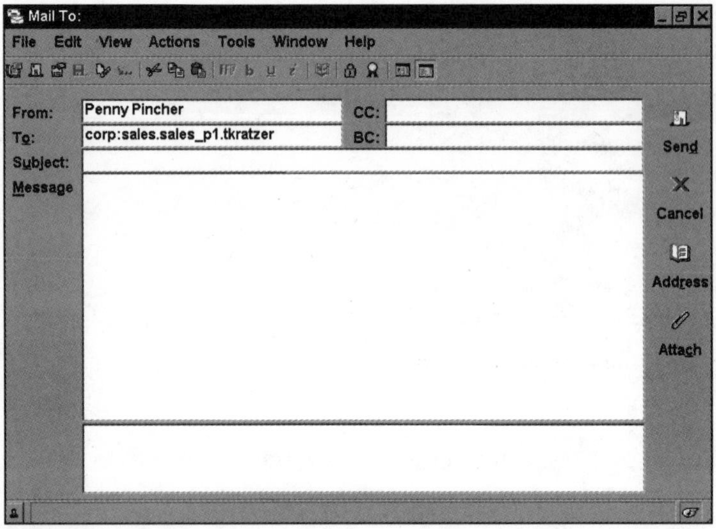

FIGURE 15.12 *Sending E-mail to an External Domain*

2. Confirm that the e-mail went through.

   Check the properties of the original sent item. Does it say that it was delivered? If so, the connection in both directions is okay. You know this because the original message was delivered (System 2 to System 1), and the delivered status message came back (System 1 to System 2).

Configuring External System Synchronization

Now you know that communication works between the two systems, so you are ready to synchronize their address books. This operation requires changes to be made on both systems.

1. Connect to System 1.
2. Choose Tools ➪ GroupWise System Operations ➪ External System Synchronization.

3. Select the Add button and fill in the GroupWise system name for the external system.

   In the example scenario, it is ACME_Mail. Pay attention to the spelling and case — this field is case-sensitive. The name acme_mail would not be correct.
4. In the External Domain field, browse to the external domain's primary domain that represents the connectivity point for System 2.
5. Select the options to send and receive from the external domain the domain, post offices, and users.

   Figure 15.13 shows a configured external domain link from System 1 to System 2.

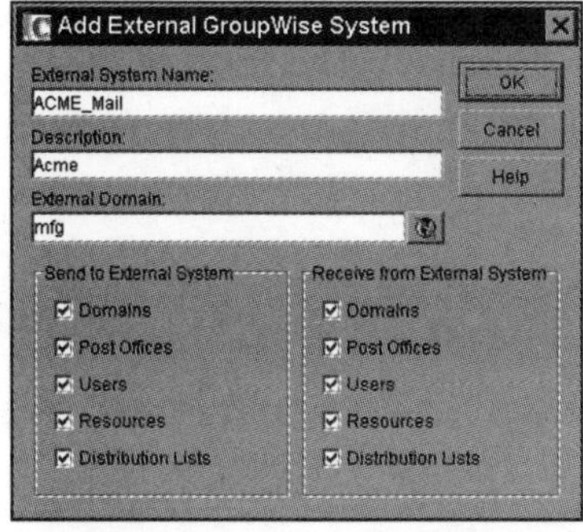

FIGURE 15.13 *Setting Up Synchronization – System 1*

6. Click OK.
7. Connect to System 2.
8. Choose Tools ➪ GroupWise System Operations ➪ External System Synchronization.
9. Select the Add button and fill in the GroupWise system name for the external system.

   In the example scenario, it is World_Wide_Widgets_Mail.

10. In the External Domain field, browse to the external domain that represents the connectivity point for System 1.

11. Select the options to send and receive from the external domain the domain, post offices, and users.

Synchronizing Systems

Now that both sides are prepared to send changes to each other, you must kick off the synchronization by having each side request all the objects it needs from the other side.

1. While connected to System 1, choose Tools ➪ GroupWise System Operations ➪ External System Synchronization.

2. Highlight the external system for System 2 and click the Request button.

   Be aware that this does generate a lot of traffic — at least one mail message per user on System 2.

3. While connected to System 2, choose Tools ➪ GroupWise System Operations ➪ External System Synchronization.

4. Highlight the external system for System 1 and select the Request button.

   Again, be ready for lots of traffic.

If all goes well, both sides should synchronize, and the post offices and users from the external system will be visible.

TIP

I have worked with external system synchronization problems several times. Based upon the experience I have had, it's quite possible that you will need to select a request of objects a few times.

Merging Two External GroupWise Systems

This walkthrough takes you through the steps of doing a complete merge of two GroupWise systems. The primary domain in System 2 will become subordinate to the primary domain in System 1, which means it will eventually be converted to a secondary domain.

NOTE

Only primary domains can be merged with an existing system, and they can only be merged if they do not own any secondary domains. If you need to merge a multi-domain system with yours, you must first have that system release all of its domains. Refer to the section, "Releasing a Secondary Domain to Create a New GroupWise System," earlier in this chapter.

The Merge Scenario

The WorldWide Widgets corporation wants to acquire the ACME corporation. (Forget, for just a moment, that you released the ACME system in an earlier walkthrough. Or perhaps you could assume that this is a real-life example of a confused corporate reorganization.)

They both have GroupWise systems. It is natural for them to merge their two GroupWise systems. This will cause the mfg domain to be a GroupWise secondary domain to the Corp primary domain. WorldWide Widgets and ACME will still keep separate trees however. Remember that System 1 is WorldWide Widgets' system, and System 2 is ACME's system.

Creating System Definitions for Merged Systems

From System 1, follow these steps to create a definition for System 2:

1. Highlight the GroupWise System object in the GroupWise view.
2. Click the right mouse button and choose New ➪ External Domain.
3. Fill out the information that will be appropriate for System 2, specifying the primary domain for System 2.

   Figure 15.14 shows the mfg domain being defined as an external domain.

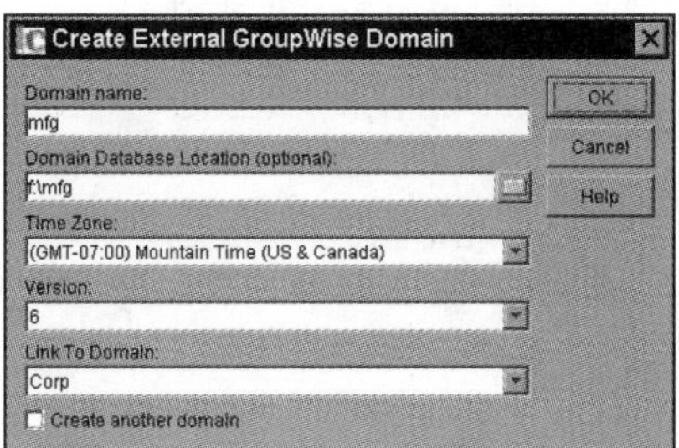

FIGURE 15.14 *Defining mfg as an External Domain*

Now there is an external domain for mfg in the World_Wide_Widgets system, as shown in Figure 15.15.

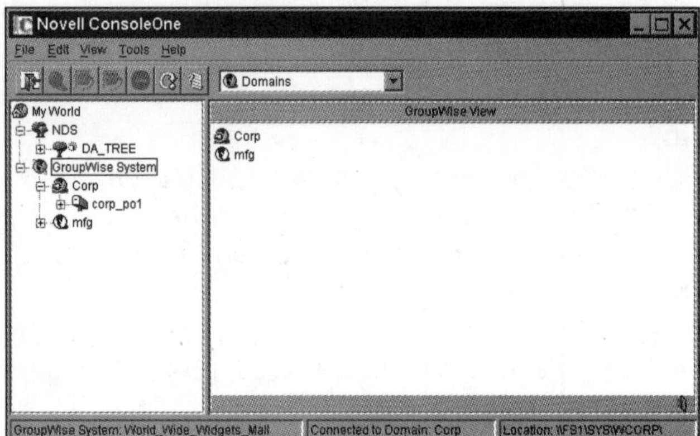

FIGURE 15.15 *Mfg Defined in the WorldWide Widgets System*

To create a definition for System 1 from System 2, follow these steps:

1. Connect to System 2 and highlight the GroupWise system object in the GroupWise view.
2. Click the right mouse button and choose New ➪ External Domain.
3. Fill out the information that will be appropriate for System 1, specifying the primary domain for System 1.

Creating MTA Connectivity for Merged Systems

To create MTA connectivity between System 1 and System 2, follow these steps:

1. While connected to System 1, choose Tools ➪ GroupWise Utilities ➪ Link Configuration.
2. Edit the link to the primary domain on System 2 (the MFG external domain), filling in the correct information so that the mfg MTA on System 1 can contact the Corp MTA on System 2.

   Figure 15.16 shows the link configuration.

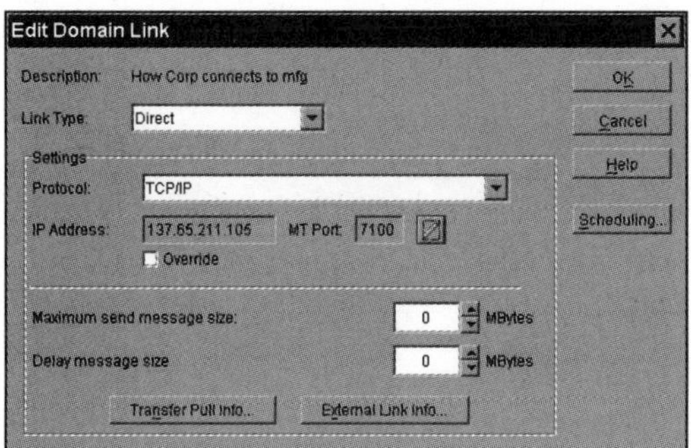

FIGURE 15.16 *Link Configuration for MTA Connectivity*

3. While connected to System 2, choose Tools ➪ GroupWise Utilities ➪ Link Configuration.
4. Edit the link to the primary domain on System 1 (the Corp external domain), filling in the correct information so that the MFG MTA on System 2 can contact the Corp MTA on System 1.

Testing Connectivity for Merged Systems

At this point, the Corp and mfg domains should be able to contact each other to transfer messages. You need to test this connectivity before proceeding.

1. Send an e-mail from a user on System 2 to a user on System 1.

   To do this, compose a message in this manner: On the To line type in the name of the external domain followed by the post office and user name all separated with dots.

   For example, you want to send to the user Admin on the post office corp_po1 off of the Corp domain in System 1. The To line of this message should read `corp.corp_po1.admin`. Figure 15.17 shows this syntax.

TIP

Suppose that the Corp primary domain did not have a post office under it. There is a post office under the Sales domain though. You can still send from System 2 to System 1. You can utilize the connection to Corp to route a message to user tkratzer in a post office under the Sales domain. Here's how the To line would read: `corp:sales.sales_p1.tkratzer`**.**

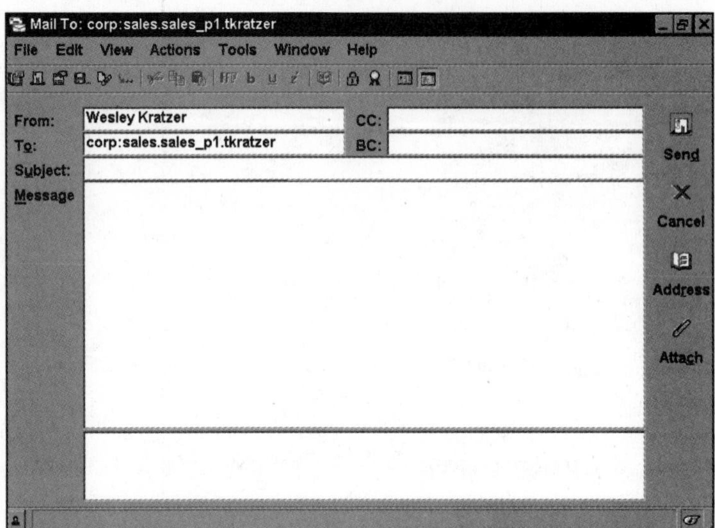

FIGURE 15.17 *Sending E-mail to an External Domain*

2. Confirm that the e-mail went through.

   Check the properties of the original sent item. Does it say that it was delivered? If so, the connection in both directions is okay. You know this because the original message was delivered (System 2 to System 1), and the delivered status message came back (System 1 to System 2).

Merging Systems

Now that you know the two systems are connected and can communicate with each other, you are ready to merge them.

1. Attach to System 1 and connect to the primary domain.

   In the scenario, this is the Corp domain.
2. Highlight the mfg domain and then choose Tools ➪ GroupWise Utilities ➪ System Maintenance.
3. Select the option to Merge External Domain as shown in Figure 15.18.

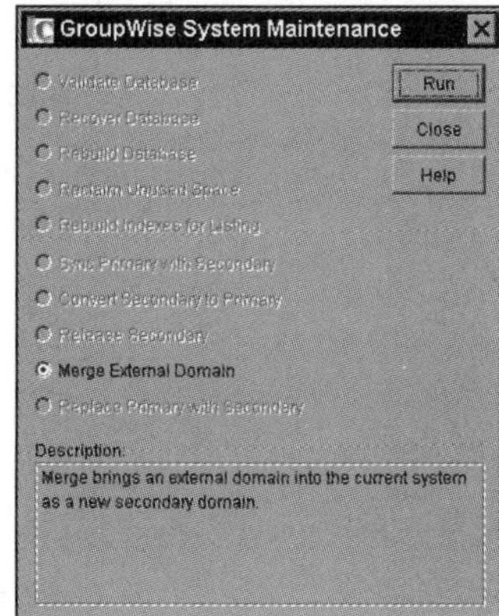

FIGURE 15.18 *Merging the External Domain mfg*

Only primary domains can be merged with an existing system, and they can only be merged if they do not own any secondary domains. If you need to merge a multi-domain system with yours, you must first have that system release all of its domains. Refer to the section, "Releasing a Secondary Domain to Create a New GroupWise System," earlier in this chapter. If you try to merge the external domain and it has secondary domains, you get an error.

4. Click the Run button.
5. The Merge Domain wizard will come up and guide you through the remainder of the merge.
6. When prompted to Merge External Systems, if the only external system defined in System 2 is System 1, then select No.
7. Do allow the Update NDS Objects option.
8. Shut down the MTA for both the primary domain and the external domain that will soon become a secondary domain.

   You do not need to bring down any POAs or other MTAs in either GroupWise system.

9. Make sure that no one is in ConsoleOne and connected to the primary domain for System 2.

   To test this, try to rename the WPDOMAIN.DB file for the primary domain for System 2 to WPDOMAIN.OLD. Then rename it back to WPDOMAIN.DB.

10. Proceed to the screen that says that you're ready to merge domain and start merging.

Synchronizing Objects

Merging two systems is rather easy. However, the merge does not broadcast the new objects brought in from System 2 to the rest of System 1. Also, the domains and post offices originally associated with System 2 don't have a clue about the objects in their new system.

In order to get all domains and post offices acquainted with the new, larger system, you must perform a top-down rebuild. This can be a big task. A top-down rebuild requires that all GroupWise domains and post offices in the entire system be rebuilt. Here are some important pointers to top-down rebuilds:

- Before rebuilding a secondary domain, synchronize it with the primary domain. See the beginning of this walkthrough for instructions on how to do this.
- Rebuilding a GroupWise domain or GroupWise post office database requires exclusive access to that database.
- For more information about rebuilding domain and post office databases, refer to Chapter 22.

Summary

The GroupWise directory is fairly flexible in allowing you to work with multiple GroupWise systems. The decision to merge systems rather than simply synchronizing them is one for you to make. There are advantages and disadvantages to each.

The advantages to merging systems include the following:

- Synchronization between domains is automatic and requires no additional configuration.
- There is a single primary domain database, allowing central administration.
- Distributed administration is still possible.

Merging systems does have its disadvantages, though:

- Some degree of central administration will always be necessary. This may not be appropriate for some organizations.
- The larger the system is, the more crowded the address book becomes.

Advantages to external system synchronization include the following:

- Administration is compartmentalized. Changes to system operations on one system do not affect the other.
- Changes to the address book are propagated across both systems. No import or export lists need to be maintained.

There are disadvantages as well to using external system synchronization:

- Synchronization must be configured. This is only a small headache, however.
- The larger the system, the more crowded the address book becomes.

CHAPTER 16

Internet Addressing

As mentioned in previous chapters, GroupWise features an option for Internet addressing. By default, when you install GroupWise, Internet addressing is not enabled. If Internet addressing is not enabled, you should take steps to enable it as soon as possible. As GroupWise evolves, certain features rely upon you having Internet addressing enabled. This chapter examines the Internet addressing standard and explores the changes that take place when Internet addressing is enabled on a GroupWise 6 system.

Defining an Internet Address

Internet addressing is the standard addressing format that is used to route and resolve Internet mail to appropriate mail hosts and user mailboxes. The format of an Internet address is `<username>@<Internet DNS domain name>`. Any e-mail message routed across the Internet must adhere to this format.

- **Internet user name:** The user name (or user ID) portion is an identifier for a mailbox in a mail system. For example, `wslick` is the user name for William Slick. The user name portion of an Internet address is typically controlled at the company or Internet service provider (ISP) level. Usually, companies or organizations specify a standard method for creating user names, often using portions of users' full names. In this book's example company, WorldWide Widgets, the naming standard for creating user names is to take the first letter of the first name and follow it with the last name.
- **Internet domain name:** The domain name portion of an Internet address is the string on the right side of the address following the @ sign. This string identifies the mail host that Internet users must reach when sending to a particular organization. For example, the user name `wslick` belongs to the domain name `worldwidewidgets.com`, so William Slick's fully qualified Internet address is `wslick@worldwidewidgets.com`.

  Usually, domain names are based on the actual company or organization name. In the example of this book, WorldWide Widgets is the company name, and the domain name that refers to WorldWide Widgets on the Internet is `worldwidewidgets.com`. When selecting a domain name, a company or organization has to pick a unique name and register that name so that no other company or organization will use that name.

- **Domain name registration:** All registered domain names can be resolved through a domain name server (DNS). Domain names are registered through an organization called Internic. A DNS resolves domain names to show the actual Internet protocol (IP) address of the mail hosts that a company or organization uses to send and receive Internet mail for that domain name. The DNS takes a domain name, which is like a zip code in the postal system, and translates that to an IP address of a mail host, which is like a local post office that handles mail for that domain.

Information regarding Internic or how to register a domain name can be found at `www.internic.org`**.**

- **Guaranteed uniqueness:** The great value of having a central body such as the Internic in charge of domain names is that all domain names are guaranteed to be unique. Since the domain names are guaranteed to be unique, fully qualified Internet addresses are also guaranteed to be unique. For example, two users that have a common user name will still be uniquely identified on the Internet, as long as the domain portion of the Internet address makes the entire Internet addresses unique. There are countless postmaster mailboxes on the Internet, but they are uniquely defined by the fact that their domain names are different.

Understanding Old-Style GroupWise Addressing Format

A basic characteristic of Internet addresses is that the address is ordered from general to specific, as the address is resolved from right to left. The most specific part of the address is the user name, on the far left. The most general part is the upper-level domain name (for example, `.com` or `.net`) on the far right. Processes that read and resolve Internet addresses read backwards compared to the way you are reading the text of this book. They start on the right-hand side and work their way to the left.

In contrast, old-style GroupWise addresses (prior to GroupWise 5.5 with Internet addressing) are resolved from left to right. They are still resolved from general to specific, though. This GroupWise address format is Domain.PostOffice.User (DPU). Note that a GroupWise domain is not quite the same as an Internet domain — GroupWise domains are named by GroupWise administrators, and they do not need to be unique worldwide. There is no central naming authority for GroupWise domains.

The fact that GroupWise domains are not unique didn't matter until companies that had common domain names began to connect to each other. To make the mail between their systems routable, each company would have to alter the name of the external domain definitions they created so that their address books would not show two Corp domains, for example.

As Internet connectivity became more and more common (almost as common as television!), GroupWise users realized that they had to know two different addressing formats — one for users on their GroupWise systems and a different one for users elsewhere on the Internet.

True Internet addresses, where every name is guaranteed to be unique, leave no question as to what domain a piece of mail should be routed to, regardless of where the piece of mail originated. To communicate through the Internet, GroupWise has had to conform to the standards of Internet addressing to allow GroupWise mail hosts to communicate with other Internet mail hosts.

Old-Style GroupWise Internet Address Resolution

By *old-style,* I am talking about any GroupWise system that does not have GroupWise Internet addressing enabled. This means all versions of GroupWise prior to GroupWise 5.5 (where the option was not available), as well as any GroupWise 5.5x or GroupWise 6x system where Internet addressing is not yet turned on.

As discussed in Chapter 10, GroupWise systems connect with the Internet through the GroupWise Internet agent (GWIA). This gateway allows GroupWise users to send e-mail to Internet users by acting as a mail host and as an address resolver. The GWIA converts GroupWise addressing formats to Internet addressing formats, and resolves Internet addresses to GroupWise addresses.

The gateway also acts as a mail host to physically send and receive mail from the Internet. The GWIA stamps the outgoing mail with an Internet-style return address. Incoming mail is converted to a GroupWise address format. For example, a message sent from `Corp.Corp_po1.wslick` to an Internet recipient will have its reply-to address changed to `wslick@worldwidewidgets.com`. An incoming mail message from the Internet will have its delivery address converted from `wslick@worldwidewidgets.com` to a GroupWise address of `Corp.Corp_po1.wslick`.

Old-Style GWIA Creation of Reply-To Addresses

When mail is passing from the GroupWise system to the Internet, the GWIA has to create an Internet-standard reply-to address from the GroupWise information so that Internet recipients of GroupWise mail will be able to reply. The gateway formulates the reply-to Internet address by using the rules shown in Figure 16.1.

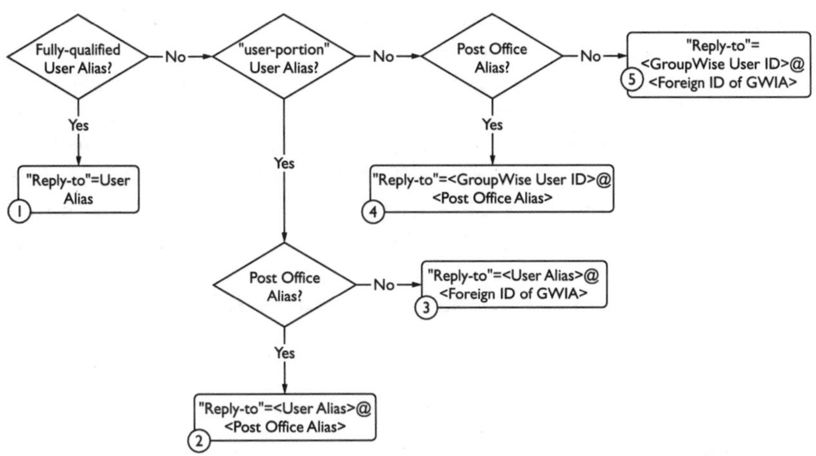

FIGURE 16.1 *Old-Style GroupWise Process for Stamping Reply-To on Outbound Messages*

Here is a look at each of these reply-to addresses in turn, with each numeral in the following list corresponding to that in Figure 16.1:

1. If there is a fully qualified user alias for the GWIA, (that is, the user alias has both a user portion and a domain portion), then the reply-to address will be set to the user alias. If Bob Snow's user alias is set to `BobSnow@bob.worldwidewidgets.com`, then that will be his reply-to address.

NOTE

If a user has more than one alias for the GWIA, the first listed alias will always be used for constructing the reply-to address.

2. If there is a user alias and a post office alias, then the reply-to address will be set to `<User Alias>@<Post Office Alias>`. For example, if BSnow's user alias is `BobSnow`, and the post office alias for his post office is `sales.worldwidewidgets.com`, then e-mail he sends will be stamped with `BobSnow@sales.worldwidewidgets.com` in the reply-to field.
3. If there is a user alias, but no post office alias, then the reply-to address will be set to `<User Alias>@<Gateway Foreign ID>`. If the GWIA has more than one gateway foreign ID set, the first one on the list will be used.

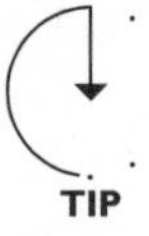

The GWIA's gateway foreign ID is defined under the properties of the GWIA. Figure 16.2 shows the Foreign ID field on the WorldWide Widgets GWIA. A GWIA can have multiple foreign IDs. The first foreign ID is the default foreign ID for the GWIA. Foreign IDs are separated (delimited) with a single space. The Foreign ID field on the GWIA cannot exceed 124 characters. If you have several foreign IDs, then do the following: Create an ASCII file in the <DOMAIN>\WPGATE\<GWIA> directory called FRGNAMES.CFG. List the main domain name, such as `worldwidewidgets.com`**, on the first line. List each of the other domain names, such as** `sales.worldwidewidgets.com`**, on a line by itself. Put a blank line at the end of the file. Restart your GWIA so that it reads this file.**

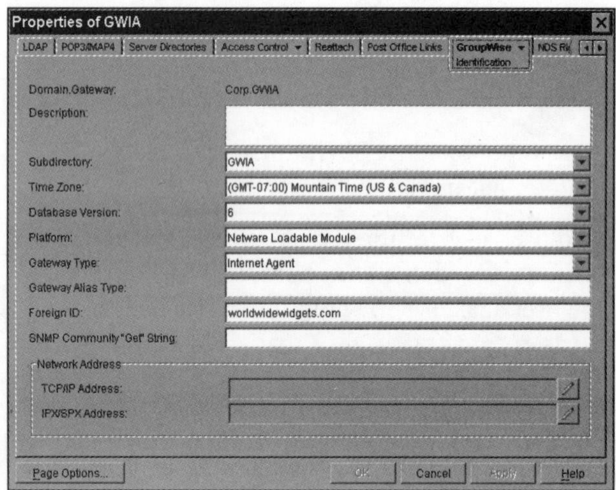

FIGURE 16.2 *The GWIA Foreign ID Field*

4. If there is no user alias, but there is a post office alias, the reply-to field will be set to `<GroupWise UserID>@<Post Office Alias>`.
5. If there is no user alias, and there is no post office alias, the reply-to address will simply be `<GroupWise UserID>@<Gateway Foreign ID>`. This is the default case. A GWIA must have a foreign ID specified, and users must have a user ID, but aliases are not required to be created.

Old-Style GWIA Resolution of Inbound Internet Addresses

Figure 16.3 shows what happens when a message is coming inbound to the GWIA.

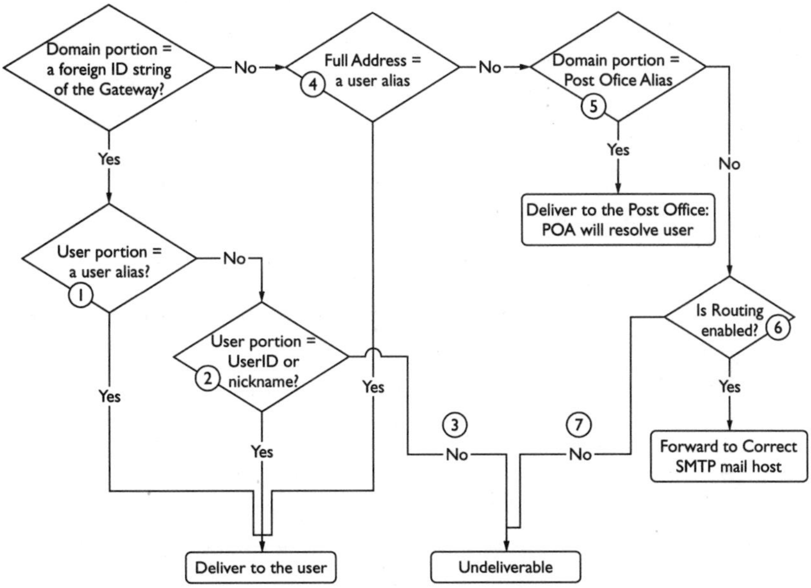

FIGURE 16.3 *Old-Style GWIA Inbound Message Resolution*

Inbound Internet mail arrives at the GWIA when a foreign mail host connects to the GWIA and sends something in on port 25. Typically, this happens because the foreign host found an MX record (DNS mail exchange) matching the GWIA up to the domain portion of an address. If DNS says that `worldwidewidgets.com` resolves to the IP address of the GWIA, then any message to any user at `worldwidewidgets.com` will get sent to that GWIA.

This means that your GWIA could receive mail that is *not* destined for your GroupWise system. The GWIA needs to be able to deal with this. The rest of this section describes how mail coming through a GWIA is resolved to a GroupWise user address.

First, the gateway compares the domain name of the message recipient with all of the foreign IDs of the gateway. This is where the GWIA is checking to see if the mail is actually destined for your system. If there is a match here, begin with Step 1. Otherwise, begin with Step 4.

1. If a match is found, then the GWIA checks to see if the user portion of the recipient address matches a user alias. If so, the message is delivered to that user.
2. If there is no user alias, the GWIA checks for matches with user IDs and nicknames. If a match is found, the message is delivered to that user.
3. If no match is found for user aliases, nor for user IDs and nicknames, then the message is undeliverable.
4. If the foreign ID string of the gateway does *not* match the domain portion of the address, the GWIA checks to see if there is a match with a fully qualified user alias (a user alias where both the user and domain portions of the address are specified). If the GWIA finds a match, the message is delivered to that user.

I have seen situations in which Step 4 of this algorithm did not work. It is just best to define all Internet domain names in the Foreign ID field or the FRGNAMES.CFG file.

5. If there is no fully qualified user alias, but there is a match between a post office alias and the Internet domain portion of the address, the GWIA will not receive the message. By default, the GWIA does not allow relaying and the Daemon portion of the GWIA will not be able to fully resolve the address, hence it will drop it.
6. If there are no alias matches, and the foreign ID did not match, then the message is not really destined for this GroupWise system. If message routing, or relaying, which is the ability for the GWIA to send mail outbound even if the destination address itself is not, is enabled, then the GWIA will attempt to pass the message on to the correct SMTP host.
7. If message relaying is not enabled, the message is undeliverable.

Pitfalls with Old-Style GroupWise Addressing

Before discussing native GroupWise Internet addressing, this section explores the limitations of the old-style addressing.

- **User training issues:** With the prevalence of consumer Internet e-mail, most users know how to address a message Internet-style. These users will want to be able to send to the Internet from GroupWise the same way they do from other e-mail applications.

Without GroupWise Internet addressing, these users must enter additional information in order to get their Internet messages out of the GroupWise system. Specifically, they must enter the domain and gateway name of the GWIA prior to the address, or they must enter the name of a foreign domain that has been associated with the GWIA. Thus, outbound messages are typically addressed `internet:user@domain`. A message simply addressed to `user@domain` will not make it out of the GroupWise system.

GroupWise addressing rules can be used in place of true Internet addressing. This will alleviate the user training issues, but won't help in other areas.

- **GWIA limitations:** Another potential problem with this traditional handling of address conversion is that the gateway may only narrowly interpret incoming mail as being part of its GroupWise system. This limitation is primarily due to the way in which the GWIA looks at its Foreign ID field/FRGNAMES.CFG file. Addresses that don't match up with this field (or with user or post office aliases) may be marked undeliverable.
- **User alias limitations:** A third problem lies in limitations of GroupWise user aliases. Only two addresses per gateway can be used to identify a GroupWise user. For example, Barbara Browbeater has a mailbox ID of `Browbeaterb` and a user alias of `Barbara.Browbeater@worldwidewidgets.com`. This means that her outgoing Internet mail will be sent out to the Internet as being from `Barbara.Browbeater@worldwidewidgets.com`, and she can receive e-mail bound for the address of either `Barbara.Browbeater@worldwidewidgets.com` or `Browbeaterb@worldwidewidgets.com`.

Benefits of GroupWise Internet Addressing

GroupWise Internet addressing offers several advantages over the old-style GroupWise addressing format.

- GroupWise addresses become true Internet addresses.
- GWIA gains flexibility as it resolves Internet addresses to GroupWise users.
- Client addressing rules may no longer be needed.
- GroupWise systems can connect to each other natively, without defining external domains.
- Future GroupWise enhancements will require Internet addressing.

Here is a discussion each of these in turn.

- **GroupWise addresses become Internet addresses:** With native Internet addressing, GroupWise addresses no longer need to be converted to Internet addressing formats when GroupWise mail is being sent out to the Internet. Instead of users being known internally to the GroupWise system as Domain.PostOffice.UserID, users will be internally known as `UserID@Internet domain name`.
- **GWIA gains flexibility:** With Internet addressing enabled, the GWIA will work very hard to match an Internet address with a GroupWise user for incoming SMTP mail. The gateway will still look for the old-style matches with aliases and foreign IDs as well as the following Internet domain name formats:
  - **Full:** `UserID.PostOffice.Domain@Internet domain name`
  - **User ID unique:** `UserID@Internet domain name`
  - **Post office unique:** `UserID.PostOffice@Internet domain name`
  - **First/Last:** `Firstname.Lastname@Internet domain name`
  - **Last/First:** `Lastname.Firstname@Internet domain name`
  - **FirstInitial/LastName:** `Firstinitial.Lastname@Internet domain name`

  The term Internet domain name is specific to GroupWise Internet addressing. The Internet domain name is an extra attribute attached to every address in GroupWise, and therefore makes GroupWise addresses comply with Internet address formats.

NOTE

Internet domain names are sometimes referred to as IDOMAINS. This term may help avoid confusion.

- **Client addressing rules are no longer needed:** When Internet addressing is enabled, client addressing rules are no longer needed to route mail messages to the Internet. Because GroupWise addresses are Internet addresses, mail addressed Internet-style will be correctly routed to the GWIA without the explicit address of the GWIA.

  Also, turning on Internet addressing will enable GroupWise users to send to other internal GroupWise users or external Internet users by simply typing the Internet address, such as `UserID@Internet domain name`. Internet addressing removes the need for addressing rules that search for an Internet-style address and replaces the address with a GroupWise gateway:internet address or with an external foreign domain:internet address.

- **Direct MTA-to-MTA connectivity between systems:** With Internet addressing enabled, you can allow any MTA on your system to connect directly to another GroupWise system. The GroupWise message transfer protocol (GWMTP) allows GroupWise users to transparently communicate over the Internet with other GroupWise users in other systems.

  GWMTP sending effectively eliminates the need to convert messages bound to other GroupWise systems. No gateway or gateway conversions are needed for the two systems to communicate. Leaving the messages in their native format also allows for native GroupWise encryption, compression, and message formats to be retained. Keeping the native message type allows appointments to be sent to users in other GroupWise systems as appointments. These items will show up correctly on calendars, can be accepted or rejected, and full status tracking is available. The native format also allows for busy searches across the Internet GroupWise systems.
- **Future GroupWise enhancements will require Internet addressing:** Upcoming enhancements will require Internet addressing to be turned on. One enhancement is the ability for the GroupWise client to mime-encode messages. Without Internet addressing, the GroupWise client will not be able to mime-encode messages.

Potential Pitfalls When Enabling Internet Addressing

GroupWise functionality is becoming entrenched in Internet addressing. It is likely that you will eventually have to enable it for full functionality. Unfortunately, enabling Internet addressing is not without a few potential hazards.

- Personal address books are converted to Internet address formats.
- Client Internet addressing rules are no longer used.
- Turning off Internet addressing isn't really an option.

This section will go over each of these in turn.

- **Address-book conversion to Internet address formats:** When Internet addressing is enabled, users' address books will be converted to Internet addressing format for the e-mail address column. This means that gateway names will be removed, as will foreign domain names.

  In some circumstances, I have seen the conversion process fail for some addresses. You may want to be alert to delivery problems for the first few weeks after Internet addressing has been enabled.

- **Legacy clients still use the old addressing format:** If your system contains a mix of 4.1, 5.2, 5.5x, and 6x post offices, your 4.1 and 5.2 users will still use the old addressing scheme. You may even have 16-bit clients, Unix clients, or Macintosh clients on your 5.5 post offices. These clients will also use the old addressing scheme.

  For these legacy clients, you will need to maintain your foreign domain names (for Internet-style addressing), as well as your addressing rules.
- **GroupWise 5.5x and GroupWise 6x clients ignore some addressing rules:** When Internet addressing is enabled, all GroupWise 5.5x and GroupWise 6x 32-bit clients will no longer use certain addressing rules. If a rule executes on address strings that contain an @ sign followed by a dot (.) and replaces it with a string that includes a colon (:), that rule will be ignored.

  For example, an addressing rule that searches for `*@*.com` and replaces that string with `inet:%1@%2.com` will be ignored by the 5.5x and 6x clients when Internet addressing is enabled.

  This should not be a problem, but it is possible on large systems that addressing rules that meet these criteria will still be needed for some reason or another.
- **Turning off Internet addressing can be painful:** The biggest disadvantage to enabling Internet addressing is that you cannot really back out of it.

Enabling Internet Addressing

There are three things you are going to have to configure to enable Internet addressing:

- Default GWIA
- Default Internet domain name
- Preferred addressing format

All of these must be configured in the Internet Addressing window shown in Figure 16.4.

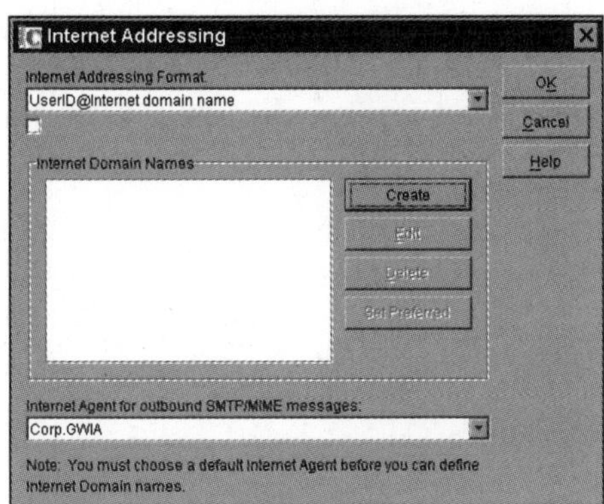

FIGURE 16.4 *The Internet Addressing Window*

Selecting the Default GWIA

First, start with the default GWIA. Before you can select the default GWIA, you must have installed the GroupWise Internet agent somewhere on your system. See Chapter 10 if you do not yet have a GWIA installed on your system.

1. Choose Tools ➪ GroupWise System Operations ➪ Internet Addressing. The window shown in Figure 16.4 comes up.
2. Populate the field labeled Internet Agent for outbound SMTP/MIME messages using the pick list.

   All GWIAs on your system should appear on this list.

NOTE

A default GWIA must be assigned so that mail that is not deliverable locally, and that cannot be resolved through GWMTP, will be automatically routed to the GWIA. This automatic routing is what allows the client Internet addressing rules to become obsolete. You don't need to specify the GWIA in the message address, because it has been specified system-wide here.

Selecting a Default Internet Domain Name

Now enter a domain name. This must be the name that your organization is known by on the Internet. It will probably be the first foreign name configured for your GWIA in the Foreign ID field/FRGNAMES.CFG.

1. From the Internet Addressing window, click Create to call up the window shown in Figure 16.5.

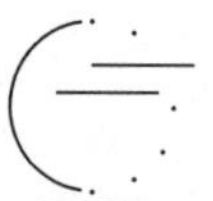
NOTE

Internet domain names cannot be created until a default GWIA has been selected.

FIGURE 16.5 *The Internet Domain Name Dialog Box*

2. Enter your organization's Internet domain name, including upper-level domain names (that is, novell.com rather than just novell).
3. Enter a description for this domain name, if desired.

   This may be useful if you plan to have more than one Internet domain name.
4. Click OK.

Choosing an Internet Addressing Format

A preferred Internet address format can be specified after a default GWIA and Internet domain name have been set. The preferred addressing format defaults to `User ID@Internet domain name`, but can be configured to one of several settings.

The Internet addressing format will then be used as the default user name format that the GWIA stamps on all outgoing mail as well as how addresses appear in the GroupWise address book. It will not be used for resolving routes on inbound e-mail. Users' Sent Items properties will also show the Created By field in this format instead of the legacy User.PostOffice.Domain format.

1. From the Internet Addressing window, pull down the Internet Addressing Format list shown in Figure 16.6.
2. Select the format that best suits your organization's needs.

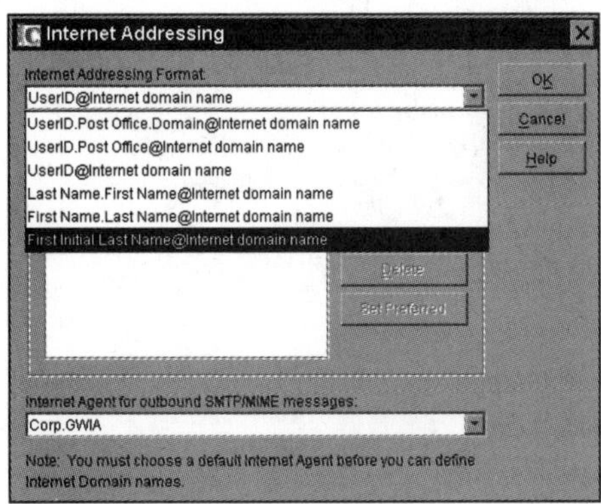

FIGURE 16.6 *The Internet Addressing Formats Selection Pull-Down Menu*

Most organizations find that `UserID@Internet domain name` works best. The reasoning behind this addressing format is discussed in the section titled "Best Practices," later in this chapter.

3. Close the Internet Addressing window.

Internet addressing is now enabled with these settings system-wide. You may choose to override some of the settings you have made here at the domain, post office, or even user level. These options are discussed in the section titled "Internet Addressing Overrides," later in this chapter.

Enabling MTA-Direct Connectivity (GWMTP)

With Internet addressing enabled, MTAs may now be allowed to connect directly to other GroupWise systems. This type of connectivity, often called GWMTP, for GroupWise message transfer protocol, allows native message format and encryption to be maintained.

Retaining the GroupWise message format between GroupWise systems is not a new concept. The same functionality is available without GWMTP, but it requires a pass-through GWIA or Async gateway. To get the same functionality with these gateways, an external domain and post office would have to be configured and maintained for every other system to which your users will send e-mail. The maintenance of these external user entries and external domains could require a lot of an administrator's time.

The big advantage of GWMTP is that the setup only has to be done once. Once it has been enabled, ongoing maintenance should be minimal. The three basic requirements to enable GWMTP are the following:

- Both systems must enable Internet addressing.
- Both systems must configure MTAs to use GWMTP.
- Both systems must publish GWMTP records to the Internet via domain name services (DNS).

This chapter has already discussed enabling Internet addressing. This next section will move directly to a walkthrough of configuring the MTA.

Allowing MTAs to Send Directly to Other GroupWise Systems

Like the heading says, the first thing you need to do is allow MTAs to send directly to other GroupWise Systems.

1. Choose Tools ➪ System Operations ➪ System Preferences to get the window shown in Figure 16.7.
2. Make sure a default routing domain is specified.

   This is the domain that will be able to talk directly to other MTAs over the Internet. You do *not* want to check the option to force all messages to this domain. Doing so can potentially be catastrophic.

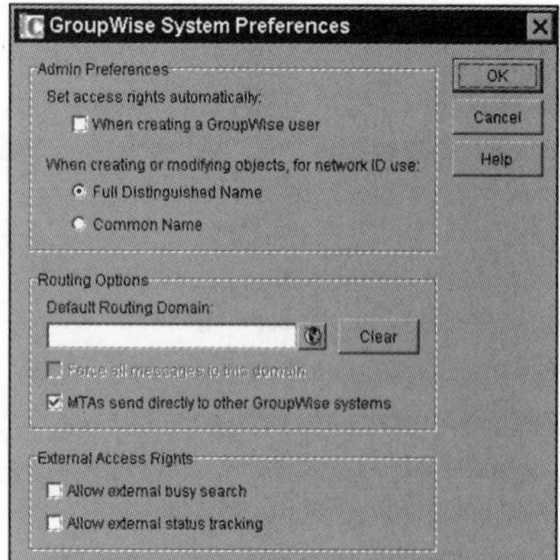

FIGURE 16.7 *The System Preferences Window*

3. Check the box labeled MTAs send directly to other GroupWise systems.
4. Close the Preferences window.

Allowing MTAs to Browse DNS

Now every MTA in your system is going to attempt to look up other GroupWise systems via domain name services (DNS). This means that every MTA must be able to see a valid domain name server. Typically, DNS requests are transmitted on port 53, so you should make sure that this port is not being filtered by your firewall. Most organizations won't have a problem with this, assuming that they allow end users to browse the Web. Web browsing also requires DNS requests, so port 53 is probably already open.

Allowing MTAs to Connect on High-Numbered Ports

You may, however, have a problem with high-numbered ports. Once the MTA finds another system's MTA on the Internet (via DNS), it will try to open a connection there using a high-numbered port.

For security reasons, many administrators do not want to have all MTAs exposed to high-numbered ports on the Internet. If you have this same concern, read about default routing domains and overrides in the next section.

Default Routing Domains and Overrides

The best way to avoid exposing all the MTAs in your system is to tell the GroupWise system to send all mail not destined to a known IDOMAIN to a default route. This would basically be all Internet mail. You rarely will want to force *all* messages (even messages going to a known IDOMAIN) to the default route. A single system-wide default routing domain is usually only advisable for GroupWise systems where there is a low volume of outbound Internet e-mail, however. On large, high-volume systems (more than 50,000 Internet messages per day) the burden on a single MTA could be too great, since all Internet-bound e-mail would pass through this MTA. Each outbound message requires a DNS lookup to determine if it is bound for another GroupWise system.

The solution is to use overrides.

1. Choose Tools ➪ GroupWise System Operations ➪ System Preferences.
2. Check the box labeled Force all messages to default routing domain.
3. Close the window.

4. Choose a second domain for routing.

   This domain will be used as an override default routing domain.

5. Choose a domain or domains to use the override routing domain instead of the system default specified in system preferences.

   In most cases, you will make this decision based on your WAN topology. For instance, all domains in one city should use a routing domain in that city.

6. Perform Steps 7 through 11 for each domain whose routing you wish to override.

7. Browse to the domain's MTA object, right-click on it, and select Properties.

8. Click on the Routing Options tab shown in Figure 16.8.

9. Click on the topmost check box in the Override column.

   This will override the default routing domain specified at the system level.

10. In the field labeled Default Routing Domain, browse to the domain you have chosen as an override routing domain.

11. Click OK to close the window and save your changes.

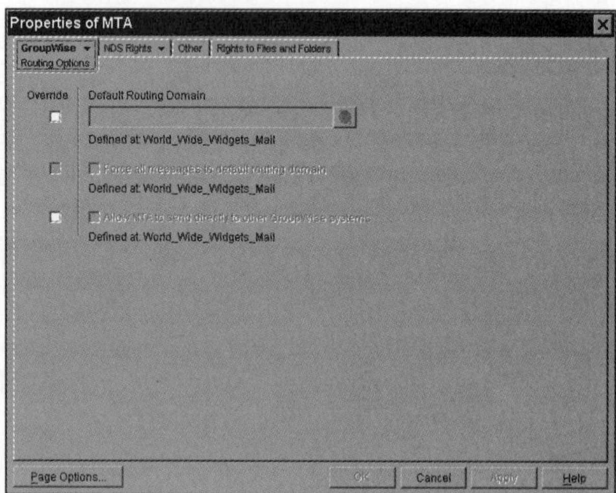

FIGURE 16.8 *The MTA Routing Options Tab*

To summarize how these default routing domains work, there are basically three options that you can set at the system level in this area:

- **MTAs send directly to another GroupWise system:** This option enables *all* MTAs system-wide to be able to perform DNS lookups. So if a user sends mail to `user@unknownIdomain.com`, then the MTA will try to do a DNS lookup on it. If it can, and it finds the appropriate DNS entries for `unknownIdomain.com`, then it sends it directly over the Internet to this other MTA. If for any reason it cannot either do a DNS lookup or find any DNS entries for `unknownIdomain.com`, then it simply hands it off to the domain that owns the default GWIA. (Unless there are any overrides anywhere, and then it obeys the override.)
- **Default routing domain:** With this option, if the MTA gets a message to an *known* IDOMAIN, then it resolves it itself (doesn't have to do a DNS lookup) to the GroupWise domain that the user is in, reads link configuration to see how to talk to this GroupWise domain, and sends the message to it. If it gets a message to `user@unknownIdomain.com`, then it once again tries to do a DNS lookup. If it fails or cannot do this, *then* it sends the message off to the default routing domain. It does *not* send all mail to this domain, only Internet mail that is destined for unknown IDOMAINs. The default routing domain gets the message, and then tries to resolve it via DNS, if this fails, it goes ahead and sends it to the default GWIA.
- **Force all messages to this domain (the default routing domain):** Finally, with this option, when an MTA gets *any* message, whether or not it is destined for a known IDOMAIN, it simply shoves it over to the forced default routing domain.

You can use the override options on any of these settings, which basically allows you to change what any particular domain is going to use that is different than what you have set under system preferences in system operations.

There are basically two ways that I recommend for setting up default routing domains so that you do not need to have all MTAs doing DNS lookups. It all depends on how many domains you are going to want or not want to do DNS lookups. If the majority of the domains should be doing DNS lookups, then follow this approach:

1. From System Operations ➪ System Preferences, click the check box that allows MTAs to send directly to other GroupWise systems.

2. Next, define a default routing domain that all Internet mail will go to if a DNS lookup fails or the MTA gets mail that is destined for unknown IDOMAINS.

   Do not check the option to force all messages through the default routing domain.

3. Go to the properties page of the MTA objects in the domains that you *do not* want to perform DNS Lookups and select Routing Options from the drop-down list.

4. From here, click the last check box in the override column (Allow MTA to send directly to other GroupWise systems), and then *uncheck* the option to perform this operation that this MTA inherited from the system level.

   Voila! This MTA is not allowed to do DNS lookups. This works great if most of your MTAs *will* do DNS lookups because you only have to do the override on the MTAs that you do *not* want to do the DNS lookups.

Now if most of your domains should *not* do DNS lookups, then you basically take the reverse approach.

1. From System Operations ➪ System Preferences, *do not* check the box to allow MTAs to send directly to other GroupWise systems.

2. Define a default routing domain that all Internet mail will go to if a DNS Lookup fails, or the MTA is not allowed to do DNS lookups and it gets mail destined for unknown IDOMAINs.

   Once again, *do not* check the option to force all messages through the default routing domain.

3. Go to the properties page of the MTA objects in the domains that you *do* want to perform DNS Lookups.

   (Obviously, you would need to make sure that you do this on the default routing domain that you defined in Step 2.)

4. Select Routing Options from the drop-down list, click the last check box in the override column (Allow MTA to send directly to other GroupWise systems), and then also check the option next to it to actually turn this feature on.

There you go. This MTA can now do DNS lookups. If it cannot find the DNS entry, it sends the message to the default routing domain.

Now a tip on how to know what each MTA is really doing: If you look at the log file for an MTA, the beginning has the configuration information. Following is an example of just the general settings at the beginning of the MTA log:

```
23:26:20 574 General Settings:
23:26:20 574   Domain Directory:                           d:\do3
23:26:20 574   Work Directory:                     d:\do3\mslocal
23:26:20 574   Preferred GWIA:                         Do1.GWIA6
23:26:20 574   Default Route:                                Do3
23:26:20 574   Known IDomains:                        *eraff.com
23:26:20 574   Known IDomains:                       *Jalene.com
23:26:20 574   Allow Direct Send to Other Systems:          No
23:26:20 574   Force Route:                                 No
23:26:20 574   Error Mail to Administrator:                 No
23:26:20 574   Display the active log window initially:    Yes
23:26:20 574   NDS Authenticated:                          Yes
[Public]
23:26:20 574   NDS User Synchronization:                   Yes
23:26:20 574   Admin Task Processing:                      Yes
23:26:20 574   Database Recovery:                          Yes
23:26:20 574   Simple Network Management Protocol (SNMP):
Enabled (index 1)
```

What you are looking for are the Default Route, Known IDOMAINs, Allow Direct Send to Other Systems, and Force Route values. These will tell you exactly how this particular MTA will act.

Remember to think of this entire process from the perspective of the MTA when it receives a message in Internet addressing format. It will first check to see if the IDOMAIN is a known IDOMAIN. If it is, and the Force Route value is No, then it will do a lookup in its index to find what GroupWise domain the user is in, because it should know about the user, and then look at its link configuration to figure out how to route the message to the internal user.

If the message is destined for a user in an *unknown* IDOMAIN, then it will once again check the Force Route value. If it is No, then it checks to see if it can do a

DNS lookup. If it can, it tries to do so. If it finds a match, it tries to connect to the destination MTA across the Internet. If no match is found, it checks the Default Route value, and if something is defined here, it sends the message to this domain. If nothing is defined here, it simply routes the message to the default GWIA.

Publish GWMTP Records to the Internet

Now your MTAs are able to route messages to other GroupWise systems on the Internet. This is half of the picture. The other half is allowing your MTAs to receive messages from other GroupWise systems. For this to happen, other systems must be able to find at least one of your MTAs using DNS.

GWMTP.TCP Record Information for the DNS Administrator

The following is information that will be useful to your DNS administrator in defining your GroupWise MTA as an entity that can be contacted on the Internet to transmit GroupWise messages to.

To resolve a foreign Internet domain name, a GWMTP-enabled MTA will do a DNS lookup for an address record for a particular Internet domain name. If the address record is found, then the MTA will look for either a service (SRV) or text (TXT) record for the GWMTP.TCP service.

A full explanation of domain name server configuration is beyond the scope of this text. What this book will try to do is provide you with enough information that you can explain to your DNS administrator what records you need.

Each GWMTP.TCP record will have several values associated with it. These are discussed briefly:

- **Name:** The service name must begin with GWMTP.TCP, for instance GWMTP.TCP.NOVELL.COM.
- **Class:** The record class may be either SRV or TXT. Choose whichever of these is easiest for you to support using the DNS tools you have available.
- **Priority:** This may be any number, but for a single-MTA system it should be 0. If you have more than one MTA, you can set one to be 0, and another to be 1. In this case, the MTA with a priority of 1 will only be used if the MTA with a 0 priority is not responding.
- **Weight:** Weight may also be any number. This value is used for load balancing. If two MTAs have the same priority but different weights, then the one with the lower weight will be preferred. If that MTA is too busy, connections will be made to the MTA with the higher weight (and the same priority) next.

- **Time to live:** Typically listed in seconds, this is the amount of time this record will be continued valid before being refreshed. If you need to make a change to an MTA's IP address or port, the time to live may be the minimum amount of time it will take your changes to propagate across the Internet DNS system.
- **IP address:** This is the IP address of the MTA.
- **Port:** This is the GWMTP port for this MTA, typically 7100. If you choose another port value here, you must also choose that value under the Network Address tab of the MTA object properties.

Internet Addressing Overrides

After Internet addressing has been enabled, customizations or overrides can be used to increase the flexibility of Internet addressing within the GroupWise system. Overrides can be enabled at the Internet Addressing tab on the detail screen of domains, post offices, and users.

Internet Domain Name Overrides

Overrides at a domain, post office, or user level may be used to specify a certain Internet domain name. For example, the sales division in the Sales GroupWise domain may want to be known as `sales.worldwidewidgets.com` rather than just `worldwidewidgets.com`. An override could be set on each domain to allow all members of each domain to have the specific Internet domain name value. If the members of a post office wanted a specific Internet domain name for their post office, an override could be done for that post office through the Internet Addressing tab on that post office object's properties window.

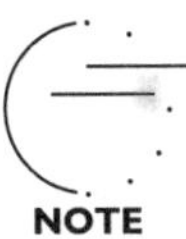
NOTE

All Internet domains that your organization wants to use need to be defined in two places. First, the Internet Addressing section under Tools ➪ GroupWise System Operations ➪ Internet Addressing. Secondly, your Internet domains should be defined for the sake of the GWIA, in the Foreign IDs field or the FRGNAMES.CFG file explained earlier in this chapter. Having all Internet domains defined in the Foreign ID field on the GWIA is not critical. If the /dia switch in the GWIA.CFG is *not* being used, the GWIA reads all IDOMAINs from the domain database to find out its identity, if you will. However, if the /dia switch is active on the GWIA, it *will not* read the domain to get the list of known IDOMAINs, and will strictly use the foreign ID names for both inbound and outbound building of reply to addresses. It will not honor the overrides on the GWIA.

The last type of Internet domain name override is at the user level. If a user or group of users wants a different Internet domain name than the one being used at the system, domain, or even post office level, you would use the Internet Addressing tab on their user objects.

Preferred Addressing Format Overrides

Domains, post office, and user objects can also have overrides to specify a specific preferred addressing format. This means that while the system default for preferred addressing format could be set to `UserID@Internet domain name`, any domain, post office, or user could have one of the other available preferred addressing formats (such as `First.Last@Internet domain name`).

TIP

Even though you select a preferred addressing format, users will be able to receive mail at *any* of the known addressing formats. This preferred format just determines what the reply-to address format will be. Hence, Billy Bob could receive mail at `billy.bob@worldwidewidgets.com`**,** `bbob@worldwidewidgets.com`**,** `bob.billy@worldwidewidgets.com`**, and so on.**

Default GroupWise Internet Agent Overrides

On a large GroupWise system, there may be more than one point at which the system connects to the Internet. Novell's corporate network is no exception: They maintain permanent Internet connections for their corporate offices in San Jose, California, and in Provo, Utah, as well as in many of their regional offices.

In these cases, it makes sense to allow regional domains to route Internet mail through a local GWIA, instead of forcing all messages through the default GWIA. Domain objects have an Internet agent for outbound SMTP/MIME messages override, allowing the system administrator to select from any GWIA defined on the system. Figure 16.9 shows the property page of a GroupWise domain object that shows this option.

MTA Overrides

The last type of overrides is found in MTA objects. MTA overrides can be used to do the following:

- Specify default routing domains on a domain-by-domain basis (rather than at the system level)
- Force all mail to be routed to the routing domain
- Specify MTA to allow GWMTP communication

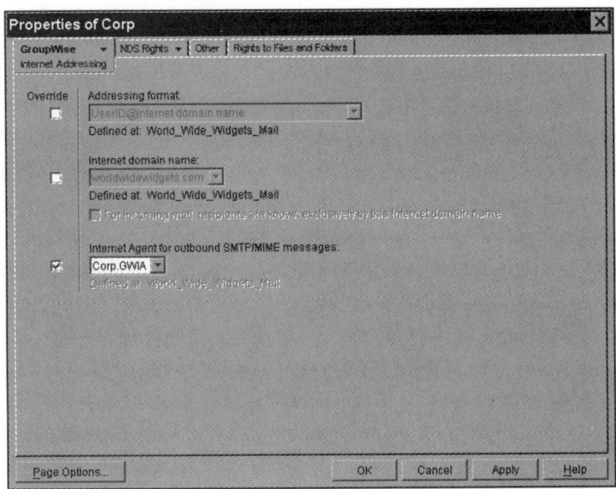

FIGURE 16.9 *Defining the Default Internet Agent for a GroupWise Domain*

A routing option override could be used to have undeliverable local mail routed through a different domain that may have GWMTP enabled. Additionally, if a routing domain is defined and an override is selected to force all messages to a default routing domain, then the domain's MTA will force all mail that is not deliverable in its local domain to be routed through the default routing domain. The last routing option, Allow MTA to send directly to other GroupWise Systems, is used to specify whether the domain MTA is allowed to communicate via GWMTP.

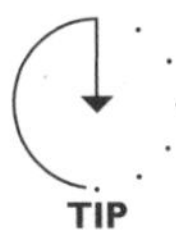
TIP

Here is the difference between a default routing domain and a default GWIA. The default routing domain is for Internet-bound e-mail that may be sendable via GWMTP. The default GWIA is for Internet-bound e-mail that cannot be sent via GWMTP. For routing purposes, it would therefore make sense to have the default GWIA reside on the default routing domain.

Mail Routing with Internet Addressing Enabled

Now that you understand the concepts behind GroupWise Internet addressing, this chapter now discusses the flow of e-mail through an Internet addressing-enabled GroupWise system.

Outbound E-Mail

Internet addressing- (or IA-) aware clients (GroupWise 5.5x and GroupWise 6x clients) allow mail with Internet addresses to be routed internally or to Internet users without the use of addressing rules or external domain definitions. Without Internet addressing enabled (and no addressing rules in use), messages sent to users with Internet-style addresses would be flagged as undeliverable when mail is sent from the client.

With Internet addressing enabled, much less lookup is done by the client on recipient addresses. Messages with Internet-style addresses are pushed on by the client to be resolved by the POA, MTA, or GWIA. Note, though, that each component in an IA-aware GroupWise system is capable of parsing Internet address information to some extent — including the GroupWise client. Each component — client, POA, MTA, GWIA — will do the best it can to resolve the address from its perspective.

If the POA cannot resolve an address, it pushes the message to the domain MTA. If the message is addressed to an Internet address, and the domain MTA cannot resolve the message to one of its post offices; or internal to the system, it will route the message to the default routing domain for a GWMTP lookup by the MTA there. If the recipient address cannot be resolved with a GWMTP DNS lookup, the message will be routed to the default GWIA for transfer to the Internet.

Inbound E-Mail

When a message arrives at a GroupWise system from the outside world, it does so in one of two ways:

- Direct MTA-to-MTA transfer via GWMTP
- SMTP/MIME transfer via the GWIA

NOTE

Messages can also come in through another GroupWise gateway, but typically those are not going to be outside world messages. Most other gateways, such as the Exchange gateway or the Lotus Notes gateway, are handing explicitly addressed messages to the GroupWise MTA, so the messages can be treated as internal to the GroupWise system.

When a message comes in via GWMTP, the MTA receiving the message will process the message by sending it to the GroupWise domain within the GroupWise system that the recipient is a member of. The recipient's domain routes the message to the recipient's POA, which delivers the message to the recipient's mailbox.

When a message comes in through the GWIA, via SMTP/MIME, it will be processed with the flow described in Figure 16.10. The GWIA will check the domain portion of the recipient address for user alias, post office alias, foreign ID, or Internet domain name matches. If GWIA does not find a match for the recipient domain address, then it will either route or relay the message to an appropriate Internet mail host for the specified domain or it will send an undeliverable message back to the sender.

Assuming a match was found (that is, the message must be delivered to this GroupWise system), the second level of resolutions involves checking the user name portion of the recipient mail address to see if a unique match can be found.

NOTE

The GWIA is fully backwards compatible for resolving traditional GroupWise addressing, in addition to using the flexible rules of Internet addressing resolution.

This next section and Figure 16.10 explore this address resolution process in more detail.

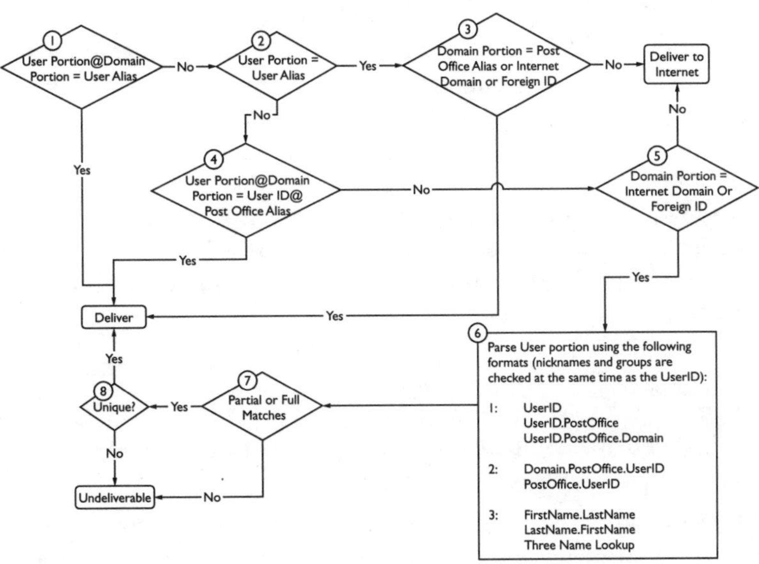

FIGURE 16.10 *GWIA Inbound Resolution with Internet Addressing Enabled*

1. Compare `user@domain` (the entire string, not just the user portion) against user aliases defined at the GWIA. If there is a match, the message can be passed directly to the MTA to be routed to the user. If there is no match, move to Step 2.
2. Compare the user portion of the address against user aliases defined at the GWIA. If there is a match, move to Step 3. If not, move to Step 4.
3. Compare the domain portion against post office aliases, Internet domain names, or foreign IDs defined for this system or assigned to the GWIA. If there is a match, the message is passed to the MTA to be delivered. If not, then the message does not belong to this GroupWise system and will be passed to the Internet.

If the message arrived at the GWIA from the MTA (that is, it came from inside the system) it will still be checked to see if it belongs on this system, using Steps 1 through 3. This is how messages addressed by non-IA-aware components to recipients on this system will be handled.

4. Does `user@domain` match up to a `UserID@Post office alias` string? If so, the message is passed to the MTA for delivery. If not, go to Step 5.
5. Compare the domain portion of the address against the Internet domain names defined on the system and against the foreign ID assigned to the GWIA. If there is a match, then move to Step 6. If not, the message is delivered to the Internet.

Steps 1 through 5 checked out aliases, which are shortcuts to address resolution. Anything that makes it to Step 6 is not going to match up to a user or post office alias, but does match up with this system's Internet name or names.

6. Once the message is known to belong to the system, a parsing engine works to try and uniquely resolve the user portion of the address with a GroupWise user. The parser engine compares the user portion of the recipient address with the following GroupWise information:
   - **U.P.D. resolution:** The address is parsed and compared against the address book for matches in UserID.PostOffice.Domain format. If the user portion has less than three segments (that is, there aren't two dots in the user portion), then it will be compared in UserID.PostOffice, or just UserID format.

- **D.P.U. resolution:** The address is parsed and compared against the address book for matches in Domain.PostOffice.UserID format. Again, if the string is not long enough, it will be compared in PostOffice.UserID format.
- **Name-based resolution:** The address is parsed and compared against the address book for matches in FirstName.LastName, LastName.FirstName, and three-part name format.

7. If there are no matches for the parsed user portion of the address, the message is undeliverable. If there are matches, even partial matches, then move to Step 8.
8. A preference filter is applied, and if, at any level of preference, the parsed address is unique, then it is delivered. Partial addresses are passed to the MTA for complete resolution at the MTA or POA level. If the parsed address is not unique, then the message is undeliverable.

Understanding the Parsing and Lookup Process

In the flow in the preceding section, the GWIA reached a point in Step 6 where it had to parse the user portion of an Internet-style address, and then do a lookup to determine if there were any matches. It is important that you understand the rules behind the parse and lookup, because they will affect the decisions you must make when implementing Internet addressing on your GroupWise system.

Every component on an IA-aware GroupWise system can do the parsing and lookup operations described following and outlined in Figure 16.11. When messages come in to the system through the GWIA, then the GWIA parses and looks up. Messages coming in through the MTA via GWMTP will have their addresses parsed and looked up by the MTA.

In the process shown in Figure 16.11, an Internet-style address has been handed to a GroupWise component, and that component has reached the point where it must parse the user portion of the address. The balance of this section explores the process.

1. GroupWise begins with a parse and lookup for matches in U.P.D. (User. PostOffice.Domain) format. If the user portion of the address has less than three components, then we will do a User.PostOffice or a User lookup. If there is one and only one match, GroupWise delivers the message. If there

is more than one match, GroupWise goes to Step 3. If there are no matches, GroupWise continues with Step 2.

2. GroupWise now parses and looks for matches in D.P.U. (Domain.PostOffice.User) format. This is the legacy addressing format used by GroupWise. Again, if there are less than three components to the user portion of the address, GroupWise will do a PostOffice.User lookup. There's no need to do a User lookup, though — GroupWise did that in Step 1. If there is one and only one match, GroupWise delivers the message. If there are multiple matches, GroupWise goes to Step 3. If there are no matches, GroupWise goes to Step 4.

3. Messages will be delivered to the closest match that is found. If one of the matches is on the same post office as the component doing the parsing and lookup, then that match will be chosen above other matches. If there is only one preferred match, the message will be delivered. If there is more than one match (that is, no preferred matches), then the message is undeliverable or ambiguous.

   If the GWIA, the POA, or the MTA reaches this point, then the message is undeliverable. If the client reaches this point, however, the user may be prompted to resolve the ambiguity.

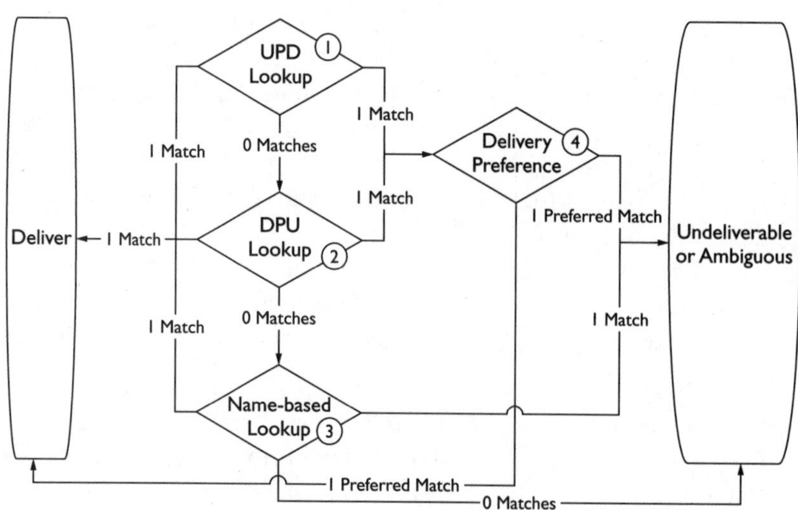

FIGURE 16.11 *The Parsing and Lookup Process*

4. GroupWise now checks the user names. GroupWise looks for matches in First.Last, Last.First, FirstInitial.Last, and three-part name format and will check all possibilities at once. If there is one, and only one, match, the message is delivered. If there is more than one match (for example, the message is addressed to James.Howard, and you have a Howard James and a James Howard on the system), then the message is ambiguous or undeliverable. No delivery preferences are applied. If there are no matches, then the message is undeliverable.

Parsing User Names

It may be helpful at this point to drill down even deeper and to look deeper at Step 4 from the preceding section. Here is the logic followed when a GroupWise component parses the user portion of the address for matches with users' full names:

1. Replace all periods left of the @ sign with spaces.
2. If there is more than one space, see Step 7.
3. Assign the text left of the space to Part_A.
4. Assign the text right of the space to Part_B.
5. Search the given and last names for all users in the GroupWise system. Compare the following combinations, and select all matches:

```
Given=Part_A
Last=Part_B

Given=Part_B
Last=Part_A
```

6. Skip to Step 11.
7. Assign the text left of the first space to Part_A.
8. Assign the text between the first space to the second space to Part_B.
9. Assign the rest of the text to Part_C.
10. Search the given and last names for all users in the GroupWise system. Compare the following combinations, and select all matches:

```
Given=Part_A
Last=Part_B Part_C

Given=Part_A Part_B
Last=Part_C

Given=Part_C
Last=Part_A Part_B

Given=Part_B Part_C
Last=Part_A
```

11. If no matches exist, skip to Step 16.
12. If a unique match is found, skip to Step 17.
13. External users who match are eliminated if internal matches exist.
14. Matches outside the local GroupWise domain are eliminated if matches exist in the local GroupWise domain.
15. If a unique match is found, skip to Step 17.
16. The message is undeliverable.
17. Deliver the message.

Parsing Scenarios

Here are a couple of example scenarios to let you see how these pieces fit together, beginning with the following:

- Message is addressed to `mike.sales@worldwidewidgets.com`.
- User Mike Sales exists in the Corp post office.
- There is a post office Sales on the system somewhere.
- No user or post office aliases exist.

Here's what will happen. The GWIA for WorldWide Widgets will decide the message belongs on this system and will attempt to resolve the user portion of the address. Now walk through the logic in the following steps:

1. The string `mike.sales` is compared against the address book for U.P.D. matches. Since there are only two parts to the string, we compare mike for user matches and sales for post office matches.
2. A partial match is found. There is a post office sales on this system.
3. The message is routed to the sales POA for resolution of the remainder of the address.
4. The sales POA looks for a user ID `mike` on the local post office and finds none. The message is undeliverable.

   Note here that having post office names that match user names can cause problems for messages addressed in First.Last or Last.First format.

And now for the second scenario, note the following:

- Message is addressed to `rip.van.winkle@worldwidewidgets.com`.
- A user with the first name Rip, and a last name Van Winkle exists in the Corp post office.
- No user or post office aliases exist.

In this case, the GWIA for WorldWide Widgets will end up attempting to resolve the user portion of the address as a three-part name.

1. The GWIA looks for a user ID `rip` on the post office `van` in the domain `winkle`. No matches are found. The names `van` and `winkle` do not match any post office or domain names on this system.
2. The GWIA looks for a user ID `winkle` on the post office `van` in the domain `rip`. No matches are found. The names `van` and `rip` do not match any post office or domain names on this system.
3. The GWIA looks for users with the following names:

   ```
   First=Rip, Last=Van Winkle
   First=Rip Van, Last=Winkle
   First=Winkle, Last=Rip Van
   First=Van Winkle, Last=Rip
   ```

4. One match is found, and the message is delivered to user Rip Van Winkle.

Best Practices

Internet addressing is going to be increasingly important to GroupWise administrators, so I encourage you to enable it. Before you do, however, you should be sure to carefully plan your Internet addressing implementation to avoid potential pitfalls. This section outlines some of the practices that administrators use successfully.

Naming Conventions

Following are a few tips to keep in mind as you plan your Internet addressing strategy:

- **Strive to make all user IDs unique throughout the GroupWise system.** GroupWise administrator will only require user IDs to be unique per post office, so you will need a separate tool to ensure that you are not duplicating a user ID.
- **Use `UserID@Internet domain name` as your preferred addressing format.** The preferred addressing format is used to build the reply-to address, and if user IDs are unique system-wide, this format allows you to move users to any post office on your system without their Internet address changing. This setting will prevent reply-to addresses that are ambiguous in cases where first- and last-name combinations are not unique.
- **If user IDs cannot be unique, avoid using Internet domain names to make an Internet address unique within the same GroupWise system.** If Internet domain names are making the user portion of a local Internet address unique, then the exclusive flag must be set on users that do not have unique user portions for their Internet addresses. This will mean that the user may only be known by the particular addressing format and Internet domain name. It also means extra work for the administrator. If user IDs cannot be unique, it will likely be easier to set user aliases for non-unique users.
- **User IDs, first names, and last names should not be the same as post office or domain names.** (See the first scenario in the section, "Parsing Scenarios," earlier in this chapter.) One easy solution for this is to include numbers or underscores in post office and domain names.

- **Users should have no more than three names embedded in their complete name.** Rip Van Winkle is okay, but Sir Rip Van Winkle is not. Think of it this way: You may have a space in either the First name or the Last name field, but never in both fields. Only the first name or last name can have a space in the name, not the first name and last name.
- **Users cannot share the same first and last name or user ID unless each of the users has a unique Internet domain name, and the exclusive flag is specified on the Internet addressing tab for each of the users.** The exclusive flag will allow each user to only be known by the specified Internet domain name, thereby guaranteeing that the users' Internet addresses are unique.
- **When used, user aliases and nicknames should be unique throughout the system.**

System Design

This section offers a few suggestions on effectively setting up GroupWise Internet addressing on your GroupWise system:

- **The GroupWise domain that owns the GWIA should not own GroupWise 4.x post offices.** Users on these post offices will lose the ability to reply to mail that arrives through the GWIA.
- **If direct MTA-to-MTA connectivity is enabled, the GroupWise domain that owns the default GWIA should be the default routing domain.** This will simplify firewall administration (only one machine needs to be outside the firewall) and reduce traffic.
- **On large systems that span wide area networks, use default GWIA and default routing domain overrides to ensure that traffic bound to the Internet takes the most efficient route.** (This assumes that your system has more than one connection to the Internet.)
- **If an external system (such as a Unix mail host) shares your Internet domain name, enable the option Forward Undeliverable Inbound Messages to Host under the SMTP/Mime Undeliverable property page of the GWIA.** See Chapter 10 for more details.
- **Ensure that all GWMTP-enabled MTAs are able to receive packets from their assigned port from the Internet and that they can send packets out to the Internet on high-numbered ports.**

Summary

GroupWise Internet addressing is an essential piece of current and future GroupWise technology. Before implementing it, however, administrators must carefully consider their naming conventions and system design. You should also take message flow and parsing into consideration. An understanding of the way the system works will help the prudent administrator design or redesign a GroupWise system so that it is easily administered and maintained.

CHAPTER 17

Maintaining the GroupWise System

Regular maintenance of your GroupWise system can be automated and should not take up much of your time as an administrator — especially if you have implemented a good system design, which Chapter 18 discusses.

If your users access the post office in client/server access mode, and you implement a few appropriate scheduled events, your chances of losing data due to damage to the information store will be minimized. This chapter covers the maintenance of the GroupWise information store and the GroupWise directory and walks you through the creation of some appropriate scheduled events.

Information Store Maintenance Concepts

The GroupWise information store — that collection of databases and directory structures discussed in Chapter 4 — is susceptible to damage, just like any other file on a file server. The information store is written to thousands of times each day, and although the odds of any individual transaction failing are astronomically low, after enough reads and writes, the odds begin to add up in favor of you seeing some problems.

For the purposes of this discussion, there are really only two kinds of damage or corruption possible:

- Structural damage
- Contents damage

It is easiest to explain these categories with an analogy. Suppose that you have a filing cabinet, and each file in each drawer contains not only its own information but also references to other files. Then one day, an angry bull moose charges through your office and dents the filing cabinet. One of the drawers will not open any more. This is structural damage.

Now, suppose that you fix the cabinet by transferring all the files you could get to from the dented cabinet into a new one. Unfortunately, you could not recover any of the files from the dented drawer. Later, when reading a file in one drawer, you see a cross-reference to a file in another drawer. You follow the cross-reference, but that referenced file is not there. This is contents damage.

Structural Maintenance

Your greatest concern regarding the GroupWise information store should be the structural health of the GroupWise databases. If there is a bull moose running around denting your databases, you need to know about it. You should take steps to ensure that all user and message databases on a post office are structurally analyzed and fixed every day. This is done via the Scheduled Events tab on the POA object.

Contents Maintenance

The contents of the GroupWise information store need to be verified on a weekly basis. The contents analysis ensures that the pointers from one record to another record are valid. The contents check and fix also ensures that master records (as discussed in Chapter 19) have pointers to the other supporting records for a message.

The Relationship between Structure and Contents

As I alluded to in the example with the filing cabinet and the moose, one common reason for content-related problems is structural damage. Take this, for example:

USERA's USER123.DB file has a pointer to record #286 in MSG17.DB. Unfortunately, a large block of MSG17.DB is damaged (for example, the server abended while the file was being written to). The next time the POA works with this file, it detects the damage, and the file is rebuilt. The damaged block could not be recovered, though, and record #286 is lost from MSG17.DB.

USERA's USER123.DB file now has a contents inconsistency. The contents analyze-and-fix routine will take the pointer in USERA's USER123.DB file and tie it off so that it points nowhere. This, in effect, makes the received item into a posted item. USERA can still read the subject line and can see who sent the message, but the message contents and any attachments are lost. USERA can contact the sender, having him or her re-send or re-compose the message, if necessary.

Contents Analysis Is Time-Consuming

A contents analysis can take a long time, especially if your post office is a large one, or if your users retain their messages indefinitely. If your information store is large, you will want to run your contents analysis over a weekend. I have encountered organizations whose GroupWise information stores were so large that a contents analysis for a single post office took well over 24 hours to run.

E-Mail Expiration

Based on what you just learned, you can see part of the logic behind not allowing your users to keep their e-mail forever. Thus, I strongly recommend that you implement an e-mail expiration policy. You may choose to expire all e-mail messages after they are 90 days old, but allow appointments to stay on the system for a full year. You may also decide to purge all deleted items (items in the trash) early each morning.

Justification for E-Mail Expiration

The downsides to allowing a GroupWise information store to grow too large are the following:

- Backup operations may not complete overnight, due to the sheer volume of data to be backed up.
- Contents analysis takes a very long time.
- QuickFinder indexing may take longer, and a QuickFinder index rebuild operation (executed from the POA console) will take much, much longer than you may have time for.
- Larger information-store databases impede post office agent performance, which will in turn mean that your users will observe poor performance from the GroupWise client.

Overcoming Hurdles to E-Mail Expiration

There are really only three reasons to keep an e-mail message longer than 90 days:

- **Sentimental reasons:** If this is the case, invite your users to use the GroupWise archive. They will still have access to the items, but they will not be impacting performance on the master mailbox.
- **Legal reasons:** If e-mail messages are considered legal documents in your company, consider writing your e-mail policy in such a way that your backup tapes can be considered the legal record of these documents.
- **As a reminder of important information:** Any e-mail message that is still being read regularly after 90 days should probably become a GroupWise document (in a GroupWise library) or should be on your company's internal Web page.

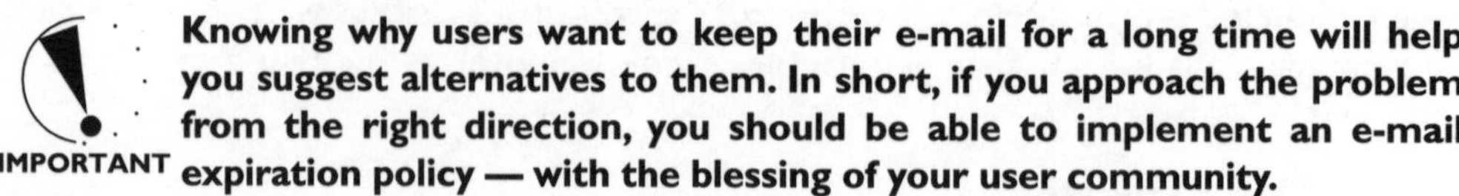
IMPORTANT

Knowing why users want to keep their e-mail for a long time will help you suggest alternatives to them. In short, if you approach the problem from the right direction, you should be able to implement an e-mail expiration policy — with the blessing of your user community.

GWCHECK/GroupWise Message Store Check

The software used to maintain and repair the GroupWise information store is commonly called *GWCHECK.* There are actually three places where this software resides:

- **The post office agent:** Each POA has the GWCHECK code built into it. The code is launched when one of the following occurs:
  - Mailbox/library maintenance is run from ConsoleOne
  - A scheduled event runs
  - The POA detects a problem with a database it is trying to work with and kicks off a GWCHECK job
- **GWCHECK.EXE:** Found in the software distribution directory ADMIN\UTILITY\GWCHECK, this is the stand-alone GWCHECK software. It runs as a Win32 application, so to run it you must have full file access to the information store from a computer with a Windows 32-bit operating system.
- **The GroupWise client:** The version of GWCHECK built into the client does not fix a user's master mailbox, but it can fix archive, caching mode, and GroupWise remote message store databases.

Benefits of Running GWCHECK on the POA

I often encourage my customers to use the POA-executed GWCHECK. Here are some very good reasons to run mailbox/library maintenance, or to use scheduled events, instead of running the GWCHECK.EXE:

- **Speed:** Assuming that the post office agent runs on the same box where the information store is located, the POA can run the GWCHECK routines at least twice as fast as GWCHECK.EXE. It can run the operation right "on the bus" rather than across a network connection.
- **Stability:** GWCHECK.EXE runs on the Windows platform and must run "across the wire." If something goes wrong on the workstation (GPF, blue screen of death, and so on), or if the LAN connection goes down, GWCHECK.EXE may do more harm than good. The POA is not as vulnerable in this way.
- **Scheduling:** The scheduled events are automatic. GWCHECK.EXE does not provide tools for automation. As an administrator, you need not manually launch regular maintenance operations if you enable scheduled events.

Benefits of Running GWCHECK.EXE

If there were no circumstances under which you might need the stand-alone GWCHECK, Novell would not have written the tool. Here are a few cases in which GWCHECK.EXE is preferred over the POA's routines:

- **Low risk to the server:** In cases where you suspect that a corrupt database is causing the POA to abend the server, you should try GWCHECK.EXE. If this routine dies while doing a database repair, it will not take the whole server with it. Fortunately, these cases are getting fewer and farther between.

- **Watch it work:** Some administrators like to see what GWCHECK is doing. The POA does not log GWCHECK operations on-screen, but GWCHECK.EXE does. When troubleshooting is being done, or a one-user GWCHECK is being done, this is fine. For regular maintenance routines though, the server-based GWCHECK routine is always better.

Getting GWCHECK Log Files

It is always a good idea to review GWCHECK logs, even if you don't want to watch the operation work. To receive a GWCHECK log from the POA, make sure that you are set up as the administrator of the domain that owns the post office against which you are running GWCHECK.

1. Highlight the domain object, right-click, and select Properties.
2. From the Identification property page, click the button to the right of the Administrator field.
3. Browse to your NDS user object and click OK.

IMPORTANT

The NDS user object you select must be grafted to a GroupWise mailbox.

The next time the POA runs a GWCHECK operation, the log file will be e-mailed to you.

Understanding Scheduled Events for Post Office Maintenance

Every post office agent object has a Scheduled Events property page. This page is used to create, schedule, and edit events for the POA.

Every scheduled event has two parts: the event and the associated action or actions. The *event* is the record that tells the POA what triggers to use. The *actions* are the operations that the POA will perform when the triggers have been set.

Triggers may include low disk space (for the disk check event type) or a particular day of the week and time of day (for the mailbox/library maintenance event type). Actions may include analyze/fix mailboxes or expire/reduce.

Events and actions created from one POA are visible by (and may be executed by) every other POA on the system.

TIP

Even though events and actions can be used by multiple post offices, I suggest making events and actions specific to each post office in your system. I've seen problems where an administrator for one post office modifies a scheduled event that has an action that is catastrophic for another post office.

Managing Scheduled Event Creation and Modification

It should be obvious (especially to administrators of large systems) that you will want to manage how administrators create and modify scheduled events.

- **Rights:** In order for a GroupWise 6 administrator to create or modify a scheduled event, or any of the listed actions, he or she must have supervisory rights to the primary domain object in NDS. If you need to control access to scheduled events, restrict administrators' access to the primary domain object.
- **Administrative procedures:** Although an administrator may be restricted from creating or modifying events or actions, even with object rights restricted, you will want to ensure that the right operations run on the right information stores. There are two ways to do this:
  - **Create different scheduled events for each post office:** Naming conventions are going to be critical here. In this case, I recommend that administrators name their events using the name of the post office the event applies to.
  - **Create standard events that work for all post offices:** Again, naming conventions are going to be important. Make sure that the name of the event describes the operation.

    In the next section, "Creating Schedule Events for Maintenance," you are encouraged to create scheduled maintenance routines one post office at a time, naming the events appropriately.

Creating Scheduled Events for Maintenance

Here is the example scenario for this section.

WorldWide Widgets wants to implement scheduled events for information-store maintenance. They have established an e-mail retention policy stating that all GroupWise messages will be retained for only 90 days, excluding calendar appointments. Furthermore, all trash items will be deleted every morning. Those users who use GroupWise remote, or use the GroupWise client in caching mode, may retain items for as long as they would like. Archiving is encouraged if users want to retain messages beyond 90 days.

This section assumes the task of creating scheduled events for CORP_PO1.

Structural Maintenance

This example begins with the structural maintenance. This event will analyze and fix the structure of all information-store databases on a daily basis.

1. Edit the POA for CORP_PO1.
2. Go to the Scheduled Events property page shown in Figure 17.1.

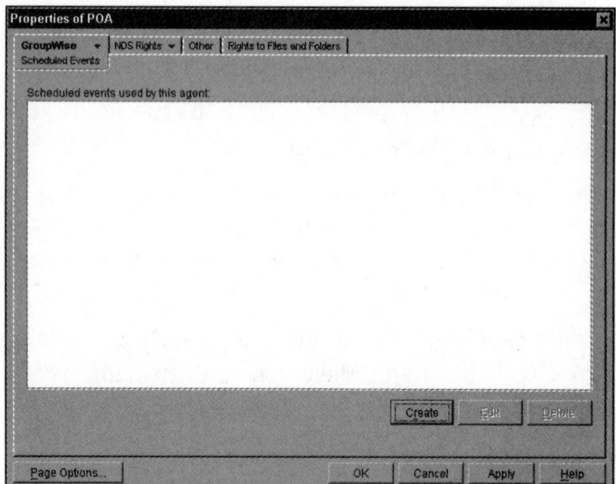

Figure 17.1 *The Scheduled Events Page for the CORP_PO1 POA*

3. Click Create and enter **CORP_PO1 - Structure - Event** as the name of the event.
4. Change the Type field to Mailbox/Library Maintenance.

5. Change the Trigger field to Daily and the Time field to 1:00 a.m.

   You now have the event name, type, time, and trigger. What hasn't been set up yet is what the event will do. You now need an action. Your scheduled event should look something like Figure 17.2.

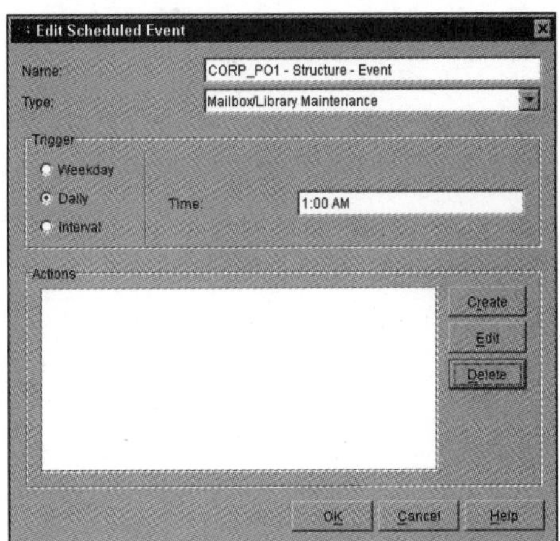

Figure 17.2 *Defining the Event*

6. Click Create.
7. Enter **CORP_PO1-Structure-Action** (the name of the action helps you associate it with the appropriate event).
8. Select the Action named Analyze/Fix Databases.
9. Put check marks in the Structure, Fix problems, User, and Message check boxes.

   Figure 17.3 shows a configured action.
10. Click the Results tab and make sure that the results are sent to the administrator.
11. Click OK twice, and you now have the first scheduled event defined.

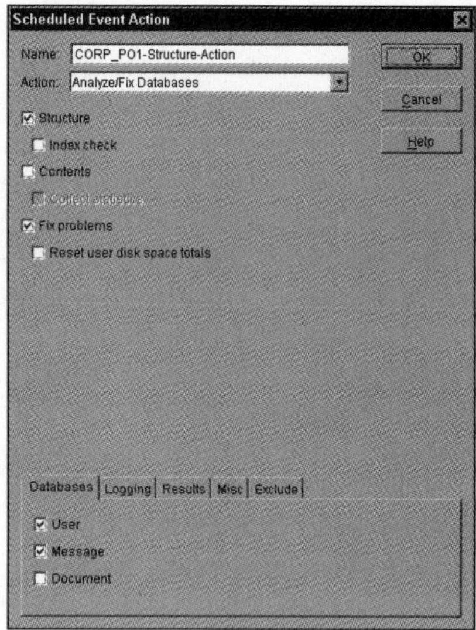

Figure 17.3 *Defining the Action*

Contents Maintenance

Now you need to make sure that the content of the CORP_PO1 information store is checked regularly.

1. Edit the POA for CORP_PO1.
2. Go to the Scheduled Events property page.
3. Click Create and enter **CORP_PO1-Contents-Event** as the name of the event.
4. Change the Type field to Mailbox/Library Maintenance.
5. Change the Trigger field to Weekday, and change the day to Saturday and the time to 3:00 a.m., as shown in Figure 17.4.
6. Click Create to create an action.
7. Make the name **CORP_PO1-Contents-Action.**
8. Select the Action named Analyze/Fix Databases.
9. Select the Contents, Fix Problems, User, and Message check boxes.

10. Click the Results tab, and make sure that the results are sent to the administrator.
11. Click OK twice, and you now have a contents check scheduled event defined.

    Figure 17.5 shows both events defined.

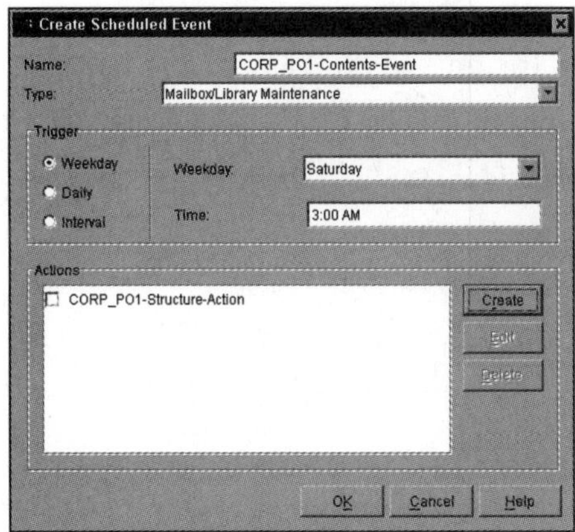

Figure 17.4 *Defining the Event*

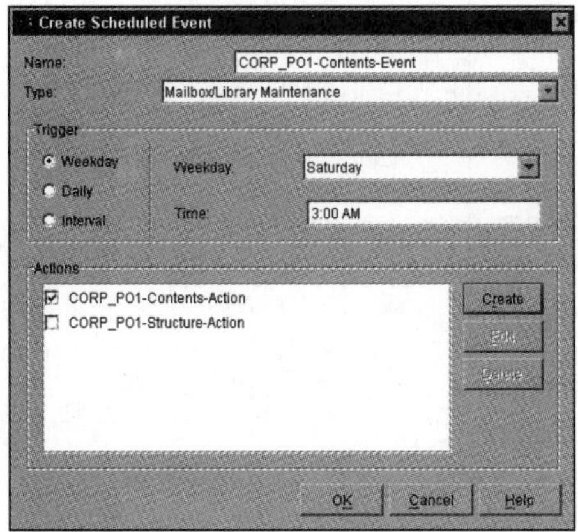

Figure 17.5 *Two Scheduled Events Defined*

Trash Deletion

Now you need to set up when to delete regularly the contents of the CORP_PO1 information store.

1. Edit the POA for CORP_PO1.
2. Go to the Scheduled Events property page.
3. Click Create and enter **CORP_PO1-Trash-Event** as the name of the event.
4. Change the Type field to Mailbox/Library Maintenance.
5. Change the Trigger field to Daily and the time to 2:00 a.m.
6. Click Create.
7. Make the name of your action **CORP_PO1-Trash-Action.**
8. Select the Action named Expire/Reduce Messages.
9. Select the Expire and Reduce Messages radio button.
10. Put check marks in the Trash older than, Received items, Sent items, and Calendar items check boxes and make sure that the Trash older than field is set to one day.

If you are using the smart purge features, as explained in Appendix A of this book, then you may want to check the Only backed-up items option. If you are not using the smart purge features, do not check this box. If you do, and you have not fully implemented a backup solution that works with the GroupWise TSA, then mail messages will not get purged, and your information store will continue to grow.

11. Make sure that the Items older than, Downloaded items older than, Items larger than, Reduce mailbox to, and Reduce mailbox to limited size check boxes are not checked, as shown in Figure 17.6.

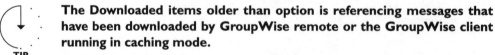

The Downloaded items older than option is referencing messages that have been downloaded by GroupWise remote or the GroupWise client running in caching mode.

12. Click OK twice, and you now have the trash deletion event defined.

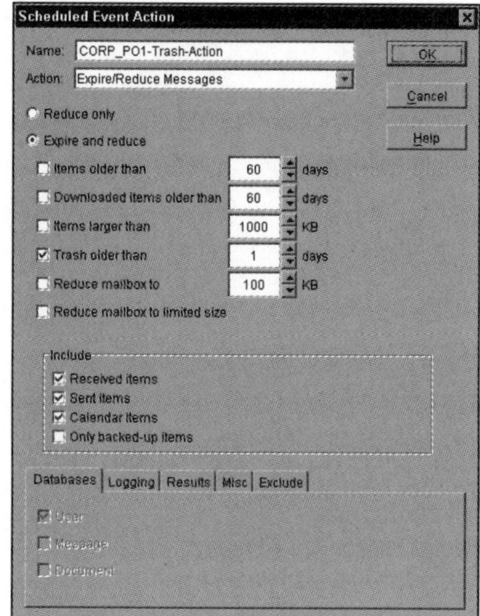

Figure 17.6 *Deleting Trash Items*

Message Expiration

Now you need to create a fourth and final event — the one that expires old mail.

1. Edit the POA for CORP_PO1.
2. Go to the Scheduled Events property page.
3. Click Create and enter **CORP_PO1-Expire-Event** as the name of the event.
4. Change the Type field to Mailbox/Library Maintenance.
5. Change the Trigger field to Weekday, and change the day to Saturday and the time to 6:00 a.m.

   Your event should now look like the one in Figure 17.7.

   Now create the action to be taken.
6. Click Create.
7. Make the name **CORP_PO1-Expire-Action.**

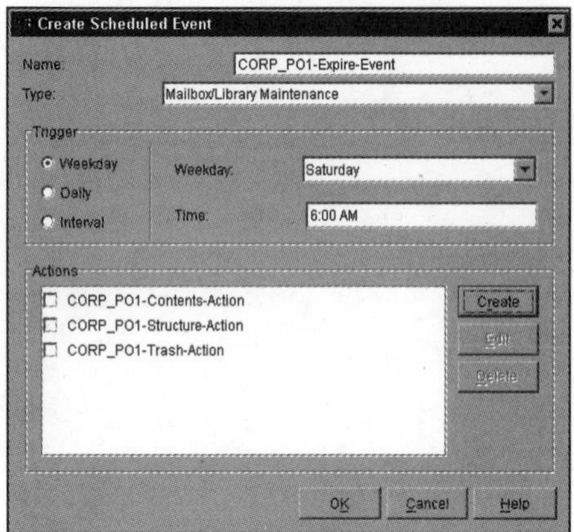

Figure 17.7 *Defining the Expire Event*

8. Select the Action named Expire/Reduce Messages.
9. Select the Expire and Reduce Messages radio button.
10. Select the following check boxes: Items older than — set this to 90 — Received items, and Sent items.
11. Make sure that the following check boxes are not checked: Downloaded items older than, Items larger than, Trash older than, Reduce mailbox to, Reduce mailbox to limited size, Calendar items, and Only backed-up items.

    Figure 17.8 shows the correct configuration.
12. Click OK twice, and you now have the last scheduled event defined.

Order and Timing of Scheduled Events

Before you run a contents analysis of a database, you ought to make sure that the structure is okay. In the preceding walkthrough, the scheduled contents analysis occurs after the structural analysis. The expire event in the example scenario was scheduled to come after the contents event.

In short, before you check contents, you should ensure that the structure is clean. Before you expire anything, you should ensure that the contents are consistent.

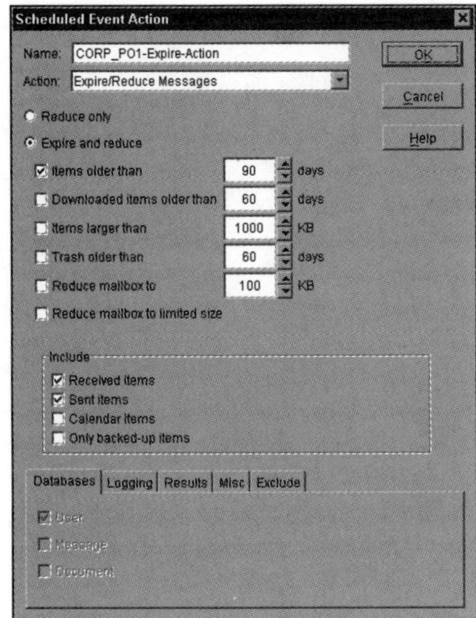

Figure 17.8 *Defining the Expire Action*

Seeing a POA's Scheduled Events from the Console Screen

You can see what scheduled events a POA intends to carry out by doing the following:

1. Go to the POA screen.
2. Select the F10 key ➪ Configuration Options ➪ Show Configuration.

   This dumps the POA's current configuration to the POA's log file.
3. Select the F9 key and view the end of the log file.

   You will see the configuration information for the POA.

Editing Scheduled Events

Take care when modifying scheduled events. Sometimes modifications do not correctly propagate down to the post office. You can check this by looking at the POA log to see what events are enabled. If the events don't match changes you made in ConsoleOne, you will either need to rebuild the post office database or delete and re-create the event or events in question.

Because of this possibility for problems, I typically recommend that if you need to edit a scheduled event, *don't*. Delete the action for the event and then the event itself. Then you can re-create the scheduled event.

GroupWise Archive Message Store Maintenance

Most users have no idea that the GroupWise 6 32-bit client has GWCHECK built into it. If a user is complaining of problems in an archive mailbox that seems like database damage, you can have them run GWCHECK on their own archive. Here's how to do it:

1. Have the user open the GroupWise mailbox.
2. Have the user hold down the Ctrl and the Shift keys simultaneously, and then choose File ➪ Open Archive while the Ctrl and Shift keys are still depressed.
3. The user will see the alert box shown in Figure 17.9.

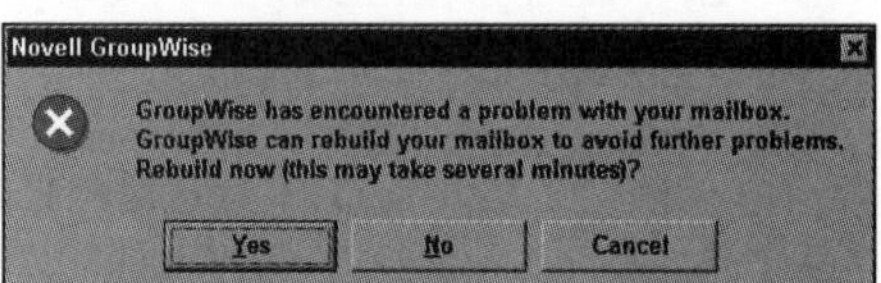

Figure 17.9 *GroupWise 32-Bit Client GWCHECK Alert*

Encourage your archive-savvy users to run these maintenance routines on their archive databases as a preventative measure. GroupWise archives are more likely to be damaged than the GroupWise information store is. Windows workstations are not quite the pillars of stability we would like them to be, and since the client writes to the archive directly, a GPF or blue screen of death can result in corrupt GroupWise archive data.

GroupWise Caching Mode and Remote Mode Maintenance

The GroupWise 6 client can be installed with a GWCHECK version that will run against a caching/remote mode mailbox. This GWCHECK is only installed and enabled if the administrator indicated that it should be. Chapter 12 talks about how to see that GWCHECK is installed and enabled. If GWCHECK is installed and enabled, your users can run GWCHECK on their caching/remote mailbox by choosing Tools ➪ Repair Mailbox. A light version of GWCHECK will launch, as shown in Figure 17.10.

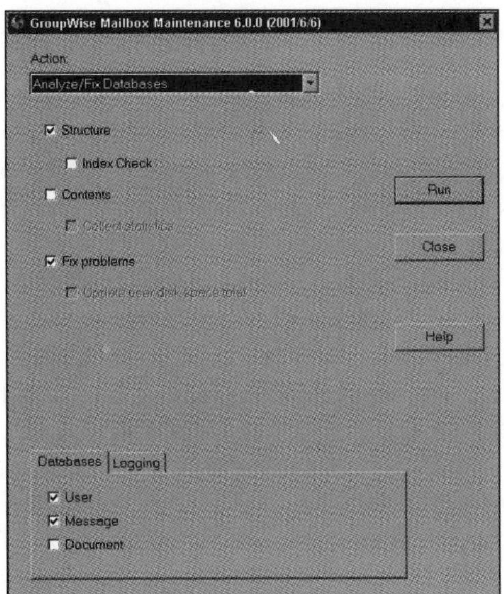

Figure 17.10 *GroupWise Caching Mode GWCHECK Screen*

Unfortunately, there's not an easy way to kick off a scheduled maintenance on users' caching and remote mode mailboxes. The users must do this themselves.

TIP

Users may also kick off a rebuild of their caching mode or remote databases by doing the following. Get out of GroupWise and then load the GroupWise client into caching or remote mode. Have the user hold down the Ctrl and Shift keys simultaneously while GroupWise is loading. Doing this will kick off a structural rebuild of their databases.

Maintaining GroupWise Directory Database Maintenance

GroupWise uses two repositories for directory information: Novell Directory Services and the GroupWise FLAIM or GDS databases (as discussed in Chapter 3).

Maintenance of Novell Directory Services (NDS) is beyond the scope of this book. Suffice it to say that if NDS is messed up, it can cause problems for GroupWise. This section will focus on maintaining the WPDOMAIN.DB and WPHOST.DB files.

My experience is that these files do not get corrupt nearly as often as information store databases. This is probably because they are not being written to as often as the information store databases. Thus it is not as critical that you run regular rebuilds of domain or post office databases.

The most important thing is that your WPDOMAIN.DB files — for all domains — are backed up regularly. Ideally, you should have this file backed up every day. Don't bother backing up the post office databases (WPHOST.DB), however. These files can be completely regenerated from the WPDOMAIN.DB file of the domain that owns the post office.

The single most important file in a GroupWise system is the primary domain's WPDOMAIN.DB file. I recommend that you run a recover-and-index rebuild of the primary domain weekly. This cannot be automated. Fortunately, you don't have to bring anything down in order to do this.

1. Connect to the primary domain by choosing Tools ➪ GroupWise System Operations ➪ Select Domain.
2. Highlight the primary domain and choose Tools ➪ GroupWise Utilities ➪ System Maintenance.
3. Select the action called Recover Database.
4. After the recover action is done, do a Rebuild Indexes for Listing action.

Summary

With the help of scheduled events, maintaining the GroupWise information store is easy. This chapter has shown you the events you will need to schedule to ensure that your GroupWise information store stays healthy.

GroupWise directory databases maintenance cannot be automated and must be done manually. Fortunately, the GroupWise directory databases are far less susceptible to damage, so they do not need to be checked regularly.

CHAPTER 18

Building Your GroupWise System Correctly

Back in 1993, when GroupWise was still WordPerfect Office, WordPerfect realized that some of the worst problems administrators had with the product were caused by poor planning. They began installing and configuring their system without knowing in advance what they wanted it to look like.

The problems caused by failing to design the system correctly only got worse as the GroupWise product matured. This chapter helps you apply much of the architectural information given to you so far as you plan your GroupWise system. I want your installation to run smoothly, and I want the system you build to meet your needs. Most of all, though, I want your system to run the way you expect it to without you having to spend a lot of time or money on technical support.

General System Configuration

There are several basic principles of GroupWise system design that you should try to adhere to. If you cannot, you should at least understand why the principle is important, so you can prepare yourself to work around the problems that your nonconformity may introduce.

E-Mail, Calendaring, and Document Management Are Mission Critical

The first principle is a simple one. The system you are going to build is going to be critical to the day-to-day work of your users. If GroupWise is down, your users will stop getting work done. If GroupWise performance is bad, your users will complain and will be less productive. If data is lost from the GroupWise system, that data will have to be re-created by users. These productivity hits will ultimately affect your bottom line. Your business will lose money when GroupWise is not running optimally.

The application of this principle is equally simple. If the system is mission-critical, if business cannot take place without it, you need to be prepared to spend money on the necessary infrastructure to support the system. This includes a solid LAN and/or WAN, a good Internet connection, and modern network file server hardware. That old NetWare 4.11 server running on the P100 box will run GroupWise, but not nearly as well as a NetWare 6 server with a XEON processor.

Mesh Message Transfer on the LAN

Message transfer agents (MTAs) can communicate via TCP/IP as they transfer messages between post offices. If you have multiple GroupWise domains on your LAN, you should probably avoid a star or hub configuration for network links. Allow every domain on the LAN to connect directly to every other domain. This will prevent bottlenecks, accelerate message transfer, and reduce the amount of network traffic.

Match WAN Message Transfer to WAN Topology

If you have more than one facility, or your offices are connected via wide area network technology (T2 or slower links), you will want to make sure that your MTA links match your WAN topology. This means that GroupWise domains should exist at the borders between the LANs. Use indirect connections between domains in one LAN and another, allowing only a single pair of domains to communicate across the WAN. This will reduce network traffic on the WAN and prevent certain kinds of MTA problems, including TCP timeout errors.

Treat the Internet as part of the WAN. After all, your users will be swapping e-mail with Internet users with great frequency. You should dedicate a domain to this WAN link. Have it host the GWIA. If you have multiple connections to the Internet, you probably will want to have multiple GWIAs.

Applying System Configuration Principles in the Real World

Here is a look at how the principles from the preceding sections can be put into practice. This section is going to examine a hypothetical organization and design a GroupWise system for that organization according to the principles outlined.

The Scenario

All-American Widgets has corporate offices in Newark, Detroit, and Salt Lake City. They have regional sales offices in Atlanta and San Francisco. They have a total of just over 11,000 employees.

In New Jersey, there are 2,500 employees, most of whom are in the sales, marketing, and engineering departments. These users are all connected to a 100MB fiber network.

In Detroit, there are 7,200 employees, all of whom are in the manufacturing division. Only about 1,000 of these users (the management team and a few stray engineers) have computers, but there are another 500 kiosks that are used by the employees on the plant floor.

There are 1,400 employees in Salt Lake City, in the service and support division. All 1,400 of them have computers, and they have a LAN similar to the one in New Jersey.

Finally, there are 15 employees in Atlanta and another 20 in San Francisco. These sales people all have mobile computers, and there's a solid network in their home office building. They do not, however, have a good network administrator.

The Newark System

It should be pretty simple to arrive at a good design for the Newark portion of the system. All-American Widgets is not going to use caching mode on the GroupWise client in a broad manner. Newark has 2,500 users, so you should have five post offices, one for every 500 users. Each post office gets its own file server.

Newark will have three domains. One domain will own the five post offices. An auxiliary domain will own the GWIA and will handle communications with the other remote sites. The third domain will be an auxiliary domain for the WebAccess gateway and Web server. So, Newark gets eight file servers, five post offices, three domains, a GWIA, and a WebAccess gateway.

The Detroit System

Detroit is a little more complex. Detroit has a much larger user base, but most of them won't be regular computer users. The Detroit site creates three post offices and two domains. One domain will have all the post offices below it. The post offices will be for the 1,000 management folk. The third post office will have 6,200 mailboxes on it. I am breaking a rule here, but I am doing so for good reason. These folks won't be using their mailboxes much. There are only 500 kiosks from which they can connect, so performance won't be a problem, and there will not be that much mail for them.

To simplify things, all the kiosks run WebAccess. That way, users don't have to worry about logging in and out of Windows to ensure that GroupWise registry settings are correct.

Detroit will need two domains. One will own three post offices. The second domain will be an auxiliary domain to house WebAccess. So, Detroit gets five file servers, three post offices, two domains, one of which will house only the GroupWise WebAccess gateway and the Web server.

The Salt Lake City System

Salt Lake City is going to look a lot like Newark, only smaller. The 1,400 users can be squeezed on to just two post offices in a single domain. Salt Lake City has its own Internet connection, and the repair technicians there will be sending a lot of Internet e-mail to customers they are supporting. A separate domain will handle WAN message transfer and will host the GWIA. Another auxiliary domain and server will host WebAccess and the Web server.

From the discussion on Internet addressing in Chapter 16, you can probably guess that All-American Widgets is going to use overrides here. The Salt Lake City users will get a different Internet domain name (probably `user@support.allamericanwidgets.com`) and will use the local GWIA as their default GWIA.

The Remote Sales Offices

Now, how do you handle the smaller offices? Here are a couple of good options. First, you could put a post office in each location, but put the domain in the corporate office. This would give these users great client/server performance when they are in the office, but would require that somebody at least know how to reboot the server and load the remote console software so that it can be maintained from the corporate office.

A second solution would be to put the sales people's mailboxes on post offices in Salt Lake City, Detroit, and/or Newark. These users would use the GroupWise client in caching mode all of the time, which won't be an inconvenience, since caching mode is optimal for users that are also on the road. This second solution is more ideal.

System Administration

With corporate headquarters in Newark, it makes sense that system administration is done from there. On a system of this size, you probably want to have a primary domain that does not own post offices. This means adding another server, and another domain, to the Newark site. This domain will be the primary domain and will have mesh links to all other Newark domains. It will connect indirectly to domains in Detroit and Salt Lake via the routing domain that owns the GWIA.

Now you see why I wanted to do all of this planning ahead of time. When you create a GroupWise system, the first thing you do is create the primary domain. But you cannot know where the primary domain is going to go until after you have the rest of the system plotted out.

Planning Your GroupWise System

Now you know the principles involved, and you've looked at how they applied to a fairly large (if hypothetical) organization. You are ready to begin planning your system.

1. First, identify how many users you are going to be providing services for. Does everyone have a computer? Will everyone get an account, regardless of whether they have a computer?
2. Divide your user base into groups, based on your network topology first, and on their departmental or workgroup affiliations second. If you have a department with users in two different remote sites, those users probably get grouped separately.
3. Take these groups of users and divide them into post offices of between 400 and 1,000 users. If you plan to put 1,000 users on a single post office, plan to spend top-dollar on file-server hardware, and be prepared for backups to take a while.
4. You should now have a list of post offices, and a rough list of which users belong to them. You are ready to begin assigning domains. On LANs, one domain can serve at least ten post offices. For systems of more than 2,500 users, though, I recommend at least three domains: one primary domain, one post office domain, and one gateway domain.
5. Determine where your LANs interface with WANs. Plan for a routing domain at each of these locations.
6. Begin drawing the links, and compare this to a map of your networks. Make sure that it makes sense. Remember, your network links should follow your WAN topology. If a packet moving from site A to site C must be transferred across a T1 line to site B, and then across a 56K line to Site C, you will want to have three domains involved, one at each site.
7. Plan your gateways, and assign them to domains accordingly. The most important of these is the GWIA. Make sure that you know which domain it is going to belong to, and where it is going to reside. Know what the foreign ID will be (that's your Internet domain name).
8. WebAccess should be running on a server that is dedicated to just run the Web server and WebAccess. Multiple WebAccess gateways should be running throughout your system.
9. Now begin assigning names to things. Remember the discussion on naming conventions in Chapter 16. Post office and domain names should have numerical characters in them to unquestionably distinguish them from user names. Try to keep names of domains and post offices short. This will make things simpler to manage.

10. Draw the system, complete with names, links, and user groups. Sleep on it. Run it by your boss. If you are the boss, run it by your spouse, significant other, fishing buddies, evil minions, or trusted lieutenants. Invite commentary and criticism. Listen.
11. Develop a standard for ports. This should include MTP ports for MTAs and POAs, as well as client/server ports for POAs. Also include live remote ports for MTAs and plan for HTTP ports for all agents. An example of this would be to have all client/server ports end in 7, such as 1657, 1667, 1677, 1687, and so on. Then if you ever have two post offices on the same server, you already know what client/server ports they will be using. An example of MTA MTP ports may be that they all end in 0, as in 7100, 7110, 7120, and so on. And make all POA MTP ports end in 1, as in 7101, 7111, 7121, and so on. It is really nice to have a standard document in relation to all the GroupWise ports that are involved in a GroupWise system.

Post Office Configuration

Most of what goes on in a GroupWise system also goes on at the post office. If you configure your GroupWise post offices correctly, your users will be far more satisfied with GroupWise.

E-Mail Policies

But I thought this was a technical book? E-mail policies may not seem technical, but they affect how you are going to configure elements of your post office. Your organization should have an e-mail policy. An e-mail policy should establish things such as the following:

- How long messages may be retained
- How large of attachments may be sent within your organization or on the Internet
- Whether users may archive their mail messages
- Whether users may use POP3, IMAP4, or NNTP
- Whether users may share address books or folders with users outside their post office

By making an e-mail policy, the GroupWise administrator can do the following:

- Set GroupWise client options to mirror e-mail policies.
- Do a better job of projecting the need for hardware resources.
- Design the GroupWise GWIA to disallow huge bandwidth eating attachments going on the Internet.
- Run reports to see who is hogging disk space, and encourage the abusers to delete certain sent- or received-mail items.

IMPORTANT

Even if your organization will allow users to retain messages for a long time, I strongly advise that your organization create a large-file-attachment policy. With GroupWise 6, you can control attachment size, right down to the post office level. So for example, you may say that users may not attach files over 50MB. Furthermore, you could have a policy that says that all files that are over 25MB must be saved off or deleted within seven days of receipt. To control attachment sizes, go into ConsoleOne, highlight a domain or post office, and choose Tools ⇨ GroupWise Utilities ⇨ Client Options ⇨ Send ⇨ Disk Space Mgmt.

Post Office Design

This section offers you a few tips to consider when designing post offices for your GroupWise system.

When and Where to Create a Post Office

Every GroupWise post office has a certain amount of cost in order for the post office to be maintained. For example, a GroupWise post office will generally reside on a server by itself. That server should have a high-quality disk subsystem and be made by a reputable hardware manufacturer. A backup solution should also be implemented for this server. It is best to make GroupWise post offices only when it is really warranted. In the past, GroupWise administrators often had to make small post offices to service regional sites. With the advancements of the GroupWise 6 WebAccess, and the GroupWise 6 client in caching mode, it's feasible to move users from small regional post offices into centralized post offices.

Where to Place Post Offices in NDS

When a user logs into GroupWise, if the NetWare client is loaded, GroupWise will look in NDS to discover information about the user's post office and POA. It is best, then, to put the GroupWise post office object in close proximity to the users associated with the post office. If the users associated with a post office are in multiple NDS contexts, just place their post office in an NDS OU that is in the same replica as the majority of the users on the post office. Users should have browse, read, and compare rights to the post office object, as well as the POA associated with the post office.

How Many Users to Place in a Post Office

If you have a good server and a fast network, GroupWise can scale nicely. The online-client/server mode of the GroupWise client can be taxing on the server when a post office has a bunch of power GroupWise users. A GroupWise post office can easily sustain thousands of mailboxes; it's the number of users logged in at the same time that scale back the practical numbers of users on a post office. Take a close look at whether it is feasible to move to a distributed processing model; by using the GroupWise 6 client in caching mode, the GroupWise client is far less chatty and taxing on the GroupWise POA. The downside to caching mode is that users need enough disk space to accommodate a complete copy of the items in their master mailbox on the server.

Other factors need to be considered when determining the number of users per server. For example, does your organization have an e-mail retention/expiration policy? If not, then the message store is bound to grow and grow. Your servers may not have enough disk space to accommodate a message store for 1,000 users that just keeps growing. GroupWise is very efficient on disk space, but let's face it, e-mail is the layman's FTP utility. When considering post offices, think about the people that will be on the post office and what their job functions are. Marketing departments are likely to have lots of presentation files. Engineering may have CAD files. So you may want to put only 250 of these kinds of folks on a post office. Production people may not deal with attachments at all, so perhaps you could put 750 of them on a post office.

Multiple Post Offices on a Server

This is a subject that somehow stirs strong emotions among GroupWise specialists. GroupWise is flexible enough to allow for more than one GroupWise post office to reside on a server. Many customers have had plenty of success with more than one post office on a server. Others have not had success using this model. Why did some fail? It often comes down to usage patterns. If you have two 700-user post offices full of power GroupWise users on one server in client-server mode, you may have performance problems. When two GroupWise POAs are loaded on a server, they are not cognizant of each other, and they have a tendency to hog the CPU if they feel they must do so. The result is that, at certain times, one of the POAs will not have the CPU time that it might need to adequately service users.

The GroupWise product suite is getting even more robust, with features such as document management and increased third-party integration. Because of this, users are more and more likely to be using GroupWise. This is good — productivity is going up; just make sure that having two post offices on a server is not degrading the potential for good productivity.

Configuring the POA Object for Optimum Performance and Function

This section discusses every setting and its relationship to a successful POA configuration. If a setting has no bearing on regular performance or function in the GroupWise system, it will not be mentioned.

Identification Property Page

This section works through the Identification property page, shown in Figure 18.1.

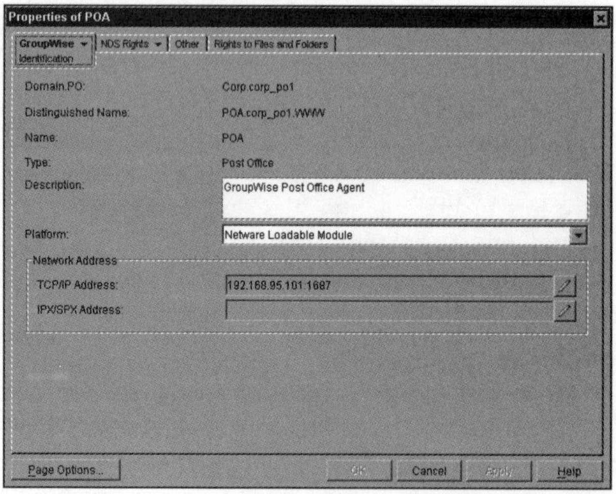

FIGURE 18.1 *The POA Identification Property Page*

- **Platform:** This isn't a Windows server bashing section. Windows servers have many advantages. However, for a post office, NetWare is a far better platform than NT. The reason: the NTFS disk subsystem. NTFS is very slow. In fact, a Windows server runs and writes data faster as a client to a NetWare server, then to its own hard disk. GroupWise runs just fine on the

Windows server platform, it's just that NTFS is so slow in comparison to NetWare that you are better off using NetWare to house GroupWise post offices.

Click on the pencil icon to the right of the TCP/IP Address line to access the next four options.

- **Network Address — IP or DNS:** The network address can be either an IP address or a DNS name. The advantage to a DNS name is that if at some time the IP address changes for a post office, the change simply needs to be made in the DNS, and the change is transparent to the users.
- **Network Address — Message Transfer Port:** Domain MTA to post office POA communication can be configured in two different manners. They are UNC and TCP/IP. The UNC method is one in which the MTA moves files to the WPCSOUT queues off of a post office. Also, in UNC mode, the MTA fetches messages from a post office using a polling cycle. The POA looks in the WPCSOUT queues periodically to see if anything needs to be processed. The polling process is far less efficient, because the MTA and the POA are not really talking to each other; they are just dropping things off in queues that each agent knows the other will look at eventually.

  TCP/IP communication between the MTA and the POA is optimal. When a POA has something for the MTA, it hands it right to the MTA, and the MTA acts on the item immediately. It's the same when the MTA needs to give something to the POA. Quick handoffs are particularly helpful in time-sensitive functions. For example, when a user does a busy search on the calendar of a user on another post office, the busy search must pass from the POA to the MTA. Since the POA speaks directly to the MTA rather than placing the busy search request in a queue, the end user has a far more interactive experience with busy search. Even if a domain and post office are on the same server, it is still optimal to configure the post office and domain to communicate via TCP/IP.

  The message transfer port (MTP) is the IP port that the POA listens on for messages from the MTA on the domain above the post office. The MTP port should be different from the HTTP port and the client/server port.
- **Network Address — HTTP Port:** The HTTP port on the POA should be filled in. This enables the POA to be monitored from a Web browser. There is some information that is available from the HTTP monitoring of the POA that is not available from the POA's console screen, such as the names of users that are logged into the POA or the version of GroupWise client that

they are using. Even if you have the /HTTP switches in the startup file of the POA, you still should fill in the HTTP port here. The GroupWise monitor program discovers the HTTP port of the POA from this field.

- **Network Address — Client/Server Port:** It's important that the POA is listening at a client/server port. Which port really doesn't matter, just as long as it's a unique port.

Agent and Log Settings Property Pages

The Agents Settings property page is shown in Figure 18.2.

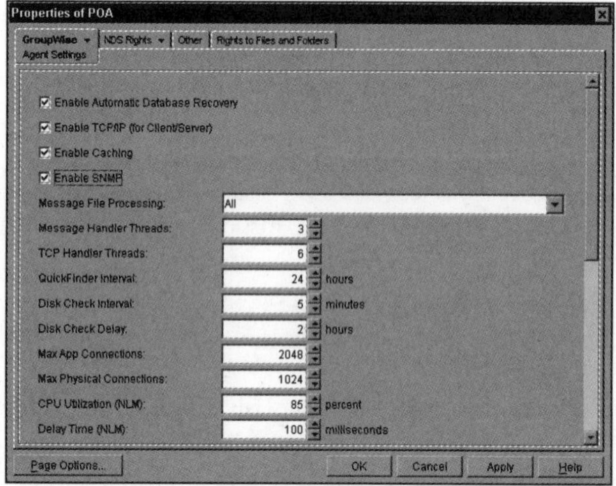

FIGURE 18.2 *The POA Agent Settings Property Page*

- **Enable Automatic Database Recovery:** If the POA discovers damage in a message-store database, having this option enabled allows the POA to kick off an immediate GWCHECK on the database.
- **Enable TCP/IP (for Client/Server):** Yep, you want this enabled for sure.
- **Enable Caching:** This is a must for better performance.
- **Enable SNMP:** If you are not using SNMP monitoring, then turn this off. It saves a little overhead. The GroupWise monitor piece is an SNMP monitoring device, so if you intend to use GroupWise monitor, do not turn this off.

- **Message File Processing:** This should be set to All. The reason for this option is that in some cases a GroupWise POA will be created for QuickFinder indexing. That POA would have message file processing set to Off. Don't set this to Low or High; if you do so, the POA will stop processing items in some of its queues.
- **Message Handler Threads:** Message handler threads should be set to about half the value of the TCP handler threads. If you have 16 TCP handler threads, than the message handler threads should be set to 8.
- **TCP Handler Threads:** This is a simple formula.

  A = Number of users

  B = The number of TCP handler threads that the POA should have allocated. The minimum value for B, though, should not go below six.

  B = A/25

  So, if a post office has 400 users, the POA should be configured with 16 TCP handler threads. If a post office has 50 users, the post office should have six threads, not two. The reason is that the POA should not be configured with less than six TCP handler threads.
- **QuickFinder Interval:** The QuickFinder indexing should happen once every 24 hours, generally in the nighttime, or when not too many users are using the post office. Couple this setting with the Enable QuickFinder Indexing checkbox and the Start QuickFinder Indexing options. Set the Start QuickFinder Indexing option to a value such as two to start the indexing at 2:00 a.m., for example. The most important thing here is that the QuickFinder indexing is not configured to go off in the middle of the workday.
- **Disk Check Interval:** Have this enabled to happen every five minutes.

  The Disk Check Interval value corresponds with any disk check event that you have defined in scheduled events on the POA. So, for example, the disk check interval kicks in every five minutes. The POA looks at the scheduled disk check events that are defined. The POA takes the appropriate action specified in the disk check events, if the disk space threshold has been crossed. I talk about the disk check events in more detail later in this section.
- **Disk Check Delay:** Go ahead and leave this at two hours. This settings means that if the POA has discovered that disk space is low, don't take the actions in the disk check event until two hours have passed. This gives you a chance to try to respond to the low disk space problem.

- **Max App Connections:** Allocate at least four application connections for each member of the post office. More is fine, but much more is not necessary. This is one of those situations where not enough is bad, more than enough is fine, much more than enough is not needed or helpful.
- **Max Physical Connections:** Allocate two physical connections per user. This is generally plenty. Setting this value to four per user is not going to cause any problems either. Just don't set it to some astronomical number, which just chews up more memory than necessary.
- **CPU Utilization:** I personally like to put this setting to 90 to 95 percent. Here's how it works: If the server crosses the CPU utilization threshold, it will not allocate more threads until the POA is below the threshold. If your POA is on a NetWare, then 95 percent is generally fine. The beauty of NetWare is that it uses the CPU very efficiently and can regularly spike in the 90s without users feeling any effect. Since GroupWise is mission-critical, it should get priority processing, greater than the default 85 percent. Having the value at 85 percent will probably be fine also, but for me, that would be the bottom threshold; I wouldn't generally recommend going below 85 percent.
- **Delay Time:** The delay time correlates with the CPU utilization option. If the CPU utilization threshold has been exceeded, the delay time is the amount of the time the POA's NLM will wait before trying to get another thread, if needed. The default of 100 milliseconds is generally more than enough. C'mon, this is NetWare; 1/10 of a second is an eternity for NetWare!
- **Enable SMP:** If you do not have a multiprocessor NetWare server, just turn this off.
- **Perform User Upkeep:** This should definitely be enabled. The Perform User Upkeep option does four things:
  - Deletes items in user's trash based upon the cleanup threshold specified under Tools ➪ GroupWise Utilities ➪ Client Options ➪ Environment ➪ Cleanup ➪ Empty Trash.
  - Advances the user's tasks to the next day.
  - Synchronizes user's frequent contact address book with the system address book. This is useful because when a user in your GroupWise system moves, this process updates users' frequent contacts address books with the new address of that user.
  - Expires items that are marked to expire on a certain day.

Perform User Upkeep should always be done sometime after midnight to be most effective. The Start User Upkeep option determines when Perform User Upkeep happens. If you enable it to happen before midnight, Perform User Upkeep will not advance task items to the next day. If task items do not get advanced, then when a user logs in in the morning, and they have a lot of tasks, the load-up time of the client takes longer.

- **Use SSL:** If you intend to monitor your POA via a web browser across the Internet, then you will want to use this option. Otherwise, don't bother.
- **HTTP Settings:** Fill in these values. The HTTP monitoring on the POA is very useful. Also, the GroupWise monitor utility uses these values to help the GroupWise monitor interface interact with the POA.

Now a brief discussion of the options available on the Log Settings property page.

- **Log File Path:** Just keep this value blank. The POA will just create the files in the <post office>\WPCSOUT\OFS directory.
- **Logging Level:** I like to put it on the Verbose setting. This helps for troubleshooting purposes.
- **Max Log File Age:** The default of seven days is generally sufficient.
- **Max Log Disk Space:** The default of 1MB is generally not nearly enough. Crank this up to 50MB. If you leave this at the default of 1MB, and the logging is on verbose, you won't even have a day's worth of logs to look at for a busy post office.

Finally, though not on either the Agent Settings or the Log Settings property pages, Chapter 17 does a really good job about explaining scheduled events, and just how to construct them. You definitely want to enable scheduled events for mailbox/library maintenance events. Chapter 17 does not talk about disk space scheduled events though, so here goes.

If you left your Disk Check interval set at five minutes back on the Agent Settings property page, a disk check event is spawned every five minutes. Also, the disk check event is defined on the Scheduled Events property page. Think this through for a moment. When do you want the red flag waved that disk space is low on a post office? As for myself, I would like to know when only 30 percent of my disk space is remaining. What action would I want take? I just want to be notified, that's all. Here's what you might do to create a notification mechanism to know when the volume that houses a GroupWise post office has dropped below 30 percent:

1. Make sure that the POA has the Disk Check interval set at a reasonable disk check number, such as five minutes.

   The Disk Check interval is a setting on the POA's Agents Settings property page. Also, make sure that the Disk Check Delay setting is set at two hours, or some other value that you think is good enough. The Disk Check Delay option means that, when the POA has hit the trigger to start the action on the disk check event mentioned in the next step, it will wait another two hours before it kicks off the disk check event.

2. Go to the POA's Scheduled Events property page and either create a new scheduled event or edit the Default POA Disk Check Event option that ships with GroupWise.

3. To create an action for the scheduled event, do the following:

   a. In the Name field, give the action a name.

   b. In the Action dropdown box, select Expire/Reduce Messages.

   c. Check the Reduce only check box, as well as the User and Message check boxes under the Databases tab.

   d. Click the Results tab, and make sure that the results are sent to the administrator.

   e. Click the Message button on the Results tab and compose a message that says something like, "The post office has dropped below 30 percent in disk space; you will receive a message every two hours until this problem is resolved."

4. To edit the disk check event, make sure that the following settings are in place:

   - **Type:** Disk Check
   - **Trigger:** 30 percent; don't bother using the Stop mail processing at option.

5. Make sure that someone is defined as an administrator for the domain that owns the post office for which you are activating this disk check event.

   This person will get the message regarding low disk space. It's generally best to make the administrator a dummy user with rules that forward messages to several people in your IS department.

Configuring the Post Office Object for Optimum Performance and Function

This section discusses every setting and its relationship to a successful post office configuration. If a setting has no bearing on performance or function in the GroupWise system, it will not be mentioned.

Post Office Settings Property Page

Figure 18.3 shows the Post Office Settings property page.

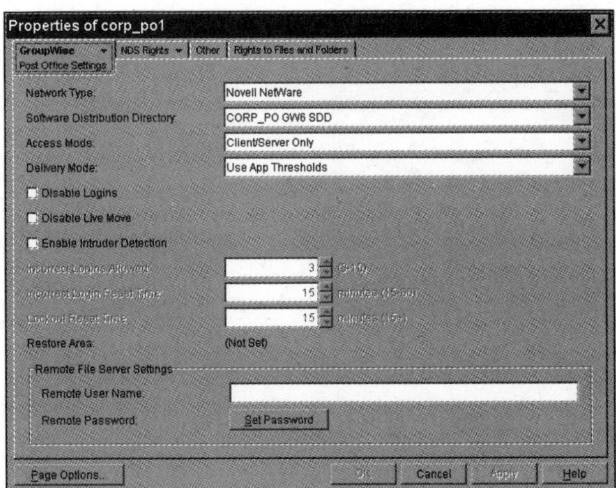

FIGURE 18.3 *The Post Office Settings Property Page*

- **Software Distribution Directory:** Chapter 12 discusses all about the software distribution directory. The value you fill in here is important, but see Chapter 12 for a full (and I mean full) explanation of the software distribution directory.
- **Access Mode:** This should be set to client/server only. Don't allow users to connect directly to the post office via a UNC connection, as this will open the message store to a much higher likelihood of corruption.
- **Disable Live Move:** Don't check this option unless you have good reason to do so. Live move is used when moving users. Live move is explained in more detail in Chapter 13.

Security Property Page

This section offers a brief discussion of the most critical element of the Security property page, shown in Figure 18.4.

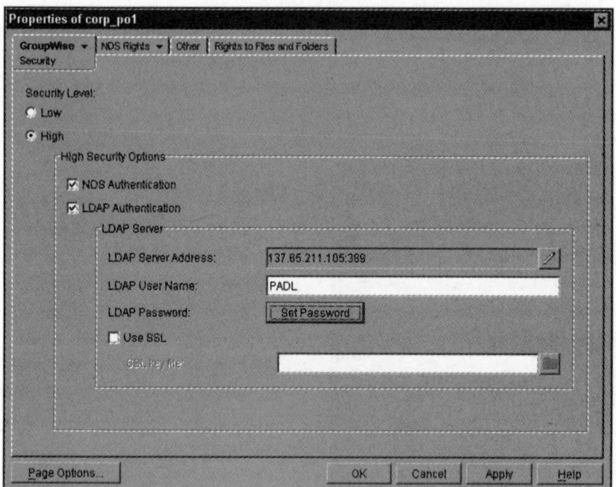

FIGURE 18.4 *The Post Office Security Property Page*

For Security Level option, you generally want it set to High, with the NDS Authentication option checked. If you have users, that do not have the Novell client installed, then you will want to make sure the user has a password on a GroupWise account, or you will want to enable LDAP authentication. The whole idea is, if the security level is high, GroupWise needs the user to authenticate through a password authentication process. The authentication will either be before the GroupWise client is started, which is the case with NDS authentication, or at the time GroupWise is loaded, which is the case with LDAP authentication or a GroupWise password.

With LDAP authentication enabled, if a user does not have the Novell client, or a user is using GroupWise WebAccess through a Web browser, the user can still use an NDS password. The POA will query NDS via LDAP in behalf of the user. A prerequisite to this functionality is that your implementation of NDS is eDirectory version 8.5 or better, with LDAP services enabled and configured.

Default WebAccess Property Page

The idea of a default WebAccess (see Figure 18.5) is important to the performance of WebAccess. But it's way too much to explain in this chapter. So, read Chapter 11 and focus on the section titled, "Configuring Multiple Agents and Application Servers for a Fault-Tolerant WebAccess System," for more information.

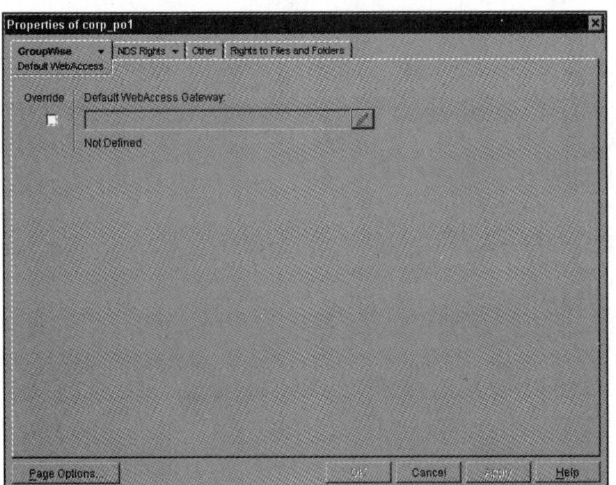

FIGURE 18.5 *The Post Office Default WebAccess Property Page*

Configuring the Post Office Client Options for Optimum Performance and Function

The GroupWise client comes with a bunch of pre-set settings. Your organization may want to control some of these settings so that your e-mail system is accomplishing its purposes. For example, if you have implemented a more robust shared address book solution, such as Concentrico's Reach for NDS product (on the CD that comes with this book), you may want to disable the use of shared address books.

GroupWise allows you to set client preferences and control features available to GroupWise clients. These preferences can be set at a domain level and excluded right down to a user level. There are a few features that, if used incorrectly, can generate more traffic in your system then you may want. Here are two client preferences to pay particular attention to:

- Wildcard addressing
- Status tracking

The client preferences can be modified in ConsoleOne by selecting a domain, post office, or user object and choosing Tools ➪ GroupWise Utilities ➪ Client Options.

- **Wildcard addressing:** Wildcard addressing is a great feature. With wildcard addressing, a user can send a message to all the recipients in a post office (that's the default), a domain, or even the GroupWise system and beyond that. The question then is do you really want your users to have that kind of power? You can turn off all users' ability to use wildcard addressing at the post office level. Then for those users who should be allowed this functionality, you can enable it for them one by one. Wildcard addressing is in Client Options under Send.
- **Status tracking:** GroupWise has a great feature called status tracking. You can see if a message got to a person, and you can see when they opened the message. Status tracking is one of the things that sets GroupWise apart from other groupware packages, so I can't knock it. Status tracking can be taken to the extreme though. If your GroupWise system's client options for status tracking is set to All information, then you are generating a tremendous amount of data that does not need to be tracked. By requiring the GroupWise system to track all information, you impact the following:
  - GroupWise remote users' downloads and uploads take longer.
  - When a user purges a large amount of messages from their trash, a tremendous amount of disk I/O is created.
  - Status messages are generated for just about every action to a message item, and rarely do people need that information.
  - Most customers will not want to enable All information. Check to see that this is not enabled somehow. Many customers will want to lock this feature down so that end users may not change the option to All information.

TIP

It's helpful to just browse through the client options and think about what settings you may want to configure or even what features you may just want to turn off.

Tuning the NetWare Server for Optimum Performance and Function

Most customers have their GroupWise post offices on NetWare servers because of NetWare's prowess in file caching. This section focuses on fine-tuning your NetWare server for optimum performance.

- **GroupWise Only Volume:** When you place a GroupWise post office on a file server, it is best to create a volume that will only house the GroupWise post office. This just makes managing e-mail simpler; for example, you'll have a good picture of just how much disk space is being taken on a post office.
- **Volume Block Size:** The NetWare volume block size should be set to 64KB. This allows the NetWare operating system to access the GroupWise databases with the most amount of efficiency.
- **Compression:** Do not enable compression on the NetWare volume dedicated for GroupWise. GroupWise already compresses the message store, and does so even better than NetWare does. It's redundant effort by the NetWare operating system to try and compress files in the GroupWise message store.
- **Immediate Purge:** GroupWise deals with a whole lot of files passing through queues off of the WPCSOUT and WPCSIN directories. Set these directories so that they are purged immediately. This allows the NetWare server to free up memory resources to optimize other parts of the NetWare server.
- **VREPAIR:** Novell's NetWare disk subsystem has been so notorious for stability that customers often forget about the notion of server maintenance. To maintain the NetWare server, make sure to run VREPAIR on the volumes of that server. This should be done on a routine basis, perhaps monthly.
- **Server Set Parameters:** Thesyntax on these settings has been confirmed for NetWare 4.x and NetWare 5.x. The values here are the minimum; if you currently have your NetWare server tuned to use higher values, you don't need to decrease the values. The STARTUP.NCF file should have the following set parameters in it:

```
Set TCP defend land attack = off
Set minimum packet receive buffers = 2000
```

The AUTOEXEC.NCF file has the following set parameters included in it:

```
Set directory cache buffer nonreferenced delay = 30
Set minimum directory cache buffers = 1200
Set maximum directory cache buffers = 4000
Set read ahead enabled = on
Set read ahead LRU sitting time threshold = 60
Set maximum file locks = 20000
Set maximum record locks = 100000
Set minimum service processes = 100
Set maximum service processes = 1000
Set new service process wait time = 0.3
Set maximum packet receive buffers = 4000
Set new packet receive buffer wait time = 0.1
```

Summary

What I really want to do here is encourage you to design your system on paper rather than in stone. Once you have created domains and named them, you cannot go back without starting over. Once users have mailboxes in one place, it is extremely tedious to move them to another place. It is especially annoying when you have to do this because your boss does not like the name of the post office, but more often than not I see this being done because post offices were too large to begin with.

Post office design is the biggest contributor to the success of your GroupWise system. There's a whole lot to good post office design, namely the following:

- E-mail policies
- POA configuration
- Post office configuration
- GroupWise client option configuration
- Server configuration

PART V

Applied Architecture

CHAPTER 19

Troubleshooting Message Flow

This chapter explores GroupWise message flow in great detail. You get to look at the processes and store files involved in message creation, as well as the replication and transfer of messages between post offices.

The goal in this chapter is to enable you to troubleshoot GroupWise message flow through an understanding of the complete *signal path* for GroupWise messages.

Understanding Message Flow at the Database Level

To begin with, here is a look at the store files. When a user creates a message, one or more GroupWise information store files are written to. The particulars depend on the type of message. This section explores this through a few scenarios.

Each of the scenarios in this chapter follows the actions of USERA. USERA's GroupWise file ID (FID) is 123. Based on this FID, USERA is assigned to place all sent items in MSG17.DB.

GroupWise Information Store Concepts

Before proceeding, here is a review of some information store concepts. Most of this information is explained in Chapter 4, but for clarity's sake, this chapter goes over it again.

GroupWise information (messages, address book info, rules, folders, and so on) is contained in the information store, which is composed of individual databases (also called store files). GroupWise information store databases are contained in each post office's OFUSER and OFMSG directories.

Databases are made of records. Every record has a particular set of fields based upon the record type. Some GroupWise fields can exceed 2K in size. Fields that do exceed 2K in size are called external BLOB (binary large object) files. BLOB files are contained in the post office\OFFILES directory.

Every item in GroupWise — whether it is a mail message, a task, a document, or anything else that can be displayed in a user's mailbox — is just a record in a GroupWise information store database. Whenever a field within a record exceeds 2K, that field is spun off to its own BLOB file outside of the database.

The User Database: USERxxx.DB

You may recall from Chapter 4 that every user has a user database. This file is named USERxxx.DB, where the xxx is replaced with the user's three-character file ID.

The easiest way to explain the user database file is that it is largely a pointer database. When USERA gets a message from USERB, the message isn't actually contained in USER123.DB. The message is contained in one of the message databases. A pointer to that message is created in the USER123.DB file.

The user database does contain records that represent complete items, however. For example, a user's folders and a user's personal calendar items are wholly contained in the USERxxx.DB file. Everything that you see from the GroupWise client is coming from the user database. You will never look at anything that is exclusively stored in the message database from the GroupWise client. Most of the things you see from the client are simply pointers to where the full message is located in the message databases.

The Message Database: MSGn.DB

Every post office has 25 message databases, numbered MSG0.DB through MSG24.DB. All messages sent between users in a GroupWise post office are contained in one of the MSGn.DB files.

Group Items versus Personal Items

When a user receives an e-mail message or an appointment, task, or note, that item is considered to be a *group item.* When a user creates an item in the calendar without sending it (that is, the item has no TO line), this is a *personal item,* also known as a *posted item.*

Message "Body" Parts

A GroupWise item is not just one record in a database. There are distinct body parts on a GroupWise message, and every body part has its own record.

Every GroupWise mail message has a handful of body parts and records. The *master record* and the *message properties record* are always present on group items (items that one user sends to another user).

- **Master record:** The master record contains fields such as TO, CC, BC, and Subject. The master record also keeps track of all of the other records associated with the original message. If the TO, CC, and BC lines contain more than 2,048 bytes of data, the master record relies on the message properties record to hold the entire contents of the TO, CC, BC, and Subject lines.
- **Message properties record:** The message properties record is used to show the properties page of a message. If the contents of this record exceed 2K (this happens often when sending to distribution lists), then only the header of this record is kept in the MSGnn.DB file. The remainder is spun off into a BLOB file in the OFFILES directory. Since the message properties record must contain the recipient list of the TO, CC, and BC lines, it becomes the master list for the TO, CC, and BC lines.

- **Message body record:** This record contains the text and attributes of the message area of a GroupWise message. If the message text is more than 2,048 bytes in length, then this record will be spun off into a BLOB file in the OFFILES directory.
- **Attachment record:** Each attachment has its own record. The attachment file itself is a field in the attachment record. If the attachment exceeds the 2,048-byte limit of the attachment field, it is spun off into the OFFILES directory.

Scenario #1: USERA Creates a Personal (Posted) Calendar Item

USERA creates a posted calendar appointment. The subject of the appointment is simply `Test`. There is no message body, nor are there any attachments. Here are some observations:

1. GroupWise puts the master record for the appointment in the USER123.DB file.
2. GroupWise creates a message body record for the body of the appointment. This also goes in USER123.DB
3. A separate alarm record is written to the USER123.DB file. This alarm record is read by GroupWise notify.

NOTE **If an attachment had been made to the appointment, then an attachment record would have been created.**

Scenario # 2: USERA Sends a Message to USERB on the Same PO as USERA

USERA creates a short message with no attachments and sends the message to USERB.

1. USERA's FID is USER123.DB. USERA's message database for outgoing messages is MSG17.DB.
2. GroupWise creates three records in MSG17.DB. In this example, the master record is record #12 in MSG17.DB, the message properties record is record #11 in MSG17.DB, and the message body record is record #13.
3. GroupWise creates a pointer in USER123.DB with a pointer to record #12 in MSG17.DB. GroupWise further indicates that this is a message sent by USERA.

4. GroupWise creates a pointer in USERB's database. USERB's FID is 789, so USERB's user database is USER789.DB. The pointer indicates that this is an inbox item. The pointer also indicates that the record is record #12 in MSG17.DB.
5. GroupWise successfully delivers the message to USERB, so GroupWise creates record #14 in MSG17.DB, which indicates that the message was delivered, and links record #14 to the master record, which is record #12. GroupWise also changes a value in the USERA's user database to indicate that the delivery happened and when it happened.

   Here is a look at what happens when USERB opens the message from USERA:
6. GroupWise creates a new record in MSG17.DB, indicating that USERB opened the message.
7. GroupWise changes a value in the pointer record in USERA's user database, indicating that the item was opened and when it was opened.

Understanding Message Flow outside the Post Office

If a GroupWise message is sent to a user on a different post office, it takes a specific route through file queues on its way to the destination post office. Understanding message flow through a GroupWise system is one of the most valuable troubleshooting tools you'll ever have.

This scenario follows a message from one post office to another. The detail at the message store level will be even more explicit than the detail previously described in this chapter.

Scenario #3: Message Flow between Post Offices

- USERA is a user on PO1, which is a post office in DOMAIN1
- USERB is a user on PO2, which is a post office in DOMAIN1
- USERA's FID is 123
- USERB's FID is 789
- The MSGnn.DB file for USERA is MSG17.DB
- All users connect to their post offices in client/server access mode
- PO1 is connected to DOMAIN1's MTA via MTP (TCP/IP) between the MTA and the POA
- PO2 is connected to directly via UNC, and so the MTA connects directly to the PO2 post office

The Message store at PO1: USERA sends a message, with the subject `Test1`, with a small message body and one attachment over 2K in size. The byte size of the file is 93,812. The message is sent to USERB.

1. The post office agent (POA) on PO1 creates the following records in MSG17.DB:
   - A master record, which is record #385 in MSG17.DB.
   - The DRN (domain record number), which is a unique identifier for the message: `3827C415.FDE`. The DRN for any GroupWise message can be viewed from the properties of a message. It will look much like this:

     ```
     Mail Envelope Properties  (3827C415.FDE : 17 : 65002)
     ```

NOTE

The `3827C415.FDE` is the DRN, the `17` is the message database that the users use, and `65002` is a number that uniquely identifies the user. Every sent message that this user sends will have `17 : 65002` in the Mail Envelope properties.

   - A message properties record, which is record #384 in MSG17.DB.
   - A message body record, which is record #382 in MSG17.DB.
   - An attachment record, which is record #383 in MSG17.DB.
   - A BLOB file called 382761a5.000 for the attachment that is created in the PO1\OFFILES\FD62 directory. The size of the BLOB file is 48,004 bytes. GroupWise compresses and encrypts BLOB files, which is why the file size decreased.
2. The POA also creates a record in PO1\OFUSER\USER123.DB with a pointer to record #385. This user database pointer record contains the following additional information:
   - The DRN for record #385
   - The date and time that the message was sent
   - To whom the message was sent
   - Other status tracking information as appropriate (delivered, opened, and so on)

The file queues at PO1

3. Since the message is destined for PO2, all records associated with the message having the DRN 3827C415.FDE are packed up into one file and placed in the PO1\WPCSIN\4 directory. The original name of the file is 482761a5.210. The file is 49,760 bytes in size. Since USERA sent the message with normal priority, it will travel through the 4 directory (where normal priority mail messages always flow.)
4. The POA on PO1 transmits the file via TCP/IP to the MTA on its message transfer protocol (MTP) port.

The file queues at DOMAIN1

5. The MTA receives the file into the DOMAIN1\MSLOCAL\GWINPROG\4 directory and names the file 00000859. It uses what's called an *MTP thread* to receive the message.
6. The MTA's MTP thread tickles the MTA's router thread (RTR) and tells him about the message in the GWINPROG\4 directory. The router thread looks at the recipient post office for the message and determines that the recipient post office is PO2.

NOTE

The DOMAIN\MSLOCAL\GWINPROG\X directories are *memory queues.* This means that an MTA will only fetch files from this directory when it is prompted to by another subprocess of the MTA. These directories do get scanned on startup or restart of the MTA, but that is the only time they get scanned. Sometimes though, you may find files stuck in the GWINPROG\X directories. If this is the case, just put them back into the DOMAIN\WPCSIN\0 directory.

7. The MTA's RTR thread puts the file in the DOMAIN1\MSLOCAL\MSHOLD\PO25B46 directory, which is the FID for PO2.

NOTE

Every GroupWise object has a FID, be it a post office, a domain, or a user. To determine the FID for a post office, view the post office with GroupWise diagnostics and look for the attribute *File ID.*

When in verbose mode, the GroupWise MTA will report the message DRN. In this case, the MTA reported the following:

```
00:24:36 RTR: DOMAIN1: 00000859 Priority 4 3827C415.FDE:17:65002
: Transfer to DOMAIN1.PO2:OFS
```

The file queues at PO2

8. The MTA's RTR thread copies the file to the PO2\WPCSOUT\OFS\4 directory. The name that it gives the file is 482769C4.210. The byte size of the file is 49,820. The size of the file increased a bit from when it was on PO1 because the route the message has taken to get to PO2 is appended to the message.

NOTE

The WPCSOUT\OFS directories are the input queues for the POA process. Every POA has an FID of OFS, and so the input queue for the POA knows to look for work to do from the MTA in the WPCSOUT\ <POA'S-FID>\X directory. The POA's FID is (or should always be) OFS. On rare occasions, the POA may have a different FID than OFS. If you discover this through GroupWise diagnostics, delete the POA and re-create it.

The message store at PO2

9. The POA picks up the file in the PO2\WPCSOUT\OFS\4 directory on its scan cycle and processes the file. The POA then commits the message to the message store at PO2.
10. The PO2 POA creates the following records in MSG17.DB:
    - A master record, which is record #4 in MSG17.DB.
    - The DRN for this master record is 3827C415.FDE, just like it was on PO1. When USERB views the properties of the message, that user will see the same DRN that the sender saw.

      ```
      Mail Envelope Properties (3827C415.FDE : 17 : 65002)
      ```

    - A message properties record, which is record #3 in MSG17.DB.
    - A message body record, which is record #1 in MSG17.DB.
    - An attachment record, which is record #2 in MSG17.DB.
    - A BLOB file called 382774cd.000 for the attachment that is created in the PO2\OFFILES\FD62 directory. The size of the BLOB file is 48,004 bytes, just the same size of the file that was originally sent.
    - A status record, which is record #5 in MSG17.DB. The status record indicates that USERB received the message. This status record must be relayed back to PO1, which is coming up in a moment.

11. The PO2 POA creates a record in PO1\OFUSER\USER789.DB with a pointer to record #4. The USER database also indicates the following:
    - The DRN for record #4
    - The date and time that the message was received
    - Who sent the message to USERB

The file queues at PO2

12. After the POA at PO2 delivered the message to USERB, it created a status message to be sent back to PO1. The status message is placed in the PO2\WPCSIN\5 directory. The name of the file is 582774cd.210. The size of the file is 820 bytes.

NOTE **The WPCSIN directory structure is the input queue for the MTA. The MTA for DOMAIN1 is configured to talk to PO2 via a UNC connection, so the MTA will pick this file up. This is different from an MTP connection in that the POA pushes information from the PO\WPCSIN\X directory up to the MTA. The POA push method through MTP is preferred, however, because it is more efficient.**

The file queues at DOMAIN1

13. The MTA's RTR thread picks up the file from the PO2\WPCSIN\5 directory and places it in the DOMAIN\MSLOCAL\GWINPROG\5 directory. It then routes the file to the DOMAIN\MSLOCAL\MSHOLD\PO15B1E\5. The name of the file is 0000085C.001, and it is 860 bytes in size.
14. The MTA's router thread tickles the MTP thread and tells the MTP thread to look in the MSLOCAL\MSHOLD\PO15B1E\5 directory for the file called 0000085C.001 to be processed.

NOTE **The MSLOCAL\MSHOLD queues are largely memory queues. This means that an MTA will fetch files from this directory only when it is given the file's specific name. The MSLOCAL\MSHOLD directories do get scanned on startup or restart of the MTA.**

The file queues at PO1

15. The MTA's MTP thread transmits the status file to the POA at PO1. The POA's MTP thread receives the status file into its WPCSOUT\OFS\5 directory. The name of the file is 582782F4.210, and it is 860 bytes in size.

The message store at PO1

16. The POA picks up the file and creates record #390 in MSG17.DB, linking that record to record #385, which is the original master record for this message.

NOTE

The last record used before the message was transmitted from PO1 to PO2 was #385. The reason the status record was # 390 is that other records were written to the MSG17.DB file. GroupWise just picks the next available record number when writing a record into a message database.

Important Architectural Concepts from Scenario #3

The previous section tracked a message as it moved between two post offices on the same domain, exposing most of the architectural methods involved in message delivery:

- Messages are either being submitted to a location or being sent out of a location.
- If the message is being submitted to a location by the MTA it is placed in a WPCSOUT\<Process-File ID> directory. This is the MTA's *output* queue.
- If the message is being sent out of a location, it is placed in the WPCSIN\X directory. This is the MTA's *input* queue.
- Every message will pass through one of the eight queue directories, numbered 0-7. Here are the purposes of these queues (another review from Chapter 4):

  0: Live, interactive request messages (busy searches, remote library queries)
  1: Remote user update requests
  2: Administration updates and high-priority mail messages
  3: Status messages from high-priority mail
  4: Normal-priority mail messages
  5: Status messages from normal-priority mail
  6: Low-priority mail messages
  7: Status messages from low-priority mail

- When messages reach an MTA, the MTA receives the file into the MSLOCAL\GWINPROG directories and then places the file into the MSLOCAL\MSHOLD\<Location-File ID> directory. The file is then either transmitted (MTP via TCP/IP) or placed (UNC connectivity) at the destination and placed in the directory that corresponds to the FID (file ID) of the process at that location that is designed to process that message.

- When a message is sent from one GroupWise post office to the next, the message will retain its DRN, no matter what post office it is sent to. If a message is sent to a gateway, the DRN is taken off by the gateway.
- When a message is sent to more than one GroupWise post office, it is written to the same numbered message database on every post office — this is determined by the sender's FID.
- Elements of a GroupWise message are broken up into separate records. Fields of certain record types can exceed 2K. If a field exceeds 2K, it becomes its own BLOB file.
- All elements of a GroupWise message are transmitted in one file when sent from one location to the next.

Scenario #4: Message Flow between Domains

USER1 on PO1 at DOMAIN1 sends a message to USER2 on PO2 at DOMAIN2. Here's the file flow. This scenario will follow this message all the way to PO2 and then follow the status message back to PO1. This scenario does not focus so much on records and databases as Scenario #3 did.

1. USER1 composes a low-priority message and sends it to USER2.
2. The POA on PO1 creates a message transport file in the PO1\WPCSIN\6 directory.
3. The POA at PO1 transmits the file from the PO1WPCSIN\6 directory to the domain MTA via TCP/IP to the MTA's port 7100.
4. The DOMAIN1 MTA receives the file and places it in the DOMAIN1\MSLOCAL\GWINPROG\6 directory.
5. The DOMAIN1 MTA moves the file to the DOMAIN1\MSLOCAL\MSHOLD\<DOMAIN2-File-ID>\6 directory.
6. The DOMAIN1 MTA transmits the file from the DOMAIN1\MSLOCAL\MSHOLD\<DOMAIN2-File-ID>\6 directory to DOMAIN2's MTA via TCP/IP, using port 7100.
7. The DOMAIN2 MTA receives the file and places the file in the DOMAIN2\MSLOCAL\GWINPROG\6 directory.

8. The DOMAIN2 MTA routes the file to the DOMAIN2\MSLOCAL\MSHOLD\<PO2-File-ID>\6 directory.
9. The MTP portion of the MTA picks up the file in the DOMAIN\MSLOCAL\MSHOLD\<PO2-File-ID>\6 directory and transmits it via TCP/IP to the PO2 POA's MTP port 7100.
10. The POA on PO2 receives the file and writes it directly into the PO2\WPCSOUT\OFS\6 directory.
11. The POA processes the message and inserts the message into the message store at PO2. The POA generates a status message and places it into the PO2\WPCSIN\7 directory.
12. The POA transmits the file in the PO2\WPCSIN\7 directory up to the DOMAIN2 MTA at TCP/IP port 7100.
13. The DOMAIN2 MTA receives the file into the DOMAIN2\MSLOCAL\GWINPROG\7 directory.
14. The MTA moves the file to the DOMAIN2\MSOCAL\MSHOLD\DOMAIN1-FILE-ID\7 directory.
15. The MTA transmits the file from the DOMAIN2\MSOCAL\MSHOLD\DOMAIN1-FILE-ID\7 directory to port 7100 on DOMAIN1's MTA.
16. The DOMAIN1 MTA receives the file into its DOMAIN1\MSLOCAL\GWINPROG\7 directory.
17. The DOMAIN1 MTA moves the file to the DOMAIN1\MSLOCAL\MSHOLD\<PO1-FILE-ID>\7 directory.
18. The DOMAIN1 MTA transmits the file to port 7100 on the PO1 POA.
19. The PO1 POA receives the file into the PO1\WPCSOUT\OFS\7 directory.
20. The PO1 POA puts the status record into the GroupWise message store on PO1.

Scenario #5: Message Flow through the GroupWise Internet Agent (GWIA)

USERA is on PO1 at DOMAIN1 and wants to send a message to `joe@acme.com` via the Internet. PO1 connects with DOMAIN1 via TCP/IP. DOMAIN1 connects with DOMAIN2 via UNC. The GWIA is located on DOMAIN2. Here is the file flow:

1. The PO1 POA writes the appropriate item records to USERA's user database and assigned message database.

2. Because the destination is not on PO1, the PO1 POA drops a transport file in the WPCSIN\4 directory.
3. The PO1 POA transmits the file from the WPCSIN\4 directory at the post office to the DOMAIN1 MTA at the MTA's MTP port.
4. The domain MTA receives the file and places it in the DOMAIN1\MSLOCAL\GWINPROG\4 directory.
5. The domain MTA routes the file to the DOMAIN1\MSLOCAL\MSHOLD\<DOMAIN2-FileID> directory.

   Note: The file ID for a domain can be determined in a couple of ways. Perhaps the easiest way is by looking at the MTA console for DOMAIN1. Choose F10 ➪ Configuration Status, highlight DOMAIN2, and press enter. The Hold directory tells you the domain file ID.
6. Because DOMAIN1 has a UNC connection to DOMAIN2, it does not transmit the message to DOMAIN2 via TCP/IP. The DOMAIN1 MTA places the message in the DOMAIN2\WPCSIN\4 directory.
7. The message is destined for the GWIA on DOMAIN2, so the file is moved to the DOMAIN2\MSLOCAL\MSHOLD\<GWIA-FileID>\4 directory.
8. The message is then moved to the DOMAIN2\WPGATE\GWIA\WPCSOUT\<GWIA-FileID>\4 directory.
9. The GWIA will convert the GroupWise message to ASCII and drop the converted file into the DOMAIN2\WPGATE\GWIA\SEND directory. This is the input queue for the GWIA's sending daemon.
10. The GWIA generates a *Transferred* status message to be sent back to USERA. The GWIA places the transferred status message in the DOMAIN2\WPGATE\GWIA\WPCSIN\5 directory.
11. The DOMAIN2 MTA picks up the file from the DOMAIN2\WPGATE\GWIA\WPCSIN\5 directory and moves it to the DOMAIN2\MSLOCAL\GWINPROG\5 directory.
12. The DOMAIN2 MTA tickles a router (RTR) thread and tells him about the file in the GWINPROG\5 directory. The RTR thread looks at the message and determines that the message is destined for DOMAIN1. The RTR thread places the message in the DOMAIN2\MSLOCAL\MSHOLD\DOMAIN1-FileID directory.

13. The DOMAIN2 MTA's RTR thread tickles the MTP thread and tells him of the file in the DOMAIN2\MSLOCAL\MSHOLD\DOMAIN1-FileID directory. The DOMAIN2 MTA transmits the file to the DOMAIN1 MTA on MTP port 7100.
14. The DOMAIN1 MTA's MTP process receives the status message into its DOMAIN1\MSLOCAL\GWINPROG\5 directory.
15. The DOMAIN1's MTA tickles a RTR thread and tells it about the file in the DOMAIN1\MSLOCAL\GWINPROG\5 directory.
16. The DOMAIN1 MTA's RTR thread routes the status message to the DOMAIN1\MSLOCAL\PO1-FileID directory.
17. The DOMAIN1 MTA's RTR thread tickles the MTP thread and tells it about the file in the DOMAIN1\MSLOCAL\PO1-FileID directory.
18. The DOMAIN1 MTA's MTP thread transmits the status message to the PO1's POA on its MTP port.
19. The POA at PO1 receives the status message into the PO1\WPCSOUT\OFS\5 directory.
20. The POA at PO1 appends the status message to the message store at PO1.

A Simplified View of Message Flow

Each of the previous three examples went into quite a bit of detail. This section outlines just the file flow for the previous scenarios. Remember, the goal here is to open up the GroupWise file system to you so that you will be able to troubleshoot problems with message delivery.

Scenario #1: PO1 to PO2 in the Same Domain

In this scenario, a user on PO1 sent a message to a user on PO2. Both PO1 and PO2 are in the same GroupWise domain.

Message: The message transport file passed through each of the following directories in order as it proceeded from PO1 to PO2 for delivery:

- PO1\WPCSIN\4
- DOMAIN1\GWINPROG\4
- DOMAIN1\MSLOCAL\MSHOLD\<PO2-FID>\4
- PO2\WPCSOUT\OFS\4

Status message: The status message transport file passed through each of the following directories as it proceeded from PO2 back to the sender's post office, PO1:

- PO2\WPCSIN\5
- DOMAIN1\GWINPROG\5
- DOMAIN1\MSLOCAL\MSHOLD\<PO1-FID>\5
- PO2\WPCSOUT\OFS\5

Scenario #2: PO1.DOMAIN1 to PO2.DOMAIN2

In this scenario, a user on PO1 sent a message to a user on PO2. PO1 and PO2 exist in different domains.

Message: The message transport file passed through each of the following directories as it proceeded from PO1 to PO2 for delivery:

- PO1\WPCSIN\4
- DOMAIN1\GWINPROG\4
- DOMAIN1\MSLOCAL\MSHOLD\<DOMAIN2-FID>\4
- DOMAIN2\GWINPROG\4
- DOMAIN2\MSLOCAL\MSHOLD\<PO2-FID>\4
- PO2\WPCSOUT\OFS\4

Status message: The status message transport file passed through each of the following directories as it proceeded from PO2 back to the sender's post office, PO1.

- PO2\WPCSIN\5
- DOMAIN2\GWINPROG\5
- DOMAIN2\MSLOCAL\MSHOLD\<DOMAIN1-FID>\5
- DOMAIN1\GWINPROG\5
- DOMAIN1\MSLOCAL\MSHOLD\<PO1-FID>\5
- PO1\WPCSOUT\OFS\5

Scenario #3: PO1.DOMAIN1 to GWIA.DOMAIN2

A user on PO1 sent a message to an Internet address. The GWIA resides on a different domain than the sender's post office.

Message: The message transport file passed through each of the following directories as it proceeded from PO1 to the GWIA. The transmission of the message via SMTP and its ultimate delivery to the Internet recipient are not described here.

- PO1\WPCSIN\4
- DOMAIN1\GWINPROG\4
- DOMAIN1\MSLOCAL\MSHOLD\<DOMAIN2-FID>\4
- DOMAIN2\GWINPROG\4
- DOMAIN2\MSLOCAL\MSHOLD\<GWIA-FID>\4
- DOMAIN2\WPGATE\GWIA\WPCSOUT\<GWIA-FID>\4

Status message: The status message transport file passed through each of the following directories as it proceeded from the GWIA back to the sender's post office, PO1. Keep in mind that this status message does not indicate that the message was delivered to the Internet recipient — only that the message was successfully transferred to the GWIA's SMTP daemon.

- DOMAIN2\WPGATE\GWIA\WPCSIN\5
- DOMAIN2\MSLOCAL\GWINPROG\5
- DOMAIN2\MSLOCAL\MSHOLD\<DOMAIN1-FID>\5
- DOMAIN1\MSLOCAL\GWINPROG\5
- DOMAIN1\MSLOCAL\MSHOLD\<PO1-FID>\5
- PO1\WPCSOUT\OFS\5

Using File Flow for Troubleshooting

The previous sections provided you with a lot of detail about the flow of messages through the GroupWise system. This information may seem a little esoteric, though. This section applies this information through some scenarios where the GroupWise administrator would need to troubleshoot problems with message flow.

Troubleshooting Scenario #1: Can't Send Internet E-Mail

The users in DOMAIN1.PO1 complain that they have noticed that they can send e-mail within the post office, but they can't send e-mail to recipients on the Internet.

- The first thing the administrator does is check the GWIA on DOMAIN3. Obviously, to send to the Internet, users have to be able to send through the GWIA. It is up and running just fine, though. As a test, the administrator sends a quick message off to his free `myrealbox.com` account. It is delivered.

- It occurs to the administrator that perhaps the users cannot send to anyone outside their post office. Rather than having one of these users send a test message, the administrator sends a message to one of the users in DOMAIN1.PO1, as well as to a user on DOMAIN2. The logic here is that by the time status messages have returned from DOMAIN2, they should also have returned from DOMAIN1.
- Checking the status of the message, the administrator sees that the message to DOMAIN1 remains in a *pending* state long after the message to DOMAIN2 showed up as being *delivered.* This means that something is blocking message flow to or from DOMAIN1.
- The administrator decides to focus on DOMAIN1.PO1 first (even though the problem may be with other post offices under that domain as well). Opening the PO1\WPCSIN\4 directory in Windows Explorer, the administrator finds nearly 300 files queued up for transport. The oldest file is nearly an hour old.
- The administrator checks the message transfer status on the POA console (see Chapter 8 for keystrokes), and the POA claims that the connection with the MTA is up and running. So the problem is not with the connection. Now the administrator gets tricky, creating a TEMP directory under the <POST OFFICE>\WPCSIN directory. This directory will become the temporary home for the queue files in WPCSIN\4 in an attempt to flush out the queue.
- The administrator attempts to copy the files from the <POST OFFICE>\WPCSIN\4 into WPCSIN\TEMP. One of the files won't go. It is a 320MB file!
- At this point, the administrator has determined the cause of the problem. Someone sent a very, very large message, and the POA and/or MTA could not handle the file. Even though these agents are multi-threaded, all threads must use the same physical connection between MTA and POA, and in this case, the network link did not have the bandwidth to manage the transfer between the post office and the domain. All other messages sitting in the WPCSIN\4 directory are being held up behind this one.

The solution here is not likely to be pretty. The administrator could try to unload the POA to get it to release the file, but it is unlikely that it will unload cleanly. This means that the server will have to be downed and the file cleared out manually. Still, with the application of good message-flow principles, the administrator was able to resolve the problem without calling technical support.

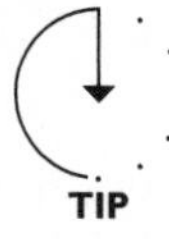

Want to find out who in that post office sent that huge file? You can contact Novell GroupWise support for a utility called the GroupWise Post Master that allows you to crack the header of these files that you find in the queues. It will tell you what the sender's user ID is, their source domain, post office, DRN, and message database. Pretty nifty. This utility was created just for such purposes so that you would not have to send the entire 320MB message in to Novell for them to tell you who the sender is. This utility does not give you the recipient list or subject line or any of the message body however.

Lessons from Troubleshooting Scenario #1

There are some basic GroupWise troubleshooting principles that I'd like you to take from this scenario:

- **The people that report problems are rarely technicians.** Don't expect their information to be accurate. Was the information from the people on PO1 accurate? Well . . . yes, they couldn't send to the Internet, but the way they described the problem you could be led to believe that they were only having problems with Internet e-mail. They were in fact having problems sending to anyone outside the post office.
- **Focus at the first point of potential failure.** In this scenario, that meant focusing on PO1. If users on PO1 are complaining of a problem, then get in as a test user on PO1 and witness the problem for yourself.
- **Think message flow.** Users say they cannot send to the Internet. What's the first place from PO1 that a message has to go in order to get to the Internet? The answer: the POST OFFICE\WPCSIN\X directories. That is the first place to start looking. If there aren't files in the POST OFFICE\WPCSIN\X directory, then keep looking upstream until you find the problem.

Troubleshooting Scenario #2: Can't Send between Post Offices

Bob on PO1 complains that he cannot send to Mary Baker on PO2. He gets the mail message back with an error D101 (user not found).

- The administrator troubleshoots by first sending to Mary Baker from his or her own mailbox on PO3. Mary gets the e-mail, and no errors are reported. Now the administrator must watch Bob send a message to Mary. Here's what happens:

- Bob starts typing Mary B . . . and the name completion fills in the rest.
- The administrator has Bob open the address book. In the GroupWise address book, Mary Baker's entry is not grayed out. The administrator has Bob tab over to the frequent contacts book. There he points out the entry for Mary Baker that has been grayed out. The administrator has Bob delete this entry from the frequent contacts list.
- Now the administrator has Bob send another message to Mary. Name completion executes as usual, and this time the message is delivered normally.

Lessons from Troubleshooting Scenario # 2

Here are a couple more GroupWise troubleshooting principles to take home:

- **Watch your users, if you can.** The devil is in the details, as they say, and it is not likely that Bob would have reported the details of name completion to his administrator.
- **Isolate the problem.** This likely means running a quick test or two. In this scenario, the administrator had to determine whether it was just Bob who couldn't send to Mary, or if it was everyone.
- **Once you've isolated the problem, apply your architectural knowledge.** In this case, an address book entry was incorrect, but it was not in the system address book. Knowing that the frequent contacts list is stored in the user database helped the administrator understand how one (and only one) user could get an error sending to one other user.

Troubleshooting Tips and Tricks

This section describes a few more troubleshooting scenarios that you may encounter, as well as how you may deal with them.

X-Locked Files

GroupWise uses a platform-independent mechanism for locking files in transit. When a transport file is in the process of being created, it is often created with a filename that starts with an X at the very beginning of the filename. This is called an *X-lock.*

Any file with an X at the beginning will not be touched by a GroupWise agent. You are most likely to see X-locked files when a big file is being transmitted, or when a link between a sending and a receiving site is slow. If you see a file with an X at the beginning of the filename, and it is fairly new (created in the last five minutes or so), it is most likely a file still in transit. If the file is more then a day old, however, it is most likely of no value and can be deleted. This was a failed attempt to transmit a file.

TCP/IP Troubles

Suppose for a moment that the POA is having difficulty talking to an MTA via MTP (TCP/IP). You suspect this because people on PO1 complain that they cannot send to anyone outside the PO. You can see that the PO1\WPCSIN\4 directory is full of files.

Where might you start? There's a set of logical places to look to determine the problem. Here's the scenario:

PO1 – POA	IP Address 192.168.95.101	MTP Port 6100
DOMAIN1 – MTA	IP Address 192.168.95.101	MTP Port 7100

1. Look at the POA and choose F10 ➪ Message Transfer Status.

   Figure 19.1 shows the message transfer status screen on the POA.

```
GroupWise POA 6.0                                    NetWare Loadable Module

                        Message Transfer Status
Directory Paths and TCP/IP Addresses
Outbound TCP/IP      192.168.95.101:7100
Inbound TCP/IP       192.168.95.101:6100
Hold                 FS1\SYS:/WCORP/PO1\wpcsin

Status               Send                          Receive
Current              Open                            Open
Last Closed          09-04-01 01:02:22
Last Closed          09-04-01 01:02:27           09-04-01 01:02:21
Last Closure Reason  TCP/IP connection failure(8908)

Messages
Written              7
Read                 10

01:02:21 0B9 Initializing worker
01:02:21 0BB Initializing worker
01:02:25 095 Guardian database: OK
```

FIGURE 19.1 *Message Transfer Status on a POA*

2. Look at the configuration status on the MTA by choosing F10 ➪ Configuration Status and look at the connection to PO1.

   Figure 19.2 shows this screen.

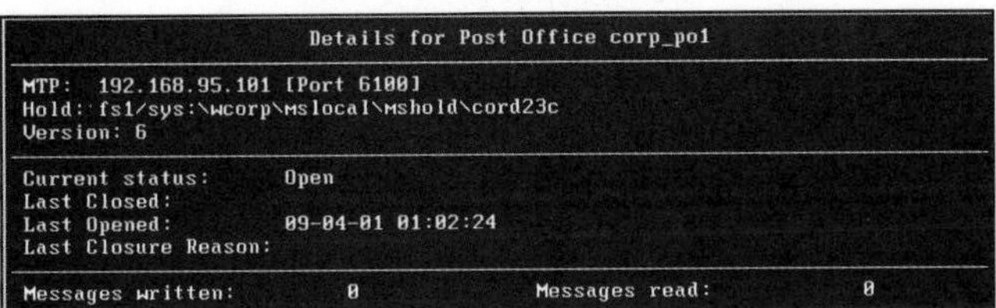

FIGURE 19.2 *Configuration Status on the MTA*

3. Confirm that the MTA is actually listening on port 7100 by loading TCPCON and choosing Protocol Information ➪ TCP ➪ TCP Connections and see that the local host is using port 7100.

   Figure 19.3 shows this screen in TCPCON.

TCP Connections Table

Type	Local Host	Port	Remote Host	Port	State
IP	0.0.0.0	427	0.0.0.0	None	listen
IP	0.0.0.0	524	0.0.0.0	None	listen
IP	0.0.0.0	1687	0.0.0.0	None	listen
IP	0.0.0.0	6100	0.0.0.0	None	listen
IP	0.0.0.0	7100	0.0.0.0	None	listen
IP	0.0.0.0	8100	0.0.0.0	None	listen

FIGURE 19.3 *TCPCON Information*

4. Confirm that the MTA will receive connections at port 7100.

   To do this, run a Telnet program. Make sure to turn on local echo in Telnet, which makes it easier to see what's going on, as in Figure 19.4.

NOTE

Figure 19.4 is from a Windows 2000 workstation. The Telnet program on Windows NT and 9x is a GUI-based telnet. Local echo is set under Terminal ⇨ Preferences.

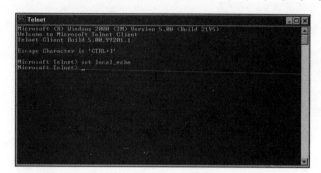

FIGURE 19.4 *Turning Local Echo On in Telnet*

5. If you get a connection to port 7100 (see Figure 19.5), type in some characters.

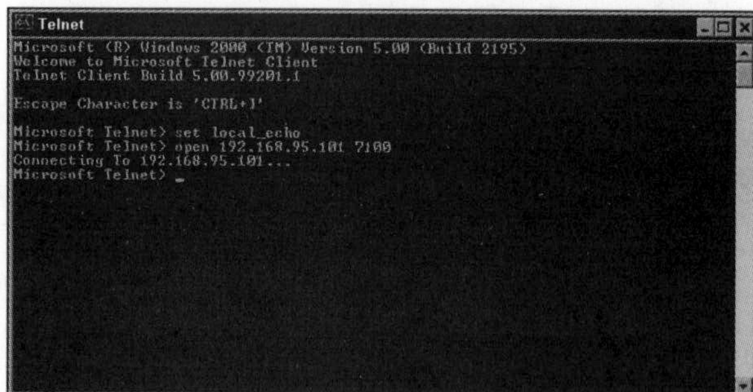

FIGURE 19.5 *Telnetting to the MTA's Port 7100*

You should then get disconnected. If you don't get disconnected then that's a problem. Perhaps you've found that the MTA is listening on port 7100, but you have no guarantee that the POA can reach the MTA on port 7100. See if the file server running the POA can ping the server running the MTA. Be sure to change the byte size on the ping packet so that it represents a "normal" sort of transmission size (try 1,000 bytes.)

6. On the file server running the POA, load ping and select the IP address for the box running the MTA, changing the packet size to 1,000 bytes.
7. Next, load the GWIP.NLM with the syntax **LOAD GWIP CONNECT 192.168.95.101 7100.**

   The GWIP.NLM can be obtained from Novell's support Web site. The name of the download file is GWIP.EXE. See Figure 19.6 for a successful GWIP session.

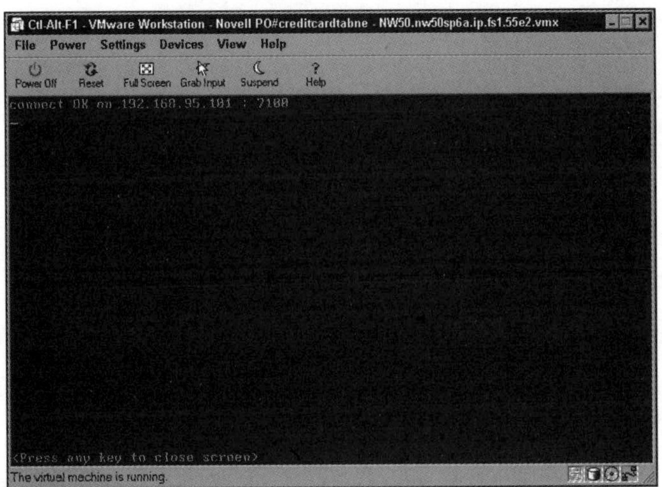

FIGURE 19.6 *A GWIP.NLM Session*

Generally, you'll find the TCP/IP connectivity problem along the way as you use these steps. If the problem continues to elude you, try doing a *reinitialize system* on the box that houses the POA and the MTA. You *can* do this while people are connected to the POA.

Best Practices

As always, there are a few things that you can do ahead of time that will make your life (and your troubleshooting) easier down the road.

- **Make sure that log files on your GroupWise agents can grow large enough and long enough to give you the diagnostic information you need when you need it.** The default max log disk space value on all GroupWise Agents is 1MB. Crank that setting up to 50 MB.
- **Look for message files in queue directories.** The mail message queue directories under a post office are the following:
  - PO\WPCSOUT\OFS\0-7: Incoming messages to the post office
  - PO\WPCSIN\0-7: Outgoing messages from the post office

The mail message queue directories under a domain are the following:

- DOMAIN\WPCSIN\0-7: These are incoming messages to the domain. These files get put into the WPCSIN\0-7 directory if another domain has UNC connectivity to this domain.
- DOMAIN\MSLOCAL\GWINPROG\0-7: When a mail message is incoming to the MTA, it is initially created in these directories.
- DOMAIN\MSLOCAL\MSHOLD\XXXXXXXX\0-7: These are outgoing messages from the domain. Wherever a mail messages goes, to a PO, to another domain, or to a gateway in this domain, it first gets routed to the DOMAIN\MSLOCAL\MSHOLD\XXXXXXXX\0-7 directory. The XXXXXXXX value corresponds with the FID of the object whose outgoing queue this represents.

TIP

In each of the DOMAIN\MSLOCAL\MSHOLD\XXXXXXXX directories, there will be a text file called MTANAME. If you open this file with any text editor, it will give you the full name of the domain or post office that this hold queue represents.

- DOMAIN\WPGATE\<gateway name>\WPCSOUT\<GATEWAY-FID>\0-7: When an MTA has a message to give to a gateway, it puts the message in this directory.
- DOMAIN\WPGATE\GATEWAY\WPCSIN\0-7: When a gateway has something to give the MTA, it puts the file in this directory.

- **If you use Windows Explorer to look at file queues, make sure Explorer is configured to give you the most accurate information.** This is important because if you don't see enough detail, you may not notice that a file in a particular queue is very large. Make sure that Windows Explorer is configured to do the following:

- Show all files
- Sort all files according to size
- Show the details for files (so that you can actually see the file size)

Summary

This chapter covered a lot of information, but it can all be distilled into three basic troubleshooting principles. When you need to troubleshoot GroupWise message flow, you need to do the following:

- Check the queue directories for "stuck" files, backlogs, and so on.
- Check the POA and MTA logs for error messages, or to track message DRNs.
- Check each of the connectivity points — TCP/IP connections between POAs and MTAs, links between MTAs on different domains, and any other links that are part of the signal path for the problem messages.

Remember, one of the easiest ways to check message flow is to send a message and then check the status on it. *Pending* status means that the flow has been blocked at some point. Any other status means that message flow is open between your mailbox and the destination mailbox.

CHAPTER 20

Moving Domains and Post Offices

Chapter 13 discusses moving user mailboxes from post office to post office. What do you do, however, when an entire post office or domain needs to be relocated? This chapter walks you through the process of moving post offices and domains to new servers (new UNC paths), as well as moving their objects around within your NDS tree.

Considerations Related to Moving a Domain

When moving domains, you are going to move a domain from one physical UNC location to another. Generally, the move is done from one file server to another. This discussion assumes that the domain will be moved from one file server to another. Here is the scenario:

- Domain to be moved is DOMAINX
- DOMAINX is a secondary domain
- DOMAINA is the primary domain in this system
- File-server name for file server where DOMAINX originally resided is FS1
- File-server name for file server where DOMAINX will reside is FS2
- Old location of DOMAINX is \\FS1\EMAIL\DOMAIN
- New location of DOMAINX is \\FS2\EMAIL\DOMAIN

Connectivity to the Primary Domain

One of the biggest concerns when moving a domain is the manner in which the new location for DOMAINX will be communicated to the rest of the system. Suppose that DOMAINX communicates to the rest of the GroupWise system via TCP/IP. The new file server, FS2, will have a different IP address than FS1 did. This needs to be communicated to the rest of the system, prior to moving DOMAINX. So the MTA object for DOMAINX must be edited, and the Network Address field should indicate the IP address for FS2. Just as soon as the IP address for DOMAINX's MTA has been changed, the rest of the system expects to communicate with DOMAINX at the new IP address.

Any changes made to the IP address for the MTA on DOMAINX should be done with ConsoleOne physically connected to the WPDOMAIN.DB for DOMAINX. If you were to change the IP address for the MTA on DOMAINX while connected to the primary domain, then your primary domain MTA would immediately restart but not be able to communicate the change to DOMAINX's MTA if DOMAINX was not running on the new file server.

Communication between DOMAINX and the primary domain is the most important communications link. If the primary domain cannot communicate with DOMAINX in order to get the information about DOMAINX's new MTA IP address, then no one is going to get the change. Make sure that DOMAINX has communication with the primary domain.

Connectivity to Post Offices

When the domain gets moved to a new IP address, the post offices have to get the information about the change of the MTA's IP address in order for the POA to communicate to the MTA.

Moving a Domain to a New Server

The following is an example task list for moving DOMAINX. There will be a running commentary as well so that the concepts applied in this walkthrough can be applied to your own domain moves.

WARNING

If the domain that you want to move houses a GroupWise WebAccess gateway, you must delete the GroupWise WebAccess gateway first before moving the domain. A GroupWise WebAccess gateway cannot be moved along with its domain. You must reinstall and reconfigure the GroupWise WebAccess gateway.

DOMAINX is being moved from the file server FS1 to the file server FS2. DOMAINX has two post offices that it communicates with via TCP/IP. Another name for TCP/IP connectivity to a POA is MTP connectivity.

As a precautionary step, you'll want to sync DOMAINX with the primary domain.

1. In ConsoleOne, connect to the WPDOMAIN.DB for the primary domain, highlight DOMAINX, and choose Tools ➪ GroupWise Utilities ➪ System Maintenance.
2. Select Sync Primary with Secondary and then click Run, as shown in Figure 20.1.

   Next, you'll want to install the GroupWise agents to FS2.
3. Go to the Software Distribution Directory\AGENTS directory and run INSTALL.EXE.

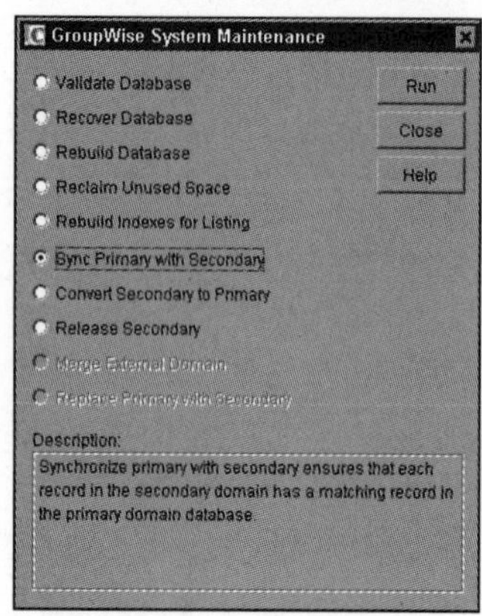

FIGURE 20.1 *Synchronizing a Primary Domain with a Secondary Domain*

4. Copy the startup file for the GroupWise MTA from \\FS1\SYS\SYSTEM to \\FS2\SYS\SYSTEM.
5. Edit the MTA startup file in \\FS2\SYS\SYSTEM and make sure that the home switch points to the new domain directory.
6. Load ConsoleOne and make sure to connect to DOMAINX in the GroupWise system view.

   To do this, go to Tools ➪ GroupWise System Operations ➪ Select Domain. Select the path to DOMAINX.

   Even though you haven't moved the domain, make sure DOMAINX and the primary domain can communicate. Use Steps 7 and 8 to confirm this.
7. Edit DOMAINX's MTA and, on the Agent Settings property page, increment the Attach Retry option by one second.
8. Connect to the primary domain in ConsoleOne, edit DOMAINX's MTA, find out if the Attach Retry value changed on DOMAINX's MTA object.

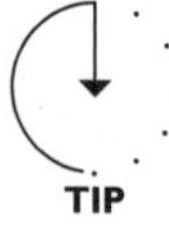

The purpose behind incrementing the Attach Retry option specifically is that this is a value that is not held in NDS. So when you see that the change that was made to this setting has actually replicated, then you know GroupWise directory replication is working.

Do not proceed to the next step, until you see this change replicate to the primary domain. Get in and out of the MTA object to see this change come through.

NOTE

If it's the primary domain that you are moving, then you can skip the focus on making sure there is communication to the primary domain because that is already happening.

9. In ConsoleOne, connect back to DOMAINX's WPDOMAIN.DB file.
10. Edit DOMAINX's MTA and change the TCP/IP address on the Network Address window to reflect the new IP address for FS2 (see Figure 20.2).

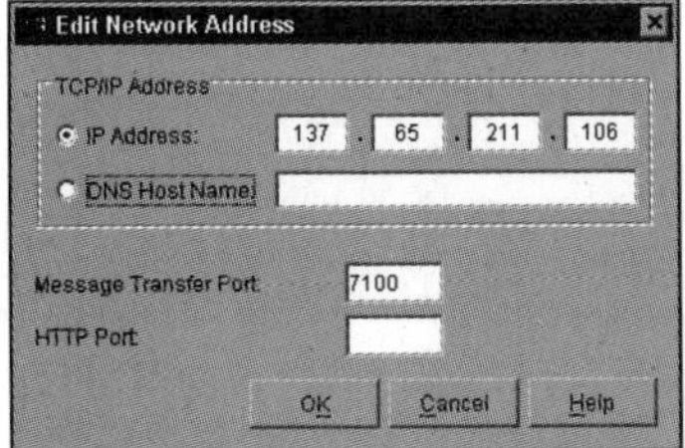

FIGURE 20.2 *Change the Network Address on the MTA*

It may sound strange to change the IP address for an MTA to reflect the IP address on a server where the MTA is not running; but don't worry, it will work. The whole idea is for the MTA that is currently running on FS1 to communicate the change in the IP address before the MTA has come down. DOMAINX's MTA will have connectivity with the rest of the MTAs in the system, but they will lose connectivity to the DOMAINX's MTA. This condition is just fine. Wait for about five minutes for this information to replicate before going to the next steps of this section.

11. Get out of ConsoleOne.
12. Bring down DOMAINX's MTA and any gateways running for DOMAINX.
13. Make sure no one is accessing the WPDOMAIN.DB.

    Here is a simple test: Try to rename the WPDOMAIN.DB file to WPDOMAIN.REN and then back to WPDOMAIN.DB. If you can't rename the file, do not proceed until you can. For NetWare servers, you can check file/open lock activity on the server monitor program to see which users still have a connection to the domain database. You then know who still has the domain database open. If the connection to the WPDOMAIN.DB happens to be 0, there is a process on the server that is holding the WPDOMAIN.DB file open.

14. Copy the domain directory from the old location to the new location.

So in other words, copy the \\FS1\EMAIL\DOMAIN\ directory to \\FS2\EMAIL\DOMAIN using one of the following options:

- You could use a backup of the domain from FS1 and then restore it back to FS2. (Gee, that's a complicated way of doing things.)
- You could use NCOPY *.* /S /E. (NCOPY is superior to COPY or XCOPY because it does a server-to-server copy, so it's faster.)
- You could use XCOPY *.* /S /E.
- You could use Windows Explorer, copy and paste the directory, and watch the flying pages!

15. Rename the WPDOMAIN.DB file on FS1 to WPDOMAIN.BAK.

16. Load ConsoleOne.

You should get an error about the fact that the domain database for DOMAINX could not be found. This is good; go to step 18.

17. Connect to the now-relocated DOMAINX domain's WPDOMAIN.DB file and when ConsoleOne asks you for the path to the domain, browse to the new UNC location for the domain.

18. Edit DOMAINX's object as shown in Figure 20.3, and change the UNC path for the domain to reflect the new path for DOMAINX.

Now you must delete the GroupWise domain from NDS without truly deleting the GroupWise domain. You must do this so that the new UNC path to the domain gets inserted into NDS; there is no other way to do this. The entire procedure for doing this is covered in the section later in this chapter called "Moving a Domain to a New Organizational Unit." You should follow every instruction in that section, however, you will not move the domain to a new organizational unit; you will simply put the GroupWise domain back into the same organizational unit it was already in. After finishing the instructions of that entire section, then proceed to the next step.

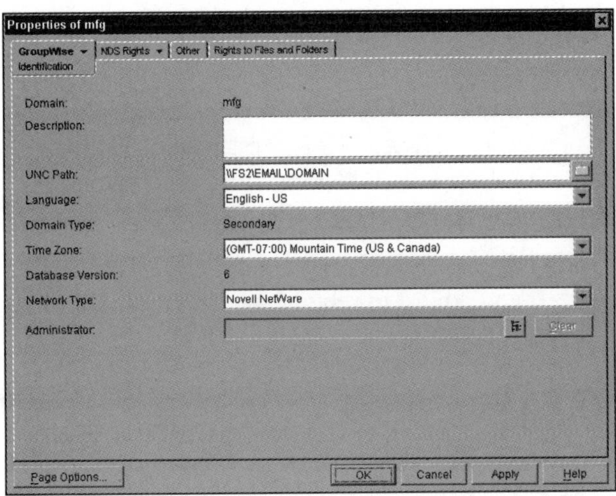

FIGURE 20.3 *Changing the UNC Path for the Newly Moved Domain*

19. Edit DOMAINX's MTA, go to the Log Settings property page as shown in Figure 20.4, and if you have specified a path, make sure it reflects the UNC path where the domain is located.

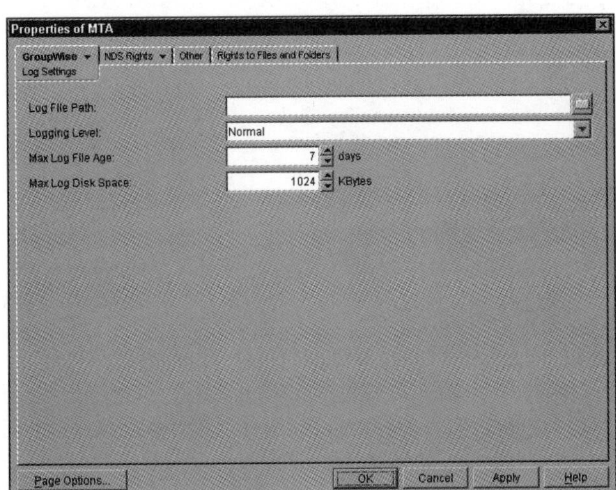

FIGURE 20.4 *Editing the GroupWise MTA's Log Settings*

20. Bring up the MTA for DOMAINX on FS2.

21. Get the POAs and the MTA talking via TCP/IP.

    You'll have to bounce the POAs. Although the IP address for the MTA may have been communicated to the POA, the POA won't restart the MTP process to use the new address. The MTP process is most likely showing the domain as closed. Bring the POA down and right back up.

    After bringing the POA back up, see if it shows the correct IP address for the MTA. To do this choose F10 ➪ Message Transfer Status.

    If the IP address is incorrect, you'll have to rebuild the WPHOST.DB file to force the information down to the post office.

TIP

If you cannot get your POA to understand that the MTA has a new IP address, or you do not want to rebuild the WPHOST.DB file, then you may want to just use the following switches in the startup file for the POA to force the POA to cooperate:

```
/MTPINIP-<IP address of the POA>
/MTPINPORT-<MTP port of the POA>
/MTPOUTIP<IP address of the MTA>
/MTPOUTPORT<IP port of the MTA>
```

22. Configure the NetWare server to run more efficiently with the new GroupWise domain by setting the following directories for immediate purge of deleted files:

```
\\FS2\EMAIL\DOMAIN\WPCSIN
\\FS2\EMAIL\DOMAIN\WPCSOUT
\\FS2\EMAIL\DOMAIN\MSLOCAL
\\FS2\EMAIL\DOMAIN\WPGATE\<gateway>\WPCSIN
\\FS2\EMAIL\DOMAIN\WPGATE\<gateway>\WPCSOUT
```

Final Notes on Moving a Domain

The example in the preceding section is not a perfect fit for every situation. For example, some sites have implemented DNS names for their MTAs rather then IP addresses. The DNS name simplifies the IP address change, because the only IP address change that will need to be changed is in the DNS's translation table.

Also, if you have a gateway below a domain that needs to be moved, you will need to see that the gateway is configured for new changes to the IP address or the new UNC path for the domain. Consider, for example, a domain with a GWIA. If you moved the domain that a GWIA is associated with, you would want to do the following:

1. Copy the GWIA's executable code to the new server.

   To install the GWIA code to a new server without using the wizard to install a new GWIA, go to the software distribution directory and run the INSTALL.EXE file from the software distribution directory with the `/copyonly` switch. Here's the syntax:

   ```
   <SDD UNC PATH>\INTERNET\GWIA\install.exe /copyonly
   ```

2. Copy the GWIA.CFG file to the new file server — this file is typically in the SYS:SYSTEM directory on a NetWare server — and modify the GWIA.CFG file so that it reflects the correct paths to the domain.
3. Modify the EXEPATH.CFG file to reflect the new path to the GWIA.CFG file.

   The EXEPATH.CFG file is in the <DOMAIN THAT OWNS THE GWIA>\WPGATE\<GWIA DIRECTORY>.

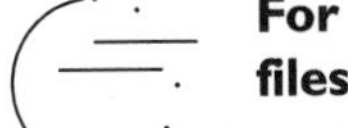

NOTE

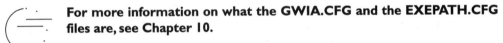

For more information on what the GWIA.CFG and the EXEPATH.CFG files are, see Chapter 10.

4. Edit the GWIA, go to the Log Settings property page, and make sure that the log path does not reflect a location at the old UNC path.

Considerations Related to Moving a Post Office

First of all, it's impossible to move a GroupWise post office to a different domain. If you are reorganizing and need to move a post office to a new domain, what you are really looking at is creating the post office anew in the new domain and moving all the users. Have a look at Chapter 13, if this is what you need to do.

This discussion talks about moving the physical location of a GroupWise post office. You are going to be moving a post office from one physical UNC location to another. Here is the information from the scenario:

- Post office to be moved is PO-X
- DOMAINA is the domain that owns the post office PO-X
- File-server name for file server where PO-X originally resided is FS1

- File-server name for file server where PO-X will reside is FS2
- Old location of PO-X: is \\FS1\EMAIL\PO
- New location of PO-X is \\FS2\EMAIL\PO

GroupWise Client Connectivity

Most customers have configured their post offices to support client/server connections from the GroupWise client to the GroupWise POA. The GroupWise client knows that it must contact the GroupWise POA via an IP address. Each time the GroupWise client loads, it reads the IP address out of one of the following locations:

- NDS
- The Windows registry where the GroupWise 32-bit client is installed
- In the USER.DB file for any GroupWise caching or remote client

If these locations don't provide the client with a valid IP address, it will check domain name services for the NGWNAMESERVER POA.

The trick is to communicate the new IP address to all GroupWise clients. If you specified the IP address for the POA using a DNS name (for example, `poa.po-x.worldwidewidgets.com`), then the change is an easy one. Just change the DNS translation table for `poa.po-x.worldwidewidgets.com` so that it reflects the new IP address of the POA when running on FS2. In this way, the settings that the clients have stored will still be correct. The client will look to DNS to resolve the host name the same way it did before the PO was moved, and DNS will give the client the new address.

If you have specified the IP address for the POA (which most customers do) using numbers (for example, 10.100.221.2), then you have to depend on the client to do an NDS lookup, or a DNS lookup for NGWNAMESERVER. This walkthrough shows you how to configure your system so that those lookups succeed.

Domain-to-Post Office Connectivity

The GroupWise MTA for DOMAINA has to know how to connect to the PO-X post office. Otherwise, messages will not move from the DOMAINA MTA to the POA running on PO-X.

GroupWise WebAccess and GWIA Connectivity

If you have GroupWise WebAccess, it needs to know about the change to PO-X's location and/or IP address. If your GWIA is configured for POP3 or IMAP4 support, it will also need to know how to get a hold of the newly moved PO-X post office. These two gateways connect directly to the post office to provide alternative types of mailbox access, as discussed in Chapters 10 and 11. If they do not know about the post office's POA's new IP address, then you will have WebAccess, POP3, or IMAP4 users who cannot get to their mail.

Libraries with Additional Document Storage Areas

If a library is contained under the post office to be moved, you may have an additional concern. Usually, you can simply copy the entire post-office structure, library directories and all, and be fine. The problem comes in when there are document storage areas (DSAs) defined outside of the post office directory.

If the DSA needs to be moved, consult Chapter 14. DSA moves can occur independently of post office moves. If the DSA does not need to be moved, all you need to do is make sure that when the POA runs at the new location, it still has full access to the DSA.

WARNING

If you move a post office to a new location but keep the DSA at the old server path, you could have problems loading your GroupWise POA. Perhaps you will get a DF17 error, and the POA will not load. You need to correct the DF17 error; but to get things up and running, you can add a `/noconfig` switch to the POA's startup file.

The Software Distribution Directory

Software distribution directories are similar to document storage areas in that they can be moved independently of the post office. You have three basic options with regard to your software distribution directory:

- **Keep the assignment the same.** This is good if the software distribution directory is on a separate server from the PO, as long as that server will still be accessible to users after the PO moves.
- **Assign the PO to a new software distribution directory.** It may be that with the PO move, a different server will be used to deliver applications to users. If there is another SDD there, it makes sense to assign that one to the PO you are moving.

WARNING

If you assign a post office to a new software distribution directory, keep in mind the BUMP and BUILD numbers. If you do not want your users to get prompted to update the GroupWise client, make sure that the BUILD number is tweaked accordingly. See Chapter 12 for more details on the BUMP and BUILD numbers.

- **Move the software distribution directory.** This should be your choice if the SDD resides on the same server as the users. In this case, you will need to copy the SDD to the new server, and edit the path of the SDD using the software directory management tool discussed in Chapters 6 and 8.

NOTE

Remember that if you need to edit the UNC path to a software distribution directory, it will increment the BUMP number, which will cause GroupWise clients to check for new client software at the SDD directory. See Chapter 12 for more information on the BUMP number.

Moving a GroupWise Post Office to a New UNC Path

Here is the scenario: The GroupWise post office PO-X is being moved from FS1 to FS2. The file server housing PO-X isn't robust enough, so you must put the GroupWise post office on its own dedicated NetWare server. The PO-X post office communicates via TCP/IP to its owning domain, DOMAINX. All users access PO-X in client/server mode.

Moving the Post Office and Creating Domain-to-PO Connectivity

A few days before the post office move, let users know that the move of the post office will happen. If everything goes well it should be rather seamless for most users. Unless you are using DNS names to identify where the POA is running, users who use GroupWise caching or remote mailboxes will need to manually change the IP address to the POA under Accounts ➪ Account Options ➪ Properties ➪ Advanced.

1. Install the GroupWise POA software to FS2.

   This can be done by running the agent install program, INSTALL.EXE, found in the AGENTS subdirectory of your GroupWise CD or software distribution directory.

2. Copy the POA's startup file from \\FS1\SYS\SYSTEM to \\FS2\SYS\SYSTEM.

   Note that you will likely be overwriting the startup file created by the installer in Step 1. This is fine.

3. Edit the POA's startup file and change the home switch to reflect the new UNC path for PO-X.

   Now you need to suspend connectivity from DOMAINA's MTA to PO-X.

4. Go to the MTA's screen at the NetWare console, press F10, and select Configuration Status.

5. Highlight the post office PO-X, press Enter, and select the Suspend option, as shown in Figure 20.5.

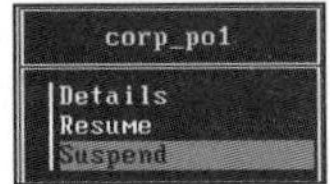

FIGURE 20.5 *Suspending MTA Connectivity to a Post Office*

6. Bring down the POA that services PO-X.

7. Rename the WPHOST.DB file in \\FS1\EMAIL\PO to WPHOST.BAK.

   Do not proceed until you have done the rename successfully. If you cannot rename the WPHOST.DB file, then there is either another POA running against the post office (maybe an indexer POA), or there are users logged in via direct mode who have a connection to it. Check file/open lock activity from the NetWare server monitor to determine who has a connection to the database.

8. Copy the contents and subdirectories of \\FS1\EMAIL\PO to \\FS2\EMAIL\PO, using one of the following options:

   - You could use a backup of the post office from FS1 and then restore it back to FS2.
   - You could use NCOPY /S /E. (NCOPY is superior to COPY or XCOPY because it does a server-to-server copy, so it's faster.)

- You could use XCOPY /S /E.
- You could use a free GroupWise backup utility from Novell called GWBACKUP, available at `http://support.novell.com`.

9. Load ConsoleOne and make sure you are connected to the WPDOMAIN.DB for DOMAINA.
10. Edit the post office object in ConsoleOne and change the UNC path to the post office as shown in Figure 20.6.

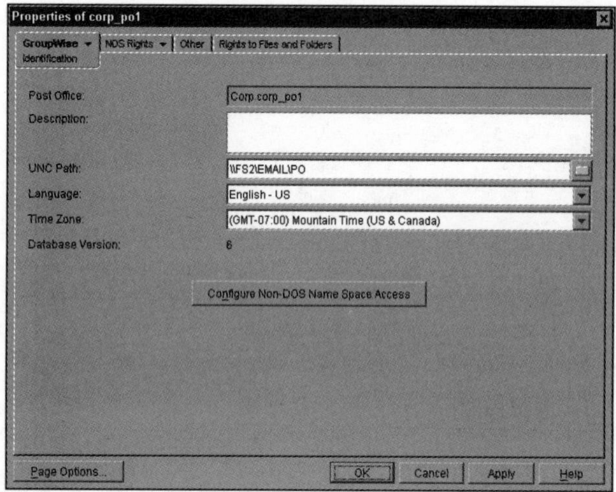

FIGURE 20.6 *Changing the UNC Path for the Post Office*

11. Edit the POA for the PO-X post office and change the IP address in the Network Address tab to reflect the IP address for FS2.

    Figure 20.7 shows this.

    Now you need to check the network links to PO-X to see if the change to the IP address made it to the link table.

12. Choose Tools ➪ GroupWise Utilities ➪ Link Configuration, select DOMAINA, and then choose View ➪ Post Office Links.

    You need to double-click the post office link to PO-X to make sure that it has the correct IP address.

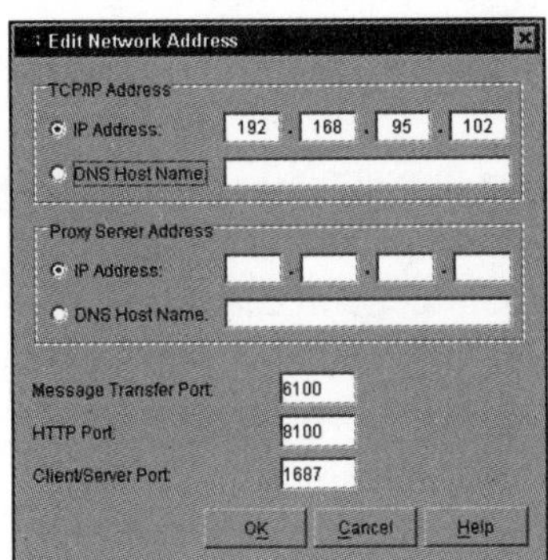

FIGURE 20.7 *Changing the IP Address for the POA*

13. Rebuild PO-X's WPHOST.DB file by highlighting the post office, choosing Tools ➪ GroupWise Utilities ➪ System Maintenance, selecting Rebuild Database, and then clicking Run.
14. Bring down the MTA for DOMAINA, and bring it right back up again.
15. Bring up the POA for PO-X on FS2 to confirm that the POA has connectivity to the domain.

    The POA for PO-X is configured for MTP, so to test connectivity you will do the following:

    - Go to the POA at the NetWare console.
    - Select F10 and then Message Transfer Status.
    - Confirm that the IP addresses are correct and that communication is established.

    Now, you can confirm WebAccess and GWIA connectivity to the post office.
16. Edit the WebAccess gateway object.
17. Select the Post Office Links property page.
18. Highlight the link to PO-X and edit it, making sure that the link reflects the new information for FS2.
19. Edit the GWIA gateway object.
20. Select the Post Office Links property page.

21. Highlight the link to PO-X and edit it, making sure that the link reflects the new information for FS2.

    Finally, you can create client connectivity.

22. Make sure that all users have browse, read, and compare NDS object rights to the post office and POA objects.

    This way, if they are running the NetWare client and are in client/server – online mode, they will discover the location to the new POA.

23. Remember that GroupWise caching and remote clients may need to manually change the IP address to the POA under Accounts ➪ Account Options ➪ Properties ➪ Advanced.

Moving a Post Office to a New Organizational Unit

As your NDS tree evolves and grows, there may come a need to move a GroupWise post office object to a new organizational unit (OU). The GroupWise software does not readily allow for this, but this section shows you how to pull it off.

To begin, you need to disable the ConsoleOne GroupWise snap-ins.

1. Get out of ConsoleOne.

2. From Windows Explorer, cut the GROUPWISE folder and its contents from the NOVELL\CONSOLEONE\<VERSION>\SNAPINS directory and paste it to C:\TEMP.

3. Reconfirm that there is no longer a GROUPWISE folder in the SNAPINS folder.

   When ConsoleOne is unsnapped from GroupWise, all GroupWise objects show up with an icon that looks like a question mark on the right-hand side of a 3D box.

4. Start ConsoleOne, and make sure that under the Tools menu, there are no GroupWise menus, as shown in Figure 20.8.

5. Delete the GroupWise POA object by highlighting and deleting the post office object, which appears to the right in Console View.

   Figure 20.9 shows the POA object.

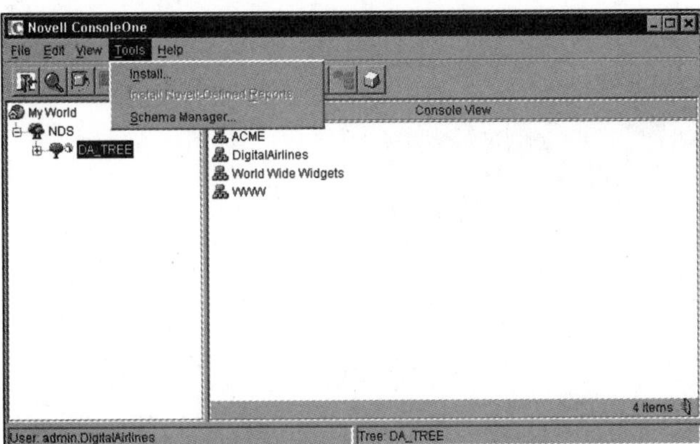

FIGURE 20.8 *ConsoleOne without GroupWise Snap-Ins*

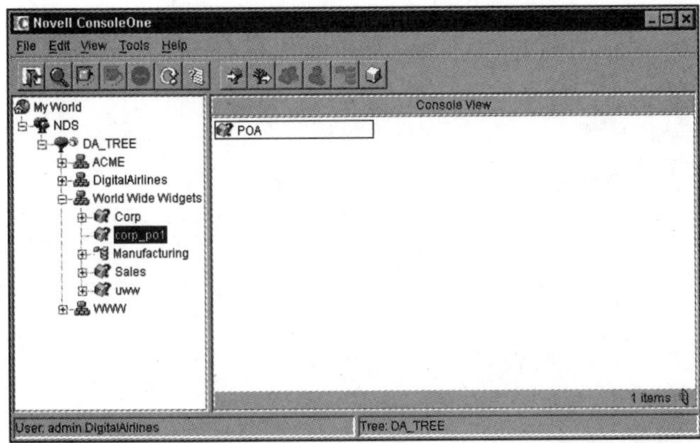

FIGURE 20.9 *The POA Object with ConsoleOne Unsnapped from GroupWise*

6. Delete any GroupWise libraries that are associated with this post office. GroupWise libraries will be in the same NDS context as the post office object, so highlight a library and delete the object, as shown in Figure 20.10.
7. Delete the post office object from NDS (see Figure 20.11).

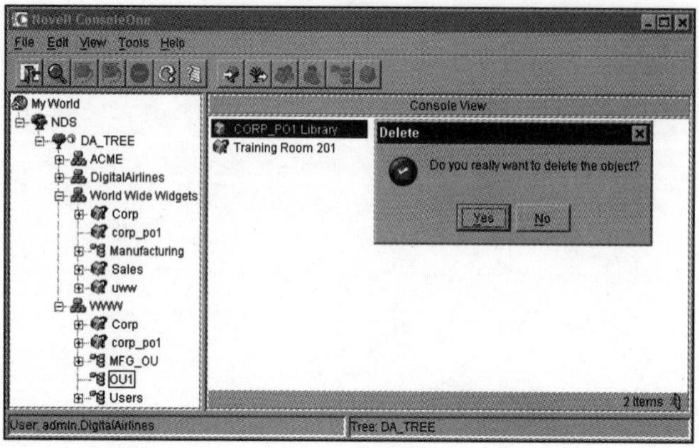

FIGURE 20.10 *Deleting the GroupWise Library Object*

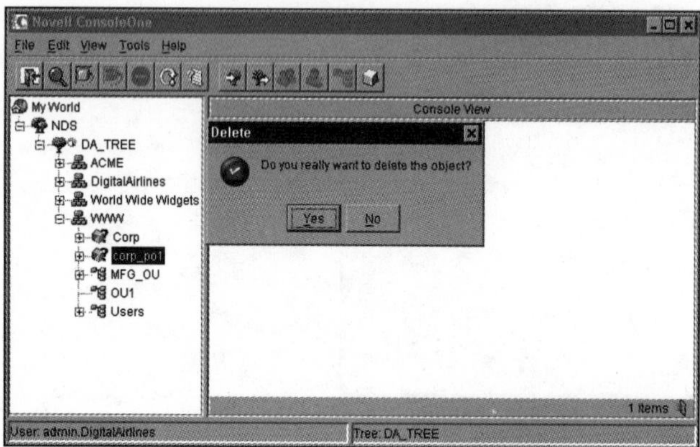

FIGURE 20.11 *Deleting the GroupWise Post Office Object*

8. Put the GroupWise snap-ins for ConsoleOne back into place by copying the GROUPWISE folder from the temporary location back to the NOVELL\CONSOLEONE\<VERSION>\SNAPINS directory.
9. Launch ConsoleOne, and the GroupWise snap-ins should now be re-enabled.
10. Go into the NDS browser view and highlight any NDS OU.

11. Choose Tools ➪ GroupWise Utilities ➪ GW/NDS Association ➪ Graft GroupWise Objects.
12. Select Domains, Post Offices, and Gateways.
13. When prompted with the Select Domain window, select the domain that owns the post office you deleted from NDS.
14. Proceed to the Post Office Context window as shown in Figure 20.12.

    Notice that the Edit Context button will not be grayed out when you highlight the post office that was deleted.

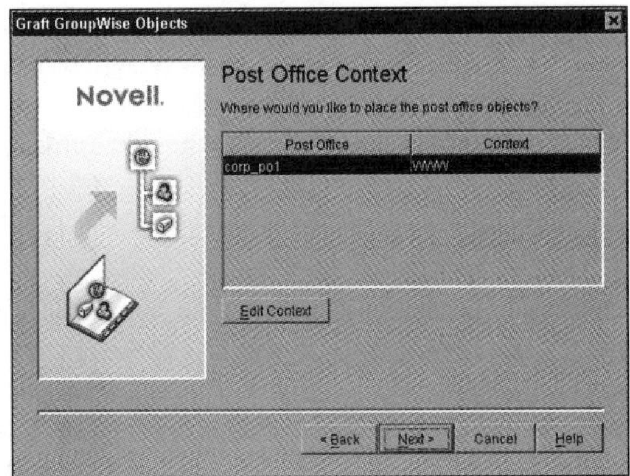

FIGURE 20.12 *Post Office Context Window*

15. Edit the context and specify the new context for the post office object.
16. Click Next and then Finish.
17. Once the graft is finished, get out of the Graft utility, and then get out of ConsoleOne and go back in.

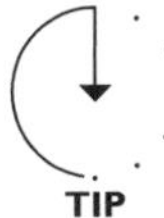

Getting in and out of ConsoleOne gives ConsoleOne a chance to re-read everything; otherwise ConsoleOne can get kind of confused after a procedure such as this.

18. Go to the NDS context that now houses your post office.
19. Now choose Tools ➪ GroupWise Utilities ➪ GW/NDS Association ➪ Graft GroupWise Objects.

20. When the graft utility comes up, graft the users associated with the post office that you just moved by selecting Users, resources, and distribution lists from the first graft screen.
21. Proceed through the graft utility and follow the prompts, choosing the post office that you just moved to a new NDS OU as the post office for which the users need to be grafted.

Moving a Domain to a New Organizational Unit

As your NDS tree changes, you may find a need to move a GroupWise domain object to a new organizational unit (OU). As with the post office OU move explained earlier in this chapter, the GroupWise software does not have a built-in function to allow for this kind of a move. You'll do this just like you moved the post office to a new OU.

WARNING

If the domain that you want to move houses a GroupWise WebAccess gateway, you must delete the GroupWise WebAccess gateway first before moving the domain. A GroupWise WebAccess gateway cannot be moved along with its domain. You must reinstall and reconfigure the GroupWise WebAccess gateway.

NOTE

When moving a GroupWise domain, the domain object must be deleted from NDS. The fact that the domain is deleted from NDS throws NDS off when trying to understand the GroupWise post office object. So when deleting a GroupWise domain object, you must also delete the post office objects along with the POAs and libraries also.

To begin, you need to disable the ConsoleOne GroupWise snap-ins.

1. Get out of ConsoleOne.
2. From Windows Explorer, cut and paste the GROUPWISE folder and its contents from the NOVELL\CONSOLEONE\<VERSION>\SNAPINS directory to C:\TEMP.
3. Reconfirm that there is no longer a GROUPWISE folder in the SNAPINS folder.

When ConsoleOne is unsnapped from GroupWise, all GroupWise objects show up with an icon that looks like a question mark on the right-hand side of a 3D box.

4. Start ConsoleOne, and make sure that under the Tools menu there are no GroupWise menus, as shown in Figure 20.13.

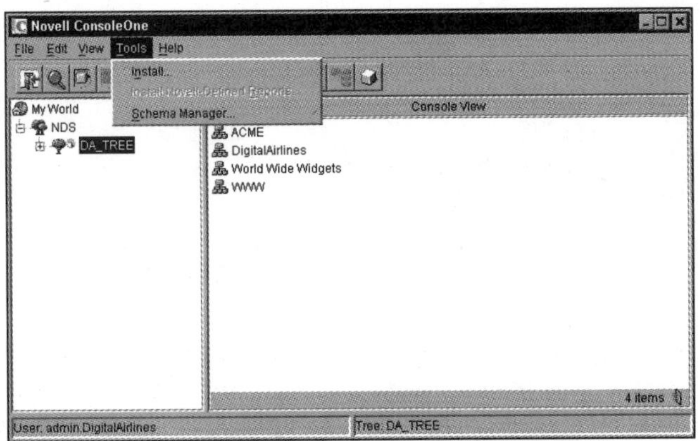

FIGURE 20.13 *ConsoleOne without GroupWise Snap-Ins*

5. Delete the GroupWise MTA object for this domain that you moved.

   To do this, find the GroupWise domain object on the right-hand side, and the MTA will show up on the left-hand side as shown in Figure 20.14.

6. Delete any gateways or provider objects that are associated with this domain.

   Gateways and provider objects are shown on the right-hand side, in the same place the MTA is.

7. Delete any GroupWise post offices that are associated with this domain.

   Refer to the section prior to this one for complete instructions on how to do this.

NOTE

The GroupWise post office object may be in a different NDS organizational unit than the GroupWise domain.

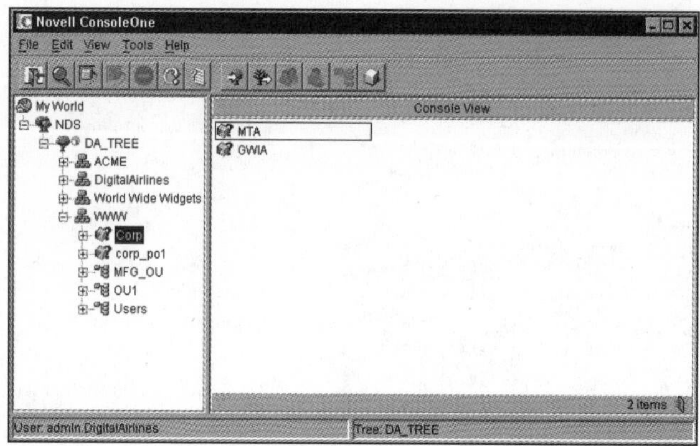

FIGURE 20.14 *The MTA Object with ConsoleOne unsnapped from GroupWise*

NOTE

You will need to delete all other objects subordinate to the domain being moved. The GroupWise post offices are not truly subordinate to the GroupWise domain in NDS. The GroupWise post office must still be deleted because NDS gets thrown off if information in the GroupWise post office points back to the deleted GroupWise domain. This *does not* mean that you need to delete the users; it just means that you'll have to delete the post office POAs subordinate to your post offices.

8. Delete the domain object from NDS (see Figure 20.15).
9. Put the GroupWise snap-ins for ConsoleOne back into place by copying the GROUPWISE folder from the temporary location back to the NOVELL\CONSOLEONE\<VERSION>\SNAPINS directory.
10. Launch ConsoleOne, and the GroupWise snap-ins should now be re-enabled.
11. Go into the NDS browser view and highlight any NDS OU.
12. Choose Tools ➪ GroupWise Utilities ➪ GW/NDS Association ➪ Graft GroupWise Objects.
13. Select Domains, Post Offices, and Gateways.
14. When prompted with the Select Domain window, select the domain that you deleted from NDS.

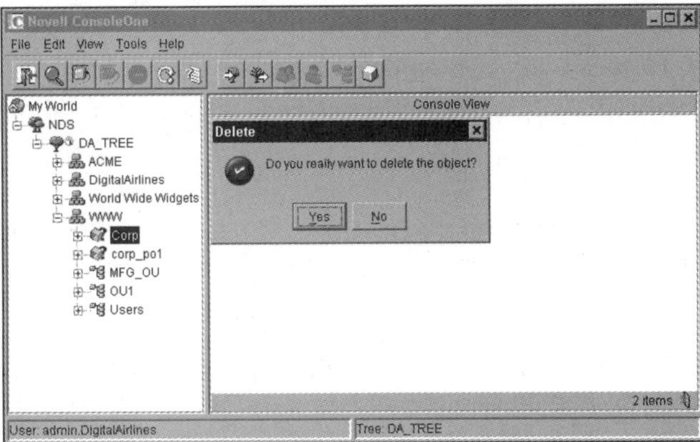

FIGURE 20.15 *Deleting the GroupWise Domain Object*

15. Proceed to the Domain Context window as shown in Figure 20.16. Notice that the Edit Context button will not be grayed out when you highlight the domain that was deleted.

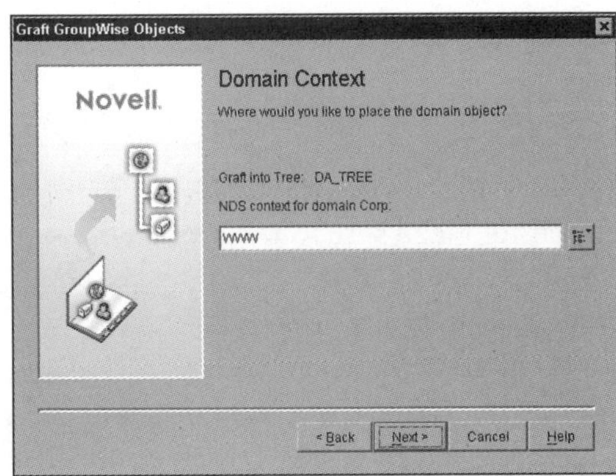

FIGURE 20.16 *Domain Context Window*

16. Edit the context and specify the new context for the domain object.
17. Now specify the context to place your post offices, and click Next and then Finish.

18. Once the graft is finished, get out of the Graft utility, and then get out of ConsoleOne and go back in.
19. Go to the NDS context that now houses your domain.
20. Now choose Tools ➪ GroupWise Utilities ➪ GW/NDS Association ➪ Graft GroupWise Objects.

NOTE

Grafting users will not put them into the same context that the domain is in. Actually, you are just re-grafting the users in their original contexts.

21. When the graft utility comes up, graft the users associated with all the post offices below the domain that you just moved to a new OU by selecting Users, resources, and distribution lists from the first graft screen.

TIP

You can just graft the users for one post office at a time, if that would be easier for you.

Make sure to specify the right context for resources and distribution lists. Any libraries will be put in the resource context that you specify.

22. Proceed through and finish the grafting of the users.

Summary

Moving things around in a GroupWise system isn't terribly difficult, but there is a lot of detail you need to pay attention to. Make sure to perform all the steps mentioned in the walkthroughs, and your domain and post office moves should be trouble-free.

CHAPTER 21

Using GroupWise Monitor

All the GroupWise 6 agents have an HTTP-monitoring functionality. GroupWise monitor takes your system beyond HTTP monitoring. Although HTTP monitoring of agents is a powerful tool, and some features are available only through HTTP monitoring, there is no alert mechanism. With the Windows-based GroupWise 6 monitor, you can be alerted of problems without having to stare at a computer screen waiting to see if a problem is happening.

Installing GroupWise Monitor

The GroupWise monitor agent can be installed on a Windows NT or 2000 computer. Although you can install the GroupWise monitor agent on a Windows 95/98/ME computer, it loses some features, and so this chapter assumes you are installing GroupWise monitor on a Windows NT/2000 computer.

Although you can install GroupWise monitor on your own workstation, I would recommend installing GroupWise monitor on an auxiliary Windows 2000 workstation or server computer that you intend to always keep running. By doing this, the GroupWise monitor can function as an agent that is monitoring your system continually.

The GroupWise Monitor software has two separate components. They are the GroupWise monitor agent and the GroupWise monitor application. Here are some details about both of these:

- GroupWise monitor agent
  - Runs only on the Windows platform
  - Provides all the features of GroupWise monitor, except it does not support HDML (handheld device markup language for wireless telephones, typically) and simple HTML support
- GroupWise monitor application
  - The application can run on any of the same platforms that the GroupWise WebAccess application can run on. It runs as a servlet, so it can run on NetWare, IIS, Unix, and so on.
  - Works only in conjunction with the GroupWise monitor agent
  - Provides the HDML and simple HTML template support for the GroupWise monitor agent

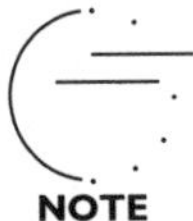
NOTE

The GroupWise monitor application cannot exist without the GroupWise monitor agent. The GroupWise monitor agent has no dependencies on the GroupWise monitor application.

Installing Windows SNMP Services

When you attempt to install the GroupWise monitor agent, you may be prompted to install SNMP services for Windows. The following are steps that I took to install SNMP services on a Windows 2000 workstation machine:

1. Go to the Control Panel.
2. Select Add/Remove Programs.
3. Select Add/Remove Windows Components.
4. Select the Management and Monitoring Tools option.
5. Select Next to allow Windows to install the SNMP.

To confirm that the SNMP service is installed and running, do the following:

1. Go to the Control Panel.
2. Select Administrative Tools.
3. Select Services.
4. Look for SNMP Service.

With SNMP services enabled, you can now proceed to the GroupWise monitor installation.

Installing GroupWise Monitor Agent

The GroupWise monitor utility is located in your GroupWise 6 <software distribution directory>\ADMIN\MONITOR directory.

1. Run the SETUP.EXE program in this directory.
2. Proceed to the GroupWise Monitor: Components screen shown in Figure 21.1.
3. Install the GroupWise monitor agent.

   Later in this chapter, you will install the GroupWise monitor application. It's generally easier to implement the agent first, and then implement the GroupWise monitor application as needed.

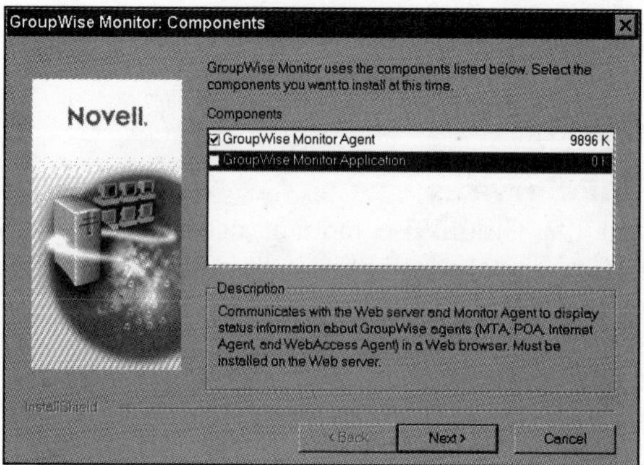

FIGURE 21.1 *GroupWise Monitor Components to Install*

The GroupWise monitor agent is sufficient for monitoring your GroupWise system. The GroupWise monitor application allows an administrator to see the information on the GroupWise monitor agent from additional interfaces such as HDML and simple HTML.

4. Specify the correct IP address and port for the GroupWise monitor utility, as shown in Figure 21.2, and then click Next.

   This IP or DNS host name is the IP address or host name of the Windows NT/2000 box on which you are installing the monitor agent.

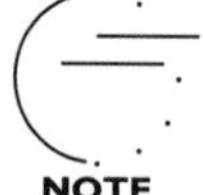

The GroupWise monitor agent utility can itself be monitored from a Web browser. That's the purpose of the Port field.

5. Specify the path to a WPDOMAIN.DB in your system, which the GroupWise monitor agent can use to read configuration information about agents in your system, and then click Next.
6. Select the language you would like for GroupWise monitor and click Next.
7. View the summary and make sure everything is correct.

   If it is not, you can use the Back button to correct things.

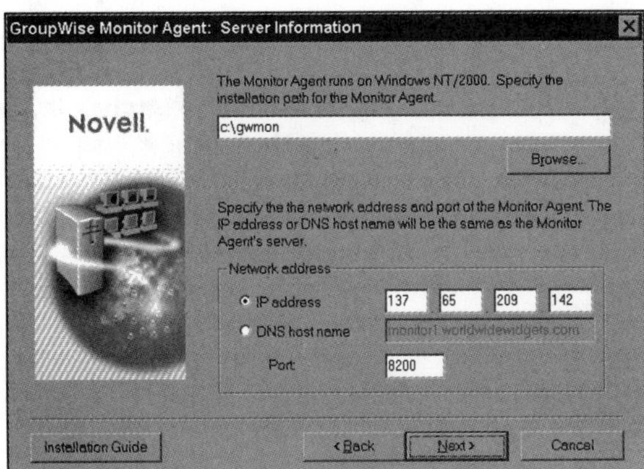

FIGURE 21.2 *GroupWise Monitor Agent Information*

Configuring Your System to Better Support GroupWise Monitor

GroupWise monitor cannot be configured from ConsoleOne. However, the information that GroupWise monitor uses to monitor your GroupWise system is spread all throughout your system. In order to make all the features of GroupWise monitor work, you must enable three things:

- HTTP monitoring of GroupWise agents
- SNMP monitoring of GroupWise agents
- Message logging on GroupWise MTA agents

Enabling HTTP Monitoring

The chapters in this book regarding the GroupWise POA, MTA, GWIA, and WebAccess components all spoke of how to enable HTTP monitoring. For more review, see each of those chapters. But in short, here's how you enable HTTP monitoring on all GroupWise agents.

1. Start ConsoleOne.
2. Go to the Network Address option of the agent you are enabling HTTP monitoring on and edit the button that looks like a pencil, to the right of the TCP/IP Address field.

3. Fill in the HTTP port value.

Make sure that the HTTP port value is in fact the HTTP port that your agent is actually listening on. If you are using the `/HTTP*` switches in the startup files of your agents, you may not be using the same values as are specified in ConsoleOne. If a GroupWise agent has `/HTTP*` switches in its startup file, those switches take precedence over the HTTP values in ConsoleOne. The GWIA keeps the `/HTTP*` switches in its GWIA.CFG file.

Enabling SNMP Monitoring

All the GroupWise agents can be monitored via SNMP, and in fact, SNMP monitoring is a default on all GroupWise agents. The GroupWise POA can be configured to disable SNMP monitoring though, so here's how to enable SNMP monitoring on the GroupWise POA.

1. Run ConsoleOne.
2. Go to the Properties of the POA object.
3. Go to the Agent Settings property page.
4. Check the Enable SNMP check box, as shown in Figure 21.3.

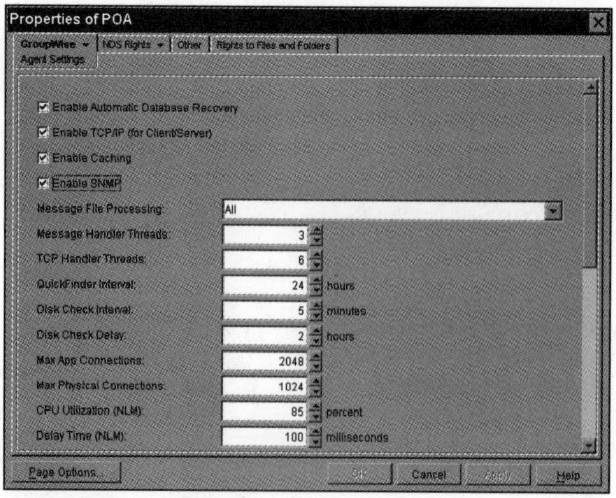

FIGURE 21.3 *Enable SNMP*

5. Now slide down to the bottom of the Agent Settings property page and input the word **public** (case-sensitive) in the SNMP Community Get String field, as shown in Figure 21.4.

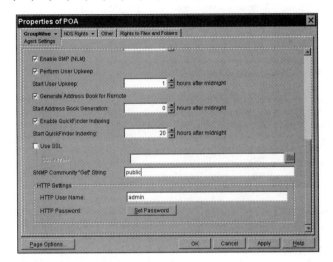

FIGURE 21.4 *SNMP Community Get String*

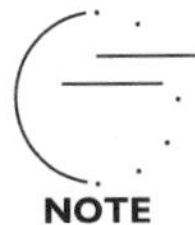

NOTE

A discussion of SNMP community get strings is outside the scope of this book. You are welcome to change the SNMP Community Get String field according to the SNMP guidelines in your organization.

Enabling MTA Message Logging

Now, to enable MTA message logging, follow these steps:

1. Run ConsoleOne.
2. Edit the properties of the MTA object.
3. Go to the Message Log Settings property page.
4. Change the Message Logging Level field so that it says Full.
5. Message logs will be placed in the <DOMAIN>\MSLOCAL\MSGLOG directory by default, unless you change the message log file path.
6. Check all check boxes.

7. Determine a value, such as 30 days, for the Delete Report After field.

Figure 21.5 shows MTA message logging enabled.

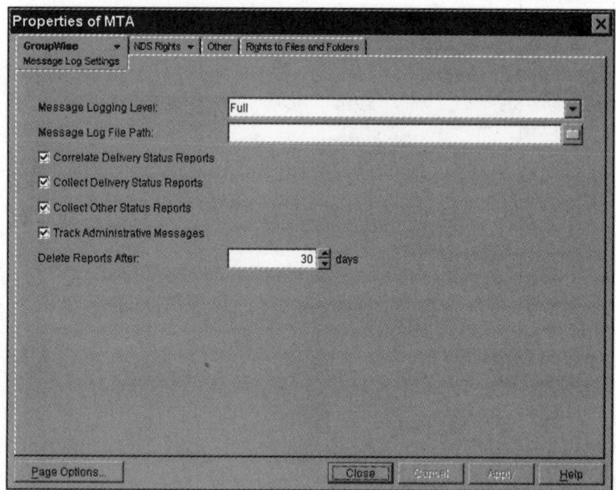

FIGURE 21.5 *Enabling MTA Message Logging*

NOTE

In previous versions of GroupWise, there was not much use for message logging, and it was often recommended by Novell support engineers to disable it. However in GroupWise 6, message logging has totally been revised, and is much more efficient and useful. The reason for enabling message logging is to give you the ability to track messages and pull reports on the GroupWise system through the GroupWise monitor component.

Starting and Using the GroupWise Monitoring Agent

The GroupWise monitoring agent is installed to the Start ➪ Programs menu tree of the Windows computer where GroupWise monitor agent was installed. By default, GroupWise monitor is installed to a folder under Start ➪ Programs ➪ GroupWise Monitor.

NOTE

With the first release of Group/Wise 6, the GroupWise monitor agent is not a Windows service.

After starting the GroupWise monitor agent, you get a listing of the agents that the GroupWise monitor agent was able to discover from your GroupWise system.

GroupWise monitor is a very powerful and configurable tool. It's kind of like a piece of soft clay. You can mold GroupWise monitor into many different things. Because of this, this chapter gives an explanation of some of the menu selections in GroupWise monitor. There are no "best practices" for configuring GroupWise monitor. So I won't tell you how to configure GroupWise monitor, or which fields to enable, I'll just explain the functional purposes of many of the features in the GroupWise monitor. It is best to explore GroupWise monitor and construct your own monitoring solution with GroupWise monitor.

The whole idea of GroupWise monitor is to allow you to view the state of your GroupWise system and notify you of problems or potential problems. The next sections talk about how to enable three kinds of notifications:

- Visual notification
- Audio notification
- Remote notification

Configuring Visual Notification: GroupWise Monitor Agent Windows Interface

The main GroupWise monitor agent screen, shown in Figure 21.6, gives you an eagle's-eye view of the state of your GroupWise system. The whole goal is to see green check marks down the left-hand side. If you see a red circle with an X through it, this is a visual alert that either an agent is down or GroupWise monitor cannot get a hold of an agent for some reason.

You can get much more information on any one of your GroupWise agents by double-clicking on the agent. A details screen comes up, as shown in Figure 21.7.

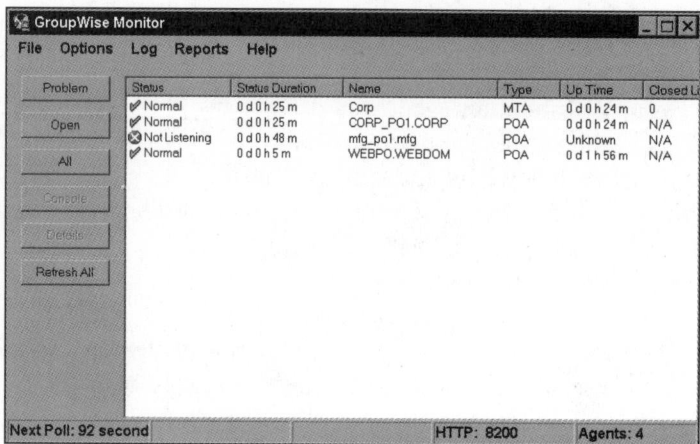

FIGURE 21.6 *The GroupWise Monitor Agent*

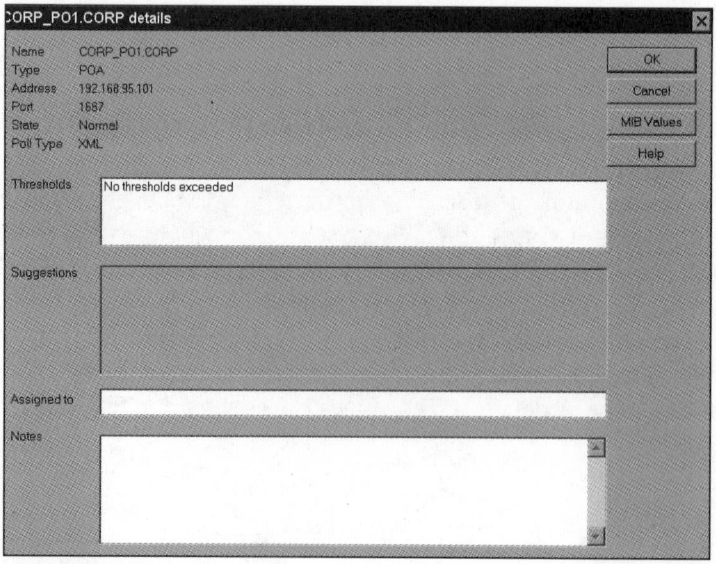

FIGURE 21.7 *Agent Details*

You can get even more details by viewing the SNMP values that the agent makes available. To do this, click on the MIB Values button. Figure 21.8 shows the MIB Values that come up on a POA agent.

Filtering

You can apply a filter so that all you see are the GroupWise POAs. To do this, choose File ⇨ Filter and uncheck all the check boxes except the POA check box.

TIP

You can start up different instances of GroupWise monitor. One could monitor just POAs; the other could monitor GroupWise MTAs. When you stop GroupWise monitor though, some of your configuration filters will be lost. You may also want to configure the second instance of the GroupWise monitor to listen at a different HTTP port. You can do this by choosing File⇨HTTP and changing the HTTP port value. Also, if you install the GroupWise monitor software to different directories, the GroupWise monitor will create a different MONITOR.XML file in that directory, which will contain the settings for that particular instance of the GroupWise monitor agent.

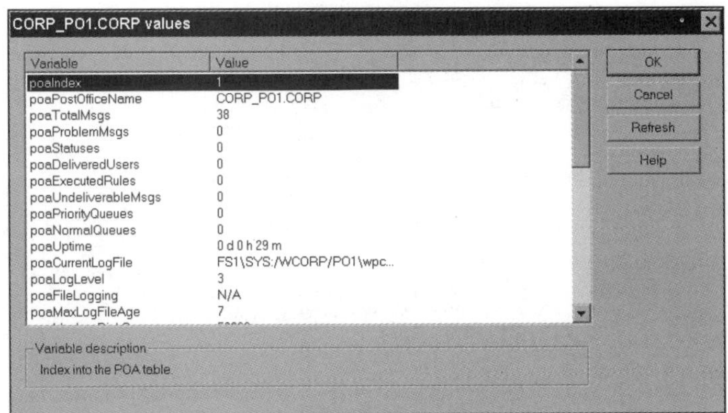

FIGURE 21.8 *SNMP/MIB Values on a POA*

Reports

With the Reports option, you can get real-time reports of configuration information, message flow, and so on. The reports features are pretty self-explanatory. What you should know though, is that the user traffic, link traffic, and message tracking features all derive information from the message logs of the GroupWise

MTAs in your system. These aren't the regular logs the MTA uses; these are the special logs that are enabled when MTA message logs are enabled. Enabling MTA message logging is explained earlier in this chapter.

User Traffic This report can track the messages sent by a particular user, within a time frame that you specify.

Link Traffic This report tracks the amount and size of messages sent between domains in your system.

Message Tracking This is a powerful feature that has a little bit of complexity. As shown in Figure 21.9, this feature requires some investigation on your part.

First here's a scenario in which you might use this feature:

- USERA on PO1.DOM1 sends a message to USERB on PO2.DOM1.
- USERB did not receive the message, and USERA shows the status of the message as pending.

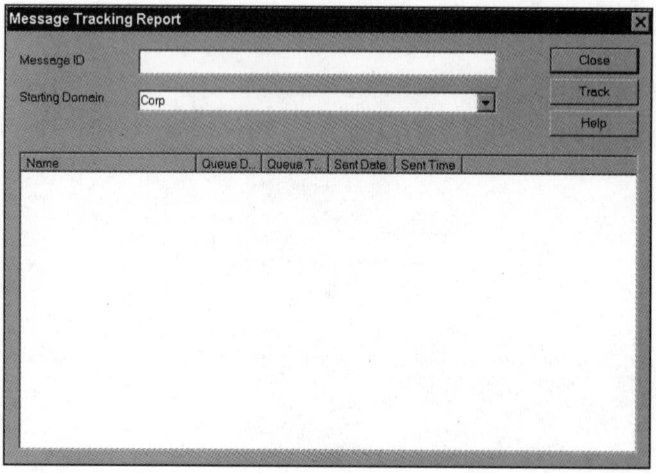

FIGURE 21.9 *Message Tracking*

You are the administrator; you want to know what happened to the message. Here is the information you would gather:

1. Have USERA go to their Sent Items folder.
2. Have USERA view the properties of the message they sent to USERB.

3. Have USERA tell you the value on the line that reads Mail Envelope Properties.

   The value you want is the 8.3 value before the first colon. Figure 21.10 shows the properties of a mail message.

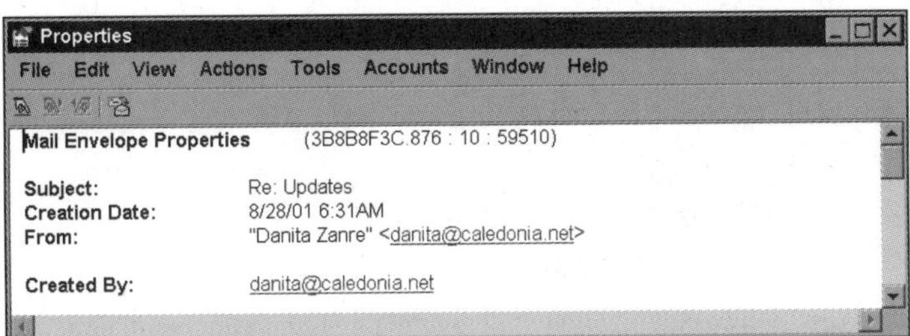

FIGURE 21.10 *Properties of a GroupWise Message*

4. After you have the 8.3 value, you have the message ID value needed for the GroupWise monitor message tracking report; put this same value in the message ID value, and select DOM1 as the starting domain.

   This value is unique to the particular message that was sent. It does not change as the message flows through the system. It is embedded inside the message file so that the MTA can log the information and tie it to this message ID.

5. Click on the Track button to generate the report.

Configuring Visual Notification: GroupWise Monitor Agent HTTP Interface

You can use GroupWise monitor, even when you are away from it, using an HTTP interface. Also, this interface allows you to define custom SNMP monitoring views of your GroupWise system. The GroupWise monitor has a Web-browser interface.

To enable HTTP monitoring and to enable the HTTP interface to give you quick access to GroupWise agents, you need to make sure the GroupWise monitor agent, and your other agents, are listening for Web-browser connections.

Each of the GroupWise agents have HTTP-monitoring functionality. See the chapters earlier in this book on the POA, MTA, GWIA, and WebAccess. These chapters discuss how to configure HTTP monitoring for that particular agent.

Specifying the HTTP Port for the GroupWise Monitor Agent The GroupWise monitor agent listens on a configurable HTTP port. This allows you to view the information that the GroupWise monitor agent is gathering from any Web browser. You do not need to be sitting at the machine that is running the GWMON.EXE program. Check to see whether this port is enabled, as well as what it is enabled for. To do this, choose File➪HTTP in the GroupWise monitor agent Windows interface, as shown in Figure 21.11.

Make sure that the HTTP port is filled in and make note of this port.

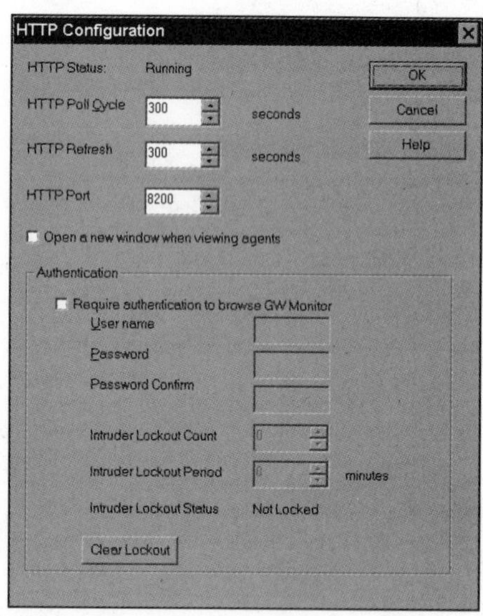

FIGURE 21.11 *GroupWise Monitor Agent HTTP Configuration*

Accessing the HTTP Interface through a Web Browser

Here is how you access the HTTP interface of the GroupWise monitor agent through your Web browser. Use the following line in your browser:

```
http://<monitor computer's IP address or DNS name>:<monitor's
HTTP port>
```

For example:

```
http://137.65.32.63:8200
```

You should get an interface similar to the one in Figure 21.12. Once you are in, you get an interface that is much like the Windows interface. There are two distinct advantages that I can see to this interface:

- HTTP access to GroupWise agents
- Custom views

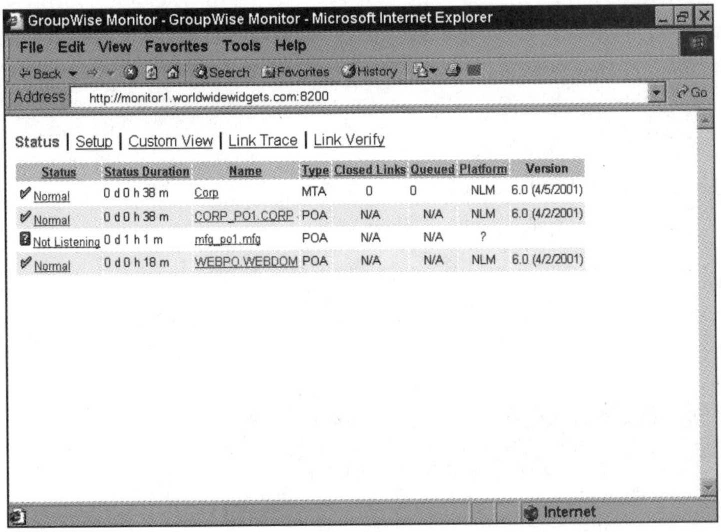

FIGURE 21.12 *GroupWise Monitor Agent Web-Browser Interface*

HTTP Access to GroupWise Agents From the main status screen in the Web browser interface of GroupWise monitor, you can click on any of the agents in the Name column, and you are immediately transported to the HTTP port of that agent and the resulting HTTP interface of that agent.

TIP

You can configure GroupWise monitor to open up the HTTP screen of agents in a new browser window. This way you always have GroupWise monitor, and you can access the HTTP interfaces of your other GroupWise agents at the same time. To do this, go back into the GroupWise monitor's Windows interface and choose File ⇨ HTTP. In the HTTP Configuration window, check the Open a new window when viewing agents option.

Custom Views With custom views, you can define the SNMP traps that you want to monitor (see Figure 21.13).

Rather than explain these traps (there's over 200 of them), do the following to understand these SNMP traps. Go to the status screen in the Web-browser interface and click an agent along the Status column. Here you will see each of the SNMP values filled in for that agent. With a little bit of thinking and matching, you should be able to determine the SNMP traps available to you. Now you can create an SNMP custom view:

1. Go back to the Custom View screen.
2. Select the SNMP traps that you are interested in.
3. Give the custom view a name by filling in the View Name field.
4. Click the green check mark next to the agents that you are monitoring.

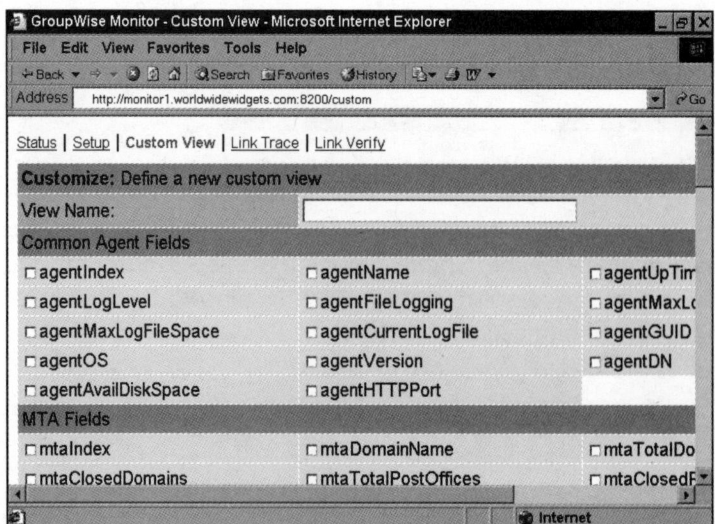

FIGURE 21.13 *GroupWise Monitor Custom Views*

Configuring Audio Notification

The GroupWise monitor agent can play sounds when certain events have happened. This is useful if the GroupWise monitor agent is in earshot of your desk. To enable audio notification, choose File ➪ Sounds, and you should see the window shown in Figure 21.14.

You can browse to find sound files that will play on the events shown in the Sound Options window.

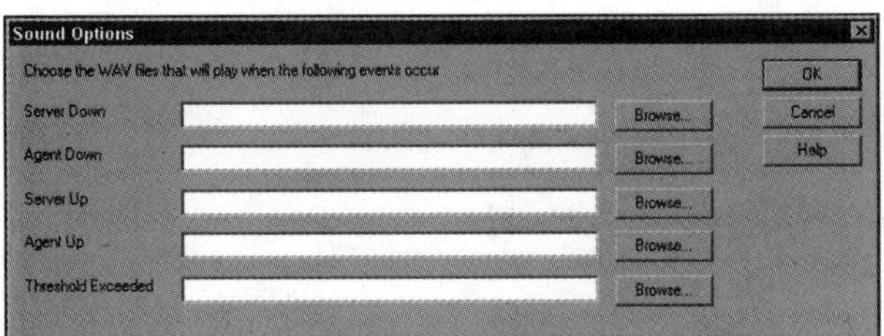

FIGURE 21.14 *GroupWise Monitor Sounds*

Configuring Remote Notification

This is a powerful notification method. With remote notification, you can have GroupWise monitor send a message to the Internet e-mail address for your pager, as well as to other e-mail addresses. Here's how you do it:

1. Go into the Windows interface of the GroupWise monitor agent.
2. Choose File ➪ Notification.
3. Select the Notification Events that you want to be notified of.
4. Fill in the Notification list with e-mail addresses to send notification to, separating each address with a comma.
5. In the Mail Domain field, specify the mail domain name for your organization.

   My organization is `worldwidewidgets.com`.
6. For the Relay address, put in the IP address for a machine that will relay the notification onto the Internet for you.

   If you have enabled relaying on the GWIA, then you can specify the IP address for your GWIA. However, if the GWIA is down, how will you be notified? You will most likely want to specify some other SMTP mailer in your system that you can relay off of. This relay value is optional. If a relay is not entered, then the GroupWise monitor agent will generate the SMTP message itself, do the DNS lookup on the domain name of the intended recipients, and deliver the mail directly. In other words, it can act as an SMTP agent in delivering the notification e-mail(s) to the intended recipients. The relay field is there in case the workstation that is running the monitor agent is not able to do the DNS lookups and connect to the destination SMTP host to deliver the mail to.

Figure 21.15 shows the GroupWise monitor configured for remote notification.

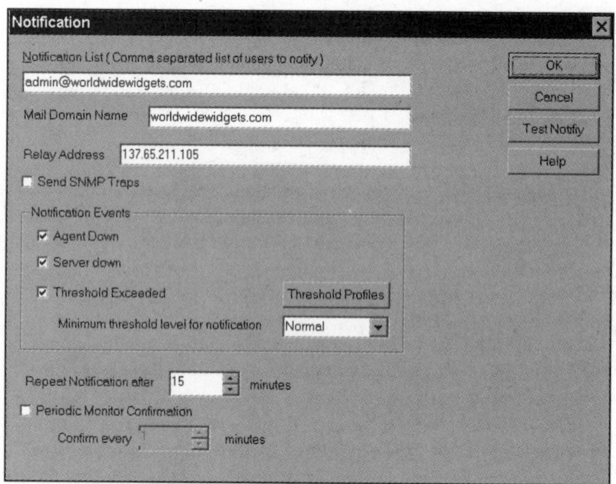

FIGURE 21.15 *Notification Window*

Installing the GroupWise Monitor Application

The primary reason you would want to install the GroupWise monitor application is if you wanted to broaden browser integration for your GroupWise monitor agent. The GroupWise monitor application can integrate the GroupWise monitor agent's interface into your Web server. A particular value to this is that you can leverage your Web server's outside availability on the Internet to broaden your access to monitoring your GroupWise agents. As if that isn't enough, the GroupWise monitor application also supports monitoring via simple HTML devices, such as a Windows CE device, or HDML-wireless devices, such as a cell phone with a micro-browser. The GroupWise monitor that comes with GroupWise 6 Support Pack 1 even includes support for the PalmPilot Web-clipping platform.

Prerequisites to Installing the GroupWise Monitor Application

The GroupWise monitor application requires that you have a Web server. The GroupWise monitor application was written to support one of four different Web servers:

- Netscape Enterprise Server for NetWare
- Netscape FastTrack Enterprise Server for Windows NT
- Microsoft Internet Information Server (IIS) for Windows NT Server
- Apache Web Server for UNIX Solaris

NOTE

There may be broader Web server support in the future.

You must have a GroupWise agent installed prior to installing the GroupWise monitor application.

Installing the GroupWise Monitor Application

Don't bother installing the GroupWise monitor application unless you have a GroupWise monitor agent installed and running.

1. Run the SETUP.EXE program in this directory.
2. Proceed to the GroupWise Monitor: Components screen shown in Figure 21.16.
3. Select only the GroupWise monitor application and click Next.
4. At the next screen, fill in the IP address and the HTTP port of the Windows NT/2000 computer that is running the GroupWise monitor agent.

   Figure 21.17 shows the screen on the GroupWise monitor agent where you can find what HTTP port the GroupWise monitor agent is using. After filling out this dialog box, click Next.

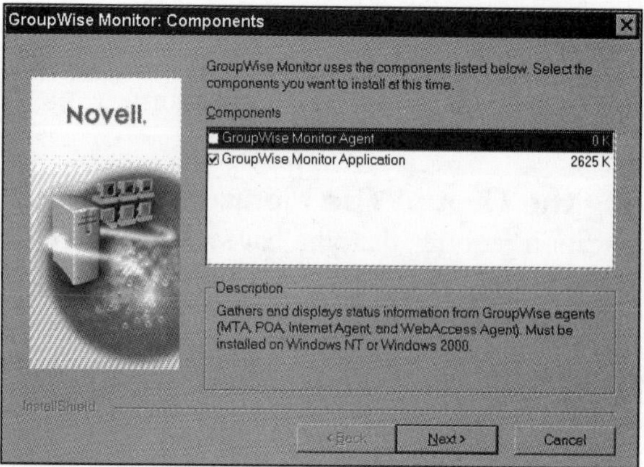

FIGURE 21.16 *GroupWise Monitor Components to Install*

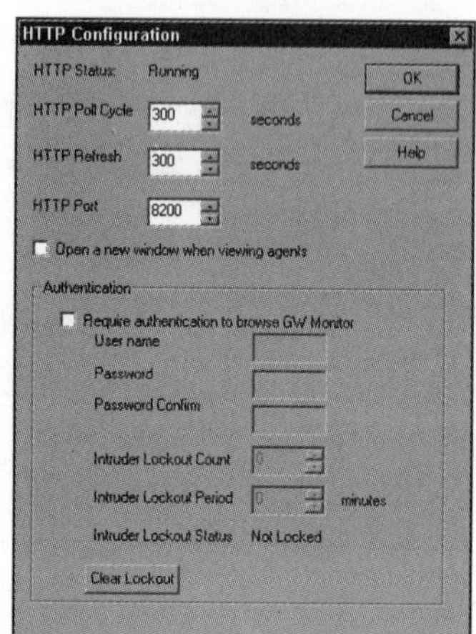

FIGURE 21.17 *GroupWise Monitor Agent HTTP Information*

5. Now the installation wizard wants to know the UNC location of your web server. The GroupWise monitor application is a Java servlet that will run on your web server. Specify the UNC path to your webserver, and click Next.

6. Figure 21.18 shows the next screen, where the installation needs the IP address for your web server. If you have SSL enabled, the GroupWise monitor application will utilize SSL. Fill in the IP address and correct port for your Web server and click Next.

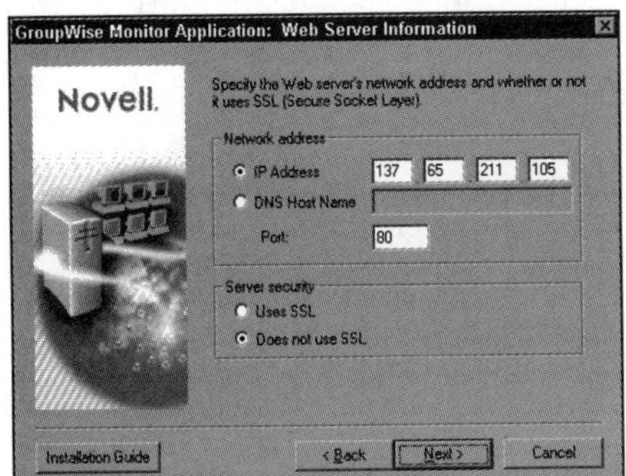

FIGURE 21.18 *Web Server Information*

7. The next screen asks if you want to make GroupWise monitor your default Web server screen. Generally, you want to answer No to this question, and click Next.

Since you will not be replacing the Web server's default Web page, you will need to access the GroupWise monitor application via the following location:

```
http://<web server name or IP address>/servlet/gwmonitor
```

8. The installation now wants to create a Novell directory on the Web server. The Novell directory is somewhat of a work directory for the GroupWise monitor application servlet. Click Next.
9. Next you are prompted which servlet gateway to use. Unless Novell has not made a servlet gateway for your Web server, it's advisable to use the Novell servlet gateway. Click Next.
10. Choose the language, and click Next.
11. Now you are prompted where in NDS to install the GroupWise monitor application configuration objects (see Figure 21.19). These objects are your administration points for the GroupWise monitor application. With these

objects, the GroupWise monitor application is represented in NDS, and you can configure it from ConsoleOne. Click Next to proceed to the summary screen.

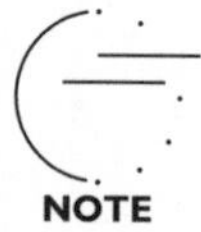

NOTE

The GroupWise monitor agent and Application are not in the GroupWise view in ConsoleOne, and they are not in the GroupWise WPDOMAIN.DB file. The GroupWise monitor agent is administered strictly from the agent itself. The GroupWise monitor application is administered from ConsoleOne in the NDS browser view.

12. You get a summary screen at the end of the installation. If everything looks all right, proceed to install the GroupWise monitor application software.

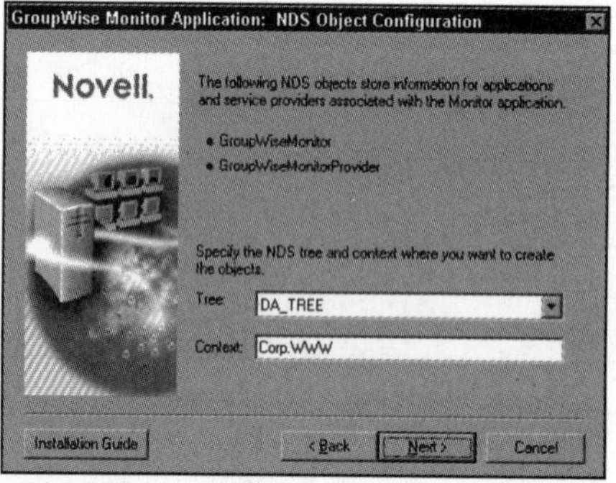
GroupWise Monitor Application: NDS Object Configuration
Novell.
The following NDS objects store information for applications and service providers associated with the Monitor application.
• GroupWiseMonitor
• GroupWiseMonitorProvider
Specify the NDS tree and context where you want to create the objects.
Tree: DA_TREE
Context: Corp.WWW
Installation Guide
< Back
Next >
Cancel

FIGURE 21.19 *GroupWise Monitor Application NDS Object Configuration*

Configuring the GroupWise Monitor Application

There really is not a whole lot to configure on the GroupWise monitor application. The GroupWise monitor application primarily needs to know the location of the GroupWise monitor agent. If ever you should need to configure the GroupWise monitor application to monitor a GroupWise monitor agent at a different IP address then you would need to configure the GroupWise monitor application. To access the GroupWise monitor application, look in the NDS location where you installed the GroupWise monitor application. You should find objects that look like the ones shown in Figure 21.20.

The MonitorProvider object is the object where you can indicate a different IP address for a GroupWise monitor agent.

The GroupWiseMonitor object has additional features such as how long a session will be terminated if it is inactive and the logout URL that a browser will be sent to when logging out of the GroupWise monitor application.

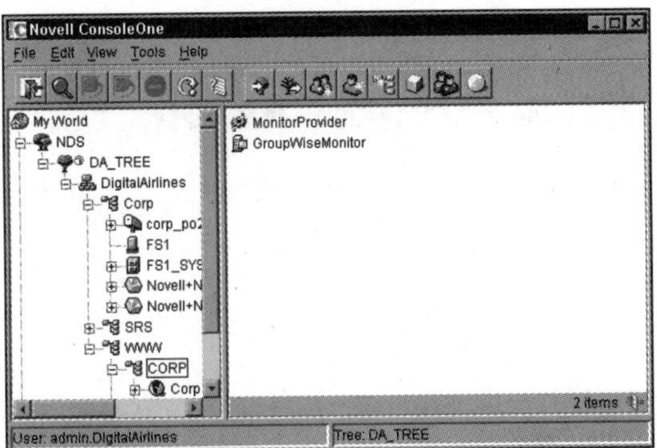

FIGURE 21.20 *GroupWise Monitor Application Components in ConsoleOne*

Starting the GroupWise Monitor Application

The GroupWise monitor application is started automatically when you start your Web server. Since the GroupWise monitor application is a servlet, you actually troubleshoot and configure the GroupWise monitor application as a part of your Web servlet and the servlet gateway. If you are using the Novell servlet gateway, the servlet-gateway administration can be accessed via browser at the following location:

```
http://<web server name or IP address>/servlet/ServletManager
```

NOTE

The servlet gateway is case sensitive with its servlets. So make sure that to access the servlet manager you do use the capital S and M as shown just previous to this note.

You will be prompted for the password to administer the servlet manager before you can administer the Novell servlet gateway.

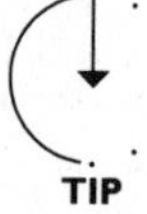

TIP

If you do not know the password needed to administer and troubleshoot the Novell servlet gateway, here's what you would do if your Novell servlet gateway is running on a NetWare server. Go to the SYS:JAVA\SERVLETS directory. Access the SERVLETS.PROPERTIES file and search for the word "password." You should find a line that specifies both the user name and password that you should use. The user name and password are case-sensitive.

Utilizing the GroupWise Monitor Applicaton

To access the GroupWise monitor application go to the following location:

`http://<web server name or IP address>/servlet/gwmonitor`

You should get a screen similar to the one shown in Figure 21.21.

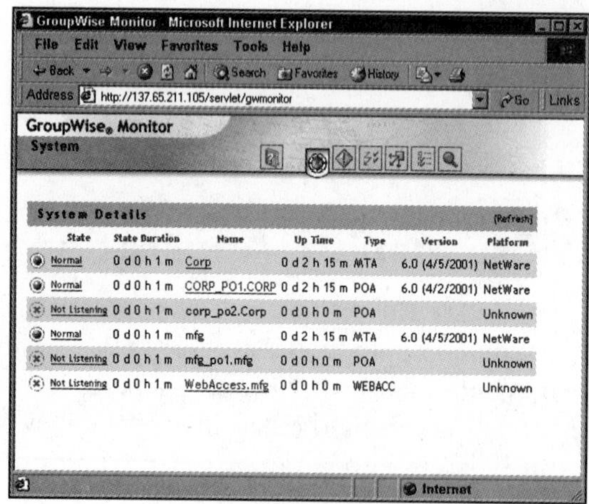

FIGURE 21.21 *GroupWise Monitor Application Client Interface (HTML Frames Version)*

If you use a phone to access GroupWise monitor, the interface looks like the one in Figure 21.22.

NOTE

The GroupWise monitor application for WML is very basic in the GroupWise 6 shipping version, but it should become more robust with successive support packs and revisions of GroupWise 6.

The navigation buttons across the top of GroupWise monitor HTML frames version allow you to switch to one of six views:

- **System:** Kind of an overall view of the agents that your GroupWise monitor agent is monitoring.
- **Problems:** This only shows you the agents that there are problems with.
- **Trace link:** This is a way of checking the status of a link from one domain MTA to another domain's MTA.
- **Check link:** This is very similar to the trace link feature.
- **Preferences:** This shows you preferences that have been set for the GroupWise monitor agent.
- **Search:** This is a way of filtering for certain agents.

The online help in GroupWise monitor gives even more detail on how you might use these features.

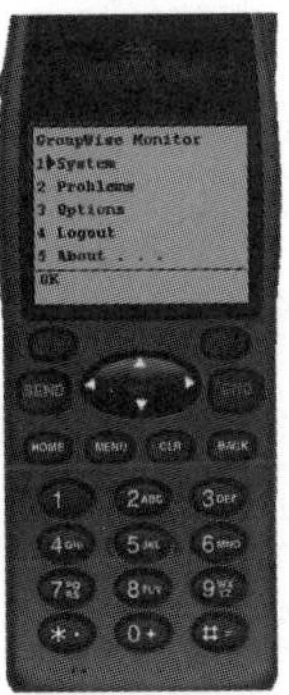

FIGURE 21.22 *GroupWise Monitor Application Client Interface (WML version)*

Summary

This chapter exposed the main functionality of GroupWise monitor. GroupWise monitor's strength is its ability to be customized and accessed from a broad variety of clients. Continue to explore GroupWise monitor, and see how you can customize it to your environment.

CHAPTER 22

Troubleshooting the GroupWise Directory

The GroupWise directory, sometimes referred to as GDS, is largely contained in the WPDOMAIN.DB and WPHOST.DB files. Typically, the most effective way to fix problems in GroupWise directory databases is by rebuilding them using system maintenance in ConsoleOne.

Using the Correct Tools

GroupWise administrators are often unclear which tools to use to fix a GroupWise problem. When a problem appears in the address book, running the mailbox/library maintenance or GroupWise check (GWCHECK) will accomplish nothing. These are the wrong tools to use to fix GroupWise address book/ WPHOST.DB problems.

Reviewing the discussion of GroupWise architecture from Part I for just a moment, there are two kinds of GroupWise databases:

- **GroupWise directory databases:** WPDOMAIN.DB and WPHOST.DB files
- **GroupWise message/information store databases:** These are the *.DB files at any post office, excluding the WPHOST.DB file.

Mailbox/library maintenance, or GWCHECK, is strictly for fixing message store databases. The tool for fixing the GroupWise directory databases is called system maintenance. As discussed in Chapter 7, you find this tool by pulling down the Tools menu and looking under GroupWise Utilities.

Fixing WPHOST.DB Files

In order to discuss repair on a post office database (WPHOST.DB), here is a look at some examples. I have described a few scenarios in this section. These scenarios will help you explore the different options for system maintenance on a WPHOST.DB file.

System Maintenance: Validate, Recover, and Rebuild

For scenario #1, a POA for a particular post office with 400 users is attempting to load. It will not load; instead, it errors out with a C022 error.

When the GroupWise POA for any post office loads up, it first interacts with the WPHOST.DB file, and then loads up the NGWGUARD.DB file. So the question is, which one of those files is to blame for the C022 error? Well, it's hard to tell.

You suspect the WPHOST.DB file could be damaged. If you rebuild the WPHOST.DB file, there's a 50 percent chance that that will fix the problem. Your WPHOST.DB file is 48MB, and in the past, rebuilding this file has taken about an hour to rebuild. That's an expensive amount of time when you only *think* the problem is the WPHOST.DB file! What do you do?

Use the Validate Database option from the System Maintenance tool (see Figure 22.1).

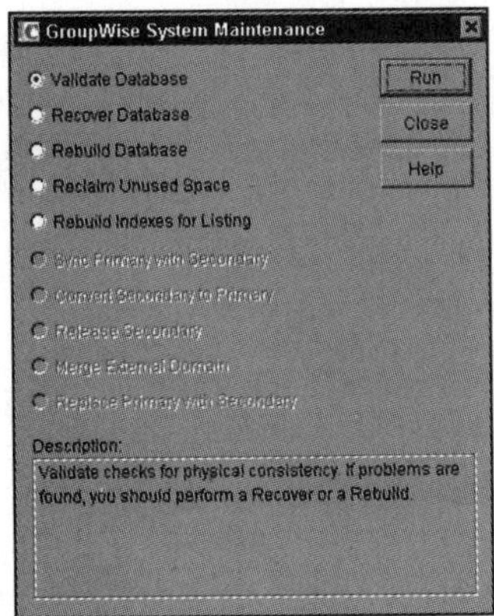

FIGURE 22.1 *System Maintenance: Validate Database*

The validate routine runs a quick structural analysis of a WPHOST.DB file to see if it is physically consistent. The validate routine usually takes under a minute.

Now, suppose that when you run the validate routine you get the error shown in Figure 22.2.

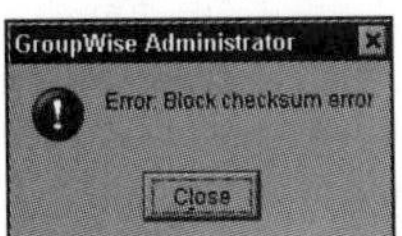

FIGURE 22.2 *Error while Validating a WPHOST.DB File*

Now you know that your theory was right. The WPHOST.DB file is damaged, and rebuilding the WPHOST.DB file is the appropriate measure.

For scenario #2, Mary Smith's name has changed to Mary Jones. You changed her name, but in one post office's address book, Mary's name will not change to Mary Jones.

In this kind of a scenario, you should be less likely to immediately suspect gross structural damage to the WPHOST.DB file. It is more likely that, for some reason, Mary's change didn't get sent down to the post office. Perhaps there is a message flow problem. The simplest thing to do is the following:

1. Synchronize Mary's object, by highlighting it, pulling down the Tools menu, and choosing GroupWise Utilities ➪ Synchronize.
2. Watch the POA for the post office where Mary's name did not change.

In this fictitious example, the POA reports a DBxx error (the xx could represent any two characters) when trying to update Mary's object. Now the question is: Is Mary the only object in this WPHOST.DB file that can't be updated? Can you change information on other users?

To troubleshoot this possibility, the administrator does the following:

1. Synchronize another user.
2. Watch the POA for the post office where Mary's name did not change.

Suppose that the POA didn't report an error when rewriting this other user object to the WPHOST.DB file. However, upon further investigation in the POA log file, you do see other DBxx errors on user objects besides Mary's.

You can conclude that there is definitely a problem with Mary's object in this one WPHOST.DB file. The problem is not specific to Mary's object record, however. It is specific to the block of records in the same location in the WPHOST.DB where Mary's object record is. A few other users' object records are also located in that damaged block in the WPHOST.DB file, which accounts for the other DBxx errors.

You can only assume that there is minor structural damage to the WPHOST.DB file at this particular post office that's getting the error.

Now, suppose that when you discover this problem, it's 10:00 a.m. on a Tuesday morning. To rebuild a WPHOST.DB file, the POA must be down so that you have exclusive access to the WPHOST.DB file.

Rebuilding the WPHOST.DB file to try and fix this problem is out of the question. It's not system critical, because users aren't complaining. You've just stumbled across a problem that you know eventually must be resolved. Suppose further that at your organization you have a very involved procedure to follow if ever you must have downtime during business hours. You want to avoid that procedure.

The system maintenance routine to run in this scenario is called recover database.

Recovering a WPHOST.DB file does not require exclusive access to the WPHOST.DB file. So you run a recover database routine. After doing so, you synchronize Mary's object, and there are no longer errors when synchronizing Mary's object.

The recover database routine quite often does not fix WPHOST.DB damage. In the preceding case, all it did was remove the damaged block of records. Your synchronization of Mary's object was required to complete the fix, because the recover routine just cut out the mushy bad part of the database, but it didn't replace the records that were lost. This is because the recover database routine only extracts information from the same WPHOST.DB file that you are trying to recover. The recover database routine is working with an information source that you already know to be questionable. If you can use the recover database routine to help you get along, that's great, but it should be considered a Band-Aid approach to get you past business hours. After hours, you should rebuild the WPHOST.DB file.

General Notes on Repairing Post Office Databases

The great thing about GroupWise architecture is that WPHOST.DB files can always be rebuilt, and with a 100 percent guarantee against data loss. This is because everything written to the WPHOST.DB file is guaranteed to have been written to its owning domain's WPDOMAIN.DB file. When rebuilding a WPHOST.DB file, GroupWise administration is doing so from the perspective of the post office's owning domain.

The system maintenance routines are not the best way to resolve all GroupWise directory problems, however. For example, if a user's record is missing or incorrect from a post office's address book, synchronizing the user may be a simpler fix. Doing a synchronize on a user's object, or any GroupWise object for that matter, repropagates that object to all GroupWise directory databases. This is far, far better than rebuilding every database on the system just to get one record right.

Fixing WPDOMAIN.DB Files

GroupWise WPDOMAIN.DB files should be approached differently than GroupWise WPHOST.DB files. Here are some concepts to keep in mind when repairing WPDOMAIN.DB files:

- Secondary domain databases are always rebuilt from the perspective of the primary domain's WPDOMAIN.DB file.
- The primary domain and its secondary domains may not always be in sync.
- In some circumstances (but rarely), going to backup for a WPDOMAIN.DB file may be the best solution.
- On some rare occasions, rebuilding a domain database may actually cause more problems than it fixes.

The best way to explore these concepts is through some scenarios.

For scenario #1, you are connected to the primary domain. You attempt to connect to DOMAINC, and when trying to do so, you get the error shown in Figure 22.3.

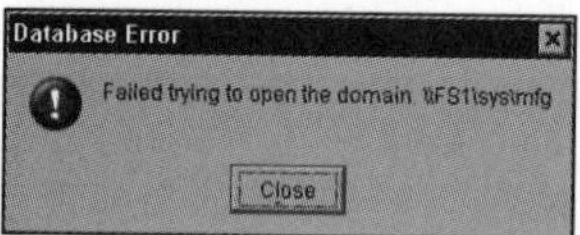

FIGURE 22.3 *Damaged WPDOMAIN.DB Error*

This error is telling you that your attempt to connect to the WPDOMAIN.DB for DOMAINC could not be changed because of a problem with the WPDOMAIN.DB for DOMAINC. Upon further investigation, you also see that the MTA for DOMAINC is not loaded. Things aren't looking good for DOMAINC's domain database.

It's a safe bet that DOMAINC's WPDOMAIN.DB file is corrupt beyond use. You could validate this theory by running a validate operation against DOMAINC. It will give some kind of an error, such as `Error opening database`. The WPDOMAIN.DB file needs to be replaced. The question then is should the WPDOMAIN.DB file be replaced from backup tape, or should it be rebuilt?

Theory tells us that everything that is in a secondary domain's WPDOMAIN.DB file is replicated up to the primary domain. If there is no reason to believe that this process of replication was impeded, then don't hesitate to rebuild the DOMAINC WPDOMAIN.DB file. The WPDOMAIN.DB for DOMAINC is rebuilt from the WPDOMAIN.DB of the primary domain.

The decision to rebuild a WPDOMAIN.DB file rather than bringing it back from backup largely depends upon your administration model. Suppose that you and one other person administer your GroupWise system. You both connect to the primary domain for all of your administration and only connect to a secondary domain occasionally. In this scenario, with an understanding of architecture, there is no reason to recover a secondary domain database from tape. The primary domain already knows about changes made to that secondary domain, because it proposed all of the changes.

Now consider the following twist: Suppose there is a damaged secondary domain that is in one of your field offices. The secondary domain is administered by someone out in the field, and their WAN link to you is often unreliable. You and the domain administrator already concur that some of the changes that have been made on the secondary domain may never have made it up to the primary domain. If the field office has a recent backup of the WPDOMAIN.DB file, their copy may be the most accurate about the objects they own.

If they recover their WPDOMAIN.DB from backup tape, then you have a new procedure to consider. You can assume that their WPDOMAIN.DB file is accurate, minus any changes that they have made in their domain since the backup. The secondary domain administrator can worry about remaking those changes. As long as they didn't add, rename, or delete any users, it's not a big deal. Unfortunately, this secondary domain's WPDOMAIN.DB database is not going to be accurate regarding the changes made to the rest of the GroupWise system. To make matters more confusing, the primary domain database is not going to be accurate regarding objects owned by this out-of-sync secondary domain.

If you rebuild this secondary domain, the field office will lose some changes that the primary domain never knew about, unless, of course, you synchronize the primary domain with the secondary domain first. Here is the procedure:

1. Highlight the secondary domain.
2. Choose Tools ➪ GroupWise Utilities ➪ System Maintenance
3. Select Sync Primary with Secondary and click Run.
4. Once that procedure is complete, you may rebuild the secondary domain database.

NOTE

You will need file access to the secondary domain to go through this procedure. Since it is a field office with unstable WAN connections, you ought to consider bringing a copy of their domain database to your local site. When you are prompted for the path to the domain database to synchronize with, and later to rebuild, you can point to your local drive, or to a location on the network.

You had to synchronize the primary domain with the secondary domain so that the primary domain knew about the changes made to the secondary domain. When a secondary domain is rebuilt, it is done from the perspective of the primary domain. The secondary domain database on disk is ignored altogether. The Sync Primary with Secondary operation took care of this for you, pushing up the secondary domain's information, on the objects it owns, to the primary domain. Then when the secondary domain is rebuilt just after the synchronize, the secondary domain will get all of those objects back correctly. The secondary domain will also have all of the correct information about the state of the GroupWise objects throughout the rest of the GroupWise system.

For scenario #2, the primary domain WPDOMAIN.DB file is corrupt beyond repair.

First of all, as a responsible network administrator, you should certainly have a backup of your primary domain. The question is whether restoring that backup is going to be the best thing to do. Typically, it is *not* the best solution.

The primary domain WPDOMAIN.DB file on your backup will quite likely be outdated, especially if your system is administered from multiple secondary domain sites. Your best hope will be a secondary domain that you feel is likely to be in sync with the primary domain. Recall the GroupWise architecture. The GroupWise primary domain broadcasts all changes made to all domains to every other domain. In theory then, if everything is in sync, a secondary domain is just as well informed about the state of the GroupWise directory as the primary domain. You now need to generate a copy of the primary domain database from a secondary domain. Here is the procedure:

1. Connect to the secondary domain that is most likely to be in sync with the primary domain.
2. Highlight the primary domain.
3. Choose Tools ➪ GroupWise Utilities ➪ System Maintenance.
4. Select the Replace Primary with Secondary option, as shown in Figure 22.4.

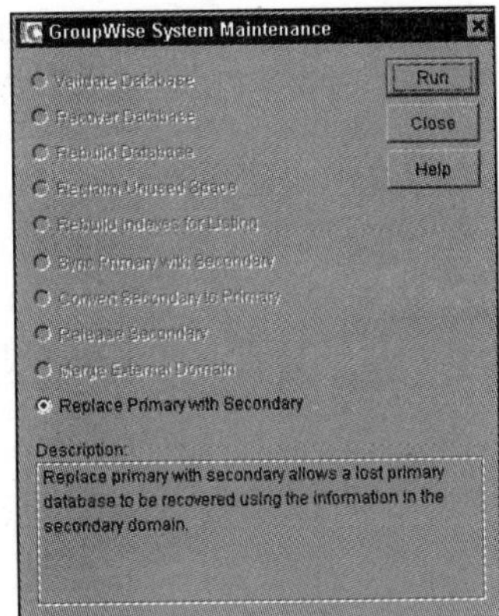

FIGURE 22.4 *Replace Primary with Secondary*

Fixing GroupWise Directory Anomalies without Rebuilds

There are other problems in the GroupWise directory that can't be readily fixed with system maintenance routines. In some cases, system maintenance routines could fix the problem, but you may want to avoid the downtime associated with rebuilding databases.

I have seen cases where an object is acting stubborn. You may need to slap it around a bit to get it to behave. Usually, these kinds of problems occur with user objects.

NOTE

Technically, user objects cannot act stubborn. I simply enjoy the anthropomorphism more than I should. The cases described here usually result when a single field in a record is out of sync, and perhaps damaged. By repeatedly attempting to rewrite that record, the field problem may be corrected.

The following are the things that can be done to a user object to get it to behave. They are listed in the order of least drastic to most drastic measures. Most of the ideas here would also apply to other GroupWise objects:

- Synchronize the user.
- Edit the user and make a minor change, click OK, and then remove the change.
- Remove GroupWise attributes on the user.
- Delete the NDS portion of a GroupWise user.

First, when zeroing in on an object, be sure to connect to the domain that owns that object. This will speed up your troubleshooting significantly, since GroupWise administration snap-ins will write the change directly, instead of passing the change through multiple MTAs.

Synchronize the User

Following are the steps for synchronizing a user object:

1. Highlight the user object.
2. Choose Tools ➪ GroupWise Utilities ➪ Synchronize.
3. Click Yes on the resulting dialog box.

This action rewrites the user's object to the WPDOMAIN.DB file, with much of the information coming from NDS. The synchronize also re-broadcasts the user's object record to all GroupWise directory databases. For a complete look at this process, refer to the synchronize section of Chapter 7.

Edit the User

This is much like synchronizing the user, but it is a different operation, and sometimes you'll have more success this way then by synchronizing the user.

1. Highlight the user object.
2. Right-click and select Properties.
3. Make an unobtrusive change to the object.

   Don't change the object name, or post office, or anything like that. Change a fax number, or something similar.
4. Click OK.

This action also re-propagates the record to every domain and post office on the system. The difference here is that there is new record data involved, which may make a difference in some cases.

Remove GroupWise Attributes

To troubleshoot using GroupWise attributes, follow these steps:

1. Highlight the user object.
2. Choose Tools ➪ GroupWise Utilities ➪ GW/NDS Association ➪ Disassociate GroupWise Attributes.

Technically, this only changes the object in NDS, but it may allow you to work with an object in spite of NDS problems that are preventing you from making changes.

Delete the NDS Portion of a User Object

To do this, I like to be unsnapped from the GroupWise snap-ins. This way you are sure that you are deleting only the NDS portion of a user object, and not the GroupWise object itself.

First, you need to disable the ConsoleOne GroupWise snap-ins.

1. Get out of ConsoleOne.
2. Copy the GROUPWISE folder and its contents from the NOVELL\CONSOLEONE\<VERSION>\SNAPINS directory to another location.
3. Delete the GROUPWISE folder temporarily.

   When ConsoleOne is unsnapped from GroupWise, all GroupWise objects show up with an icon that looks like a question mark on the right-hand side of a 3D box.
4. Start ConsoleOne, and make sure that under the Tools menu there are no GroupWise menus, as shown in Figure 22.5.
5. Highlight the user in question and delete that user's NDS object.
6. Put the GroupWise snap-ins for ConsoleOne back into place by copying the GROUPWISE folder from the temporary location back to the NOVELL\CONSOLEONE\<VERSION>\SNAPINS directory.

After the dust has settled from deleting the user's NDS object, you will want to create the user's NDS object again. Don't create the user's NDS object from a template that associates them with a GroupWise account though. The GroupWise account is already created. The balance of these steps helps you establish the NDS account again, and associate it with the GroupWise account.

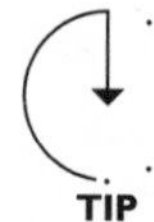

Before trying to create the NDS user object, wait for a while, at least 15 minutes, if not an hour.

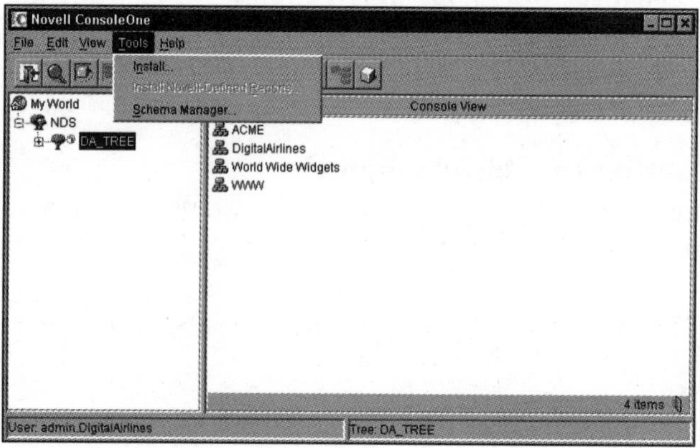

FIGURE 22.5 *GroupWise Snap-Ins Disabled*

7. Load ConsoleOne, and be sure to be connected to the WPDOMAIN.DB file for the domain that this deleted user is a member of.

   Create the user in the exact NDS OU that you deleted the user from before.
8. Edit the NDS object, and go to the GroupWise Account page.
9. Select the browse button that looks like a globe, to the right of the Post Office field.
10. Select the post office that the user is a member of.
11. Select Apply, and you should get the Possible Match Found prompt similar to the one in Figure 22.6.

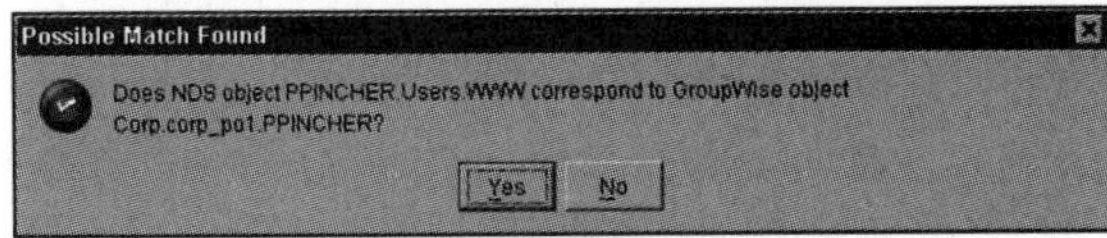

FIGURE 22.6 *Possible Match Found*

How GroupWise Directory Changes and Objects Get Replicated

When troubleshooting the GroupWise directory, it's helpful to understand how changes replicate in the GroupWise directory. The following is an exhaustive discussion on how one object got replicated.

Short Explanation

GroupWise object replication basically moves up from a secondary domain to the primary domain and from the primary domain to all other domains. Each domain is responsible for replicating objects to their respective post offices.

Objects, and changes to objects or records, in the GroupWise directory get replicated in the very same manner.

Long Explanation

Now for the long explanation, consider the following scenario:

- USERA = User
- DOMAINB = secondary domain
- PO2 = PO off of DOMAINB
- DOMAINA = primary domain
- PO1 = PO off of DOMAINA
- DOMAINC = secondary domain
- DOMAIND = secondary domain

A GroupWise administrator is connected to DOMAINB. The administrator creates USERA. USERA is added to PO2. Here's what happens:

1. USERA's record is committed to the WPDOMAIN.DB file for DOMAINB by the NetWare administrator.
2. USERA's record is broadcast to PO2 by DOMAINB's MTA.
3. USERA's record is broadcast to DOMAINA's MTA by DOMAINB's MTA.
4. PO2's POA accepts USERA's record and commits it to PO2's WPHOST.DB file.
5. DOMAINA's MTA accepts USERA's record and commits it to DOMAINA's WPDOMAIN.DB file.
6. DOMAINA's MTA broadcasts USERA's record to its post office PO1.
7. PO1's POA accepts USERA's record and commits it to PO1's WPHOST.DB file.
8. DOMAINA broadcasts USERA's record to all other domains in the system besides DOMAINB. This includes DOMAINC and DOMAIND.
9. DOMAINC accepts the broadcast of USERA and does everything that DOMAINA did with the object, except it does not broadcast USERA to anyone outside its domain. That is DOMAINA's job.
10. DOMAIND does exactly what DOMAINC does.

Very, Very Long Explanation

The following is a very detailed scenario that shows the file flow and the logic of a user object creation. The names of the files are only relevant to the operation that took place on a test system. The names of the files created on your system will be different.

- USERA = User
- DOMAINB = secondary domain
- PO2 = PO off of DOMAINB
- DOMAINA = primary domain
- PO1 = PO off of DOMAINA
- DOMAINC = secondary domain
- DOMAIND = secondary domain

For this scenario, communication between all domains and post offices is via TCP/IP.

1. Connected to DOMAINB, the administrator creates a user object, USERA, under DOMAINB, PO2.
2. The change is committed to the DOMAINB WPDOMAIN.DB file.
3. There are two files created in the DOMAINB\WPCSIN\2 directory:

   File one is called A7D93EDD.000.

   File two is called A7D93EDD.001.
4. File one is picked up by DOMAINB's MTA and copied to the GWINPROG\2 directory using a router thread (RTR), and moved to the input queue for the MTP portion of the MTA.

   DOMAINB's MTA log reports the following:

   ```
   RTR: DOMAINB: 00000800: Routing
   comm3/sys:\domainb\mslocal\gwinprog\2\00000800


   RTR: DOMAINB: 00000800: Originator: DOMAINB.Domain Message
   Server [ADS]
   RTR: DOMAINB: 00000800 Priority 10  :0:0 : Transfer to DOMAINA


   RTR: DOMAINB: 00000800: Message queued:
   comm3/sys:\domainb\mslocal\mshold\dom3859\2\00000800.001
   ```
5. The MTP portion of the DOMAINB MTA finds the file and transmits it to DOMAINA, the primary domain. Note that the name of the thread is DOMAINA-IPS0 but that this is a thread created by DOMAINB's MTA.

   DOMAINB's MTA log reports the following:

   ```
   MTP: DOMAINA-ipS0: Connection established. 151.155.106.66
   MTP: DOMAINA-ipS0: Transmitting file
   comm3/sys:\domainb\mslocal\mshold\dom3859\2\00000800.001
   ```
6. A new copy of the message is also made for PO2, and queued up to the MTP process of the DOMAINB MTA.

   DOMAINB's MTA log reports the following:

   ```
   RTR: DOMAINB: 00000801: Routing
   comm3/sys:\domainb\mslocal\gwinprog\2\00000801
   ```

continued

```
RTR: DOMAINB: 00000801: Originator: DOMAINB.Domain Message
Server [ADS]

RTR: DOMAINB: 00000801 Priority 10  :0:0 : Transfer to
DOMAINB.PO2:ADS

RTR: DOMAINB: 00000801: Message queued:
comm3/sys:\domainb\mslocal\mshold\po23a0e\2\00000801.001
```

7. DOMAINB's MTA transmits the file to PO2 and reports the following in the log:

```
MTP: PO2-ipS0: Transmitting file
comm3/sys:\domainb\mslocal\mshold\po23a0e\2\00000801.001
```

8. PO2's POA MTP process reports the following about receiving the message from the domain:

```
MTP: Receiver thread started: 1 running
MTP: DOMAINB: Attention packet received
MTP: DOMAINB: Accepting connection
MTP: DOMAINB: Returning acknowledge (0)
MTP: DOMAINB: File transfer request received

MTP: DOMAINB: Received file:
COMM3\SYS:/DOMAINB/PO2\wpcsout\ofs\2\A7d950d6

MTP: DOMAINB: Returning acknowledge (3)

Processing a7d950d6.000
Domain Message Server.DOMAINB
Admin message processed: OK
MTP: DOMAINB: File transfer request received

MTP: DOMAINB: Received file:
COMM3\SYS:/DOMAINB/PO2\wpcsout\ofs\2\A7d950d8

MTP: DOMAINB: Returning acknowledge (3)
```

```
Processing a7d950d8.000
Domain Message Server.DOMAINB
Admin message processed: OK
```

9. The POA places the administration files in the WPCSOUT\ADS\2 directory. They are called 37D950D6.000 and 37D950D8.000.

10. The delivery thread on the POA then tickles the admin thread of the POA (this does not show in the log — the event takes place in the POA stack, behind the scenes).

    The admin thread reports the following:

    ```
    ADM: Completed: Update object in Post Office - User
    DOMAINB.PO2.USERA (Administrator: (T2-TREE) tkratzer.Novell,
    Domain: DOMAINB)
    ADM: Completed: Update object in Post Office - MTA DOMAINB
    (Administrator: (ACME) tkratzer.ACME1, Domain: DOMAINB)
    ```

    Meanwhile, on DOMAINA (the primary domain) . . .

11. DOMAINA's MTA is receiving the file from DOMAINB's MTA.

    DOMAINA's MTA log reports the following:

    ```
    MTP: DOMAINB: Received file:
    comm3/sys:\domaina\mslocal\gwinprog\2\00000801


    RTR: DOMAINA: 00000801: Routing
    comm3/sys:\domaina\mslocal\gwinprog\2\00000801
    ```

12. DOMAINA's MTA identifies the message as an administrative message and queues the message up to its admin thread in the WPCSOUT\ADS\2 directory.

    DOMAINA's MTA log reports the following:

    ```
    RTR: DOMAINA: 00000801: Originator: DOMAINB.Domain Message
    Server [ADS]


    RTR: DOMAINA: 00000801 Priority 10  :0:0 : Transfer to
    DOMAINA.Domain Message Server:ADS


    RTR: DOMAINA: 00000801: Message queued:
    comm3/sys:\domaina\wpcsout\ads\2\B7d94d48.00!
    ```

13. DOMAINA's MTA tickles the admin thread, and the admin thread reports the following:

    ```
    ADM: Completed: Update replica User DOMAINB.PO2.USERA
    ```

14. DOMAINA's MTA then queues the message up to its post office, PO1.

    It does this in the exact manner in which the DOMAINB MTA queued up the change to PO2.

15. DOMAINA's MTA then broadcasts the administration message to both DOMAINC and DOMAIND in the same manner that DOMAINB broadcast the administration message up to DOMAINA.

16. DOMAINC and DOMAIND's MTAs broadcast the administration message to their post offices, just as DOMAINB broadcast its administration message to PO2.

A very simple operation in GroupWise administration becomes a file that must be replicated to all other GroupWise directory databases.

Best Practices for Working with the GroupWise Directory

For a large GroupWise system, here are some good rules:

- **If you perform large operations, such as grafting or modifying multiple users on a domain, GroupWise administrator should be connected to the domain that owns the objects being modified.** If you do not do this, you will generate about 50 percent more administration traffic between domains than you need to. This means that not all of your administration will be done through the primary domain.
- **If your system has a lot of administration messages flowing through it, implement the 2nd Mail Priority Router on the primary domain MTA.** To do this, edit the MTA object, go to the Agents Settings page, and check the box named 2nd High Priority Router. This will provide an additional thread for processing admin messages, making bottlenecks at the MTA a little less likely.
- **Design your GroupWise system so that your primary domain is only doing administrative work.** If the primary domain is housing the GWIA,

or is a routing hub for all other domains, then it may not be efficient enough in servicing GroupWise administration changes. It is even ideal to see to it that the primary domain has no post offices off of it.

Bulletproofing the GroupWise Directory

The following practice is not widespread, but it is definitely worth mentioning. This idea came about when a customer's primary domain WPDOMAIN.DB file went bad. The idea of going to backup just wasn't all that pleasing because of all the changes made in the system since they did their last backup. The customer needed to re-create the primary domain from a secondary domain.

The system maintenance feature, Replace Primary with Secondary, is a lifesaver, but it raises an important question: How do you guarantee the integrity of a secondary domain database, ensuring that you'll have a fail-safe backup if your primary domain goes bad?

Here is a way to do just that:

1. Create a secondary domain called BACKUP-PRIMARY-DOMAIN, host it somewhere in your network, in close reach of the primary domain.

   Ideally, it should be on a separate server, but on the same LAN segment as the server hosting the primary domain.

   You need to disable others from connecting to this WPDOMAIN.DB file with ConsoleOne. You do this by tricking all domains into thinking that this secondary domain is at a different UNC path, than it really is. Steps 2 and 3 help you do this.
2. While connected to the primary domain, change the UNC path to the secondary domain BACKUP-PRIMARY-DOMAIN to make it invalid.
3. Restrict NDS object rights to this domain so that only a few people even have NDS rights to this domain object.
4. Establish MTA to MTA links so that only the primary domain can speak to this domain.
5. Make the link a TCP/IP link between the two domains.

IMPORTANT **In order to connect to the BACKUP-PRIMARY-DOMAIN domain, you will always need to choose Tools ➪ GroupWise System Operations ➪ Select Domain, and then manually attach to the WPDOMAIN.DB for this domain. Doing a right-mouse-click and then clicking Connect won't work because the UNC path to the BACKUP-PRIMARY-DOMAIN is incorrect.**

The system now has, in effect, a fully replicated version of the primary domain database, which is only about one minute out of sync with the primary domain. Should the primary domain database get irretrievably corrupted (in the case of a major disk failure, for instance), you will have a secondary domain database that is the best possible candidate for use in a Replace Primary with Secondary operation. Just connect manually to the WPDOMAIN.DB for the BACKUP-PRIMARY-DOMAIN and then perform the Replace Primary with Secondary system maintenance routine.

Understanding the Administration System

The administration of the GroupWise system goes hand-in-hand with the GroupWise directory. The administration system of GroupWise consists of two separates sets of software components:

- GroupWise administrator snap-ins to ConsoleOne
- The admin threads of the MTA and the POA

The GroupWise Snap-Ins

The GroupWise administration snap-ins are often misunderstood. Administrators are quite often cognizant of the version of the GroupWise client, or the version of the GroupWise agents. There is often little emphasis put on determining the version of GroupWise administration.

The version of administration is especially important when you have implemented a patch or a new version of GroupWise, and you really want to leverage the new fixes or features in that patch or new version. As discussed in Chapter 7, in order to determine the version of GroupWise administration you are using, do the following:

1. Load ConsoleOne.

2. Choose Help ➪ About Snapins, and you should see a screen as shown in Figure 22.7.

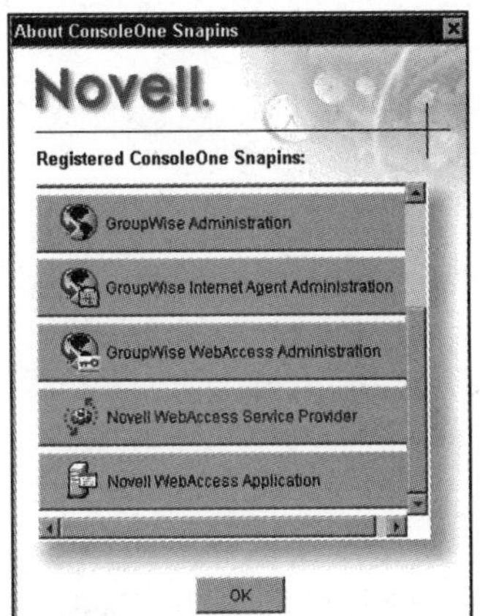

FIGURE 22.7 *About Snapins in ConsoleOne*

3. Click on a snap-in to see its version information.

Is this the version you want to be running? If this is the right version, is this version of the GroupWise snap-ins on every file server or workstation where ConsoleOne is running?

A lot of Novell's customers have a huge GroupWise installation that is managed by several administrators. It is important that everyone who runs ConsoleOne is using the latest GroupWise snap-ins, or at least the latest ones that have been approved for your organization. If this is not the case, someone may be causing problems in the GroupWise system — problems due to bugs that may already have been addressed in a later patch of the GroupWise administrator snap-ins.

Understanding the GroupWise Admin Thread

Before GroupWise 5.5 and GroupWise 6, the admin thread was actually a separate agent. It was the administration agent, or ADA, in GroupWise 5.0 through 5.2. In GroupWise 4.1, the admin server was called ADS. It is helpful to know this because as you explore the GroupWise system, you will actually see the terms ADA and ADS used. In GroupWise 6, ADS, ADA, and ADM all mean the admin thread.

In GroupWise 6, the admin thread is just a sub-process of the MTA and the POA. In the MTA and POA log files when the admin thread runs, it is logged as ADM. This chapter discussed this earlier, and this concept is also discussed in Chapters 8 and 9.

The admin thread on an MTA or POA is responsible for updating its respective directory database. This admin thread has two input queues:

- **The ADS directory queue:** The first input queue for the admin thread is the WPCSOUT\ADS\2 directory off of a post office or domain. The admin thread comes to life every minute. For example, when an POA's admin thread discovers a file in the PO\WPCSOUT\ADS\2 directory, it makes a change in the WPHOST.DB file. If a domain MTA's admin thread discovers a file in the WPCSOUT\ADS\2 directory, it makes the appropriate change to the WPDOMAIN.DB file.
- **The Tickle queue:** The admin thread will also come to life when it gets a tickle from the POA or MTA that owns the thread. In GroupWise 6, although the admin thread comes to life every minute, when an MTA or POA gets an administration message via a TCP/IP connection, it queues the message up to the admin thread by a routine in memory. At the GroupWise domain/MTA level, quite often administration files do not even go into the WPCSOUT\ADS\2 directory because they are just handed off to the admin thread while they are in the GWINPROG directory off of the MSLOCAL directory.

Summary

There are a variety of ways to fix a GroupWise directory problem. You need to determine what the problem is and determine the most expedient solution. With an understanding of the architecture, you will be better able to troubleshoot these problems and find the best solutions.

Always remember that the GroupWise synchronization process is complex, and that several GroupWise agents may need to be involved in order to replicate an object. Make sure every agent is communicating correctly before going further.

CHAPTER 23

Troubleshooting GroupWise

Every application, or suite of applications, has its own particular set of error messages. GroupWise is no exception. As you administer your GroupWise system, you will inevitably see some of these errors. This chapter discusses the logic behind these errors and gives you some procedures to help you quickly arrive at the root of the problem that is plaguing you.

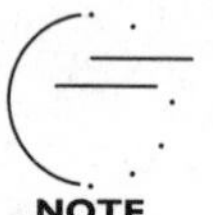

NOTE

For information specific to troubleshooting GroupWise message flow, refer to Chapter 19.

Using the Scientific Method

Before beginning, it may not be a bad idea to review the scientific method. Most high-school science students learn that this method has four important steps:

1. Observe
2. Hypothesize
3. Predict, based upon the hypothesis
4. Test the hypothesis

The scientific method provides you with a very effective plan for troubleshooting. Too often, administrators are so wound up in their search for a solution, they shoot from the hip, hoping perhaps to stumble on the answer. Sometimes this works.

Sometimes, though, you'll encounter a real stumper of a problem, and the standard bag of tricks isn't going to help. These stumpers are where the scientific method is going to help out.

Observation Tools

The most important part of the scientific method is the observation phase. For the scientific method to work well for you, you need to know about a good set of observation tools. Only by using tools to carefully observe the conditions that are generating the errors will you be able to make meaningful predictions. Here are some tools that will allow you to take a close look at components in your GroupWise system.

Windows Workstations/Servers

The following tools are for Windows-based systems:

- **WINIPCFG (Win95/98 only):** This utility tells you vital information about IP configuration of the local machine.
- **IPCONFIG:** This command-line version of the WINIPCFG utility tells you vital information about IP configuration of the local machine.
- **PING:** The PING tool allows you to send small packets via TCP/IP to any host on the network or internetwork (or Internet, for that matter). If you can't connect to the POA, perhaps you should see if you can ping it.
- **TELNET:** The TELNET tool allows you to open a TCP/IP connection on any port, to any host on the network or Internet. If you can't connect to the POA with the GroupWise client, perhaps you should see if you can connect to port 1677 (the client/server port) of the POA using the TELNET tool.
- **REGMON:** This utility tells you what calls are being made to the registry. It takes a while to get savvy with this utility, but once you do it's great for determining what registry entries are causing a problem. Registry Monitor can be obtained from `www.sysinternals.com`.
- **FILEMON:** This utility is similar to REGMON, except that it will tell you every file on a Windows platform that is accessed. This utility may also be obtained from `www.sysinternals.com`.

NetWare Servers

These tools will work on your NetWare-based systems:

- **PING.NLM:** This is the NetWare version of the PING tool. It allows you to choose the packet size, and will even keep some simple statistical tallies as you ping hosts from the server console.
- **GWIP.NLM:** This tool is a little better than a ping, and almost as good as a TELNET. Since there is no true TELNET tool for a NetWare server, GWIP.NLM is an excellent addition to your troubleshooting toolkit. It can be obtained from `support.novell.com`. Go to the file finder and do a search for GWIP.NLM.
- **TCPCON.NLM:** Load TCPCON and then go to Protocol Information ➪ TCP ➪ TCP Connections. You can see if a GroupWise agent is actually listening on a port.

- **MONITOR.NLM:** Here you can get an idea of how your system resources are faring. Look at things such as the Disk Cache Utilization ➪ LRU Sitting time. (This is the menu tree on a NetWare 5.x server.) This value should be well above 15 minutes. You can also see which server processes are taking up the most CPU time. This is a very powerful and complex tool.

GroupWise Error Codes

Now that you have a few more observation tools in your scientific method toolbox, you need to know what the error codes mean. Most problems reported by GroupWise components are accompanied with some kind of a four-character error code, such as `8201` or `C05D`. These codes map to certain kinds of problems. Rather than memorizing the individual mappings, however, it is useful to learn the families, or classes, of error codes.

82xx Errors

The 82xx class of errors indicates some sort of file access or file I/O problem. Perhaps the POA is trying to access a database at a given path, but the database is not there (`8209, path not found`). Perhaps file-system rights have not been granted to an MTA that is attempting to poll a remote post office (`8201, access denied`).

89xx Errors

You will generally see 89xx errors in conjunction with TCP/IP communication problems. For example, if a POA goes down, the GroupWise Client will report an 8908 error. If the MTA times out on a communication with a POA, it may report an 8912 or an 8913 error. The 89xx error suite also includes many errors outside of the realm of TCP/IP communications, but the non-TCP/IP errors do not crop up much.

Cxxx Errors

The Cxxx errors typically point to database structural integrity problems. For example, a user gets C022 errors when creating any item in GroupWise. The error means that database integrity has been compromised. Maybe the error is a C04F error, which means that the database checksum did not add up correctly. In either case, you know from the error class that structural damage has been done to a GroupWise store file.

There are two Cxxx-class errors that are a little bit different: C05D and C067. Both of these errors indicate structural damage to the information/message store, rather than just to one store file. This means that one or more store files are not correctly registered in the GroupWise guardian database. C05D means that a registered store file could not be found. C067 means that a store file could not be created, because an unregistered version exists on disk.

Dxxx Errors

The Dxxx class of errors points to database content problems. The problem may be a missing record, which will return a D107 error. In the case of a missing user record (when the POA tries to deliver to a user who does not exist in the address book), you might see a D101 error. The problem might not be that a record is missing, though. It may simply be that the data does not match what the GroupWise component was expecting to see, like when the entered password does not match the one required (`D109, access denied`).

Exxx Errors

The Exxx class of errors changes the rules a bit. Instead of mapping to a kind of database problem or I/O problem, E-class error messages indicate that the problem was found while using a document-management feature. The error state may actually indicate a normal situation, such as when a user tries to access a document that he or she has not been given rights to (E51B). It may also indicate a content problem with the document-management databases. A missing document record will return an E811 error.

Using the Error Classes

If you know what each error class means, you will still be missing an important piece of the puzzle. Most GroupWise errors tell you what kind of a problem was encountered, but do not tell you which component had the problem. For instance, if the GroupWise client is encountering structural problems working with the GroupWise archive, it will probably report a C022 or C04F error. Those are the same errors the POA would use to report problems with a message database in the post office directory. The same exact error can be reported by two different components, and it can be caused by a problem in any of several different areas.

The only way you can know which component has the problem is by applying some of the architectural information available in the rest of the book. Here are some questions you can ask yourself that may help you out:

- **What component reported the error?** For instance, if the POA reports a C022, you will see the error in the log. Check the log to see if there is any other information about the problem. Generally, the POA will report which database it's having a problem with.

- **What components do not report the error?** Suppose the client reports an error, but the POA does not. This would narrow things down quite a bit for you. The databases that a client has exclusive access to over the POA are the archive databases and the caching mode and remote databases.
- **What pieces are touched by the component(s) that report(s) the error?** If you know, for instance, that the client reported an error, but the POA did not, you would need to then know what pieces the Client touches that the POA does not. In client/server access mode, the problem would likely be the GroupWise archive. In direct access mode, the problem could be the master mailbox or the archive.

The Complete List of GroupWise Error Messages

As of this writing, Novell has not published a complete list of the error codes used by all GroupWise components. Fortunately, the errors you are likely to see have been well documented, and appear online at Novell's support connection Web site.

The Novell Support Connection When you see an error message, you can look it up in the knowledge base at `http://support.novell.com`. The odds are really, really good that you are not the first person to see this message. This method is good for looking up messages one at a time, as you encounter them.

GroupWise Magazine GroupWise has its own magazine. It's a great tool for administrators and users alike. I also write for this magazine. To access this magazine, go to one of the following locations:

`www.gwmag.com`

`www.novell.com/coolsolutions/gwmag/`

Use the Support Connection

Now that I've told you about how to apply the scientific method with the GroupWise error classes, I am going to take it all back. Don't troubleshoot if you don't have to!

Novell has a world-class support site. Use the knowledge base at `http://support.novell.com` before you begin racking your brains. In most cases, the exact set of conditions you are seeing has already been documented by Novell Technical Services, and one or more ready-made solutions await you. Why reinvent the wheel?

- **Boolean search tips:** As you use Novell's support connection Web site, there are a couple of things you can do to make your searches faster and more productive.
  - **Use quotation marks:** If you are looking for a literal error message, put that string in quotation marks. This will pull up only the documents that include the string you entered.
  - **Use the Boolean AND:** If you are looking for keywords (GWIA and virus, for instance) be sure to put the word AND (capitalized) between them. This tells the search engine to look for documents that have both words, not just one or the other.
- **Changes to the support connection:** For years, Novell customers have needed to be Boolean search experts to quickly find the information they were looking for. At the time of this writing, Novell is employing new technology as documents are created, in hopes of allowing for a new, friendlier interface.Novell has implemented this new technology at the following location:

  `http://solutionet.novell.com`

  For the foreseeable future, however, those of you who employ these Boolean search tips will still be able to find things the way you are used to finding them.

Using Three-Step Mailbox Troubleshooting

On a large system, you may see mailbox-related errors often enough that you don't want to take the time to actually troubleshoot each one. Well, a GroupWise administrator I worked with passed along a gem. This administrator takes a standard approach to every problem they get with a user mailbox, no matter what the error is. This approach fixes about 80 percent of their problems right off the bat.

The nice thing about this approach is that the operations you will be performing are not invasive or destructive. These actions can be performed on a healthy mailbox with no ill effects. This means that almost no matter what the problem you are having, you can take these steps safely.

So, when are you going to use this procedure? Here are some possible cases:

- One user gets errors trying to send new messages.
- Everybody gets errors trying to send to one particular user.
- A user reports that messages he/she has read are showing up as being unread.

This list could go on and on. Suffice it to say that if you think the problem is related in any way to the GroupWise message/information store, this procedure is a good place to start.

There are three things that need to be done, and they need to be done in order:

1. Synchronize the user.
2. Run a structural rebuild on the user database using GWCHECK (server-based, or stand-alone — see Chapter 17 for more details).
3. Run an analyze/fix of the contents of the user database (do not include the message database).

The logic behind these steps is simple. First, make sure that the user object you want to work on is correctly represented in the post office database. The synchronize operation takes care of that.

Second, make sure that the user database for this user is structurally clean, with no damaged blocks or records for you to choke on. The structural rebuild operation takes care of this.

Finally, you want to make sure that all records in the user database correctly point to records elsewhere in the information store. The analyze/fix operation does this for you.

The rest of this section walks through each of these operations in turn.

- **Synchronize the user:** The synchronize function, covered in Chapter 7, broadcasts a user's GroupWise object to your entire GroupWise system. Synchronizing is a fairly quick operation. To synchronize a user, do the following:
  1. Load ConsoleOne.
  2. Highlight the user in GroupWise view or in NDS browser view.
  3. Choose Tools ➪ GroupWise Utilities ➪ Synchronize.
- **Run a structural rebuild on the user's database:** Now that the user object has been synchronized, you are ready to issue a structural rebuild on that user's database.

1. Load ConsoleOne.
2. Highlight the user in GroupWise view or in NDS browser view.
3. Choose Tools ➪ GroupWise Utilities ➪ Mailbox/Library Maintenance.
4. In the Action dropdown list, select Structural Rebuild.
5. Under the Databases tab, select the User check box, making sure that the Message option is unchecked.

Figure 23.1 shows these menu recommendations.

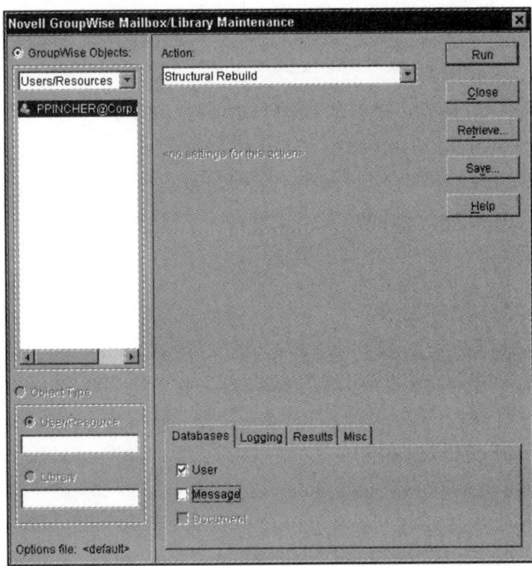

FIGURE 23.1 *Performing a Structural Rebuild*

Administrators are sometimes reluctant to do a structural rebuild on a user. They have a mistaken notion that a structural rebuild of a user database is a drastic, potentially destructive operation. It is not! A structural rebuild does not throw messages out of the folders or into the root of the cabinet. These administrators are mistaking structural rebuild for re-create user database, which is an entirely different function. (Re-creating a user database will throw messages out of folders.)

- **Run an analyze/fix on the contents of the user database:** When the POA analyzes the contents of a user database, it validates all the pointers in the database. The contents analysis also cleans up a user's personal address book. Here are the steps for running this operation:

1. In ConsoleOne, highlight the user in GroupWise view or in NDS browser view.
2. Choose Tools ➪ GroupWise Utilities ➪ Mailbox/Library Maintenance.
3. From the Action dropdown list, select Analyze/Fix Databases.
4. Select the Contents and Fix Problems check boxes, as well as the User check box under the Databases tab, making sure to uncheck all other check boxes.

   See Figure 23.2 for an example of these menu selections.

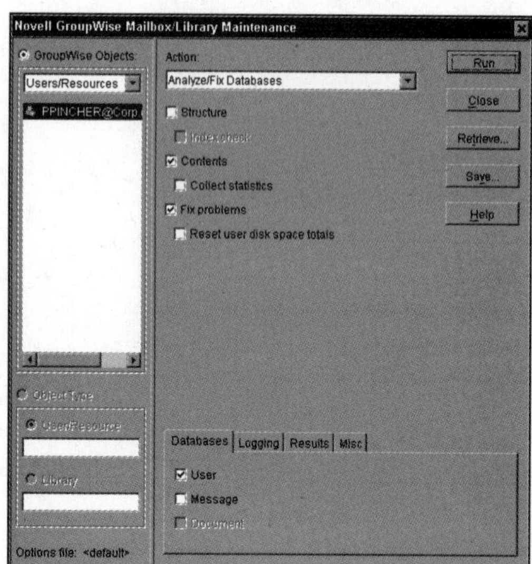

FIGURE 23.2 *Running a Contents Analyze-and-Fix Operation*

Determining Problem Specificity

The steps in the preceding section could have taken care of a mailbox problem. If they did not, then some very simple troubleshooting begins. Here is a systematic approach.

Determine If the Problem Is Machine-Specific

As the administrator, can you duplicate the problem from your own machine? Log in to the network as yourself and access the problem user's account by using the /@u-? switch. For troubleshooting purposes, have an extra GroupWise icon on your desktop. The icon should have a /@u-? switch after the GRPWISE.EXE. See Figure 23.3 for an example of this.

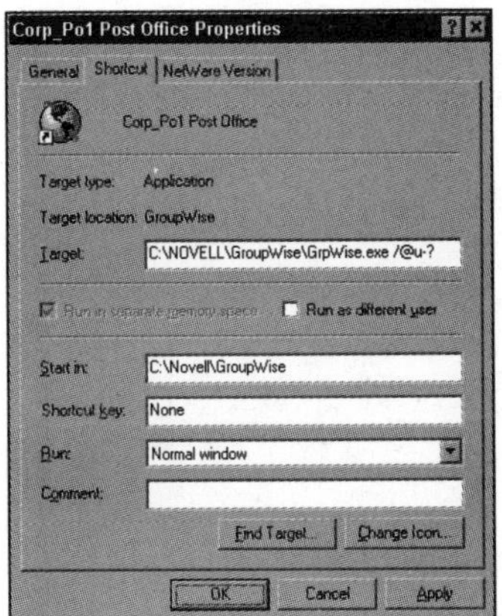

FIGURE 23.3 *An Extra GroupWise Troubleshooting Icon*

You must have GroupWise notify and the other GroupWise client software, such as the address book, unloaded in order to get into someone else's GroupWise account (the client suite can only connect to one account at a time). You will also need to get the user's password in order to enter their mailbox when using the /@u-? switch.

The user may not have a password or may have forgotten the password. With NDS single sign-on authentication, users often have no need to remember their GroupWise password. If the user has not set a password, and you have set your post office security level to high or high NDS, then you'll get the error shown in Figure 23.4.

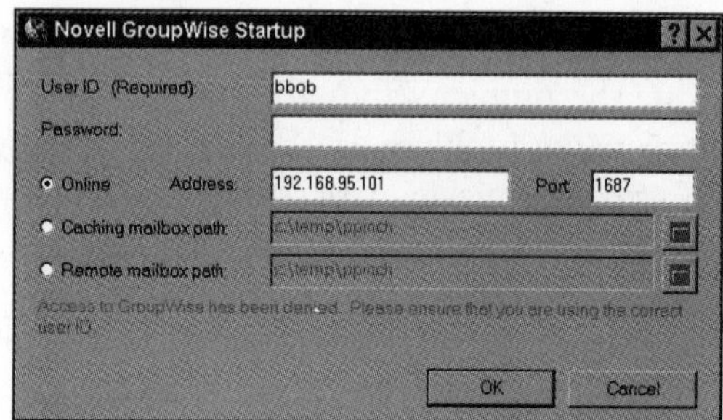

FIGURE 23.4 *GroupWise Error Trying to Login*

If you get this error, then you will need to reset the user's GroupWise password as follows:

1. Load ConsoleOne.
2. Edit the properties for the user whose password needs to be reset.
3. Go to the GroupWise Account page.
4. Select Change GroupWise Password.
5. Change the user's password, click OK once, and then click Cancel. (That second OK button is grayed out, but the password will get changed.)

Now that you are in the user's account, can you duplicate the problem? If you can, then you have isolated the problem to the user's mailbox. Jump down to "Troubleshooting User-Specific Problems" later in this chapter.

Troubleshooting Machine-Specific Problems

Suppose, however, that you can't duplicate the problem from your own machine. If this is the case, you would say that the problem is machine-specific.

Perhaps something has corrupted the GroupWise installation. At this point, I don't have a nice, numbered list of steps, but I do have a few suggestions:

Uninstall/Reinstall

One option is try uninstalling and reinstalling a few components:

- **Uninstall GroupWise and then reinstall GroupWise.** After the uninstall, remove the NOVELL\GROUPWISE directory completely.
- **Reinstall Windows messaging.** Windows messaging can be reinstalled from the GroupWise 6 software distribution directory by running WMS.EXE from the CLIENT\WIN32\WMS directory in your software distribution directory. For Windows 95, 98, and ME, run WMS from the 95 directory. For Windows NT/2000 and XP, run WMS.EXE from the NT directory.
- **Uninstall Windows messaging.** This can be hard to do on some machines because, although Windows messaging is installed, there's no uninstall option in the Windows Control Panel. This may sound funny, but you may have to run WMS.EXE to install Windows messaging before the Windows Control Panel will allow you to uninstall it.
- **Change Windows messaging profile information.** Delete the GroupWise profiles and then re-add them. The Windows messaging profile information is typically in the Control Panel under the Mail or Mail/Fax option. Sometimes this option isn't available. If you can load the GroupWise client, go to the address book and choose File ➪ Services.

Troubleshooting TCP/IP from the Workstation

Perhaps the problem looks like a TCP/IP communication problem between the client and the POA (89xx-class errors). Here are some things to do to troubleshoot:

1. Ping the server running the POA. If you can't PING successfully, fix that problem before going further.
2. Telnet to the POA. Run Windows Telnet by entering **telnet** from the Run prompt under the Start menu.
3. When using Telnet, turn on Local Echo.
4. Connect to the POA; the host name should be the DNS name or IP address of the POA, and the port should be 1677, or whatever your client/server port is. Figure 23.5 shows a Telnet session.

```
C:\WINNT\System32\command.com
Microsoft (R) Windows 2000 (TM) Version 5.00 (Build 2195)
Welcome to Microsoft Telnet Client
Telnet Client Build 5.00.99201.1

Escape Character is 'CTRL+]'

Microsoft Telnet> set local_echo
Microsoft Telnet> open 192.168.95.101 1677
Connecting To 192.168.95.101...
Microsoft Telnet> _
```

FIGURE 23.5 *Telnet to the POA*

5. Upon successfully connecting to the POA's client/server port, you should be allowed to type characters and press Enter several times. Also, after holding the Enter key for several seconds, you should get disconnected from the POA. When you get connected, and hold down the Enter key for several seconds, and get disconnected, that's exactly the behavior you want from the POA. If you can't get the connection to the POA as the client/server port, then you've got some kind of a TCP/IP problem.

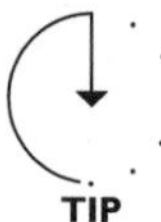

TIP

If you get a connection to the POA, and hold down the Enter key, and never get disconnected, then that's actually an indication of a TCP/IP problem (for some reason, the POA cannot talk back to the client to close the connection).

If there are TCP/IP problems then it would be appropriate to verify the TCP/IP settings or reinstall the TCP/IP services on the user's workstation. It may also be a good idea to break out the LAN sniffer and see if there is a network problem on this network segment.

Troubleshooting User-Specific Problems

If the problem can be reproduced on multiple machines, your problem is likely user-specific. Before you can classify a problem this way, however, you need to make sure the problem isn't specific to the post office or network segment.

A good test would be to go to a machine on the same network segment, or same network switch as the machine that seems to be giving the user problems. From that machine, log in as a different user than the problem user, but one who is on the same post office as the problem user. Does the problem persist? If so, the problem really isn't user-specific, and it's not machine-specific; it's either post office-specific or network-specific.

Components Specific to Users

Imagine that a problem looks like it really is user-specific. It is still ideal to try and troubleshoot the problem away from the user's machine. There are just a few things that are truly specific to a user:

- **The user's object entry in the GroupWise directory:** Only the user interfaces with their object entry in WPHOST.DB file.
- **The user's master mailbox:** The USERXXX.DB database file in the GroupWise information store at the post office, and any other store files it references for item content.
- **The user's caching mode or remote databases:** If the user happens to use caching mode or remote, these files will be on the user's local drive. If you troubleshoot from a different workstation, GroupWise remote databases should not come into play.
- **The user's archive databases:** If the user is archiving to a local drive, then troubleshooting from a separate workstation should isolate the problem.

Isolating GroupWise Archive Problems

The GroupWise client interacts with the archive databases on three different occasions:

- When the GroupWise client first loads
- When reading items from the archive mailbox
- When archiving a message item

The simplest way to try and determine if a problem is an archive problem is to rename the user's archive directory. To determine a user's archive directory, do the following:

1. In the GroupWise client, go to Tools ➪ Options ➪ Environment ➪ File Location.
2. Write down the archive directory path.

3. Determine the user's three-character FID.

   In the GroupWise client, this information can be found under Help ⇨ About GroupWise. It's the three characters in the parentheses following the user's name, as shown in Figure 23.6.

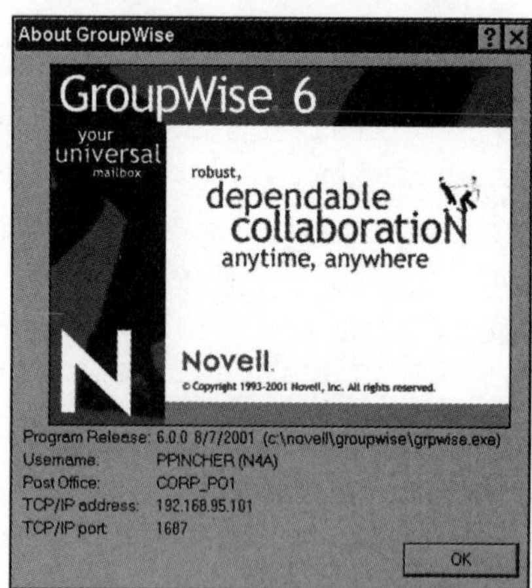

FIGURE 23.6 *The GroupWise FID as Shown from the GroupWise Client*

   The archive directory is the file location of the archive plus OFxxxARC (where xxx is the user's FID). So if the user's archive directory is C:\ARCHIVE and the user's FID is 123, then the archive directory is C:\ARCHIVE\OF123ARC.

It is always a good idea to back up GroupWise archives before working with them. In fact, Novell recommends that GroupWise archives be placed on network drives so that they are backed up automatically.

4. Rename this directory.

If this solves the problem, then you know that the problem was with the user's GroupWise archive. You can now name it back, and start taking steps to repair it using the stand-alone GWCHECK for Windows (GWCHECK.EXE).

TIP

The GroupWise Client has GWCHECK within it. If you want to run a GWCHECK on an archive database do the following. Hold down the Ctrl and the Shift keys simultaneously, and then choose File ⇨ Open Archive, while the Ctrl and Shift keys are still depressed.

Isolating GroupWise Master Mailbox Problems

Generally, a problem is either in a user's database or one of the message databases on the post office. The most likely culprit for problems is the USERxxx.DB file for the user. The contents of a USERxxx.DB file are the one thing that users can really mess up. For instance, a user can create a personal group with invalid addresses. If a user is complaining of a problem, and the problem is user-specific, begin by looking for things such as the user's preferences and address book for clues on what is causing the problem.

If you already ran a structural rebuild on this user's user database and you've reached this point, you may want some additional confirmation that you are looking in the right place. One way to do this is by renaming the user's user database. This is a common troubleshooting step.

1. Make sure the user is out of GroupWise.
2. Rename the user's USERxxx.DB file to USERxxx.OLD.

NOTE

You may have to bring the POA down to release this file. Just unload the POA, and then while the POA is unloading, go to the Console prompt and immediately reload the POA. Users who are in GroupWise will automatically reconnect to the POA, and there is generally a negligible interruption of service for end users.

3. Using the stand-alone GWCHECK utility, specify the following, as shown in Figure 23.7:
   - **Database Type:** Post Office
   - **Database Path:** Specify the path to post office that the user is on
   - **Post Office Name:** Specify the name of the post office that the user is on
   - **Object Type:** User/Resource
   - **User/Resource:** The problem user's USERxxx.DB file
   - **Action:** Structural Rebuild (Not a structure Analyze/Fix Databases!)
   - **Databases:** User

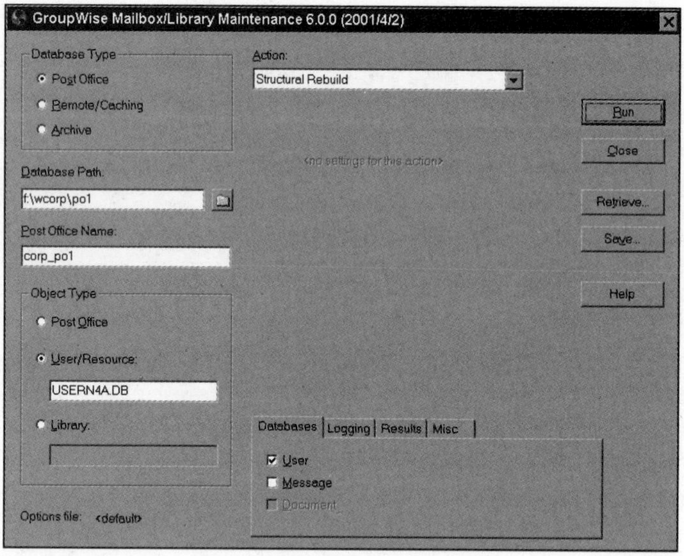

FIGURE 23.7 *GWCHECK to Drop a USERXXX.DB File from the Guardian Database*

4. Click Run.

   When GWCHECK runs it will report, among other things, an error 26. This error is good. It means that GWCHECK will remove the registration of problem user's USERxxx.DB from the NGWGUARD.DB file. By doing this, you have cleared the way for the system to allow you to create a new USERxxx.DB file for this user.

TIP

You may have to bring the POA down again. When you go to load the GroupWise client, you could get a C05D error. A C05D error means that the USERxxx.DB file is registered in the NGWGUARD.DB file but is not on the disk. You just unregistered the USERxxx.DB file from the NGWGUARD.DB file, but the POA has it cached in memory. Bringing down the POA and bringing it right back up fixes things.

5. Run GroupWise as the problem user.

   The e-mail box will be empty. Do the same action that caused a problem before. Does the problem still exist? If not, you know that the problem was wholly contained in the USERxxx.DB file that was renamed to USERxxx.OLD. If the problem does still exist, then you are looking at a problem with the post office database, or perhaps you have not correctly ruled out machine- or network-specific problems.

6. Whether or not the problem was isolated to the user database you renamed, you should now rename the new USERxxx.DB file to something else, and rename the USERxxx.OLD file back to USERxxx.DB.

   Again, you may need to unload and reload the POA to force the release of the file.

Proceed to the next section for more ideas on how to proceed, now that you know the problem is in the USERxxx.DB file.

Fixing Master Mailbox Problems

Suppose that in Step 5 in the preceding section, you isolated the problem to this user's user database. Now what should you do?

- If you didn't synchronize the user object, do so now.
- If you didn't run a structural rebuild on the user's database, do so now.
- If you didn't run a contents check on the user's database, do so now.
- Run a Reset Client Options operation on this user from Tools ➪ GroupWise Utilities ➪ Mailbox/Library Maintenance.
- Run an index check on the user's database.
- Rid the user of the personal address book(s) and the entries in the frequent contacts address book list.

  You can export each of these books from the client, and then delete all the entries in each of these address books. When you have finished your testing and troubleshooting, you can re-import these entries.

  To export an address book go, into the GroupWise address book and choose File ➪ Export. Make sure that you are not exporting the GroupWise system address book. Just export the frequent contacts and the user's personal address books.

If none of the steps above resolve the problem, and the problem is really causing the user some headaches (which is to say, you cannot tell the user just to ignore the problem), then you've got two options:

- **Use the Re-create User Database option.** This routine could possibly fix the problem, but things will be pretty disorganized when the user goes back into their mailbox. All of their items will be thrown into the root of the mailbox Cabinet folder. The user's personal calendar items will also be lost.

- **Archive everything.** Archive everything that the user has, and then give the user a brand new, empty user database. Then unarchive the items into the new database.

Generate a Fresh User Database without Losing Items

This walkthrough gives you the tools to give a user a new USERxxx.DB file without losing their GroupWise messages and calendar items. I refer to the user in this walkthrough as USERA.

NOTE

This process is fairly involved, and should only be undertaken when all other troubleshooting has failed to clean up errors that you have positively identified as user-specific.

- **Define a new archive directory:** If the user already has an archive directory, you do not want to append to that archive. Just create an archive directory that will be used temporarily. Load the GroupWise client as USERA. Set or change the archive path to be C:\TEMPARC. Figure 23.8 shows this.

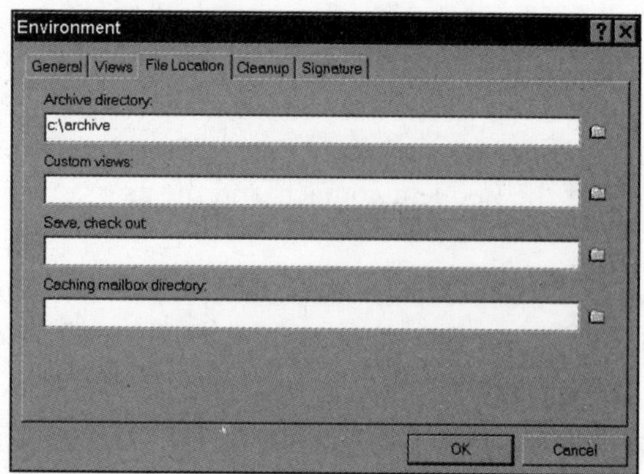

FIGURE 23.8 *Setting a New Archive Path*

If an archive mailbox already exists, you will get a message like the one in Figure 23.9 asking you to move the contents of the existing archive. Click No.

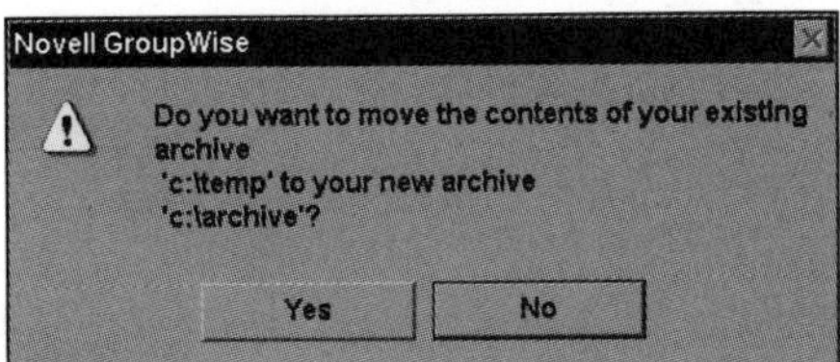

FIGURE 23.9 *Prompt to Move Archive Contents*

- **Find all items in the mailbox:** Now you need to be able to grab every single item in the master mailbox. To do this, use the GroupWise find feature. Choose Tools ➪ Find. Keep the Find dialog box just the way it looks in Figure 23.10. Do not check or uncheck any of the boxes that come up by default. Just click OK.

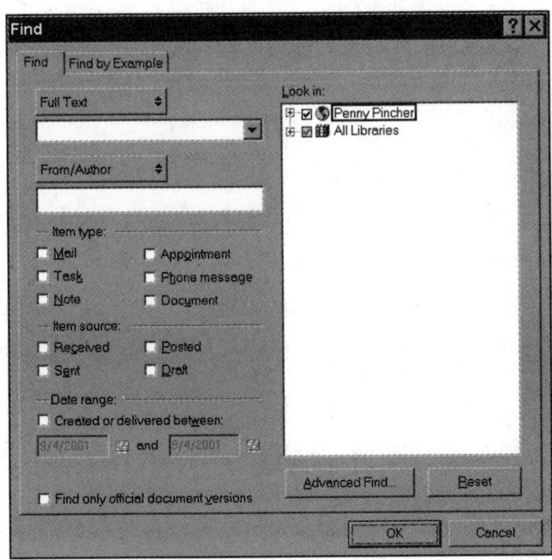

FIGURE 23.10 *A Find Everything Query*

As shown in Figure 23.11, this query will find everything in USERA's mailbox. This find will not only include the user's inbox items but also USERA's personal calendar items, draft messages, and sent items.

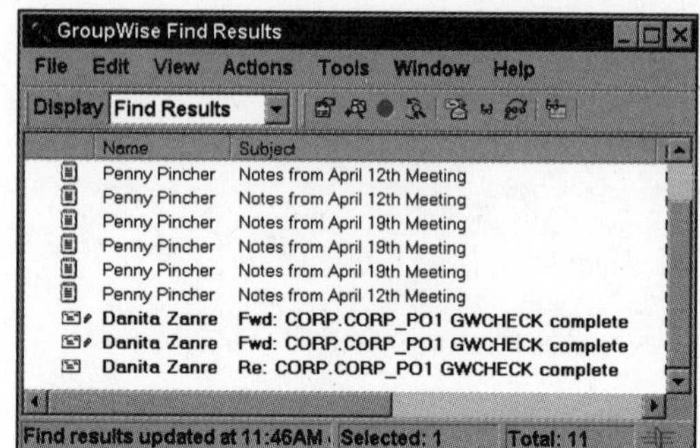

FIGURE 23.11 *Results of a Find Everything Query*

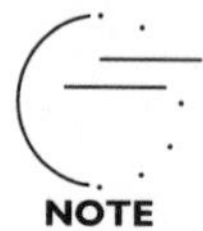

If users have a lot of items in their mailboxex, or they have folders such as NNTP folders, you could potentially get an error saying that there are too many items to display in the Find Results window. To avoid this, when you specify the query, make sure to uncheck NNTP folders, and maybe even specify a date range. Then, archive the items in the Find Results window and increment the date range back so that you get more items to archive.

- **Archive all items:** From the Find Results folder, you can now mark the items to be archived. Select a couple of hundred items at a time, and then choose Actions ➪ Archive.

Documents in GroupWise libraries will not be archived. This is fine. They will be retained in the library. The user can do a search for the documents later.

- **Export personal address books:** Load the GroupWise address book. Inside the address book, go to the personal address book and choose File ➪ Export. A dialog box will come up asking what to select as shown in Figure 23.12. Select Entire Address Book.

  Export each of the address books that the user has. You can even export the frequent contacts list, if you would like.

Export Question

Do you want to export the address items that are currently selected or export the entire address book?

Entire Address Book... | Selected Items... | Cancel

FIGURE 23.12 *Exporting an Address Book*

- **Delete shared folders:** The shared folders that USERA may have created for others need to be unshared. The folders that USERA has shared have a hand with a blue sleeve with the hand pointed to the right.

  1. Highlight the folder to be unshared and right-click on it.
  2. Select Sharing.
  3. Click the Not shared radio button.
  4. Click OK.
  5. Enter a brief message explaining that the shared folder has been unshared, perhaps telling recipients of the folder when you plan to re-share it, and click OK.

  Make note of the folders that have been shared with USERA by someone else. USERA will need to ask the owner of those folders to re-share the folder. To determine who owns a shared folder, highlight the shared folder and choose Properties ➪ Sharing, as shown in Figure 23.13.

  After noting the shared folders, delete the shared folders that were shared with USERA. Only USERA deletes these shared folders from USERA's mailbox.

- **Delete shared address books:** Make sure to unshare the shared address books that USERA shared, and make note of shared address books that USERA received from others.
- **Note USERA's proxy access list:** See if USERA has given proxy access to someone else. Take note of who has access. To view the proxy access that other people have to USERA, go to Tools ➪ Options ➪ Security ➪ Proxy Access.

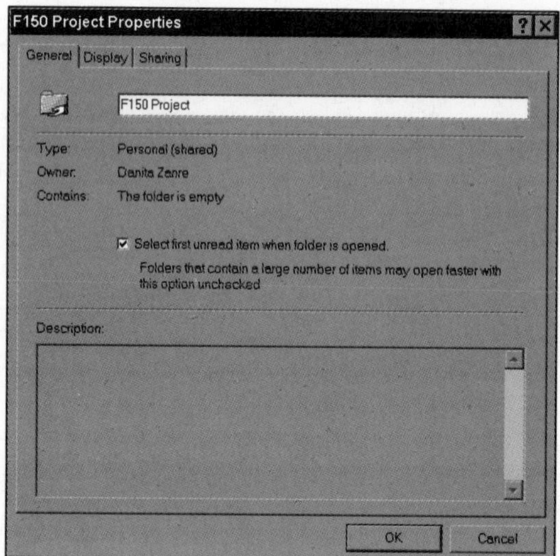

FIGURE 23.13 *Seeing Who Owns a Shared Folder*

- **Archive the user's trash:** This may seem like a funny idea, but some users don't want to lose their trash. And it makes for a smoother outcome to this process for the user if you do retain the trash. There isn't a way to archive the trash bucket, but here's what you could do. Drag and drop the items from the trash bucket to a newly created temporary folder called Trash. Then archive all the items in the Trash folder. When you unarchive the user's items, the folder you designated for trash will come back. Then drag the items back into the trash and delete the temporary trash folder you created.
- **Note USERA's FID:** Determine what USERA's FID is. If GroupWise is loaded, and you're logged in as USERA, choose Help ➪ About GroupWise. The FID is in parentheses next to the user's name.
- **Rename USERA's user database:** Now you need to rename USERA's user database file. You know that USERA's FID is 123. The file you are looking for, USER123.DB, will be found in the OFUSER subdirectory of the user's post office directory. Rename the file to USER123.OLD.

NOTE

As discussed earlier in the chapter, the POA may need to be unloaded before this database can be renamed.

- **Drop USERA's user database from the guardian database:** USERA's database has been renamed, but it must still be dropped from the NGWGUARD.DB file. Configure GWCHECK to run as shown in Figure 23.14.

  1. Run the standalone GWCHECK utility.
  2. Specify the following:
     - **Database Type:** Post Office
     - **Database Path:** Specify the path to post office that USERA is on
     - **Post Office Name:** Specify the name of the post office that the USERA is on
     - **Object Type:** User/Resource
     - **User/Resource:** USER123.DB
     - **Action:** Structural Rebuild (Not a structure Analyze/Fix Databases!)
     - **Databases:** User
  3. Click Run.

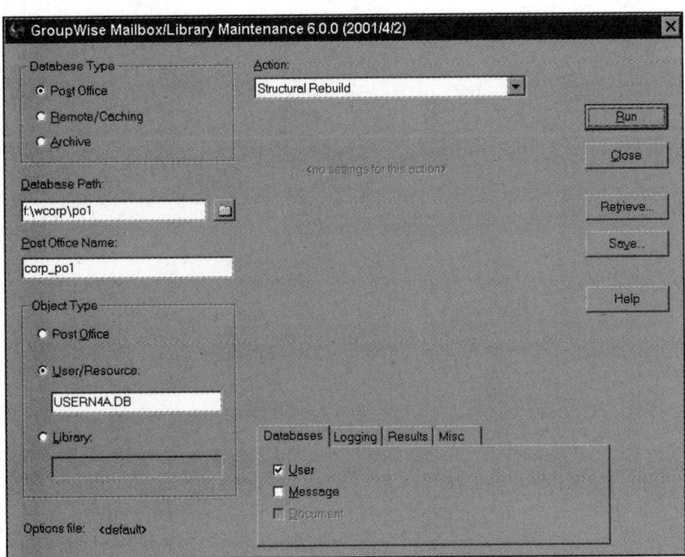

FIGURE 23.14 *Using GWCHECK to Drop a USERxxx.DB File from the Guardian Database*

The GWCHECK log will indicate an error 26; you should expect and want this error. See Figure 23.15.

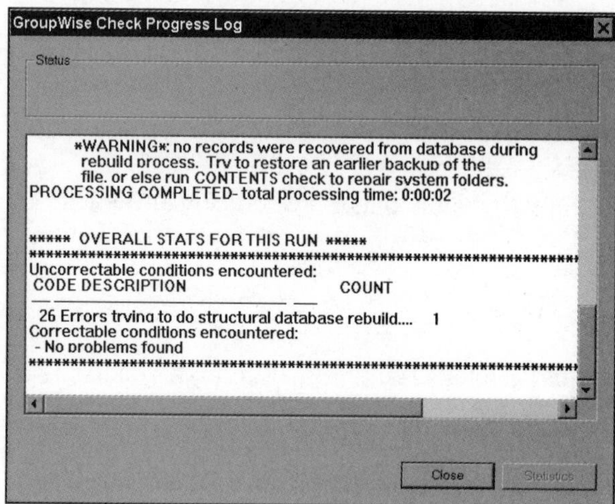

FIGURE 23.15 *GWCHECK Gives an Error 26*

- **Access and test the clean mailbox:** It's time for a sanity check. Launch GroupWise as USERA (using the /@u-? switch). The mailbox should be empty. Make sure that you can no longer duplicate the problem the user was having. If you can still duplicate the problem, then this whole exercise is pointless. You probably did not correctly determine the specificity of the problem.

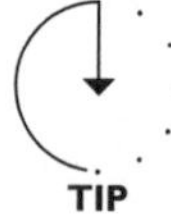
TIP

Remember, if you get a C05D error loading the GroupWise client, then you just need to bring the POA for this post office down and back up again.

- **Restore items from the archive:** Assuming the problem can no longer be duplicated, it is time to begin the process of moving items back into the master mailbox.
  1. Choose Tools ➪ Options ➪ Environment ➪ File Location.
  2. Set the archive path to be C:\TEMPARC.

3. Open up the archive mailbox by choosing File ➪ Open Archive.
4. Stay in the archive mailbox and exit GroupWise with the archive mailbox open.

   You are doing this so that a QuickFinder index of the archive database can be made.

NOTE

GroupWise may take a little while to exit. This is because the QuickFinder indexing piece of GroupWise is indexing the GroupWise archive database as you exit. You want this to happen, because you will need to use the archive index in order to use the find feature to restore the items you have archived.

5. Launch the GroupWise client again, and open the archive mailbox.
6. If you made a trash folder, unarchive those items first; then go into the master mailbox and delete the items so that they are moved to the trash again.
7. Choose Tools ➪ Find, and then click OK.

   The find feature will find all the items in the archive mailbox.
8. Highlight a few hundred items at a time, and then choose Actions ➪ Archive.

   This will un-archive all the items and place them back into the master mailbox.

- **Restore other items:** At this point, the user should have 90 percent of their stuff back. The remaining 10 percent is address-book information, certain preferences, and folders or address books shared with other users. The following tasks may be completed in whatever order you see fit:
  - **Repopulate USERA's personal address book.** Do this by re-importing *.NAB files that were exported earlier. To import, go to the address book and choose File ➪ Import. You may also have to create address book tabs before doing the import.
  - **Set the archive path back to the original archive path that USERA had, if they had an archive path.** Do not select the option to move items.
  - **Set up proxy access.**
  - **Set up shared folders.**

- **Request shared folders from others who have shared folders with USERA.**
- **Set up shared address books.**
- **Request shared address books from others who have shared address books with USERA.**

Summary

This chapter emphasized using the scientific method as a means of troubleshooting. The scientific method is this:

1. Observe
2. Hypothesize
3. Predict, based upon the hypothesis
4. Test the hypothesis

This chapter also emphasizes that problems are generally one of the following:

- User-specific
- Machine-specific

CHAPTER 24

Using Wireless and Handheld Devices with GroupWise 6 WebAccess

This chapter discusses wireless access to the GroupWise mailbox. It also discusses using handheld devices to access the GroupWise mailbox.

If you read Chapter 11 regarding WebAccess, you should be familiar with the concepts of WebAccess and what the different components are that make up WebAccess. If you have not already read Chapter 11, you should go back and read it before getting into this chapter. Things will make better sense if you have the background from Chapter 11 under your belt first. This chapter will help you better understand how access from wireless and handheld devices works through WebAccess. It will also give you an understanding of how modular and flexible GroupWise WebAccess is in regards to providing future support for all sorts of different devices and protocols. This is one of the major advantages to the GroupWise WebAccess architecture.

Understanding Templates

GroupWise 6 WebAccess uses templates that facilitate access to the GroupWise mailbox from many different devices. Think of templates as a skeleton document that the WebAccess application stuffs the data into before displaying it to the connected client's device. This data is the data from the user's mailbox that is delivered to the application from the WebAccess agent. If you are using a wireless phone to access your GroupWise mailbox through WebAccess, the application recognizes what type of device it is communicating with. As a result, when the data is received from the user's mailbox, the application will place this data (the mail items, for example) into a template that has been designed to work with wireless phones using the wireless access protocol (WAP).

The use of templates at the application level allows Novell development engineers to easily add support for additional devices. No coding changes need to occur at the agent level. The only changes that need to be made is to tell the WebAccess application to understand what data coming from a certain device looks like, and then develop the templates to place the data into before it is delivered back to the device.

The WebAccess templates are stored under the JAVA directory on the Web server. On a NetWare server, this directory is at SYS:\JAVA\SERVLETS\COM\NOVELL\WEBACCESS\TEMPLATES.

Out-of-the-Box Templates Included in GroupWise 6

The templates that ship with GroupWise 6 support the following devices or browsers:

- Any Web browser that supports HTTP 1.1 or 1.0.
- Any Web browser that uses simple HTTP. This is usually what a Windows CE device's browser will use.
- Any wireless phone that supports WML (wireless markup language) through the WAP protocol (wireless access protocol).

If you were to look at the template directories, you would note the following directories:

- **Frames:** The Frames directory contains the templates that most of the standard Web browsers will use (Netscape and Internet Explorer, for example).
- **HDML:** The HDML directory contains the templates that handheld devices use. HDML stands for the handheld device markup language. It is similar to HTML, but scaled down for handheld-device use.
- **Simple:** The Simple directory contains the templates for devices that use the simple HTML interface. These would be devices using the Windows CE operating system.
- **WebClip:** The WebClip directory is incomplete with the shipping version of GroupWise 6 WebAccess. As of the writing of this book, Novell had released an enhancement pack to the wireless piece for GroupWise 6. It provides full functionality using the WebClip templates. WebClipping technology is used with the Palm OS products.
- **WML:** The WML directory includes the wireless markup language templates and are used by wireless phones primarily.

Obtaining Updated WebAccess Templates

Because of the architecture of the WebAccess system, it is very simple for Novell to update and enhance the wireless templates that work with WebAccess. Usually, these updates simply update the actual templates, as well as the WEBACC.CFG file that tells the WebAccess application what types of templates to use for different devices or protocols. Because the templates are very modular, Novell does not have to wait for a full service-pack release to update them or add additional device support. Novell can release just updates to the wireless components. As of the writing of this book, there is one released update to the WebAccess templates. Just go to `http://support.novell.com` and search for the filename GW6WEP1.EXE. This is the GroupWise 6 Wireless Enhancement Pack, Version 1. If you have upgraded to a subsequent support pack to GroupWise 6, such as Support Pack #1, it is not necessary to download this WebAccess template update.

Managing Templates through the GroupWise WebAccess Object

There are a few things that you as an administrator can configure regarding templates. Administering the GroupWise templates is done by going to the properties of the GroupWise WebAccess object in ConsoleOne. From the Application property page, shown in Figure 24.1, select Templates from the drop-down list. From here, you can administer and configure how the templates are configured.

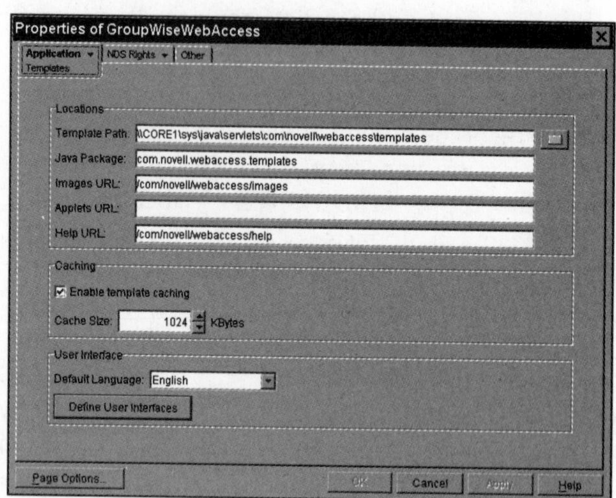

FIGURE 24.1 *WebAccess Application Templates Property Page*

- **Template Path:** This is the path to the template directories. Under this path, you will see a directory representing each of the installed templates.
- **Java Package:** A Java package name is a directory path that uses the period (.) instead of a slash (\) to separate components of the path. Hence, this is really just a path that you are looking at here. Basically, this points to the same directory as the Template Path field, identifying the location of the template string tables. Unless you are a developer and creating your own custom templates, you will never need to modify this path.
- **Images URL:** This is the path to the image files. This is referring to a path under the Web server where the image (*.gif) files that the different templates will display are located.
- **Applets URL:** This field allows you to define the path to any custom applets that you may be using. It is possible to use Java applets for some of the WebAccess components. This is most commonly seen if you want to develop custom address-book or calendar views.
- **Help URL:** This is the path under the root of the Web server to the location of the help files. You can move the help files to a different location, if desired.
- **Caching:** This option allows the WebAccess application to cache the templates in RAM the first time they are used, which increases performance.
- **Cache Size:** This value determines how much RAM the server will use to cache the templates. The default setting is large enough to contain all the default templates. Unless you have created custom templates, you should not need to modify this setting.
- **Default Language:** This identifies the default language that will be presented to end users when they hit your Web server's home page, and you have selected to use the default WebAccess home page.

Defining User Interface and Browser Integration

This section is an explanation of what the Define User Interfaces window, shown in Figure 24.2, allows you to do. It will go through each of the three property pages here and explain what they mean in relation to the templates.

User Interfaces

The User Interfaces tab in Figure 24.2 allows you to define the available templates. You can add additional references to templates, if needed.

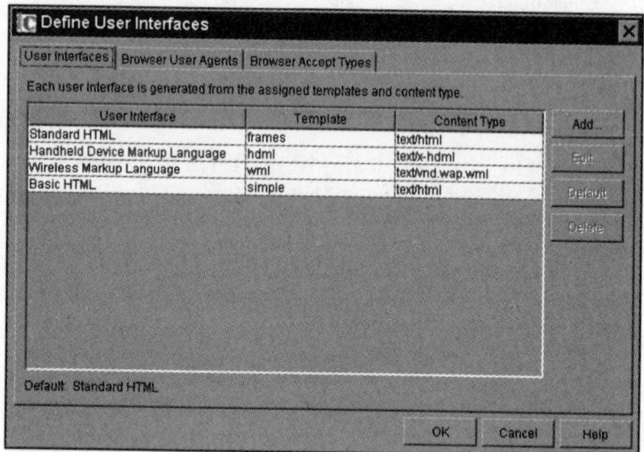

FIGURE 24.2 *User Interfaces*

- **User Interface:** This defines the name of the template. This value just makes it easy to put a simple name in to define the template.
- **Template:** This is the actual name of the directory under the Template directory, as defined earlier.
- **Content Type:** This defines what type of possible content this template can serve up. In other words, it defines what type of content the receiving device can handle.

Browser User Agents

The Browser User Agents tab shown in Figure 24.3 lets you associate a user interface or template with a particular type of Web browser. The WebAccess application makes this association based on the browser identifying itself to the WebAccess application. This could include the platform, version of browser, and so on. In other words, if a browser's user agent information includes Windows CE (this would be in the header of the data sent to the WebAccess application), the application will use the basic HTML interface (or the simple templates) and not the default frames, which are defined under the User Interfaces tab.

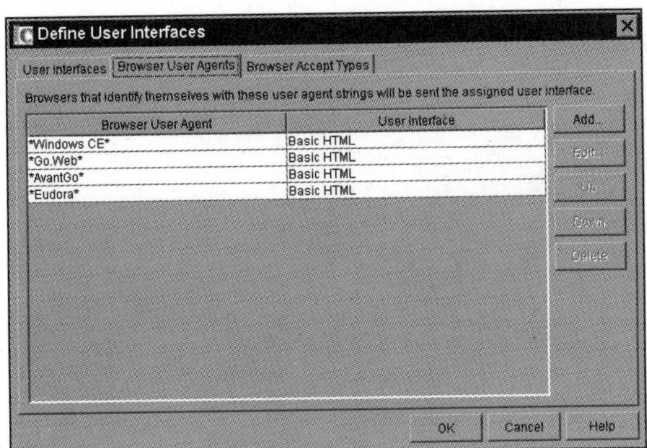

FIGURE 24.3 *Browser User Agents*

- **Browser User Agent:** This column is where you identify what a browser can use to identify itself to the WebAccess application.
- **User Interface:** This column defines the template or user interface that will be delivered to the device when a match is made from the Browser User Agent list.

Browser Accept Types

The Browser Accept Types tab shown in Figure 24.4 also lets you associate a user interface or template with a particular type of Web browser. However, this association is based on the content type the browser will accept, not the browser identifying itself. For example, if a browser accepts text/html (one of the predefined entries), the WebAccess application will use the standard HTML interface (or the Frames templates). Most browsers will accept multiple content types, including text/html or text/plain. This identifies what type of information the browser can understand.

Many browsers accept more than one content type, such as both text/html and text/plain.

- **Browser Accept Type:** This identifies what format the data can be in when the browser receives it.
- **User Interface:** This defines the templates that deliver this type of content to the browser.

Define User Interfaces

User Interfaces | Browser User Agents | Browser Accept Types

The browser will be sent the interface based on the best match for the browser's preferred format.

Browser Accept Type	User Interface
text/x-hdml	Handheld Device Markup Language
text/vnd.wap.wml	Wireless Markup Language

Add... Edit... Delete

OK Cancel Help

FIGURE 24.4 *Browser Accept Types*

So, in a nutshell, what the Define User Interfaces window allows you to do is identify and configure what set of templates are associated with different types of browsers — everything from standard browsers to wireless phones.

NOTE

If you edit and make changes in the Define User Interfaces window, this information is written to the WEBACC.CFG file. The WebAccess application does not dynamically read this file. To get the changes to take effect, the WebAccess application must be shut down and restarted. This can be done by shutting down the Web server, as well as the Java virtual machine. On NetWare, you can issue the NSWEBDN command, followed by a JAVA – EXIT command. Simply restart the Web server with a NSWEB command, and the Web server will automatically load the WebAccess application or servlet.

Understanding How the WebAccess Application Detects What Templates to Use

Here is a discussion on how the WebAccess application knows what templates to actually use for the different types of browsers and devices that it supports.

When a device is directed to the URL that points to the SERVLET/WEBACC location on the Web server, it sends a small packet that contains header information about the browser that is being used. The WebAccess application then reads the cached information from the WEBACC.CFG file. This is where it determines what type of browsers it can support.

If the information from the browser contains the Browser User Agent name (Windows CE, AvantGo, and so on), then it knows right off to use the associated template listed in the User Interface column.

If the browser has not provided the Browser User Agent name, then the WebAccess application will look for what type of data the browser can understand. This information is what is configured in the Browser Accept Types options. If the browser identifies that it can understand text/x-hdml, then the WebAccess application knows that it is probably talking to a wireless phone that is expecting data in the x-hdml format. It then checks the User Interface value and knows what templates to use when corresponding with the device.

If the WebAccess application still is not sure what type of device it is communicating with, then it will go to the User Interface value and use the default template here.

This should help you to understand how the WebAccess application understands what device or browser it is communicating with, as well as what set of templates to use when communicating to this device.

Accessing Your GroupWise Mailbox from a Windows CE Device

GroupWise wireless requires a Windows CE device that supports IE version 4.0 or better. To determine the version of IE that comes with a Windows CE device, go to the Control Panel and the System icons.

To access the GroupWise WebAccess system from a handheld device running Windows CE, you must first have some way to get online with the device. There are a couple options you have to get online with your Windows CE device. You can use a modem with the Windows CE device and dial a traditional ISP to get Internet access. You can also use a wireless LAN card with the Windows CE device, which would put you on a corporate network, if this service is available to you.

Once you are online and have access to the Web server where the GroupWise WebAccess application is running, you can enter the URL to your WebAccess server. The Windows CE device should tell the Web server that it is a Windows CE device, and the WebAccess application will use the simple templates to display the mail. Figure 24.5 shows an example of what the simple interface looks like.

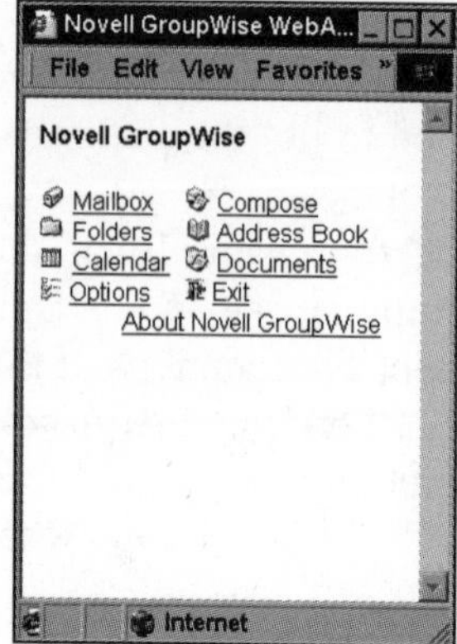

FIGURE 24.5 *WebAccess Simple HTML Interface*

Notice that you do not get all the graphics that the traditional GroupWise WebAccess frames view gives you.

You will also notice that the simple templates are designed to fit on a much smaller screen. This is very helpful when using a Windows CE device because it eliminates much of the scrolling across the screen to view the entire contents of the mailbox.

If you need to test if the simple templates are working, you can tell the WebAccess application what templates you would like to use via the URL line. Here is an example of how to specifically tell the WebAccess application that you would like to use the simple templates:

```
http://<yourwebserverver DNS
name>/servlet/webacc?User.html=Simple
```

NOTE

The `User.html=Simple` is case-sensitive.

When you hit return, the WebAccess application will display the login page using the simple templates.

As you can see, it is pretty simple to use a Windows CE device to access WebAccess. The WebAccess application will detect what type of device is communicating with it, and use the appropriate simple templates.

Accessing Your GroupWise Mailbox from a Wireless Phone

To access the GroupWise mailbox from a wireless phone, there are a few prerequisites that must be met first.

First, the phone must support the wireless application protocol (WAP). WAP is a wireless protocol that was designed to allow wireless applications to work across different wireless network technology types. It was developed by the WAP Forum, which consisted of various wireless venders. Think of WAP as the vehicle that carries the data to your cell phone.

To clarify why GroupWise WebAccess uses WML and HDML templates instead of a WAP template, you can think of WAP as the vehicle that brings WML or HDML content to a wireless device. WML (wireless markup language) and HDML (handheld device markup language) are the actual text documents that display content, and they sit on top of the WAP protocol. Hence, GroupWise uses the WML and HDML templates to create the content, which is delivered over the WAP protocol to the wireless device.

If you have a WAP-enabled phone, then the next step is to make sure that the phone service provider provides WAP service to the phone. Otherwise, you have this nice gadget that is acting like a traditional cell phone. You will not be able to access the GroupWise mailbox from it because you are not subscribed to this service.

With a WAP phone and a subscription from the cellular phone service provider, you should be able to access the WebServer where your GroupWise WebAccess application is running. On the phone's browser, you would enter the URL to the Web server that is running the WebAccess application.

NOTE

If the Web server does not have any WML or HDML pages to display, you will not be able to see the HTML Web page that is the default from a WML/HDML device. You need to enter the /SERVLET/WEBACC portion of the URL to direct the phone browser directly to the WebAccess application, for example, `<yourwebserververver DNS name>/servlet/webacc`**.**

When your phone accesses the SERVLET/WEBACC page, you will be presented with a prompt to enter the GroupWise user ID. After you key this in and select

OK, you will be prompted for the GroupWise password. After keying this in, you will then be given a simple menu option consisting of Mail, Appointments, Tasks, Address Book, Compose, Documents, Options, and Logout. You can scroll through them to perform different tasks. Figure 24.6 shows GroupWise wireless on a cell phone.

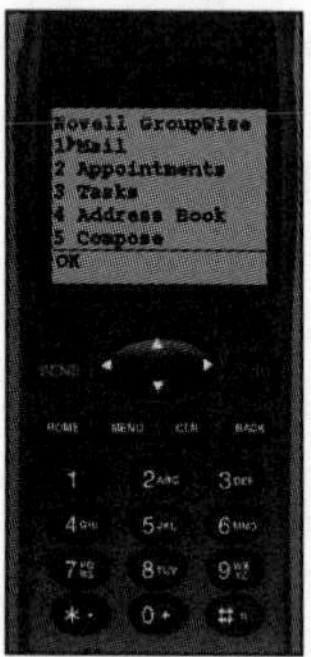

FIGURE 24.6 *WebAccess Simple WML Interface*

As an administrator, you can test WebAccess to verify that you can access your mailbox from a WAP-enabled cell phone. Instead of just telling the Web browser to use the WML or HDML templates, you must use a WAP phone emulator. The reason for this is that the standard browsers out there do not support the WML or HDML protocols. WML was specifically designed for small handheld or wireless devices, and is not supported by the traditional Web browsers.

To test with a WAP emulator running on any Windows OS platform, just go to `www.openwave.com` and download the OpenWave software developer kit (SDK). Don't worry about having to know how to program, because you are downloading a SDK. It has a very simple install that you can install the WAP phone emulator. Once installed, you can enter the URL in the GO field and hit return. It should connect you to the URL that you specified and allow you to log into the WebAccess mailbox.

Accessing Your GroupWise Mailbox from a Palm OS Device

The shipping version of the GroupWise 6 WebAccess component does not allow you to access the GroupWise mailbox from a Palm OS device. However, as of the writing of this book, Novell has released an updated version of the WebAccess templates that fully supports access to the GroupWise mailbox from devices running the Palm OS.

So the first step is to either install the GW6WEP1.EXE patch to your WebAccess system or apply the Service Pack 1 for GroupWise 6, which will contain these updated templates for the Palm OS as well.

The way that the Palm OS accesses the WebAccess system is by using a proprietary method called WebClipping. WebClipping must be supported by the device running the Palm OS. If your Palm OS device does not have the built-in wireless functionality, then you can purchase a product such as Palm's Mobile Internet Kit and a modem and install the WebClipping software that gives you the ability to dial an ISP, and then use the WebClipping software to connect to the WebAccess server.

There is an additional piece that you must have in place to access WebAccess from the Palm OS. It is a PQA file. This PQA file must be installed on to the Palm OS device. It contains the IP address or URL of the Web server. To access the GroupWise mailbox from a Palm OS device, install the GROUPWISE.PQA file, which is created by the GW6WEP1.EXE update patch. Install this *.PQA file to your Palm OS, WebClipping-enabled device. Then run this application from the Palm OS. You will be prompted to enter the GroupWise user ID and password. When you connect, the data is actually transmitted to the URL inside the GROUPWISE.PQA application.

NOTE

The GROUPWISE.PQA file is specific to a certain instance of GroupWise WebAccess. The *.PQA file holds encryption key information that ties it to the GroupWise WebAccess application that the GW6WEP1.EXE software was pointed to when generating the *.PQA file.

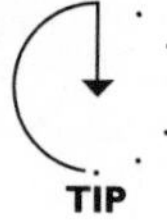
TIP

The GroupWise.PQA file is placed on your Web server by the installation software for WebAccess and Wireless. On my server, which is a NetWare server running Netscape Enterprise Web Server, the GRPWISE.PQA file was at the following path: `\\FS1\SYS\Novonyx\suitespot\docs\com\novell\webaccess\palm`**.**

Information Regarding SSL-ized Connections from Handheld Devices

Many installations of GroupWise WebAccess are using SSL to encrypt the data between the browser and the WebAccess application. This is advisable for security reasons. There are a few issues regarding this and using handheld or wireless devices to access WebAccess.

In order for the Web server to communicate with a Web browser, they must exchange certificates. As a result, the device that is accessing the WebAccess system, must be able to support certificates. Most of the handheld and wireless devices come preconfigured with a set list of trusted root certificate authorities. What this means is that if you have used Novell's certificate server to generate a certificate for the Web server, you will not be able to use the handheld devices to access WebAccess. You must request and install a certificate from one of the certificate vendors that the device has in its trusted root list.

TIP

Verisign is the most-supported certificate authority.

If using a cellular phone to access WebAccess that has SSL enabled on the Web server, you must check with the cellular phone service provider to make sure that their gateway has your Web server's certificate issuer on its trusted root list. Otherwise, the data will not pass through the cellular phone's network and down to your cell phone.

Just be aware of these issues. The safest thing is to have the Web server use a certificate that was obtained from a vendor that is in the trusted root list of the devices that will be used to access the WebAccess system.

Summary

In summary, this chapter describes how WebAccess works with some of the more popular handheld and wireless devices on the market. There are many other devices that also work with WebAccess. If they support HTML, simple HTML, WML, HDML, or WebClipping, then they should be able to be used to access the GroupWise mailbox through WebAccess.

The wireless and handheld device support in GroupWise 6 WebAccess components is very impressive, and adds a lot of value for your end users.

CHAPTER 25

GroupWise Developer APIs

This chapter was written by Sean Kirkby, a software developer at Concentrico, Inc. Sean has worked with the GroupWise product since it was known as WordPerfect Office 3.0, and has created custom GroupWise solutions for years.

Concentrico, Inc., is a premier GroupWise support and solution provider. Concentrico has used the various GroupWise APIs to create the Reach for NDS product line, a collection of tools that connect and synchronize GroupWise systems with contact management systems such as GoldMine, Act!, Maximizer, Siebel, and others.

Concentrico's experience with the GroupWise APIs eminently qualifies them to provide the content for this chapter.

Covering such a large topic as the GroupWise APIs in such a small space as a single chapter poses challenges. The purpose of this chapter is to introduce GroupWise administrators to the wide range of solutions that GroupWise will support as a collaboration platform. Often, system administrators and decision makers are unaware of how tightly integrated GroupWise can become with their other systems, processes, and applications. Hopefully, this chapter will change that.

Although this chapter is to serve as an introduction to the many GroupWise APIs, we will cover two of the easiest-to-use and most useful APIs in more detail, with sample code.

Note that while solutions to GroupWise customization problems can be developed using a variety of programming languages and on a variety of operating platforms, the sample code in this chapter was developed using Borland Delphi 5.0 and Microsoft Visual Basic 6.0, and is designed to run on Microsoft 32-bit Windows operating systems.

Prerequisite Knowledge

In order to be able to use the GroupWise APIs, it is important that you be familiar with the GroupWise client and its capabilities. You should, for instance, be familiar with shared folders, query folders, personal folders, the calendar, and the various item types (mail message, phone message, appointments, tasks, notes, and document references). You should be familiar with the GroupWise query process, the various ways to log in to a mailbox, and so on.

Delphi and Visual Basic

In order to follow the examples in this chapter, you should have a working knowledge of either Delphi 5 or Visual Basic 6. If you have a copy of either (or both!), you will find it easier to follow the examples as you run them in your own environment.

Microsoft's Component Object Model (COM) and OLE Automation

Finally, you should note that of all of the GroupWise APIs, the three most-often used APIs are heavily dependent on Microsoft's component object model, or COM, and OLE automation. These are the GroupWise object API (referred to as GWOAPI in this chapter), the custom third-party object API (referred to as C3PO in this chapter), and the token commander.

You do not need to be an expert in OLE automation to use these APIs, but the more you know about it, the easier it is to use the GroupWise APIs.

Fortunately, Delphi and Visual Basic can hide a lot of the implementation details inherent in COM and OLE automation. If you know how to access Microsoft Office objects from Delphi or Visual Basic, then you will find parts of the GroupWise API to be quite easy to understand.

If you are new to COM, OLE automation, and creating ActiveX DLLs and components, it will be worth your time to orient yourself to their use and creation within the context of your development environment (Delphi or Visual Basic). Note that you can also use C++ to use the GroupWise APIs, but it is a much more complicated process. Your code is easier to control, but there will be roughly ten to thirty times the amount of code to accomplish the same tasks when compared to Delphi and Visual Basic. Creating COM and OLE automation servers in C++ takes some time to master.

There are many resources for learning about COM and automation on the World Wide Web. A quick search using any popular search engine for terms such as COM, OLE, automation, and tutorial will likely inundate you with URLs to tutorials, both good and bad.

Structure of This Chapter

There are many ways to customize access to GroupWise — so many, in fact, that they could comprise a book all on their own.

The GroupWise API documentation found in the Novell Developer Kit and online takes a *reference* approach to documenting the APIs. This is useful if you already know what APIs exist and what they can be used for.

In this section, we take a *solutions* approach to the APIs, identifying types of customization solutions you may want to create for or with GroupWise, and discussing which API is best suited to that task.

We only have room in this chapter for an in-depth look at two of the APIs that are easiest to learn, yet provide a very powerful platform for customizations. The other solutions will briefly discuss the API you would use, and provide references for learning more.

The following types of custom solutions are discussed in this chapter:

- Access GroupWise data from custom windows applications
- Automate the GroupWise client
- Other methods for accessing GroupWise data
- Add your own buttons or menus to the GroupWise client
- Trap and handle events in the GroupWise client
- Create custom items in the GroupWise database
- Access GroupWise data from the Web
- Connect GroupWise to other messaging systems
- Automatically create, delete, and modify GroupWise accounts
- Connect to the GroupWise document management system
- The future of customizing GroupWise (XML integration services)

Access GroupWise Data from Custom Windows Applications

Often, GroupWise administrators need to be able to access e-mail messages, calendar data, documents, or address book data from a non-GroupWise application. But the GroupWise databases are encrypted with a proprietary, non-published encryption method — they are not open for developers to access.

Fortunately, Novell provides a number of methods for accessing this data through its various GroupWise APIs. We will consider one of these methods in detail, in the context of a scenario that outlines a business problem that we would like to solve.

Scenario

Suppose that you work for a consulting firm that uses GroupWise to schedule its consultants for appointments with its clients.

In your current process, the amount of time the consultant spends with a client is documented in an e-mail and sent to a manager for approval. The manager then sends it to the accounting department, who enters it into the accounting system.

But you have found that the process often leaves billable work undocumented, and a lot of time is being spent duplicating information. The appointment has already been entered into GroupWise along with the amount of time worked, but the consultant must remember to create an e-mail with this same information and send it to his manager in order for it to be billed. Often, consultants forget to create e-mails for appointments that they have completed, and sometimes they enter the information in their e-mail inaccurately. In addition, the accountant must re-enter the same data into the accounting system, once the manager has approved it.

"Why can't a program be written to take the appointment information out of GroupWise and automatically put it into the accounting system?" you wonder. The good news is that such a program *can* be written.

This section uses a sample application that allows the user to select a folder from the GroupWise mailbox and calculate the time represented by appointments in that folder. In order to do this, you write a program that can access the data in GroupWise.

Novell provides a number of methods for accessing data in a GroupWise mailbox. Each of the GroupWise APIs has advantages and disadvantages, and for nearly every project, one of the GroupWise APIs will stand out as the clear choice to solve the problem. In this case, the GroupWise object API is the best choice. A quick survey of the capabilities and features of the other APIs will bear this out.

The GroupWise Object API

The GroupWise object API (GWOAPI) is, by far, the most powerful and feature-rich method currently publicly available for accessing GroupWise data on the Windows platform. While it is feature-rich, it is platform-dependent (it will only work on Win32 OSs), and depending on what you need to do, it can introduce performance concerns.

But for the most part, it is a great tool for creating applications that access GroupWise data.

In order for the GWOAPI to work, you must have the GroupWise 32-bit client installed.

To use the GWOAPI, you must request a copy of the GroupWise application object from the Windows operating system. Windows then requests this object from the GroupWise client executables, and it is returned to your program.

Applications that allow your program to request an object from them through Windows are known as *automation servers*. There are many automation servers in addition to GroupWise, such as Microsoft Word or Excel. When you request an automation server object, you must tell Windows which automation server it should get the object from.

Every automation server (including GroupWise) has a unique *program identifier*, or *ProgID*. When you request an object from an automation server, you must specify the server's ProgID. The ProgID for the GroupWise application object is NovellGroupwareSession.

The GroupWise application object has a number of methods and properties that you use to gain access to the data in a GroupWise mailbox. In many cases, methods and properties of the GroupWise application object return other objects that have their own methods and properties. These methods and properties also often return other objects, and so on. The GWOAPI is largely a big hierarchy of objects that represent data in the GroupWise mailbox.

All of these objects are documented in the GWOAPI documentation, which you can access online or download and install on your machine (the installed version is an Adobe Acrobat .PDF file).

To access the GWOAPI documentation online, browse to `http://developer.novell.com/ndk/doc_groupwise.htm` and select the GroupWise Object API link (the View link allows you to see it online, and the Download link allows you to download and install the documentation locally).

The secret to successfully working with the GWOAPI is to keep the documentation readily available. There are quite a few objects defined in the GWOAPI, and it isn't practical for you to memorize them all! You will find yourself referring to the GWOAPI documentation quite often.

You will find all of the objects in the GWOAPI documented under the Reference ➪ Objects section of the GWOAPI documentation.

The Basic Solution

The actual solution to the scenario described earlier requires an application that interfaces with two systems: GroupWise and the accounting system. Since there are many accounting systems, we won't endeavor to select a single one to work with in the sample application. In fact, the example won't interface with any kind of system besides GroupWise. The example focuses on how to connect to GroupWise and access its data. Once you have done that, you can easily apply that data anywhere and any way you wish, including automatically adding it to an accounting system. How you do that will, of course, depend on the accounting system you are interfacing with.

The sample assumes that a consultant keeps appointments for any particular client in a separate folder. You would like to allow the user to select such a folder, and have your application calculate how much time is documented in that folder using appointment items. It is assumed that every appointment in a client's folder represents a billable item. This is not a requirement of the GWOAPI or this application; it is merely an assumption we are making to help keep the sample simple and focused.

For this example, we will develop a simple GWOAPI application that has the following basic logic:

In Pseudo-Code

```
Attach to the GroupWise Application
Log into a GroupWise Mailbox
Retrieve a list of folders and display it to the user

Wait for user to select a folder

When user selects folder

      Retrieve Folder Object from mailbox
      Find all appointments in Folder Object

      For each appointment in Folder
            TotalTime = TotalTime + appointment.duration
      End For

      Display TotalTime to user

End When
```

We will discuss each element of the pseudo-code in the following sections.

Attach to the GroupWise Application

All GWOAPI applications start the same way: They must attach to the GroupWise application. The GroupWise client doesn't need to be loaded, but it must be installed.

When the GroupWise client is installed, it registers an automation server called NovellGroupwareSession. In order to attach to the GW application, we must create a NovellGroupWareSession automation server object. Doing this returns an object of type *Application* (defined in the GWOAPI objects reference).

In this sample program, this object will be a global object, as it will be used in various parts of the program.

The following code shows how to connect to the GroupWise application:

In Delphi

```
// in order to create OLE Automation objects in Delphi, you
   must include the
// "ComObj" unit in your "Uses" clause


// we assume that the application's main form class is
   TForm1.
// we create the OLE Automation object when the form is
   created
// (i.e. in the form create event handler)


implementation


{$R *.DFM}


uses
      ComObj;


Var
  // the OLE Automation object is actually a Variant in
     Delphi
  // this will be global to this unit
  vGWApp : Variant;
```

```
// here is the form create event handler...
// it is called when the form is created, and it creates our
   GW application object
procedure TForm1.FormCreate( Sender: Tobject );
begin

vGWApp := CreateOLEObject( 'NovellGroupwareSession' );

end;
```

In Visual Basic

```
' objGWApp is a global variable in this class file
Dim objGWApp as Object

' this is the "form load" event handler
' this is where we create the OLE Automation object
Private Sub Form_Load()

   Set objGWApp = CreateObject("NovellGroupwareSession")

End Sub
```

After you have the application object, you need to log in to a GroupWise mailbox.

Log In to a GroupWise Mailbox

The GroupWise client is a collection of applications and services that work together. Any GroupWise client application (that is, the actual client, the address book, Notify, and so on) will access the GroupWise mailbox through the *GroupWise object request broker* (GWORB), which is a software component that does not have an interface. The GWORB is like a gatekeeper for all GroupWise applications — it manages their access to the mailbox.

When you log in to a mailbox, it is actually the GWORB that authenticates to GroupWise. The GWORB only has to authenticate once. Every GroupWise application checks to see if the GWORB is loaded and authenticated when it loads. If the GWORB is loaded, then the application simply uses the mailbox that the GWORB is connected to.

This is why the GroupWise client will simply load without prompting for a user ID or password if Notify is already running. If Notify loads when Windows starts up, then when Notify loads, it loads the GWORB and authenticates to your mailbox (you may have to enter login information when Notify loads first, depending on your mailbox and workstation settings).

The GWOAPI works like another client application (similar to Notify and the GroupWise client itself).

In order for your application to log in to a mailbox, you simply call the *Login()* method on the Application object (see the documentation for the Application object in the GWOAPI reference). This method returns another object of type *Account*. Through the Account object, you can access the data in a GroupWise mailbox.

The Login method may take a number of parameters. You can pass the user ID and password, or you can pass a command-line string. (This isn't necessarily the command line that was passed to your application, though it could be. The string could contain any command-line parameters that are valid for the GroupWise client, such as `/@u-?` or `/ipa-myserver.mydomain.com`.)

You can also pass a parameter that indicates whether or not the Login method should be allowed to prompt for login information if it can't find it.

GWORB always tries to determine which mailbox to log in to based on information it can find in these locations:

- On the command line or other login parameters passed to it by an application
- In the local registry
- From NDS
- From a POA acting as the GroupWise name server
- By prompting the user for the information

If you call the Login() method with no parameters, then GWORB will look in the registry or NDS for login information (that is, user ID, post office location, and so on). If it can't find it there, then it will try to connect to a GroupWise name server. If that fails, then it will prompt the user for the information.

This process is followed no matter what application is asking the GWORB to authenticate to a mailbox.

In general, the GWOAPI does not have an interface of any kind — it does not display dialog boxes, for example. For instance, you can't use the GWOAPI to open a mail message and display it to the user using the GroupWise client dialog displays. Rather, you get the data elements of a particular mail message and do with it what you would like, including creating your own dialog to display the data and showing it to the user. The GWOAPI (mostly) does not provide any user interfaces of any kind.

There is one exception to this rule, however, and that is with the Login method. Unless you specify that it should not, the Login method will present the user with the generic GroupWise login prompt if it needs to (that is, if it can't find login information in the registry or NDS). But this can be suppressed (see the Application.Login documentation in the GWOAPI reference).

Because of the way the GWORB works, if another GroupWise application has already logged in to a mailbox, then when your application calls the Login() method, it will automatically connect to the mailbox that the GWORB is logged in to, even if you specify a different user ID (such as with the /@u switch).

If you need your application to connect to a specific mailbox, even if another GroupWise application is logged in to a different mailbox, then you would use the Application.MultiLogin method. We won't cover this method here, but you can learn about it in the documentation. The MultiLogin method could be used, for example, to allow a manager to log in to a consultant's mailbox and locate and approve appointments for billing, even if the manager has his own GroupWise client running, logged into his own mailbox.

For our purposes, we can assume that each user will be locating and approving appointments in their own mailbox, and that they either already have GroupWise running, or have logged in at least once before.

So, we can just call the Login() method with no parameters.

Like the Application object, the Account object will be a global variable so that all the functions in the application can access it, and you only have to log in one time.

The following code shows how this is done:

In Delphi

```
implementation

{$R *.DFM}

uses
      ComObj;

Var
  vGWApp, vGWAcct : Variant;
```

```
procedure TForm1.FormCreate( Sender: Tobject );
begin

        vGWApp := CreateOLEObject( 'NovellGroupwareSession' );

        vGWAcct := vGWApp.Login;

end;
```

In Visual Basic

```
Dim objGWApp as Object
Dim objGWAcct as Object

Private Sub Form_Load()

    Set objGWApp = CreateObject("NovellGroupwareSession")

    Set objGWAcct = objGWApp.Login

End Sub
```

Next, you need to get a list of folders and present it to the user.

Retrieve a List of Folders and Display It to the User

This application will use a simple *listbox* control to display folders to the user. You could use a more elaborate *treeview* control, but in order to keep focus on the scenario and the basics of the solution, we will use the more simple listbox control.

In the GWOAPI, there are two objects that you can use to get a complete list of folders: the *Folder* object and the *Folders* (plural) object.

When you look at a list of folders in the GroupWise client, every item you see there is represented in the GWOAPI as a Folder object (except the trash — see the documentation about the *Trash* object). Folder objects have a property called Folders that returns a Folders object.

A Folders object is a list of folders that are immediately owned by the Folders (plural) object's parent (that is, the Folder object that you got the Folders object from).

The Folders object has a property and a method that is very useful. The property is the Count property, which returns the number of folders it contains, and the method is the *Item()* method, which takes an index number and returns the folder at that index (for example, Item(3) returns the third folder in the list).

Starting your quest for a complete list of folders, get the root folder object from the Account object. The Account object has a property called RootFolder that returns a folder object that represents the top-most folder in the mailbox. (This is the folder that is named with the user's display name.) Then access the Root folder's Folders property, which contains all of the folders that the Root folder contains (this will include the Mailbox folder, the Calendar folder, the Cabinet folder, and so on, unless they have been moved by the user). Then simply iterate through each of the Root folder's children, looking for folders they each contain.

In order to do this, you need to create a recursive function that takes two parameters:

- The folder object to start with
- The starting folder's parent's full path name

Note that Folder objects don't provide a method or property that returns their full path (the folder name and each of its ancestor folder names delimited by a backslash). If you want to get a folder's full path, you have to build it yourself, which is why you pass the folder's parent's full path to your function.

Because the algorithm for processing each folder and its children is identical for every folder, you can use recursion to make the job easier. So the function will be a recursive function that calls itself over and over until it reaches the last folder.

For each folder, add it with its full path name to the list box control. The code for doing this follows:

In Delphi

```
procedure TForm1.GetFolderList(vThisFolder : Variant;
sParentFolderName : String);
var
  i : Integer;
  vFolders : Variant;
  vChildFolder : Variant;
  sThisFolderName : String;
begin

  // create this folder's full path name using its name and
     its parent's full path name
  if sParentFolderName = '' then
```

```
      sThisFolderName := vThisFolder.Name
    else
      sThisFolderName := sParentFolderName + '\' +
  vThisFolder.Name;

    // add it to the list box
    ListBox1.Items.Add( sThisFolderName );

    // update the display so they know something is happening
    ListBox1.Refresh;

    // get this folder's "Folders" collection
    vFolders := vThisFolder.Folders;

    // for each of its child folders, call the GetFolderList
       method recursively
    for i := 1 to vFolders.Count do begin

      // get the child folder
      vChildFolder := vFolders.Item( i );

      // send it with its parent's full path name to
         GetFolderList
      GetFolderList( vChildFolder, sThisFolderName );

    end;

  end;
```

In Visual Basic

```
Private Sub GetFolderList(objThisFolder As Object,
sParentFolderName As String)

    Dim i As Integer
    Dim objFolders As Object
```

```
    Dim objChildFolder As Object
    Dim sThisFolderName As String

    ' create this folder's full path name
    If sParentFolderName = "" Then
        sThisFolderName = objThisFolder.Name
    Else
        sThisFolderName = sParentFolderName & "\" &
objThisFolder.Name
    End If

    ' add it to the list box
    List1.AddItem (sThisFolderName)

    ' update the display so they know something is happening
    List1.Refresh



    ' get this folder's "Folders" collection
    Set objFolders = objThisFolder.Folders

    ' for each child folder, call the GetFolderList method
      recursively
    For i = 1 To objFolders.Count

        ' get the child folder
        Set objChildFolder = objFolders.Item(i)

        ' send it with its parent's full path name to
          GetFolderList
        Call GetFolderList(objChildFolder, sThisFolderName)

    Next i

End Sub
```

Because the function is recursive, you only need to call it once to get the entire list of folders. Add a button to the main form that invites the user to click it in order to get the list of folders. Then, you only have to call GetFolderList() from the button's click event handler. The button event handlers are shown in the following code:

In Delphi

```
// the button object is named "Button1"
procedure TForm1.Button1Click(Sender: TObject);
begin
  // sometimes long folder lists can take a while to
     process...
  // so we change the mouse cursor to an hourglass until we
     are done
  Screen.Cursor := crHourGlass;
  Application.ProcessMessages;

  // clear the list box
  ListBox1.Clear;

  // we start with the RootFolder which we get from vGWAcct.
  // RootFolder has no parent, so its "parent's name" is an
     empty string
  GetFolderList( vGWAcct.RootFolder, '' );

  // change the mouse back to show we are done.
  Screen.Cursor := crDefault;
  Application.ProcessMessages;
end;
```

In Visual Basic

```
' the button object is named "Command1"
Private Sub Command1_Click()

    ' sometimes long folder lists can take a while to
      process...
    ' so we change the mouse cursor to an hourglass until we
      are done
```

```
    Screen.MousePointer = vbHourglass
    Refresh

    ' clear the list box in case the user clicks the button
      again
    List1.Clear

    ' we start with the RootFolder which we get from vGWAcct.
    ' RootFolder has no parent, so its "parent's name" is an
      empty string
    Call GetFolderList(objGWAcct.RootFolder, "")

    ' change the mouse back to show we are done.
    Screen.MousePointer = vbDefault
    Refresh

End Sub
```

At this point, when the application runs, you can click the button, and it will show you a list of folders in your mailbox.

The application then waits for the user to do something. The design of the application is to allow the user to select a folder. When the user does this, you find the folder object in the mailbox, find all of the appointments in that folder, and add up the durations of each of them and display it to the user.

You can create an event handler for the click event on the list box control so that when the user clicks on an item in the list box, the application can perform its magic.

The List Box Click Event Handler

The basic logic for the event handler, taken from the pseudo-code in the section, "The Basic Solution," earlier in this chapter, is the following:

In Pseudo-Code

```
When user selects folder

      Retrieve Folder Object from mailbox
      Find all appointments in Folder Object
```

```
        For each appointment in Folder
              TotalTime = TotalTime + appointment.duration
        End For

        Display TotalTime to user

End When
```

In order to accomplish this, you will create two functions that will help you with your solution:

- A FindFolder function that will search the GroupWise mailbox for the Folder object that corresponds to the list box item the user clicked
- A FormattedTotalTime function that will take the total amount of time and format it into a string that can be displayed to the user

When these functions are created (see the upcoming section, "Locating a Folder in the Mailbox"), you can use them in your list box click event handler. You haven't created the FindFolder and FormattedTotalTime functions yet, but when you have done so, the list box click event handler will look like this:

In Delphi

```
procedure TForm1.ListBox1Click(Sender: TObject);
var
  vFolder, vApptList, vAppointment : Variant;
  i : Integer;
  rTotalTime : Double;
begin

  rTotalTime := 0.0;

  // find the folder object
  vFolder := vFindFolder( ListBox1.Items[ListBox1.ItemIndex]
);

  // call the "FindMessages" method on the folder to get all
     the appointments
  vApptList := vFolder.FindMessages( '(APPOINTMENT)' );
```

```
// notify the user we are about to start a potentially long
   process
  Screen.Cursor := crHourGlass;
  Application.ProcessMessages;

  // for each appointment...
  for i := 1 to vApptList.Count do begin

    // get the appointment object
    vAppointment := vApptList.Item( i );

    // add the appointment duration to the total time
    rTotalTime := rTotalTime + vAppointment.Duration;

  end;

  // notify the user that we are done
  Screen.Cursor := crDefault;
  Application.ProcessMessages;

  // set our label caption to the formatted total time string
  lblTotalTime.Caption := sFormattedTotalTime( rTotalTime );


end;
```

In Visual Basic

```
Private Sub List1_Click()
    Dim objFolder As Object
    Dim objApptList As Object
    Dim objAppointment As Object
    Dim i As Integer
    Dim rTotalTime As Double

    rTotalTime = 0#
```

```
' find the folder object
    Set objFolder =
objFindFolder(List1.List(List1.ListIndex))

    ' call the "FindMessages" method on the folder to get all
      the appointments
    Set objApptList = objFolder.FindMessages("(APPOINTMENT)")

    ' notify the user we are about to start a potentially
      long process
    Screen.MousePointer = vbHourglass
    Refresh

    ' for each appointment...
    For i = 1 To objApptList.Count

        ' get the appointment object
        Set objAppointment = objApptList.Item(i)

        ' add its duration to the total
        rTotalTime = rTotalTime + objAppointment.Duration

    Next i

    ' notify the user we are done
    Screen.MousePointer = vbDefault
    Refresh

    ' set our label caption to the formatted total time
      string
    lblTotalTime.Caption = sFormattedTotalTime(rTotalTime)

End Sub
```

Note that a new control was also added to the form. It's a label control named lblTotalTime. This will be used to display the total time to the user.

There are three topics of interest in this example:

- How to locate a folder in the mailbox, given its full path name
- How to search for items (in this case, appointments) in a folder
- How to deal with date and time information obtained from GroupWise

We will discuss these next.

Locating a Folder in the Mailbox

You have already seen how to iterate through the entire list of folders in GroupWise. You could use this same method to locate a folder, if you know the folder's name (not the full path name, but just the folder's name), but this would present two problems:

- It is possible to have two folders with the same name, as long as they are not in the same parent folder, so just having the folder's name is not enough to guarantee that a particular folder is the one you want — you need the full path of the folder, including all of its ancestors' names.
- Having to iterate through the entire tree of folders is a waste of processor time.

Because the design of the application allows you to have the full path name of a folder when the user selects one (you stored the full path in the list box, not just the folder name), you can use a much more efficient, more accurate algorithm for locating the folder you want.

This algorithm works because the Folders object has a method called *ItemByName()*, which takes a string as a parameter and searches its Folders collection for a folder by that name.

In order to accomplish this, you can create a new function that takes the full folder path string as its only parameter, and searches the GroupWise mailbox for the folder using the ItemByName() method.

The FindFolder method code is listed as follows:

In Delphi

```
// in Delphi, our function returns a Variant which is the
   folder object we want
//
```

```
// the sFolderPath parameter will have the format of
//
//    "RootFolder\SomeFolder\SubFolder..."
//
function TForm1.vFindFolder(sFolderPath: String): Variant;
var
  vGWFolder : Variant;
  sTemp : String;
begin

  // this gets the root folder name out of the list b/c we
     will start our search with it
  sFolderPath := Copy( sFolderPath, Pos( '\',sFolderPath)+1,
Length(sFolderPath) );

  // get the root folder object to start the search with.
  vGWFolder := vGWAcct.RootFolder;

  // if the root folder is the one we want, then the original
  // sFolderPath would = RootFolder.Name, and taking the root
     folder name
  // out of sFolderPath would leave us with an empty string.
     If the
  // resulting sFolderPath has more text in it, then the
     folder we want is
  // somewhere under the root folder and we have to keep
     looking
  if sFolderPath <> '' then begin

      // as long as there are subfolders to get...
      while Pos( '\', sFolderPath ) <> 0 do begin
```

```
            // get the next folder name
            sTemp := Copy( sFolderPath, 1, Pos( '\',
sFolderPath ) -1 );
            // take it out of sFolderPath
            sFolderPath :=
Copy(sFolderPath,Pos('\',sFolderPath)+1,Length(sFolderPath));

            // get the folder object
            vGWFolder := vGWFolder.Folders.ItemByName( sTemp );

        end; // while

        // we are at the last folder in the chain
        vGWFolder := vGWFolder.Folders.ItemByName( sFolderPath
);

    end; // if

    // return what we found
    Result := vGWFolder;

end;
```

In Visual Basic

```
' in Visual Basic, our function returns an Object which is
  the folder object we want
'
' the sFolderPath parameter will have the format of
'
'    "User Name\Some Folder\Sub Folder..."
'
Function objFindFolder(sFolderPath As String) As Object
    Dim objGWFolder As Object
    Dim sTemp As String
```

```
    Set objFindFolder = objGWAcct.RootFolder

    ' this gets the root folder name out of the list b/c we
      will start with it
    sFolderPath = Mid(sFolderPath, InStr(sFolderPath, "\")
+ 1)

    ' get the root folder to start with.
    Set objGWFolder = objGWAcct.RootFolder

    If sFolderPath <> "" Then



        Screen.MousePointer = vbHourglass
        Refresh

        ' as long as there are subfolders to get to...
        While InStr(sFolderPath, "\") <> 0

            ' get the next folder name
            sTemp = Left(sFolderPath, InStr(sFolderPath, "\")
- 1)

            ' take it out of the string
            sFolderPath = Mid(sFolderPath, InStr(sFolderPath,
"\") + 1)

            ' get the next folder object
            Set objGWFolder =
objGWFolder.Folders.ItemByName(sTemp)

        Wend
```

```
        Screen.MousePointer = vbDefault
        Refresh

        ' we are at the last folder in the chain
        Set objGWFolder =
objGWFolder.Folders.ItemByName(sFolderPath)


    End If

    Set objFindFolder = objGWFolder

End Function
```

In the event handler, when the user clicks on the list box, you get the text of the item they clicked on, which is the full path name of the folder they are interested in. You can then pass this text to the FindFolder function, which returns the folder object from GroupWise.

Searching for Items in a Folder

Once you have the Folder object for which the user wants to calculate time, you need to locate all of the appointments in that folder and sum their durations. Only appointment items have duration properties, so you can't simply go through every item and try to add its duration. Some of the items may be tasks, or mail messages, or document references. Trying to access the duration property of one of these types will generate an exception. So you want to only work with appointment objects in the folder, which means you have to locate them and separate them out.

To do this, you will use GroupWise's built-in search engine.

GroupWise employs a very powerful indexing and searching engine to allow for searching of mailboxes and libraries. The technology it uses is called QuickFinder.

The GroupWise object API allows programmers to query a GroupWise mailbox or library in much the same way you do through the GroupWise client — by specifying the attributes of the items you want to locate.

There are numerous ways to perform queries within GroupWise through the object API. One way is to create a Query object (see the GWOAPI documentation under Reference ➪ Objects ➪ Query) and use it to initiate the query. Query objects have a QueryMessages property that returns a MessageList object, which is the list of Message objects (or one of its descendants, including Mail, Appointment, Task, Note, Phone, and DocumentReference) that match the query. A Query object has a Locations property, which is a list of folders, mailboxes, and libraries to perform the search in. You could create a Query object and set its Location property to include only the folder you want to search.

Another way to perform a query is to use the FindMessages method on a Folder object, which returns a MessageList object. The FindMessages method limits the query to items contained by the Folder object on which you execute FindMessages. This approach seems to be more direct and intuitive for this purpose, so you will use the FindMessages method on the Folder object, rather than create a Query object and add the folder object to its Locations property.

Like other collection objects in the GWOAPI, the MessageList object has a Count property and an Item() method.

In order to perform a query, whether through a Query object or through a Folder object's FindMessages method, you must indicate to the QuickFinder query engine which messages you are interested in. You do this by supplying a string that indicates the properties and values of those properties that matching messages should have. This string is called a filter expression, and it must follow a carefully documented syntax.

Filter Expressions

A *filter expression* is a formula that indicates how to find the messages you care about. The syntax of a filter expression is documented in the GWOAPI documentation under Reference ➪ Filter Expression Syntax. However, the documentation has very few examples and is a bit esoteric.

To help you learn what a particular filter expression should look like in order to perform the query you want, we have included a utility for seeing numerous examples of query expressions. Included in the examples for this chapter is an executable called GWQueryStringViewer that allows you to select a Query folder from the GroupWise mailbox, and it will display the corresponding filter expression used by the GroupWise client to execute the query. In order to get an accurate view of what a filter expression should look like, use the GroupWise client to create the query you would like to perform in your custom GWOAPI application, save the results to a query folder, and use GWQueryStringViewer to see the filter expression that the GroupWise client saved with the Query folder.

Some examples of valid filter expressions are listed in the following table:

FILTER EXPRESSION	RESULTS
`(APPOINTMENT)`	Any item that is an appointment
`(MAIL AND FROM MATCHES "Sean Kirkby")`	All mail messages where the From text is Sean Kirkby
`(BOX_TYPE=OUTGOING)`	All sent items
`(TASK AND BOX_TYPE = OUTGOING AND NOT COMPLETED)`	All sent tasks that have not been marked completed by the recipient

Note that filter expressions must begin with an open parenthesis, but the entire query does not need to be enclosed in parentheses. For instance, the following is a valid filter expression:

```
(TASK AND BOX_TYPE = OUTGOING) OR (APPOINTMENT AND
DELIVERED_DATE = TODAY)
```

This expression would return all sent tasks *and* all appointments delivered today (sent or received). Note that the two groups of criteria are joined with the `OR` operator, but the entire expression is *not* enclosed in parentheses.

For these purposes, you simply want to find all the appointments, so the filter expression `(APPOINTMENT)` will do the trick.

Refer to the list box click event handler code earlier in this chapter to see how you use the Folder.FindMessages method and the `(APPOINTMENT)` filter expression to get a list of all appointments (and only appointments) in the folder.

Working with Date and Time Objects

The third aspect of the sample time calc application is accessing and manipulating the durations of the appointments in a folder.

Once you have the Folder object you are interested in, and once you have queried that folder for a list of appointments and received a MessageList object in return, you can now iterate through the appointments and add up the time each one takes.

As the preceding section shows, the FindMessages method of a Folder object returns a MessageList object. In the list box click event handler, you simply iterate through the MessageList object using the Count property and Item() method. You are guaranteed that 100 percent of the items in the MessageList object are appointments because of the filter expression you used, so you really don't need to do any checking to make sure they are appointments.

If you had no such guarantee, you would definitely want to verify that each item is an appointment, because appointments have properties that other message types don't have — namely, properties that identify the beginning and ending dates and times, and duration of the appointment, among others.

Since you don't have the MessageList object until run-time, and since the MessageList object can contain messages of various types (that is, they don't have to all be the same type), there really isn't a guarantee that the MessageList doesn't have non-appointment objects in it — except for the fact that the MessageList was generated by a query using a filter expression that ensures that only appointments come back.

Date and time values in the world of COM and OLE automation are typically stored as double values that have an integral portion and a fractional portion. This number, by convention, represents the number of days that have elapsed since midnight on December 30, 1899. By examining an OLE date/time variable stored as a double, you will have a value that indicates a specific point in time, right down to the millisecond. The fractional portion represents the fractional number of days — in other words, the number of hours, minutes, seconds, and milliseconds.

An example would be the double value of `37966.791666667`, which is 37,966 days and 19 hours after December 30, 1899, which corresponds to 7:00 p.m. on December 11, 2003.

Appointment objects in the GWOAPI have a Duration property that is a double value. While it is a double, and as such, does represent a number of whole and fractional days, it is stored as a double, and not as a date value. Technically, date values are stored as doubles, but they are identified as dates. This is important when retrieving the value, especially when you consider the type of variable you retrieve the value into.

Appointment objects also have StartDate and EndDate properties. The GWOAPI documentation indicates that their values are date values. They are actually stored as doubles, but can be retrieved into special date variables in Delphi and Visual Basic without any conversion.

If you access the StartDate and EndDate properties using a variant (in Delphi) or object (in Visual Basic) variable, the date value is automatically converted to a string representation of the date and time (if the StartDate or EndDate properties are being accessed in a context that requires a string), even though it is stored as a double value. This is not true of the Duration property, since its type is indicated as double.

For instance, if an appointment begins at 12:00 p.m. on 9/7/1998, you could perform the following operations on the StartDate property of the appointment:

```
sMyString := vAppointment.StartDate \\ sMyString would be
"9/7/1998 12:00 PM"
dblMyDouble := vAppointment.StartDate \\ dblMyDouble would be
36045.5
```

If the appointment were an hour long, then you could do the following:

```
sMyString := vAppointment.Duration \\ sMyString would be
"4.16666666666667E-02"
dblMyDouble := vAppointment.Duration \\ dblMyDouble would be
0.0416666666666667
```

If this same value (`0.0416666666666667`) were identified as a date, then converting it to a string would give you `12/31/1899 1:00 AM`, rather than `4.16666666666667E-02`.

In this case, you are dealing with the Duration property, and you simply want to add them. So you use a local double variable to store the sum, and later to pass to the FormattedTotalTime() method.

Refer to the list box click event handler, and you will see how you iterate through the message list and total the durations of all the appointments.

Once you have the total, you pass it to the formatting function, which simply breaks it down into days, hours, and minutes. (We don't care about seconds or milliseconds, and an application that was used in real-life would probably round the minutes up to a boundary such as 15 or 30 minutes since most consultancies charge at 15- or 30-minutes interval — but we won't worry with that here.)

You start by using the integral portion of the double value. Initially, the integral portion represents the number of whole days. If the value were, for instance, `1.6513888888889`, then you would break it down like this:

- The integral portion of the original value is 1, meaning one full day. So you store that, and subtract it from the original value.
- That leaves you with a fractional number of days: 0.6513888888889. To find out how many hours that is, you multiply by 24 (there are 24 hours in a day, and 0.6513888888889 days). That gives a value of 15.6333333333333.
- The integral portion of this value is the number of whole hours, namely 15. So you store that and subtract it from the value, which leaves a value of 0.6333333333333.

- This represents the fractional number of hours. To convert it to minutes, you multiply by 60 (there are 60 minutes in an hour, and 0.6333333333333 hours). This gives us a total of 38.0. The integral portion of this is the number of whole minutes, namely 38.
- So you take these values and build a string that makes sense to the user: 1 day, 15 hours, 38 minutes.

Conclusion

And thus you have a simple GWOAPI application that allows the user to select a GroupWise folder and calculates the total amount of time represented by appointments in that folder. You have solved the customer's problem!

Well, not really — not 100 percent, at least. You still have to push this data into the accounting system.

And, you should somehow indicate in GroupWise that the appointments you counted have already been billed. You also have to modify the calculation scheme to *not* include appointments that have been billed already. Doing this will involve the use of FieldDefinition objects and Field objects, both of which are documented with the GWOAPI documentation. Taking this into account is beyond the scope of this example, but the documentation should get you on the right path.

Automate the GroupWise Client

We will examine this simple API in the context of a simple business need, described next.

Scenario

A small law firm uses Microsoft Word to prepare client documents. They also use GroupWise to collaborate with their clients, with opposing counsel, and others.

Some of the law firm's employees spend much of their day working in Microsoft Word, but frequently have to send e-mail reminders or requests for information to others. Often, routine parts of documents they are working on must be cut-and-pasted into the body of the e-mail (such as a case or matter number, an address or phone number, and so on).

In addition, some of the e-mail messages they send must contain lengthy disclaimers, which are identical every time they send them.

They have requested the ability to initiate the sending of these messages from within Word, without having to switch to GroupWise first. Furthermore, they would like the ability to automatically include certain disclaimers at-will, and to extract pieces of information from the document they are working on and automatically paste them into the e-mail before it is sent.

This will save the employees a lot of time and strain.

The Token Commander

The token commander is an OLE automation object provided by the GroupWise client that allows you to send commands to the client interface, controlling it in various ways. You acquire a copy of the token commander object in the same way that you acquire a copy of the GroupWise application object in the GroupWise object API. The ProgID for the token commander is GroupWiseCommander. The examples in the section, "Getting the Token Commander," show how to get a copy of the token commander.

The token commander has only one method, Execute(), and it has no other methods. You use the Execute() method to send tokens, or commands, to the GroupWise client interface. Note that the token commander does not actually interface with GroupWise data. Instead, it interfaces with the GroupWise *client*. For this reason, not only does the client have to be installed in order for the token commander to work but also it must be running.

Using the Execute() method of the token commander, you send commands to the GroupWise client that cause it to do things automatically that you could otherwise do manually with your mouse and keyboard. For instance, if you want to send a message with the GroupWise client, you would choose File ➪ New ➪ Mail, or click the New Mail button on the toolbar, or press the Ctrl+M shortcut on the keyboard. All of these cause a New Mail dialog box to appear, where you can type the names of recipients, provide a subject and message body, and attach files.

The token commander can also cause the New Mail dialog box to appear. You simply send the client a special token (a string that represents a command). In this case, the token you would use is NewMail(). We will cover how to use this token and other tokens later in the example for this section.

For now, simply understand that if you sent the NewMail() token to the client using the token commander's Execute() method, a New Mail dialog box would appear, ready and waiting to receive input from the user.

Other tokens would allow you to automatically select recipients, create subject and message bodies, add attachments, or even simulate the user typing on the keyboard.

You can find documentation for the token commander at `http://developer.novell.com/ndk/doc_groupwise.htm` under the GroupWise Tokens category. The token commander documentation includes documentation for every token you can send, listed alphabetically.

Using the token commander, you can automate the keystrokes and mouse movements that a user would normally use to perform routine and repetitious actions in GroupWise.

Next, we will look at the basic structure of the solution to the scenario outlined for this section.

The Basic Solution

After interviewing users at the law firm, it is determined that two basic e-mail types should be supported, each with their own disclaimer, and each requiring different information from the document that is open.

It is decided that this solution will simply query the user and allow them to select a message type. It will then create a new message dialog box, add the disclaimer to the message body, harvest the necessary information from the currently open document, add that to the message body, and then allow the user to enter a subject, select recipients, add attachments, and send the message.

The following pseudo-code outlines the basic logic of the application:

In Pseudo-Code

```
Get copy of Token Commander

Wait for user to select a message type

When user selects a message type
   Create new message dialog

   if type = 1 then begin
      Add disclaimer_1 to message body
   end if

   if type = 2 then begin
      add disclaimer_2 to message body
   end if
```

```
   Exit application
End When
```

After the message dialog box is created, and the pertinent information added to it, the application exits and the user is left with the modified new message dialog box to add recipients, a subject, add to the message body if needed, and send the message.

Each step in the pseudo-code is examined in the following sections.

Getting the Token Commander

In order to use the token commander in your application, you simply create a GroupWiseCommander OLE automation object. The ProgID for the token commander is GroupWiseCommander. The following examples show how to do this:

In Delphi

```
// in order to create OLE Automation objects in Delphi, you
   must include the
// "ComObj" unit in your "Uses" clause

// we assume that the application's main form class is
   TForm1.
// we create the OLE Automation object when the form is
   created
// (i.e. in the form create event handler)

implementation

{$R *.DFM}

uses
      ComObj;

Var
  // the OLE Automation object is actually a Variant in
     Delphi
  // this will be global to this unit
  vGWCommander : Variant;
```

```
// here is the form create event handler...
// it is called when the form is created, and it creates our
   Token Commander
procedure TForm1.FormCreate( Sender: Tobject );
begin


      vGWCommander := CreateOLEObject( 'GroupWiseCommander'
);


end;
```

In Visual Basic

```
' objGWCommander is a global variable in this class file
Public objGWCommander as Object

' this is the "form load" event handler
' this is where we create the OLE Automation object
Private Sub Form_Load()

   Set objGWCommander = CreateObject("GroupWiseCommander")

End Sub
```

In order for the token commander to work, the GroupWise client must be loaded and running. If the client is not running, then when you try to get a copy of the token commander, the token commander will try to load the client for you. If the client fails to load, an exception is generated.

Note that this requirement does not refer to simply being *authenticated* to GroupWise — it's not good enough to just have Notify loaded and be logged in. The actual GroupWise client must be running for the token commander to work.

The token commander sends commands to the GroupWise client using DDE. The commands are often very dependent on the current state of the GroupWise client when they are received by GroupWise.

Using DDE and tokens to control the GroupWise client is a method that dates back to the GroupWise 4.x days when DDE was a new development technology under Windows 3.1. GroupWise 4.1 used to support a macro engine that would process the tokens in a script, making it possible to repetitively automate many functions in GroupWise by simply creating a sequential list of tokens. This is still possible using the same tokens, although there is not a macro processing engine in GroupWise 5.x or 6.0 that can process the tokens in order. The tokens must be passed to GroupWise from within a COM controller, such as this sample application.

After you have a copy of the token commander, you must find out what kind of message the user wants to send.

Waiting for User to Select a Message Type

You will do this by simply listing the possibilities as radio buttons (since there are only two). In a more complex solution, you could list message types in a database or an .INI file, along with the name of a file that contains the disclaimer or default text for the message body, and so on.

But in this case, you will simply hard-code the options into the application.

Examine either the Delphi and Visual Basic sample code (or both!) to see the radio buttons that give the user the choice.

This application requires the user to click a button to actually create the message.

When the user clicks the button, you will examine the radio buttons to find out what kind of message you should create. This is a bit of a misnomer — in every case, you will be creating a mail message, but in each case, the default disclaimer text added to the message will be different.

Creating the Message

Once the user has selected the message type, you can create the message and add the default text that matches the type that the user selected.

To do this, you use the token commander to send a create new mail message token to the client, followed by a set the message body text to token.

To issue tokens, or commands, to the client using the token commander, you will use the Execute() method of the token commander. The Execute() method takes two parameters and returns an integer value. It might be called like this:

In Visual Basic

```
iReturnVal = vGWCommander.Execute("NewMail()", sReturnString)
```

The Execute() method returns 0 if the call to Execute() failed for some reason, and it returns a non-zero value if the call succeeds.

Basically, calling Execute() causes the first parameter to be converted to a DDE token, and it passes that token (using DDE) to the DDE server in the GroupWise client.

Each of the tokens is like a function call itself. You pass a string representation of the token function call, along with its parameters, to the Execute() method.

For instance, the SetItemText() token takes three required parameters and one optional parameter. This token allows you to set the value of a text field on any particular item in the mailbox. You pass the function a string that represents the message ID of the item you want to modify, an enumerated value that indicates which field of the item to modify (TO: field, subject, message body, and so on), and you pass a string that will either replace the current contents of the field being modified or append to the current contents. Whether the field is appended to or replaced depends on the fourth (optional) parameter, which indicates whether an append or a replace should happen. If it is not provided, replace is assumed.

The syntax of the token is:

```
SetItemText( string; integer; string[; integer] )
```

The first string is the message ID of the item to modify. The first integer indicates which field to modify (the enumerated values for each modifiable field are documented with the token commander reference entry for the SetItemText() command). The second string is the new text value. The third integer indicates whether to append or replace the field (1 for append, 0 for replace).

In order to issue the SetItemText() command to the client, you have to pass it, along with its parameters, to the Execute() method of the token commander.

An example of this is shown in the following code:

In Delphi

```
. . .
   iResult := vGWCommander.Execute(
'SetItemText("X00";10;"New message body")', sResult )
. . .
```

In Visual Basic

```
. . .

iResult=objGWCommander.Execute("SetItemText(""X00"";10;""New
message body"")",sResult)
. . .
```

In passing token commands to the Execute() method, any token-command parameter that is a string must be enclosed in double-quotes. Token-command parameters must be separated by semicolons.

Note the X00 message ID string. Every message item in a GroupWise mailbox has a unique identifier. Often, token commands need a message ID string so that the client knows which item to perform the command with. The SetItemText() token command is a good example. You can request that the client modify the message body of a mail message, but you must indicate *which* message to modify!

If a mail message is open in the client, then any application that issues the ItemMessageIDByView() token command will receive a string that represents the unique message ID for that mail message. This can be used to acquire the message ID for token commands that need it (such as the SetItemText() token command).

However, GroupWise items aren't assigned a unique message ID until they are actually saved to a database (that is, either sent or received). In this example, you are working with a *new* item that has not been sent yet. Therefore, it does not have a unique message ID. Passing the ItemMessageIDByView() command causes the value X00 to be returned (that's X with two zeros after it). The message ID X00 is reserved for items that are being created, that have not been sent yet.

So when you send the SetItemText() command, you indicate a message ID of X00 so that the message body of the newly created mail message will be modified. Of course, if you pass this command and no newly created items exist (that is, no items with a message ID of X00), then the token command will fail to execute, and you will get an error result back.

To perform the function this application must perform, you will use both the NewMail() token command and the SetItemText() token command. You will issue these token commands as a result of the user pressing the Create button on the form. The button's click event handler will check to see what kind of message the user selected, then add the appropriate text to the message body.

These are demonstrated in the following sample code, which is taken from the sample projects:

In Delphi

```
procedure TForm1.Button1Click(Sender: TObject);
var
  iResult : Integer;
  sResult : String;
begin

  // create the new mail message dialog
  iResult := vGWCommander.Execute('NewMail()', sResult);

  // check to see which disclaimer to include
  // send the "ItemSetText()" command with "X00" as the
     message ID
```

```
  // "10" is the enumerated value for the message body field
  if rbMessageType1.Checked = TRUE then

    iResult :=
vGWCommander.Execute('ItemSetText("X00";10;"Disclaimer #1")',
sResult)

  else

    iResult :=
vGWCommander.Execute('ItemSetText("X00";10;"Disclaimer #2")',
sResult);

  // exit the application, leaving the user with the new mail
     dialog
  Application.Terminate;

end;
```

In Visual Basic

```
Private Sub btnCreate_Click()
    Dim iResult As Integer
    Dim sResult As String

    ' create the new mail message dialog
    iResult = objGWCmndr.Execute("NewMail()", sResult)

    ' check to see which disclaimer to include
    ' send the "ItemSetText()" command with "X00" as the
      message ID
    ' "10" is the enumerated value for the message body field
    If rbMessageType1.Value = True Then
```

```
        iResult =
objGWCmndr.Execute("ItemSetText(""X00"";10;""Disclaimer
#1"")",sResult)

    Else

        iResult =
objGWCmndr.Execute("ItemSetText(""X00"";10;""Disclaimer
#2"")",sResult)

    End If

    ' exit the application, leaving the user with the new
      mail dialog
    End

End Sub
```

Note that in these examples, you are assigning the return value of the Execute() method to the integer iResult. Typically, you would examine iResult to see if it was 0 or non-zero, indicating failure or success of the call. To keep these examples simple, you won't do that here. But it is a good idea to check for failures in your own code. If the Execute() method fails to execute a token command, it does *not* generate an exception. It simply returns 0 and puts an error message string in the sResult variable.

Note also that some token commands return values. Some return strings, others return numbers or dates. In all cases, the return value is converted to a string and placed in the sResult variable. You could pass a variant (for Delphi) or object (for Visual Basic) variable as the second parameter to the Execute() method. In this way, if the token command returns a number, and the Execute() method puts a string representation of that number in your return variable, you can still access it as a number. (Variants and objects can automatically be converted to a number or date or string by the compiler, depending on the expression they are being used in.)

Conclusion

This is a very simple example of how to use the token commander. Elaborate solutions can be created that are very creative. For example, a very patient person could create an OLE automation server that mimics all of the token commands and simply passes the correct token command to the token commander when the mimicked methods are called. In addition, this automation server could implement its own exception handling scheme, automatically raising exceptions for your code to handle if a 0 value is returned by the Execute() method, for example. There are quite a few tokens, providing all sorts of capabilities. You should read through the documentation to become familiar with them.

You can build on this sample application to allow for more message types, allowing default disclaimers or other default text to reside in text files that the user can modify, if you want. In addition, you can add other features, such as automatically including certain recipients or certain attachments based on the selected message type.

Other Methods for Accessing GroupWise Data

There are other methods for accessing data in a GroupWise mailbox without using the GroupWise object API. This section will discuss a few of them, along with their benefits.

POP3 and IMAP4

GroupWise provides access to mailbox data using POP3 and IMAP4, two popular Internet protocols. Of course, this is beneficial to those users who want to be able to access GroupWise mailbox data using a commercial or publicly available POP3 or IMAP4 client.

But these protocols can also be used in a custom solution.

Suppose you want to create a custom-built knowledge management application that periodically retrieves users' e-mail from GroupWise, indexes it, and stores it in a searchable database. Suppose, further, that for scalability reasons you choose not to implement your indexing agent on Windows. A more suitable platform such as Linux, Unix, or NetWare is chosen.

The problem, then, is how do you access GroupWise data in mailboxes from a non-Windows OS? You can't use the GWOAPI since it only works on Windows.

POP3 or IMAP4 would be good solutions for this. When messages are downloaded via POP3, they are marked to indicate that they are already downloaded, and your POP3 client on the indexing agent can be configured to ignore those that have already been downloaded.

Since POP3 and IMAP4 are well-documented protocols, you can develop custom applications that can access data in GroupWise quite easily. Both protocols are TCP-based and both support a simple set of commands. You can read about POP3 and IMAP4 commands at these Web sites:

```
POP3: http://www.ietf.org/rfc/rfc1939.txt
IMAP4: http://www.ietf.org/rfc/rfc2060.txt
```

Note that with both IMAP4 and POP3, only mail message types are supported. You can access other message types, but they are converted to mail messages as they are retrieved. Additional attributes (such as start date and end date, task priority, and so on) are not retrieved — they are lost.

While POP3 and IMAP4 are not the most feature-rich methods for accessing GroupWise data, they do have one major benefit: You can use them to access GroupWise messages from nearly any platform. Thus, a Unix application can easily be written to access GroupWise mailbox data. A Java servlet can be written to access GroupWise message data and integrate it into a Web page. Platform independence is possible when using these methods.

MAPI

GroupWise supports extended MAPI, Microsoft's messaging API, which can be used to access and manipulate data in a GroupWise mailbox.

Extended MAPI allows you to access GroupWise folders and messages, as well as address-book data. Although MAPI is a very old standard, it is still in use today by nearly every major productivity application on the market.

You can learn more about MAPI from Microsoft's Web site by browsing to `http://msdn.microsoft.com/library/default.asp` and searching for MAPI. You should find a link to the MAPI Programmers Reference.

Although MAPI does provide decent access to the GroupWise mailbox, it lacks robust support for native GroupWise item types such as appointments. Furthermore, developing applications that use true MAPI are not as easy as developing OLE automation clients, since MAPI is not available through an automation Server.

Add Your Own Buttons or Menus to the GroupWise Client

Suppose you wanted to add a button to the GroupWise toolbar that allowed you to launch the GWOAPI application you created. This way, the application would appear to be tightly integrated with GroupWise, and users would be able to run it right from the GroupWise interface.

To add buttons to the toolbar, you need to use the C3PO API.

Custom Third-Party Objects (C3POs)

The C3PO API is an innovative API that allows you to modify the GroupWise client and its behavior. C3PO stands for *Custom Third-Party Objects.* The name can make it difficult to understand what the API is used for and how it works.

Of course, adding a single button to a toolbar that launches an external application when clicked is a bit simplistic. Far more complicated and useful solutions can be created.

Consider, for example, the solution you created using the GWOAPI. Using the C3PO API, you could expand on that solution, providing much more functionality and tighter integration with the GroupWise client.

You could, for instance, create a new type of appointment, based on the default appointment, that not only allows you to keep track of the appointment's duration, but also allows you to specify a specific project code, or customer ID when the appointment was created, allowing you to create more useful and accurate reports. In addition, an attribute could be created that allows you to categorize the work (consulting, troubleshooting, custom development, and so on), which could be used to figure the price per hour, for example. Finally, the C3PO could allow you to select the folder right in the GroupWise client, without having to create a separate interface or dialog box. The solution can be so tightly integrated with the GroupWise client that new GroupWise users wouldn't know that it was a custom solution!

Like the GWOAPI, C3POs depend heavily on OLE automation. But C3POs are different in that they are developed as OLE automation *servers,* rather than *controllers.* The GroupWise client has an automation controller called the C3PO Manager that is designed to make use of C3POs that are developed according to the C3PO specification. You create an automation server, assign it a unique ProgID, then register it with GroupWise so that the C3PO manager knows about it, and what its ProgID is.

When the GroupWise client loads, the C3PO manager gets a copy of your C3PO server from the operating system, and makes calls to your automation server that give you a chance to add your own buttons and menus to the client, along with custom code to be executed when your buttons or menus are selected.

If you develop C3POs, you will likely develop ones that will use the GWOAPI for access to data in the mailbox. This means that your C3POs will typically be both OLE automation servers *and* OLE automation controllers.

C3POs allow you to do a number of things:

- Add buttons to any of the toolbars in GroupWise.
- Add menu items to any of the menus in GroupWise.
- Add menu items to any of the contextual or pop-up menus in GroupWise.
- Detect and respond to a limited number of events in GroupWise (such as when a message is received, opened, deleted, and printed, or when GroupWise starts up or the user wants to exit).
- Create custom item types based on the standard GroupWise message types (that is, you can create a custom appointment that has all of the capabilities of regular appointments, plus your own custom capabilities) — you can even associate custom opened and not opened icons with your custom items.

Even though C3POs *allow* you to do all of these things, your own C3PO doesn't have to do *all* of them. You can develop a C3PO that simply adds a new button to the toolbar and launches an external program when it is clicked. You can develop a C3PO that creates a new item type based on appointments, and that also adds a menu item to the File ➪ New menu to allow the user to create items of your new type from the menu. You can create a C3PO that adds a standard disclaimer to each message that is sent without forcing the user to remember to type it or otherwise include it.

Any single C3PO can do any number of these things, including all of them.

You can view Novell's C3PO documentation at `http://developer.novell.com/ndk/doc_groupwise.htm` under the heading of GroupWise C3PO.

A Tutorial and Sample Projects

The C3PO API is a very powerful way to customize GroupWise. It allows you to modify the interface by adding buttons and menus; it allows you to monitor and handle events, such as when a message is opened; and it allows you to create custom items.

Lack of time and resources prevent us from providing an in-depth view of creating C3POs and providing sample projects in this chapter. But you can download an easy-to-follow tutorial at the following location:

`http://www.Concentrico.net/GW6AdminGuide/Tutorials`

The folks at Concentrico maintain an in-depth tutorial on how to create C3POs, complete with sample projects to aid you in your efforts to learn to create GroupWise add-ons.

Trap and Handle Events in the GroupWise Client

As a user works in the GroupWise client, it is often useful for your software to know when the user performs some action in GroupWise, such as opening or deleting a mail message, or when a new message is delivered, or when the user wants to exit GroupWise.

GroupWise provides two APIs that allow you to monitor and handle certain events.

C3POs

In addition to adding buttons and menus to the GroupWise client, C3POs allow you to monitor and handle certain events that occur in GroupWise.

For instance, consider the solution you created using the GroupWise token commander, which allowed users to select from a list of mail message types, automatically adding an appropriate disclaimer when the message was sent. With C3POs, you could present that same list to users when they try to create a new mail message. If they click on the New Mail button on the toolbar, or choose File ➪ New ➪ Mail, your C3PO can trap that event and pop up a dialog box giving the user a chance to select what kind of mail message they want to send.

This gives your C3PO a chance to add text to a message body or add recipients to a distribution list. The list of events that C3POs can handle is documented with the C3PO documentation. Note that C3POs have an object called an EventMonitor that can only monitor four defined events (OnReady, OnShutdown, OnDelivery, and OnOverflow). There are certainly more events you would want to monitor (such as printing an item, deleting an item, sending an item, and so on).

These other events *can* be monitored, but they are handled through the CommandFactory object in the C3PO API. They are not referred to as events, but rather commands.

Refer to the C3PO documentation for more information.

Oddly, the C3PO API doesn't provide a way for you to trap a send event, indicating that the user has pressed the Send button. But there is another API that allows you to trap events, known as the third-party handler API.

Third-Party Token Handler DLL (TPH DLL)

The third-party handler API, also known as the TPH API, allows you to create a token handler DLL that the GroupWise client loads. When the user works in the GroupWise client, tokens are generated that represent the various actions the user takes. If any TPH DLLs are loaded, the GroupWise client sends the tokens to the handlers before acting on them itself.

Each handler is allowed to examine the token and determine if it wants to do something in response to it — that is, whether it wants to handle it or not.

After viewing a token, the TPH DLL can decide to forward the token back to the client or not. If the TPH DLL does not want the default client action to take place (that is, if the TPH DLL is designed to supplant the default client action, rather than add to it), it can indicate to the client that the token has been handled and no further processing should take place.

Multiple TPH DLLs may be installed, and every token is passed to each of them one after another. If any TPH DLL indicates that the token has been handled, no other TPH DLLs will receive the token.

Tokens represent nearly every action in the GroupWise client. For instance, when the user elects to create a new message, the BFTKN_SEND_STDMAIL token is generated and passed to the chain of TPH DLLs.

When the user actually presses the Send button, the BTKN_SEND token is generated.

Each token is identified by a (hopefully) unique value. The TPH include files that are included with the GroupWise token sample code download defines named constants for most tokens that the client will generate. However, there are not definitions for *every* token generated. There are some tokens that you may wish to handle that are not defined in the include files or documented anywhere else.

To help you identify token values that may not be defined or documented, Concentrico has created a utility called GroupWise Token Viewer, or GroupWise TV. This utility is included with the other Concentrico code bundled with this book.

It is a combination C3PO and TPH DLL that acts on every token it receives. It is registered as a C3PO, is loaded when the GroupWise client loads, and displays either the defined constant name or token value for every token that is generated. This allows you to see token values for tokens that have no defined name.

Note that this utility produces output based on defined constants available from Novell at the time the utility was created (January 2000).

The GroupWise token sample code download can be found at the following URL:

```
http://developer.novell.com/ndk/sample_groupwise.htm
```

The TPH specification is documented with the GroupWise tokens documentation, found at the following URL:

```
http://developer.novell.com/ndk/doc_groupwise.htm
```

Access GroupWise Data from the Web

Suppose your employer has just deployed an HTML-based corporate portal that employees access frequently. You have been getting requests from different departments to allow users to see their calendar data in the portal. In addition, some departments want to be able to search for and view documents from the departmental library through the portal.

How would you do this?

There is actually more than one way to accomplish this. If your Web server runs on a Windows platform and supports some type of plug-in, you could create a native Windows application that logs into and accesses a GroupWise account using the GWOAPI. But this can be clunky and may lack scalability.

A better way would be to use the WebAccess gateway.

GroupWise ships with the WebAccess gateway, which is actually an alternative client, allowing users to view their mailbox data using a Web browser.

The WebAccess gateway is actually a framework that you can utilize to access GroupWise data and present it in a customized fashion, along with other data (if you want).

The WebAccess gateway consists of four types of components: a Java servlet, template files, the WebAccess agent, and a provider, which is a Java class that can be called by a servlet.

You can customize the WebAccess interface in two basic manners:

- Modifying the templates the servlet uses to create the final text (HTML or XML) documents
- Creating custom providers the servlet uses to access data from other sources

The servlets, templates, and providers all reside on one machine, typically a Web server. The WebAccess Agent, also known as the GroupWise interface agent, or GWINTER for short, may run on the Web server, but can also run on a separate box.

The servlets can run on NetWare, Windows NT/2000, or Unix, and the agent can run on NetWare or Windows NT/2000. This allows you to run the servlets on one box (probably outside a firewall, if you are providing access over the Internet), while running the agent on another box (inside the firewall). In addition, this gives you more flexibility concerning what platforms are needed. Of course, users can run any modern browser from any supported platform.

The WebAccess gateway installs two servlets known as WebAcc for Web Access and WebPub for Web Publisher. The WebAcc servlet is used to gain access to GroupWise mailbox data (folders, items, address book data, and so on). The WebPub servlet is used to provide public access to documents in GroupWise libraries.

Each servlet has a configuration file. Providers are registered for each servlet in the servlet's configuration file. The WebAcc servlet is installed with two providers configured: the GroupWise provider and the LDAP provider. The WebPub servlet is installed with one provider configured: the Web Publisher provider.

The GroupWise and Web Publisher providers communicate with the Web Access agent, which governs access to the GroupWise system. The WebAccess agent provides login and other services, similar to the object API. By communicating with the WebAccess agent, these providers can issue requests and receive data from a mailbox or library. The providers then pass the data back to the servlet, which combines it with template files. This results in an HTML or XML document that is sent back to the browser.

The LDAP provider works in a similar fashion, but it communicates with LDAP servers directly. It doesn't go through the WebAccess agent.

Novell provides extensive documentation concerning how to interact with the servlets, how to modify the templates, or how to create your own providers. The documentation can be found at the following URL:

```
http://developer.novell.com/ndk/doc_groupwise.htm
```

Look under the GroupWise WebAccess Customization heading.

Connect GroupWise to Other Messaging Systems

Suppose you just began work for a government organization that is using a mainframe-based messaging system for about 60 percent of the government workers, while the remaining 40 percent use GroupWise. The mainframe system is a homegrown system that was created seven years ago, but it seems to be stable and working. There are plans to migrate the users on that system into GroupWise, but in the meantime your management has asked you to figure out how to connect the two systems.

How would you do that?

So far, all of the APIs we have looked at are client-side APIs. This means that the solutions you create have to be installed on each user's workstation (except for the WebAccess solutions).

This problem, however, requires some way to be able to send messages out of the GroupWise system into another system, and to retrieve messages from the other system into GroupWise.

If the other system supports one of the messaging standards that GroupWise supports (for example, IMAP4 and POP3), you could just connect them using that. But in this case, the system in use was created before these Internet standards were in widespread use, and the team responsible for creating it has long since left the organization.

Because it is a homegrown system, there is no commercial solution. You will have to create one. Fortunately, in this case (let's assume), the mainframe system is running on ADABASE and can easily be modified.

Of course, there are many complexities involved on the mainframe side of this solution that have nothing to do with GroupWise. But for these purposes, we are interested in how to connect such a solution to the GroupWise system.

The two options we have are to retro-fit the ADABASE system with a standard such as SMTP or create a custom gateway that connects to both GroupWise and the ADABASE system. We will assume that the first option is not practical.

In this case, we will use the GroupWise API gateway.

The GroupWise API gateway has been a part of the GroupWise gateway family since GroupWise 4.x. It installs like any other gateway, and messages can be addressed to it like any other gateway. You can create an external foreign domain and link to it through the API gateway, allowing you to add post offices and users that are reached through the gateway.

Unlike GWIA or the X.400 gateway, however, the API gateway does not support any single messaging standard. Instead, it converts outbound messages to text files, and accepts text files as inbound messages which it converts to native GroupWise messages.

The text file format is well-documented and provides nearly every messaging feature you would need, including support for calendar items.

In this solution, you would create a custom application that sends and receives messages to and from the GroupWise system using the API gateway, and also communicates with the ADABASE system through its own mechanisms.

API gateway messages have two parts: the message header and attachment files. In API gateway messages, the message body is actually stored as an attachment. So every message that has a message body will be comprised of at least two files: the header and a file that contains the body.

The gateway is pretty straightforward to install and administer, and the documentation is fairly complete. The API gateway is free and can be downloaded from the following Web site:

`http://developer.novell.com/ndk/gwgateway.htm`

It will run on DOS, NetWare, or OS/2. The NetWare and OS/2 versions are multi-threaded and 32-bit, so they perform much better than the DOS version. But the DOS version can be handy if you just need a gateway to test your application with.

The documentation for the API gateway can be found online at the following URL:

`http://developer.novell.com/ndk/doc_groupwise.htm`

Look under the GroupWise API Gateway heading.

Automatically Create, Modify, and Delete GroupWise Accounts

Suppose you work for an organization with a high turnover rate for GroupWise accounts, such as a university that provides GroupWise accounts for its students. You have been asked by your boss to provide an automated way to create and manage GroupWise accounts in order to streamline the university's provisioning process.

There are two methods you could use to do this: the admin object API and the API gateway.

In addition to providing message conversion capabilities, the API gateway also provides GroupWise Directory Service (or GDS) services. You can export the entire list of users or any portion of it. You can create new GroupWise accounts or delete them. You can also modify GroupWise accounts.

However, be aware that the GDS is tightly integrated with Novell Directory Services (or NDS), and the only way to keep them in sync is to make modifications to the GDS using the GroupWise snap-in for ConsoleOne or NWAdmin (depending on your version of GroupWise) or to use the admin object API. Any changes made to the GDS through back doors such as the API gateway will *not* be reflected in NDS.

For this reason, the admin object API is the better solution.

The admin object API is very similar to the GWOAPI discussed earlier in this chapter. It is accessed as an OLE automation server. Its ProgID is NovellGroupwareAdmin.

The top-level object for the admin object API is the System object. You call the Connect() method on the System object, passing the path of a domain database. After connecting to a valid domain, you can access domains, post offices, users, and a host of other attributes on the System object that give you access to the GDS.

Using this API, you can create, delete, and modify any GroupWise object, ensuring that changes are synchronized to NDS.

In order for the admin object API to work, you must have the GroupWise client installed, as the OLE automation server is installed with the client.

For this reason, this solution is platform-dependent — it will only work on Windows.

You can find documentation for the admin object API at the following URL:

`http://developer.novell.com/ndk/doc_groupwise.htm`

Look under the heading GroupWise Administrative Object API.

Connect to the GroupWise Document Management System

Suppose you are developing an application that you would like to integrate with popular document management systems (DMSs). You would like your application to be able to natively store and access its documents in a DMS without severely limiting which DMSs your customers can use.

Of course, GroupWise has document management capabilities, and you can access them through the GroupWise object API. But you would like to be able to develop your integrations to a single standard, without having to develop proprietary APIs such as the GWOAPI.

How can you do this?

The answer lies in the fact that GroupWise is an ODMA-compliant DMS. This means that it supports the open document management API, an API developed by a consortium many years ago.

ODMA is a standard API that defines how compliant DMSs and compliant clients must be developed. It was originally developed by a consortium of industry players (including SoftSolutions, which was acquired by WordPerfect, which was acquired by Novell . . .).

The API was later maintained by the Association for Information and Image Management, or AIIM (`http://www.AIIM.org`).

The future of ODMA is uncertain, but most office productivity suites and document management systems continue to support it. There are a number of other standards that provide similar benefits, and thus may supplant ODMA. But for the time being, it is a good choice for standardizing access to DMSs from your application (especially if you want to ensure that GroupWise is supported!).

The ODMA has been revised a number of times, and there are currently three released versions of the API: 1.0, 1.5, and 2.0. Each successive version provides greater functionality than the last.

You should be aware, however, that GroupWise only supports version 1.0 of the standard. There are indexing and searching capabilities exposed in version 1.5 and version 2.0 that GroupWise will not support.

Nevertheless, ODMA provides most of the functionality you need to be able to access documents in a compliant DMS, modify its properties, check documents out, support versioning, and so on.

On the Windows platform, ODMA-compliant DMSs provide their own DLL that exposes standard ODMA functions that clients would need to access. GroupWise supplies its own ODMA32.DLL file for this purpose. Your client application can call the ODMA functions without trepidation or regard to the DMS in use, because compliant DMSs all support the ODMA functions in the same manner (or they wouldn't be compliant!). These functions allow GroupWise to provide the user with its own interface for navigating its libraries, for example, when the user elects to open a document in your application. You can see this at work in any ODMA-compliant application, such as the applications in Microsoft Office.

The GroupWise SDK documentation site contains a link to the ODMA documentation, but it does not contain the documentation itself. Nor are there any examples. ODMA is a standard, and GroupWise supports it fully (for version 1.0), so samples provided by AIIM in the ODMA documentation will suffice for GroupWise. The actual location of the documentation within AIIM's Web site has been a bit fluid. The link from Novell's SDK documentation is kept up to date with the ODMA documentation location, so it is a good idea to access it through Novell's Web site.

You can access the ODMA documentation at the following URL:

```
http://developer.novell.com/ndk/doc_groupwise.htm
```

Look under the heading of GroupWise ODMA.

The Future of Customizing GroupWise: XML Integration Services

At Novell's BrainShare conference in Salt Lake City, held in March of 2000, Novell provided a number of classes on a new technology that it dubbed XIS (pronounced ek-sis). The acronym stands for XML Integration Services.

XIS is an XML-based event system that allows you as a developer to create event publishers that push events into XIS, or to create event consumers that can subscribe to events created by publishers, and that are notified when such events take place.

Along with classes on XIS, Novell provided classes on how the next version of GroupWise would be XIS-enabled both at the client and on the backend, allowing developers to create applications that took advantage of this publish-and-subscribe API.

This was big news to the GroupWise development community because it meant that there would finally be a true server-side API that allowed developers to participate in the communication between GroupWise clients and GroupWise servers. This is something that has been lacking in the GroupWise API set from the beginning.

With XIS, developers would be able to examine the data stream between the POA and the client, for instance, and to even modify it — injecting their own data into the stream, changing existing data, or disallowing transfers altogether.

At BrainShare 2000, some of the GroupWise development team showed working sample applications, demonstrating how XIS could be used to provide access to the local file system from within GroupWise (for example), or how the GroupWise client could be used to access other DMS systems that were either ODMA or WebDAV-compliant.

When GroupWise 6 was finally released in April of 2001, however, support for XIS was not exposed.

Nevertheless, multiple sources within Novell have indicated that support for XIS is a goal of theirs, and we remain hopeful that it will be exposed. It is encouraging that, although XIS is not exposed in the current release of GroupWise, the documentation for XIS is still being maintained and is still available online.

Documentation for the XIS system can be viewed online at the following URL:

```
http://developer.novell.com/ndk/doc_groupwise.htm
```

Look under the heading of XML Integration Services. There are also a number of tools to aid in developing XIS applications.

Summary

GroupWise is certainly a powerful collaboration platform out-of-the-box. But, as with nearly every commercial application, it serves a broad base of needs. There is almost always a need beyond what it can do out of the box.

Well-designed applications provide developers with the tools necessary to customize the application to fit their customers' needs. Without these capabilities, a system's usefulness is very limited, if not nonexistent.

Fortunately, GroupWise provides a number of powerful methods for integrating it into your environment more tightly. All it takes is a good place to start, access to good information, and some time to experiment.

The products developed by many Novell partners such as Concentrico are good examples of how the value of GroupWise can be dramatically increased.

Visit `http://www.novell.com/products/groupwise/partners/` for lists of partners who develop products that work with GroupWise.

APPENDIX A

Managing Your GroupWise Message Store: Smart Purge, Backup, and Restore

To control the size of a message store, administrators may use the expire option in mailbox/library maintenance or GWCheck to remove items based on their age, type, item size, or mailbox size. The problem with this option is that it's a little too arbitrary, and important items sometimes get expired. Overzealous housekeeping by users occasionally purges important items from the store, too.

Though recovery of individual items from backup is possible, there's no guarantee that an expired or purged item has ever been backed up. As a result, administrators and users are reluctant to expire or purge items from the store, so it grows and grows and grows. That's where the new backup, restore, and smart purge features in GroupWise 6 come to the rescue.

Understanding What Smart Purge Is

Smart purge is designed to ensure that items are never expired or purged from the message store until there is at least one backup of them, ensuring that restoration is possible.

By default, users are permitted to *purge items not backed up*. Administrators can use client options at the user, post office, or domain level to either prompt users when they try to purge (empty) an item that has not been backed up or disable this option to prevent items being purged until they are backed up.

The smart purge feature relies on the users' mailboxes (USERxxx.DB) being time-stamped when they are backed up. That time stamp is set by either of three utilities: the GroupWise backup target service agent (TSA), GWTSA.NLM; the GroupWise time-stamp utility, GWTMSTMP.NLM or .EXE; or the ConsoleOne time-stamp utility. These utilities are described later in this appendix.

Once the backup time stamp is set in a user database, items in that mailbox will only be purged or expired if their time stamps predate the backup time stamp, that is, they were present in the mailbox at the time specified by the backup time stamp.

Using the GroupWise 6 Target Service Agent

This section discusses domain and post office backup using the GroupWise 6 target service agent (TSA), GWTSA.NLM.

GWTSA.NLM is automatically installed to the server's SYS:\SYSTEM directory during the MTA/POA installation. This installation also creates a GWTSA.NCF file configured for the domains and post offices selected during the agent installation, and it adds a disabled command to run this NCF file to AUTOEXEC.NCF.

There are six command-line parameters for GWTSA that can be used in the load command in GWTSA.NCF:

- `/help`: Lists the command line parameters
- `/home-< volume:\path >`: Multiple home switches can be set, one to each domain and post office to be backed up by this GWTSA. Multiple home switches are only used if you have multiple agents (and the databases these agents service) running on the same physical NetWare server.
- `/log`: Enables GWTSA logging
- `/ll-< normal|verbose >`: Log level setting; default is normal
- `/tempdir=< vol:\path >`: Temp directory used to copy files during backup. This should not be the SYS, volume if possible.

NOTE

The /tempdir parameter is not listed by /help.

- `/lang-< languageID >`: Default is US

SMDR.NLM needs to be loaded before loading GWTSA. SMDR will autoload SMS.NLM and other SMS NLMs. When loaded, GWTSA.NLM registers itself with SMS. TSA-compliant backup software can then be loaded and will use GWTSA to do open-file backup of the domains and post offices for which GWTSA has been configured.

A few important points on GWTSA:

- GWTSA it is only available as an NLM.
- The GWTSA.NLM can only be used to back up local domains and post offices, that is, it cannot access another server.
- Only one instance of GWTSA can be loaded per server.

What GWTSA does includes the following:

- Converts databases and files to SDIF format for third-party backup software.
- Adds backup time stamps to user databases.
- Restores data, converting SDIF format provided by third-party backup software to GroupWise databases and files.

Using GWTSA to Back Up a Domain or Post Office

The backup sequence for backing up a domain or post office is the following:

1. Run the backup process, ensuring open files are being backed up.
2. Add the backup time stamp to the user databases by either of the following methods:
   - GWTMSTMP.NLM
   - ConsoleOne time-stamp utility

TIP

If your backup software is unable to integrate with GWTSA, you can still use the smart purge feature, but you will have to manually set the backup time stamp on the user databases using the ConsoleOne time-stamp utility. Note that you will need to ensure that your backup solution can handle open files.

Using GWTMSTMP.NLM

To add a backup time stamp using GroupWise's time-stamp utility, you need to run the GWTMSTMP utility to set the backup time stamp to the current time and date. The command line is the following:

```
GWTMSTMP.NLM /ph-< path to post office > /set
```

There are seven command line parameters for GWTMSTMP:

- `/?`: Lists the command line parameters.
- `/ph-< path to post office >`: Points to the post office. This parameter is required.
- `/set`: Sets the backup time stamp. Defaults to the current date and time if `/date` and `/time` are not specified.
- `/get`: Displays the current backup time stamp of the specified user database. If no user ID is specified, all user databases are listed. This is the default action if only the `/ph` parameter is used.
- `/@u-< userID >`: Specifies a user ID for the `/set` or `/get` parameters.

- `/time-< H:M am/pm >`: Specifies time to set the backup timestamp. Used in conjunction with the `/set` parameter.
- `/date-< M/D/YYYY >`: Specifies date to set the backup timestamp. Used in conjunction with the `/set` parameter.

Using the ConsoleOne Time-Stamp Utility

To add a backup time stamp using ConsoleOne, do the following:

1. Select the post office object.
2. Choose Tools ➪ Backup/Restore Mailbox.
3. On the Backup tab, select the Backup radio button and click OK.

   The POA will set the backup time stamps on the user databases.

Remote/Cached Mailbox Backup

This feature allows the user to make a backup copy of cached or remote mailboxes.

- Automated backup can be configured in the client with the Tools ➪ Options ➪ Environment ➪ Backup Options tab, which is also only available when the client is in caching or remote mode. Users can set the following:
  - Whether mailbox backup should be automated
  - Which directory the mailbox should be backed up to
  - When, that is, how often, the mailbox should be backed up
  - Whether the user should be prompted before mailbox backup is done
- Immediate backup can be forced in the client with the menu option Tools ➪ Backup Mailbox, which is only available when the client is in caching or remote mode. Users can set the following:
  - Which directory the mailbox should be backed up to
  - Whether the user should be prompted before mailbox backup is done

Using Restore

In previous versions of GroupWise, the process of restoring lost items or mailboxes was a complex task left entirely to administrators. GroupWise 6 allows users to restore items from the client, and provides a simple method for restoration of mailboxes by administrators.

Understanding Restore Areas

Administrators can now keep a backup copy of the post office online, allowing users access to it from the client to restore items. Administrators can also access the backup copy of the post office to restore mailboxes to the live post office. This is done in ConsoleOne through Tools ⇨ GroupWise System Operations ⇨ Restore Area Management.

Administrators can do the following:

- Create one or more restore areas for a system.
- Automate access by assigning post office or user objects as members of a restore area.
- Assign a post office as a member automates access for all users in that post office.

To make this all work, you must ensure the following:

- Users have read and write file-system rights to access the restore area.
- Even where neither the post office nor the users are members, users who have file-system rights to the restore area directory can still access the restore area from the client by navigating to it manually.

Restoring Data Using GWTSA

GroupWise post office data can be restored to either the post office, overwriting the live data, or to a restore area to provide for mailbox or item restoration as described near the end of this appendix. GWTSA.NLM is loaded as for the backup sequence described in the section, "Using GWTSA to Back Up a Domain or Post Office," earlier in this appendix, and third-party backup software is used to restore the required data.

NOTE

When loading GWTSA.NLM to restore data to a restore area, a `/home` switch pointing to the restore area must be included.

Restoring Data without GWTSA

GroupWise post office data that has been backed up without GWTSA is in native file format, so it does not need GWTSA to convert it. It can be restored to either the post office, overwriting the live data, or to a restore area to provide for mailbox or item restoration as described near the end of this appendix.

It is also possible to manually copy the entire post office to a restore area periodically, using this data for mailbox or item restoration. The POA would need to be down to do this.

Where Should Data Be Restored To?

Restore to the post office, overwriting the live data when you specifically want to replace the existing data with the backup data. You would most likely do this in cases where there has been major corruption or data loss in the live data. Data added to the store after the backup was done will be lost with this type of restoration. The POA would need to be down to do this.

Restore to a restore area to provide for mailbox or item restoration in situations where the live data is intact, but some items are missing. No data is lost due to this type of restoration.

Restoring a Mailbox

Administrators can restore all messages to a user's mailbox from a restore area using ConsoleOne:

1. Highlight the user object in the right pane.
2. Choose Tools ➪ GroupWise Utilities ➪ Backup/Restore Mailbox.
3. Only the Restore tab is available, where you click Yes to restore all messages for this user.

Restoring Individual Items to a Mailbox

In the backup copy of the mailbox, the user has partial functionality to access items, including read, search, and undelete. Users can selectively restore any items from the backed-up mailbox, with the exception of documents.

From the client, in online mode, users can do the following:

- Use File ➪ Open Backup to access the backup copy of their mailbox from the restore area.
- If neither the post office nor the users are members of the restore area, users will have to manually browse to the restore area directory from the client to access it.

When the backup is opened, only those items that exist in the backup and do not exist in the master mailbox will be listed.

- Items in master mailbox trash are considered to be missing from the master mailbox.
- Right-clicking an item in the backup provides the option to restore it to the master.
- Archived items are no longer in the master mailbox and are considered to be missing from it.

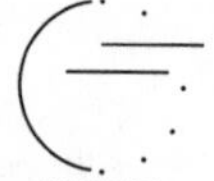

NOTE

Restoring an item copies it to the master mailbox. The item remains in the backup.

Restoring Individual Items to a Remote/Cached Mailbox

The item restore procedure is the same for a cached/remote mailbox as for an online mailbox. The main differences are the following:

- Responsibility for backup of a cached/remote mailbox lies with the user.
- Access to the backup is available when the client is offline.

NOTE

Restored items will synchronize back to the master mailbox.

APPENDIX B

What's on the CD-ROM?

This appendix provides you with information on the contents of the CD that accompanies this book. For the latest and greatest information, please refer to the ReadMe file located at the root of the CD. Here is what you will find:

- System Requirements
- Using the CD with Windows
- What's on the CD
- Troubleshooting

System Requirements

Make sure that your computer meets the minimum system requirements listed in this section. If your computer doesn't match up to most of these requirements, you may have a problem using the contents of the CD.

For Windows 9*x*, Windows 2000, Windows NT4 (with SP 4 or later), Windows Me, or Windows XP:

- PC with a Pentium processor running at 120 Mhz or faster
- At least 32 MB of total RAM installed on your computer; for best performance, I recommend at least 64 MB
- Ethernet network interface card (NIC) or modem with a speed of at least 28,800 bps
- A CD-ROM drive

Using the CD with Windows

To install the items from the CD to your hard drive, follow these steps:

1. Insert the CD into your computer's CD-ROM drive.
2. A window will appear with the following options: Install, Explore, eBook, Links and Exit.

   Install: Gives you the option to install the supplied software and/or the author-created samples on the CD-ROM.

Explore: Allows you to view the contents of the CD-ROM in its directory structure.

eBook: Allows you to view an electronic version of the book.

Links: Opens a hyperlinked page of Web sites.

Exit: Closes the autorun window.

If you do not have autorun enabled or if the autorun window does not appear, follow the steps below to access the CD.

1. Click Start ➪ Run.
2. In the dialog box that appears, type ***d*:\setup.exe**, where *d* is the letter of your CD-ROM drive. This will bring up the autorun window described above.
3. Choose the Install, Explore, eBook, Links, or Exit option from the menu. (See Step 2 in the preceding list for a description of these options.)

What's on the CD

The following sections provide a summary of the other software and materials you'll find on the CD.

Applications

Recently, Novell GroupWise has garnered significantly more third-party support. In fact, Concentrico.net even provides custom GroupWise development. The CD that accompanies this book includes a few popular GroupWise third-party solutions. Here is a review of the solutions that these products provide.

Reach QuickInfo, from Concentrico.net

For GroupWise users, sometimes just getting a phone number from the GroupWise address book is tedious. And then you have to squint when you look at the phone number. Concentrico's Reach QuickInfo puts the GroupWise address book information in quick reach by putting the QuickInfo icon in the Windows tool tray. QuickInfo is also available from just about any GroupWise toolbar. With QuickInfo, looking up a phone number can be done in about a quarter of the time it would take to find a phone number in the GroupWise address book. Once you have an address, you can use the More button to see all of the information on the address book entry.

The product included on this CD is a 60-day demo version. For more information on Reach QuickInfo, go to `www.concentrico.net`.

Reach for NDS, from Concentrico.net

Concentrico's Reach for NDS product line acts as a middleware platform for GroupWise. It acts as a conduit for information in different systems to be displayed in, synchronized with, and available to the GroupWise system.

Synchronize Corporate Data with GroupWise

With Reach for NDS, you can create custom shared address books and synchronize them with your accounting system. This allows users in GroupWise to have access to customers and vendors that are listed in the accounting system. If an accounts payable clerk changes a vendor's phone number or e-mail address in the accounting system, that data will automatically change in the GroupWise shared address book. If a new customer is added to the accounting system, that same new customer will automatically appear in the GroupWise shared address book.

Furthermore, Reach for NDS's handy features allow you to better manage your communications with customers, vendors, partners, and so on. With Reach for NDS, you can access all messages sent to and received from any address-book entry.

Synchronize Contact Management Systems with GroupWise

You can also use Reach for NDS to synchronize full-featured contact-management systems with GroupWise shared address books or with the GroupWise calendar. For instance, you can synchronize Act! contact data, appointments, and tasks with the GroupWise address book and calendar. You can also synchronize other popular contact-management systems such as GoldMine, Maximizer, Siebel, and many others.

The product included on this CD is a 30-day demo version. For more info on Reach for NDS, go to `www.concentrico.net`.

GWFaxWare, from Tobit Software

GWFaxWare (also known as FaxWare for GroupWise) is Novell's recommended fax solution for GroupWise. Faxing is still a technology that is prevalent in many organizations. FaxWare is well integrated with GroupWise and drives down the costs of using faxing technology.

FaxWare for GroupWise consists of FaxWare 6.0, the Fax-to-SMTP gateway (MailGate/PostMan), and a fax plug-in for the GroupWise client. Faxes can be sent and received from the standard GroupWise client, through the GroupWise

WebAccess client, through GroupWise Wireless, or through the stand-alone FaxWare client software (InfoCenter).

The product included on this CD is a full version with a five-user license. For more information on GWFaxWare, go to `www.groupwisesolutions.com` or call toll-free (866) 329-0101.

GroupWise Anti-Virus Agent, from The Messaging Architects/GroupWise Solutions

The GroupWise Anti-Virus Agent (GWAVA) is a powerful anti-virus and e-mail content-security solution, specifically developed to provide advanced, around-the-clock protection for GroupWise 5.x@nd6.x servers and your network.

Finally! An NLM-based virus-protection solution for GroupWise, GWAVA was created in close partnership with Novell. GWAVA integrates with the GroupWise MTA and runs as an NLM. You can implement GWAVA on the domain that services your GWIA, and you can go even further and integrate GWAVA on other GroupWise domains in your system.

I have personally set up GWAVA in a customer's environment; this is powerful software!

The product included on this CD is a 30-day demo version. For more information on GWAVA, go to `www.groupwisesolutions.com`.

Acrobat Reader 5.0, from Adobe

You can find out more about this freeware program at `www.adobe.com`.

Shareware programs are fully functional, trial versions of copyrighted programs. If you like particular programs, register with their authors for a nominal fee and receive licenses, enhanced versions, and technical support. *Freeware programs* are copyrighted games, applications, and utilities that are free for personal use. Unlike shareware, these programs do not require a fee or provide technical support. *GNU software* is governed by its own license, which is included inside the folder of the GNU product. See the GNU license for more details.

Trial, demo, or evaluation versions are usually limited either by time or functionality (such as being unable to save projects). Some trial versions are very sensitive to system date changes. If you alter your computer's date, the programs will "time out" and will no longer be functional.

eBook version of *Novell's GroupWise 6 Administrator's Guide*

The complete text of this book is on the CD in Adobe's Portable Document Format (PDF). You can read and search through the file with the Adobe Acrobat Reader (also included on the CD). However, you won't be able to print out the text.

Troubleshooting

If you have difficulty installing or using any of the materials on the companion CD, try the following solutions:

- **Turn off any anti-virus software that you may have running.** Installers sometimes mimic virus activity and can make your computer incorrectly believe that it is being infected by a virus. (Be sure to turn the anti-virus software back on later.)
- **Close all running programs.** The more programs you're running, the less memory is available to other programs. Installers also typically update files and programs; if you keep other programs running, installation may not work properly.
- **Reference the ReadMe:** Please refer to the ReadMe file located at the root of the CD-ROM for the latest product information at the time of publication.

If you still have trouble with the CD, please call the Hungry Minds Customer Care phone number: (800) 762-2974. Outside the United States, call 1 (317) 572-3993. You can also contact Hungry Minds Customer Service by e-mail at `techsupdum@hungryminds.com`. Hungry Minds will provide technical support only for installation and other general quality control items; for technical support on the applications themselves, consult the program's vendor or author.

Index

continued

E

F

G

M

continued

N

O

P

continued

V

W

X

Z

Hungry Minds, Inc. End-User License Agreement

READ THIS. You should carefully read these terms and conditions before opening the software packet(s) included with this book ("Book"). This is a license agreement ("Agreement") between you and Hungry Minds, Inc. ("HMI"). By opening the accompanying software packet(s), you acknowledge that you have read and accept the following terms and conditions. If you do not agree and do not want to be bound by such terms and conditions, promptly return the Book and the unopened software packet(s) to the place you obtained them for a full refund.

1. **License Grant.** HMI grants to you (either an individual or entity) a nonexclusive license to use one copy of the enclosed software program(s) (collectively, the "Software") solely for your own personal or business purposes on a single computer (whether a standard computer or a workstation component of a multi-user network). The Software is in use on a computer when it is loaded into temporary memory (RAM) or installed into permanent memory (hard disk, CD-ROM, or other storage device). HMI reserves all rights not expressly granted herein.

2. **Ownership.** HMI is the owner of all right, title, and interest, including copyright, in and to the compilation of the Software recorded on the disk(s) or CD-ROM ("Software Media"). Copyright to the individual programs recorded on the Software Media is owned by the author or other authorized copyright owner of each program. Ownership of the Software and all proprietary rights relating thereto remain with HMI and its licensers.

3. **Restrictions On Use and Transfer.**

   (a) You may only (i) make one copy of the Software for backup or archival purposes, or (ii) transfer the Software to a single hard disk, provided that you keep the original for backup or archival purposes. You may not (i) rent or lease the Software, (ii) copy or reproduce the Software through a LAN or other network system or through any computer subscriber system or bulletin-board system, or (iii) modify, adapt, or create derivative works based on the Software.

(b) You may not reverse engineer, decompile, or disassemble the Software. You may transfer the Software and user documentation on a permanent basis, provided that the transferee agrees to accept the terms and conditions of this Agreement and you retain no copies. If the Software is an update or has been updated, any transfer must include the most recent update and all prior versions.

4. **Restrictions on Use of Individual Programs.** You must follow the individual requirements and restrictions detailed for each individual program in Appendix B of this Book. These limitations are also contained in the individual license agreements recorded on the Software Media. These limitations may include a requirement that after using the program for a specified period of time, the user must pay a registration fee or discontinue use. By opening the Software packet(s), you will be agreeing to abide by the licenses and restrictions for these individual programs that are detailed in Appendix B and on the Software Media. None of the material on this Software Media or listed in this Book may ever be redistributed, in original or modified form, for commercial purposes.

5. **Limited Warranty.**

(a) HMI warrants that the Software and Software Media are free from defects in materials and workmanship under normal use for a period of sixty (60) days from the date of purchase of this Book. If HMI receives notification within the warranty period of defects in materials or workmanship, HMI will replace the defective Software Media.

(b) **HMI AND THE AUTHOR OF THE BOOK DISCLAIM ALL OTHER WARRANTIES, EXPRESS OR IMPLIED, INCLUDING WITHOUT LIMITATION IMPLIED WARRANTIES OF MERCHANTABILITY AND FITNESS FOR A PARTICULAR PURPOSE, WITH RESPECT TO THE SOFTWARE, THE PROGRAMS, THE SOURCE CODE CONTAINED THEREIN, AND/OR THE TECHNIQUES DESCRIBED IN THIS BOOK. HMI DOES NOT WARRANT THAT THE FUNCTIONS CONTAINED IN THE SOFTWARE WILL MEET YOUR REQUIREMENTS OR THAT THE OPERATION OF THE SOFTWARE WILL BE ERROR FREE.**

(c) This limited warranty gives you specific legal rights, and you may have other rights that vary from jurisdiction to jurisdiction.

6. **Remedies.**

(a) HMI's entire liability and your exclusive remedy for defects in materials and workmanship shall be limited to replacement of the Software Media, which may be returned to HMI with a copy of your receipt at the following address: Software Media Fulfillment Department, Attn.: *Novell's GroupWise 6 Administrator's Guide,* Hungry Minds, Inc., 10475 Crosspoint Blvd., Indianapolis, IN 46256, or call 1-800-762-2974. Please allow four to six weeks for delivery. This Limited Warranty is void if failure of the Software Media has resulted from accident, abuse, or misapplication. Any replacement Software Media will be warranted for the remainder of the original warranty period or thirty (30) days, whichever is longer.

(b) In no event shall HMI or the author be liable for any damages whatsoever (including without limitation damages for loss of business profits, business interruption, loss of business information, or any other pecuniary loss) arising from the use of or inability to use the Book or the Software, even if HMI has been advised of the possibility of such damages.

(c) Because some jurisdictions do not allow the exclusion or limitation of liability for consequential or incidental damages, the above limitation or exclusion may not apply to you.

7. **U.S. Government Restricted Rights.** Use, duplication, or disclosure of the Software for or on behalf of the United States of America, its agencies and/or instrumentalities (the "U.S. Government") is subject to restrictions as stated in paragraph (c)(1)(ii) of the Rights in Technical Data and Computer Software clause of DFARS 252.227-7013, or subparagraphs (c) (1) and (2) of the Commercial Computer Software - Restricted Rights clause at FAR 52.227-19, and in similar clauses in the NASA FAR supplement, as applicable.

8. **General.** This Agreement constitutes the entire understanding of the parties and revokes and supersedes all prior agreements, oral or written, between them and may not be modified or amended except in a writing signed by both parties hereto that specifically refers to this Agreement. This Agreement shall take precedence over any other documents that may be in conflict herewith. If any one or more provisions contained in this Agreement are held by any court or tribunal to be invalid, illegal, or otherwise unenforceable, each and every other provision shall remain in full force and effect.